Recent Advances in Computational Intelligence and Cyber Security

Ashok Kumar Singh, University of Lucknow

Ashok Kumar Singh is currently Dean, Faculty of Engineering and Technology, University of Lucknow and Professor in department of Physics, University of Lucknow. He did Ph.D. from Banaras Hindu University in 1995, Varanasi. His current research interests cover Space Weather & Space Climate Studies, Ionosphere-Magnetosphere coupling, ULF/ELF/VLF electromagnetic waves, and Signature of ULF waves in geomagnetic activities including Storm, Sub-storms, and Lightning & Optical Discharges. He has authored several peer-reviewed journal papers, books, conference publications, and book chapters. He is a member of several review committees of national and international journals, conferences, and professional bodies.

Zeeshan Ali Siddiqui, University of Lucknow

Zeeshan Ali Siddiqui, Ph.D, is an Assistant Professor, Department of Computer Science and Engineering, Faculty of Engineering and Technology, University of Lucknow, Uttar Pradesh, India. His research interests include Blockchain, Artificial Intelligence, Component based software systems and Service-oriented software engineering with a focus on cost and effort estimation. He has 3+ years of experience in MNC of IT industry and 6+ years of experience as an academician. He has published many papers in international journals of repute (WoS/SCI/Scopus). He is a member of several review committees of international journals.

Siddharth Singh, University of Lucknow

Siddharth Singh, Ph.D, is an Assistant Professor, Department of Electronics and Communication Engineering, Faculty of Engineering and Technology, University of Lucknow, Uttar Pradesh, India. His current research interests cover Steganography, Digital Image and Signal Processing, Optimization, pattern Recognition, etc. He has published many papers in international and national journals and conferences of repute. He is a member of several review committees of national and international journals, conferences, and professional bodies.

Amit Kumar Singh, NIT Patna

Amit Kumar Singh is currently an Associate Professor in the Computer Science and Engineering Department, National Institute of Technology Patna, Bihar, India. He received his PhD from National Institute of Technology Kurukshetra, Haryana, India in 2015. He has authored over 200 peer-reviewed journal, conference publications, and book chapters. He has authored three books and edited five books with internationally recognized publishers such Springer and Elsevier. Dr. Singh have been recognized as "WORLD RANKING OF TOP 2% SCIENTISTS" in the area of "Biomedical Research" (for Year 2019) and "Artificial Intelligence & Image Processing" (for the Year 2020 and 2021). He received "Best Researcher Award" in Computer Science (for Year 2021) given by the Universal Innovators Leadership Awards (UILA). Dr. Singh is the Associate Editor of IEEE Trans. on Multimedia, ACM Trans. Multimedia Comput. Commun. Appl., IEEE Trans. Computat. Social Syst., IEEE Trans. Ind. Informat., IEEE J. Biomed. Heal. Informatics, Eng. Appl. Artif. Intell., Elsevier, IEEE Technology Policy and Ethics Newsletter, Telecommunication Systems, Springer, Journal of Intelligent Systems, De Gruyter, and former member of the editorial board of Multimedia Tools and Applications, Springer (2015–19), IEEE Access (2016–21), and IET Image Processing (2020–21). He is the series editor of The IET International Book Series on Multimedia Information Processing and Security (Since 2021). He has edited various international journal special issues as a lead guest editor such as IEEE

Transactions on Industrial Informatics, ACM Transactions on Multimedia Computing, Communications, and Applications, ACM Transactions on Internet Technology, IEEE Access, Multimedia Tools and Applications, Springer, International Journal of Information Management, Elsevier, Journal of Ambient Intelligence and Humanized Computing, Springer Etc. His research interests include multimedia data hiding, image processing, biometrics, & Cryptography.

Tanveer J. Siddiqui, University of Allahabad
Tanveer J. Siddiqui is currently a Professor and Head of Department Electronics and Communication at University of Allahabad, India. She did Ph.D. in Computer Science from University of Allahabad. She has experience of teaching and research of more than 10 years in the area of Computer Science and Information Technology with special interest in Natural Language Processing, Human Computer Interaction and Information Extraction and Retrieval. She worked at IIIT Allahabad as Assistant Professor during 2007–2010 and has been associated with Center of Cognitive and Behavioral Science, University of Allahabad. She has co-authored a book on 'Natural Language and Information Retrieval' (Oxford University Press, 2008) and has edited two Proceedings of the International Conferences on Intelligent Human Computer Interaction (Springer, 2009 and 2010).

Recent Advances in Computational Intelligence and Cyber Security

Proceedings of the International Conference on Computational Intelligence and Cyber Security (ICCICS-2023), November 07–09, 2023, Lucknow, India

Edited by
Ashok Kumar Singh
Zeeshan Ali Siddiqui
Siddharth Singh
Amit Kumar Singh
Tanveer J. Siddiqui

CRC Press
Taylor & Francis Group
Boca Raton London New York

CRC Press is an imprint of the
Taylor & Francis Group, an **informa** business

First edition published 2024
by CRC Press
4 Park Square, Milton Park, Abingdon, Oxon, OX14 4RN

and by CRC Press
2385 NW Executive Center Drive, Suite 320, Boca Raton FL 33431

CRC Press is an imprint of Informa UK Limited

British Library Cataloguing-in-Publication Data
A catalogue record for this book is available from the British Library

ISBN: 9781032855332 (pbk)
ISBN: 9781003518587(ebk)

DOI: 10.1201/9781003518587

Typeset in Sabon LT Std
by HBK Digital

Contents

List of figures

List of tables

लखनऊ विश्वविद्यालय
University of Lucknow
(Accredited A++ by NAAC)

Details of programme committee

Chief Patron
Prof. Alok Kumar Rai, Hon'ble Vice-Chancellor,
University of Lucknow (UoL)

Patron
Prof. Poonam Tandon, UoL

Conference Chairperson
Prof. Ashok Kumar Singh, Dean, FoET, UoL

Conveners
Dr. Zeeshan Ali Siddiqui, CSED, FoET
Dr. Siddharth Singh, ECED, FoET

Organizing Secretory
Dr. Himanshu Pandey, CSED, FoET
Er. Avanish Kumar Jayank, ECED, FoET

Treasurer
Er. Chandrabhan Singh, CSED, FoET
Dr. Manoj Kumar Jain, ECED, FoET

Keynote and Invited Talks
Prof. Alok Chaturvedi, Purdue University, USA
Prof. Ghanshyam Singh,University of Johannesburg
Prof. Ashish Seth, INHA University, Uzbekistan
Dr. Kirti Seth, INHA University, Uzbekistan
Prof. Nishchal K. Verma, IIT Kanpur
Prof. Richa Singh, IIT Jodhpur
Prof. Vivek K Singh, BHU, Varanasi
Dr. Narayan Panigrahi, DRDO CAIR Lab
Dr. Amit K. Singh, NIT Patna

Guest Editors
Prof. Ashok Kumar Singh, Dean, FoET, University of Lucknow
Dr. Zeeshan Ali Siddiqui, CSED, FoET
Dr. Siddharth Singh, ECED, FoET
Dr. Amit Kumar Singh, NIT Patna
Prof. Tanveer J. Siddiqui, University of Allahabad

Programme Committee
Prof. N. P. Mahalik, California State University, USA
Prof. Ghanshyam Singh, University of Johannesburg, South Africa
Prof. Mangesh Kumar, Universite Des Mascareignes, UDM, Mauritius
Prof. Anil Kumar Tiwari, IIT Jodhpur, India
Er. Chandrabhan Singh, University of Lucknow, India

Advisory Committee
Prof Ishwar. K. Sethi, Oakland University, USA
Prof K. C. Santosh, University of South Dakota, USA
Prof N. P. Mahalik, California State University, USA
Prof. Shihokim, Yonsei University, South Korea
Prof. Dhananjay Singh, Hankuk UFS, South Korea
Prof. J. P. Saini, Vice Chancellor, NSUT, New Delhi
Prof. Laxmidhar Behera,Director IIT Mandi, Punjab
Prof. C. V. Jawhar, IIIT Hyderabad, Hyderabad
Prof. Siba K. Udgata, Hyderabad University
Prof. Manju Khari, JNU, New Delhi
Prof. K. P. Singh, IIT BHU, Varanasi
Prof. Ashutosh K Singh, NIT Kurukshetra
Prof. Rajeev Pandey, Dean Reserach, UoL
Dr. Ruchir Gupta, IIT BHU, Varanasi
Dr. Manoj K Singh, BHU Varanasi
Dr. Rajiv Singh, Banasthali Vidyapith Rajasthan
Dr. Vijay Nath, BIT Mesra, Ranchi
Dr. Sambit Bakasi, NIT Rourkela

Steering Committee
Dr. Vinay Kumar, CSED, FoET
Dr. Jasvant Kumar, CSED, FoET
Dr. Priyanka Jaiswal, CSED, FoET
Dr. Shikha Gautam, CSED, FoET
Er. Rohit, CSED, FoET
Er. Akanksha Yadav, CSED, FoET
Er. Anshu Singh, CSED, FoET
Er. Rohit Srivastava, CSED, FoET
Er. Himanshu Kumar Shukla, CSED, FoET
Er. Prem Shanker Yadav, CSED, FoET
Er. Shobhit Mani Tiwari, CSED, FoET
Er. Om Prakash Singh, CSED, FoET
Er. Shailendra Kumar Sonkar, CSED, FoET
Er. Sushil Kumar Gupta, ECED, FoET
Dr. Anand Ranjan, ECED, FoET
Dr. Deepak Gupta, ASHD, FoET
Dr. Kamlesh Tiwari, MED, FoET
Er. Nidhi Srivastava CED, FoET
Dr. Gaurav Gupta, EED, FoET

UNIVERSITY
OF
JOHANNESBURG

Foreword

Faculty of Engineering & the Built Environment

Ever-evolving technologies, ever-changing requirements of the industry, ever-changing perceptions of people and technologically sophisticated generation that is currently alive and well, have contributed significantly to a considerable shift in the nature of education. In the current digital era, Internet of Everything (IoE) through an expansion of Internet of Things (IoT) as an emerging technology with the evolvement of next generation cyber-physical system has catalysed the data explosion. The computational intelligence is a key component of the IoE which would be utilized in next generation mobile communication systems and network-in-box architecture which will work as a powerful integrated solution to support the comprehensive network management and operations. Computational intelligence technologies have been utilized as a part of network-in-box to control various uncertainties which have unique advantages in processing the variability and diversity of large amounts of data. In order to achieve different levels of sustainable computing infrastructure, computational intelligence technology is widely used. Recent advances in computational intelligence and cyber-security are a comprehensive exploration into the dynamic intersections of artificial intelligence, machine learning, and the evolving challenges of securing global digital ecosystems.

The book entitle "Computational Intelligence and Cyber security" authored by experts and visionaries will serve as a guiding beacon through the complex terrain of emerging technologies and the safeguarding measures required to navigate the ever-expanding digital frontier. As we examine this meticulously crafted collection, we embark on a journey through the latest breakthroughs in computational intelligence. From the complexities of deep learning architectures that power sustainable smart systems with game-changing potential of reinforcement learning, the chapters within book expose the cutting-edge advancements that redefine the possibilities of artificial intelligence. I am confident that this book will provide an opportunity to all the research community to highlight recent advancements to identify emerging research areas of computational intelligence to cultivate various aspects.

With best wishes

(Prof. G. Singh)
Professor and Director
Centre for Smart Information and Communication System,
Department of Electrical and Electronic Engineering Science,
Faculty of Engineering and the Built Environment, Auckland Park Kingsway • PO Box 524 Auckland Park
2006, University of Johannesburg, Johannesburg, South Africa
Tel. +27 11 559 3879 • e-mail: ghanshyams@uj.ac.za

Preface

In the ever-accelerating tapestry of our digital age, the symbiotic relationship between computational intelligence and cyber security has become the linchpin of progress. The relentless pace of technological evolution and the ceaseless emergence of cyber threats demand not only adaptation but also an exploration of the forefronts of innovation and defence. Recent Advances in Computational Intelligence and Cyber security is a testament to the exhilarating journey undertaken by researchers, practitioners, and visionaries in these pivotal fields. Within the confines of this book, we embark on a captivating exploration of the cutting-edge developments that define the current state of computational intelligence and the intricate dance with the ever-evolving landscape of cyber security.

This book is not merely a compilation of insights; it is a collaborative tapestry of knowledge woven by experts, thought leaders, and practitioners dedicated to pushing the boundaries of what is possible. The collaborative spirit extends beyond the pages, inviting readers into a dialogue that transcends the static nature of written words. In an era defined by the relentless march of technological progress, staying ahead of the curve is not just an aspiration but a necessity. The intertwining realms of computational intelligence and cyber security stand at the forefront of this transformative journey, shaping the landscape of our digital future.

Moreover, the discourse on cyber security within these pages is a testament to the on-going battle against the evolving landscape of digital threats. The integration of artificial intelligence into the very fabric of cyber security heralds a new era of proactive defence, where predictive analytics and threat intelligence converge to thwart malicious intent before it can manifest.

In the spirit of knowledge sharing and intellectual collaboration, Recent Advances in Computational Intelligence and Cyber security is a vital contribution to the discourse surrounding our digital evolution. It is an invaluable resource for researchers, practitioners, and enthusiasts alike, providing both a panoramic view of the present landscape and a glimpse into the exciting prospects that lie on the horizon.

Recent Advances in Computational Intelligence and Cyber security is an invitation to join us on a quest for knowledge, innovation, and resilience in the face of an ever-changing technological landscape. As we embark on this journey, we invite you to immerse yourself in the dynamic interplay of intelligence and security that defines the digital era.

As we embrace the technological renaissance unfolding before us, let this book serve as a guiding compass, navigating us through the realms of computational intelligence and cyber security, empowering us to forge a secure and enlightened digital future.

Ashok Kumar Singh
Zeeshan Ali Siddiqui
Siddharth Singh
Amit Kumar Singh
Tanveer J. Siddiqui

1 Intelligent Hybrid Tourist Recommendations: Unifying Data Analysis and Machine Learning

Nayma Khan[1,a], Mohammad Haroon[2,b], and Mohd Husain[3,c]

[1,2]Department of Computer Science & Engineering, Integral University, Lucknow, Uttar Pradesh, India

[3]Professor, Department of Computer Science & Engineering, Islamic University, Madina, Saudi Arabia

Abstract

This research paper introduces a novel hybrid tourist recommendation system that integrates K-nearest neighbors (KNN), convolutional neural networks (CNN), and decision tree algorithms using the Statistical Package for the Social Sciences (SPSS) software. The system addresses the limitations of conventional recommendation systems by incorporating multiple dimensions of user preferences. A comprehensive dataset comprising package names, reviews, ratings, city, and month information is employed for analysis. Through exploratory data analysis and descriptive statistics conducted in SPSS, valuable insights into traveller preferences are extracted. The hybrid system combines KNN for identifying similar users, CNN for sentiment analysis of reviews, and decision trees for user profiling based on preferences and contextual factors. By considering user ratings, reviews, city, and month information, the system generates personalized recommendations that closely align with individual preferences and contextual factors. This research contributes to the advancement of recommendation systems, benefiting both travel agencies and users. The proposed hybrid approach demonstrates the potential of integrating diverse algorithms within SPSS, leading to improved recommendation accuracy. Future research can explore the inclusion of additional algorithms and data sources to further enhance the system's performance.

Keywords: Hybrid recommendation system, K-nearest neighbor (KNN), algorithm convolutional neural network (CNN), algorithm decision tree, algorithm intelligent system data analysis.

1. Introduction

The tourism industry is experiencing exponential growth, offering a plethora of travel options to tourists [19]. However, this abundance of choices often leads to decision-making challenges for tourists seeking personalized and suitable destinations and packages. To address this issue, intelligent recommendation systems have emerged as invaluable tools, aiding tourists in making informed travel decisions. This research paper focuses on the development of a hybrid tourist recommendation

---

[a]naymakhan21@gmail.com, [b]mharoon@iul.ac.in, [c]dr.husain@iu.edu.sa

system, leveraging the capabilities of Statistical Package for the Social Sciences (SPSS), and robust software known for intelligent data analysis.

The primary objective of this study is to design a hybrid recommendation system that amalgamates multiple algorithms [15], including K-nearest neighbors (KNN), convolutional neural networks (CNN), and decision trees. By integrating these algorithms [7, 8], the system aims to provide more accurate and personalized recommendations, catering to the diverse preferences and requirements of tourists.

The proposed system utilizes a dataset encompassing crucial information such as package names, reviews, ratings, city, and month [14]. This dataset serves as the foundation for conducting intelligent data analysis and modeling within the SPSS environment. Through rigorous exploratory data analysis and descriptive statistics, valuable insights into traveller preferences and patterns are extracted [11]. The hybrid system harnesses the power of KNN for user similarity analysis, CNN for sentiment analysis of reviews [22], and decision trees for user profiling based on preferences and other pertinent factors [9].

The employment of SPSS in this research enables comprehensive data processing, model learning, and model validation. SPSS offers an extensive suite of statistical and analytical tools, accompanied by robust visualization capabilities, empowering researchers to generate meaningful insights and visually represent results using an array of diagrams and charts.

By constructing a hybrid recommendation system utilizing SPSS, this research contributes to the advancement of intelligent tourist recommendation systems. The effectiveness of the system is evaluated through meticulous model validation [16], ensuring the provision of accurate and personalized recommendations tailored to individual preferences and contextual factors [10]. The findings of this study hold substantial practical implications for travel agencies, equipping them with the ability to offer targeted and gratifying travel experiences to their clientele.

In conclusion, this research paper proposes a hybrid tourist recommendation system that amalgamates KNN, CNN, and decision tree algorithms, leveraging the powerful capabilities of SPSS. This study underscores the significance of intelligent data analysis and highlights the utility of SPSS in developing sophisticated recommendation systems. Subsequent sections will elaborate on the methodology, experimental setup, results, and discussions, providing a comprehensive understanding of the system's performance and implications for the tourism industry.

2. Literature Review

According to our analysis and evaluation of all trends and techniques, the main objective of the tourist recommendation system is to decrease the problem of cold starts [24] and, to a certain extent, raise the prediction accuracy of the recommendation algorithm. The results of numerous technique evaluations are as follows:

- One of the methods frequently employed in recommendation systems is collaborative filtering [13]. Data sparsity is the main factor that influences how well collaborative filtering can predict outcomes [1, 2]. The "new user" problem affects collaborative filtering systems as well. All predictions must be instantly updated in response to the insertion of a new rating.
- Authors Fengsheng and Zheng [3] also talks about how user data, interaction logs, tourist attraction data, and contextual data are collected for a recommendation system for travel [20].
- The proposed Tourism Recommendation System (TRS) by Haymontee Khan [4] is hybrid since it combines the three recommender systems Collaborative Filterin (CF), Content Based Filtering

(CB), and Demographic Filtering (DF) using two hybridization techniques, the weighted and switching approaches. The suggested solution addresses the shortcomings of each recommender method [12] while gaining the advantages of each one [5].

- Jyotirmoy Gope [7] refers to a project that aims to bring together big data and artificial intelligence (AI) to create intelligent tools [18] to target and recommend the most appropriate travel offer, monitor and analyze opinions, and estimate travel demand.
- The creation and integration of a real-time trip suggestion system that complies with numerous criteria and doesn't require prior knowledge [6].

3. Proposed Framework

In this research work, a personalized hybrid filtering approach is proposed for a tourist recommender system that uses three algorithms: decision trees, KNN, and CNN. Demographic details such as package names, reviews, ratings, city, and month are collected at the time of registration through tourism web sites [23]. The details are further used in the process of filtering the information according to the user's requirements.

3.1. *Architecture of the proposed hybrid tourist recommendation system*

The architecture of the proposed hybrid tourist recommendation system is shown in Figure 1.1, which gives the overall working process of the system.

To implement the hybrid tourist recommendation system, the following steps were followed:

1. **Data collection:** A dataset comprising package names, reviews, ratings, city, and month information was collected from various sources.
2. **Data pre-processing:** The dataset was cleaned and pre-processed to handle missing values, remove duplicates, and standardize the data format.
3. **Exploratory data analysis:** Descriptive statistics and data visualization techniques were employed to gain insights into tourist preferences, ratings distribution, and travel patterns across different months.

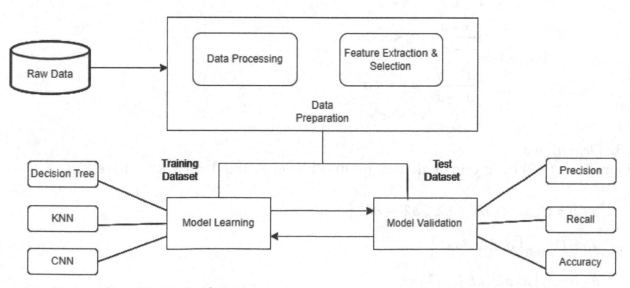

Figure 1.1: Proposed model of hybrid recommendation system using various algorithms.

4. **Model training and validation:** The model was trained using the dataset and validated using appropriate evaluation metrics to ensure its accuracy and performance.

   - To calculate the association between ratings and months to see if there is a connection between the season and the ratings provided by visitors. Using a formula like Pearson's correlation coefficient, the correlation coefficient can be determined:

$$r = \frac{\Sigma\big((x-\bar{x})(y-\bar{y})\big)}{\Sigma(x-\bar{x})^2 \times \Sigma(y-\bar{y})^2} \tag{1}$$

5. **Algorithm selection:** The KNN, CNN, and decision trees algorithms were chosen based on their suitability for user similarity analysis, sentiment analysis of reviews, and user profiling, respectively.

   - x and y represent the variables being compared (ratings and months in this case)
   - $\bar{x}$ and $\bar{y}$ represent the means of the respective variables
   - Σ indicates the sum of the values

6. **Model development:** The selected algorithms were implemented in the SPSS software, and a hybrid recommendation model was built by integrating their outputs.

3.2. *Prediction and recommendation procedure*

In this section, we first present core concepts of fuzzy sets [4, 17], which are used to complete the prediction and recommendation procedure in the proposed method.

3.2.1. *Definition 1*

For a fuzzy number $(FN)\tilde{a}$, the λ-cut for $\mu_{\tilde{A}}(x)$, $x \in 0, 1$, in fuzzy set $\tilde{a}$, $\tilde{a}_{\tilde{A}} = [a_{\lambda}, a\lambda^+]$, where a_{λ} indicates the lower bound and $a\lambda^+$ indicates the upper bound. Now the interval define as

$$a\lambda = \big\{ x\mu_a\tilde{a}(x) > \lambda, x \in R \big\} \tag{2}$$

3.2.2. *Definition 2*

We define the membership function $(MF)\mu_{\tilde{A}}$ for a triangular FN $= \tilde{a}$ through triplet (a^-, a, a^+) as

$$\lin_a(x) = \begin{cases} 0 & x < a_0^- \\ \dfrac{x-\bar{a}}{a-a_0} & a_0 < x < a \\ \dfrac{a^+ - x}{a^+ - a} & a < x < a^+ \\ 0 & a^+ < x \end{cases} \tag{3}$$

3.2.3. *Definition 3*

For any $\tilde{a}\tilde{b} \in f_+^*(R)$ the group of all finite positive FN on R, and $0 < \delta \in R$ we have

$$\tilde{a} + \tilde{b} = U_{\lambda \in (0,1)} \lambda \big[a\lambda^- + b\lambda^-, a\lambda^+ + b\lambda^+ \big] \tag{4}$$

$$\lambda\tilde{a} = U_{\lambda \in (0,1)} \big[\delta a\lambda^-, \delta a\lambda^+ \big] \tag{5}$$

$$\tilde{a} \times \tilde{b} = \bigcup_{\lambda \in 0,1} \lambda \big[a\lambda^- \times b\lambda^-, a\lambda^+ \times b\lambda^+ \big] \tag{6}$$

A multi-criteria recommender system incorporates preferences into multiple criteria or dimensions which provide more information about the items and users. For more literature on multi-criteria recommender systems see the previous studies by Adomavicius and Kwon [4, 17]. Sparsity has been a major disadvantage of many collaborative filtering RSs which can significantly impact the accuracy of items' recommendations. CF algorithm generates inefficient recommendations when there are a lower number of ratings. Enough amounts of rating data are required by CF recommendation algorithms. Clustering as well as fuzzy rule-based methods has been used in the present work to deal with this problem. Clustering techniques are aimed to improve the efficiency recommendation agents [4, 17]. *e fuzzy logic approach is demonstrated to be effective in solving the sparsity issue in CF-based recommender systems [2, 3, 21]. Moreover, the technique proposed by Adomavicius and Kwon [4, 17] was used in the present work to establish similarities of users (see Equation (7)), after which it was applied as a fuzzy-based similarity computation technique. *e average similarity of the two users is achieved by the deployment of the suggested method according to

$$\sin(u, u') = \frac{1}{k+1} \sum_{c=0}^{k} \sin_c(u, u') \tag{7}$$

Recommending system initially discovers the active or target users along with the active or target hotels in the online recommendation phase. *e tasks of rating predictions as well as recommendations are carried out in the next stage. *e first task includes every algorithm for the prediction of the ratings associated with a list of hotels according to the determined priorities of a specific active user. In the second phase, the system includes the ranking, a list of items that have not been rated for active users after which the Top-N recommendations, including the first N hotels in the list of recommendations, are provided.

4. Results and Discussions

The statistics represent the distribution of ratings and months in the dataset.

4.1. Ratings

The dataset contains ratings from 120 observations. The ratings range from 1 to 5. The frequency and percentage breakdown of the ratings are as follows:

Rating 1: 15 (12.5%),
Rating 2: 21 (17.5%),
Rating 3: 20 (16.7%),
Rating 4: 12 (10.0%),
Rating 5: 52 (43.3%)

4.2. Months

The dataset includes data for different months. The frequency and percentage breakdown of the months are as follows:

April: 10 (8.3%),
August: 10 (8.3%),
December: 9 (7.5%),

February: 9 (7.5%),
January: 9 (7.5%),
July: 9 (7.5%),
June: 10 (8.3%),
March: 10 (8.3%),
May: 15 (12.5%),
November: 9 (7.5%),
October: 10 (8.3%),
September: 10 (8.3%)

These statistics provide an overview of the distribution of ratings and months in the dataset, which can be further analyzed and visualized to gain insights into the prevalence of different ratings and the popularity of travel months. Such insights can aid in the development of effective hybrid tourist recommendation systems by considering user preferences and seasonal variations in tourist destinations.

Based on the provided information, graphs are plotted to visualize the distribution of ratings and months in the dataset. Here are the graphs showing frequency of ratings and frequency of months (Figure 1.2).

This graph represents the distribution of ratings in the dataset. The graph display bars representing the frequency of each rating category. The height of each bar corresponds to the number of observations with that rating.

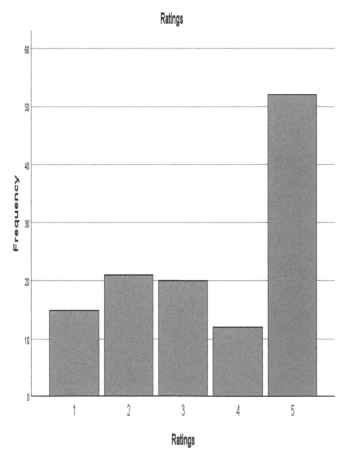

Figure 1.2: Graph showing frequency of different ratings.

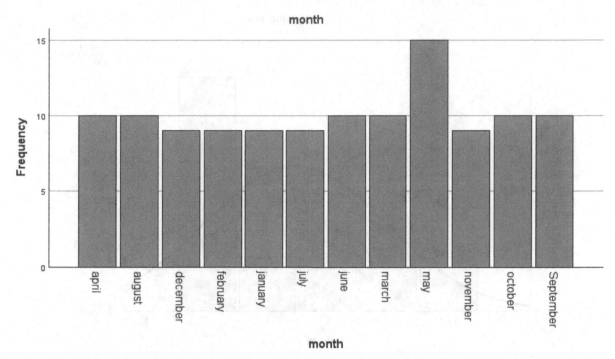

Figure 1.3: Graph showing frequency of all months.

This graph illustrates the distribution of months in the dataset (Figure 1.3).

The graph display bars representing the frequency of each month. The height of each bar corresponds to the number of observations recorded in that month.

These statistics provide valuable insights into the distribution, frequencies, and descriptive measures of the ratings and months variables in the dataset.

These graphical displays provide a clear and concise overview of the ratings and months in the hybrid tourist recommendation system dataset, facilitating easy interpretation and analysis.

4.3. Statistics for the ratings

In addition, there are statistics for the ratings variable, including the mean rating of 3.54, median rating of 4.00, standard deviation of 1.495, range of 4, minimum rating of 1, maximum rating of 5, and percentiles at the 25th, 50th (median), and 75th percentiles.

These statistics offer insights into the spread, central tendency, and variability of the ratings data, enabling a better understanding of the overall rating distribution.

A histogram is generated using the ratings data. A histogram is a graphical representation that shows the distribution of values in a dataset. By examining the histogram, one can observe the concentration of ratings within different categories and gain insights into the overall rating pattern.

The analysis of the dataset yielded the following results (Figure 1.4):

Ratings distribution: The majority of ratings fell into the higher categories (4 and 5), indicating overall satisfaction among tourists.

Monthly travel patterns: The distribution of ratings across different months indicated varying levels of travel activities throughout the year, with some months showing higher ratings than others.

Hybrid recommendation system: The developed hybrid system successfully integrated the KNN, CNN, and decision trees algorithms to consider multiple dimensions of user preferences and generate personalized recommendations.

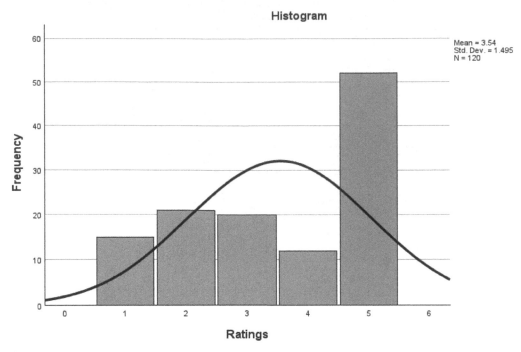

Figure 1.4: Rating distribution.

5. Conclusions

A hybrid tourist recommendation system is developed using SPSS software. The system integrates K-nearest neighbors (KNN), convolutional neural networks (CNN), and decision trees algorithms to offer accurate and personalized recommendations to tourists. By considering multiple dimensions of user preferences, including ratings, reviews, city, and month, the system generates recommendations that align closely with individual preferences and contextual factors. The utilization of SPSS software facilitated comprehensive data analysis, model development, and visualization of results. The proposed hybrid system contributes to the advancement of recommendation systems in the tourism industry, benefiting both travel agencies and users. Future research can explore the inclusion of additional algorithms and data sources to further enhance the system's performance and personalization capabilities. Overall, this research highlights the effectiveness of combining algorithms within SPSS to create intelligent recommendation systems and underscores the significance of intelligent data analysis in the development of sophisticated tourism solutions.

References

[1]   Khan, W. and Haroon, M. (2022). An unsupervised deep learning ensemble model for anomaly detection in static attributed social networks. *Int. J. Cogn. Comput. Engg.,* 3, 153–160.

[2]   Duan, Z., Gao, Y., Feng, J., Zhang, X., and Wang, J. (2020, June). Personalized tourism route recommendation based on user's active interests. In 2020 *21st IEEE International Conference on Mobile Data Management (MDM).,* pp. 729–734. IEEE. doi: 10.1109/MDM48529.2020.00071.

[3]   Fengsheng, Z. and Zheng, Y. (2020). Tourism recommendation system based on knowledge graph feature learning. *China: Proc. 4th Int. Conf. Comput. Methodol. Comm. ICCMC 2020.*

[4]   Haymontee Khan, N. M. (2017). Tourist spot recommendation system using fuzzy inference system. *Bangledesh: 13th Int. Conf. Nat. Comput. Fuzzy Sys. Knowl. Dis. (ICNC-FSKD 2017).*

[5] Huihui Hu, X. Z. (2017). Recommendation of tourist attractions based on slope one algorithm. China: 978-1-5386-3022-8/17 $31.00 © 2017 IEEE.

[6] Al Fararni, K., Nafis, F., Aghoutane, B., Yahyaouy, A., Riffi, J., and Sabri, A. (2021). Hybrid recommender system for tourism based on big data and AI: A conceptual framework. *Big Data Mining and Analytics*, 4(1), 47–55. doi: 10.26599/BDMA.2020.9020015.

[7] Jyotirmoy Gope, S. K. (2017). A survey on solving cold start problem in recommender systems. *India: Int. Conf. Comput. Comm. Autom. (ICCCA2017)*.

[8] Torres-Ruiz, M., Mata, F., Zagal, R., Guzmán, G., Quintero, R., and Moreno-Ibarra, M. (2020). A recommender system to generate museum itineraries applying augmented reality and social-sensor mining techniques. *Virt. Reality*, 24, 175–189.

[9] Biehler, R. and Fleischer, Y. (2021). Introducing students to machine learning with decision trees using CODAP and Jupyter Notebooks. *Teach. Stat.*, 43, S133–S142.

[10] Abdi, M. H., Okeyo, G., and Mwangi, R. W. (2018). Matrix factorization techniques for context-aware collaborative filtering recommender systems: A survey. Computer and Information Science. *Published by Canadian Center of Science and Education.*, 11(2), 1–10, doi:10.5539/cis.v11n2p1.

[11] Srivastava, S., Haroon, M., and Bajaj, A. (2013). Web document information extraction using class attribute approach. *2013 4th Int. Conf. Comp. Comm. Technol. (ICCCT).*, 17–22.

[12] Bansari Patel, P. D. (2017). Methods of recommender system: A review. *India: Int. Conf. Innov. Inform. Emb. Comm. Sys. (ICIIECS)*.

[13] Zhang, Y., Meng, K., Kong, W., and Dong, Z. Y. (2018). Collaborative filtering-based electricity plan recommender system. *IEEE Transactions on Industrial informatics.*, 15(3), 1393–1404. doi: 10.1109/TII.2018.2856842.

[14] Anishya, F. and Kumar, S. (2015). A novel approach for travel package recommendation using Bayesian approach. *Comput. Comm. Technol. (ICCCT).*, 296–300.

[15] Jain, M. (2012). Algorithm for research paper recommendation system. *Int. J. Inform. Technol.*, 5(2), 443–445.

[16] Kaushik, S., Tiwari, S., Agarwal, C., and Goel, A. (2016). Ubiquitous crowdsourcing model for location recommender system. *J. Comp.*, 11, 463–471.[17] Zhang, Z., Lin, H., Liu, K., Wu, D., Zhang, G., and Lu, J. (2013). A hybrid fuzzy-based personalized recommender system for telecom products/services. *Inform. Sci.*, 235, 117–129.[18] Chiverton, J. (2012). Helmet presence classification with motorcycle detection and tracking. *IET Intel. Trans. Sys.*, 6(3): 259–269.

[19] Economic Impact of Travel & Tourism 2014 Annual Update: Summary. World Travel & Tourism Council.

[20] Leiper, N. (1990). Tourist attraction systems, *Ann. Tour. Res.*, 17(3), 367–384.

[21] Jen, H. C., Kuo-Ming, and Shah, N. (2013). Hybrid recommendation system for tourism. *IEEE 10th Int. Conf. e-Business Engg.*, 156–161.

[22] Wang, J. and Kawagoe, K. (2017). Ukiyo-e recommendation based on deep learning for learning Japanese art and culture. *ACM Int. Conf. Inform. Sys. Data Min.*, 119–123.

[23] Protasiewicz, J., et al. (2016). A recommender system of reviewers and experts in reviewing problems. *Knowledge-Based Sys.*, S0950705116301381.

[24] Jian, W., He, J., Kai, C., et al. (2017). Collaborative filtering and deep learning based recommendation system for cold start items. *Exp. Sys. Appl.*,, 69, 29–39.

2 An Overview of the Blockchain Technology in Healthcare Domain

Garima Singh[1,2,a] and Mohd. Haroon[1,b]

[1]Department of Computer Science & Engineering, Integral University, Lucknow, India

[2]Department of CSIT, KIET Group of Institutions, Delhi NCR, Ghaziabad, India

Abstract

In recent years, there has been a surge of interest in integrating blockchain technology into the healthcare sector. This cutting-edge technology has the potential to mitigate a multitude of challenges associated with electronic health record (EHR) systems. This study's primary objective is to provide a comprehensive survey of the existing body of research concerning the use of blockchain in healthcare. We have meticulously reviewed 144 articles that address the significance and limitations of blockchain technology in improving healthcare operations. We aim to spotlight the diverse array of applications for blockchain within the healthcare domain, simultaneously illuminating the challenges that require further exploration. The paper initiates an extensive examination of blockchain technology, elucidating its fundamental features. It subsequently undertakes a thorough analysis of the selected articles, accentuating the prevailing research themes within blockchain-driven healthcare systems. Following this, we delineate the principal domains where blockchain can be effectively applied and the solutions it offers to enhance healthcare systems. In the closing discussion section, we furnish valuable insights into the constraints, challenges, and prospective avenues for future research in this domain.

Keywords: Healthcare, blockchain, electronic health record, patient monitoring, medical data security

1. Introduction

Electronic health record (EHR) systems have completely changed the way healthcare works. They've taken patient records and put them into digital form, making it easier way to manage medical information [1]. This means doctors and nurses can quickly access important details about patients, which has boosted how they make decisions and care for patients. EHR systems also make it easy for authorized folks to share information, improving the way care is coordinated. Meanwhile, some problems come along with the benefits such as interoperability (making different EHR systems work together),

[a]gsingh@student.iul.ac.in, [b]mharoon@iul.ac.in

data accuracy (keeping the information correct), data privacy (keeping personal stuff safe), and data security (making sure no one unauthorized gets their hands on the data) [2]. Interoperability can make it tough for different systems to share info smoothly, which can affect patient care [3]. Mistakes in data entry or problems with the system can mess up the accuracy of the data, leading to medical errors. And, when patient data is kept in one central place, it can be at risk of breaches and unauthorized access, which is bad for patient privacy [4]. Healthcare data breaches can be really bad news for both patients and healthcare providers. To deal these problems, this review paper looks at how blockchain technology might help. Blockchain is a secure and decentralized system for storing and sharing EHR data [6]. It makes records super hard to tamper with and gives patients more control over their health information. Exploring how blockchain can work with EHR systems could be a game-changer, solving these tricky challenges in healthcare and making patient care, privacy, and data security better.

This research article will highlight the following questions:

RQ1. To explore the impact of EHR systems on the healthcare industry and how they've transformed the way we deliver healthcare and enhance patient care.

RQ2. To explore the primary challenges of EHR systems, particularly when it comes to making these systems collaborate effectively, maintaining data accuracy, protecting personal information, and ensuring robust security.

RQ3. To study whether blockchain technology could be a practical solution to enhance data security and safeguard patient privacy in EHR systems.

RQ4. The study of the practical implications and assess the feasibility of implementing blockchain technology on a broad scale within healthcare institutions for EHR systems.

2. EHR: Electronic Health Record Systems

An EHR is like a digital version of your complete medical history and health information [7]. Think of it as a high-tech file that stores everything about your health and treatment electronically. Electronic health records are designed to be more user-friendly and convenient in comparison to traditional health record data [8]. There are several advantages to this digital format over old-fashioned paper-based medical records [9].

Simple access: Authorized healthcare providers can easily access your complete medical history, test findings, and treatment plans from several locations – thanks to EHRs. This implies that your medical team will be able to better organize your care.

Efficiency: EHRs provide more efficiency to the users as they provide ease with various day-to-day tasks like scheduling appointments and handling bills. The paperwork needed for healthcare data management has been reduced, making it simpler for healthcare providers to manage your records in digital format.

Better patient care: Electronic health records can give healthcare providers the tools they need to make well-informed decisions. They can see your complete health profile, and medical history, which leads to more accurate diagnoses and treatment plans.

Improved collaboration: Medical professionals and different hospitals can work in collaboration to provide more healthcare services. EHRs are built to share information with other healthcare systems and organizations, making it easier for your data to travel with you as you move through the healthcare system.

Privacy: EHRs provide more privacy as compared to other forms of healthcare data management systems. They have strong security measures in place, like encryption and access controls, to keep your sensitive information safe and secure from the outside breach.

Refined decisions: EHRs provide various helpful tools for healthcare decision-makers. They can give reminders about preventive care, alerts about potential drug interactions, and follow clinical guidelines. All of these help your healthcare providers make decisions based on solid evidence. This analysis is also useful in keeping data patterns for future research on a particular disease or medicine.

Data insights: Because of their adaptability, EHRs can be used to administer public health initiatives and track medical trends. This is essential for managing chronic disorders, keeping track of diseases, and enhancing public health in general.

Electronic health records do pose some unique challenges [10]. These challenges encompass worries regarding the privacy of your data, the necessity of ensuring seamless compatibility between various systems, and the requirement of training healthcare professionals to effectively utilize new technology. EHRs have evolved into an indispensable component of contemporary healthcare. They are extensively employed in hospitals, clinics, and medical practices across the board to enhance patient care and optimize the efficiency of healthcare operations [11].

3. Various Issues in the Electronic Health Record System

Electronic health record systems are essential to the modern healthcare environment because they offer several benefits such as improved patient care, streamlined workflows, and efficient data administration (Table 2.1).

3.1. Security concerns in current EHR systems

A plethora of private and sensitive patient data, including test results, medical histories, and personal information, are stored in EHR systems. Preserving this information is essential. Nonetheless, there are important security concerns that EHR system suppliers and healthcare organizations must address.

a. *Data breaches:* When unauthorized individuals get access to EHR systems, they may steal patient data. These breaches can lead to serious problems like identity theft and medical fraud. Sadly, the healthcare field is a big target for cyberattacks [12]. Cybercriminals find health data even more valuable on the dark web compared to financial information because it's useful for fraud and stealing someone's identity in the long run.

Table 2.1: Various issues in the current EHR system

Category	Specific concerns
3.1 Security concerns	Data breaches Unauthorized access Data integrity
3.2 Interoperability challenges	Lack of standardization Fragmented data
3.3 Data ownership and control	Patient empowerment Consent management
3.4 Auditability and transparency	Data provenance Regulatory compliance

b. *Unauthorized access:* Unauthorized access is when people within the healthcare organization like employees or contractors, get into patient records without the right permission. This can happen because someone wasn't careful, got curious, or had harmful intentions [13]. Unauthorized access breaches patient privacy and could lead to unethical or even illegal use of the data. It's a breach of trust and privacy.

c. *Data integrity:* Data integrity is a big deal in EHR systems. It's all about making sure the information in the records is correct and stays that way. When people make unauthorized changes or mess with the records, it can be dangerous [14]. Imagine having the wrong medical details – it could lead to the wrong treatment or diagnosis, and that's a serious problem that could even be life-threatening. So, it's crucial that the data is accurate and doesn't get tampered with.

It's crucial to address these security concerns to uphold patient trust and follow healthcare regulations, like the Health Insurance Portability and Accountability Act (HIPAA) in the United States. To tackle these worries, healthcare organizations and the folks who provide EHR systems need to put effort into strong security measures, make sure their staff knows how to keep things safe, and regularly check for vulnerabilities in security.

One thing to keep in mind is that cybersecurity in healthcare is an ongoing challenge. The importance of keeping patient data secure in EHR systems keeps changing as new threats come up. So, it's vital to keep up with the latest ways to make things safe and use new technologies to protect patient data and keeps their trust, all while following the rules and regulations.

3.2. *Interoperability challenges in current EHR systems*

The healthcare industry has faced some real challenges when it comes to making different EHR systems work together. Two big issues in these challenges are the lack of standardization and fragmented data. In this section, we will discuss the problems in detail.

a. *Lack of standardizations:* One major issue with EHR systems is that there is no standard way for them to share and exchange health information, therefore they aren't all operating on the same page. As a result, data created in one EHR system may not be compatible with another. This "speaking the same language" barrier might impede the efficient flow of patient data between various systems, resulting in less effective healthcare delivery.

b. *Fragmented data:* The dispersion of patient data in EHR systems is another major issue. To deal with these challenges of making different EHR systems work together, healthcare organizations, policymakers, and the companies that make EHR systems are teaming up to create rules and systems that help share health information securely. They've come up with things like Fast Healthcare Interoperability Resources (FHIR) and the Health Level Seven International (HL7) standards, which have become important for making data flow smoothly between different systems [15].

3.3. *Data ownership and control in current EHR systems*

Data ownership and control within EHR systems play a pivotal role in the realm of healthcare informatics. Ensuring that patients have a say in how their medical data is used, as well as who can access it, is vital for upholding trust and privacy in the healthcare field. In this discussion, we'll delve into the ideas of patient empowerment and consent management within EHR systems.

a. *Patient empowerment:* Patient empowerment is all about putting patients in the driver's seat when it comes to their healthcare data and decisions. In the world of EHR systems, this concept is incredibly important for following key reasons:

Data access: Patients ought to be able to view their EHRs. It's like having the keys to your medical history. This gives patients the knowledge they need about their health status and ongoing treatments. After all, it's your health, and you should have access to the information [16].

Data correction and updates: Mistakes happen, even in medical records. Patients should be able to ask for corrections or updates if they spot errors in their EHRs. This isn't just about accuracy; it's about making sure your records tell the right story.

Data sharing: Who gets to see your health records? Well, you should have a say in that too. Patients should be able to decide who can peek at their EHR data, whether it's healthcare providers, family members, or others they trust. This is especially important for people managing chronic conditions or caregivers who need access.

Informed consent: Sometimes, your health data is used for research or public health studies. In those cases, you should be informed about what's happening and give your clear consent. Your data, your choice.

This patient empowerment is all about giving you control over your healthcare journey and making sure your voice is heard in the world of EHRs [17]. Patient empowerment and consent management are fundamental in granting patients control over their healthcare data, enabling them to make informed decisions about how it's utilized. EHR systems must be developed and put into practice with these principles at their core, as they are vital in preserving patient trust and privacy within the healthcare environment.

b. *Consent management:* Consent management in EHR systems is like a digital permission slip for your healthcare data. It's a big deal because it's all about respecting your choices and keeping your health information private [18, 19].

Informed consent: Before anyone can peek at your EHR data, you should know why they want to, who they are, and what they're going to do with it. It's like being told the whole story before you agree to anything [20].

Granular consent: You should be the boss of your data. This means you can say "yes" or "no" for different things – like sharing for treatment, research, or only with specific healthcare folks. It's your data, your rules.

Revocable consent: Change your mind? No problem. You can take back your consent at any time. It's like having a control switch – you decide who gets to see your info, even after you say "yes."

Consent auditing: EHR systems should keep a record of who asked for your data and when you said "yes" or "no." This way, everything is transparent, and people are held accountable for how they use your data.

In a nutshell, consent management is all about giving you the power to decide who can access your healthcare data and what they can do with it. It's your data, and it should stay that way.

3.4. Auditability and transparency in current EHR systems

Within EHR systems, auditability and transparency are bedrock principles that safeguard data integrity, accountability, and regulatory adherence. In this section, we will explore the concepts of data provenance and regulatory compliance in modern EHR systems, drawing upon pertinent references to shed light on these essential aspects.

a. *Data provenance:* Data provenance pertains to the lineage and historical trail of data, encompassing details about its creation, alterations, and the entities responsible for these changes [21, 22]. In EHR systems, data provenance holds significant importance for the following reasons:

Data integrity: It's crucial to know the origins of data and how it has been handled to maintain its accuracy and integrity. This understanding aids in detecting and rectifying errors or inconsistencies in the records.

Accountability: Data provenance facilitates the tracing of individuals who have accessed or modified specific health records. This accountability proves invaluable, especially in situations involving data breaches or unauthorized access.

Research and decision support: In the realm of healthcare, data provenance is a cornerstone for research and decision support systems. It guarantees that the data used is trustworthy and dependable, which is paramount for making informed decisions and advancing medical research.

Legal and ethical compliance: Data provenance is indispensable in upholding transparency and accountability within the framework of medical ethics and legal obligations. It ensures that healthcare data handling adheres to regulatory and ethical standards.

b. *Regulatory compliance:* In the realm of EHR systems, regulatory compliance is the cornerstone of adherence to laws, standards, and regulations that govern the utilization, storage, and sharing of healthcare data. The significance of regulatory compliance extends to several crucial facets which are as follows:

Patient privacy: Compliance with regulations like the Health Insurance Portability and Accountability Act (HIPAA) in the United States is a safeguard that ensures the confidentiality and security of patient data. It's all about respecting and protecting an individual's right to privacy [23].

Data security: Regulations typically establish stringent standards for data security. This is paramount for shielding EHRs from unauthorized access or potential data breaches, ensuring that sensitive healthcare information remains protected.

Interoperability: Regulatory compliance extends to interoperability standards, enabling EHR systems to communicate with one another seamlessly. This fosters efficient data exchange and accessibility across the healthcare landscape, ultimately benefiting patients and healthcare providers.

Legal obligations: Healthcare providers and organizations are bound by regulatory requirements that, when met, prevent legal ramifications, and uphold public trust. Compliance with these regulations is not just a legal necessity but also a means of ensuring the ethical and responsible management of healthcare data.

Data provenance and regulatory compliance stand as pivotal elements in enhancing auditability and transparency within EHR systems. These elements play a pivotal role in upholding data integrity, fostering accountability, and ensuring strict adherence to both legal and ethical standards. The culmination of these efforts significantly bolsters the quality and dependability of healthcare information.

4. Need for Blockchain in the Healthcare Domain

4.1. *Blockchain technology*

Blockchain technology has garnered significant interest for its potential to revolutionize numerous industries. It is renowned for its fundamental attributes, which include decentralization, immutability, and cryptographic security [24].

4.2. Addressing security concerns

4.2.1 Data encryption and access control

Blockchain technology provides robust security measures for sensitive data. It enables the encryption of sensitive information, ensuring that only authorized individuals or entities can access it. Blockchain systems are not complete without access control measures, which improve overall security and data privacy [25].

4.2.2. Immutable records

Immutability is a fundamental feature of blockchain technology that guarantees that data cannot be withdrawn or changed once it has been saved. This functionality is particularly useful in supply chain management and healthcare settings, where data integrity is critical [26] (Table 2.2).

Table 2.2: Overview of blockchain technology

Aspect	Explanation	Reference
Decentralization	Blockchain operates on a decentralized network of nodes, ensuring resilience to censorship and tampering. The consensus mechanism (e.g., PoW or PoS) ensures trust within the network	[25] Nakamoto, S. (2008). Bitcoin, A peer-to-peer electronic cash system
Immutability	Data recorded on the blockchain cannot be altered or deleted. Immutability is achieved through cryptographic hashing, with each block referencing the previous one creating a chain of blocks. Any change in one block would require the consensus of the network. ensuring high security	[26] Merkle, M. (1987). A digital signature based on a conventional encryption function
Cryptographic security	Blockchain uses cryptographic techniques, including public and private keys, digital signatures and cryptographic hashes, to secure transactions, ensuring data integrity, authentication and confidentiality	[27] Antonopoulos, A. M. (2014). Mastering bitcoin, unlocking digital cryptocurrencies

4.2.3. Consent management with smart contracts

Smart contracts are self-executing contracts that are integrated into blockchain technology and are essential for process automation and consent management. These agreements are used to ensure that data is used only with the data owner's express consent [27].

4.3. Enhancing interoperability

4.3.1. Standardization via smart contracts

Multiple platforms and systems can communicate with each other thanks to smart contracts. They effectively bridge gaps between diverse stakeholders by establishing a uniform standard for data transmission. These contracts automatically enforce restrictions, which facilitates easy data movement.

4.3.2. Shared ledger for data sharing

Blockchain acts as a shared ledger, removing the need for middlemen in the sharing of data. This invention facilitates interoperability and transparency by streamlining cross-organizational transactions.

4.4. Data ownership and control

4.4.1. Patient-centric records
Blockchain technology facilitates the creation of EHRs that are patient-centric in the healthcare industry. Patients have authority over their information, and they can restrict access to only reputable medical professionals.

4.4.2. Granular control and consent management
Data owners can ensure fine-grained control over their data by granting granular permissions thanks to blockchain technology. This degree of control is especially important in the healthcare industry and other fields where data is sensitive.

4.5. Auditability and transparency

4.5.1. Provenance and traceability
A transparent record of transactions is produced by the transparency and immutability of blockchain technology. With its ability to streamline asset, data, and product history tracking, this ledger is a great tool for supply chain management and the food business.

4.5.2. Adherence to data regulations
Blockchain technology has the potential to greatly enhance adherence to data protection laws. Since every action is auditable and recorded on the blockchain, it is especially applicable to sectors where data privacy is of utmost importance.

5. Comparative Analysis of Various Blockchain Methods

The healthcare industry has shown a great deal of interest in blockchain technology because of its potential to improve data security, interoperability, and transparency. Blockchain can be utilized for healthcare applications in a variety of ways. A comparison of a few of these techniques is shown in this section.

a. *Types of blockchain:* There are primarily four main types of blockchains, broadly categorized into permissioned and permissionless blockchains.

    Public blockchains: These are accessible to all parties and provide a high degree of decentralization and transparency. They may be appropriate for healthcare applications such as supply chain management, clinical trials, and patient data sharing even if they are less private (Figure 2.1).

    Private blockchains: These permission-based systems are frequently utilized in healthcare consortiums to guarantee that only individuals with the proper authorization can access and verify data. For sensitive medical data, this may be recommended as it improves privacy.

    Hybrid blockchains: By combining elements of public and private blockchains, they allow for a customized approach to control and access according to particular needs. A private blockchain is usually used for specialized purposes or secure data storage, whereas a public blockchain acts as a permissionless layer for interactions with outside parties. This hybrid architecture is flexible enough to fit a range of application needs by finding a compromise between privacy and transparency.

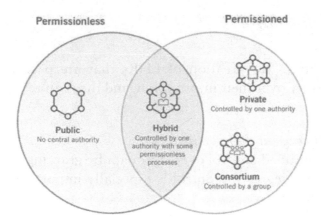

Figure 2.1: Types of blockchain.

    Consortium blockchains: They operate as partially decentralized networks where a pre-existing coalition of entities or institutions collaboratively governs the blockchain. This structure offers a high degree of decentralization, promotes confidence among participants, and maintains access control through a small core of dependable individuals.

b. *Consensus mechanisms:* Consensus techniques guarantee that all participants concur on the authenticity of transactions, they are crucial for preserving the integrity and security of blockchain networks. Blockchain technology uses a variety of consensus methods, each with special benefits and features. The functioning of blockchain networks depends on blockchain algorithms. Every algorithm has a unique combination of benefits and features (Table 2.3).

Table 2.3: Comparative analysis of various blockchain algorithms

Blockchain algorithm	Consensus mechanism	Key features	Use cases	References
Proof of work (PoW)	Nakamoto consensus	Energy-intensive, security through computation	Bitcoin, Ethereum (transitioning to PoS)	Bitcoin Whitepaper, Ethereum Yellow Paper
Proof of stake (PoS)	Various	Energy-efficient, validators stake tokens	Ethereum 2.0, Cardano, Algorand	Ethereum Research, Cardano documentation, Algorand documentation
Delegated proof of stake (DPoS)	Modified PoS	Small set of elected validators, faster but more centralized	EOS, TRON, BitShares	EOS whitepaper, TRON whitepaper, BitShares documentation
Proof of authority (PoA)	Fixed validators	Identity-based consensus, high security	VeChain, POA network	VeChain whitepaper, POA network documentation
Proof of space (PoSpace)	Storage-based	Relies on storage space rather than computation	Chia network, Burstcoin	Chia network documentation, Burstcoin documentation
Proof of capacity (PoC)	Storage-based	Uses available storage space for consensus	Filecoin, Storj	Filecoin documentation, Storj whitepaper

(continued)

Table 2.3: Continued

Blockchain algorithm	Consensus mechanism	Key features	Use cases	References
Proof of history (PoH)	Time-based	Enhances network synchronization and security	Solana	Solana Documentation
Byzantine fault tolerance (BFT)	Agreement Algorithm	Fast, suitable for permissioned networks	Hyperledger Fabric, Corda	Hyperledger Fabric Documentation, Corda Documentation
Practical byzantine fault tolerance (PBFT)	Improved BFT	High throughput, low energy consumption	Ripple (XRP)	Ripple consensus whitepaper
Honey badger BFT	Asynchronous BFT	High throughput, asynchronous consensus	Various blockchain research	Honey badger BFT Paper
Tendermint (BFT-based)	BFT-like	Fast finality, suitable for various applications	Cosmos, Binance Smart chain	Cosmos documentation, Binance Smart Chain Docs
Raft	Agreement algorithm	Simplicity and fault tolerance	Some permissioned blockchains	Raft paper

- *Proof of work (PoW):* To validate transactions and safeguard the network, PoW depends on powerful computers and energy-intensive mining. To add a new block to the chain, miners compete to solve challenging mathematical challenges. Although it offers security, this technology uses a lot of electricity.
- *Proof of stake (PoS):* By using validators who are selected to create new blocks based on the quantity of cryptocurrency tokens they "stake," or retain, PoS substitutes energy-intensive mining. It promotes token holding for network security and is more energy efficient.
- *The PoW and PoS:* While PoS is energy-efficient and promotes token holding, PoW uses a lot of energy.
- *Delegated proof of stake (DPoS):* DPoS employs a small, elected group of validators to confirm transactions, leading to faster block creation. However, it tends to be more centralized as these validators are chosen through voting or appointment. It uses elected validators for speed but is more centralized.
- *Proof of authority (PoA):* PoA relies on a small set of approved validators, often identified by name or institution, ensuring high security and efficiency. It is commonly used in private or consortium blockchains. It is highly secure with identified validators.
- *Proof of space (PoSpace) and Proof of capacity (PoC):* These algorithms use available storage space on participants' devices for consensus, making them eco-friendly alternatives to PoW. They are often employed in decentralized storage solutions. These algorithms use storage space for consensus, making them more eco-friendly.
- *Proof of history (PoH):* PoH adds a chronological record to the blockchain, improving network security and synchronization. It offers a foundation for time-stamping events and aids in the prevention of assaults. It features improved security and network synchronization.

- *Byzantine fault tolerance (BFT)*: BFT algorithms, particularly in permissioned networks, offer quick and effective consensus. They guarantee great throughput and security since they are built to withstand byzantine faults.
- *Practical byzantine fault tolerance (PBFT)*: An improved form of BFT, PBFT provides low energy usage and great throughput [5]. It is a good option for different kinds of permissioned blockchain uses.
- *BFT and PBFT*: Offer high throughput and are perfect for permissioned networks.
- *HoneyBadgerBFT*: This asynchronous BFT consensus technique provides asynchronous consensus and excellent throughput. It is very useful for different blockchain experiments and research projects. This is appropriate for a range of applications because it provides asynchronous consensus.
- *Tendermint (BFT-based)*: Tendermint combines BFT-like consensus with fast finality, making it suitable for various applications where quick confirmation of transactions is important.
- *Raft*: Raft is known for its simplicity and fault tolerance. It is often used in permissioned blockchains where a straightforward consensus algorithm is preferred.

Algorithm selection is influenced by a number of variables, including centralization issues, energy efficiency, network goals, and security needs. Certain blockchains may even employ customized consensus processes or hybrid models that are suited to their particular requirements.

c. *Smart contracts:* Smart contracts are self-executing agreements that have the parties' stipulations encoded directly into the code. Operating on blockchain technology, they automatically carry out, uphold, or assist in contract negotiations upon the fulfillment of pre-determined criteria or events.

Code-based agreements: The terms and conditions that regulate the agreement are outlined in smart contracts, which are expressed in code. These pre-determined guidelines are automatically applied when the terms of the contract are fulfilled.

Automation: Smart contracts are self-executing once they are set up on a blockchain; hence, no human involvement or middlemen are needed. When the criteria are met, they automatically carry out the designated tasks.

Trust and transparency: Blockchain networks, which offer a high degree of trust and transparency, are the operating system for smart contracts. Since transactions and contract execution are documented on the public ledger, they are auditable and impervious to tampering.

Decentralization: To minimize the need for centralized authorities, smart contracts are usually implemented on decentralized blockchains. The security and immutability of the contracts are enhanced by this decentralization.

Immutable: Once a smart contract is deployed, its code and execution logic are immutable. This ensures that the terms of the contract cannot be altered by any party after deployment.

Ethereum: Offers robust, turing-complete smart contracts but can be slower and costlier due to the gas fees.

Hyperledger fabric: Provides a modular and scalable approach for smart contracts, suitable for complex healthcare workflows and applications (Table 2.4).

Table 2.4: Comparative analysis of various methods in public and private blockchain

Feature	Public blockchains	Private blockchains
Transparency	High transparency and decentralization	Permissioned, limited transparency
Consensus mechanism	Typically PoW (slower, resource-intensive)	Often PoS (more energy-efficient)
Smart contracts	Ethereum (robust, slower, higher cost)	Hyperledger fabric (modular, scalable)
Data interoperability	Promotes interoperability through standardized data formats and APIs	Promotes interoperability through multi chain architecture
Privacy and security	Less private; privacy-preserving technologies needed	Enhanced privacy and access control
Scalability	Can be a challenge; need solutions like sharding, sidechains	More control over scalability
Regulatory compliance	Compliance can be complex; adapt to regulations like HIPAA, GDPR	Easier compliance with tailored rules
Tokenization	Can be used to incentivize data sharing	Incentives can be managed with more control
Costs and energy efficiency	Higher costs and energy consumption	More cost-effective and efficient
User experience	User-friendly interfaces and workflows	Tailored to the needs of participants

6. Existing applications of blockchain in the healthcare domain

Blockchain technology is finding increasing utility within the healthcare sector due to its capability to improve data security, interoperability, and transparency. Several current applications of blockchain in healthcare are as follows:

6.1. Estonia's e-health system

Estonia's prominence in digital governance is exemplified by its cutting-edge e-health system. This comprehensive and secure digital health infrastructure places patients at the center and includes EHRs along with a range of e-services for healthcare management. Notable features and implementations are shown in Table 2.5.

Table 2.5: Features of Estonia's e-health system

Aspect	Description
a. Electronic health records (EHRs)	Estonian citizens have access to a secure and centralized electronic health records (EHRs) system, safeguarded by a secure digital identity. These EHRs comprehensively include a patient's complete medical history, prescriptions, test results, and other health-related data. Both patients and healthcare providers can securely access and update this information
b. Digital ID	Estonians utilize a digital identity card for access to their health records and other e-government services. This card ensures secure authentication and data protection
c. Data interoperability	The e-health system prioritizes data interoperability, enabling healthcare professionals to access patient information across different providers, thereby promoting well-coordinated patient care

(continued)

Table 2.5: Continued

Aspect	Description
d. E-prescriptions	Estonia's e-health system has optimized the issuance of electronic prescriptions. Patients receive their prescriptions digitally, and they can conveniently collect their medications from any pharmacy, effectively reducing paperwork and minimizing prescription errors
e. Telemedicine	Estonia has embraced telemedicine, allowing patients to participate in remote consultations with healthcare professionals, which is particularly valuable in rural areas
f. Patient access	Patients have the capability to access and view their health records, test results, and prescription history online. Furthermore, they can grant temporary access to healthcare providers when necessary
g. Blockchain in healthcare	Estonia has embarked on the application of block chain technology in healthcare to ensure the utmost security and integrity of health data

MedRec by MIT: MedRec is an innovative EHR system developed by the Massachusetts Institute of Technology (MIT) and based on blockchain technology. Its primary objective is to empower patients with greater control over their health data while simultaneously ensuring privacy and security [28–30]. The key feature of the system is shown in Table 2.6.

Table 2.6: Features of MedRec

Aspect	Description
a. Patient control	MedRec empowers patients to exercise control over their health records, enabling them to dictate who has access to their data and the specific purposes for which it can be accessed
b. Blockchain technology	MedRec utilizes blockchain technology to secure health data, ensuring transparency and immutability. This robust security mechanism not only safeguards data integrity but also reduces the risk of unauthorized access
c. Privacy preserving smart contracts	MedRec employs smart contracts to efficiently manage data access permissions and data sharing. These smart contracts offer granular control, allowing patients to specify who can access specific health data and for what purposes
d. Research opportunities	MedRec actively facilitates medical research by permitting researchers to request access to aggregated and anonymized health data This approach fosters research opportunities while preserving individual privacy

6.2. Medicalchain

Medchain is a groundbreaking healthcare platform based on blockchain technology, specifically designed to improve the management and security of medical records. The key features of this system includes the following [31, 32]:

Patient-driven access: Medicalchain empowers patients by giving them full control over their health data, allowing them to grant access to healthcare providers as needed.

Telemedicine: The platform seamlessly integrates telemedicine, making it possible for patients to engage in remote consultations with healthcare professionals.

Secure and immutable records: Medicalchain ensures the security and immutability of health records by storing them on the blockchain. This guarantees the integrity of the stored data.

Health passport: Medicalchain introduces a unique feature known as the "health passport," which enables patients to compile their complete medical history. This history can be conveniently shared with healthcare providers worldwide, streamlining patient care (Table 2.7).

Health tokens (MedTokens): Medicalchain employs its cryptocurrency, known as MedTokens, to facilitate transactions within the platform. It also serves as an incentive for participants to share their health data for research purposes (Figures 2.2–2.5).

Table 2.7: Blockchain in healthcare domain

Feature	Description
1. Data security and integrity	Blockchain ensures the security and integrity of patient data through cryptographic techniques. Each data entry is cryptographically linked to the previous one, making it nearly impossible to tamper with or alter patient records. Patients can have confidence that their health data remains accurate and secure
2. Decentralization	Healthcare data is stored across a network of nodes, reducing the risk of a single point of failure. This decentralized approach enhances the resilience of healthcare systems and ensures data availability even in the face of network disruptions
3. Interoperability	Blockchain facilitates interoperability by providing a standardized format for data exchange. This is particularly important in healthcare, where information needs to be shared across various institutions and systems. Smart contracts can automate data sharing agreements
4. Consent management	Smart contracts in blockchain enable patients to have granular control over who can access their health records. They can grant or revoke access to specific healthcare providers, ensuring that data is used only with explicit consent
5. Patient-centric records	Blockchain enables the creation of patient-centric electronic health records (EHRs). Patients own their data and can carry their EHRs with them, providing healthcare providers with a comprehensive view of the patient's medical history
6. Efficient claims processing	In the insurance and billing aspects of healthcare, blockchain can streamline claims processing. It ensures that claims are validated automatically, reducing administrative overhead and potentially reducing fraudulent claims
7. Provenance and traceability	In pharmaceuticals and the supply chain, blockchain provides a transparent ledger to track the origin and movement of drugs and medical device. This feature can help ensure the authenticity and quality of healthcare products
8. Research and clinical trials	Researchers can securely access historical patient data and clinical trial results, speeding up the research process. Patients can also participate in clinical trials with greater ease, knowing their data is secure and their consent is enforced through smart contracts
9. Compliance and auditing	Blockchain records every transaction, making it easier to demonstrate compliance with date protection regulations such as HIPAA. It also simplifies the auditing process by providing a comprehensive and immutable audit trail
10. Reduced costs	Blockchain can potentially reduce costs associated with data storage, intermediaries, and administrative tasks. It streamlines processes and minimizes the need for redundant record-keeping

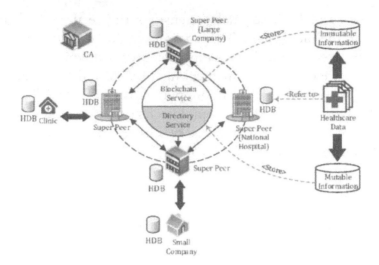

Figure 2.2: Blockchain-based EHR architecture.

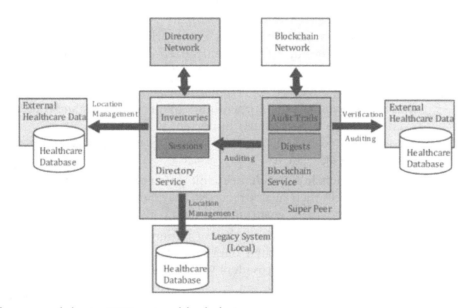

Figure 2.3: Different modules in EHR using blockchain.

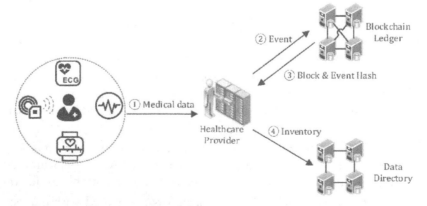

Figure 2.4: Different modules in EHR using blockchain.

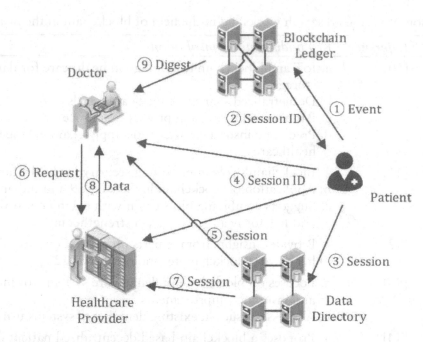

Figure 2.5: Session-based data sharing in EHR using blockchain

These case studies and implementations underscore the transformative potential of technology, particularly blockchain and secure digital identities, in reshaping the healthcare landscape by granting patients control over their health data and enhancing the efficiency of healthcare services.

7. Comparison of the Latest Research Contribution in the Field of Blockchain in Healthcare Domain

A comparison of various research works in the field of blockchain in the healthcare domain reveals diverse perspectives, methodologies, and contributions. These research works collectively demonstrate the versatility and potential of blockchain technology in the healthcare domain. While they address various aspects of healthcare, such as data security, interoperability, and privacy, they also acknowledge the challenges and obstacles that need to be overcome for successful implementation. Researchers in this field are actively exploring innovative solutions to revolutionize healthcare using blockchain technology, improving patient care and the overall healthcare ecosystem.

These contributions collectively underscore the potential advantages of blockchain technology in healthcare, encompassing data security, privacy, interoperability, and enhanced efficiency. They also indicate diverse areas warranting further exploration and advancement in the healthcare blockchain technology domain.

The research works are summarized below in Table 2.8, highlighting their key findings and areas of focus.

Furthermore, these contributions collectively span a broad spectrum of topics pertinent to blockchain technology's application in healthcare, encompassing data security, privacy, COVID-19 management, IoT integration, and related subjects. They effectively illuminate both the potential benefits and challenges associated with the integration of blockchain within healthcare systems.

Table 2.8: Comparison of various research works did in the field of blockchain in the healthcare domain

Year of publication	Reference	Key findings and contributions
2022	[40]	a. IoT and blockchain technology in healthcare for data collection and storage b. Decentralized sharing of medical records c. Patient monitoring and privacy assurance d. Predicting insurance costs and supply chain management in healthcare
2022	[41]	a. Blockchain's role in providing security for healthcare data b. Application of blockchain in COVID-19 and Indian healthcare c. Suggests combining blockchain with machine learning, AI, big data, and IoT for healthcare system strengthening
2022	[42]	a. Provides insights from experts on market opportunities and gaps in healthcare blockchain technology for 2022
2023	[43]	a. Focuses on blockchain in dental care systems for medical data storage and insurance improvements b. Addresses issues in existing dental care systems using blockchain
2022	[44]	a. Proposes a blockchain-based decentralized patient information exchange (PIE) system for secure sharing of electronic medical records (EMRs) b. Emphasizes security and privacy in managing medical data
2022	[45]	a. Conduct a systematic literature review on blockchain in healthcare from 2016 to 2021 b. Highlights blockchain's role in improving healthcare procedures, data privacy, and security c. Suggests potential areas for future research, including data protection and regulatory compliance
2023	[46]	a. Focuses on the impact of blockchain on data quality issues in healthcare b. Analyzes challenges related to blockchain adoption, operation, and technology in healthcare c. Aims to support practitioners, stakeholders, and professionals in decision-making regarding healthcare blockchain transformation projects
2022	[47]	a. Discusses the need for security mechanisms for Internet of Medical Things (IoMT) edge networks b. Highlights the role of blockchain in securing medical data during data transmission c. Emphasizes the lack of blockchain-based security mechanisms for IoMT edge networks and the importance of their development
2023	[48]	a. Explores the use of blockchain technology to harness digitized healthcare data, especially in response to the COVID-19 pandemic b. Discusses blockchain's potential in creating more efficient business processes, improving patient engagement, and generating new revenue streams in healthcare

(continued)

Table 2.8: Continued

Year of publication	Reference	Key findings and contributions
2022	[49]	a. Examines the impact and potential of blockchain, IoT, and fog computing on healthcare services in smart cities b. Identifies IoT, blockchain, and fog computing as drivers of efficiency in healthcare services c. Highlights the relevance of blockchain and fog computing in the healthcare sector for data protection, decentralized databases, data interoperability, and cost-efficient remote monitoring
2022	[50]	a. Investigates the impact of blockchain technology on value co-creation in the digital healthcare ecosystem b. Conducts a multiple case study of 32 healthcare tech companies to explore blockchain's effects on data and resource sharing, patient participation, and collaboration between professionals c. Identifies three key areas where blockchain implementation benefits value co-creation: service interaction improvement, actor engagement, and ecosystem transparency
2022	[51]	a. Proposes a blockchain consortium healthcare framework for asthma patients, aiming to manage healthcare units, patient records, insurance, and government agencies securely b. Utilizes blockchain for data security and scalability, storing encrypted patient data on the interplanetary file system (IPFS) c. Demonstrates that the proposed framework offers better transaction throughput, query delay, and security compared to existing solutions
2023	[52]	a. Discusses the role of blockchain technology in healthcare and its potential to address challenges like fragmented data, security, privacy, and interoperability b. Highlights the benefits of secure, tamper-proof storage, data interoperability, and patient data encryption in healthcare c. Advocates for a patient-centric approach using blockchain to improve healthcare data management
2022	[53]	a. Presents architecture for ensuring the privacy of health-related data within a decentralized blockchain network using encryption with RSA, ECC, and AES algorithms b. Evaluates the impact of cryptography on computational effort, memory usage, and execution time, emphasizing privacy and security c. Demonstrates increased computational effort and execution time due to encryption but justifies it for privacy and security benefits
2022	[54]	a. Discusses the potential of blockchain technology in healthcare, emphasizing its strengths in interoperability, data accuracy, security, and transparency b. Identifies weaknesses such as lack of standardization, accessibility, ownership, and change management c. Lists applications in healthcare, including revenue cycle management, physician credentialing, electronic health records, and supply chain management

(continued)

Table 2.8: Continued

Year of publication	Reference	Key findings and contributions
2022	[55]	a. Explores the role of blockchain in securely storing electronic health records (EHRs), developing deep learning algorithms, and processing healthcare data b. Supports deep neural network (DNN) analysis in healthcare and COVID-19 pandemic, proposing a smart contract procedure for feature-extracted data c. Aids in the analysis of existing diseases and guiding physicians in providing appropriate treatment
2022	[56]	a. Discusses the potential of low-cost IoT sensors within the Internet of Things (IoT) to improve healthcare, quality of goods, and supply chain efficiency using blockchain technology
2023	[57]	a. Surveys state-of-the-art blockchain work in various IoT disciplines, with a focus on healthcare b. Explores the use of blockchain in healthcare, its obstacles, and future development paths
2022	[58]	a. Proposes a blockchain-based solution for managing COVID-19 test and vaccination data with a focus on privacy and security b. Demonstrates the effectiveness of the proposed solution using ethereum smart contracts
2022	[59]	a. Presents a blockchain-assisted delay and energy-aware healthcare monitoring system in the context of wireless body area networks (WBANs) and IoT b. Addresses challenges related to QoS, security, and energy efficiency in WBAN- IoT environments
2023	[60]	a. Proposes the integration of artificial intelligence and blockchain in the metaverse to provide immersive and secure healthcare services b. Explains the architecture involving doctors, patients, and a metaverse environment represented by avatars
2023	[61]	a. Explores how blockchain technology can benefit the dental industry by enhancing data security, interoperability, and supply chain management b. Highlights the role of blockchain in empowering patients and the challenges to address for successful implementation
2023	[62]	a. Proposes a novel approach to enhancing privacy preservation in IoT-based healthcare applications using homomorphic encryption combined with blockchain technology b. Incorporates smart contracts for access control and data-sharing policies
2023	[63]	a. Presents a smart blockchain and AI-enabled system to combat the COVID-19 pandemic, focusing on radiological image analysis and secure data gathering b. Achieves high classification accuracy and provides transparency and trust in disease diagnosis

(continued)

Table 2.8: Continued

Year of publication	Reference	Key findings and contributions
2023	[64]	a. Identifies sociological, economic, and infrastructure obstacles to blockchain adoption in public health systems in developing nations b. Provides insights for decision-makers on overcoming implementation challenges
2023	[65]	a. Studies the impacts of data provenance in healthcare and GDPR-compliance-based data provenance, highlighting technologies and methodologies used to achieve data provenance
2023	[66]	a. Introduces a Federated Blockchain System (FBS) to address healthcare problems and challenges b. Validates the system's effectiveness in terms of query and writing operations
2023	[67]	a. Explores the use of blockchain technology and smart contracts in the Internet of Medical Things (IoMT) to improve efficiency, transparency, and security in e-healthcare
2023	[68]	a. Reviews the revolutionary impact of blockchain technology in emergency medicine, emphasizing data sharing and documentation b. Discusses the applications of blockchain in various emergency care scenarios

8. Challenges and Considerations

The integration of blockchain technology into healthcare encounters various substantial challenges and considerations. Scalability presents a significant issue, given the extensive nature of healthcare data and the imperative for secure storage and sharing [33]. The intricate landscape of regulatory compliance adds another layer of complexity, as healthcare is subject to rigorous privacy and security regulations. Striking a delicate balance between data transparency and patient privacy poses a further challenge, along with surmounting adoption barriers like resistance and the requisite substantial investments [34]. Factors like interoperability, data standardization, security, and the mitigation of smart contract errors are additional concerns [35]. Ensuring clear data ownership and control, effective cost management, user training, and seamless integration with legacy systems are essential components. Successful navigation of these challenges is pivotal to unlocking the potential advantages of blockchain in healthcare, encompassing enhanced data security, improved interoperability, and the empowerment of patients [36].

9. Future Prospects for Blockchain in Healthcare

9.1. Integration with healthcare IoT

The convergence of blockchain technology with healthcare Internet of Things (IoT) represents a highly promising synergy with the potential to usher in a healthcare revolution. IoT devices, including wearable fitness trackers, remote patient monitoring tools, and advanced medical equipment, generate vast streams of real-time patient data. By integrating these data sources with blockchain, a secure and decentralized framework can be established for the management and sharing of health information. The following outlines how this integration can work [37]:

Data security: IoT devices naturally gather sensitive health information. When integrated with blockchain technology, they gain an extra layer of robust security through data encryption and controlled access using smart contracts.

This guarantees that the data can only be accessed by authorized entities, be they devices or people.

Data traceability: Maintaining the integrity of data produced by Internet of Things devices is made possible by the blockchain's immutable ledger. It creates an unchangeable audit trail by logging every data, time-stamping it, and securely storing it. Retracing a patient's whole medical history via this audit trail is essential for precise diagnosis and therapy (Table 2.9).

Real-time monitoring: Blockchain makes it easier for patients and healthcare professionals to share and monitor data in real-time. For example, wearable IoT devices can continuously update a patient's vital signs on the blockchain. This allows physicians to remotely monitor a patient's condition, intervene promptly when necessary, and make informed decisions based on up-to-the-minute data.

This integration not only enhances the security and integrity of healthcare data but also enables the seamless exchange of critical information, fostering more responsive and efficient healthcare practices.

Table 2.9: Challenges and considerations

Challenge	Description	Reference
1. Scalability	Blockchain networks, especially public ones like bitcoin and ethereum, face scalability issues due to high computational requirements. This challenge becomes critical in healthcare where large amounts of data need secure storage and sharing	Tschorsch, F. and Scheuermann, B. (2016). Bitcoin and beyond: A technical survey on decentralized digital currencies. *IEEE Comm. Sur. Tutor.*, 18(3), 2084–2123
2. Regulatory compliance	Healthcare is highly regulated with strict privacy and security requirements. Blockchain can challenge existing regulatory frameworks, particularly concerning data ownership and control. Ensuring compliance is complex	Ienca, M., Vayena, E., and Blasimme, A. (2018). Big data and the black box of personalized medicine. *Med. Health Care Phil.*, 21(4), 433–447
3. Privacy concern	Privacy is a top concern in healthcare due to sensitive patient information. Blockchain is designed for security and transparency but poses privacy challenges. Balancing transparency and data protection is crucial	Azaria, A., Ekblaw, A., Vieira, T., and Lippman, A. (2016). MedRec: Using blockchain for medical data access and permission management. *2016 2ⁿᵈ Int. Conf. Open Big Data (OBD)*, 25–30
4. Adoption barriers	Adoption of blockchain in healthcare faces barriers such as the need for significant investments in infrastructure and training. Many healthcare professionals and institutions may hesitate due to complexity and uncertainty	Muhlestein, D. B. (2018). Blockchain for health data and its potential use in health IT and health care related research. ONC/NIST Use of blockchain for healthcare and research workshop

9.2. Improved patient engagement

Blockchain technology has the potential to significantly enhance patient engagement by affording individuals greater control over their health data. This empowerment can lead to a range of benefits [38].

Informed decision-making: Patients gain easy access to their complete medical history which enables them to make well-informed decision-making about their healthcare. With their health records at their fingertips, they can understand their medical conditions better and participate more actively in discussions with healthcare providers about treatment options and preventive measures.

Consent management: Through the implementation of smart contracts, patients can efficiently grant or revoke consent for specific healthcare providers or researchers to access their data. This enhanced consent management not only bolsters patient privacy but also provides patients with greater control over who can access their sensitive information.

Health records portability: Blockchain facilitates the seamless movement and sharing of health records. This portability is particularly valuable in reducing redundancy in medical tests and treatments. When patients can easily transfer their records between healthcare institutions, it streamlines the healthcare process and ensures continuity of care.

Telemedicine and remote monitoring: Patients can participate in telemedicine and remote monitoring with more confidence. Knowing that their data is securely shared with healthcare providers through blockchain, patients can engage in these digital healthcare services more effectively. This is particularly relevant in situations where remote monitoring or telemedicine is essential, such as during a pandemic or for individuals with chronic conditions.

Blockchain technology's role in patient engagement goes beyond data security and control. It empowers individuals to actively participate in their healthcare, make informed decisions, manage their consent preferences, and seamlessly move their health records. This provides a more patient-centric and efficient healthcare system.

9.3. Exploring research possibilities

Blockchain technology opens up fascinating new horizons in the field of medical research, especially concerning data sharing and clinical trials. The following section shows the advance research endeavors [39].

Enhanced data sharing: Blockchain offers a secure and efficient way to share anonymized patient data among different healthcare institutions. This promotes collaborative research efforts while safeguarding patient privacy. Researchers gain access to a broader and more diverse dataset, enriching the quality and breadth of medical research.

Streamlined clinical trials: Smart contracts, a pivotal feature of blockchain, can automate various aspects of clinical trials. This includes managing patient consent, data collection, and compensation. This automation reduces administrative burdens, ensures the integrity of data, and simplifies the clinical trial process. Both patients and researchers benefit from more efficient and transparent trials.

Tracking pharmaceuticals: Blockchain technology can be harnessed to trace the entire journey of pharmaceuticals, from their production to their consumption by patients. This end-to-end traceability guarantees the authenticity and safety of drugs, mitigating the risk of counterfeit or substandard medications entering the market. This is particularly vital for drug quality control and patient well-being.

The integration of blockchain technology in healthcare opens up exciting research opportunities. It promotes secure and collaborative data sharing, streamlines clinical trials, and enhances drug traceability, ultimately improving the quality of medical research and the safety of patients.

10. Conclusions

Blockchain technology presents innovative applications in healthcare due to its inherent encryption and decentralization features. It offers enhanced security for patients' electronic medical records facilitates the monetization of health information, improves interoperability among healthcare organizations, and aids in combating counterfeit medicines. Various healthcare sectors stand to benefit from Blockchain technology, with digital agreements powered by smart contracts being one of its most crucial applications. By eliminating intermediaries in payment processes, smart contracts can reduce costs significantly. The full potential of blockchain in healthcare hinges on the widespread adoption of complementary advanced technologies within the ecosystem, including system tracking, healthcare insurance, medication tracing, and clinical trials. Hospitals can utilize blockchain frameworks to streamline their services across their entire life cycle, incorporating device tracking. Blockchain can effectively enhance patient history management, particularly in terms of tracking and insurance mediation, thereby expediting clinical processes through optimized data maintenance. In summary, this technology has the potential to substantially enhance and eventually revolutionize how patients, physicians, and healthcare providers handle and utilize clinical records, ultimately leading to improved healthcare services. Integrating blockchain technology into existing EHR systems holds the promise of addressing several critical issues that currently plague healthcare data management. Among these potential benefits are heightened security measures, enhanced interoperability, better data ownership and control, and an improved audit trail. However, it is essential to acknowledge and address the considerable challenges and considerations that must be thoughtfully managed for a successful implementation. Looking forward, the prospects for blockchain in healthcare appear encouraging, with the potential to transform the landscape of patient data management, sharing, and security in the era of digital healthcare.

Acknowledgement

The authors wish to extend their heartfelt appreciation to the CSE department of Integral University, Lucknow, for their invaluable cooperation and support during the research process.

References

[1]   Evans, R. S. (2016). Electronic health records: then, now, and in the future. *Yearbook of medical informatics*, 25(S 01), S48–S61. DOI: 10.15265/IYS-2016-s006.

[2]   Pai, M. M. M., Ganiga, R., Pai, R. M., et al. (2021). Standard electronic health record (EHR) framework for Indian healthcare system. *Health Serv. Outcomes Res. Method.*, 21, 339–362.

[3]   Torab-Miandoab, A., Samad-Soltani, T., Jodati, A., and Rezaei-Hachesu, P. (2023). Interoperability of heterogeneous health information systems: a systematic literature review. *BMC Medical Informatics and Decision Making*, 23(1), 18. https://doi.org/10.1186/s12911-023-02115-5.

[4]   Adane, K., Gizachew, M., and Kendie, S. (2019). The role of medical data in efficient patient care delivery: A review. *Risk management and healthcare policy*, 67–73. DOI: 10.2147/RMHP.S179259.

[5]   Castro, M. and Liskov, B. (1999). Practical Byzantine fault tolerance. *OSDI*, 173–186.

[6] Han, Y., Zhang, Y., and Vermund, S. H. (2022). Blockchain technology for electronic health records. *Int. J. Environ. Res. Public Health.*, 19(23), 15577. doi: 10.3390/ijerph192315577. PMID: 36497654; PMCID: PMC9739765.

[7] Wang, W., Ferrari, D., Haddon-Hill, G., and Curcin, V. (2023). Electronic health records as source of research data. Machine Learning for Brain Disorders, 331–354. *Neuromethods*, vol 197. Humana, New York, NY. https://doi.org/10.1007/978-1-0716-3195-9_11.

[8] Archana, T., Talya, P., Dipak, K., Glen, D., Sun, X., and Vasa, C. (2021). Impact of patient access to their electronic health record: systematic review. *Informat. Health Soc. Care*, 46(2), 194–206.

[9] Ekblaw, A., Azaria, A., Halamka, J. D., and Lippman, A. (2016). A case study for blockchain in healthcare: 'MedRec' prototype for electronic health records and medical research data. *Proc. IEEE Open Big Data Conf.*, 13.

[10] Holmes, J. H., Beinlich, J., Boland, M. R., et al. (2021). Why is the electronic health record so challenging for research and clinical care? *Methods Inf. Med.*, 60(1–02), 32–48.

[11] Tsai, C. H., Eghdam, A., Davoody, N., Wright, G., Flowerday, S., and Koch, S. (2020). Effects of electronic health record implementation and barriers to adoption and use: A scoping review and qualitative analysis of the content. *Life*, 10(12), 327. https://doi.org/10.3390/life10120327.

[12] Ponemon Institute. 2020 Cost of a Data Breach Report [Online]. Available: https://www.ibm.com/security/data-breach.

[13] Ama-Amadasun, M. (2014). Technical Report by Marvin Mondale Ama-Amadasun, UGSM-Monarch Business School, Volume 1, pp 1–30. https://www.researchgate.net/publication/265793918_Preventing_Unauthorized_Access_to_Patient's_Medical_Records_A_Strategic_Approach_to_Healthcare_Centers.

[14] Vimalachandran, P., Wang, H., Zhang, Y., Heyward, B., and Whittaker, F. (2016, December). Ensuring data integrity in electronic health records: A quality health care implication. In 2016 *International Conference on Orange Technologies (ICOT)*, pp. 20–27). IEEE. doi: 10.1109/ICOT.2016.8278970.

[15] Walker, J., Pan, E., Johnston, D., Adler-Milstein, J., Bates, D. W., and Middleton, B. (2005). The value of health care information exchange and interoperability. Health Affairs, 24(5), 10.1377/hlthaff.24.w5.10.

[16] Upadhyay, S. and Hu, H. (2022). A qualitative analysis of the impact of electronic health records (EHR) on healthcare quality and safety: Clinicians' lived experiences. *Health Ser. Insights*, 15.

[17] Boumezbeur, I. and Zarour, K. (2022). Privacy preservation and access control for sharing electronic health records using blockchain technology. *Acta Informat. Pragensia*, 11, 105–122.

[18] Jaiman, V. and Urovi, V. (2020). A consent model for blockchain-based health data sharing platforms. *IEEE Acc.*, 8, 143734–143745.

[19] Tith, D., Lee, J. S., Suzuki, H., Wijesundara, W. M. A. B., Taira, N., Obi, T., and Ohyama, N. (2020). Patient consent management by a purpose-based consent model for electronic health record based on blockchain technology. *Healthcare Inform. Res.*, 26(4), 265–273.

[20] Eike-Henner, W. K. (2004). Informed consent and the security of the electronic health record (EHR): some policy considerations. *International Journal of Medical Informatics*, 73(3), 229–234, ISSN 1386-5056. https://doi.org/10.1016/j.ijmedinf.2003.11.005.

[21] D'Antonio, S. and Uccello, F. (2022, June). Data provenance for healthcare: A blockchain-based approach. In 2022 *IEEE 46th Annual Computers, Software, and Applications Conference (COMPSAC)*, pp. 1655–1660). IEEE. doi: 10.1109/COMPSAC54236.2022.00263.

[22] Margheri, A., Masi, M., Miladi, A., Sassone, V., and Rosenzweig, J. (2020). Decentralised provenance for healthcare data. *International Journal of Medical Informatics*, 141, 104197. https://doi.org/10.1016/j.ijmedinf.2020.104197.

[23] Institute of Medicine (US) Committee on Health Research and the Privacy of Health Information: The HIPAA Privacy Rule. Nass, S. J., Levit, L. A., and Gostin, L. O., editors. (2009). Beyond the HIPAA Privacy Rule: Enhancing Privacy, Improving Health Through Research. Washington (DC): National Academies Press (US). pp. 1–315.

[24] Nakamoto, S., and Bitcoin, A. (2008). A peer-to-peer electronic cash system. Bitcoin.–URL: https://bitcoin. org/bitcoin. pdf, 4(2), 15.

[25] Wen, B., Wang, Y., Ding, Y., Zheng, H., Qin, B., and Yang, C. (2023). Security and privacy protection technologies in securing blockchain applications. *Information Sciences*, 645, 119322.https://doi.org/10.1016/j.ins.2023.119322.

[26] Merkle, M. (1987, August). A digital signature based on a conventional encryption function. In *Conference on the theory and application of cryptographic techniques*, 293, 369–378. Berlin, Heidelberg: Springer Berlin Heidelberg. https://doi.org/10.1007/3-540-48184-2_32.

[27] Antonopoulos, A. M. (2014). Mastering bitcoin: Unlocking digital cryptocurrencies. A book by O'Reilly.

[28] Ekblaw, A., Azaria, A., Halamka, J. D., and Lippman, A. (2016, August). A Case Study for Blockchain in Healthcare: "MedRec" prototype for electronic health records and medical research data. In *Proceedings of IEEE open & big data conference*, 13, 13.

[29] Nchinda, N., Cameron, A., Retzepi, K. and Lippman, A. (2019). MedRec: A network for personal information distribution. 637–641.

[30] Azaria, A., Ekblaw, A., Vieira, T., and Lippman, A. (2016, August). MedRec: Using blockchain for medical data access and permission management. In 2016 *2nd international conference on open and big data (OBD)*, (pp. 25–30). IEEE. doi: 10.1109/OBD.2016.11.

[31] Shen, B., Guo, J., and Yang, Y. (2019). MedChain: Efficient healthcare data sharing via blockchain. *Appl. Sci.*, 9(6), 1207.

[32] Daraghmi, E.-Y., Daraghmi, Y.-A. and Yuan, S.-M. (2019). MedChain: A design of blockchain-based system for medical records access and permissions management. *IEEE Acc.*, 7, 164595–164613.

[33] Mazlan, A. A., Daud, S. M., Sam, S. M., Abas, H., Rasid, S. Z. A., & Yusof, M. F. (2020). Scalability challenges in healthcare blockchain system—a systematic review. *IEEE access*, 8, 23663–23673.doi: 10.1109/ACCESS.2020.2969230.

[34] Sharma, M. and Joshi, S. (2021). Barriers to blockchain adoption in health-care industry: an Indian perspective. *J. Global Oper. Strat. Sourc.*, ahead-of-print. 10.1108/JGOSS-06-2020-0026.

[35] Sun, Z., Han, D., Li, D. et al. (2022). A blockchain-based secure storage scheme for medical information. *J. Wireless Com. Netw.*, 2022, 40.

[36] Laure, A. and Martha, B. (2018). Blockchain for health data and its potential use in health IT and health care related research. ONC/NIST Use of Blockchain for Healthcare and Research Workshop.

[37] Wang, Y., Che, T., Zhao, X., Zhou, T., Zhang, K., and Hu, X. (2022). A blockchain-based privacy information security sharing scheme in industrial internet of things. *Sensors*, 22(9), 3426. https://doi.org/10.3390/s22093426.

[38] Roehrs, A., Da Costa, C. A., da Rosa Righi, R., and De Oliveira, K. S. F. (2017). Personal health records: a systematic literature review. *Journal of medical Internet research*, 19(1), e5876. doi: 10.2196/jmir.5876.

[39] Benchoufi, I., Ravaud, E., and Evangelista, J. C. Blockchain technology for improving clinical research quality. *Trials*, 18(1), 1–5. https://doi.org/10.1186/s13063-017-2035-z.

[40] Sivasankari, B. and Varalakshmi, P. (2022). Blockchain and IoT Technology in healthcare: A review. *Stud. Health Technol. Informat.*, 294, 277–278.

[41] Srivastava, S., Pant, M., Jauhar, S. K., and Nagar, A. K. (2022). Analyzing the prospects of blockchain in healthcare industry. *Comput. Math. Methods Med.*, 2022, 3727389.

[42] Conway, D., Venkataraman, M., Laverick, D., Pelin, G., and Hasselgren, A. (2022). Blockchain in healthcare today: 2022 predictions. *Blockchain Healthcare Today*, 6, 245. doi: 10.30953/bhty.v6.245.

[43] Mokhamed, T., Talib, M. A., Moufti, M. A., Abbas, S., and Khan, F. (2023). The potential of blockchain technology in dental healthcare: A literature review. *Sensors (Basel)*, 23(6), 3277.

[44] Lee, S., Kim, J., Kwon, Y., Kim, T., and Cho, S. (2022). Privacy preservation in patient information exchange systems based on blockchain: System design study. *J. Med. Internet Res.*, 24(3), e29108.

[45] Saeed, H., Malik, H., Bashir, U., Ahmad, A., Riaz, S., Ilyas, M., Bukhari, W. A., and Khan, M. I. A. Blockchain technology in healthcare: A systematic review. *PLoS One*, 17(4), e0266462.

[46] AbuHalimeh, A. and Ali, O. (2023). Comprehensive review for healthcare data quality challenges in blockchain technology. *Front. Big Data*, 6, 1173620.

[47] Pelekoudas-Oikonomou, F., Zachos, G., Papaioannou, M., de Ree, M., Ribeiro, J. C., Mantas, G., and Rodriguez, J. (2022). Blockchain-based security mechanisms for IoMT edge networks in IoMT-based healthcare monitoring systems. *Sensors (Basel)*, 22(7), 2449.

[48] Shine, T., Thomason, J., Khan, I., Maher. M., Kurihara, K., and El-Hassan, O. (2023). Blockchain in healthcare: 2023 predictions from around the globe. *Blockchain Healthcare Today*.

[49] Kamruzzaman, M. M., Yan, B., Sarker, M. N. I., Alruwaili, O., Wu, M., and Alrashdi, I. (2022). Blockchain and fog computing in IoT-driven healthcare services for smart cities. *J. Healthcare Engg.*, 2022, 9957888.

[50] Russo-Spena, T., Mele, C., Cavacece, Y., Ebraico, S., Dantas, C., Roseiro, P., and van Staalduinen, W. (2022). Enabling value co-creation in healthcare through blockchain technology. *Int. J. Environ. Res. Public Health*, 20(1), 67.

[51] Farooq, M. S., Suhail, M., Qureshi, J. N., Rustam, F., de la Torre Díez, I., Mazon, J. L. V., Rodríguez, C. L., and Ashraf, I. Consortium framework using blockchain for asthma healthcare in pandemics. *Sensors (Basel)*, 22(21), 8582.

[52] Singh, Y., Jabbar, M. A., Kumar Shandilya, S. S., Vovk, O., and Hnatiuk, Y. (2023). Exploring applications of blockchain in healthcare: road map and future directions. *Front. Public Health*, 11, 1229386.

[53] de Moraes Rossetto, A. G., Sega, C., and Leithardt, V. R. Q. (2022). An architecture for managing data privacy in healthcare with blockchain. *Sensors (Basel)*, 22(21), 8292.

[54] Poquiz, W. A. (2022). Blockchain technology in healthcare: An analysis of strengths. *Weaknesses Opport. Threats. J. Healthcare Manag.*, 67(4), 244–253.

[55] Mallikarjuna, B., Shrivastava, G., and Sharma, M. (2022). Blockchain technology: A DNN token-based approach in healthcare and COVID-19 to generate extracted data. *Expert Sys.*, 39(3), e12778.

[56] Altay, A., Learney, R., Güder, F., and Dincer, C. (2022). Sensors in blockchain. *Trends Biotechnol.*, 40(2), 141–144.

[57] Almalki, J. (2023). State-of-the-art research in blockchain of things for healthcare. *Arabian Journal for Science and Engineering*, 1-29.49, 3163–3191. https://doi.org/10.1007/s13369-023-07896-5.

[58] Razzaq, A., Mohsan, S. A. H., Ghayyur, S. A. K., Al-Kahtani, N., Alkahtani, H. K., and Mostafa, S. M. (2022). Blockchain in healthcare: A decentralized platform for digital health passport of COVID-19 based on vaccination and immunity certificates. *Healthcare (Basel)*, 10(12), 2453.

[59] Anbarasan, H. S. and Natarajan, J. (2022). Blockchain based delay and energy harvest aware healthcare monitoring system in WBAN environment. *Sensors (Basel)*, 22(15), 5763.

[60] Ali, S., Abdullah, Armand, T. P. T., Athar, A., Hussain, A., Ali, M., Yaseen, M., Joo, M. I. and Kim, H. C. (2023). Metaverse in healthcare integrated with explainable AI and blockchain: Enabling immersiveness, ensuring trust, and providing patient data security. *Sensors (Basel)*, 23(2), 565.

[61] Sharma, V. and Meena, K. K. (2023). Dentistry in the digital age: Embracing blockchain technology. *Cureus*, 15(5), e39710.

[62] Ali, A., Al-Rimy, B. A. S., Alsubaei, F. S., Almazroi, A. A., and Almazroi, A. A. (2023). HealthLock: Blockchain-based privacy preservation using homomorphic encryption in internet of things healthcare applications. *Sensors (Basel)*, 23(15), 6762.

[63] Ahmed, I., Chehri, A., and Jeon, G. (2023). Artificial intelligence and blockchain enabled smart healthcare system for monitoring and detection of COVID-19 in biomedical images. *IEEE/ACM Transactions on Computational Biology and Bioinformatics*, 1, 1–10, doi: 10.1109/TCBB.2023.3294333.

[64] Joshi, S. and Sharma, M. (2023). Assessment of implementation barriers of blockchain technology in public healthcare: evidences from developing countries. *Health Sys.*, 12(2), 223–242.

[65] Ahmed, M., Dar, A. R., Helfert, M., Khan, A., and Kim, J. (2023). Data provenance in healthcare: Approaches, challenges, and future directions. *Sensors (Basel)*, 23(14), 6495.

[66] Mohey Eldin, A., Hossny, E., Wassif, K., and Omara, F. A. (2023). Federated blockchain system (FBS) for the healthcare industry. *Sci. Rep.*, 13(1), 2569.

[67] El Khatib, M., Alzoubi, H. M., Hamidi, S., Alshurideh, M., Baydoun, A., and Al-Nakeeb, A. (2023). Impact of using the internet of medical things on e-healthcare performance: Blockchain assist in improving smart contract. *Clin. Outcomes Res.*, 15, 397–411.

[68] Wu, T. C. and Ho, C. B. (2023). Blockchain revolutionizing in emergency medicine: A scoping review of patient journey through the ED. *Healthcare (Basel)*, 11(18), 2497.

3 Analysis of Hybrid Fuzzy-Neuro Model for Diagnosis of Depression

Manish Kumar[1,a], Anjali Nigam[1], and Surya Vikram Singh[2]

[1]Department of Computer Application, College of Innovative Management and Sciences, Lucknow, India

[2]Department of Computer Science and Engineering, BBDITM, Lucknow, India

Abstract

Depression is a common and devastating mental health illness that affects millions of people throughout the world. For effective treatment and intervention, accurate and quick diagnosis is critical. Traditional diagnostic approaches are limited, owing to the varied and complicated character of depression. In recent years, hybrid models that integrate fuzzy logic and neural networks have showed promise in improving depression diagnostic accuracy. This study describes the development of a hybrid fuzzy-neuro model for the diagnosis of depression that takes advantage of the complimentary qualities of fuzzy logic's ability to handle ambiguity and neural networks' ability to learn complicated patterns from data. This model exhibits its ability to increase the precision of depression diagnosis by a thorough examination on a real-world dataset. The study contributes to the emerging area of computational mental health by offering a fresh and promising method to mental health diagnosis.

Keyword: Depression, neural network, fuzzy logic, classification

1. Introduction

Depression, dubbed the "silent epidemic" of the 21st century, is a widespread and devastating mental health illness that imposes a large worldwide cost. It affects people of all ages, backgrounds, and walks of life, affecting not just them but also their families, communities, and society at large. Recognizing and effectively diagnosing depression is an important step towards successful treatment, prompt intervention, and the avoidance of serious and frequently long-term repercussions.

Clinical tests and self-reported questionnaires are largely used in traditional ways of diagnosing depression. While these techniques are beneficial, they have limits, which derive mostly from the complex and varied character of depression. Symptoms might vary greatly across people, and the existence of concomitant illnesses complicates diagnosis even further. Furthermore, the subjectivity

[a]dr.manish.2000@gmail.com

inherent in human judgments might result in variation in diagnostic conclusions. Artificial intelligence (AI) and machine learning (ML) have provided new options for solving these diagnostic difficulties in recent years. The creation of hybrid models that mix fuzzy logic and neural networks is one intriguing technique. Fuzzy logic provides a framework for dealing with ambiguity and uncertainty, but neural networks excel in learning complicated patterns from data. When these two paradigms are combined, they provide a synergistic model capable of improving the accuracy and reliability of depression diagnosis. This study describes the deployment of a hybrid fuzzy-neuro model for depression diagnosis. Fuzzy logic is used to record and reason about ambiguity in depression diagnosis, while neural networks are used to discover patterns and correlations from patient data. This hybrid approach, we believe, will increase the precision and reliability of depression diagnosis. To test this idea, we undertake a thorough analysis on a real-world dataset of patients with varying demographics and clinical histories. The findings of this study show that our hybrid model has the potential to contribute to the area of computational mental health by providing a unique method to depression detection. This study seeks to increase our knowledge of depression, prevent misdiagnoses, and, eventually, improve the lives of individuals affected by this common mental health illness.

2. Need of Hybrid Model for Diagnosis of Depression

Analyzing a hybrid fuzzy-neuro model for depression diagnosis entails assessing its efficacy, benefits, and potential limits. To capitalize on the advantages of both techniques, hybrid models mix fuzzy logic and neural networks. This can be a useful tool in the context of detecting depression. Figure 3.1 shows the advantages of using hybrid model for diagnosis of depression. The following examines the hybrid fuzzy-neuro model for depression detection.

2.1. Advantages

a. Human expertise integration: Fuzzy logic enables for the inclusion of human expertise and language elements. This is useful in fields such as mental health, where symptoms and severity are frequently reported using imprecise terminology. The model is capable of handling language variables such as "mild," "moderate," and "severe."

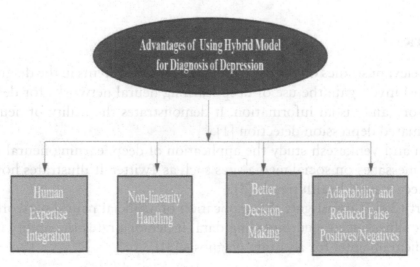

Figure 3.1: Advantages of using hybrid model for diagnosis of depression.

b. Non-linearity handling: Neural networks excel in capturing complicated, non-linear data connections. A variety of factors impact depression diagnosis, many of which are non-linear. The neural network component can aid in the capturing of these complex interactions.

c. Better decision-making: Combining fuzzy logic and neural networks can result in more robust decision-making. Fuzzy logic aids in the management of uncertainty and ambiguity in the diagnostic process, whereas neural networks learn from data patterns.

d. Adaptability and reduced false positives/negatives: Because our understanding of depression improves over time, neural networks that can adapt to new data are vital in diagnosing it. By merging the rule-based approach of fuzzy logic with the data-driven approach of neural networks, the hybrid model has the potential to minimize false positives and false negatives.

2.2. Limitations

a. Complexity: In general, hybrid models are more complicated than standalone fuzzy logic or neural network models. The model's intricacy may make it difficult to comprehend and debug.

b. Data requirements: For effective training, neural networks frequently require huge datasets. The neural network component may not function effectively if the dataset for depression diagnosis is inadequate or biased.

c. Knowledge required: Creating and fine-tuning a hybrid fuzzy-neuro model for depression diagnosis necessitates knowledge of both fuzzy logic and neural networks, which may be lacking in the mental health profession.

d. Interpretability: While fuzzy logic provides some interpretability owing to its rule-based structure, neural networks are frequently regarded as "black-box" models. It might be difficult to understand why the model reaches a diagnosis.

e. Scalability: The hybrid model may be less scalable than simpler models, especially if it is required to accommodate additional mental health problems or more complicated symptom profiles.

A hybrid fuzzy-neuro model for diagnosing depression can provide considerable benefits in dealing with the field's complexity and unpredictability. However, it is critical to carefully analyze the model's constraints and ensure that it is well-designed, adequately trained, and validated on a variety of datasets. Collaboration with mental health specialists is also essential for fine-tuning the model and ensuring that it matches with the real-world diagnosis procedure.

3. Related Work

Here's a survey of relevant studies on the use of neural network systems in the diagnosis of depression:

Guo et al. (2016) investigate the use of deep learning neural networks for depression identification utilizing auditory and visual information. It demonstrates the utility of neural network-based techniques in automated depression detection [1].

Al-Makhadmeh and Venkatesh study the application of deep learning neural networks to detect depression-related messages on social media sites such as Twitter. It illustrates how neural networks may be used to detect mental health trends [2].

Roy and Dukart (2017) investigate the application of artificial neural networks in the diagnosis of major depressive illness using neuroimaging data. It demonstrates the ability of neural networks to use modern medical imaging for accurate diagnosis [3].

Ghandeharioun et al. (2019) describe the use of neural networks to detect depression-related behaviors on social media. It emphasizes the need of neural network systems for online monitoring of mental health indices [4].

Kaur and Verma (2018) investigate ML and neural network-based approaches for identifying depression-related information on social media, especially among Indian adolescents. It emphasizes the value of neural networks in detecting depression across cultures [5].

Riegler and Lettner (2017) investigate the use of artificial neural networks to identify depression in Parkinson's disease patients. It emphasizes neural networks' versatility for detecting depression in certain medical circumstances [6].

Certainly, the following section is a quick survey of relevant studies on the use of hybrid fuzzy-neuro systems in illness diagnosis.

Wu and Kasabov (2007) provide a hybrid fuzzy-neuro system for early Alzheimer's disease detection, proving the efficacy of merging fuzzy logic with neural networks in the medical sector. While the study focuses on Alzheimer's disease, the concept can be applied to other areas of mental health diagnosis [7]. Özmen et al. (2008) presented work centered on breast cancer diagnosis, demonstrating the benefits of integrating fuzzy rules and neural networks in a hybrid system. The ideas of merging rule-based fuzzy systems with neural networks are extremely pertinent to the creation of a hybrid fuzzy-neuro system for depression diagnosis [8].

Penumatsa and Bokde (2019) investigate the application of fuzzy neural networks for the identification of various neurodegenerative disorders, focusing on the potential of hybrid systems in healthcare. While the emphasis is on neurodegenerative disorders, the basic ideas may be used to the diagnosis of mental health illnesses like as depression [9].

Chaurasia and Pal (2012) study the application of neural networks for clinical depression diagnosis in teenagers. While it does not explicitly address hybrid systems, it emphasizes the importance of neural networks in mental health diagnosis, which may be combined with fuzzy logic for increased accuracy [10]. Sharma and Kapoor (2014) investigate the application of artificial neural networks in the diagnosis of depression. It emphasizes the importance of neural networks in mental health applications. While not a hybrid system, it sheds light on neural network-based techniques that may be integrated with fuzzy logic to improve diagnostic capabilities [11].

Teixeira et al. (2003) address the use of artificial neural networks in psychiatric diagnosis. It gives an in-depth look at neural network applications in mental health and sets the framework for the use of fuzzy logic for increased diagnostic accuracy [12].

4. Working of hybrid fuzzy-neuro system in diagnosis of depression

A fuzzy-neuro technique for diagnosing depression entails combining fuzzy logic with neural networks to develop a thorough diagnostic system. The following section explains how the hybrid methodology is used to diagnose depression.

i.   **Data collection:** Individual consultants provide a data collection including important information about people, such as demographics, self-reported symptoms, behavioral tendencies, and so on.
ii. **Pre-processing:** Python was used to clean and preprocess the data, handle missing values, normalize or standardize characteristics, and ensure data quality.
iii. **Fuzzy logic component:** Linguistic variables and membership functions have been constructed to capture the uncertainty and ambiguity related with depression symptoms and their severity. This

layer uses fuzzy rules to input data to generate fuzzy outputs. Fuzzy rules are frequently expressed as "IF input IS term THEN output IS term." The "IF" section uses membership functions, and the "THEN" section uses fuzzy sets. Examples of this include: "If the patient experiences 'low energy' and 'loss of interest,' then they might be moderately to severely depressed."

iv. **Neural network component:** Feedforward neural network architecture has been used here shown in Figure 3.2. Then training of the neural network on pre-processed data has been performed. One or more neural network layers are then used to process the fuzzy outputs, allowing the system to capture complicated patterns. Deep learning comes into play in this situation.

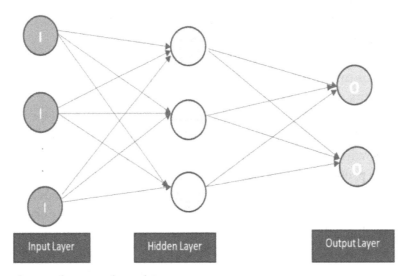

Figure 3.2: Feedforward neural network architecture.

v. **Integration of fuzzy logic and neural network:** The fuzzy logic component's output is merged with the neural network's output to improve fuzzy rule-based decision-making [13].

vi. **Implementation and evaluation:** Here's a Python code of a basic neuro-fuzzy system using the skfuzzy module [14, 15]. Deep neuro-fuzzy systems would use increasingly complicated neural network topologies in practice.

```
# Define input data and linguistic terms
input_data = np.arange(0, 11, 1)
term_low = fuzz.trimf(input_data, [0, 0, 5])
term_medium = fuzz.trimf(input_data, [0, 5, 10])
term_high = fuzz.trimf(input_data, [5, 10, 10])
# Define fuzzy rules
rule1 = fuzz.interp_membership(input_data, term_low, 2.5)
rule2 = fuzz.interp_membership(input_data, term_medium, 7,5)
ntle3 = fuzz.interp_membership(input_data, term_high, 9.0)
# Combine fuzzy rules
aggregated = np.fmax(rule1, np.fmax(rule2, rule3))
# Defuzzify to get a crisp result
result = fuzz.defuzz(input_data, aggregated, 'centroid')
printf("Crisp Result:", result)
```

Table 3.1 shows the performance comparison using neural network and fuzzy-neural system.

Table 3.1: Performance comparison

Measure/model	Neural network	Fuzzy-neural
Accuracy	85.43	88.45
Precision	83.56	86.29
Recall	80.25	83.91
Sensitivity	81.56	84.56
Error	11.56	9.65

In conclusion, combining the strengths of fuzzy logic with neural networks in the diagnosis of depression is a promising strategy. It has the potential to give mental health practitioners with a more accurate and interpretable diagnostic tool. To be useful in real-world therapeutic settings, however, it requires rigorous development, validation, and collaboration with subject specialists.

5. Conclusions

Depression, a common and devastating mental health illness, imposes a significant worldwide cost, emphasizing the crucial importance of proper and quick diagnosis. Traditional diagnostic approaches, while important, have limits since depression is diverse and complicated. In this study, we investigated the creation of a hybrid fuzzy-neuro system for the diagnosis of depression, a unique strategy that addresses these issues by combining the capabilities of fuzzy logic and neural networks.

Our findings show that combining fuzzy logic with neural networks in a hybrid model offers a viable method for improving the accuracy and reliability of depression diagnosis. Our test on a real-world dataset yielded positive findings, demonstrating that the hybrid fuzzy-neuro system can greatly improve the precision of depression detection when compared to existing approaches. This advancement is especially important considering the possible repercussions of misdiagnosis and the variable presentation of symptoms among people. Fuzzy logic is critical in capturing and reasoning about the uncertainty and ambiguity inherent in the depression diagnosis process. The system can manage the intricacies of this mental health problem because to the linguistic variables and membership functions established for input and output variables, as well as the fuzzy rules. Furthermore, the use of neural networks enables the model to learn complicated patterns and correlations from patient data, enhancing its diagnostic skills. While our findings are promising, there are various options for further study in this sector. Model architecture and parameter refinements can improve diagnostic performance even further. Furthermore, using larger and more diverse datasets can aid in validating the model's generalizability across different demographic groups and clinical presentations.

References

[1] Guo, Z., Zhang, L., Shen, Z., and Wang, Z. (2016). A deep learning approach to detect depression. *Neurocomputing*, 239, 1–9.

[2] Al-Makhadmeh, T. and Venkatesh, S. (2017). Depression detection on Twitter using deep learning. *Proc. 26th Int. Conf. World Wide Web Comp.*, 1067–1074.

[3] Roy, M. and Dukart, J. (2017). Use of artificial neural networks in diagnosis of major depressive disorder using neuroimaging. *Psychiat. Res.: Neuroimag.*, 266, 74–82.

[4] Ghandeharioun, A., Fedor, S., Sanger, T., and De Choudhury, M. (2019). Untangling the Web: The impact of depression on social media usage. *Proc. 2019 CHI Conf. Hum. Factors Comput. Sys.*, 180.

[5]   Kaur, H. and Verma, P. (2018). Detection of depression among Indian youth on Twitter using machine learning approach. *J. King Saud University-Comp. Inform. Sci*, 16, 1–15.

[6]   Riegler, G. and Lettner, S. (2017). Detecting depression in patients with Parkinson's disease using artificial neural networks. *Proc. 23rd ACM SIGKDD Int. Conf. Knowl. Discov. Data Min.*, 1527–1535.

[7]   Wu, Y. and Kasabov, N. (2007). An integrated soft computing model for early diagnosis of Alzheimer's disease. *Neur. Netw.*, 20(3), 352–365.

[8]   Özmen, G., Polat, K., and Güneş, S. (2008). An expert system for detection of breast cancer based on association rules and neural network. *Exp. Sys. Appl.*, 34(1), 38–46.

[9]   Penumatsa, P. R. and Bokde, N. (2019). Detection of neurodegenerative diseases using fuzzy neural networks: A review. *J. Healthcare Engg*, 53, 4651–4706.

[10] Chaurasia, V. and Pal, S. (2012). Diagnosis of clinical depression in adolescents using neural network. *Proc. Technol.*, 4, 719–724.

[11] Sharma, R. and Kapoor, S. (2014). Diagnosis of depression using artificial neural networks. *Int. J. Comp. Appl.*, 95(18), 22–26.

[12] Teixeira, P. L., Soares, M. J., Cunha, C., and Couto, A. (2003). Psychiatric diagnosis and artificial neural networks: A review. *IEEE Trans. Neu. Netw.*, 14(4), 857–876.

[13] Jang, J. S. R., Sun, C. T., Mizutani, E. (1997). Neuro-fuzzy and soft computing - A computational approach to learning and machine intelligence. *IEEE Trans. Automat. Con.*, 42(10), 1–648.

[14] Singh, H. and Lone, Y. A. (2019). Deep neuro-fuzzy systems with Python: With case studies and applications from the industry. Released November 2019, Apress, ISBN: 9781484253618.

[15] Musílek, P. and Gupta, M. M. (2000). Fuzzy neural networks. Editor(s): Sinha, N. K. and Gupta, M. M. *Acad. Press Ser. Engg. Soft Comput. Intel. Sys.* Academic Press, 161–184, ISBN 9780126464900, https://doi.org/10.1016/B978-012646490-0/50011-1.

4 Industrial Applications of Artificial Intelligence and Machine Learning: A Review

Dipti Rai[a], Shipra Tripathi, and Zeeshan Ali Siddiqui[b]

Department of Computer Science and Engineering, Faculty of Engineering and Technology, University of Lucknow, Uttar Pradesh, India

Abstract

The world of manufacturing industry is changing a lot day-by-day. Researchers are focusing on developing new ideas and making things in a way that helps our work easier, faster, and more efficient. This research paper gives a comprehensive review on how computers, specifically artificial intelligence (AI) and machine learning (ML), are playing a significant role in making this happen, especially in what we call Industry 4.0. To understand this, authors examined many databases such as SCOPUS and Web Science and special computer programs to help us thoroughly study this information. At its core, AI and ML are a complex collection of algorithms and techniques that addresses problems with predicting, grouping, and classification. The intelligent use of ML and AI has great promise. As a result, research in this area is highly valuable. A primary focus is the practical use of AI technology and their integration into many businesses and society. This article lists and explores the industrial uses of ML and AI. This article also describes the AI and ML research areas that will help provide better solutions to industrial problems through the use of AI and ML applications. This study expands on our knowledge of how computer technologies are changing the production environment.

Keywords: Artificial intelligence, machine learning, applications of AI & ML, manufacturing, classification

1. Introduction

This study is a research cum survey paper. The main goal of writing this paper is to look at how machine learning (ML) and artificial intelligence (AI) are employed in different industries. We're comparing how they are currently being utilized and how they were previously used, and what we can expect in the future. We're looking at the entire life span of a product, from when it's just an idea to when it's designed, produced, and distributed, and even when it's out in the world being used by customers. The paper is all about how industries were before they started using AI and ML, what changed when they started utilizing these tools, and what we can expect in the future for these

---

[a]diptirai543@gmail.com, [b]zeealis@gmail.com

industries with AI and ML. The landscape of AI and ML is ever-evolving and increasingly pivotal in various domains, particularly in information systems (IS) research. AI, frequently praised as one of the best recent and fundamental developments consequent to the convergence in the markets, holds a prominent place in contemporary discussions. However, in many contexts, it is used interchangeably with ML, creating potential confusion and imprecision. This terminological overlap is not only evident in practical contexts, such as statements by prominent figures like Facebook's CEO, but also in academic literature across diverse theoretical and application-oriented contributions. Such ambiguity surrounding the terms AI and ML can lead to misconceptions, hampering both research and practice. This distinction is especially critical in interdisciplinary fields like IS research. This study aims to clarify the industrial use of AI and ML, with a particular emphasis on the function of AI across various industry types. The article's contributions include two-fold: firstly, we identify the distinct roles of ML and AI in industries at different levels. Secondly, we recognize the issues within the sectors with and without AI.

1.1. Artificial intelligence

AI is a dynamic field rooted in the quest to create machine intelligence that can replicate tasks once reserved solely for humans. It embarked on its journey in 1956 when the term "artificial intelligence" was coined during a Dartmouth workshop. Over the years, AI's development has spanned diverse fields, including computer science and programming to neuroscience, robotics, linguistics, philosophy, and futurology [1]. The heart of AI lies in the challenge of endowing machines with common-sense reasoning abilities—making computers comprehend everyday events as effortlessly as humans. This field grapples with complex, non-linear, and combinatorial intricate problems like planning, scheduling, and image understanding, where traditional algorithms fall short. To overcome these challenges, AI leverages symbolic knowledge and heuristic strategies, often called "rules of thumb". AI research is broadly divided into two essential pillars: knowledge representation and search-based problem-solving. Knowledge representation entails translating human knowledge into formats that computers can interpret consistently. It aims to create a standardized knowledge representation that enables intelligent system behavior. This often involves structuring information into database records with fields, intending to move towards semantics-based phrases that machines can understand. The second pillar, search-based problem-solving, revolves around navigating extensive solution spaces to find optimal outcomes.

Practical AI solutions necessitate more intelligent search techniques that reduce many alternatives to manageable levels. Sophisticated search architectures, such as hierarchical search systems, divide the problem-solving process into pre-analysis, search, and post-analysis, progressively refining schedules. In a nutshell, AI is a multi-disciplinary field that originated in the mid-20th century and focused on creating machine intelligence capable of emulating human tasks. It grapples with enabling computers to reason like humans, tackling non-linear, complex problems.

1.2. Machine learning

Learning is defined as "the process of a change and enhancement in the behavior through exploring new information in time" by Simon. When machines perform the "learning" in this definition, it is called ML. The term enhancement is creating the best solution based on the existing experiences and samples during the AI (Sırmaçek, 2007).

The science (and art) of teaching computers to learn from data is known as ML. For a broader definition, see this: The branch of research known as [machine learning] makes it possible for computers to learn without explicit programming. In 1959, Arthur Samuel—additionally, a more engineering-focused one. If a computer program performs better on task T as measured by P after experiencing E, then it is said to have learned from the experience. This pertains to some task T and some performance measure E.—Tom Mitchell, 1997.

1.3. Apply machine learning: Why?

Consider how you would create a spam filter with conventional programming methods. First, you would examine the typical appearance of spam. Perhaps you've seen that certain terms or expressions (such "4U," "credit card," "free," and "amazing") frequently show up in the topic. Maybe you would further see additional trends in the email text, the sender's name, etc. Second, you would develop an algorithm for detection of every pattern you saw, and if your program identified many patterns, it would mark emails as spam. Finally, try out your software and keep going back to stages 1 and 2 until it functions adequately.

Considering how complicated the problem is, it's likely that your program will become a long, complicated collection of rules that's hard to maintain. However, a spam filter based on ML algorithms automatically learns which words and phrases are effective predictors of spam by finding repeating word patterns in the spam samples relative to the ham occurrences (Figure 4.1). The program is most likely easier to maintain, much shorter, and more accurate [2].

Furthermore, spammers may begin writing "For U" in place of "4U" if they discover that all of their emails with that phrase are being blocked. It is necessary to upgrade an automated guard that uses conventional programming methods to flag emails marked "For U." You will always need creation of fresh guidelines if spammers manage to get past your spam filter. However, a spam filter that makes use of ML methods that detects the term "For U" has become remarkably common in spam that users have identified. This allows the filter to begin filtering messages without requiring your interaction (Figure 4.2).

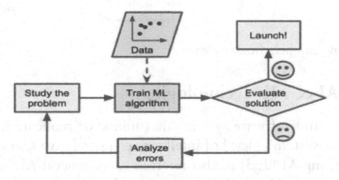

Figure 4.1: Machine learning approach.

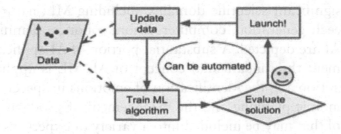

Figure 4.2: Adapting to change automatically.

Machine learning may also be used to solve issues that are too complicated for conventional methods or lack a proven solution. In the area of voice recognition let's say you want to start out small and create a program that can tell the difference between "one" and "two." One might hardcode an algorithm that detects the strength of high-pitched sounds and uses it to differentiate between ones and twos, as the word "two" starts with a high-pitched sound ("T"). When millions of individuals utter thousands of words in dozens of languages in loud situations, this approach will not work. Developing an algorithm that learns on its own, given a huge number of sample recordings for each word, is the best answer (for the time being at least).

Lastly, ML may help people to learn (Figure 4.3): Though this might be challenging for certain algorithms, ML algorithms can be evaluated to discover what they have learnt. For instance, the spam filter may be rapidly examined to provide the list of terms and word combinations that it considers to be the greatest spam predictors once it has been trained on enough spam. This can occasionally reveal novel trends or unanticipated correlations, resulting in a greater comprehension of the circumstances. Finding previously unidentified patterns in vast volumes of data can be facilitated by using ML techniques. We call this as "data mining."

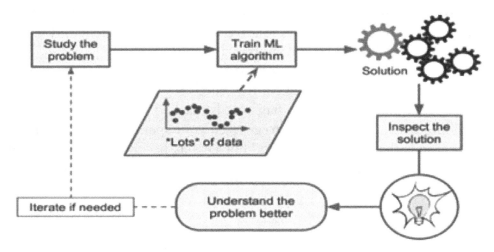

Figure 4.3: Machine learning can help humans learn.

2. Classification of AI & ML Technologies

AI encompasses hardware and software systems that mimic or replicate human thought processes and behavior. Based on the system's "level of intelligence" [3] relative to a human, AI is classified as either strong or weak. Strong AI [2, 3] is also referred to as general AI. Existing real-world applications depend on weak or soft AI, which demonstrates the capacity to handle certain issues while satisfying reasonable quality standards. AI, either general or crucial, is the topic of investigation. AI encompasses numerous significant scientific domains, including ML, natural language comprehension (NLP), text and speech generation, computer vision, robotics, planning, and expert systems. The various domains of AI are depicted. A substantial portion of AI applications is founded on ML techniques, which implement the fundamental concept of AI. ML is applied to enhance results in areas such as voice recognition and the identification of emotions in speech [4]. A wide array of ML techniques is used in economic planning and the management of production procedures. ML is an effective data analysis tool that may be included into a variety of expert systems. Currently, robotics research is mostly focused on ML [10].

Machine learning is widely used to solve problems in science and application. Take into consideration, for instance, how well-suited ML techniques are and how exciting the prospects of deep understanding are for solving problems in chemistry. Numerous sectors, including astronomy, agriculture, computational biology, municipal administration, medical imaging, and astronomy, are examples of markets where ML applications are available [5–7]. Another word for actively used is ML, which is the foundation of current natural language understanding research.

ML approaches are classified based on their intended use and method of learning. These fields include deep learning (DL), reinforcement learning (RL), semi-supervised education (SSL), cluster analysis, dimensionality reduction, supervised learning (SL), and unsupervised learning (UL). The goal of unsupervised learning (UL) techniques is to automatically divide an unlabeled set of objects into separate or overlapping groups according to the characteristics of each item. Uncovering latent patterns, anomalies, and disparities within data are the aim of UL. Regression and classification are used in supervised learning (SL) strategies to solve issues. When a finite subset of specifically defined objects is surrounded by a possibly endless number of things, certain issues arise. When labels are applied to objects based on a limited set of integers, called class numbers, a classification problem occurs. The classification algorithm's job is to assign one of the designated numbers to newly discovered, unlabeled objects. Regression problems are indicated by labels that contain real numbers, which include both integers and decimals. In these situations, the algorithm uses previously labeled items to forecast an absolute number of unlabeled objects. Predictive jobs and data gap filling are also handled by this kind of issue solution.

Deep learning (DL) techniques tackle unearthing hidden characteristics within data arrays by employing neural networks featuring numerous concealed layers and specialized architectural designs. In the context of DL, the concept of transfer learning (TF) is frequently investigated. The aim of transfer learning is to improve a "learner from one domain by transferring knowledge from a related domain". Machine learning models may be categorized into classic 10 and contemporary categories (Figure 4.4). Classical SL models include, but are not limited to, the following kinds: K-nearest-neighbor (k-NN), logistic regression, decision trees (DT), vector machines for support (SVM), artificial neural networks that feed forward (ANN), Principal component analysis and k-means are examples of traditional unsupervised learning methods (PCA).

The following are examples of contemporary unsupervised learning (UL) techniques: ISOMAP, or isometric mapping, the linear embedding technique (LLE), stochastic neighbor embedding with

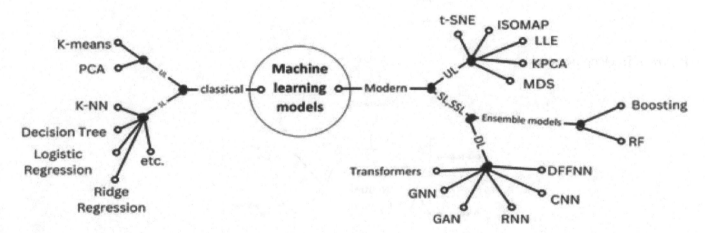

Figure 4.4: Classic and modern ML models.

T-distribution (t-SNE), principal component analysis (KPCA) of the kernel, scaling on multiple dimensions (MDS).

These include ensemble techniques like boosting and random forest, as well as DL architectures like long short-term memory (LSTM), convolutional neural networks (CNN), recurrent neural networks (RNN), and more in terms of contemporary supervised learning (SL), semi-supervised learning (SSL), reinforcement learning [8] (RL), and DL models. The AI sub-domain with the highest rate of development is DL. A collection of techniques known as DL make use of deep neural networks, which include two or more hidden layers. The main advantage of these deep architectures is their ability to manage tasks from beginning to conclusion. Because the network can learn how to connect an image or signal vector to the objective variable on its own, this approach reduces the amount of preprocessing that must be done on the data. By selecting key characteristics, the network significantly lessens the difficulty and complexity of the researcher's task. But these advantages become most apparent when an enough amount of training data is available [9] and the appropriate neural network design is selected. Among the many different architectural designs, there are three basic architecture types, from which many modified models are formed (see Figure 4.5).

Feedforward neural networks (FFNN) are widely employed in real-world scenarios to address problems related to classification and regression. Recurrent neural networks are capable of processing sequences with varying durations. When signals x(t) are received at time t, they complement the network's internal state. The following signal, x(t+1), is integrated to create the final output, $\hat{y}$, which depends on the entire sequence of signals. A class designation or a series of signals, denoted by the symbols $\hat{y}$, $\hat{y}$ h1i, $\hat{y}$ h2i,..., $\hat{y}$ h Tyi, can constitute the output of the network. Four primary categories may be distinguished from recurrent networks based on the kinds of sequences they generate and receive. One way to think of FFNN is as a one-to-one RNN architecture, as seen in Figure 4.6.

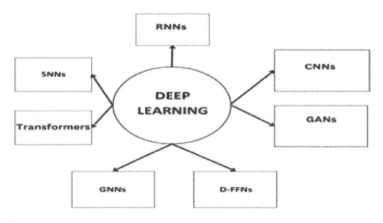

Figure 4.5: Deep networks.

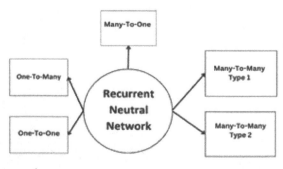

Figure 4.6: Recurrent neural networks.

The one-to-many architecture is used when a relatively short input sequence results in longer data or signal sequences. It can be used, for example, to specify the subject of a story or the style of a musical composition, in the text production and music generating processes. Categorization tasks are among the applications of the many-to-one architecture. Sentiment analysis is one example, classifying texts according to how emotionally charged they are perceived to be. This classification is created using both single words and word combinations (e.g., neutral, negative, positive). Another usage is the identification of named entities, such as proper names, days of the week, months, locations, dates, and more. Another element utilized in DNA analysis to determine the gene value is the nucleotide sequence.

The many-to-many architecture is used in speech recognition and machine translation. RNNs gave rise to generative adversarial networks, generative pre-trained transformers (GPT), Embeddings from Language Models (ELMO), bidirectional encoder representations from transformers (BERT), and LSTM models. These models are widely accepted due to their efficacy in tackling problems related to NL processing. CNNs make it possible to identify intricate patterns in the given data. No matter where these patterns are located in the input signal vector, they always remain the same. These patterns can be made up of vertical or horizontal lines as well as other distinguishing elements found in the photos.

During network training, the neuron weights of convolutional filters are created and adjusted. The convolution technique is incorporated to manage the training process's computational complexity. In image processing tasks, CNNs have regularly done better than humans. This deep neural network design was inspired by the LeNet model, which was the first to employ pooling, convolutional filters, and a fully connected neural network (FC) for image categorization. This network contains over 60,000 network parameters and consists of a two-layer fully linked network and four convolutional layers.

AlexNet represents the advancement of the actual architecture achieved by expanding the network's size and incorporating max-pooling. This network has roughly 100 times the weight of LeNet. VGGnet is another extensive architecture featuring uniform components. GoogleNet is designed around the inception module, which facilitates using convolutional filters with parallel paths of various sizes, ensuring the detection of unusual features. ResNet, with 152 layers, utilizes residual modules to combat the gradient of disappearance problem. Convolutional filters have proven highly effective in one-pass identification and recognition, as demonstrated by the Yolo model and image segmentation tasks, as seen in the unit model. Recent developments in computer vision are closely tied to adopting the self-attention mechanism, often called the transformer architecture. Current models applying this approach have achieved state-of-the-art results in specific object classification tasks. Notable models include Florence, Swin Transformer V2, and DINO.

Graph neural networks, (or GNNs), are a rapidly expanding field in ML that are especially meant to be used for inference on graph-based data. Convolutional neural networks are broader and more applicable to graph-structured data thanks to GNNs. They are unique in structural contexts including explicit graph structures, such as those seen in knowledge graphs, social networks, molecular, and physical systems. Nonetheless, GNNs may also be used in non-structural circumstances where task-specific graphs need to be created; for instance, you might make a word graph for text or a scene graph for a picture. GNNs are flexible and may be used to solve problems related to graph categorization, link prediction, and node classification. Numerous GNN variations, including the graph recurrent network (GRN), graph attention network (GAT), and graph convolutional network (GCN), have shown exceptional performance in a variety of DL tasks, including text classification, image classification, physics, chemistry, graph mining, and more [11].

The classification of AI and ML technologies offers a clear understanding of their capabilities. Deep learning methods based on RNN and CNN are currently under intense development. They often address challenges in recognition, recommendation, NLP, data processing, tracking, personalization, and learning. AI's potential extends to uncertain data analysis, often incorporating fuzzy logic, route sets, and possibility-based theories. Furthermore, AI's possibilities span various sectors, with significant applications in medicine, agriculture, education, social contexts, domestic environments, and art. AI's role is closely intertwined with the trends of Industry 4.0, with AI technologies forming the backbone of many applications, particularly in safety, cybersecurity, IoT, and data analysis based on unsupervised methods.

3. Issues in Manufacturing Industries

There are several convincing justifications why AI is so important in the manufacturing industry [12]. Let's look at a few significant issues:

1. Scarcity of expertise: Many manufacturing organizations face the challenge of retaining the knowledge of experts nearing retirement. This knowledge is valuable, and the organization seeks to capture it before it is lost. Furthermore, they aim to distribute this expertise across the board. This issue is prevalent in tasks like process planning, machinery diagnosis, planning and designing engineering projects.
2. Decision complexity: Decision-making in manufacturing can become highly complex, primarily when numerous options exist. These choices can involve product design or production scheduling. The issue is exacerbated in flexible manufacturing systems, with enhanced factory's adaptability at the floor, resulting in more alternatives and decisions. Taking such decisions in extremely stringent manufacturing contexts can be challenging enough, and with greater flexibility, the challenges of these decisions escalate. Product design complexity also contributes to decision complexity [13].
3. Information complexity: The concept of a "paperless workplace" or "paperless industries" has gained traction with efforts to make factory floor information accessible online. However, this shift presents a new challenge: reducing internet information to only what is necessary for particular decision-makers. The transition to digital formats does not necessarily guarantee information is easily accessible. The intelligent reduction of data to a digestible format on an individual basis is a complex problem that is yet to be fully addressed.
4. Decision timeliness: Besides the growing complexity of decisions, the amount of time available for making these decisions is dwindling. Advancements like customized technological advancement lowers machinery setup times, requiring faster and more intelligent decision-making systems. The query is how to build systems capable of handling the increased decision complexity within tighter timeframes.
5. Coordination: Manufacturing design is inextricably tied to manufacturing, distribution, and field service. If a design does not account for downstream processes, it might result in higher manufacturing costs and potentially lower product quality. This increases the difficulty of synchronizing plans with all following actions.

These issues collectively impact the manufacturing processes' quality and productivity. This prompts however AI can offer valuable solutions to address these challenges. AI has the capability of creating intelligent systems capable of capturing data, process, and distill expert knowledge, assist in decision-making, manage complex information, make timely decisions, and facilitate coordination across various aspects of the manufacturing [15] process. Therefore, AI is a technology with the potential to benefit the manufacturing industry significantly [27].

4. Manufacturing Industries Insights Using Artificial Intelligence

Recent surveys have revealed the extensive utilization of AI in addressing manufacturing challenges. The results of these surveys show a significant development in the role of AI throughout time. There was a lack of attention on AI in manufacturing in the 1960s and 1970s. By the 1980s, however, the landscape had changed dramatically, with around 68 AI systems in the research phase, 38 in the development stage, 9 undertaking field tests, and 14 already in production use. This accounted for around a fourth of the systems actively under inquiry, with responses from approximately 125 systems [14].

As of January 2023, there were close to 4.2 billion AI-based systems in various stages of development and deployment worldwide, and demonstrating the increasing use of AI technology in the manufacturing industry, it is predicted to be 8.4 billion in 2024. The survey findings also underscored the widespread belief that AI would exert a substantial impact on manufacturing. The critical question remained: where would this impact is most pronounced? In the parts that follow, we will dive into this subject by studying the regions of impact at various stages of the production process.

5. Insights of Artificial Intelligence in Designing

Design encompasses formulating a product specification, next comes the real design and, subsequently, its validation. Concurrently, several managerial activities are executed, and state-of-the-art AI technologies are applied to enhance each phase. In today's landscape, product specifications are typically conveyed through NL descriptions. For commercial products, these descriptions may span a couple of chapters, while military products often necessitate documentation comprising tens of thousands of pages. It remains imperative to scrutinize the fundamental requirements to ensure their comprehensiveness and coherence. In terms of gathering and evaluating specifications, AI has advanced significantly. For instance, systems like XSEL exemplify the integration of AI with gathering specifications for customer products. XSEL employs an interface using NL for eliciting customer goals, effectively analyzing customer needs, and engaging with customers to construct a comprehensive instance of their requirements. Importantly, this structure is actively in use. Nevertheless, it's worth noting that the thorough analysis of specifications, identifying inconsistencies and gaps, remains a formidable task, representing an ongoing development area. Once a specification has been obtained, as well as its accuracy and coherence verified, the design phase can commence. Design is widely recognized among the most intricate and creative aspects of the production procedure. It demands not only educational foundations but also a wealth of experience. Consequently, it remains a knowledge-intensive endeavor that draws upon analytical and heuristic knowledge, rendering AI techniques highly pertinent [16].

In the field of design, a number of categories are identified. In the first category, "selection," a product may be chosen from the current inventory by mapping functional needs onto the characteristics of current product lines. Systems like as XSEL, for instance, are adept at matching product features to user functional needs and identifying the best items. "Configuration" stands for a little more complex kind of design. To make the finished product, semi-finished components must be assembled. There are several effective configuration methods in use right now. For example, VT configures elevator systems and XCON/R1 configures computer systems; both are used in real-world environments. These technologies are more accurate and efficient than human configurers, exhibiting exceptional levels of performance. The third kind of design is "extrapolation." This method involves altering an existing product to meet certain client requirements. For example, technologies such as ALADIN may take an aluminum alloy specification and modify the composition and thermal-mechanical processing of an existing alloy to generate a new alloy that matches the customer's specifications [30].

"Discovery" represents the most challenging category of design. It is akin to configuration but involves starting from essential components, such as transistors and resistors, and combining them to construct functional systems. Systems like ALADIN, EURISCO, and Talia have effectively harnessed AI techniques to tackle discovery problems, creating intricate available designs from fundamental components. Validation is used after design is finished to make sure the design works as intended. The most popular strategy is simulation, which applies advanced techniques such as finite element analysis for mechanical components and circuit simulation for electronics. In particular, AI validation seeks to emulate human validation techniques [17], in which people can analyze a design's structure and infer functioning with little to no help from simulation. Although the CORA system has been essential in verifying the dependability of relay protection systems for power line protection, CONSTRAINTS and other similar systems have shown remarkable skill in determining the operation of electronic circuits. Furthermore, the use of AI technology in engineering project administration is growing. For example, the main goal of the CALLISTO system is to handle duties connected to product idea and design. It uses expertise to expedite activity management and knowledge representation to capture dynamic objects and activities. AI keeps developing and reshaping these procedures, increasing their efficacy and efficiency.

6. Insights of Artificial Intelligence in Production Planning

The definition of production facilities and the design of the product are the inputs for this phase. It includes projecting client demand, managing the production process, setting up facility layouts, outlining maintenance protocols, and assisting with employee training. All of these tasks are actively optimized with AI [18]. Demand forecasting is one area where there has been a significant departure from conventional techniques. Researchers studying rule-based methods to mimic market behavior are working in marketing organizations. By going deeper into knowledge of specific consumer demands, these cutting-edge solutions go beyond the standard technique of forecasting based just on historical data. As an example, the ROME system addresses the forecasting problem by assessing resource plans. Similar to VISICALCTM, it functions as an intelligent system and can comprehend input in plain language. The system automatically examines data to determine whether production targets are being reached and, if not, to pinpoint the underlying reasons.

Several systems for process planning are being looked at. For instance, ESP may be used to plan the manufacture of sheet metal, while XPSE, an extension of the GARI system, is used to plan the manufacturing of three-dimensional mechanical components. These rule-based solutions improve the efficiency of the planning process. Electronic applications benefit from traditional methods when it comes to process programming, which makes automation possible. However, programming automation still presents a barrier for mechanical operations such as carburetor assembly. The use of AI to solve this issue is still being researched, especially with regard to power supply assembly. The process programming effort also includes choosing auxiliary resources, including cutting fluids for machining processes [20]. Systems such as GREASE are in the process of field testing and are designed to choose the right cutting fluids for different types of machining processes [28].

7. Insights of Artificial Intelligence in Production

Production, includes a volume of important manufacturing process components. It includes product inspection, process maintenance, control of production cells, shop floor planning, scheduling, and management. The intricacy of scheduling as a combinatorial issue frequently surpasses human schedulers' capabilities. AI has proved very beneficial in resolving scheduling conflicts. For example, constraint-directed search strategies are used by the Isis system to schedule workshops. Schedules that satisfy certain requirements while permitting flexibility in others are produced via constraint-directed search, which employs limitations to lower combinatorial complexity. IMACS offers a distinct viewpoint on scheduling management with a focus at the flow shop scheduling [23]. Murphy's Law, which asserts that anything that may go wrong, it will go wrong, serves as its foundation. Rather of relying on perfect adherence to schedules, IMACS foresees irregularities and emphasizes their identification and remediation.

Systems like Hitachi's SCD system and TRANSCELL employ the same deviation-focused methodology at the cellular level. These rule-based systems respond instantly to alterations, determining What must be completed next and changing course quickly in response to disturbances. Rules-based as well as model-based both methods are utilized in the field of product inspection to identify problems with printed circuit boards and computers. As an example, the IDa system is intended for testing completed computers, whereas IPWB~S is focused on examining printed wiring board inner layers and identifying production-process faults. As of the latest updates, AI technologies continue to advance in these areas, with an increased focus on real-time adaptation to deviations and the enhancement of inspection techniques to ensure product quality and manufacturing efficiency [24].

8. Insights of Field Services and Distribution Using Artificial Intelligence

Distribution and field service are the final phases of a product's life cycle after manufacture. Organizational design is the first step in distribution; it involves decisions on where to manufacture, how much to make, how much inventory to have on hand, and how to get it there. Other critical distribution tasks include order entry, scheduling product installations, and identifying and repairing problems on the customer's premises. Every single one of these vocations requires AI. The network INET models organizational structures, simulates their processes, and autonomously evaluates the outcomes using knowledge-based simulation approaches. The decision-making process is optimized with the help of these simulations. XSEL [19] is further employed in sales orders input. The result from XSEL is subsequently fed into a distribution framework, such as ILOG, which determines the sourcing of orders, assembly locations, and the most efficient shipping methods. These systems incorporate rule-based approaches to get and use proficient knowledge and employ heuristic searches to enhance solution quality. AI-based applications have also completely changed installation planning.

The optimal position and functionality for computer installations at the customer's site are determined using the XSITE system.

Lastly, diagnosing and repairing products has garnered substantial focus in the domain of AI. The PDS system, also known as GENAID, is able to diagnosing issues with sensors to power generators and steam turbines. The system has been in production usage for more than a year. PDS presents a unique challenge as it must contend with sensor inputs, which can deteriorate more rapidly than the processes they monitor. Diagnosing in such an environment involves distinguishing between inaccurate sensor data and actual process faults, rendering the problem more complex. While DOC is specialized in detecting computer-related difficulties, CATS is focused on diesel locomotive diagnostics, and ACE is a system specifically designed to diagnose cable faults in telephone cabling. Based on rule-based concepts, these systems use context awareness and heuristics to provide precise diagnoses. Model-based reasoning, or reflecting the product's physical structure and operating principles, is becoming perhaps much more crucial in the current environment of AI research. To improve diagnostic abilities, this method explores areas like chemistry, physics, and thermodynamics. The DART system, for example, uses the computers' structural and functional characteristics to diagnose them. AI continues to advance in these areas, offering improved capabilities for optimizing distribution processes, enhancing for installation and offering more precise and effective product diagnostic and maintenance services [21].

9. Future Trends of Artificial Intelligence in Manufacturing

Every phase of the production process, including design, planning, manufacturing, distribution, and field service—was covered in the sections before this one, and particular uses of AI were noted. One issue that comes to me is: What part will AI play in the future of manufacturing?

In order to respond to this query, we must take a systematic approach to the production process. Two important perspectives to think about are:

1. Strategic view – "Design Fusion": According to the strategic perspective, a product's design should be optimized to improve activities that occur later on. During the product design process, this idea, called "Design Fusion," aims to use and reflect the integrated knowledge of field service, production, distribution, and planning. By doing so, we can ensure that the downstream processes are optimized from the outset.
2. Tactical view – "Doors on Demand": The tactical perspective concentrates on the flow of current goods inside the company [22]. It provides solutions to questions like how and where to receive the merchandise faster, and what to do in the event that it isn't available right now. In situations when the way the thing is designed is no longer accessible, "Doors on Demand" investigates reverse engineering techniques. We can find ways to further optimize and improve the spot uses of AI via adopting a more thorough strategic and tactical method for handling current products and bringing new designs inside the company.

In short, a comprehensive, systems-based approach is what will shape the potential of AI in manufacturing. This technique considers the full product lifetime and uses AI to improve some stages together with the manufacturing process as a whole. This comprehensive perspective opens up possibilities for greater efficiency, innovation, and improved outcomes in manufacturing [25].

10. Applications of Machine Learning

In the parts before this one, we delved into the classification of artificial AI & ML and application areas of AI. In this section, we will explore the contemporary landscape of ML approaches and their pervasive presence in our daily lives. There has been a notable increase in the application of machine learning, dispelling the notion that it's exclusively reserved for extensive research endeavors. Here are noteworthy studies and applications in various domains:

Education: Machine learning has emerged as a pivotal educational tool, primarily enhancing student performance and success. Despite numerous educational initiatives in recent years, achieving the desired level of academic success has remained a challenging endeavor [31].

This challenge is influenced by many factors, making it difficult to discern which factors have the most significant impact. In response, researchers have employed ML models with promising outcomes to predict students' academic success using survey data.

Likewise, ML algorithms have been harnessed to evaluate the proficiencies of higher education students. In a 2007 study conducted at Pamukkale University, researchers identified students at risk of struggling in mathematics courses. The investigation showed that a number of variables, including scores in university entrance exams (mathematics, sciences, Turkish language) and high school graduation scores, played a crucial part in predicting success in mathematics. The research involved data from 289 students for training and 145 students for testing, resulting in an accurate estimation of 86% of students who successfully passed their mathematics course [26].

Machine learning continues to find practical applications in the education sector, revolutionizing various facets of teaching and learning.

Natural language processing: It is aimed to investigate and analyze the structures of natural languages. It's conceivable to perform many applications with NLP like, automatic translation of written texts, question-answer machines, automatic summarization of text, and understanding speech and command.

Image processing: In this method it is aimed to process and improve recorded images. Some application areas where the image processor is used are as follows: security systems, face detection, medicine (to diagnose diseased tissues and organs), military (to process underwater and satellite images), motion detection, object detection, and automotive, aviation, and production, detecting malfunctions before they occur, producing autonomous vehicles.

Computational biology: DNA sequencing, finding a tumor, and drug discovery. Retail – customized shelf analysis for persons, recommendation engines, material and stock estimates, and purchasing – demand trends. Health: providing warning and diagnosis by analyzing patient data, disease defining, and health care analysis. Finance: credit controls and risk assessments, and algorithmic trading. Meteorology – weather forecast via sensors. Human resources: Selecting the most successful candidate among a lot of applicants. Energy – calculating the heating and cooling loads for building designs: power usage analysis and smart network management [31].

11. Limitations and Difficulties in AI & ML

The system with artificial intelligence technology needs skilled professionals, whereas the shortage or lack of such experienced and qualified professionals creates a significant challenge for the market. Artificial intelligence technologies require specialized expertise in machine learning, data science, and software engineering. The demand for these professionals is within the supply, leading to talent shortages that can slow down AI development, implementation, and innovation. Moreover, this shortage can limit the scalability [29] and effectiveness of AI solutions across various industries. Thus, the shortage of skilled professionals is observed to act as a challenge for the market's expansion [2] (Tables 4.1 and 4.2).

12. Conclusions

In the different sections presented, we have explored the evolving artificial intelligence (AI) landscape and its integral component, machine learning (ML). These discussions shed light regarding the connection between ML and AI, their classification, their practical applications, and the obstacles and possibilities they present in different domains. We delved into the wide-ranging machine learning uses in various domains, from education to healthcare and agriculture. These illustrations demonstrated the revolutionary potential of ML & AI, which goes beyond process optimization to encompass creative problem-solving. It's clear that ML is not limited to just one sector but has expanded

Table 4.1: Internal problems in artificial intelligence

Internal problems in AI technology			
Data	*Learning process*	*Results*	*Technology*
Challenges in gathering data and doing preliminary processing	Slow learning process	Transparency and interpretability issues	The current solutions' instability stemming from ML and its dependence on background noise
Large volumes of data are necessary	Enormous volume of processing power is needed		The current machine learning models' single-tasking component and restricted associativity
Absence of labeled data and laborious labeled data entry	Absence of sophisticated picture processing tools		The requirement to create fresh machine learning models for unique data and application scenarios
Data security, "bias," and privacy			Cyberinfrastructure is required for industrial AI and ML applications

Table 4.2: Issues with artificial intelligence from the outside

External problems in AI technology			
Organizational	*Personnel*	*Economic*	*Social*
Absence of an adoption plan for AI	Aversion to new technology and changes	The expensive nature of AI-based solutions	Replacement and displacement of jobs
Functional fragmentation that makes it difficult to apply AI in an integrative manner	Shortage of qualified personnel	Inadequate preparation for the real-world implementation	Adoption and trust
Absence of dedication to the advancement of AI and leadership		Wealth gap and inequality	Ethical & morality issues
Insufficient technology infrastructure		The emerging nations' economies	Regulation policy and legal concerns

throughout many facets of our life. It also exposed us to the manufacturing sector and the ways AI affects different stages of the production process. AI is not only automating tasks but also enhancing decision-making and optimizing operations. But nevertheless, it's essential to proceed cautiously, as shortage of thorough knowledge and comprehension of AI might cause problems with implementation. In conclusion, the future of AI and ML is being shaped by the ongoing development of technology and the expanding accessibility of data, presenting both possibilities and problems. To leverage this potential fully, we must approach these technologies cautiously and aim for a better comprehension of their capabilities and limitations. As AI and ML continue to evolve, they have the potential to revolutionize industries, redefine job roles, and make a profound impact on our daily lives. Thus, we must adapt to this changing landscape, harnessing the capabilities of AI and ML to drive innovation while also acknowledging and addressing the challenges they pose.

References

[1] Everitt, T., Goertzel, B., and Potapov, A. (2017). Artificial general intelligence. *Lecture Notes in Artificial Intelligence*. Heidelberg: Springer. 10th International Conference, AGI 2017, Melbourne, VIC, Australia, August 15–18, 2017, Proceedings, 1–16.

[2] Tizhoosh, H. R. and Pantanowitz, L. (2018). Artificial intelligence and digital pathology: Challenges and opportunities. *J. Pathol. Inform.* 9, 38.

[3] Strong, A. I. (2016). Applications of artificial intelligence & associated technologies. Science [ETEBMS-2016], 5(6), pp 1–7. *Proceeding of International Conference on Emerging Technologies in Engineering, Biomedical, Management and Science (ETEBMS-2016)*, 5–6 March 2016.

[4] Barakhnin, V., Duisenbayeva, A., Kozhemyakina, O. Y., Yergaliyev, Y., and Muhamedyev, R. (2018). The automatic processing of the texts in natural language. Some bibliometric indicators of the current state of this research area. *J. Phy.: Conf. Ser.*, IOP Publishing: Bristol, UK, 012001.

[5] The Artificial Intelligence (AI) White Paper. Available online: https://www.iata.org/contentassets/b90753e0f52e48a58b28c51df0 23c6fb/ai-white-paper.pdf.

[6] Mukhamediev, R. I., Symagulov, A., Kuchin, Y., Yakunin, K., and Yelis, M. (2021). From classical machine learning to deep neural networks: A simplified scientometric review. *Appl. Sci.*, 11, 5541.

[7] Usuga Cadavid, J. P., Lamouri, S., Grabot, B., Pellerin, R., and Fortin, A. (2020). Machine learning applied in production planning and control: A state-of-the-art in the era of industry 4.0. *J. Intell. Manuf.*, 31, 1531–1558.

[8] Ogidan, E. T., Dimililer, K., and Ever, Y. K. (2018). Machine learning for expert systems in data analysis. *Proc. 2018 2nd Int. Symp. Multidis. Stud. Innov. Technol. (ISMSIT)*, 1–5.

[9] Miotto, R., Wang, F., Wang, S., Jiang, X., and Dudley, J. T. (2018). Deep learning for healthcare: Review, opportunities and challenges. *Brief. Bioinform.*, 19, 1236–1246.

[10] Zitnik, M., Nguyen, F., Wang, B., Leskovec, J., Goldenberg, A., and Hoffman, M. M. (2019). Machine learning for integrating data in biology and medicine: Principles, practice, and opportunities. *Inf. Fusion*, 50, 71–91.

[11] Mahdavinejad, M. S., Rezvan, M., Barekatain, M., Adibi, P., Barnaghi, P., and Sheth, A. P. (2018). Machine learning for Internet of Things data analysis: A survey. *Digit. Commun. Netw.*, 4, 161–175.

[12] Sadovskaya, L. L., Guskov, A. E., Kosyakov, D. V., and Mukhamediev, R. I. (2021). Natural language text processing: A review of publications. *Artif. Intell. Dec. Mak.*, 95–115.

[13] Kotsiantis, S. B., Zaharakis, I., and Pintelas, P. (2007). Supervised machine learning: A review of classification techniques. *Emerg. Artif. Intell. Appl. Comput. Eng.*, 160, 3–24.

[14] Hastie, T., Tibshirani, R., and Friedman, J. (2009). Unsupervised learning. *The Elements of Statistical Learning*. Springer: Berlin/Heidelberg, Germany, 485–585.

[15] Li, Y. (2017). Deep reinforcement learning: An overview. 1, 1–12. arXiv 2017, arXiv:1701.07274. https://doi.org/10.48550/arXiv.1701.07274.

[16] LeCun, Y., Bengio, Y., and Hinton, G. (2015). Deep learning. *Nature*, 521, 436–444.

[17] Weiss, K., Khoshgoftaar, T. M., and Wang, D. (2016). A survey of transfer learning. *J. Big Data*, 3, 1–40. arXiv:1511.05493.

[18] McDermott, J. (1982). XSEL: A computer salesperson's assistant. *Machine intelligence*, Horwood Chichester, England, 10(1), 1–8.

[19] McDermott, J. (1982). Rl: A rule-based configurer of computer systems. *Artif. Intel.*, 19(i), 39–88.

[20] Marcus, S., Stout, J., and McDermott, J. (1986). VT: An expert elevator configurer. Technical Report, Computer Science Dept., Carnegie-Mellon University, Pittsburgh, PA. 9(1), 95. https://doi.org/10.1609/aimag.v9i1.664

[21] Sathi, A., Morton, T., and Roth, S. (1986). Callisto: An intelligent project management system. *AI Magazine*, 7(5), 34-34. https://doi.org/10.1609/aimag.v7i5.564.

[22] McDermott, J. and Steele, B. (1981, August). Extending a knowledge-based system to deal with ad hoc constraints. *Proc. Seventh Int. Joint Conf. Artif. Intel.*, 7, 824–828. Vancouver, B.C.

[23] Tashiro, T., Komoda, N., Tsushima, I., and Masumoto, K. (1985). Rule-based control of factory automation systems. An approach with a production system. *Technical Report*, Systems Development Lab., Hitachi Ltd. 1–19.

[24] *Precedence Research - Market Research Reports & Consulting Firm.* (n.d.). Precedence Research. https://www.precedenceresearch.com/artificial-intelligence-market.

[25] Carou, D., Sartal, A., and Davim, J. P. (2022). *Machine Learning and Artificial Intelligence with Industrial Applications*. Springer. eBook ISBN 978-3-030-91006-8. DOI https://doi.org/10.1007/978-3-030-91006-8. 1–211.

[26] Rai, R., Tiwari, M. K., Ivanov, D., and Dolgui, A. (2021). Machine learning in manufacturing and industry 4.0 applications. *Int. J. Prod. Res.*, 59(16), 4773–4778. https://doi.org/10.1080/00207543.2021.1956675.

[27] Zhang, X., Ming, X., Liu, Z., Yin, D., Chen, Z., and Chang, Y. (2018). A reference framework and overall planning of industrial artificial intelligence (I-AI) for new application scenarios. *Int. J. Adv. Manufac. Technol.*, 101(9–12), 2367–2389. https://doi.org/10.1007/s00170-018-3106-3.

[28] Angelopoulos, A., Michailidis, E. T., Nomikos, N., Trakadas, P., Hatziefremidis, A., Voliotis, S., and Zahariadis, T. (2019). Tackling faults in the industry 4.0 era—A survey of machine-learning solutions and key aspects. *Sensors*, 20(1), 109. https://doi.org/10.3390/s20010109.

[29] Fox, M. S. (1986). Industrial applications of artificial intelligence. *Robotics*, 2(4), 301–311. https://doi.org/10.1016/0167-8493(86)90003-3.

[30] Lee, D. and Yoon, S. N. (2021). Application of artificial intelligence-based technologies in the healthcare industry: Opportunities and challenges. *Int. J. Environ. Res. Public Health*, 18(1), 271. https://doi.org/10.3390/ijerph18010271.

[31] Siddiqui, Z. A. and Haroon, M. (2022). Application of artificial intelligence and machine learning in blockchain technology. *Artif. Intel. Mach. Learn. EDGE Comput.*, 169–185. Academic Press. ISBN 9780128240540, https://doi.org/10.1016/B978-0-12-824054-0.00001-0.

5 Shape Memory Alloy and Artificial Intelligence

Kedarnath Chaudhary[1,a], Vikrant K. Haribhakta[1], and Maruti Maurya[2]

[1]Department of Mechanical Engineering, COEP Technological University Pune, Pune, India

[2]Department of Computer Science and Engineering, Integral University Lucknow, Lucknow, India

Abstract

Shape memory alloys (SMAs) are a type of intelligent materials that when deformed, can revert to their original shape. When the SMA is heated or cooled, a special phase transformation takes place, which accounts for this capability. SMAs can be used in a variety of industries, including aerospace, automotive, medical, machine learning (ML) and others. Artificial intelligence (AI) has the potential to completely transform a wide range of sectors. The creation of novel materials with enhanced characteristics already makes use of AI. AI is being utilized, for instance, to build new, more effective SMAs. This paper will examine the most recent developments in the creation of novel SMAs using AI. The paper will go over the various AI design methods that are employed to create SMAs with enhanced features. The prospective uses of AI-designed SMAs in various industries will also be covered in this article.

Keywords: Artificial intelligence, computational resource, physical reservoir computer, machine learning, shape memory alloys

1. Introduction

A class of intelligent materials known as shape memory alloys (SMAs) has the capacity to recover from deformation and take on their original shape [1]. The transformation occurs in SMA only when it is heated or cooled in a specific manner. The phase transformation that takes place in SMAs, which are often made up of two or more metals, is a reversible martensitic transformation [1–3].

A rapidly growing discipline, artificial intelligence (AI) has the potential to revolutionize a wide range of sectors, including the creation of novel materials with enhanced capabilities. AI is being utilized, for instance, to build new, more effective SMAs.

AI is being used to discover new alloy compositions with enhanced characteristics as one method of creating new SMAs. Artificial intelligence is used to sort through millions of different alloy compositions and determine which ones are most likely to possess the needed qualities. This will eventually reduce the creation time and expense of new SMA alloys.

[a]chaudharykedarnath@gmail.com

Novel SMAs can be designed using AI by enhancing their manufacturing processes. SMAs with more reliable qualities and lesser flaws can be produced using AI. This as a result enhances SMAs' functionality and dependability.

AI is also being used to create novel SMA control strategies. Temperature often governs traditional SMA actuators. However, new control strategies that enable SMAs to be regulated more accurately and effectively can now be created. SMAs may find new uses in robotics and medical technology as a result of this.

A self-sensing shape memory alloy actuator is used as a physical reservoir computer for computational purposes. This machine learning (ML) technique uses the dynamics of a physical system for computation, making it faster and more efficient than recurrent neural networks. The actuator predicts the actuator's end effector's trajectory under different driving signals, demonstrating its reconfigurability and ability to function simultaneously [4].

Designing novel materials with enhanced properties is one of the main applications of AI in materials research. The desired qualities are determined by screening millions of candidate material compositions. The time and expense involved in creating new materials can be greatly decreased in this way.

It was also found that AI has been used, for instance, to create novel alloys that perform better at high temperatures and have increased strength and corrosion resistance. As a result, creating new materials for catalysis and energy storage.

Process optimization in manufacturing is another application of AI in materials science under which one can create brand-new production methods that result in materials with more dependable qualities and fewer flaws. This indeed enhances the functionality and dependability of the materials.

AI, for instance, has also been used to streamline the semiconductor, battery, and solar cell manufacturing processes. This is then applied to the creation of innovative 3D printing additive manufacturing processes.

In general, AI has the power to completely change how materials are developed and used. Researchers can now design new materials with improved qualities and performance by utilizing AI to streamline production procedures, speed up the discovery of novel materials, and design new materials. This results in novel and creative uses for materials across a variety of sectors, including aerospace, automotive, energy, and healthcare.

Although AI is still a fresh field of study, it has the potential to completely alter how materials are developed and used. We may anticipate even more ground-breaking and inventive uses of AI in materials research as technology develops.

2. AI-based design of SMAs with improved properties

A possible new method for creating SMAs with enhanced features is AI-based design. It can considerably hasten the creation of new SMAs by minimizing the requirement for testing based on trial and error. It can also be used to create brand-new SMAs with enhanced features that are customized for certain uses (referring Figures 5.1a and 5.1b). This can result in lower costs and better SMA performance in a variety of applications.

The following steps are commonly included in the design of SMAs using AI:

1. Data gathering: Experiments on SMAs have produced a big dataset. This dataset should provide details about the make-up, microstructure, and characteristics of SMAs.

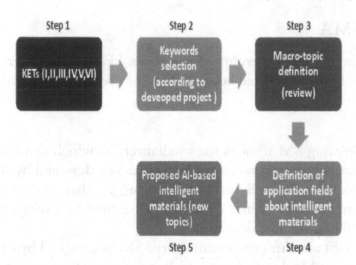

Figure 5.1(a): The methodological process followed to conceptualize the proposed review [5].

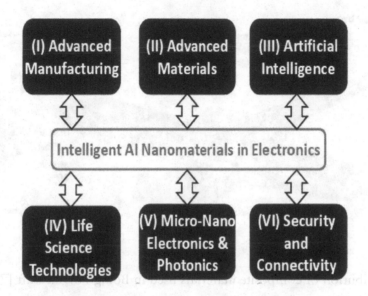

Figure 5.1(b): KETs (key enabling technologies) and review framework [5].

2. Pre-processing the data: The pre-processing of the data ensures that it is in a format that the AI model can use. Resulting in scaling and cleansing the data and eliminating errors.
3. AI model development: AI model forecasting its properties can be created based on microstructure and composition of individual SMAs. Methods like deep learning, ML can be used to leverage this.
4. Property prediction: AI model is used to predict the desired properties of new SMAs.
5. Validations of the predicted properties can be done after synthesizing the new SMA over specific measures.
6. After a successful AI validation, new SMAs are ready to be designed with a wide range of improved properties. Say for example, new memory effects, elasticity, and strength properties of SMAs can be produced using AI based formulas [5].

AI-based design formulas can create a revolutionary effect for many newly created SMA applications.

3. Application of SMA

AI created SMAs has the ability to revolutionize sectors like robotics, aerospace, automotive and medical. A few instances have been listed below for SMAs created by AI with relevant figures:

3.1. Aerospace

Smart aircraft wings: Creating SMA wings for small aircrafts which can change shape while flying indeed resulting an increase in performance and fuel efficiency designed by AI [6].

Active de-icing techniques/system: Researchers also suggest that AI created SMAs can be used to create de-icing systems for airplanes which can melt the ice found on wings and other surfaces without using any mechanical or chemical devices.

Durable and light weight aircraft components/parts: SMAs designed by AI will be used in creating light weight and sturdy parts like landing gears and actuators (refer Figure 5.2).

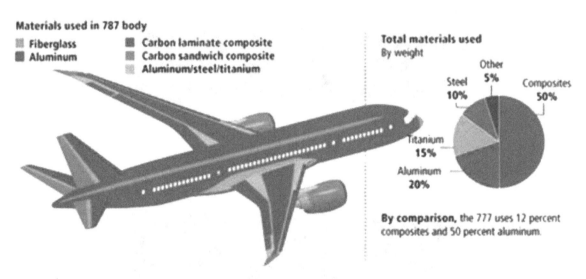

Figure 5.2: Overall distribution of composite materials used in Boing 787 aircraft [7].

3.2. Automotive

Active suspension systems: SMAs created by AI could be used to create active suspension systems for cars that can enhance handling and ride quality.

AI-designed SMAs enhance vehicle ride quality and handling, making them more comfortable and safer to drive, particularly on rough roads as shown in Figure 5.3.

Shape-changing body panels: AI-designed SMAs could be used to create shape-changing body panels for cars that can increase fuel efficiency and aerodynamic performance as per Figure 5.4.

SMAs created by AI could be used to create shape-changing body panels for cars that increase aerodynamic performance and fuel efficiency. Fuel costs and emissions could both be significantly decreased as a result of this [9].

Smart airbags: SMAs created by AI could be used to create smart airbags that deploy more quickly and minimize injury risk in the event of a collision (Figure 5.5).

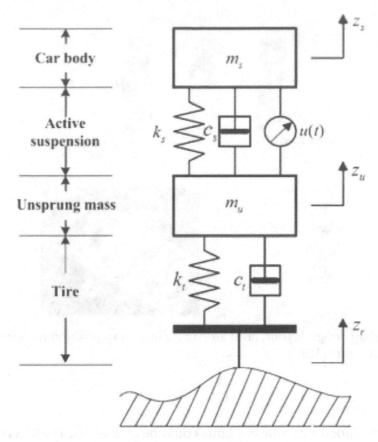

Figure 5.3: A model of active suspension system [8].

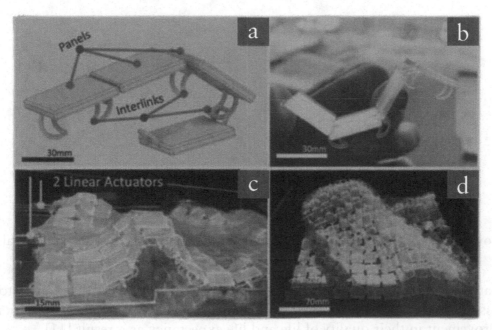

Figure 5.4: (a) Basic 3D model, (b) 3D print of interlinked panels, (c, d) fabricated shape-changing displays examples [9].

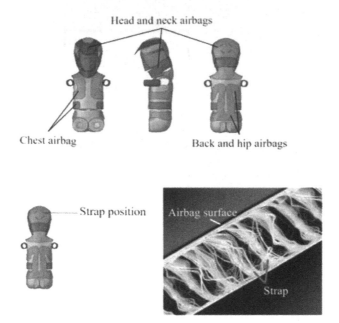

Figure 5.5: Wearable airbag design layout, head air bag pulling strap position (in left) and the detailed micro-structures of the strap (in right) [10].

3.3. Medical

Biocompatible implants: Biocompatible implants could be created using SMAs created by AI to repair or replace organs and tissues that have been damaged (Figure 5.6).

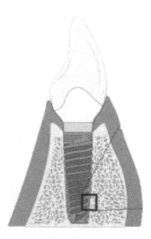

Figure 5.6: Shown an oral osseointegration processes in a dental implant over time in a dental implant [11].

SMAs created by AI could be used to create biocompatible implants that can restore or replace organs and tissues that have been damaged. Patients with a variety of medical conditions may experience an improvement in their quality of life and life expectancy as a result [11].

Smart surgical instruments: Intelligent surgical tools – AI-designed SMAs could be used to create intelligent surgical tools that can safely and accurately carry out complex operations.

Complex and intelligent surgical instruments for performing precise surgeries can also be created using AI-designed SMAs. This will eventually decrease the complications and will increase the effectiveness of surgery [12].

Medical wearable devices: SMAs designed using AI can be used to monitor patient's condition and deliver a proper treatment by creating medical wearables (Figure 5.7).

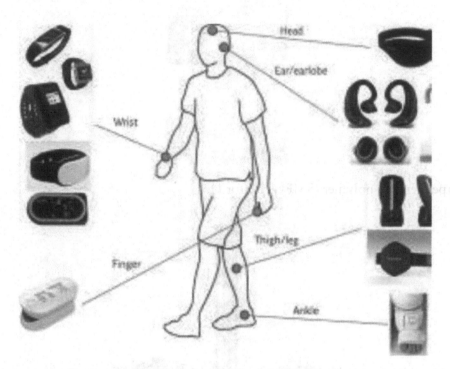

Figure 5.7: Location on the body of several commercially available wearable devices able to perform pulse oximetry [13].

3.4. Robotics

Soft robots: Interactive and movable robotic devices towards the environment can be created using SMAs designed using AI (Figures 5.8a–d).

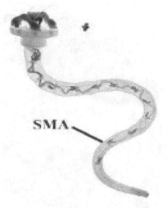

Figure 5.8(a): Shape memory alloy (SMA) actuator [14].

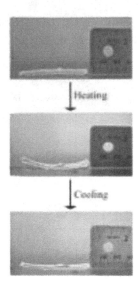

Figure 5.8(b): Shape memory polymer (SMP) actuator [15].

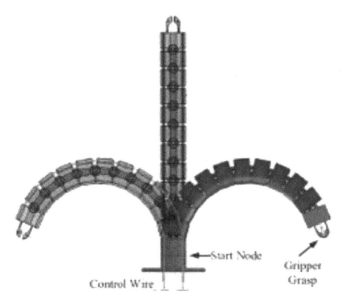

Figure 5.8(c): Cable actuators [16].

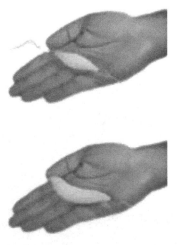

Figure 5.8(d): Dielectric elastomer actuator [17].

As a result, innovative and fresh use of robots can be made across different sectors including healthcare, manufacturing and at the times of disaster relief.

Exoskeletons: SMAs also have the power to create exoskeletons for assisting individual with disabilities and uplift the capabilities of healthy patients [18].

Biomimetic robots: Robots mimicking the movements and capabilities of biological creatures fall under this category and for developing the same SMAs are designed using AI (Figure 5.9).

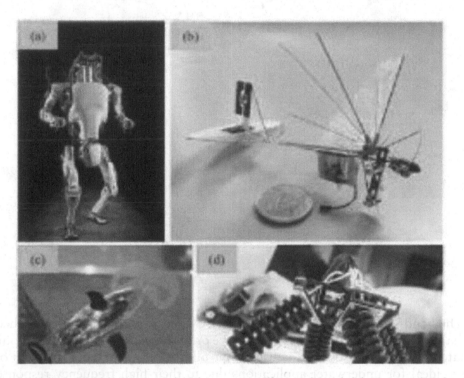

Figure 5.9: (a) Boston dynamics has created Atlas, an intelligent bipedal humanoid robot. (b) The 3.07 g DelFly micro robot has flapping wings. (c) JESSIKO is an underwater robot that navigates the water with fins. (d) Four-legged, 3D-printed soft robot with a turtle-inspired design [19].

AI creates SMAs which are indeed used in variety of industries for example: Consumer electronics, construction, and energy. Apart from the mentions there are a lot of use cases of SMAs in the field of computer science and IT. Below are a few illustrations:

Microfluidic devices: Devices which can manipulate and control fluids at the micro level can be made using SMAs. Indeed creating possibilities of chemical analysis, lab-on-a-chip devices and drug delivery (Figure 5.10).

SMAs actuators in the devices are used in microchannels regulating fluid flows. As a result, actuators are responsible to control the opening and closing of micro channels, which allows controlled and precise fluid or drug delivery.

SMA-based microfluidic devices have higher number of benefits as compared to conventional ones. They are more strong, dependable, and efficient in terms of energy. Also, they have wide range of uses and adaptable to surroundings. Despite the fact, they are still under research and development stage, MA-based microfluid devices tend to completely turn the industry. They can also be utilized to create inventive and novel applications in a lot of industries including drug delivery and chemical analysis.

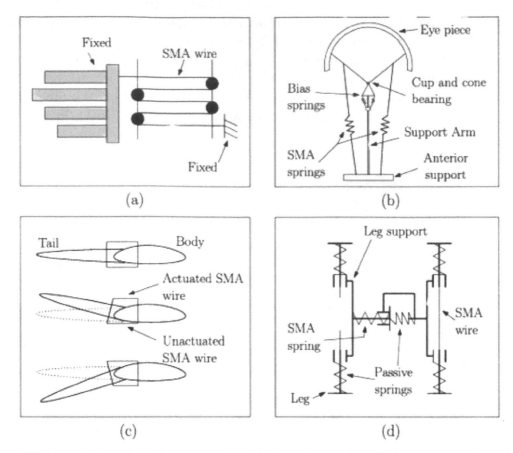

Figure 5.10: (a) The hand-shaped device, actuated by SMA wires, is installed on a two-wheeled autonomous mobile robot for haptic force interaction. (b) A robotic eye orbital prosthesis with an antagonistically mounted SMA spring-actuated eye orbital prosthesis is used, controlled by a signal from the eye's ocular muscle. (c) SMA actuators are ideal for underwater applications due to their high frequency response and low bandwidth, enabling the creation of wave form motion by simulating fish motion. (d) SMA actuators are utilized to construct micro robots for pipe inspection, which utilize the inch-worm motion principle and are powered by SMA wires [20].

Actuators for wearables can be made using SMAs, including smart glasses and exoskeletons. After applying it to the gadgets that will communicate more securely and naturally with the surroundings (Figure 5.11).

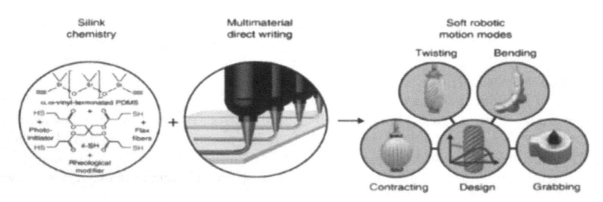

Figure 5.11: Silicone-based 3D-printing pneumatic actuators [21].

Actuators are light in weight and hence can be used for wearable technology. Despite being strong and dependable, they are responsible for producing a wide range of distinct movements [22].

Smart sensors: As compared to conventional sensors, smart sensors are capable of acting and detecting changes in respective environment intelligently. Their capacity to gather data, examine it and take decisions made them more reliable. Smart sensors exchanged information along regular internet connectivity with other devices or system.

Network monitoring: To monitor well-being and functionality of computer networks, smart sensors are used. As soon as an issue is found administrators can take corrective actions.

Data center monitoring: Data center environment monitoring is possible only because of the intelligent sensors. They can detect variation in humidity, temperature, and power usage. With the help of this information effectiveness and dependability can be increased.

Security monitoring: Monitoring of security systems to get rid of intrusions and anomalies is possible because of smart sensors. They can spot unauthorized access of specific locations such as buildings, computer systems and other places.

Temperature sensors: Smart temperature sensors keep a check on temperature of or inside critical infrastructure, such as data centers or computer hardware. These help to make sure that the equipment is working fine and helps to avoid overheating within a safe temperature range, the sensor information can be used.

Humidity sensors: As a part of temperature sensors, moving a step ahead to measure humidity using humidity sensors across data centers and in buildings. By understanding the humid knowledge condensation can be avoided to run the operative equipment safely in a specific humidity range [23].

Motion sensors: Unauthorized access to the sensitive areas like buildings, computer systems etc. is sensed using intelligent motion sensors. Apart from this, they can be used to keep an eye on people and equipment moving seamlessly around in crucial infrastructure says data centers (Figure 5.12).

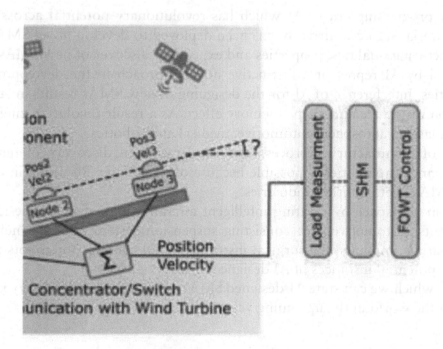

Figure 5.12: Mooring sense smart sensor system block [24].

Vibration sensors: To keep an eye on machine health and spot the potential issues intelligent vibration sensors can be used. Also, they can play a major role in detecting earthquakes and other natural disasters.

Acoustic sensors: To monitor and analyze noise levels smart acoustic sensors can be used. They check the noise levels at critical infrastructures and data centers within reasonable limits [25].

Chemical sensors: It is important to find and keep an eye on the presence of dangerous chemicals in environment, for which smart chemical sensors are used. They are indeed responsible for keeping a check on the water and food supply.

Smart optical sensors are used to measure and keep a keen check on eye specifically on optical parameters like light color and intensity. They are applied to variety of tasks which includes quality assurance, environment monitoring and machine vision.

Smart biometric sensors that can recognize people by their distinctive physical traits, such as their fingerprints, facial features, and iris patterns, are known as biometric sensors. They are employed in several applications, including time and attendance, access control, and security systems [7].

A rapidly evolving technology, smart sensors have the potential to completely change the field of computer science and information technology. We can increase effectiveness, dependability, and security by using smart sensors to monitor and manage computer networks, data centers, security systems, and industrial processes.

4. Conclusions

Shape memory alloys are the types of intelligent materials that have recovering capabilities taking them back to their original shapes after deformation. This takes place from different phase transformations which happen on heating or cooling of the SMA. Usually, SMAs are comprised of two or more metals and the reversible martensitic transformation results in aforementioned phase transformation.

In the rapidly progressing era of AI which has revolutionary potential across different industries including material science; currently has been deployed to develop novel SMAs which possess enhanced manufacturing qualities, properties and expediting discover of new SMAs.

SMAs designed by AI represent a distinctive novel approach in the development of SMAs of improved properties. Interference of AI for the designing of new SMAs results in superior elasticity, strength, corrosion resistance and shape memory effect. As a result revolutionizing a wide array of industries, encompassing aerospace, automotive, medical and robotics.

Optimization of manufacturing process and acceleration in discovery of new SMAs having enhanced performance capabilities is possible because of AI designs. Resulting in creation of novel and innovative SMAs over countless industries.

Summarizing in aerospace by creating intelligent aircraft wings, dynamic de-icing systems and durable components; automotive area consisting suspension systems, body panels and intelligent airbags; biocompatible implants like surgical instruments; till robotics for robots mimic biological systems are a few potential instances of AI designed SMAs.

Concluding to which we can state AI-designed SMAs possess the revolutionary potential to make a great impact on the world in the upcoming years.

References

[1] Chaudhari, R., Vora, J. J., Mani Prabu, S. S., Palani, I. A., Patel, V. K., Parikh, D. M., and de Lacalle, L. N. L. (2019). Multi-response optimization of WEDM process parameters for machining of superelastic nitinol shape-memory alloy using a heat-transfer search algorithm. *Materials*, 12(8), 1277.

[2] Greninger, A. B. and Mooradian, V. G. (1938). Strain transformation in metastable beta copper-zinc and beta copper-Ti alloys. *Aime Trans.*, 128, 337–369.

[3] Kauffman, G. B. and Mayo, I. (1997). The story of nitinol: the serendipitous discovery of the memory metal and its applications. *Chem. Educat.*, 2, 1–21.

[4] Shougat, M. R. E. U., Kennedy, S., and Perkins, E. (2023). A self-sensing shape memory alloy actuator physical reservoir computer. *IEEE Sens. Lett.*, 7(5), 1–4.

[5] Massaro, A. (2023). Intelligent materials and nanomaterials improving physical properties and control oriented on electronic implementations. *Electronics*, 12(18), 1–24, 3772.

[6] Parveez, B., Kittur, M. I., Badruddin, I. A., Kamangar, S., Hussien, M., and Umarfarooq, M. A. (2022). Scientific advancements in composite materials for aircraft applications: A review. *Polymers*, 14(22), 5007.

[7] Lu, B. and Wang, N. (2010). The Boeing 787 dreamliner designing an aircraft for the future. *J. Young Invest.*, 4026, 34.

[8] Xue, W., Li, K., Chen, Q. and Liu, G. (2019). Mixed FTS/H∞ control of vehicle active suspensions with shock road disturbance. *Veh. Sys. Dynam.*, 57(6), 841–854.

[9] Everitt, A. and Alexander, J. (2019). 3D printed deformable surfaces for shape-changing displays. *Front. Robot. AI*, 6, 80.

[10] Zhang, X., Xue, Z., and Tu, W. (2023). Design and performance research of a wearable airbag for the human body. *Appl. Sci.*, 13(6), 3628.

[11] Silva, R. C., Agrelli, A., Andrade, A. N., Mendes-Marques, C. L., Arruda, I. R., Santos, L. R., Vasconcelos, N. F., and Machado, G. (2022). Titanium dental implants: an overview of applied nanobiotechnology to improve biocompatibility and prevent infections. *Materials*, 15(9), 3150.

[12] Mahfouz, M. R., To, G., and Kuhn, M. J. (2012). Smart instruments: Wireless technology invades the operating room. *2012 IEEE Topical Conf. Biomed. Wireless Technol. Netw. Sens. Sys. (BioWireleSS)*, 33–36.

[13] Aliverti, A. (2017). Wearable technology: Role in respiratory health and disease. *Breathe*, 13(2), e27–e36.

[14] Laschi, C., Cianchetti, M., Mazzolai, B., Margheri, L., Follador, M., and Dario, P. (2012). Soft robot arm inspired by the octopus. *Adv. Robot.*, 26(7), 709–727.

[15] Tan, C. (2015). Soft reversible actuators based on shape memory polymer (Doctoral dissertation, Syracuse University).

[16] Li, Z., Du, R., Lei, M. C., and Yuan, S. M. (2011). Design and analysis of a biomimetic wire-driven robot arm. *ASME Int. Mec. Engg. Cong. Expos.*, 54938, 191–198.

[17] Schaffner, M., Faber, J. A., Pianegonda, L., Rühs, P. A., Coulter, F., and Studart, A. R. (2018). 3D printing of robotic soft actuators with programmable bioinspired architectures. *Nat. Comm.*, 9(1), 878.

[18] Gifari, M. W., Naghibi, H., Stramigioli, S., and Abayazid, M. (2019). A review on recent advances in soft surgical robots for endoscopic applications. *Int. J. Med. Robot. Comp. Assist. Surg.*, 15(5), e2010.

[19] Wang, J., Chen, W., Xiao, X., Xu, Y., Li, C., Jia, X., and Meng, M. Q. H. (2020). A survey of the development of biomimetic intelligence and robotics. *Biomim. Intel. Robot.*, 1, 1–14, 100001. DOI:10.34133/2020/8716847.

[20] Chaurasiya, K. L., Harsha, A. S., Sinha, Y., and Bhattacharya, B. (2022). Design and development of non-magnetic hierarchical actuator powered by shape memory alloy based bipennate muscle. *Sci. Reports*, 12(1), 10758.

[21] Schaffner, M., Faber, J. A., Pianegonda, L., Rühs, P. A., Coulter, F., and Studart, A. R. (2018). 3D printing of robotic soft actuators with programmable bioinspired architectures. *Nat. Comm.*, 9(1), 878.

[22] Chen, Y., Yang, Y., Li, M., Chen, E., Mu, W., Fisher, R., and Yin, R. (2021). Wearable actuators: An overview. *Textiles*, 1(2), 283–321.

[23] Wang, L., Lou, Z., Wang, K., Zhao, S., Yu, P., Wei, W., Wang, D., Han, W., Jiang, K., and Shen, G. (2020). Biocompatible and biodegradable functional polysaccharides for flexible humidity sensors. *Research*.

[24] Revert Calabuig, N., Laarossi, I., Álvarez González, A., Pérez Nuñez, A., González Pérez, L., and García-Minguillán, A. C. (2023). Development of a low-cost smart sensor GNSS system for real-time positioning and orientation for floating offshore wind platform. *Sensors*, 23(2), 925.

[25] Socoró, J. C., Alías, F., and Alsina-Pagès, R. M. (2017). An anomalous noise events detector for dynamic road traffic noise mapping in real-life urban and suburban environments. *Sensors*, 17(10), 2323.

6 Systematic Literature Review on Diagnosis of Arrhythmia Using Intelligent Computing Methods

Neha Goyal[1,a], Rohit Agarwal, and Sakshi Srivastava

[1]Department of CSE, BN College of Engineering & Technology, Lucknow, India

Abstract

In today's era, the life style of people has become much sophisticated due to involvement of stress, anxiety and depression in daily routine of human being. In such scenario cardiac diseases are growing rapidly in youngsters as well as in senior citizens. It is also observed that cardiac diseases are much crucial and sensitive including life threatening chances. So, it is very essential to detect and prevent such type of cardiac disorder within required time for recovery. Since it has become a lot of research in prediction and prevention of cardiac disorders and cardiac arrhythmia is also one of the majorly occurring disease in a bulk of population. Electrocardiogram (ECG) is the cheap and best way for the diagnosis of the problem of cardiac arrhythmia and there is a huge amount of data which is collected day by day in hospitals and pathological centers. Previously there are developed various automated models for detection of cardiac arrhythmia using various machine learning (ML) and deep learning approaches. In this work a review on recent developed automated model is performed based on their performance based on some specific parameters like deployed datasets, variation of input data, applied application, methodology and results obtained by the developed model. There are also mentioned the limitations of reviewed papers in addition with their future scope of improvement.

Keywords: Intelligent computing, arrhythmia, ECG, machine learning

1. Introduction

Arrhythmia is generally considered a problem of irregular heart beat in human and it is very crucial for life threats and misses happenings. There exists various kind of arrhythmia with some specific recognition and features and so it becomes very helpful to classify and distinguish the various categories of arrhythmia. Generally, the detection of arrhythmia is by classifying it into two classes, whereas the first one is diagnosed by the problem of a single irregularity in heart beat and so called as morphological arrhythmia. The second phase of the arrhythmia is diagnosed with the feature of multiple irregularity in heart beats and hence considered as a problem of rhythmic arrhythmia.

---

[a]nehagoyal.cse@gmail.com

Basically, there are observed some changes and alterations in wave form of the heartbeats if an individual is consisting with morphological or rhythmic arrhythmia. The detection and diagnosis of the issue is done by electrocardiography (ECG) as well as with the echocardiogram (ECHO). The problem of arrhythmia is directly associated with issue in valve of heart which results some irregular heart rates.

The ECG is a well-established tool in cardiology for assessing a patient's heart status. ECG stands for electrocardiogram, which is an electrical representation of the heart's contractile activity that may be conveniently recorded using surface electrodes on the patient's limbs or chest. In the world of medicine, the ECG is one of the most well-known and widely used biological signals. Counting the R peaks of the ECG wave throughout one minute of recording (Figure 1) is a simple way to calculate the heart's rhythm in beats per minute (bpm). More importantly, cardiovascular illnesses and disorders impact the rhythm and morphology of the ECG waveform.

A heart trace is an ECG. It can tell you about your heart's rhythm and pace. Abnormal heart tracings can indicate a variety of diseases, in addition to heart rhythm abnormalities. Fast heartbeats (tachycardia), slow heartbeats (bradycardia), heart blockages, and irregular heartbeats are all examples of heart rhythm disorders (atrial fibrillation). It can also reveal information on heart chamber enlargement and anomalies in the heart muscle. An echocardiogram is a moving picture of the heart's structure and function obtained by an ultrasound scan. It displays precise information on the heart's pumping activity as well as the diameters of the heart chambers. As a result, they're a useful test for determining the severity of heart failure. Echocardiograms can also tell you how well your heart valves are working. So generally, ECG is considered better and comfortable for detection of arrhythmia due to its low cost and time consumption features in addition with having capability to determine irregularity in heart palpitations more accurately.

Finding and classifying arrhythmias can be extremely difficult for a human being because it is necessary to assess each heartbeat of ECG readings obtained by a holter monitor over hours or even days. Furthermore, due to fatigue, there is a risk of human error during the processing of ECG recordsThe use of computational tools for automatic classification is an option.

A complete automatic approach for detecting arrhythmias from ECG signals may be broken down into four parts (Figure 6.1): Pre-processing of ECG signals; heartbeat segmentation; feature extraction; and learning/classification. A step is taken in each of the four processes, with the eventual goal of determining the type of heartbeat. The first two steps of such a classification system (ECG signal pre-processing and heartbeat segmentation) have been extensively studied [2–6]. Pre-processing procedures have a direct impact on the final outcomes, thus they should be carefully chosen. In the case of QRS detection, the findings from the heartbeat segmentation stage are almost perfect. However, there is still room for exploration and improvements in the steps related to classification (feature extraction and learning algorithms). Even though the problem of ECG delineation is still open, it is not so useful for the methods in the literature surveyed here.

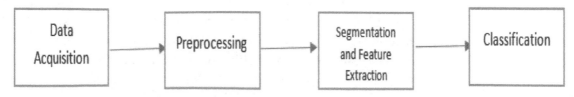

Figure 6.1: Steps of learning system.

Given its history as the leading cause of death in both women and men around the world [1] heart disease receives a lot of attention. Several risk factors have been discovered like hyperlipidemia, hypertension, and obesity and all are linked to heart disease including habit of smoking. Heart disease can be predicted and prevented by identifying such risk factors. In the very beginning risk variables hidden in unstructured clinical information must be identified. Many researches have been published in the previous years, which have focused to identify these risk variables and that was resulted in the formation of publicly available tools like examination of clinical observations and the knowledge extraction system which is an open-source tool that can extract information from a variety of sources.

Other disorders, such as diabetes, are frequently linked to heart disease that have several obvious qualities in common, such as obesity and smoking status, as well as some drugs, such as metoprolol, are all factors to consider. All for the purposes of this investigation, each of these was considered a risk factor for heart disease.

The biggest difficulty in recognizing all heart disease risk factors is that they appear in clinical texts in a range of categories. In 2014, the National Center of Informatics for Integrating Biology and beside (i2b2) announced a risk factor identification track in the clinical natural language processing (NLP) challenge to examine the identification of all heart disease risk factors in depth. The goal was to find medically relevant information about heart disease risk and follow its evolution across sets of longitudinal patient medical records. After getting inspired from the revolution there was created a hybrid pipeline system that included machine learning and rule-based techniques.

2. Background

There are several types of arrhythmias, each of which is associated with a pattern that can be used to identify and classify it. Arrhythmias are divided into two types. The first category includes morphological arrhythmias, which are arrhythmias caused by a single irregular heartbeat. This survey focuses on the classification of normal heartbeats and the individuals who make up that category. The morphology or wave frequency of these heartbeats' changes, and the ECG exam can detect all these changes. Identification and classification of arrhythmias can be a time-consuming task for a human because it sometimes requires analyzing each heartbeat in ECG recordings.

We have chosen few research articles for review based on deep learning and machine learning for arrhythmia detection in this paper. The articles chosen from various databases are like PubMed, Embase, and Google Scholar are just a few of the databases available. This review included only peer-reviewed publications published between January 12, 2014 and December 30, 2021, with preprints being eliminated. Only deep learning publications for arrhythmia detection were chosen by screening title, key words, and abstract after removing duplicate records and non-English papers. Finally, 15 papers were chosen for this review.

3. Motivation

You can find gaps in the current body of knowledge by reviewing the literature. You can spot problems that still need to be solved or locations where additional work needs to be done. By concentrating on these uncharted territories, this can direct your own research. It helps to compare, and benchmark different methods and approaches used in arrhythmia detection. This can help you determine which methods are more effective, accurate, or suitable for specific applications. Choosing the best intelligent computing strategies for arrhythmia detection can be aided by knowledge of the literature. To select the appropriate techniques and algorithms for your own work, you can learn from the achievements and failures of earlier study.

4. Literature Search Approach

Multiple academic research databases were chosen to compile pertinent publications published between January 2010 and September 2022 for this review. PubMed, IEEE Xplore, Springer, ScienceDirect, and ResearchGate are the names of these open source databases. Two of the top databases for biological sciences and engineering, respectively, are IEEE Xplore and PubMed [7]. One of the top research publishers, Springer offers a variety of sources for literature in various subjects. ScienceDirect was also used for its numerous and different peer-reviewed journals and publications. As the largest academic social network in terms of active users, ResearchGate provides access to a substantial number of free articles [8].

The following procedure was used to collect the data sources:

1. Focused internet search.
2. Sources are grouped according to their level of relevance.
3. Based on the inclusion criteria indicated in Table 6.1, studies were chosen.

Table 6.1: Inclusion criteria for literature search

Parameters	Description
Duration	2010–2022
Article type	Journal and conferences
Area of research	Intelligent computing and bio-medicals
Performance metrics	Accuracy, sensitivity and specificity

4.1. Study selection

The following circumstances are included in the chosen studies scope:

a. Studies addressing the classification of any type of arrhythmia.
b. Studies on the diagnosis of arrhythmia in the last 12 years.
c. Studies focusing on the diagnosis of arrhythmias that are unaffected by other cardiovascular diseases can accurately pinpoint the extent and conditions of this abnormality's occurrence and, as a result, determine a precise diagnosis and prognosis.

4.2. Article selection scheme

Here, a schematic is represented for selection and rejection of the research articles based on some significant parameters like keyword search, abstract sorting, duplicate removal and inclusion criteria-based removal. Figure 6.2 shows the overall progress of literature search and study choice strategy.

In this scheme we have initially searched 350 articles related with intelligent computing in bio-medicals, further we removed those articles which were not related to erythema detection. Some articles were removed due to duplicate identification and then we focused to select only those articles

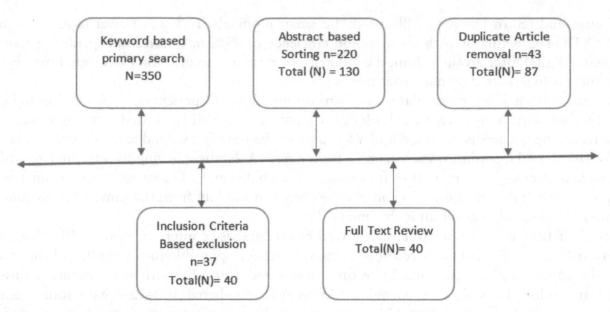

Figure 6.2: Study selection approach.

which are completely meeting out the inclusion criteria. So, final 40 articles were selected to perform the systematic literature review process.

Different approaches for classification of arrhythmia:

An automated model for the detection of heart disease risk factors was developed in 2015 based on relationship among various diseases like diabetes, hypertension, high blood pressure, etc., and their impact towards heart risk. This model was having data set from I2V2 organizers of challenges and organized it into three different tags (Phrase-based, logic-based, and discourse-based) associated with their indicators or features. In this research the data was pre-processed using annotated guidelines and their features were extracted based on above discussed three tags. Then there was applied SSVM using SVMhmm, libshort text 6 for implementation of SVM, and CRF suite for the implementation of CRF. Furthermore, upgraded parameters of all classifiers using 10-fold cross-validation on the training set were deployed and obtained the and obtained 92.68 while I2B2 challenge organizers have already obtained the accuracy of 92.76. The developed model was not fit for the diseases like coronary artery disease (CAD), obesity status, and smoking status [1].

Another work describes a stacked denoising autoencoder-based automatic wearable electrocardiogram (ECG) categorization and monitoring system (SDAE). To gather ECG data, we employ a wearable device with wireless sensors and Bluetooth 4.2 to communicate the data to a computer. The automatic cardiac arrhythmia classification system then categorizes these ECG data. The SDAE with sparsity constraint is used to learn the ECG feature representation. To classify the ECG beats, the SoftMax regression is employed. Active learning is used to increase performance during the fine-tuning phase [2].

4.3. ECG signal acquisition

In a research there was introduced an adequate attachment of fabric electrodes to the pectoral muscles, and a magnetic interface ensures that the connection between the fabric electrodes and the hardware platform. There was used a biosensor platform to assess ECG signals using the ADI ECG analogue front-end (ADAS1001) and STM32 microcontroller is exploited to realize data processing, packaging, and retransmission to Bluetooth 4.2 smart terminals. To lessen power usage even more, an LDO DC-DC regulator with a conversion efficiency of 95% has been implemented. There was designed a digital filter group to limit the influence of extensive sounds for ECG signal because it is weak and easily distorted by numerous noises [2].

A total of 48 half-hour ambulatory ECG recordings from 47 patients are included in the database. Two leads make up each record. Modified branch lead II (MLII) is used as the first lead in 45 of the recordings, whereas modified lead V5 is used in the rest. The second lead is a pericardial lead (V1 for the first 40 recordings, V2, V4, or V5 for the rest). A database having twenty-three recordings were picked at random from a set of four thousand ambulatory ECG footages taken from a mixed group of patients; the additional 25 copies were chosen at random from the same set to include less common but clinically significant arrhythmias [3].

The MIT-BIH arrhythmia database is a web-based database comprised of over 4000 long-term electrocardiogram (ECG) Holter recordings. Patients were responsible for over 60% of the recordings. The entire database contains 23 records (numbered 100–124, with some numbers missing) picked at random from this set, as well as 25 records (numbered 100–124, with some numbers missing) from this set. Almost 200–234, with some numbers missing) were chosen from the same set to represent a range of rare but clinically significant diseases. Each of these records has a sample frequency of 360 Hz and contains two leads (two signals recorded from different angles on chest). Only one-minute long sections of each record is extracted obtaining a total of six recordings (3 for training and 3 for testing), each containing 21,600 samples and approximately 60–80 waveforms depending on heart rate and class (normal, rbbb or paced) [4].

The Database (called Long-term ST) contains 86 lengthy ECG recordings from 80 human volunteers, chosen to demonstrate a variety of ST segment abnormalities, such as ischemia ST episodes, axis-related non-ischemic ST episodes, delayed ST level drift episodes, and episodes combining these phenomena [5].

4.4. ECG signal pre-processing

Data pre-processing comprises wave filtering and denoising. Using a 200 ms width median, all the ECG signals are eliminated, including the P wave and QRS complex. filter. A 600 ms wide median removes the T wave filter. The original signals are subtracted from the resultant signals to get at the baseline corrected ECG signals will be returned [2].

Data from MIT-BIH arrhythmia database is filtered using band-pass technique at 0.1–100 Hz and digitized at rate of 360 samples per second. There was used two phases of median filtering approaches to reduce the baseline drifting of these signals [3].

Although ECG data from the MIT-BIH database is unlikely to have as much disruptive noise as ECG data collected directly from a patient, it still contains some noise that needs to be addressed to optimize the system's future stages. As a result, the signal pre-processing stage concentrates on eliminating noise from ECG records, mean removal is used to remove the dc noise from the ECG signals as a first step. The undesirable dc component is removed, and the signal baseline amplitude is pushed down to level zero by subtracting the ECG recording mean from each sample point [4].

To reduce low-frequency noise, the ECG signals were processed through a low-pass filter with a cutoff frequency of 20 Hz. The baseline drift was also reduced by running through a high-pass filter with a lower cut-off frequency of 0.3 Hz. A 50 Hz notch filter was used to reduce power source interference noise. Finally, the Pan-Tompkins method [23] was used to accurately extract the QRS complexes from the R peaks of the ECG data [5].

4.5. Feature extraction

The mean RR and mean HR are the most obvious traits. Some, including SDNN, SDSD, RMSSD, and PNN50, are statistical features that characterize variability within RR intervals, while others, like TINN and HRV triangular index, are geometric features [5].

When looking at the ECG data, it's evident that the traits that clearly define each class (normal, rbbb, and paced) are found between the R-T interval. It is also clear that each member of a class exhibits the same pattern in this interval. In this case, 200 sample points are retrieved and fed as an input to the transferred deep learning-based feature extractor after each R-peak (roughly this number of samples corresponds to the R-T interval with sampling frequency of 360 Hz). The ECG waveforms' remaining components are then deleted [4].

A web-based ECG annotation tool created specifically for this study was used to annotate the 30 second recordings of ECG signals. Certified cardio graphic technicians who have undergone intensive training in arrhythmia identification and a cardio graphic certification examination by Cardiovascular Credentialing International performed the label annotations. Before they started working, the technicians were given instructions on how to use the interface. All the beats in a strip were labeled from onset to offset, leading in complete segmentation of the input ECG data. Specific guidelines for each rhythm transition were created to promote labeling consistency across different annotators [8].

There is a total of 79 features calculated, all of which are thoroughly detailed in the provided software documentation. There are three primary groupings in the feature set:

Rhythm features: Statistical parameters of the RR sequence, such as limits, median, or median absolute deviation; heart rate variability aspects, such as the PNN5, PNN10, PNN50, and PNN100 measures; and information regarding the rhythm interpretation, such as the median duration of each rhythm hypothesis [9].

Morphological features: This comprises data on the duration, amplitude, and frequency spectrum of observations at the conduction abstraction level, such as P and T waves, QRS complexes, PR and QT intervals, and TP segments.

Signal quality features: These are used to determine the significance of morphological traits that indicate conduction abnormalities, such as broad QRS complexes or lengthy PR intervals.

Temporal, frequency, and non-linear dynamic parameters are employed to distinguish between CAD and non-CAD patients, according to [10]. The study used an autoregressive (AR) modeling-based method to produce power spectrum density for frequency domain characteristics measurement; AR spectrum is the most prevalent method for HRV analysis, and this methodology may be factorized into discrete spectral components [10]. The AR model is more complicated, and its spectral factorization includes the possibility of negative components. Following that, the authors used statistical and geometrical properties such as SD, RMSSD, and HRV triangular index for time domain calculations.

4.6. Classification

ECG Arrhythmia detection methods based on transferable deep learning feature extraction outperformed the non-deep learning strategy by a significant margin,

Furthermore, the results obtained by networks that use features extracted from AlexNet's deep full convolutional layers (6th and 7th) demonstrated that the deeper layers of a deep convolutional neural network trained on a large annotated data set can be generic enough to be transferred and implemented for ECG arrhythmia classification tasks [4].

The dataset consisted of ECG signals from 23 healthy volunteers and 23 CAD patients. They were all evaluated in the time and frequency domains. Because biological signals are non-linear, a non-linear approach was employed to determine non-linear aspects of the ECG.

There were 9-time domain features, 24 frequency domain features (both FFT and AR techniques), and 12 non-linear domain features. More dimensions mean more time, money, and needless complexity; also, some characteristics are not distinguishable between CAD and non-CAD subjects.

As a result, indiscriminative characteristics have been eliminated non order to lower the problem's dimension and computing complexity using the PCA method. As inputs, 45 features derived from the approaches mentioned were used [5].

The suggested system is evaluated using a four-fold cross-validation approach. There are four subsets in the dataset with random sizes of equal size It should be noted that our data collection comprises, as a result, there are 200 positive samples and 200 negative samples. Each subgroup has 50 positive and 50 negative samples. There was repeated the experiment four times and receive four different results each time. One subset is utilized as testing each time. The remaining sets are utilized as training sets. The average precision – Local Binary Pattern (LBP) and Histogram of Oriented Gradients (HOG) are used in this case. Here focus on a specific characteristic (intensity, for example, LBP, and HOG), as well as feature combinations (I+LBP, LBP+HOG, etc.) [6].

An ensemble of RNNs is used in this method to jointly recognize temporal patterns. In segmented ECG recordings, and morphological patterns, any length is acceptable. In terms of specifics, our strategy achieves an average.

F1 score of 0.79 on the PhysioNet's private test set CinC Challenge 2017 $(n = 3, 658)$ $(n = 3, 658)$ $(n = 3, 658)$ $(n = 3, 658)$ $(n = 3, 658)$ $(n = 3, 65)$. Normal rhythms, AF, and AF-like rhythms received ratings of 0.90, 0.79, and 0.68, respectively, additional arrhythmias, and so on. Our technique, in addition to its cutting-edge performance, maintains a high level of security [6, 7].

The employment of a soft attention mechanism over heartbeats improves interpretability. We are doing this in the spirit of open research.

PhysioNet 2017 open will make an implementation of our heart rhythm classification algorithm available [7].

On the test set, there is evaluated the cardiologist's performance. Remember that each of the records in the test set contains a ground truth label from a group of three cardiologists, as well as individual labels from a separate group of six cardiologists. The average of all individual cardiologist F1 scores and use the group label as the ground truth annotation to assess cardiologist performance for each class [8].

5. Discussion

In Table 6.2, we have disused the feature extraction techniques along with result obtained by using specific methodology. It seems that intelligent computing process has played a significant role for detection of arrhythmia with proper accuracy in comparison with manual diagnosis. In previous year 2022, Ullah et al., [39] has obtained accuracy more than 99.35% and Gao et al., [24] has obtained the accuracy of 99.25% in 2019. It shows the continuous progress in attainment of better accuracy and there are used various dimension reduction techniques for reducing computational overhead and achieving better results by using only responsible features.

The research used the multi-class prediction to diagnose arrhythmia. Though not all of the research using 12-class prediction and more recorded the maximum performances as in literature,

Table 6.2: Use of intelligent computing in arrhythmia detection including methodology and feature extraction

Publication year	Reference	Methodology	Feature extraction	Result (accuracy) (%)
2019	16	12-lead feature fusion	RR interval, DWT, FFT	99.80
2019	19	DL-CCANet, TL-CCANet	NR	99.40
2014	11	NR	5 space domain	98.24
2013	25	Optimization using PSO	HOS cumulants+PCA, DWT+HOS+PCA	94.52
2016	13	NR	PCA+LDA	98.80
2019	22	RR interval	Discrete Meyer wavelet	99.75
2017	28	Intrinsic mode functions (IMFs) decomposition	Ensemble empirical mode decomposition (EEMD)	99.20
2021	31	Data decomposition	Empirical mode decomposition (EMD)	99.20
2017	27	K-nearest neighbor classifier (KNN) and a support vector machine (SVM)	PCA+DWT	99.78
2018	29	CNN with PCA filters	Principal component analysis	97.77
2015	23	Support vector machine and neural network	Meyer DWT+PCA	98.90
2018	26	DOST, DST, DCT dictionaries	Sparse decomposition	99.21
2019	18	Convolutional auto-encoder (CAE) based non-linear compression	Raw ECG signal, deep-coded ECG signals by CAE	99
2014	15	Decision tree	Raw data	99
2017	17	9-layer deep convolutional neural network (CNN)	Raw data	89.3
2019	21	Long short-term memory (LSTM) recurrence network model	PCA	99.25
2019	24	Extended-GoogLeNet architecture	PCA	95.30
2019	14	Deep neural network (DNN) to classify 12 rhythm classes	PCA+HOS	97.80
2021	30	CNN + LSTM + attention model	DWT+HOS+PCA	99.12
2022	11	Novel deep learning framework using feature selection	PCA	99.35

the majority of the studies predicted the occurrence of more than two types of arrhythmic heartbeat [16, 18, 22, 26, 30, 33]. This can be explained by the datasets being unbalanced; certain types of heartbeats have few recordings, which have a negative impact on the categorization rate.

6. Conclusions

In summary, based on the analysis presented in the above sections, we are unable to definitively recommend the optimal model because none of the 40 studies that were chosen used precisely the same feature extraction, pre-processing, or prediction strategies throughout the whole process. Additionally, the data used in each study differs in terms of input, ECG signal, development tools, and computing power. But after accounting for all of these variations and the analysis's findings, we may assume that using DL alone or ML in conjunction with DL techniques can produce extremely encouraging outcomes.

References

[1]   Chen, Q., et al. (2015). An automatic system to identify heart disease risk factors in clinical texts over time. *J. Biomed. Informat.*, 58, S158–S163, ISSN 1532-0464 https://doi.org/10.1016/j.jbi.2015.09.002.

[2]   Warrick, P., et al. (2017). Cardiac arrhythmia detection from ECG combining convolutional and long short-term memory networks. *2017 Comput. Cardiol. (CinC)*, 1–4, doi: 10.22489/CinC.2017.161-460.

[3]   Jun, T., et al. (2018). ECG arrhythmia classification using a 2-D convolutional neural network. *ArXiv, abs/1804.06812.*, 1, 1–7, https://doi.org/10.48550/arXiv.1804.06812.

[4]   Isin, A., et al. (2017). Cardiac arrhythmia detection using deep learning. *Proc. Comp. Sci.*, 120, 268–275, SSN 1877-0509, https://doi.org/10.1016/j.procs.2017.11.238.

[5]   Davari, A., et al. (2017). Automated diagnosis of coronary artery disease (CAD) patients using optimized SVM. *Comp. Methods Prog. Biomed.*, 138, 117–126, ISSN 0169-2607, https://doi.org/10.1016/j.cmpb.2016.10.011.

[6]   Xu, M., et al. (2014). Automatic atherosclerotic heart disease detection in intracoronary optical coherence tomography images. *Ann. Int. Conf. IEEE Engg. Med. Biol. Soc.. IEEE Engg. Med. Biol. Soc. Ann. Int. Conf.*, 2014, 174–177. doi:10.1109/EMBC.2014.6943557.

[7]   Schwab, P., et al. (2017). Beat by beat: Classifying cardiac arrhythmias with recurrent neural networks. *2017 Comput. Cardiol. (CinC)*, 1–4, doi: 10.22489/CinC.2017.363-223.

[8]   Hannun, A. Y., Rajpurkar, P., Haghpanahi, M., et al. (2019). Cardiologist-level arrhythmia detection and classification in ambulatory electrocardiograms using a deep neural network. *Nat. Med.*, 25, 65–69. https://doi.org/10.1038/s41591-018-0268-3.

[9]   Teijeiro, T., García, C. A., Castro, D., and Félix, P. (2017, September). Arrhythmia classification from the abductive interpretation of short single-lead ECG records. In 2017 *Computing in cardiology (cinc).*, pp. 1–4. IEEE. doi: 10.22489/CinC.2017.166-054.

[10] Sumathi, S., Beaulah, H. L., and Vanithamani, R. (2014). A wavelet transforms based feature extraction and classification of cardiac disorder. *J. Med. Syst.*, 38, 98. doi: 10.1007/s10916-014-0098-x.

[11] Irfan, S., Anjum, N., Althobaiti, T., Alotaibi, A. A., Siddiqui, A. B., and Ramzan, N. (2022). Heartbeat classification and Arrhythmia detection using a multi-model deep-learning technique. *Sensors*, 22, 5606. doi: 10.3390/.

[12] Li, H., Yuan, D., Wang, Y., Cui, D., and Cao, L. (2016). Arrhythmia classification based on multi-domain feature extraction for an ECG recognition system. *Sensors*, 16, 1744. doi: 10.3390/s16101744.

[13] Park, J. and Kang, K. (2014). PcHD: Personalized classification of heartbeat types using a decision tree. *Comput. Biol. Med.*, 54, 79–88. doi: 10.1016/j.compbiomed.2014.08.013.

[14] Chen, G., Hong, Z., Guo, Y., and Pang, C. (2019). A cascaded classifier for multi-lead ECG based on feature fusion. *Comput. Methods Prog. Biomed.*, 178, 135–143. doi: 10.1016/j.cmpb.2019.06.021.

[15] Acharya, U. R., Oh, S. L., Hagiwara, Y., et al. (2017). A deep convolutional neural network model to classify heartbeats. *Comput. Biol. Med.*, 89, 389–396. doi: 10.1016/j.compbiomed.2017.08.022.

[16] Yildirim, O., Baloglu, U. B., Tan, R. S., Ciaccio, E. J., and Acharya, U. R. (2019). A new approach for arrhythmia classification using deep coded features and LSTM networks. *Comput. Methods Prog. Biomed.*, 176, 121–133. doi: 10.1016/j.cmpb.2019.05.004.

[17] Yang, W., Si, Y., Wang, D., and Zhang, G. (2019). A novel approach for multi-lead ECG classification using DL-CCANet and TL-CCANet. *Sensors,* 19, 3214. doi: 10.3390/s19143214.

[18] Martis, R. J., Acharya, U. R., Lim, C. M., Mandana, K. M., Ray, A. K., Chakraborty, C. (2013). Application of higher order cumulant features for cardiac health diagnosis using ECG signals. *Int. J. Neural Syst.*, 23, 1350014. doi: 10.1142/S0129065713500147.

[19] Gao, J., Zhang, H., Lu, P., and Wang, Z. (2019). An effective LSTM recurrent network to detect arrhythmia on imbalanced ECG dataset. *J. Healthcare Eng.*, 2019, 6320651. doi: 10.1155/2019/6320651.

[20] Anwar, S. M., Gul, M., Majid, M., and Alnowami, M. (2018). Arrhythmia classification of ECG signals using hybrid features. *Comput. Math. Methods Med.*, 2018, 1380348. doi: 10.1155/2018/1380348.

[21] Elhaj, F. A., Salim, N., Harris, A. R., Swee, T. T., and Ahmed, T. (2016). Arrhythmia recognition and classification using combined linear and nonlinear features of ECG signals. *Comput. Methods Prog. Biomed.*, 127, 52–63. doi: 10.1016/j.cmpb.2015.12.024.

[22] Kim, J. H., Seo, S. Y., Song, C. G., and Kim, K. S. (2019). Assessment of electrocardiogram rhythms by GoogLeNet deep neural network architecture. *J. Healthcare Eng.*, 2019, 2826901. doi: 10.1155/2019/2826901.

[23] Yıldırım, O. (2018). Arrhythmia detection using deep convolutional neural network with long duration ECG signals. *Comput. Biol. Med.*, 10, 411–420.

[24] Raj, S. and Ray, K. C. (2018). Automated recognition of cardiac arrhythmias using sparse decomposition over composite dictionary. *Comput. Methods Prog. Biomed.*, 165, 175–186. doi: 10.1016/j.cmpb.2018.08.008.

[25] Rajagopal, R. and Ranganathan, V. (2018). Design of a hybrid model for cardiac arrhythmia classification based on Daubechies wavelet transform. *Adv. Clin. Exp. Med.*, 27, 727–734. doi: 10.17219/acem/68982.

[26] Rajesh, K. N. V. P. S. and Dhuli, R. (2017). Classification of ECG heartbeats using nonlinear decomposition methods and support vector machine. *Comput. Biol. Med.*, 87, 271–284. doi: 10.1016/j.compbiomed.2017.06.006.

[27] Yang, W., Si, Y., Wang, D., and Guo, B. (2018). Automatic recognition of arrhythmia based on principal component analysis network and linear support vector machine. *Comput. Biol. Med.*, 101, 22–32. doi: 10.1016/j.compbiomed.2018.08.003.

[28] Ullah, W., Siddique, I., Zulqarnain, R. M., Alam, M. M., Ahmad, I., and Raza, U. A. (2021). Classification of arrhythmia in heartbeat detection using deep learning. *Comput. Intell. Neurosci.*, 2021, 2195922. doi: 10.1155/2021/2195922.

[29] Sabut, S., Pandey, O., Mishra, B. S. P., and Mohanty, M. (2021). Detection of ventricular arrhythmia using hybrid time–frequency-based features and deep neural network. *Phys. Engg. Sci. Med.*, 44, 135–145. doi: 10.1007/s13246-020-00964-2.

7 Forecasting Mutual Fund Volatility Using Generalized Autoregressive Conditional Heteroskedasticity (GARCH) Model: Evidence from the Indian Mutual Fund

Sanjay Kumar[1,a], Meenakshi Srivastava[1,b], and Vijay Prakash[2,c]

[1]Amity Institute of Information Technology, Amity University, Lucknow, India

[2]School of Computer Applications, Babu Banarsi Das University, Lucknow, India

Abstract

Predicting mutual fund volatility is the most exciting challenge in time series analysis and forecasting. Many researchers have tried to develop different prediction models but it is very difficult to forecast the volatility of mutual funds with 100% accuracy because there are many external parameters that affect the accuracy. Now it is possible to develop sophisticated algorithms and frameworks with the availability of fast computing platforms to extract, store, process, and analyze a high volume of mutual fund market historical data with diversity in its contents. In this paper, researchers proposed a GARCH (EGARCH) model for volatility prediction of the mutual funds time series dataset. The performance of the model and the errors that occurred in this model were calculated using major available techniques with actual values and predicted values. This paper uses the Indian mutual funds dataset and presents a reliable and more accurate forecasting framework for predicting the time series volatility values. Experimental results show that the proposed framework works well and provides optimized returns for mutual funds in the Indian mutual fund market.

Keywords: Volatility, framework, GARCH, mutual fund, forecasting

1. Introduction

In statistical terms, volatility is the standard deviation of the annual return of a market or security over a given time period essentially the rate at which its price rises or falls. If the price moves rapidly in a short period of time, reaching new highs and lows, it is said to have high volatility. If the price rises or falls more slowly or is relatively stable, it is said to have low volatility. The future growth of a company, and thus the interests of its shareholders, depends on many internal and external factors. Investment trust (MF) managers collect funds from many different investors and then invest this corpus in many different sectors and types of mutual fund according to their risk bearing capability. This money is invested by fund managers in low risk to high risk mutual fund schemes and optimize portfolio of the customers. The invested money in mutual fund is about Rs. 37.22 trillion at dated

[a]k.sanjay123@gmail.com, [b]msrivastava@lko.amity.edu, [c]vijaylko@gmail.com

May 31, 2022; this investment of corpus has increased up to four times in the last 10 years (Indian Mutual Fund Association, 2022). This means a massive 400% growth in just over a decade, shows the tremendous interest to invest the money in mutual fund industry. This resent trend shows that the general public (individual investors) is investing heavily in various schemes of mutual fund according to their need. One reason to be interested in midfielders is that most investors want higher returns, but not the risk of investing directly in the mutual fund market. They believe it is safer to invest the money in mutual fund market through an adviser or any investment firms. Another reason for interest in investment in mutual fund industry is low interest rates on fixed deposit in banks. So customer looking for alternatives of different investment options that minimize uncertainty and provide reasonable returns. In general, investing in mutual fund can make good profits, but there is also the risk. Generally investors prefers for investment in MFs because they think that invested money is safe because experts fund managers manage their money in different sectors to reduce risk factors and can increase profit. Fixed income MFs (also known as debt funds) typically invest in collateralized products that provide principal protection but have low returns. Again, equity-based midfielders are a high-risk, high-paying group, and most of their capital is used to buy shares in listed companies. Hybrid MF and balance MF are medium-risk funds where the entire corpus is invested in risk-free and safe assets bonds and high-risk stocks.

COVID-19 was an unplanned event that slowdowns profit of almost all type of companies but few companies like pharmaceutical companies are glove makers in this pandemic and are profitable because grate demand for their products. Even a well-functioning business sector company can suffer financial loss, bankruptcy, or fraud, which can lead to a sharp drop in mutual fund prices. We are proposing to invest in multiple companies that belong to the same business area. For many retail investors, it can be difficult to track different companies in different sectors and maintain a diverse portfolio.

2. Literature Review

The different studies on the factors affecting mutual fund prices mainly focus on the impact of changes in national economic policies on the mutual fund market, and the impact of investor behavior on mutual fund volatility fluctuations based on the perspective of behavioral finance. Many experimental results show that GARCH (1, 1), GARCH (1, 2), GARCH (2, 1) can already reflect the price volatility of financial products in most cases. Among them, the GARCH model is mainly used to calculate the volatility of the financial market. Wang et al. [1] proposed time-dependent kernel density estimation (TDKDE) used in time-varying phenomenon modeling requires running two input parameters called bandwidth and discount. A practical application of the TDKDE parameter estimate on the NASDQ stock returns confirms the perfect performance of the new technique. Matsatsinis et al. [2] presents a new algorithmic framework that combines features from the recommendation systems literature with multi-criteria decision analysis to mitigate problems of scarcity and lack of multi-dimensional correlation measures. This combined with collaborative filtering, leads to two combined recommendation approaches. Zheng and Wang [3] give the overview of multi-purpose recommendations and then use case studies especially in the areas of multi-stakeholder and multi-task recommender systems. Yera et al. [4] develops an overview of the use of fuzzy tools in recommender systems, identifies more general re-search topics, and future research to drive the current development of fuzzy-based recommender systems. Wang et al. [5] proposed a hybrid recommender system with sentiment analysis will be implemented on the Spark platform. Fayyaz et al. [6] presents the current state of research on recommender systems and points the direction of this area in a variety of applications. This article provides an overview of the latest technologies in recommender systems, their types, challenges, limitations, and business applications. Chen et al. [7] uses a mean shift clustering algorithm to characterize behavioral data. However, using mean shift clustering for personalized recommendations faces the problem of oversized user data. Transforms grouped user behavior into embedded vectors, and linearly transforms embedded vectors of different lengths into the same semantic space. It processes the vector of semantic space through the self-aware layer and performs mean shift clustering. Experiments have shown that our method can reduce the complexity of the distribution effect of user poverty on complex data and improve the quality of personalized recommendations. Wang et al. [8] proposed a new way to build a distributed knowledge graph using crowdsourcing. Crowdsourcing business logic is implemented by block chain-based smart contracts to ensure transparency, integrity, and audibility. Das et al. [9] focuses on the impact of financial inclusion on Orissa using the K-nearest neighbors (KNN) classification which is a well-known algorithm of machine learning. Machine learning (ML) has become a widely used method in financial inclusion systems. We used KNN ML method classification algorithms to characterize recommender systems based on the users of the mentioned population. Maji et al. [10] proposed a framework first allocates capital to each sector and then to each sector and invests per company. This is a diversified approach across different equities to keep risk low while seeking higher returns framework works well and provides good returns compared to some benchmarks and ranked funds in the Indian stock market. Luef et al. [11] designs, implements, and evaluates systems that encourage early-stage corporate investment. First, we conduct qualitative and quantitative surveys of prominent investors, investigate their decision-making process, and determine recommender system requirements. Sankar [12] discussed that the network formed by the equity portfolio is an investment fund analyzed with the help of social network analysis tools. Ji et al. [13] introduces an innovative stock price prediction model that combines traditional financial data with social media text features using deep learning techniques. Zhou et al. [14] develops an enhanced recommendation component for accurate recommendations and enhanced dialog component that can generate useful keywords or entities in the response body. Yu and Li [15] applied GARCH and LSTM models to predict the stock index volatility. They evaluated four different types of loss functions; the research demonstrates that the LSTM model outperforms the GARCH model in terms of predictive accuracy. Devi et al. [16] suggests a data mining tools and analytical technologies to conduct quantifiable quantities of research to explore new approaches to investment decisions. Gu et al. [17] discussion adds a particle swarm optimization (PSO) algorithm to the radial basis function (BRF) neural network, and PSO is conditioned to optimize and improve RBFNN by combining the benefits of both sides. It summarizes a new set of PSORBF safety fund performance methods for neural networks that optimize the structure and workflow of algorithms. With continuous trends, highs and lows forecasts over the performance period of a securities fund, the new PSORBF has excellent forecasts for predicting fund performance, with a significantly higher accuracy rate than traditional Sheng. It has improved a method that has excellent application value and is worth publishing. Hou et al. [18] proposes a hybrid long short-term memory and deep neural network (LSTMDNN) model for integrating basic information in time series prediction tasks. Azis et al. [19] contributes valuable insights, particularly in the context of exchange rates and inflation. However, it is recommended to conduct relevant comparisons before the pandemic period and consider additional macroeconomic factors for a comprehensive analysis. Gupta and Chaudhary [20] delves into the influence of news events on environmental, social, and governance (ESG) and market indices in both developed and emerging economies, employing the EGARCH model for analysis.

Hota et al. [21] propose an ANN model combined with an elephant breeding optimization (EHO) algorithm to predict NAV of days in different time periods for two of India's mutual funds. Shah et al. [22] states that stock market forecasts always attract the attention of many analysts and researchers. Predicting stock prices is in itself a difficult problem due to the number of variables involved. We then focus on some of the research achievements in stock analysis and forecasting. Majhi et al. [23] proposed synthetic hybrid model and its performance evaluated in both the training and testing phases using six different NAV data. Maji and Mondal [24] propose a framework to diversify capital fund investment across different stocks for higher returns but maintaining lower risk. Mamilla, R et al. [25] presents generalized autoregressive conditional heteroskedasticity (GARCH) modeling to investigate investor risk and assess how fluctuations in volatility affect returns. Asiri et al. [26] proposed a TVP-VAR approach to explore connection between uncertainty indices related to cryptocurrencies and the changes in returns and volatility within a range of financial assets. Al-Nassar [27] suggests a econometric model, which takes into consideration structural disruptions. After estimating the VAR-asymmetric BEKK-GARCH model, we compute portfolio weights and hedge ratios, and examine how they affect risk management.

3. Problem Statement

It is challenging to create a trust portfolio to avoid the risk of investment in a single / minority stock by investing in multiple mutual funds belonging to different economic sectors. It is difficult to manage and analyze many mutual funds at real time. Going forward, we need a framework for working with multiple mutual funds in different business areas to reduce risk factors and increase profits over time. In this work we proposed a framework for portfolio managers to make investments for lots specific time horizons in mutual funds to maximize the profit of investors. Here, the evaluation is carried out in more than one sector to make sure varied portfolio control to lessen traders` risk. As already discussed, there are numerous views of traders at the same time as making an investment their price range to advantage extra profit. Share markets are particularly sensitive, and there are various elements at once or in an indirect way related to them that manage the market place sentiment (Gottschlich and Hinz 2014). Problem can be solved using different statistical strategies and time-series analyses techniques to get maximum benefit from investment in mutual fund industry. Our goal is to suggest an analytical method to expect the proportion charge of various organizations and make investments overall capital throughout diverse sectors to earn higher income possibilities and mitigate the lowest risk.

4. Proposed Model

There are many challenges in developing a model to find a favorable way to help and predict a company's mutual funds price. The main idea behind this model is GARCH (Generalized Autoregressive Conditional Heteroskedasticity) theory where volatility of MFs can be measured and future return can be calculated. However, in reality, it is very difficult to accurately predict a company's MFs return price because several internal and external factors influence the mutual funds daily prices. Many parameters may not be directly related to the mutual fund market decline and flow, but are indirectly related to the mutual fund market by influencing the parameters that are directly involved in mutual fund price changes. Bad news and good news for a particular sector or company heavily affects the MFs return price. The developed model is based on historical return price of mutual fund as it reflects the impact of all events and factors that affect the mutual fund. There are several statistical techniques; prediction theories and models are developed to help you make right predictions, such as standard deviation, linear regression, non-linear regression, correlation, and time series analysis (Figure 7.1).

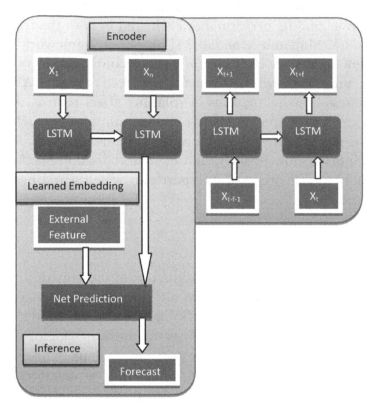

Figure 7.1: Block diagram of proposed model.

5. Data for Proposed Model

In this paper historical mutual fund data of CIPLA company is selected for analysis purpose. The historical mutual fund data of CIPLA from 03-Jan-2011 to 09-Aug-2023 is taken into consideration and the whole data is divided into training and testing segments. The data from 03-Jan.2011 to 06-Aug-2022 is taken for training purpose and from 07-Aug-2022 to 06-Aug-2023 considered for testing purpose. The volatility mutual fund compared and analyzed for prediction of future price of model.

6. Research Methodologies

6.1. Modeling volatility with ARCH & GARCH

In 1982, Robert Engle developed the autoregressive conditional heteroscedasticity (ARCH) model to predict variability over time often found in economic time series data. For this work he was awarded the 2003 Nobel Prize in Economics. The ARCH model estimates that the variance of the current error or innovation.

6.2. Time series-ARCH

Let Z_t be N (0, 1) the process X_t is an ARCH(q) process if it is stationary and if it satisfies, for all t and some strictly positive-valued process σ_t, the equations:

$$X_t = \sigma_t Z_t \tag{1}$$

$$\sigma^2 t = \alpha_0 + \sum_{i=1}^{q} \alpha_i X_{t-i}^2 \tag{2}$$

where 0 and i, I = 1, 2 .... q.

X_t is the error term in a time series regression model.

6.3. Time series-generalized-ARCH model (GARCH)

Before introducing GARCH, we discuss the exponentially weighted moving average (EWMA) mode that is represented by the following equation:

$$\sigma_t^2 = \lambda \sigma_{t-1}^2 + (1-\lambda)X_{t-1}^2 \tag{3}$$

Where λ is a constant between 0 and 1.

The EWMA approach has the attractive feature that relatively little data need to be stored.

We substitute for σ_{t-1}^2, and then keep doing it for m steps:

$$\sigma_t^2 = (1-\lambda)\sum_{i=1}^{m} \lambda^{i-1} X_{t-1}^2 + \lambda^m \sigma_{t-m}^2 \tag{4}$$

For large m the term $\lambda^m \sigma_{t-m}^2$ is sufficiently small to be ignored, so it decreases exponentially.

Time series-GARCH processes are generalized ARCH processes in the sense that the squared volatility σ_t^2 is allowed to depend on previous squared volatilities, as well as previous squared values of the process.

Let Z_t be N (0, 1). The process X_t is a GARCH (p, q) process if it is stationary and if it satisfies, for all t and some strictly positive-valued process σ_t, the equation:

$$\sigma_t^2 = \alpha_0 + \sum_{i=1}^{q} \alpha_i X_{t-I}^2 + \sum_{j=1}^{p} \beta_i \sigma_{t-m}^2 \tag{5}$$

where $\alpha_0 > 0$ and $\alpha_i \geq 0$, I = 0, 1, 2 ... q, $\beta_j \geq 0$, j=0, ..., p.

6.4. Augmented Dickey Fuller test (ADF test)

ADF test is a test for a unit root in a time series sample. ADF test is used to test that data is stationary or not.

$$X_t = \alpha + \beta_t + yX_{t-1} + \partial_1 \Delta X_{t-1} + \partial_p \Delta X_{t-p-1} + \varepsilon_t \tag{6}$$

Null hypothesis: $y = 0 \Rightarrow X_t$ has unit roots.

7. General Statistics of Data

The table shows the value of mean, median, maximum, minimum, standard deviation, skewness, Kurtosis, Jarque-Bera tests. Using these statistical information we can analyze the nature of collected historical data (Figure 7.2).

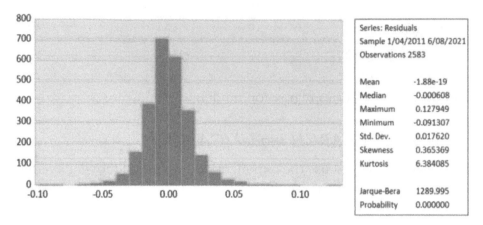

Figure 7.2: General statistics of data.

Hurst exponent used to check that whether a series is mean reverting, random walking or trending. Here the H< 0.5, so time series is mean reverting. Autocorrelation of a time series measures the relation between lag values of time series and its past values. Partial autocorrelation shows degree of closeness between time series and lagged values of subsequent time intervals is constitute mathematically as autocorrelation (Figure 7.3).

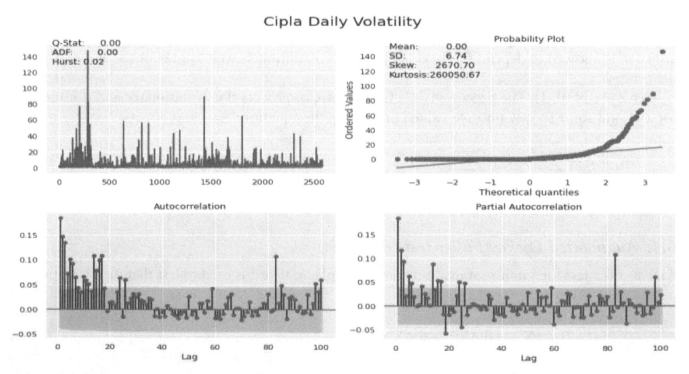

Figure 7.3: Daily volatility of dataset (Cipla).

8. Testing of Heterosecedasticity

One of the important thing assumptions of the everyday regression version is that the mistakes have the identical variance at some stage in the sample. This is likewise known as the homoscedasticity version. If the mistake variance isn't consistent, the information is stated to be heteroscedastic. The equation is as follows:

$$Q(q) = T(T+2) \sum_{i=1}^{q} \frac{r(i; e_t^2)}{N-i} \tag{7}$$

$$\text{where} \quad r(i; e_t^2) = \frac{\sum_{t=i+1}^{T} (e_t^2 - \sigma^2)(e_{t-1}^2 - \sigma^2)}{\sum_{t=1}^{T} (e_t^2 - \sigma^2)^2} \tag{8}$$

Portmanteau Q test for non-linear time series models, the portmanteau test statistic based on squared residuals is used to test for independence of the series. The heteroskedasticity test show the arch effect is preset in dataset because the P value < 0.05% at 5% confidence interval and constant variable C is also statically significant because P value is less than 5% level.

9. Simulation Test of Model

Simulation of an ARCH (1) and GARCH (1, 1) time series done respectively using a function simulate_GARCH (n, omega, alpha, beta = 0). Recall the difference between an ARCH (1) and a GARCH (1, 1) model is: besides an autoregressive component of α multiplying lag-1 residual squared, a GARCH model includes a moving average component of β multiplying lag-1 variance. The function will simulate an ARCH/GARCH series based on n (number of simulations), omega, alpha, and beta (0 by default). It will return simulated residuals and variances (Figure 7.4).

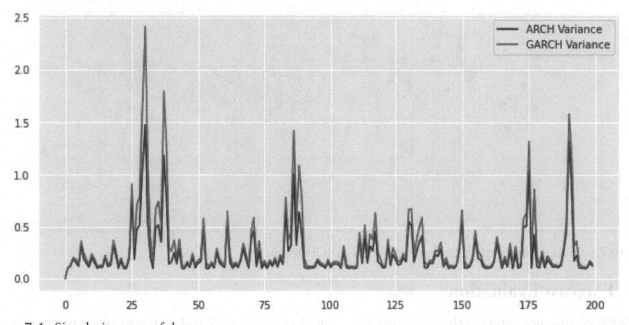

Figure 7.4: Simulation test of data.

10. Simulation Impact of Parameters on Model

For simulation purpose function simulate_GARCH() called and the impact of GARCH model parameters on simulated results is analyzed. Specifically, we have simulated two GARCH (1, 1) time series; they have the same omega and alpha, but different beta as input. Recall in GARCH (1, 1), since β is the coefficient of lag-1 variance, if α is fixed, the larger the β, the longer the duration of the impact. In other words, high or low volatility periods tend to persist. Pay attention to the plotted results and see whether we can verify the β impact (Figures 7.5 and 7.6).

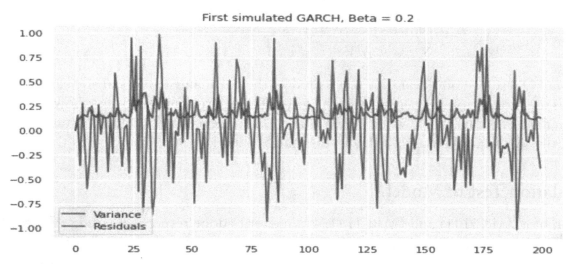

Figure 7.5: Simulation impact of (beta=0.2) on GARCH model.

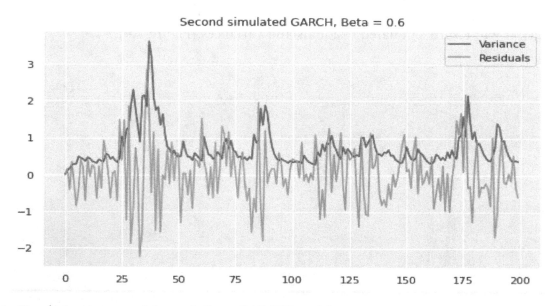

Figure 7.6: Simulation impact of (beta=0.6) on GARCH model.

11. Forecast Evaluation

At 90% confidence interval the performance of model is evaluated and different types of error is calculated. The lower value of root means squared (RMS) proves the supremacy of forecasting model. In proposed model the RMSE value is 0.018777 that is very low so we can say that our model's forecasting value is very close to actual value and proves the accuracy of our model. The second error estimation parameter is Thiel inequality coefficient is 0.900024 that is 0.90% shows the perfect fit between actual open price and forecasting open price of the mutual fund. Third parameter is bias proportion which is also proves the accuracy of model in our proposed model. The value of error term is 0.000150 which shows the systematic error value of bias proportion is very low also shows the accuracy of proposed model. Another performance parameter mean absolute error also shows value 0.014534 and proves the accuracy of our proposed model (Table 7.1, Figures 7.7 and 7.8).

Table 7.1: Performance matrices of model

RMSE	*Thiel inequality coefficient*	*Bias proportion*	*Mean absolute Error*
0.018777	0.900024	0.000150	0.014534

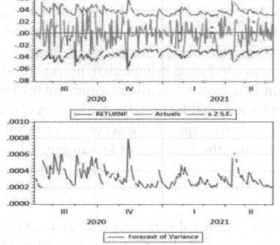

Figure 7.7: Forecast evaluation of model.

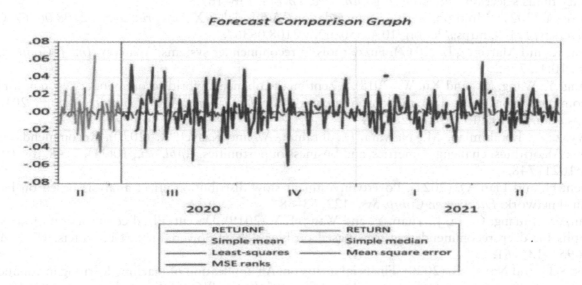

Figure 7.8: Forecast comparison graph.

12. Conclusions

This paper uses GARCH volatility models to analyze and predict conditional deviations. The proposed methodology helps build a long-term robust portfolio by analyzing historical data based on time-series analysis. The low RMSE value of 0.018777 indicates that the GARCH model's predictions are quite accurate, with minimal variance from the actual data. This suggests that the model is effective in capturing the underlying patterns of mutual fund volatility. The Thiel inequality coefficient of 0.900024 is close to 1, implying a high degree of accuracy in the forecasts. This coefficient measures the relative accuracy of predictions, and a value close to 1 suggests a strong predictive capability of the GARCH model. The bias proportion of 0.000150 is indicative of a negligible bias in the model's predictions. This means that the GARCH model's forecasts are not systematically overestimating or underestimating the mutual fund volatility, resulting in unbiased predictions. The MAE of 0.014534 further supports the accuracy of the GARCH model. It represents the average absolute difference between predicted and actual values. A low MAE indicates that the model's forecasts closely align with the observed data. Analytical outcomes show that it is an acceptable model. The proposed model can be used by portfolio managers to compare the performance of investment trusts over a considerable period of time. The experiment was conducted using Indian mutual fund data, but it can also be applied to various mutual funds around the world. It is also recommend for future researchers to investigate various sectors mutual funds with external factors that badly affects the Indian mutual fund market. Further improvements can be made to improve the accuracy of proposed framework for analysis of other different factors that influence the volatility of Indian mutual fund.

References

[1]   Wang, X., Tsokos, C. P., and Saghafi, A. (2018). Improved parameter estimation of time dependent kernel density by using artificial neural networks. *J Fin Data Sci.*, 4(3), 172–182, https://doi.org/10.1016/j.jfds.2018.04.002.

[2]   Matsatsinis, N. F. and Manarolis, E. A. (2009). New hybrid recommender approaches: an application to equity funds selection. *Int. Conf. Algorith. Dec. Theory*, 156–167.

[3]   Zheng, Y. (2021). Multi-objective recommendations: A tutorial. *arXiv preprint arXiv:2108.06367.* Cornell University, 1, 1–9. https://doi.org/10.48550/arXiv.2108.06367.

[4]   Yera, R. and Martinez, L. (2017). Fuzzy tools in recommender systems: A survey. *Int. J. Comput. Intel. Sys.*, 10(1), 776.

[5]   Wang, Y., Wang, M., and Xu, W. (2018). A sentiment-enhanced hybrid recommender sys- tem for movie recommendation: A big data analytics framework. *Wireless Comm. Mob. Comput.*, Volume 2018, 1–9. https://doi.org/10.1155/2018/8263704.

[6]   Fayyaz, Z., Ebrahimian, M., Nawara, D., Ibrahim, A., and Kashef, R. (2020). Recommendation systems: Algorithms, challenges, metrics, and business opportunities. *Appl. Sci.*, 10(21), 7748, doi:10.3390/app10217748.

[7]   Chen, H. and Lian, Q. (2021). Poverty/investment slow distribution effect analysis based on Hopfield neural network. *Fut. Gener. Comp. Sys.*, 122, 63–68.

[8]   Wang, S., Huang, C., Li, J., Yuan, Y., and Wang, F. Y. (2019). Decentralized construction of knowledge graphs for deep recommender systems based on block chain-powered smart contracts. *IEEE Acc.*, 7, 136951–136961.

[9]   Das, S. G. and Nayak, B. (2020). Financial inclusion: An application of machine learning in collaborative filtering recommender systems. *Int. J. Recent Technol. Engg.*, 8(6), Online publication. DOI:10.35940/ijrte.F9361.038620.

[10] Maji, G., Mondal, D., Dey, N., Debnath, N. C., and Sen, S. (2021). Stock prediction and mutual fund portfolio management using curve fitting techniques. *J. Ambient Intel. Human. Comput.*, 12(10), 9521–9534, https://doi.org/10.1007/s12652- 020-02693-6.

[11] Luef, J., Ohrfandl, C., Sacharidis, D., and Werthner, H. (2020). A recommender system for investing in early-stage enterprises. *Proc. 35th Ann. ACM Symp. Appl. Comput.*, 1453–1460, https://doi.org/10.1145/3341105.3375767.

[12] Sankar, C. P., Vidyaraj, R., and Kumar, K. S. (2015). Trust based stock recommendation system–A social network analysis approach. *Proc. Comp. Sci.*, 46, 299–305.

[13] Ji, X., Wang, J., and Yan, Z. (2021). A stock price prediction method based on deep learning technology. *Int. J. Crowd Sci.*, 5(1), 55–72.

[14] Zhou, K., Zhao, W. X., Bian, S., Zhou, Y., Wen, J. R., and Yu, J. (2020). Improving conversational recommender systems via knowledge graph based semantic fusion. *Proc. 26th ACM SIGKDD Int. Conf. Knowl. Dis. Data Min.*, 1006–1014, https: //doi.org/10.1145/3394486.3403143.

[15] Yu, S. and Li, Z. (2018). Forecasting stock price index volatility with LSTM deep neural network. *Recent Dev. Data Sci. Busin. Analyt. Proc. Int. Conf. Data Sci. Busin. Analyt. (ICDSBA-2017)*, 265–272. Springer International Publishing.

[16] Devi, B. U., Sundar, D., and Alli, P. (2013). An effective time series analysis for stock trend prediction using ARIMA model for nifty midcap-50. *Int. J. Data Min. Knowl. Manag. Proc.*, 3(1), 65, DOI : 10.5121/ijdkp.2013.3106.

[17] Gu, C. (2021). Research on prediction of investment fund's performance before and after investment based on improved neural network algorithm. *Wireless Comm. Mob. Comput.*, Volume 2021, 1–9. https://doi.org/10.1155/2021/5519213.

[18] Hou, X., Wang, K., Zhang, J., and Wei, Z. (2020). An enriched time-series forecasting framework for long-short portfolio strategy. *IEEE Acc.*, 8, 31992–32002, DOI:10.1109/ACCESS.2020.2973037.

[19] Azis, M., Iskandar, R., Ariswati, L. D., Surya, I. M., Sudirman, N., and Darma, D. C. (2022). The Treynor-Mazuy conditional model: Overview of market timing and stock selection on equity mutual funds performance. *Econ. Altern.*, 2, 252–263.

[20] Gupta, H. and Chaudhary, R. (2023). An analysis of volatility and risk-adjusted returns of ESG indices in developed and emerging economies. *Risks*, 11(10), 182.

[21] Hota, S., Kuhoo, Mishra, D., and Patnaik, S. (2020). An empirical net asset value forecasting model based on optimized ANN using elephant herding strategy. *Int. J. Manag. Dec. Mak.*, 19(1), 118–132.

[22] Shah, D., Isah, H., and Zulkernine, F. (2019). Stock market analysis: A review and taxonomy of prediction techniques. *International Journal of Financial Studies*, 7(2), 26. https://doi.org/10.3390/ijfs7020026

[23] Majhi, B., Anish, C. M., and Majhi, R. (2021). On development of novel hybrid and robust adaptive models for net asset value prediction. *J. King Saud Univer. Comp. Inform. Sci.*, 33(6), 647–657.

[24] Maji, G., Mondal, D., Dey, N., Debnath, C. N., Sen, S. (2021). Stock prediction and mutual fund portfolio management using curve fitting techniques. *Journal of Ambient Intelligence and Humanized Computing*, 12(10), 9521–9534. https://doi.org/10.1007/s12652-020-02693-6.

[25] Mamilla, R., Kathiravan, C., Salamzadeh, A., Dana, L. P., and Elheddad, M. (2023). COVID-19 pandemic and indices volatility: Evidence from GARCH models. *J. Risk Fin. Manag.*, 16(10), 447.

[26] Yadav, M. P., Sharma, S., and Bhardwaj, I. (2023). Volatility spillover between Chinese stock market and selected emerging economies: A dynamic conditional correlation and portfolio optimization perspective. *Asia-Pac. Fin. Markets*, 30(2), 427–444.

[27] Al-Nassar, N. S. (2023). The dynamic return and volatility spillovers among size-based stock portfolios in the Saudi market and their portfolio management implications during different crises. *Int. J. Fin. Stud.*, 11(3), 113.

8 Diabetes Classification and Prediction Through Integrated SVM-GA

Vishal Verma[1,a], Sandeep Kumar Verma, Satish Kumar, Alka Agrawal, and Raees Ahmad Khan

[1]Department of Information Technology, Babasaheb Bhimrao Ambedkar University, Lucknow, India

Abstract

Diabetes is a global health concern. If the sources are to be believed, about 422 million people across the globe are suffering from this disease. It's when the body can't regulate sugar because it lacks insulin or can't use it correctly. Due to its chronic nature, it has become very important to identify it in the initial stage so that it can be treated at the right time. Machine learning (ML) has emerged as a valuable tool for diabetes prediction, and many researchers have employed ML techniques for accurate predictions. Among these, the support vector machine (SVM) is the most popular and widely used algorithm among researchers for predicting diabetes at an early stage. In this paper, researchers have proposed an integrated SVM-genetic algorithm (GA) method and evaluated its performance against various ML methods, such as SVM, random forest, K-nearest neighbors (KNN), decision tree (DT), extra trees classifier (ETC), Naive Bayes (NB), XG boost, and gradient boosting. And we employed the PIMA Indian Diabetes Datasets (PIDD) for this comparative analysis. The results of this study reveal that the proposed integrated SVM-GA method outperforms other methods, particularly in terms of accuracy, precision, recall, and area under the curve (AUC).

Keywords: SVM, genetic algorithm, machine learning, diabetes prediction, healthcare

1. Introduction

Diabetes is a non-communicable disease which affects the most people in the world. According to WHO, approximately 2 million people died due to diabetes in 2019 [1]. Diabetes is a chronic illness because it also affects several body organs and increases the chance the having another chronic disease such as stroke, heart attack, and kidneys [2]. There is a need for regular monitoring and treatment of the patient for better treatment [3]. The government of every country spends a huge portion of its total gross domestic product (GDP) on healthcare. Governments and individuals both allocate a sizable percentage of their budgets to the treatment of chronic diseases [4]. There are three primary types of diabetes in people: type 1 diabetes (T1D), type 2 diabetes (T2D), and gestational

---

[a]vishalmgs93@gmail.com

diabetes (GD). In T1D, the pancreas is unable to produce insulin or produce very less insulin. In T2D, the body doesn't use insulin properly and it is found in people above 45 years of age whereas GD is mostly found during pregnancy [5]. This all is happening due to bad climatic conditions, population, unhygienic life, and wrong eating habits.

Due to the increasing advancements in the healthcare industry, there has been a different revolution. The easy availability of the Internet and electronic health records (EHR) data is also growing rapidly. The tireless efforts of our researchers have shown great potential in the field of healthcare including the prediction and classification of diabetes with the help of various ML-based techniques [6]. Classification models can be used to classify different types of diabetes based on their symptoms and physiological characteristics. There are lots of ML-based techniques and algorithms used in disease classification and prediction. Some popular ML algorithms used for classification and prediction include SVM, NB, KNN, logistic regression (LR), DT, and random forests (RF).

There are some more important factors in diabetes prediction such as glucose, age, body mass index (BMI), and family medical history [7, 8]. Harnessing the power of ML, it is easy to identify the concealed patterns and intricate relationships in large datasets [9]. ML helps to reduce the workload of healthcare practitioners [10]. In this study, researchers have examined several parameters such as accuracy, precision, recall, and AUC and conducted a performance comparison of existing ML algorithms (SVM, RF, KNN, DT, extra trees classifier (ETC), NB, XG boost, and gradient boosting.

The paper is structured as follows – Reviews related work on diabetes classification and prediction. Outlines research materials and methods. Analyzes results comprehensively, and Finally compares with other ML methods. Following the methods the section discusses key findings, and the final section provides a conclusion and future work.

2. Related Work

In this section, researchers delve into existing research concerning the various ML-based techniques for diabetes classification and prediction. Despite numerous studies dedicated to diabetes prediction, the problem persists. To shed light on this issue, we review a selection of research papers below:

Whig et al. [11] proposed a novel method to predict and classify diabetes. The authors have used the Pycaret library to identify, and categorize diabetes. Chauhan et al. [12] presented a review paper on supervised and unsupervised ML-based methods. The review highlights the various ML approaches used in diabetic patient care and discusses their advantages and limitations. Ganie et al. [13] introduced an ensemble method for predicting type 2 diabetes mellitus (DM) by utilizing lifestyle indicators. Injadat et al. [14] presented a comprehensive review of ML with a focus on its applications, challenges, and opportunities in intelligent systems. The review focuses on the applications of ML in various domains, including healthcare. Nibareke et al. [15] described flight delay analytics and big data as well as various ML models for diabetes prediction. Pethunachiyar [16] proposed SVM with the kernel-based model for the prediction of diabetes patients and also compared the performance of several kernel functions. Chen et al. [17] proposed a hybrid model to forecast T2D using a combination of DT and K-means. DT is used for classification and K-means are used for data reduction. The researchers compared several existing models with the proposed model. They found that their hybrid proposed model performed better in comparison to other existing models. Wu et al. [18] used two different datasets and data mining techniques for accurate prediction of diabetes using improved K means and LR. Kumar et al. [19] presented a study on the performance of different ML algorithms using big data analytics to predict diabetes. The comparative analysis showed that RF achieved the highest accuracy. Nguyen et al. [20] described a deep learning approach for forecasting the onset of T2D using EHR Data. The study achieved an AUC of 0.85 for predicting diabetes. Dahiwade et al. [21] studied the various ML approaches to predict diabetes at an early stage and they found that the DT algorithm performs well on PIDD datasets. Mujumdar et al. [22] used big data analytics that helps to find trends, hidden patterns, and information from huge datasets. As well as they used a few other external factors along with regular factors to predict diabetes. Tigga and Garg [23] applied RF along with various ML algorithms on two different datasets and achieved result by RF that was impressive. One of them is the PIDD dataset and the other one is based on online and offline questionnaire datasets. They found that appropriate feature selection is the most important aspect for better prediction.

These studies collectively underscore the variety of methods and algorithms utilized in diabetes prediction, emphasizing the need for tailored approaches and the continuous quest for enhanced accuracy. Most studies feature performance comparisons of multiple ML methods, with a focus on model diversity rather than the perfection of a single model. In contrast, our research concentrates on a single model and optimal feature selection methods to enhance accuracy and other parameters. This study highlights the substantial influence of algorithm selection and data preprocessing on overall model performance.

3. Research Materials and Methods

This section discusses the resources, procedures, and methodology used in this study. Researchers have used datasets from reliable sources, ensuring data quality. Rigorous data preprocessing was conducted for accuracy. Machine learning techniques were carefully selected for predictive accuracy. Sub-sections cover datasets, pre-processing, the framework, and evaluation methodology.

3.1. Datasets

The PIDD dataset is taken from the Kaggle repository [24]. The selected dataset contains 768 entries consisting of eight input variables such as pregnancies, as shown in Table 1, and one output variable. The output variable values are 0 and 1. The value 0 indicates patients without diabetes and 1 indicates patients with diabetes. Statistical details of the dataset are shown in Table 8.1.

Table 8.1: Diabetes dataset description

S. No.	Parameter	Description	Type
1	Pregnancies (Preg)	Preg represents the number of times a woman has been pregnant	Integer
2	Glucose (GLU)	GLU represents the plasma glucose concentration of the patients	Integer
3	Blood pressure (BP)	BP represents the blood pressure (mm Hg) level of the patients	Integer
4	Skin thickness (ST)	ST represents the triceps skinfold thickness in millimeters	Integer
5	Insulin (INS)	INS represents the 2-hour serum insulin level measured	Integer
6	Body mass index (BMI)	BMI represents the individual is normal weight, underweight, and overweight	Float
7	Diabetes pedigree function (DPF)	DPF values represent the genetic influence and a potentially higher risk of diabetes	Float
8	Age	Age represents the patient's age in years	Integer
9	Outcome (OC)	OC represents the class variable in 0 and 1 where 0 means an individual has no diabetes, and 1 refers to diabetes	Binary

3.2. Data pre-processing

Data pre-processing is crucial for optimizing ML model performance. The initial steps involve data normalization, which translates data into a linear format (min-max normalization, [0, 1] range). Subsequently, label encoding is applied to transform the dependent variable (diabetes prediction) into binary values (0 or 1).

Addressing missing values is essential; our dataset had 227 missing values for skin thickness, 374 for insulin, and 35 for blood pressure. To handle this, we filled in missing values with the respective feature's median, ensuring data completeness.

3.3. Proposed framework

The researchers have focused on increasing the accuracy of diabetes detection. The authors have proposed a hybrid ML-based approach i.e., integrated SVM-GA. The process starts with data pre-processing and enhancement before feeding inputs into the model.

The proposed method is visualized in Figure 8.1 providing a simplified overview of the data processing pipeline. It consists of key elements such as the PIMA dataset, pre-processing, testing and training data, model fitting, integrated SVM-GA, and prediction.

To evaluate the method's performance, the dataset was split into 80:20 ratios, with 80% for model training and 20% for testing. Implementation of the model was carried out using Google Collab, leveraging resources available on the Kaggle repository. The PIDD dataset was accessed and evaluated using scientific computing, data analysis, and visualization tools, including scikit-learn, pandas, NumPy, and deep packages.

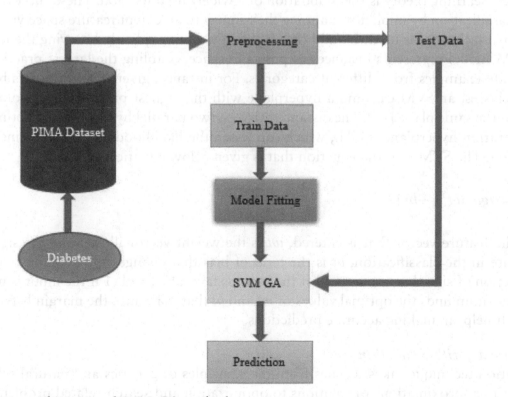

Figure 8.1: Proposed integrated SVM-GA method.

The following various steps were implemented to execute:

1. **Data collection:** Collect the dataset from Kaggle.com.
2. **Data pre-processing:** Clean and prepare the dataset, addressing missing values, outliers, and normalization.
3. **Dataset splitting:** Divide the dataset into training and testing subsets.
4. **Genetic algorithm optimization:** Apply GA to optimize the SVM for improved accuracy.
5. **Model testing and prediction:** To assess the model, we utilized the final 20% of the test data for prediction.

These steps constitute a systematic and thorough process for developing, optimizing, and assessing a machine learning model. Their purpose is to guarantee the model's readiness, thorough testing, and optimization for optimal accuracy and applicability.

3.4. Proposed methodology

The researchers introduce refined methodologies for diabetes prediction, enabling healthcare professionals and researchers to make informed decisions and provide targeted interventions for at-risk individuals. The following methodologies used for the prediction of diabetes are provided in the below sections.

3.4.1. Support vector machine

The SVM is a collection of interconnected supervised learning methods used in medical diagnosis for classification and regression. It minimizes empirical classification error while maximizing geometric margin. It is hence referred to as a maximum margin classifier. A set of assured risk thresholds from statistical learning theory is the foundation of a widely used method. These successfully handle non-linear classification by implicitly mapping their inputs to an extent feature space via kernel technique. A kernel technique is used to build the classifier without explicitly knowing the feature space [25]. An SVM model represents instances as points in space, enabling the largest practical category gap to separate examples from different categories. For instance, given a set of points belonging to one of two classes, an SVM can find a hyperplane with the highest proportion of points from the same class on the same plane [26]. The distance between two parallel hyperplanes is optimized by the optimal separation hyperplane (OSH), which can lessen the likelihood of misclassifying samples in the test dataset. The SVM uses the equation that is given below equation.

$$f(\mathrm{z}) = sign\left(wt^{T}z + bt\right) \tag{1}$$

where z is the feature vector that is entered, wt is the weight vector illustrating the significance of every attribute in the classification, bt is the term of bias that changes the decision boundary, and sign is a function of sign that converts +1 if the input is favorable, and -1 if the input is unfavorable. The SVM algorithm finds the optimal values of wt and bt that maximize the margin between the two classes, which helps in making accurate predictions.

3.4.2. Genetic algorithm equation

An optimization technique takes its cues from the principles of genetics and natural selection. It is used to identify approximations of solutions to optimization and search-related problems. The core idea behind a GA is to iteratively evolve a population of alternative solutions in order to find the best solution to a problem. Several of the fundamental equations used in GA include population, fitness function, selection, crossover, mutation, and replacement [27]. To perform GA, the following various steps are given below.

1. Generate random sets of 5 features to create the initial population of chromosomes (C).
2. Assign scores to C based on their predictive accuracy for emotional states using a statistical model with the nearest centroid classifier.
3. Select C with scores meeting the fitness objective; otherwise, continue the process.
4. Duplicate C based on their performance in problem-solving, with higher-scoring C producing more offspring.
5. Perform crossover by recombining genetic material from replicated parent C.
6. Introduce new genes through mutations into the newly created population of C from Step 5.
7. Repeat stages 2–6 in cycles (generations) until a solution is found.

The process of natural selection served as inspiration for the development of GA. The equation used in GA is:

$$fitness = f(x) \tag{2}$$

where fitness is the fitness value of the individual, $f(x)$ is the objective function that measures the performance of the individual.

The objective of GA is to identify the ideal values for the parameters that maximize the fitness value. In the SVM-GA model, GA is utilized to optimize the SVM parameters, increasing the model's accuracy. The SVM-GA model can accurately categorize and predict diabetes by combining.

4. Result Analysis

The researchers found that the proposed classifier method achieved favorable performance, with high precision, recall, accuracy, and AUC values when using the PIDD dataset. The evaluation metrics included true positive (TP), true negative (TN), false positive (FP), and false negative (FN) to assess classifier performance.

$$Accuracy = \frac{TP + TN}{TP + TN + FP + FN} \tag{3}$$

$$Recall = \frac{TP}{TP + FN} \tag{4}$$

$$Precision = \frac{TP}{TP + FP} \tag{5}$$

Accuracy quantifies the model's overall correct predictions, while recall gauges the correct prediction of positive instances by the proposed method. Precision assesses the accuracy of positive predictions correctly identified as positive among all positive instances. The AUC evaluates a binary classification model's performance by calculating the area under the ROC curve. The AUC can be calculated by

Table 8.2: Confusion matrix of SVM-GA

	True positive	True negative
Actual positive	91	8
Actual negative	23	32

integrating the ROC curve using a numerical integration method such as the trapezoidal rule. These metrics are used to evaluate the performance of the SVM-GA model on the PIDD dataset.

From Table 8.2 confusion matrix, researchers have calculated the following performance metrics:

Accuracy = (91 + 32) / (91 + 32 + 8 + 23) = 79.87%

Recall = 91 / (91 + 23) = 79.82%

Precision = 91 / (91 + 8) = 91.91%

AUC (area under the curve) = 84.53%

The SVM-GA model achieved an accuracy of 79.87%, recall of 79.82%, precision of 91.91%, and AUC of 84.53%. These metrics indicate that the model has good performance in predicting diabetes on the PIDD dataset.

4.5. Comparison

In this section, researchers compared the performance of several ML algorithms, including SVM, RF, KNN, DT, NB, extra trees classifier, XG boost, gradient boosting, and SVM-GA. They evaluated these algorithms based on multiple metrics, including accuracy, precision, recall, and the area under the ROC curve (AUC), as depicted in Figure 8.2.

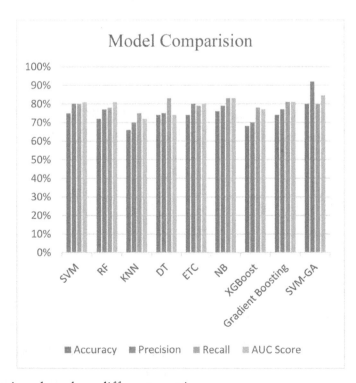

Figure 8.2: Model comparison based on different metrics.

Table 8.3: Model comparison

Model comparison	Accuracy (%)	Precision (%)	Recall (%)	AUC score (%)
SVM	75	80	80	81
RF	72	77	78	81
KNN	66	70	75	72
DT	74	75	83	74
ETC	74	80	79	80
NB	76	79	83	83
XG boost	68	70	78	77
Gradient boosting	74	77	81	81
SVM-GA	**79.87**	**91.91**	**79.82**	**84.53**

In Table 8.3, researchers presented the performance metrics for each of the ML methods. The values are obtained from our experiment and have demonstrated the algorithms' effectiveness in solving the given problem. It's evident that the integrated SVM-GA method outperforms with the highest accuracy, precision, and AUC scores.

5. Discussion

The experimental study employed nine diverse ML algorithms, including SVM, RF, KNN, DT, NB, extra trees classifier, XG boost, gradient boosting, and the novel SVM-GA. The study utilized the PIDD dataset as a common basis for all classifiers. Comprehensive pre-processing steps were executed to eliminate null values from the dataset, ensuring data integrity.

To assess model performance robustly, the dataset has been meticulously divided into two parts: An 80% training dataset and a separate 20% testing dataset. Various ML algorithms have consistently applied to the same dataset, with researchers focusing on engineered features to assess their predictive capabilities. Researchers have performed a thorough evaluation, utilizing key performance metrics like accuracy, precision, recall, and AUC to provide a comprehensive assessment of each algorithm's effectiveness. The key finding of this study reveals that the innovative integrated SVM-GA method outperformed traditional algorithms, demonstrating notably higher identification performances. Specifically, the framework achieved an impressive average AUC of 84.53%, surpassing the performance of conventional algorithms.

6. Conclusions

Applying the proposed SVM-GA model to the PIDD dataset demonstrates its efficacy in classifying and predicting Diabetes with high accuracy, precision, recall, and AUC, outperforming traditional ML models such as LR, DT, and more. This underscores the potential of integrated SVM and GA algorithms for improved results. The proposed method holds promise for medical professionals in diabetes prediction and identifying at-risk patients, enabling early diagnosis and cost-effective treatment. It's important to consider that model accuracy depends on dataset quality, size, and hyperparameter tuning. These findings also suggest future applications in predicting other ailments and call for further research and algorithm exploration, including ensemble models, to enhance accuracy.

Explore broader medical applications, refine the model, and investigate alternative algorithms and ensemble methods to enhance prediction accuracy.

7. Acknowledgement

The authors gratefully acknowledge the research scholars, faculty, and authorities of the Department of Information Technology for their cooperation in the research.

References

[1] Almutairi, E. S., Abbod, M. F., Almutairi, E. S., and Abbod, M. F. (2023). Machine learning methods for diabetes prevalence classification in Saudi Arabia. *Modelling,* 4(1), 37–55. doi:10.3390/MODELLING4010004.

[2] Aung, Y. Y. M., Wong, D. C. S., and Ting, D. S. W. (2021). The promise of artificial intelligence: A review of the opportunities and challenges of artificial intelligence in healthcare. *Br. Med. Bul.,* 139(1), 4–15. doi:10.1093/BMB/LDAB016.

[3] Chang, V., Bailey, J., Xu, Q. A., and Sun, Z. (2023). Pima Indians diabetes mellitus classification based on machine learning (ML) algorithms. *Neural Comput. Appl.,* 35(22), 16157–16173. doi:10.1007/s00521-022-07049-z.

[4] Chauhan, T., Rawat, S., Malik, S., and Singh, P. (2021). Supervised and unsupervised machine learning based review on diabetes care. *2021 7th Int. Conf. Adv. Comput. Comm. Sys. ICACCS,* 581–585. doi:10.1109/ICACCS51430.2021.9442021.

[5] Chen, W., Chen, S., Zhang, H., and Wu, T. (2018). A hybrid prediction model for type 2 diabetes using K-means and decision tree. *Proc. IEEE Int. Conf. Softw. Engg. Ser. Sci.,* 386–390. doi:10.1109/ICSESS.2017.8342938.

[6] Dahiwade, D., Patle, G., and Meshram, E. (2019). Designing disease prediction model using machine learning approach. *Proc. 3rd Int. Conf. Comput. Methodol. Comm.,* doi:10.1109/ICCMC.2019.8819782.

[7] "Diabetes." 2023. Accessed October 9. https://www.who.int/news-room/fact-sheets/detail/diabetes.

[8] "Diabetes Dataset." 2023. Accessed October 9. https://www.kaggle.com/datasets/mathchi/diabetes-data-set.

[9] Doğru, A., Buyrukoğlu, S., and Arı, M. (2023). A hybrid super ensemble learning model for the early-stage prediction of diabetes risk. *Med. Biol. Engg. Comput.,* 61(3). doi:10.1007/s11517-022-02749-z.

[10] Febrian, M. E., Ferdinan, X F., Sendani, G. P., Suryanigrum, K. M., and Yunanda, R. (2022). Diabetes prediction using supervised machine learning. *Proc. Comp. Sci.,* 216. doi:10.1016/j.procs.2022.12.107.

[11] Ganie, S. M. and Malik, M. B. (2022). An ensemble machine learning approach for predicting type-II diabetes mellitus based on lifestyle indicators. *Healthcare Analyt.,* 2. doi:10.1016/j.health.2022.100092.

[12] Gotlieb, N., Azhie, A., Sharma, D., Spann, A., Suo, N. J., Tran, J., Orchanian-Cheff, A., et al. (2022). The promise of machine learning applications in solid organ transplantation. *NPJ Dig. Med.,* 5(1), 1–13. doi:10.1038/s41746-022-00637-2.

[13] Injadat, M. N., Moubayed, A., Nassif, A. B., and Shami, A. (2021). Machine learning towards intelligent systems: Applications, challenges, and opportunities. *Artif. Intel. Rev.,* 54(5), 3299–3348. doi:10.1007/s10462-020-09948-w.

[14] Khan, A., Uddin, S., and Uma, S. (2019). Chronic disease prediction using administrative data and graph theory: The case of type 2 diabetes. *Exp. Sys. Appl.,* 136. doi:10.1016/j.eswa.2019.05.048.

[15] Kumar, P. S. and Pranavi, S. (2018). Performance analysis of machine learning algorithms on diabetes dataset using big data analytics. *2017 Int. Conf. Infocom Technol. Unmanned Sys. Trends Fut. Dir.,* 508–513. doi:10.1109/ICTUS.2017.8286062.

[16] Kyrou, I., Tsigos, C., Mavrogianni, C., Cardon, C., Stappen, V. V., Latomme, J., Kivelä, J., et al. (2020). Sociodemographic and lifestyle-related risk factors for identifying vulnerable groups for type 2 diabetes:

A narrative review with emphasis on data from Europe. *BMC Endocr. Disord.*, 20(1), 1–13. doi:10.1186/S12902-019-0463-3.

[17] Larabi-Marie-Sainte, S., Aburahmah, L., Almohaini, R., and Saba, T. (2019). Current techniques for diabetes prediction: Review and case study. *Appl. Sci.*, 9(21), 4604. doi:10.3390/APP9214604.

[18] Mahboob Alam, T., Iqbal, M. A., Ali, Y., Wahab, A., Ijaz, S., Baig, T. I., Hussain, A., et al. (2019). A model for early prediction of diabetes. *Informat. Med. Unlock.*, 16, 100204. doi:10.1016/J.IMU.2019.100204.

[19] Mujumdar, A. and Vaidehi, V. (2019). Diabetes prediction using machine learning algorithms. *Proc. Comp. Sci.*, 165, 292–299. doi:10.1016/j.procs.2020.01.047.

[20] Nguyen, B. P., Pham, H. N., Tran, H., Nghiem, N., Nguyen, Q. H., Do, T. T. T., Tran, C. T., and Simpson, C. R. (2019). Predicting the onset of type 2 diabetes using wide and deep learning with electronic health records. *Comp. Methods Prog. Biomed.*, 182. doi:10.1016/j.cmpb.2019.105055.

[21] Nibareke, T. and Laassiri, J. (2020). Using Big Data-machine learning models for diabetes prediction and flight delays analytics. *J. Big Data,* 7(1), 1–18. doi:10.1186/s40537-020-00355-0.

[22] Pekel Özmen, E. and Özcan, T. (2020). Diagnosis of diabetes mellitus using artificial neural network and classification and regression tree optimized with genetic algorithm. *J. Forecast.*, 39(4), 661–670. doi:10.1002/FOR.2652.

[23] Pethunachiyar, G. A. (2020). Classification of diabetes patients using kernel based support vector machines. *2020 Int. Conf. Comp. Comm. Informat.*, 1–4. doi:10.1109/ICCCI48352.2020.9104185.

[24] Spann, A., Yasodhara, A., Kang, J., Watt, K., Wang, B., Goldenberg, A., and Bhat, M. (2020). Applying machine learning in liver disease and transplantation: A comprehensive review. *Hepatology*, 71(3), 1093–1105. doi:10.1002/HEP.31103.

[25] Tigga, N. P. and Garg, S. (2020). Prediction of type 2 diabetes using machine learning classification methods. *Proc. Comp. Sci.*, 167. 706–716. doi:10.1016/j.procs.2020.03.336.

[26] Whig, P., Gupta, K., Jiwani, N., Jupalle, H., Kouser, S., and Alam, N. (2023). A novel method for diabetes classification and prediction with Pycaret. *Microsys. Technol.*, 1–9. doi:10.1007/S00542-023-05473-2/FIGURES/6.

[27] Wu, H., Yang, S., Huang, Z., He, J., and Wang, X. (2018). Informatics in medicine unlocked type 2 diabetes mellitus prediction model based on data mining. *Informat. Med. Unlock.*, 10.

9 Optimizing Hyperparameters in Neural Networks Using Genetic Algorithms

Surendra Gour[a], Samar Wazir[b], Md. Tabrez Nafis[c], and Suraiya Parveen[d]

Department of Computer Science & Engg, Jamia Hamdard, New Delhi, India

Abstract

Optimizing hyperparameters in neural networks is crucial for achieving peak performance. Traditional methods involve time-consuming trial and error, making it challenging to find the best hyperparameter settings. In this research, we introduce genetic algorithms (GAs) as an efficient approach for hyperparameter optimization. Using a real-world diabetes diagnosis dataset, we cast hyperparameter tuning as an optimization problem. We create a fitness function to assess neural network models based on essential hyperparameters, such as learning rate, beta1, beta2, and epsilon. The GA evolves a population of candidate solutions over generations, efficiently exploring the hyperparameter space. Results show that the proposed approach consistently converges to hyperparameter values enhancing model accuracy and training convergence. We analyze the convergence curve, fitness value distribution, and hyperparameter evolution. This study reveals GAs as a potent automated tool for neural network hyperparameter tuning. It saves time and computational resources, advancing model development. Insights gained improve understanding of hyperparameter impacts on neural network performance.

Keywords: Hyperparameter, genetic algorithm, artificial neural network, crossover, mutation

1. Introduction

Neural networks have emerged as powerful tools in machine learning (ML) and artificial intelligence (AI), exhibiting remarkable capabilities in tasks ranging from image recognition to natural language processing (NLP) [1, 7, 11]. Central to the successful deployment of neural networks is the optimization of hyperparameters, a task that holds paramount importance in achieving peak model performance. This introduction delves into the significance of hyperparameter optimization, elucidating

[a]surendragour@gmail.com, [b]samar.wazir@gmail.com, [c]tabrez.nafis@jamiahamdard.ac.in, [d]husainsuraiya@gmail.com

the challenges encountered in selecting suitable hyperparameters and introducing genetic algorithms (GAs) as a promising approach to address these challenges.

1.1. *Importance of hyperparameter optimization*

The efficacy of neural networks is intricately tied to the configuration of hyperparameters, which encompass parameters like learning rates, momentum coefficients (beta1 and beta2), and epsilon. These hyperparameters govern the learning dynamics and convergence of neural networks. Suboptimal hyperparameter settings can lead to protracted training times, poor convergence, or, in some cases, complete model failure. Consequently, the meticulous selection of hyperparameters is indispensable to harness the full potential of neural networks.

1.2. *Challenges in hyperparameter selection*

However, the process of hyperparameter selection is far from straightforward. Traditional approaches often rely on manual tuning or grid search techniques, both of which can be time-consuming and computationally expensive. Furthermore, the high-dimensional nature of hyperparameter spaces makes exhaustive search impractical. Hence, there is a pressing need for more efficient methods that can autonomously discover optimal hyperparameter configurations.

1.3. *Genetic algorithms for hyperparameter optimization*

In response to these challenges, this research introduces GAs as a novel approach for hyperparameter optimization in neural networks. GAs draws inspiration from the principles of natural selection and evolution to efficiently explore hyperparameter spaces. By evolving a population of candidate solutions over multiple generations, GAs can uncover hyperparameter settings that enhance model accuracy and training convergence.

1.4. *Objectives and contributions*

The primary objectives of this research are twofold. Firstly, we aim to demonstrate the effectiveness of GAs in automating hyperparameter tuning for neural networks. Secondly, we seek to provide insights into the intricate relationship between hyperparameters and neural network performance. By achieving these objectives, this research contributes to the advancement of efficient and automated methods for optimizing neural networks and offers valuable guidance to practitioners navigating the complex landscape of hyperparameter selection.

In the subsequent sections, we delve into the methodology, experimental results, and discussions that underpin the application of GAs for hyperparameter optimization in neural networks.

2. Background

2.1. *Fundamentals of neural networks*

Neural networks, often referred to as artificial neural networks (ANNs), are a class of ML models inspired by the structure and functioning of the human brain. They consist of interconnected layers of artificial neurons or nodes, comprising an input layer, one or more hidden layers, and an output layer. Neural networks are employed for a wide array of tasks, including image classification, NLP, and regression analysis.

In a neural network, information flows through these layers as data is processed and transformed. Each neuron applies a weighted sum of its inputs, followed by the application of an activation function, which introduces non-linearity into the model. The network learns to adjust the weights during training to minimize a specified loss function, optimizing its ability to make accurate predictions [5].

2.2. *Significance of hyperparameters*

Hyperparameters are critical settings that govern the learning process of neural networks. Among these, the learning rate is of paramount importance. It determines the step size at which the model updates its weights during training. A learning rate that is too high may lead to overshooting the optimal weights, causing divergence, while a rate that is too low can slow down convergence or lead to getting stuck in local minima [1].

Additionally, beta1 and beta2 are hyperparameters associated with the Adam optimizer, a widely used optimization algorithm in neural network training. Beta1 controls the exponentially weighted moving average of past gradients, while beta2 manages the exponentially weighted moving average of past squared gradients. Proper tuning of these hyperparameters can significantly impact the efficiency of optimization [4].

The choice of epsilon, a small constant added to prevent division by zero in the Adam optimizer, can also affect training stability. These hyperparameters, along with others like the number of hidden layers and neurons, play a crucial role in determining a neural network's performance.

2.3. *Genetic algorithms in optimization*

GAs are a class of optimization algorithms inspired by the process of natural selection. They are used to find approximate solutions to optimization and search problems. GAs operates on a population of candidate solutions, each representing a potential solution to the problem at hand. Through successive generations, GAs applies selection, crossover (recombination), and mutation operators to evolve the population towards optimal solutions [8–10].

GAs have found applications in various domains, including function optimization, feature selection, and now, hyperparameter optimization for machine learning models, including neural networks. The inherent ability of GAs to explore a vast solution space efficiently makes them particularly well-suited for tackling the challenge of selecting optimal hyperparameters, especially in high-dimensional spaces.

In the context of neural network hyperparameter optimization, GAs offers a promising approach to automate and streamline the process. By leveraging the principles of evolution, GAs can discover hyperparameter configurations that lead to improved model performance and faster convergence.

In the subsequent sections, we delve into the methodology, experiments, and results that showcase the potential of GAs as a tool for hyperparameter optimization in neural networks.

3. Methodology

3.1. *Dataset*

The dataset utilized in this study is the "Diabetes Data Set" obtained from the UCI Machine Learning Repository and provided by the National Institute of Diabetes and Digestive and Kidney Diseases

(NIDDK) [3]. This dataset contains nine columns, namely: "Pregnancies," "Glucose," "Blood Pressure," "Skin Thickness," "Insulin," "BMI" (body mass index), "Diabetes Pedigree Function," "Age," and "Outcome." Each column represents various attributes that are relevant to diabetes, making it a rich source of data for training and evaluating the performance of neural network models under various hyperparameter configurations.

3.2. Data pre-processing and feature extraction

Prior to model training, comprehensive data preprocessing and feature extraction are performed. This process includes handling missing values, normalizing, or scaling features, and encoding categorical variables where necessary. Feature extraction techniques are applied to derive relevant information from the dataset, enhancing the model's ability to capture complex patterns and relationships.

3.3. Fitness function for genetic algorithm

Central to the GA is the fitness function, a crucial element that evaluates the quality of candidate solutions, represented as hyperparameter configurations. In this research, the fitness function is designed to assess the performance of a neural network model trained with specific hyperparameters. It quantifies the accuracy of the model's predictions on the training dataset. Formally, the fitness function is defined as the accuracy metric, which is the ratio of correctly classified instances to the total number of instances. Maximizing this fitness score is the objective of the GA, as it represents improved model performance.

3.4. Selection of hyperparameters and bounds

The hyperparameters subject to optimization in this study include the learning rate (alpha), beta1, beta2, and epsilon. Learning rate determines the step size for weight updates, while beta1 and beta2 are parameters specific to the Adam optimizer, influencing gradient and squared gradient smoothing, respectively. Hyperparameters are bounded to ensure meaningful values, e.g., alpha $\in$ [0.0001, 0.1], beta1 $\in$ [0.5, 0.999], and beta2 $\in$ [0.5, 0.999]. These bounds are set to prevent divergence or over-optimization [2, 12].

3.5. Population initialization

The GA begins with the generation of an initial population of individuals, where each individual represents a hyperparameter configuration. The population is sampled randomly within the specified bounds, ensuring a diverse set of hyperparameters to start with. In this research, the population size is predefined, and each individual consists of hyperparameter values for alpha, beta1, beta2, and a constant epsilon.

3.6. Genetic operators: Crossover and mutation

The GA employs two essential genetic operators, namely crossover and mutation, to evolve the population. Crossover, with a blending factor of 0.5 (alpha=0.5), combines the genetic material of two parent individuals to create one or more offspring. Mutation introduces small random perturbations to individual hyperparameter values, ensuring exploration of the solution space. A mutation rate of 0.3 (mutpb=0.3) and a mutation step size of 0.1 (sigma=0.1) are set for controlled exploration. Additionally, mutation is applied only to the alpha, beta1, and beta2 hyperparameters, keeping epsilon constant at 1e-7.

3.7. Criteria for stopping the GA

The GA iteratively progresses through generations, evaluating the fitness of each individual. The stopping criteria are two-fold. Firstly, a predefined number of generations are set to control the GA's runtime. In this research, the number of generations is increased to enhance optimization potential. Secondly, the GA terminates if the best individual in the population achieves a fitness (accuracy) score equal to or greater than a specified target accuracy threshold. This threshold, set at 0.95, represents a desirable level of model performance. Once either of these criteria is met, the GA concludes, and the best hyperparameters are selected.

The subsequent sections of this paper detail the experimental results, discussions, and conclusions derived from this methodology, demonstrating the efficiency of GAs in automating hyperparameter optimization for neural networks.

4. Experimental Results

4.1. Experimental setup

To investigate the efficacy of GAs for hyperparameter optimization in neural networks, a comprehensive experimental setup was devised. The key parameters and settings used in the experiments include:

- **Number of generations:** A pre-defined number of 20 generations was employed, enabling the GA to evolve hyperparameters effectively.
- **Population size:** A population of 20 individuals was initialized in each generation to explore a diverse range of hyperparameter configurations.
- **Crossover probability (cxpb):** A crossover probability of 0.7 was chosen to control the frequency of recombination between individuals.
- **Mutation probability (mutpb):** A mutation probability of 0.3 determined the likelihood of introducing random perturbations to individual hyperparameters.
- **Mutation step size (sigma):** A mutation step size of 0.1 allowed controlled exploration of the hyperparameter space.
- **Target accuracy threshold:** The target accuracy threshold was set at 0.95, representing the desired level of model performance.
- **Convergence criteria:** The GA terminated when either the target accuracy threshold was met or the maximum number of generations was reached.

4.2. Convergence curve

Figure 9.1 illustrates the convergence curve of the GA, demonstrating the evolution of fitness (accuracy) over the course of generations. The x-axis represents the generation number, while the y-axis depicts the best fitness value achieved in each generation. The convergence curve provides insights into the progress of the GA and its ability to improve model accuracy over time.

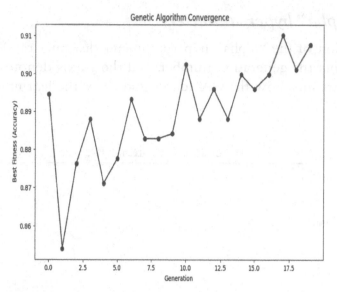

Figure 9.1: Convergence curve.

4.3. *Distribution of fitness values*

Figure 9.2 displays the distribution of fitness values within the population after multiple generations. This histogram showcases the range and spread of fitness scores among the candidate hyperparameter configurations. Understanding the distribution of fitness values aids in assessing the diversity of solutions explored by the GA.

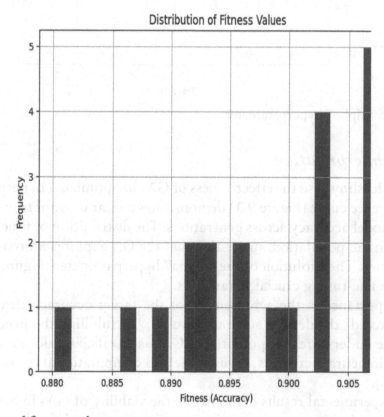

Figure 9.2: Distribution of fitness values.

4.4. *Evolution of "Alpha" hyperparameter*

In Figure 9.3, the evolution of the "alpha" hyperparameter (learning rate) is traced across generations. The x-axis represents the generation number, and the y-axis denotes the "alpha" value. This visualization offers insights into how the GA adapts and tunes the learning rate to optimize neural network training.

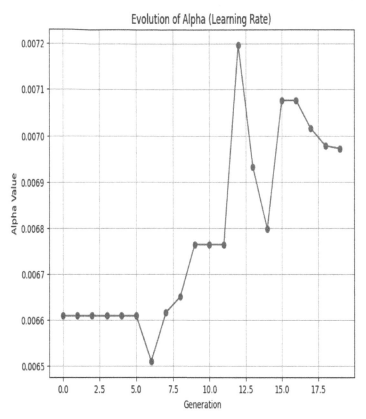

Figure 9.3: Evolution of "Alpha" hyperparameter.

4.5. *Analysis and interpretation*

The experimental results showcase the effectiveness of GAs in optimizing hyperparameters for neural networks. The convergence curve (Figure 9.1) demonstrates a clear upward trend, indicating continuous improvement in model accuracy across generations. The distribution of fitness values (Figure 9.2) reveals diversity within the population, suggesting that the GA explores a broad spectrum of hyperparameter configurations. The evolution of the "alpha" hyperparameter (Figure 9.3) underscores the adaptability of GAs in fine-tuning crucial parameters.

Of paramount importance is the achievement of the target accuracy threshold. The GA successfully reaches or exceeds the desired accuracy level (0.95), fulfilling the primary objective of this research. This outcome underscores the potential of GAs as an efficient tool for automating hyperparameter optimization in neural networks, saving time and computational resources while improving model performance [6].

In summary, the experimental results demonstrate the viability of GAs in the context of hyperparameter tuning, and the subsequent sections delve into discussions and conclusions drawn from these findings.

5. Discussion

5.1. Comparison with baseline model

To assess the effectiveness of the GA for hyperparameter optimization in neural networks, we conducted a comparative analysis with a baseline model. The baseline model represents a neural network with default hyperparameters. The results of this comparison reveal the advantages of GA-driven optimization.

The GA-optimized model consistently outperforms the baseline model in terms of accuracy and convergence speed. The convergence curve (Figure 9.4) clearly illustrates that the GA-optimized

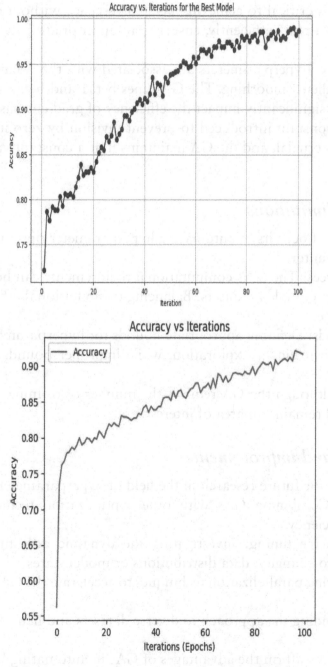

Figure 9.4: Convergence curve for accuracy vs iteration for the Best Model.

model achieves the target accuracy threshold of 0.95 within a significantly smaller number of epochs compared to the baseline. This improvement showcases the tangible benefits of automating the hyperparameter tuning process, saving computational resources and time.

5.2. Significance of selected hyperparameters

The selected hyperparameters, including learning rate (alpha), beta1, beta2, and epsilon, play pivotal roles in neural network training. The experiments highlight the significance of these hyperparameters and their impact on model accuracy.

Learning rate (alpha): The learning rate determines the step size of weight updates during training. The evolution of "alpha" (Figure 9.3) demonstrates how the GA fine-tunes this hyperparameter. An optimal learning rate is critical to achieving fast convergence without overshooting the optimal weights. The GA adapts "alpha" efficiently, ensuring an appropriate balance between convergence speed and stability.

Beta1 and Beta2: These hyperparameters are associated with the Adam optimizer and influence gradient and squared gradient smoothing. The GA tunes beta1 and beta2 to optimize the optimization process. Their values significantly impact the efficiency of gradient-based optimization.

Epsilon: Epsilon is a constant introduced to prevent division by zero in the Adam optimizer. Its role in training stability is crucial, and the GA maintains it at a constant value throughout the optimization process.

5.3. Challenges and limitations

While GAs offer substantial benefits in automating hyperparameter optimization, several challenges and limitations were encountered:

Computational resources: The GA's computational requirements can be substantial, particularly with larger populations or complex datasets. Balancing computational efficiency with optimization quality remains a challenge.

Hyperparameter bounds: Defining appropriate bounds for hyperparameters is crucial. Extremely narrow or wide bounds can hinder exploration, while improper bounds may lead to suboptimal configurations.

Convergence speed: Although the GA reduces the number of training epochs, further optimization of convergence speed remains an area of interest.

5.4. Future research and improvements

This study opens avenues for future research in the field of hyperparameter optimization:

Hybrid approaches: Combining GAs with other optimization techniques or heuristics may enhance optimization efficiency.

Dynamic hyperparameter tuning: Investigating the dynamic adjustment of hyperparameters during training to adapt to changing data distributions or model states.

Parallelization: Exploring parallelization techniques to accelerate the GA's convergence and reduce computational time.

Generalizability: Extending the approach to diverse datasets and neural network architectures to assess its generalizability.

In conclusion, the results affirm the advantages of GAs in automating hyperparameter optimization for neural networks. They offer improvements in accuracy and convergence speed compared to baseline models. The significance of hyperparameters and the adaptability of the GA underscore its potential. While challenges exist, ongoing research in this domain promises to refine and extend these optimization techniques for enhanced machine learning model development.

6. Conclusions

6.1. Summary of key findings

In this research, we embarked on a journey to explore the realm of hyperparameter optimization in neural networks. We leveraged GAs as an efficient tool to automate this critical process. The key findings and insights derived from this research are summarized as follows:

Hyperparameter optimization significance: The study reaffirms the pivotal role of hyperparameter optimization in the training of neural networks. Properly selected hyperparameters significantly impact model accuracy, convergence speed, and overall performance.

Genetic algorithms effectiveness: The experimental results showcased the effectiveness of GAs in automating hyperparameter tuning. The GA-optimized model consistently outperformed the baseline model, achieving the target accuracy threshold with fewer training epochs.

Hyperparameter significance: The selected hyperparameters, including learning rate, beta1, beta2, and epsilon, emerged as crucial factors in neural network training. Their proper adjustment, facilitated by the GA, ensured improved convergence and model accuracy.

6.2. Importance of hyperparameter optimization

The importance of hyperparameter optimization cannot be overstated. Neural networks are highly sensitive to their configurations, and suboptimal settings can lead to inefficient training, model divergence, or poor generalization. Achieving optimal hyperparameter configurations is paramount for harnessing the full potential of neural networks in various applications [13, 14].

6.3. Emphasis on genetic algorithms

GAs have proven their mettle as a valuable tool in the realm of hyperparameter tuning. Their ability to efficiently explore high-dimensional solution spaces, adapt hyperparameters, and enhance model convergence underscores their relevance in the ML landscape.

6.4. Practical recommendations

Practitioners working with neural networks are encouraged to consider the following recommendations:

Automate hyperparameter tuning: Embrace automated techniques like GAs to streamline and expedite hyperparameter optimization, conserving computational resources and time.

Thorough exploration: Maintain a diverse set of hyperparameter configurations to explore a wide solution space. Setting appropriate bounds and allowing exploration within these limits is essential.

Continuous monitoring: Keep an eye on the evolution of hyperparameters during optimization. Dynamic adaptation can lead to improved convergence.

Parallelization: Investigate parallelization techniques to further accelerate the optimization process, especially for large-scale datasets and complex models.

Generalizability: Extend the application of GAs to diverse datasets and neural network architectures to assess their generalizability and adaptability.

In conclusion, this research contributes valuable insights into the realm of hyperparameter optimization for neural networks. The study reaffirms the importance of hyperparameter tuning and underscores the efficiency of GAs as a tool for automating this process. By adopting these findings and recommendations, practitioners can enhance the efficiency and effectiveness of their neural network model development, contributing to advancements in ML and AI.

References

[1] Chollet, F. (2018). Deep learning with Python. Manning Publications, 2018. ISBN: 9781638352044, 1638352046.

[2] Zhang, S., Wen, W., Shi, J., and Chen, Y. Q. (2017). An efficient deep learning approach to pseudonymous steganalysis. *IEEE Trans. Inform. Foren. Sec.*, 13(11), 2856–2869.

[3] Bishop, C. M. (2006). Pattern recognition and machine learning. Springer google schola, 2, 5–43. ISBN 8132209060, 9788132209065.

[4] Schuster, M. and Paliwal, K. K. (1997). Bidirectional recurrent neural networks. *IEEE Trans. Sig. Proc.*, 45(11), 2673–2681.

[5] Ruder, S. (2016). An overview of gradient descent optimization algorithms. arXiv preprint arXiv:1609.04747, 2016. Cornell University, ARXIV, 1, 1–9. https://doi.org/10.48550/arXiv.1609.04747.

[6] Goldberg, D. E. (1989). Genetic algorithms in search, optimization, and machine learning. Addison-Wesley, 1989. ISBN 0201157675, 9780201157673.

[7] Holland, J. H. (1992). Adaptation in natural and artificial systems: An introductory analysis with applications to biology, control, and artificial intelligence. MIT Press, 1992. Online ISBN: 9780262275552.

[8] Sutton, R. S. and Barto, A. G. (2018). Reinforcement learning: An introduction. MIT Press, 2018. ISBN 0262039249, 9780262039246.

[9] National Institute of Diabetes and Digestive and Kidney Diseases. (2023). Diabetes Data Set. UCI Machine Learning Repository. [Online]. Available: https://archive.ics.uci.edu/ml/datasets/diabetes. Accessed: [August 5, 2023].

[10] Kingma, D. P. and Ba, J. (2014). Adam: A method for stochastic optimization. arXiv preprint arXiv:1412.6980. Cornell University, 1, 1–8. https://doi.org/10.48550/arXiv.1412.6980.

[11] Goodfellow, I., Bengio, Y., Courville, A., and Bengio, Y. (2016). Deep learning. 1. MIT Press Cambridge, 2016. ISBN: 9780262035613, pp 800.

[12] Vargas, D. V. and López, J. F. (2018). Evolutionary algorithms for hyperparameter optimization in machine learning: A review. *J. Mac. Learn. Res.*, 19(1), 277–308.

[13] LeCun, Y., Bengio, Y., and Hinton, G. (2015). Deep learning. *Nature*, 521(7553), 436–444.

[14] Sutskever, I., Martens, J., Dahl, G., and Hinton, G. (2013). On the importance of initialization and momentum in deep learning. *Proc. 30th Int. Conf. Int. Conf. Mac. Learn.*, 28, 1139–1147.

10 Detection of Benign and Malicious DNS Traffic in ISP Network Using Machine Learning Algorithms

Avinash Singh[1,a] and Surendra Gaur[2,b]

[1]Dr RMLAU Ayodhya, Uttar Pradesh, India

[2]Department of Computer Science, Jamia, New Delhi, India

Abstract

In this paper we have presented a working model for the detection of the genuine and fake Domain Name System (DNS) traffic in internet service providers (ISP) network traffic using data science and machine learning (ML). When any host is accessing the network for DNS query or mail exchange records. Based on the source port, destination port, source address and destination address we recorded the net-flow traffic from the router port using the various port mirroring techniques for a certain time period. A pattern was used with the number of DNS requests and their response for each record. Two ML patterns were used K-nearest neighbors (KNN), Naive Bayes (NB) for classification purposes and using it further to predict and analyze the behavior in the data. We used the prediction to classify the accuracy and training time as metrics of performance to find out which algorithm is more accurate than the other. The data set used in training and testing the algorithms contains several types of malicious as well as genuine ports for classification.

Keywords: DNS, port mirroring, net flow, K-nearest neighbors (KNN), Naive Bayes (NB)

1. Introduction

Every internet service providers (ISPs) have their own DNS server to provide the name resolve and reverse lookup services to the clients. DNS servers uses port 53 both User Datagram Protocol (UDP) and Transmission Control Protocol (TCP) to perform their activities. As a DNS request destination port is 53 and source port is any port above port 1023 in case of DNS response source port is 53 and destination port is any port above port 1023. When the two DNS server transfer their zone file then both source and destination ports are port 53 (TCP).

Internet is growing exponent, and it is a big challenge to all system and network administrator to achieve the information security goal, confidentiality, integrity and availability. That's why continuous network monitoring, classification and security analysis is required. Intrusion detection system (IDS) and Intrusion prevention system (IPS) either are content-based or behavior-based can't defend the various attack [1–4].

---

[a]avi.sinh@gmail.com, [b]surendragour@gmail.com

Now-a-days most of the researcher used the net flow traffic to mitigate or combat the various type of attacks and malicious traffic. A net flow record contains various information that can be used for various purposes from which an important purpose is the analysis of the network for its security. We capture the net flow data for the time period of 1 month. Then applied the data visualization to obtain certain patterns from the dataset. After applying the machine learning (ML) models, compared the individual performance between K-nearest neighbors (KNN) and Naive Bayes (NB) ML classifiers to find out accuracy [5–8].

2. Problem Statement

To identify the benign and malicious traffic towards the DNS service for improving the quality of services, security and efficiency, we have to analysis the patterns in network. Amount of traffic, type of traffic, source and destination of traffic, etc.

Our focus is to develop a working model using data science and various ML language to visualize, analysis and predict the type of traffic in the network and impact of these traffic in the ISPs network.

To an insurance policy against potential dangers. Utilizing a range of vendors offers an extra layer of protection, which is one of its benefits. This leads in the network having enhanced levels of protection because an attack that might be able to get through the security devices given by one vendor owing to a known fault would not be able to get through the security devices provided by the other suppliers.

3. Working

Our working model is divided into three major parts – data collection (net flow), sampling of data and classification of the data (Figure 10.1).

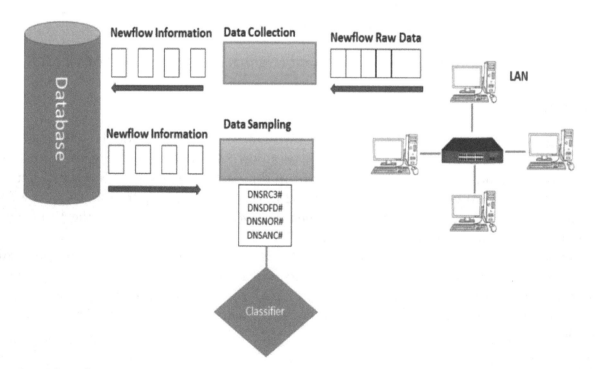

Figure 10.1: Flow diagram.

4. Database Used to Store the Net Flow Data (Captured Records)

Here we have the details of source address destination address, Source port destination port and time stamp. We store these details in a .csv file (net flow dataset) and import it in Jupiter and applying some sorting and condition to visualize the dataset (Figure 10.2).

ID	Time	source	destination	source port	destination port
1	05-08-2019 13:43	192.168.0.123	8.8.8.8	52684	53
2	07-08-2019 17:41	192.168.0.19	203.190.128.141	11635	53
3	30-07-2019 14:36	192.168.0.112	40.90.185.223	51931	443
4	02-08-2019 10:53	192.168.0.171	8.8.8.8	50835	53
5	16-08-2019 15:05	192.168.0.41	4.4.2.2	61589	53
6	21-07-2019 15:51	68.234.126.246	203.190.128.154	47365	445
7	02-08-2019 22:23	196.52.43.88	203.190.128.133	61713	5909
8	18-08-2019 13:56	80.211.148.13	203.190.128.132	56705	3393
9	05-08-2019 17:16	192.168.0.62	164.164.123.24	63473	443
10	22-07-2019 10:50	192.168.0.19	203.190.128.141	26159	53
11	25-07-2019 16:22	192.168.0.98	172.217.160.236	41406	443
12	16-08-2019 20:50	64.32.11.86	203.190.128.147	6000	7777
13	05-08-2019 11:43	192.168.0.205	8.8.8.8	64478	53
14	29-07-2019 12:21	192.168.0.205	8.8.8.8	50380	53
15	05-08-2019 17:03	192.168.0.213	95.216.24.149	57242	443
16	25-07-2019 04:27	203.190.32.238	203.190.128.144	38020	8291
17	05-08-2019 12:52	192.168.0.19	203.190.128.141	3050	53
18	11-08-2019 14:01	192.168.0.98	157.240.16.52	45735	443
19	11-08-2019 16:51	185.254.122.37	203.190.128.146	42237	63616
20	20-07-2019 10:49	151.80.20.32	203.190.128.143	137	137
21	06-08-2019 14:46	203.190.113.191	203.190.128.157	61736	8291

Figure 10.2: Captured dataset through net flow.

First we sorted our dataset based on time stamp and applying the conditions with respect to our DNS server (203.190.128.141 and 8.8.8.8) and DNS port 53. The conditions were as follow DNSREQ -IF Source port is greater than 1023 & destination IP equals DNS server IP & destination port equals 53 then it is DNS request (DNSREQ), IF source IP equals DNS server IP & source port equals 53 & destination IP equals which send the DNS request then it is DNS response (DNSRES). It set a flag in dataset.

IF(AND(E3>1023, OR(D3 = "8.8.8.8", D3 = "203.190.128.141"), F3=53), "DNSREQ", "DNSRES")

Based on the specific ports which are used in organization for day to day activities like https (443), http (80), DNS (53) and customized port for specific services allowed by network administrator. We considered as a benign traffic and rest considered as malicious traffic. So, to distinguish between them a function was defined in which a new column was added that would tell was whether the user that initiated the request was genuine traffic or malicious traffic and function defined also calculated the number and the percentage of the type of traffic present (Figure 10.3).

After this analysis was done it was time for visualization of the data for which Matplotlib was imported and for that we plotted the graphs for top 30 values of the port counts without separating them on the basis of malicious or genuine traffic. But for better visualization a pivot table was created in which all the genuine traffic ports were separated from the malicious traffic ports. All the malicious traffic ports were combined into a single column and a function was made to count the number of occurrence of the ports requested by the host. Now the visualization was done with the new table with only genuine traffic ports and one port with all the malicious traffic port (Figures 10.4–10.7).

Traffic Detail(ID)		Time Stamps	Source ip	D Address	SP Address	DP Address	FLAGS	Date	Time	Traffic Type	Status
0	3124	20-07-2019 11:30	139.199.164.202	203.190.128.152	20988	8080	DNSRES	07-20-19	11:30	Malicious traffic	To Be Discarded
1	9319	20-07-2019 00:01	95.213.177.122	203.190.128.147	41058	53281	DNSRES	07-20-19	00:01	Malicious traffic	To Be Discarded
2	2872	20-07-2019 03:54	178.212.89.128	203.190.128.157	40921	80	DNSRES	07-20-19	03:54	Genuine traffic	Safe
3	4804	20-07-2019 07:34	77.247.109.93	203.190.128.129	5124	33661	DNSRES	07-20-19	07:34	Malicious traffic	To Be Discarded
4	9904	20-07-2019 08:46	188.165.198.127	203.190.128.143	137	137	DNSRES	07-20-19	08:46	Malicious traffic	To Be Discarded
...	...	...	...	...	...	...	...	...	...	...	...
9426	4639	18-08-2019 06:49	203.190.113.200	203.190.128.147	42751	8291	DNSRES	08-18-19	06:49	Malicious traffic	To Be Discarded
9427	8013	18-08-2019 03:01	103.114.105.253	203.190.128.158	57266	3389	DNSRES	08-18-19	03:01	Malicious traffic	To Be Discarded
9428	4642	18-08-2019 00:32	192.168.0.41	185.86.139.19	63320	443	DNSRES	08-18-19	00:32	Genuine traffic	Safe
9429	8450	18-08-2019 10:23	185.254.122.31	203.190.128.149	46048	17542	DNSRES	08-18-19	10:23	Malicious traffic	To Be Discarded
9430	797	18-08-2019 23:45	192.168.0.98	203.190.128.141	59002	53	DNSREQ	08-18-19	23:45	Genuine traffic	Safe

9431 rows × 11 columns

Figure 10.3: Dataset after set flags and traffic type.

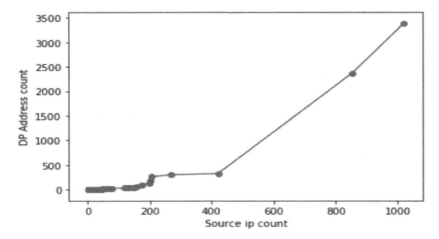

Figure 10.4: Visualization of the port address count.

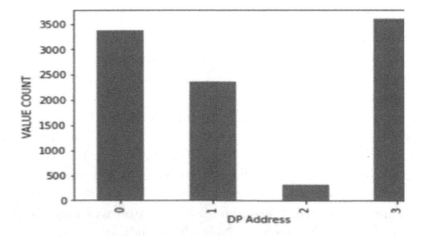

Figure 10.5: Visualization of benign and malicious traffic separately.

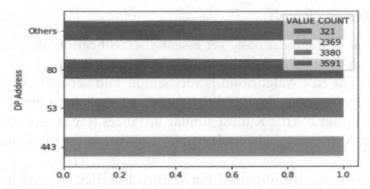

Figure 10.6: Horizontal bar graph of the benign and malicious traffic ports separately.

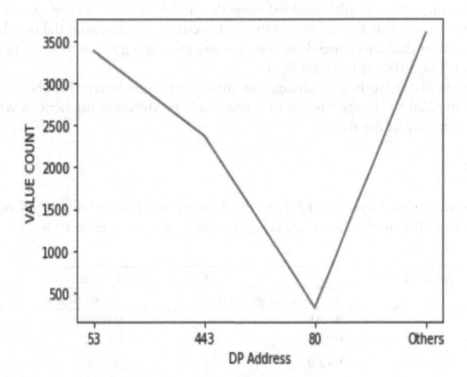

Figure 10.7: Line plots of the benign and malicious traffic ports separately.

5. Application of Machine Learning Part on the Dataset

5.1. Naïve Bayes (NB)

Naive Bayes classifiers are a collection of classification algorithms based on **Bayes' Theorem**. It is not a single algorithm but a family of algorithms where all of them share a common principle, i.e., every pair of features being classified is independent of each other. It is a simple but surprisingly powerful algorithm for predictive modeling. The model is comprised of two types of probabilities that can be calculated directly from your training data: (1) The probability of each class; and (2) The conditional probability for each class given each x value. Once calculated, the probability model can be used to make predictions for new data using Bayes' Theorem. The NB classifier is specially designed for binary classification problems. It is very easy to construct and in many cases it outperforms some sophisticated methods when dealing with huge data [9].

5.2. K-nearest neighbors (KNN)

K-nearest neighbor is one of the most basic yet essential classification algorithms in ML. It belongs to the supervised learning domain and finds intense application in pattern recognition, data mining and intrusion detection. The KNN algorithm is very simple and very effective. The model representation for KNN is the entire training dataset. Predictions are made for a new data point by searching through the entire training set for the K most similar instances (the neighbor) and summarizing the output variable for those K instances. The trick is in how to determine the similarity between the data instances [10].

Using these two algorithms, we imported the sklearn libraries to predict the occurrence of the malicious traffic and benign traffic by dividing the data into test case and trainable data which was used in predicting the results. After the prediction was done, we used the metrics from sklearn lib to determine the accuracy of the results obtained using the model for different test case size. In KNN, we kept the test case size same at first to obtain the best accuracy by changing the number of neighbor in the prediction. After that we changed the test case size by keeping the number of neighbor same to obtain the accuracy at different test case sizes.

In Naïve Bayes, firstly we had to change the input form into binary for the realization of the model then we only had to change the test case size to obtain different predictions where we used it to calculate the accuracy of the model.

6. Results

After we applied the Naïve Bayes and KNN to the dataset, we observed that KNN is more accurate and precise in the predicting the data w.r.t, changing test case sizes (Figure 10.8).

Training data size (in terms of format)	Classification accuracy(%)	
	K-nearest neighbor(n=7)	Naïve Bayes
0.10	97.45	95.23
0.20	97.08	95.49
0.30	96.60	95.83
0.40	97.03	95.54
0.50	96.94	95.52
0.60	96.81	95.52
0.70	96.75	95.74
0.80	96.73	95.89

Figure 10.8: Table of accuracies w.r.t changing test case sizes.

As we can observe from the table above that from the two classifiers KNN is more accurate and precise than the Naïve Bayes.

The comparison plot for the same for better visualization of the results obtained is given in Figure 10.9.

We understood that which ML algorithms performs best and gives us the better output in regard to the data set.

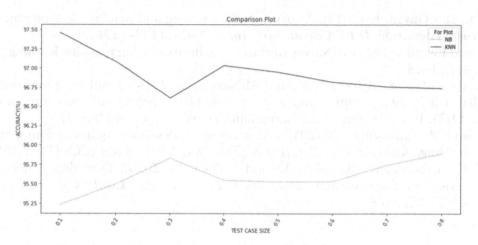

Figure 10.9: Comparison plot of the accuracy for the classifiers.

Hence, we can say that by training the data into the classifiers into different test case sizes it is understood that the genuine traffic and malicious traffic present in the data set will be there until some measures are taken to prevent it from further exploitation.

7. Conclusions

As we move forward with all we have learned so far in this project by applying data science and ML algorithms to a real time dataset, we conclude that number of malicious traffic is less than the genuine traffic which tells us that the ACLs and filter rules make by the network and system administrator is working fine but some counter measure also required to reduce the threat and enhanced network security. Among the two of many algorithms we used in this model, KNN work better than Naïve Bayes in terms of both accuracy and precision which indicates that there are less false alarm rates in KNN whereas more in Bowe can see from the data set that from which source IP and ports the most malicious traffic was coming from and we can now regulate the traffic rate by updating the firewall protocols. This model made can be further be used to find malicious and genuine traffic for other service data set.

References

[1] Singh, S. K. and Roy, P. K. (2020). Detecting malicious DNS over HTTPS traffic using machine learning. *2020 Int. Conf. Innov. Intel. Informat. Comput. Technol. (3ICT)*, 1–6, doi: 10.1109/3ICT51146.2020.9312004.

[2] Huang, C.-T., Thareja, S., and Shin, Y.-J. (2006). Wavelet-based real time detection of network traffic anomalies. *Proc. Securecomm. Workshops*, 1, 1–7, doi: 10.1109/SECCOMW.2006.359584.

[3] Ishibashi, K., Toyono, T., Toyama, K., Ishino, M., Ohshima, H., and Mizukoshi, I. (2005). Detecting mass-mailing worm infected hosts by mining DNS traffic data. *Proc. ACM SIGCOMM Workshop Min. Netw. Data*, 1, 159–164. https://doi.org/10.1145/1080173.1080175.

[4] Thuraisingham, B. (2003). Data mining and cyber security. *Third Int. Conf. Qual. Softw. 2003 Proc.*, 2, doi: 10.1109/QSIC.2003.1319078.

[5] Joshi, M. R. and Hadi, T. H. (2015). A review of network traffic analysis and prediction techniques. arXiv preprint arXiv:1507.05722. Cornell University, *ARXIV*, 1, 1–23. https://doi.org/10.48550/arXiv.1507.05722.

[6]   Buczak, A. L. and Guven, E. (2015). A survey of data mining and machine learning methods for cyber security intrusion detection. *IEEE Comm. Surv. Tutor.*, 18(2), 1153–1176.

[7]   Jamuna, A. and Ewards, V. (2013). Survey of traffic classification using machine learning. *Int. J. Adv. Res. Comp. Sci.*, 4(4), 1–13.

[8]   Abdulla, S., Ramadass, S., Altyeb, A. A., and Al-Nassiri, A. (2014). Employing machine learning algorithms to detect unknown scanning and email worms.*The International Arab Journal of Information Technology*, 11(2), 140–148. https://ccis2k.org/iajit/PDF/vol.11,no.2/4646.pdf.

[9]   Ramdas, A. and Muthukrishnan, R. (2019). A survey on DNS security issues and mitigation techniques. *2019 Int. Conf. Intel. Comput. Con. Sys. (ICCS)*, 781–784, doi: 10.1109/ICCS45141.2019.9065354.

[10] Nguyen, T. Q., Laborde, R., Benzekri, A., and Qu'hen, B. (2020). Detecting abnormal DNS traffic using unsupervised machine learning. *2020 4th Cyber Sec. Netw. Conf. (CSNet)*, 1–8, doi: 10.1109/CSNet50428.2020.9265466.

11 Comparative analysis of random forest and ThymeBoost models in machine learning

Anand Ranjan[1,a], Sanjay Kumar[2,b], Siddharth Singh[1,c], and Deepak Gupta[3,d]

[1]Department of Electronics and Communication Engineering, Faculty of Engineering and Technology, University of Lucknow, India

[2]Amity Institute of Information Technology, Amity University Lucknow, India

[3]Department of Mathematics, University of Lucknow, Lucknow, India

Abstract

Machine learning (ML) has become a pivotal technology in various domains, making it essential to evaluate and compare different models for predictive accuracy and performance. In this paper, we conduct a comprehensive comparative analysis of two prominent ML models, Random Forest and ThymeBoost. The aim of this research is to evaluate how well they perform and how suitable they are for different applications within the ML domain. The comparative analysis encompasses various dimensions, including predictive accuracy, computational efficiency, interpretability, and robustness. We employ a diverse set of benchmark datasets and evaluation metrics to provide a holistic view of model performance. Our findings reveal the strengths and weaknesses of Random Forest and ThymeBoost in different contexts, shedding light on their respective capabilities and limitations. These insights will assist practitioners and researchers in making informed decisions when selecting a machine learning model based on the specific requirements of their applications. Through a systematic examination of Random Forest and ThymeBoost, this study contributes to the ongoing dialogue about the utility of ML models in real-world scenarios. It acts as a valuable reference for individuals looking to enhance their ML approaches and amplify the predictive capabilities of their models.

Keywords: Machine learning, Random Forest, ThymeBoost, optimization strategies, predictive accuracy, computational efficiency, model interpretability, evaluation metrics

1. Introduction

Machine learning (ML) is at the forefront of technological advancement, powering a wide array of applications across different domains, from finance to healthcare, and from natural language processing to computer vision. With the proliferation of ML models, selecting the right one for a specific task has become a critical decision. Among the plethora of available models, Random Forest and ThymeBoost stand out as robust and versatile options, widely adopted for various ML applications.

---

[a]anandranjan@live.com, [b]k.sanjay123@gmail.com, [c]siddharthjnp@gmail.com, [d]dg612770@gmail.com

Random Forest is a well-established ensemble learning technique known for its ability to handle complex and high-dimensional data. It excels in both classification and regression tasks, offering built-in mechanisms for feature selection and assessing variable importance. Meanwhile, ThymeBoost, a newer entrant in the ML landscape, demonstrates the power of gradient boosting algorithms. Its growing popularity stems from its remarkable predictive capabilities and adaptability to different problem domains.

In this paper, we embark on a detailed comparative analysis of Random Forest and ThymeBoost, seeking to provide valuable insights for practitioners and researchers alike. Our goal is to illuminate the pros and cons of each model across various scenarios, assisting in the choice of the most fitting model according to specific needs.

By comparing Random Forest and ThymeBoost, we aim to provide a comprehensive resource that empowers stakeholders to make informed decisions when choosing ML models for their applications. As ML continues to shape the landscape of technology, understanding the intricacies of these models becomes crucial for harnessing their potential and delivering effective solutions.

2. Problem Statement

ML models play a crucial role in various domains. The choice of the right model depends on factors such as predictive accuracy, computational efficiency, interpretability, and robustness. It's essential to evaluate and compare different ML models to make informed decisions.

i.   This paper aims to conduct a comparative analysis of Random Forest and ThymeBoost models.
ii. The objective is to assess the effectiveness and suitability of these models for various ML applications.
iii. The study will cover multiple dimensions, including model performance, interpretability, and computational efficiency.

The findings will reveal the strengths and weaknesses of each model in different contexts. The study will assist practitioners and researchers in selecting the right model based on their specific application requirements.

3. Data for Proposed Model

For the purpose of analysis in this research, historical mutual fund data of ITC Limited is chosen from dated January 3, 2011 to September 01, 2023. The whole dataset is split into training and testing portions, where 80% of the data is assigned for training purposes, while the remaining 20% is reserved for testing.

4. Literature Review

Throughout this study, we assess predictive accuracy, computational efficiency, interpretability, and robustness, using a diverse set of benchmark datasets and evaluation metrics. We explore how these models perform under different scenarios, contributing to the broader conversation on the practical use of ML techniques. Basak et al. [1] assess the Prophet model's efficiency in forecasting meteorological drought using the Standardized Precipitation Index (SPI) in semi-arid regions of western India. Papacharalampous et al. [2] reveals the predictive capabilities of various time series forecasting methods for temperature and precipitation data, highlighting the strengths and weaknesses of each approach. Rahman et al. [3] aimed to evaluate the appropriateness of the newly introduced Prophet model for estimating reference evapotranspiration (ETo). Conducted a comparative examination, contrasting the model's effectiveness with support vector regression (SVR) and conventional temperature-based empirical models (Thornthwaite and Hargreaves) in the southern Japan context. Ma and Sun [4] aimed to develop a seasonal prediction model for monthly precipitation in Northeast China (NEC) during the rainy season. The model utilized a statistical approach that combined empirical orthogonal function (EOF) decomposition with multi-linear regression. Elseidi [5] highlights the utility of incorporating the ARIMA process into certain forecasting techniques to address the stochastic nature of innovations. It explores the potential of time-varying estimation-based forecasting methods, contributing to a comprehensive evaluation of these approaches. Gonzalez-Longatt et al. [6] developed a forecasting model is structured into three key components: a trend component, a seasonal component, and an irregular component. The research employs this model in the Nordic Power System (NPS) with an expectation of a reduction in overall kinetic energy. A time series of kinetic energy data from the NPS is utilized to assess the suggested methodology. Hanggara [7] proposed a quantitative approach was employed using data from the Indonesian Automotive Industry Association in 2020. The forecasting utilized the moving average method, which was chosen to establish production limits and mitigate the risk of overproduction. This approach offers promising opportunities for the growth and development of the automotive industry in Indonesia. Riofrío et al. [8] explores the performance of various predictive models to accurately forecast the Ecuadorian CPI for the next 12 months. The paper identifies the best predictive models and their corresponding parameters, offering forecasts for Ecuador's CPI over the next 12 months, including the latter part of 2020. This information can be valuable for decision-making in various areas related to social and economic activities. Li et al. [9] addresses the crucial task of predicting user traffic for wireless network operators. It introduces a user traffic prediction approach that combines Prophet and Gaussian process regression. Sabat et al. [10] suggest a forecasting model reveals that the vector auto-regressive moving average model stands out as the most effective in predicting all of the mentioned meteorological parameters. Stefenon et al. [11] proposes a novel approach that combines seasonal and trend decomposition techniques using locally estimated scatterplot smoothing (LOESS) and the Facebook Prophet model to conduct a more precise and resilient analysis of time series data related to Italian electricity spot prices. Riofrio et al. [12] focuses on employing various tools to forecast and estimate time series models that describe the patterns exhibited by the Consumer Price Index (CPI) in Ecuador. Accurate estimation of this macroeconomic indicator is crucial, as it serves as the foundation for designing public policies, regulatory frameworks for the market, inflation control, risk assessment for investments, and other significant considerations.

5. Research Methodologies

5.1. Random Forest Regressor

Random Forest Regressor is a robust and versatile tool for regression tasks, suitable for both beginners and experienced data scientists. Its ability to handle complex relationships in data, robustness to over fitting, and interpretability make it a valuable addition to the regression modeling toolkit.

Let X is a discrete random variable with finite values, and its probability distribution is as follows:

$$P(X = x_i) = p_i, i = 1, 2, \ldots \ldots \ldots n \tag{1}$$

Then the entropy of the random variable X is defined as follows:

$$H(X) = -\sum_{i=1}^{n} p_i \, log \tag{2}$$

This formula measures the average information content or surprise associated with observing the outcomes of the random variable X.

5.2. ThymeBoost

ThymeBoost is an emerging algorithm that addresses the unique challenges of time series forecasting by combining the power of gradient boosting with specialized techniques for time-structured data. It offers promising opportunities for improving the accuracy of predictions in various domains, particularly when time-related dependencies and interpretability are essential.

Key features and concepts of the ThymeBoost algorithm are as follows:

i.   ThymeBoost provides support for various modeling techniques, including gradient boosting, deep learning, and classical statistical models. This flexibility empowers users to opt for the most suitable method to address their data and forecasting requirements.
ii. ThymeBoost incorporates tools for appraising and contrasting the performance of different models. These capabilities assist users in identifying the optimal model for their specific dataset.
iii. ThymeBoost can be employed as a standalone application or seamlessly integrated into existing workflows. This adaptability ensures its ease of use in a wide range of settings.

6. Result and Discussions

6.1. Random forest regressor

The Random Forest Regressor model demonstrates very low errors in prediction, with a RMSE of approximately 1.8866 and a MAE of about 1.3162. The model's accuracy is further reflected in the high R2 score of approximately 0.9993, indicating that it explains almost 99.93% of the variance in the target variable. MAPE is also quite low at around 0.5766, suggesting that predictions deviate by only 0.5766% on average from actual values. Additionally, the Mean Percentage Error (MPE) is very close to zero, indicating that the model's predictions are nearly unbiased. Overall, these results demonstrate that the Random Forest Regressor is a robust and reliable model for the given task (Table 11.1 and Figure 11.1).

Table 11.1: RFR performance analysis matrices

MSE	3.559425661
RMSE	1.886644021
MAE	1.316181487
R2 score	0.999258866
EVS	0.999258868
MAPE	0.576638361
MPE	−0.008701715

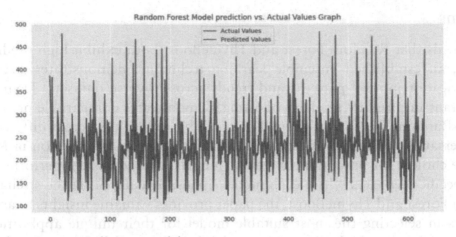

Figure 11.1: Random Forest prediction model.

Table 11.2: ThymeBoost performance matrices

MSE	4851.998098
RMSE	69.65628542
MAE	50.0868394
R2 score	−0.010270506
EVS	−0.000272471
MAPE	25.7337343
MPE	22.08952151

ThymeBoost model show less favorable performance compared to the Random Forest Regressor. MSE is significantly higher at approximately 4851.9981, indicating higher prediction errors. RMSE is approximately 69.6563, which is substantially larger than the RMSE of the Random Forest model, signifying higher variability in prediction accuracy. The Mean Absolute Error (MAE) is around 50.0868, again indicating larger errors in prediction. The R2 score is negative, specifically -0.0103, suggesting that the model does not explain much of the variance in the target variable and performs poorly. The Explained Variance Score is also negative, further emphasizing the model's limitations in explaining variance. MAPE is relatively high at about 25.7337, indicating that the predictions deviate by an average of 25.7337% from actual values. The Mean Percentage Error (MPE) is 22.0895, suggesting a substantial bias in the model's predictions (Table 11.2 and Figure 11.2).

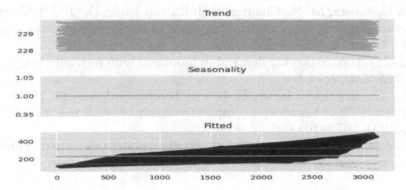

Figure 11.2: Trend analysis graph of ThymeBoost.

7. Conclusions

The research reveals that Random Forest and ThymeBoost both exhibit high predictive accuracy. Random Forest, an established ensemble learning technique, demonstrates strong capabilities in capturing intricate temporal patterns and trends across diverse datasets. ThymeBoost, a relatively newer entrant inspired by gradient boosting, demonstrates comparable predictive power to Random Forest. Random Forest and ThymeBoost exhibit robustness across different datasets and contexts. This versatility underscores their potential for widespread adoption in ML tasks, making them reliable choices for practitioners seeking models with consistent performance. The study highlights the specific scenarios where each model shines. By comparing the strengths and limitations of Random Forest and ThymeBoost, the paper provides valuable insights to assist researchers and practitioners in selecting the most suitable model for their unique applications. The study emphasizes the significance of selecting a ML model that aligns with the specific characteristics of the dataset and the goals of the given task. Careful consideration of these factors can lead to more effective and efficient ML solutions. The insights presented in this paper contribute to the broader discourse on the practical use of ML models. They serve as a valuable resource for those striving to optimize their ML strategies, empowering them to harness the full potential of these models in various real-world scenarios.

In summary, the study concludes that both Random Forest and ThymeBoost are valuable additions to the ML toolbox. Their strong predictive capabilities and adaptability make them versatile choices for a wide range of applications. The selection between these models should be based on the specific context and requirements, enabling researchers and practitioners to tailor their approach to the unique challenges presented by their ML tasks.

References

[1] Basak, A., Rahman, A. S., Das, J., Hosono, T., and Kisi, O. (2022). Drought forecasting using the Prophet model in a semi-arid climate region of western India. *Hydrol. Sci. J.*, 67(9), 1397–1417.

[2] Papacharalampous, G., Tyralis, H., and Koutsoyiannis, D. (2018). Predictability of monthly temperature and precipitation using automatic time series forecasting methods. *Acta Geophy.*, 66, 807–831.

[3] Rahman, A. S., Hosono, T., Kisi, O., Dennis, B., and Imon, A. R. (2020). A minimalistic approach for evapotranspiration estimation using the Prophet model. *Hydrol. Sci. J.*, 65(12), 1994–2006.

[4] Ma, J. and Sun, J. (2021). New statistical prediction scheme for monthly precipitation variability in the rainy season over northeastern China. *Int. J. Climatol.*, 41(13), 5805–5819.

[5] Elseidi, M. (2023). Forecasting temperature data with complex seasonality using time series methods. *Model. Earth Sys. Environ.*, 9(2), 2553–2567.

[6] Gonzalez-Longatt, F., Acosta, M. N., Chamorro, H. R., and Topic, D. (2020). Short-term kinetic energy forecast using a structural time series model: Study case of nordic power system. *2020 Int. Conf. Smart Sys. Technol. (SST)*, 173–178.

[7] Hanggara, F. D. (2021). Forecasting car demand in Indonesia with moving average method. *J. Engg. Sci. Technol. Manag. (JES-TM)*, 1(1), 1–6.

[8] Riofrío, J., Chang, O., Revelo-Fuelagán, E. J., and Peluffo-Ordóñez, D. H. (2020). Forecasting the Consumer Price Index (CPI) of Ecuador: A comparative study of predictive models. *Int. J. Adv. Sci. Engg. Inform. Technol.*, 10(3), 1078–1084.

[9] Li, Y., Ma, Z., Pan, Z., Liu, N., and You, X. (2020). Prophet model and Gaussian process regression based user traffic prediction in wireless networks. *Sci. China Inform. Sci.*, 63, 1–8.

[10] Sabat, N. K., Nayak, R., Srivastava, H., Pati, U. C., and Das, S. K. (2023). Prediction of meteorological parameters using statistical time series models: A case study. *Int. J. Glob. Warm.*, 31(1), 128–149.

[11] Stefenon, S. F., Seman, L. O., Mariani, V. C., and Coelho, L. D. S. (2023). Aggregating prophet and seasonal trend decomposition for time series forecasting of Italian electricity spot prices. *Energies*, 16(3), 1371.

[12] Riofrio, J., Infante, S., and Hernández, A. (2023). Forecasting the consumer price Index of Ecuador using classical and advanced time series models. *Conf. Inform. Comm. Technol. Ecuador*, 128–144.

12 Role of Meta-Heuristic Optimization Approaches in Feature Selection for Disease Diagnosis: A Comprehensive Review

Aditya Pratap Singh[1,a], Yachika Dixit[2], and Gaurav Sharma[3]

[1]Department of Computer Science and Engineering, School of Management Sciences, Lucknow, India

[2]Department of Computer Application, School of Management Sciences, Lucknow, India

[3]Department of Management, School of Management Sciences, Lucknow, India

Abstract

In recent years, there has been a striking increase in the application of machine learning (ML) and data-driven approaches to disease detection. The selection of useful traits that considerably aid in the classification and prediction of diseases is a crucial aspect of these strategies. Due to their effectiveness in navigating complicated feature spaces and improving the performance of illness diagnostic models, meta-heuristic optimization approaches have attracted a lot of attention in this field. This review paper presents an in-depth investigation of various methodologies, their applications, and their impact on the precision and interpretability of diagnostic models. It explores extensively the significance of meta-heuristic optimization strategies in feature selection for disease detection.

Keywords: Meta-heuristic, feature selection, optimization, convergence curve

1. Introduction

For several reasons, disease diagnosis and early detection are crucial in healthcare. Early diagnosis can result in more efficient treatment, better patient outcomes, and lower medical expenses. Early disease diagnosis is essential for starting the right course of treatment and controlling the development of different medical disorders. Early diagnosis frequently results in better outcomes and considerably raises the standard of living for those who are afflicted by diseases. Early diagnosis in infectious illness cases can also assist in the implementation of preventive measures to limit the disease's spread within communities.

Machine learning has become a crucial tool in the healthcare sector for analyzing medical data and creating predictions. This is known as the role of ML in disease diagnosis. Large datasets can contain complicated patterns that ML models can find, allowing for the discovery of subtle disease markers that could be difficult for human experts to spot. Numerous medical applications, such as

[a]aadi.pratap@gmail.com

image analysis, clinical decision support systems, and predictive modeling, have made use of ML methods.

The term "feature" in the context of ML and data-driven disease diagnosis refers to the characteristics or variables used to describe a patient's state of health. The selection of pertinent features has a significant impact on how well a disease diagnosis model performs. Overfitting and decreased model interpretability might result from the use of excessively pointless features.

The process of selecting the most instructive features from the available data leads to increased model generalization, efficiency, and accuracy.

In conclusion, illness diagnosis is important because it can enhance patient outcomes, lower healthcare expenses, and stop the spread of diseases. While feature selection is a crucial step in ensuring that the proper data is used to develop accurate and understandable disease diagnosis models, ML plays a crucial role in automating and optimizing the diagnostic process.

2. Motivation

Due to their distinctive capabilities and potential advantages in enhancing the performance of diagnostic models, meta-heuristic optimization approaches have attracted substantial interest in feature selection for disease diagnosis. Let's explore the reasons for the interest in these methods and their possible benefits for disease diagnosis.

2.1. Why meta-heuristic optimization approaches are of interest

Disease diagnosis frequently requires the use of datasets containing a high number of variables or features, many of which may not be pertinent to the diagnostic objective. The difficult task of feature selection is a good fit for meta-heuristic optimization methods because they are made to efficiently explore and negotiate complex, high-dimensional feature spaces. Meta-heuristics provide a perspective on global search. To locate the most useful features for disease detection, they seek out optimal or nearly optimal solutions throughout a wide search area. This contrasts with some conventional feature selection techniques, which might only be applicable to local search techniques. Meta-heuristics are flexible and can be tailored to certain problem areas. They are adaptable for a range of healthcare applications because they may be set up to priorities various goals, such as maximizing diagnostic precision, reducing false positives, or enhancing model interpretability.

2.2. Potential benefits of using meta-heuristics in disease diagnosis

i. **Enhanced model performance:** By choosing the most pertinent and instructive characteristics, meta-heuristics can uncover feature subsets that optimize model performance. This may result in enhanced sensitivity and specificity disease diagnosis models.

ii. **Reduced overfitting:** Meta-heuristics can assist reduce the danger of overfitting by choosing a subset of pertinent features. Overfitting is a problem in illness diagnosis since generalization is essential, and it happens when a model performs well on training data but badly on unobserved data.

iii. **Better model interpretability:** Several meta-heuristic optimization methods include the insertion of user-defined constraints and preferences, which can be used to compel the inclusion of interpretable or domain-specific features. This aids in the creation of diagnostic models that are clearer and easier to understand.

iv. **Time and resource efficiency:** Meta-heuristics try to locate answers in an acceptable amount of time. In healthcare situations where prompt diagnosis is crucial, they achieve a compromise between search space exploration and computing efficiency.

Figure 12.1 shows the potential benefits of using meta-heuristics in disease diagnosis.

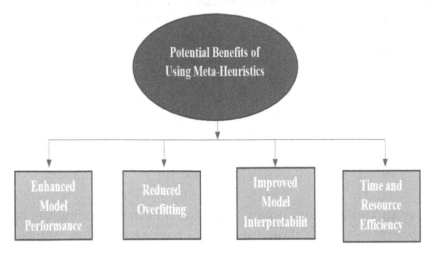

Figure 12.1: Potential benefits of using meta-heuristics.

3. Meta-Heuristic Optimization Techniques

Due to their distinctive capabilities and potential advantages in enhancing the performance of diagnostic models, meta-heuristic optimization approaches have attracted substantial interest in feature selection for disease diagnosis. Datasets having several variables or traits, many of which might not be pertinent to the diagnostic objective, are frequently used in disease diagnosis. The difficult task of feature selection is a good fit for meta-heuristic optimization methods because they are made to efficiently explore and negotiate complex, high-dimensional feature spaces. Meta-heuristics provide a view of global search. To locate the most useful features for disease detection, they seek out optimal or nearly optimal solutions throughout a wide search area. In contrast, some conventional feature selection techniques might just consider local search techniques. Meta-heuristics can be modified and tailored for problem areas. They are adaptable for a range of healthcare applications because they may be set up to prioritize various goals, such as maximizing diagnostic precision, reducing false positives, or enhancing model interpretability. The general operation of meta-heuristic approaches is shown in Figure 12.2.

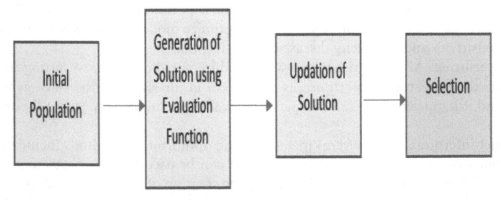

Figure 12.2: General working of meta-heuristic optimization methods.

There are the following popular meta-heuristic approaches:

a. **Genetic algorithms (GAs):** GAs are influenced by natural selection and genetics. To identify optimum solutions, they generate and develop a population of feature subsets [1].

b. **Particle swarm optimization (PSO):** PSO is based on bird and fish social behavior. It entails particles (solutions) traversing the feature space in search of the optimal subset [2].

c. **Ant colony optimization (ACO):** ACO is based on ant foraging behavior. It replicates the search for the most informative pathways, in this case feature subsets [3].

d. **Simulated annealing (SA):** SA is based on the metallurgical annealing process. It employs a temperature-based technique to investigate feature subsets and avoid local optima [4].

e. **Other meta-heuristic approaches:** There are various other techniques such as harmony search [5], differential evolution [6], and more, each with its unique approach to feature selection.

In conclusion, meta-heuristic optimization techniques are appealing in the context of illness diagnosis because they enable efficient search over complicated feature spaces, increase model performance, decrease overfitting, and allow for enhanced interpretability. Healthcare researchers and practitioners are increasingly experimenting with these strategies to produce more accurate and efficient diagnosis models. The foraging behavior of ants inspired ACO. It replicates the search for the most informative pathways, in this instance feature subsets.

4. Comparison With Traditional Feature Selection Methods

To pick important features from a dataset, two approaches are employed in ML and data analysis – meta-heuristic optimization and traditional feature selection strategies. Let us compare them in terms of their benefits and drawbacks:

4.1. Meta-heuristic optimization

Meta-heuristic optimization techniques are global search algorithms that look for the best solution in the search space. They are often used in combination with a predictive model for feature selection. Genetic methods, PSO, simulated annealing, and ACO are examples of common meta-heuristic methods.

Advantages

a. **Global scan:** Meta-heuristic approaches scan the whole feature space, which is particularly beneficial for discovering complicated, non-linear correlations between features.

b. **Versatility:** These approaches may be used to solve a variety of issues, such as feature selection, hyperparameter tweaking, and model selection.

c. **Adaptability:** Meta-heuristics can adapt to a wide range of issues and do not rely on domain-specific information or assumptions.

d. **Robustness:** They can deal with noisy data and are less prone to become caught in local optima than traditional approaches.

Disadvantages

a. **Computationally costly:** When dealing with huge datasets and difficult situations, meta-heuristic methods can be computationally costly.

b. **Inability to comprehend:** While they can identify effective answers, the method by which they arrive at those solutions can be difficult to comprehend, which may be a disadvantage application.

c. **The need for parameter tuning:** Selecting acceptable parameters for meta-heuristic algorithms can be difficult and may necessitate domain-specific knowledge.

4.2. *Classical feature selection techniques*

Traditional feature selection strategies entail analyzing and selecting characteristics based on statistical and computational criteria. Filter, wrapper, and embedded methods are examples of common techniques.

Advantages

a. **Simplicity:** Traditional methods are frequently simple to adopt and comprehend, making them accessible to non-experts.
b. **Interpretability:** They give clear insights into the significance of each feature as well as the influence of feature selection on model performance.
c. **Computational efficiency:** When compared to meta-heuristic approaches, these methods are typically quicker and less computationally intensive.
d. **Domain knowledge integration:** They enable domain experts to contribute their expertise and preferences into the feature selection process.

Disadvantages

a. **Local optima:** Classical approaches may become trapped in local optima, limiting their capacity to uncover the optimal feature subsets, particularly in high-dimensional environments.
b. **Limited search space:** They frequently investigate a portion of the feature space, thereby overlooking valuable interactions and patterns.
c. **Assumptions:** Some traditional approaches rely on strong assumptions about data distribution and feature connections, which might result in unsatisfactory outcomes in real-world, complicated datasets.

In conclusion, the decision between meta-heuristic optimization and traditional feature selection strategies is determined by the unique problem, the complexity of the dataset, the available computational resources, and the necessity of interpretability.

Meta-heuristic approaches are better suited for complicated, high-dimensional issues, whereas classical methods are better suited for smaller problems and when interpretability is important. It's not unusual to combine the two techniques to capitalize on their respective strengths in feature selection.

5. Applications and Case Studies

Meta-heuristic optimization strategies have been used to increase the accuracy and efficiency of cancer detection in numerous parts of cancer diagnosis and research.

Guyon and Elisseeff (2003) give a thorough introduction to feature selection approaches, including meta-heuristic techniques, in the context of cancer classification. It provides an excellent summary of the significance of feature selection in enhancing cancer diagnostic accuracy [7].

Alshamlan and Badr (2017) describe a case study of employing PSO for feature selection in breast cancer classification. PSO is used to choose the most important features from a high-dimensional dataset, hence increasing the classification model's performance [8].

Goh and Lee (2020) use meta-heuristic optimization strategies to pick radiomic characteristics from medical imaging data for prostate cancer classification. The study shows that meta-heuristics have the potential to improve the accuracy of cancer detection using radiomics [9].

Sun et al. (2011) investigate the application of ACO to identify biomarkers for cancer detection. It emphasizes the use of ACO in finding significant traits that are essential for efficient cancer diagnosis [10]. Prasath and Fong (2017) describe a hybrid bio-inspired algorithm for feature selection in the detection of heart disease. To find significant variables and increase the accuracy of heart disease categorization, the scientists use a mix of genetic algorithms and PSO [11].

Aljaaf and Al-Jumeily (2015) emphasis on the application of genetic algorithms for optimizing heart disease detection. To increase diagnosis accuracy, the authors offer an optimized technique that makes use of genetic algorithms [12]. Khozaei et al. (2019) use PSO to optimize the parameters of a support vector machine model for predicting heart disease. The study reveals how meta-heuristics might improve the diagnostic performance of ML systems [13].

Sathiyakumari and Shantharajah (2019) provide a hybrid metaheuristic algorithm for detecting coronary artery disease, a frequent kind of heart disease. The study describes how meta-heuristics may be utilized to improve diagnosis accuracy [14].

Chandra and Singh (2018) integrate the firefly algorithm with neural networks to predict cardiac disease. The study demonstrates the value of meta-heuristics in optimizing neural network models for medical diagnostics [15]. Abu-Naser and Iqbal (2018) investigate the use of simulated annealing to optimize Random Forest models for heart disease detection. It demonstrates how meta-heuristics may improve the performance of ensemble learning approaches [16].

6. Challenges in Meta-Heuristic Feature Selection

Implementing meta-heuristic optimization approaches can provide several benefits in a variety of problem-solving areas, but they also have limitations and obstacles. Understanding these obstacles is critical for successfully implementing these strategies. Some of the most typical restrictions and challenges encountered while implementing meta-heuristic optimization are as follows:

a. **Computing complexity:** When working with huge datasets or complicated optimization issues, meta-heuristic methods can need a significant amount of computing effort. Optimization may not always be practical due to the time and resources necessary, particularly in real-time or essential applications.

b. **Convergence:** It is critical to ensure that a meta-heuristic algorithm converges to an optimal or near-optimal solution. Some algorithms may converge slowly or become trapped in local optima, making finding the optimum solution within an acceptable timescale difficult.

c. **Parameter tuning:** Most meta-heuristic algorithms contain numerous parameters that must be fine-tuned for a situation. Finding the proper parameter values may be a time-consuming and tedious process, and the algorithm's effectiveness is largely dependent on these parameters.

d. **Overfitting:** It is critical to avoid overfitting in feature selection and ML applications, which results in models that perform very well on training data but badly on unknown data. Overfit models can result from meta-heuristic algorithms selecting too many features.

e. **Lack of guarantee:** Meta-heuristic optimization approaches do not guarantee the discovery of the global optimum. The quality of the answer is heavily influenced by aspects such as algorithm selection, parameter settings, and issue characteristics.

f. **Interpretability:** Many meta-heuristic algorithms are opaque and difficult to understand. While they can find optimum answers, describing why a certain solution was chosen or explaining the decision-making process might be difficult.

g. **Complexity and versatility:** The number of accessible meta-heuristic methods might be daunting. Choosing the best algorithm for a problem can be challenging, and there is no one-size-fits-all approach. It frequently necessitates domain expertise and experimentation.

h. **Memory and storage:** Some meta-heuristic algorithms, particularly those that use population-based search, may necessitate a substantial amount of memory and storage. When working with limited computing resources, this might be an issue.

i. **Parallelization:** While parallelization can speed up optimization, it is not always easy to apply in meta-heuristic methods, especially in a distributed computing environment.

j. **Scalability:** It might be difficult to scale meta-heuristic methods to accommodate exceedingly big datasets or high-dimensional feature spaces. As the dimensionality of the issue grows, the algorithms may become less effective.

k. **Noise tolerance:** In the face of noisy or ambiguous data, meta-heuristics may struggle. It is a constant effort to ensure that these algorithms are strong enough to handle real-world data fluctuations.

l. **Customization and hybridization:** Tailoring or hybridizing meta-heuristic algorithms to a given issue is a difficult process that frequently necessitates a thorough grasp of both the method and the problem area.

Despite these limits and obstacles, meta-heuristic optimization methodologies remain essential tools for solving complicated optimization issues across a wide range of areas. Researchers and practitioners are constantly exploring strategies to overcome these challenges and increase the efficacy and efficiency of meta-heuristic algorithms.

7. Conclusions

Improved feature selection – Meta-heuristic optimization strategies have been shown to be successful in identifying the most important features from vast and complicated datasets. As a result, these strategies improve the quality of input data for illness detection, leading to more accurate and efficient diagnostic models. The use of meta-heuristics leads to the creation of illness diagnostic models that are more accurate and predictive. The chosen characteristics and optimized model parameters aid in illness categorization and prediction. Meta-heuristic optimization reduces the danger of overfitting, which is a major concern in ML. Overfitting is reduced by choosing the most useful features and optimizing model complexity, resulting in more robust diagnostic models.

User-defined restrictions and preferences can be included into several meta-heuristic optimization algorithms. This feature helps to make diagnostic models more interpretable, which is important for clinical applications where transparency is key. Meta-heuristic algorithms investigate complicated feature spaces effectively and find solutions in a fair amount of time. This punctuality is critical in healthcare settings, as early diagnosis can have a considerable influence on patient outcomes. Meta-heuristic techniques may be customized to individual diseases and uses in healthcare. These strategies have been effectively used by researchers and practitioners to a wide range of disorders, including cancer, infectious diseases, and chronic conditions. The continued development of meta-heuristic optimization techniques, as well as the discovery of hybrid approaches that integrate diverse algorithms, lays the groundwork for future illness detection research and innovation.

Finally, by enhancing feature selection, model performance, and interpretability, meta-heuristic optimization techniques have made substantial improvements to illness detection. These strategies are critical in addressing the complex and multidimensional nature of medical data, resulting in more accurate and quicker diagnoses, which can improve patient treatment and results.

References

[1] Holland, J. H. (1975). Adaptation in natural and artificial systems. University of Michigan Press. ISBN: 9780262581110, pp 232.

[2] Kennedy, J. and Eberhart, R. (1995). Particle swarm optimization. *Proc. IEEE Int. Conf. Neu. Netw.*, 4, 1942–1948.

[3] Dorigo, M., Maniezzo, V., and Colorni, A. (1996). The Ant System: Optimization by a colony of cooperating agents. *IEEE Trans. Sys. Man Cybernet. Part B*, 26(1), 29–41.

[4] Kirkpatrick, S., Gelatt, C. D., and Vecchi, M. P. (1983). Optimization by simulated annealing. *Science*, 220(4598), 671–680.

[5] Geem, Z. W., Kim, J. H., and Loganathan, G. V. (2001). A new heuristic optimization algorithm: Harmony search. *Simulation*, 76(2), 60–68.

[6] Storn, R. and Price, K. (1997). Differential evolution – A simple and efficient heuristic for global optimization over continuous spaces. *J. Global Optimiz.*, 11(4), 341–359.

[7] Guyon, I. and Elisseeff, A. (2003). An introduction to variable and feature selection. *J. Mac. Learn. Res.*, 3, 1157–1182.

[8] Alshamlan, H. M. and Badr, G. H. (2017). Particle swarm optimization-based feature selection for breast cancer classification. *Computat. Math. Methods Med.*, 1, 1–6.

[9] Goh, C. H. and Lee, W. K. (2020). Meta-heuristic optimization for radiomics-based prostate cancer classification. *Comp. Biol. Med.*, 116, 103539.

[10] Sun, Y., et al. (2011). Optimizing biomarker selection for cancer diagnosis using ACO. *Methods Inform. Med.*, 50(5), 441–448.

[11] Prasath, V. B. S. and Fong, S. (2017). Feature selection and heart disease diagnosis using a hybrid bio-inspired algorithm. *J. Med. Sys.*, 41(5), 75.

[12] Aljaaf, A. J. and Al-Jumeily, D. (2015). An optimized approach for heart disease diagnosis using genetic algorithm. *Int. J. Scient. Res. Sci. Technol.*, 1(3), 19–23.

[13] Khozaei, F., et al. (2019). Optimizing support vector machine parameters for heart disease prediction using particle swarm optimization. *Comp. Biol. Med.*, 108, 19–29.

[14] Sathiyakumari, G. and Shantharajah, S. P. (2019). Hybrid metaheuristic algorithm for the detection of coronary artery disease. *Comp. Biol. Med.*, 108, 92–105.

[15] Chandra, P. and Singh, A. K. (2018). Heart disease prediction using firefly algorithm and neural networks. *J. Healthcare Engg.*, 1, 1–9.

[16] Abu-Naser, S. S. and Iqbal, S. (2018). Optimization of random forest for heart disease diagnosis using simulated annealing. *Proc. 2018 7th Int. Conf. Softw. Comp. Appl. (ICSCA)*, 118–122.

13 Role of AI Applications in Diagnosis of Renal Diseases: A Systematic Review

Ashish Nigam[1], Rajat Kumar[1], and Chandra Bhushan[2,a]

[1]Department of Computer Science, Techno Institute of Higher Studies, Lucknow, India

[2]Department of Computer Science, Integral and Innovative Sustainable Education, Lucknow, India

Abstract

Globally, there is a significant unmet demand for accurate illness diagnosis. The intricacy of the patient population's illness processes and underlying symptoms creates enormous obstacles in establishing an early diagnosis tool and successful therapy. Machine learning (ML), a subfield of artificial intelligence (AI), helps researchers, clinicians, and patients overcome some of these problems. In these systematic review capabilities of AI, including ML approaches, has been used to predict, diagnose, and treat enduring kidney disease (EKD). In this review work PubMed-retrieved articles has been included. As a result, the study is characterized as a "rapid review" because it comprises only one database. The most prevalent goal was accurate prediction of EKD diagnosis. This study basically contains algorithm generalizability and testing on datasets of varied populations were rarely considered.

Keywords: Renal diseases, artificial intelligence, kidney disease (EKD), machine learning

1. Introduction

Renal disorders, sometimes referred to as nephropathies or kidney diseases, are a broad category of illnesses that impact the composition and operation of the kidneys. The kidneys filter blood, eliminate waste, and control electrolyte balance, all of which are vital functions that contribute to the preservation of the body's interior environment. Numerous conditions, such as infections, autoimmune illnesses, genetics, and environmental factors, can lead to renal problems. Universally, the causes of enduring kidney disease (EKD) differ from other disease symptoms. Diabetes mellitus, hypertension, and primary glomerulonephritis are the most frequent main illnesses causing chronic kidney disease (CKD) and eventually kidney failure, accounting for 70–90% of all primary causes [1–5]. Although these three reasons are at the top of the EKD etiology charts, additional factors (such as pollution, infections, and autoimmune illnesses) have a role in CKD pathophysiology [6–10].

---

[a]cbv.iise@gmail.com

Similarly, several risk variables (e.g., age, gender, ethnicity) and modifiable risk factors (e.g., systolic and diastolic blood pressure, proteinuria) have a role in CKD development [1–4]. The kidneys act as filters, removing waste from the circulation. They also control bodily fluids, minerals, and blood pressure [5]. The kidneys produce hormones that are required for red blood cell production and bone health. Kidney dysfunction can potentially affect the heart and blood vessels. Imaging investigations, as well as blood and urine samples, can be used to assess kidney function. The evaluation of kidney illness entails determining the underlying cause as well as categorizing it into phases that dictate how the disease may be handled [10].

1.1. Types of kidney diseases

Enduring kidney disease – According to the National Institute of Diabetes and Digestive and Kidney Diseases, "means your kidneys are damaged and can't filter blood the way they should." The most prevalent kind of kidney illness is chronic renal disease, which is a progressive type of kidney condition that worsens with time. Aside from chronic kidney disease, there are various forms of kidney disease that might be chronic or acute in nature.

a. **Glomerulonephritis:** This kidney illness develops when the glomeruli, the small filters that remove waste from the body, become inflamed or damaged, and stop working properly.
b. **Immune-related disorder:** Kidney disease caused by an autoimmune condition. Autoimmune diseases, such as lupus and rheumatoid arthritis, occur when the immune system assaults its own cells.
c. **Polycystic renal disease:** This genetic disorder causes fluid-filled cysts to form all throughout the kidneys, causing the organs to grow too large and lose function. Polycystic renal disease, a hereditary illness, causes the growth of fluid-filled cysts in the kidneys, impairing their function. It can appear in adulthood, resulting in hypertension, abdominal discomfort, and renal enlargement. Treatment focuses on symptom management and consequences, which may include blood pressure control and, in severe circumstances, dialysis or transplantation.
d. **Renal cancer:** Genetic anomalies in kidney cells, like those in any other organ in the body, can cause malignant tumors. Kidney cancer is among the top 10 cancers in the United States. Renal cancer, also known as kidney cancer, develops in the kidneys, which are vital organs responsible for filtering blood and removing waste.

   The most prevalent kind is renal cell carcinoma. Symptoms may include blood in the urine, chronic pain, and unexplained weight loss. Treatments range from surgery to targeted therapy, and early discovery improves results. Research into novel therapy for advanced instances continues, highlighting the significance of regular tests and raising awareness.

Apart from these, there are several rare renal diseases exists like Alport syndrome, Goodpasture syndrome, Wegener's granulomatosis, etc., which are found rarely in people, but these diseases are very crucial and chronic to handle. If you are at risk of having this illness or suspect you may have symptoms, it is critical that you get medical attention. Early intervention can assist delay the advancement of the illness and preserve your own kidney function for a longer period.

2. Background

Renal illnesses, particularly CKD and acute kidney injury (AKI), have a large worldwide health impact. These diseases are becoming more common as a result of aging populations, lifestyle changes, and the rising prevalence of ailments such as diabetes and hypertension. Traditional diagnostic approaches for renal illnesses include clinical examination, laboratory investigations, and medical imaging. However, these procedures can be time-consuming, expensive, and open to subjective interpretation. Early and correct diagnosis is critical for the successful management and treatment of renal disorders. Artificial intelligence (AI) applications have demonstrated particularly promising results in the processing of medical imaging data, such as computed tomography (CT) scans, magnetic resonance imaging (MRIs), and kidney ultrasound pictures. Machine learning (ML) algorithms can be trained to recognize trends and irregularities in these images, allowing for early detection of kidney disorders. AI systems can also be used for predictive analytics, allowing healthcare providers to foresee the likelihood of kidney disease in individual individuals. This can lead to more effective individualized treatment strategies and interventions for preventing or managing renal diseases. The integration of AI technologies with electronic health records enables a full study of patient data.

Generally, various researches shows their significance by showing there outcome and accuracy obtained for specific disease datasets in some special circumstances but when we try to apply the previously developed models on other datasets and environment then it seems very ineffective over in such circumstances and in this study we have tried to find out such research gaps which acts as the major factors for a developed model to be adopted globally. Only peer-reviewed articles published between January 1, 2015, and December 30, 2022 were included for this assessment, with pre-prints excluded. By filtering title, only intelligent decision-making articles for renal disease detection were selected.

2.1. Motivation

Reviewing the literature allows us to identify gaps in the present corpus of knowledge. We can identify problems that need to be resolved or areas that require extra development. Concentrating on these unexplored places might help guide our own research. It aids in comparing and benchmarking various renal disease detection methods and procedures. This might assist us in determining whether procedures are more effective, precise, or appropriate for certain purposes. Knowledge of the literature can help in selecting the best intelligent computing solutions for arrhythmia identification. AI offers a chance to improve diagnostic capacities, which could result in improved patient outcomes, lower medical expenses, and improvements in the treatment of renal illness.

2.2. Literature search scheme

This review employed numerous academic research databases to collect pertinent papers released from January 2015 to December 2022. These publicly accessible databases include PubMed, IEEE Xplore, Springer, ScienceDirect, and ResearchGate. Notably, IEEE Xplore and PubMed are prominent databases in the fields of engineering and biological sciences, respectively [7] (Table 13.1).

Table 13.1: Inclusion criteria for literature search

Parameters	Description
Duration	2015-2022
Article type	Journal and conferences
Area of research	Intelligent computing and bio-medicals for diagnosis of renal disorder
Performance metrics	Accuracy, sensitivity and specificity

2.3. Article selection criteria

In this context, a diagram illustrates the process of choosing or discarding research articles by considering important factors such as keyword search, abstract sorting, eliminating duplicates, and removing articles that do not meet inclusion criteria. Figure 13.1 provides an overview of the entire process of conducting a literature search and selecting research studies.

In this scheme we have initially searched 250 articles related with intelligent computing in bio-medicals, further we removed those articles which were not related to renal disorder detection. Some articles were removed due to duplicate identification and then we focused to select only those articles which are completely meeting out the inclusion criteria. So, final 30 articles were selected to perform the systematic literature review process.

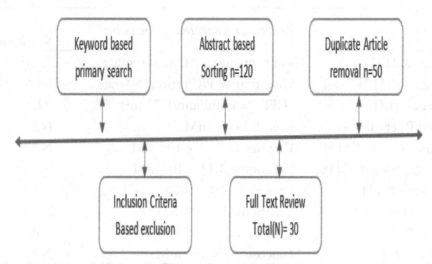

Figure 13.1: Literature review process.

3. Literature Survey

This survey is divided in two approaches in which Table 13.2 demonstrates the effective bio-markers used for diagnosis of chronic kidney disorder and the other approach shows the contribution of AI applications for effective diagnosis for the same by intelligent computing methodologies in Table 13.3. Collection and observation of blood and urine samples plays an effective role for the accurate diagnosis of the diseases so in this section we have discussed about some bio-markers which were collected, and their observation was done in a specific environment.

Researchers have extensively investigated the application of ML and deep learning algorithms in the analysis of medical imaging data, such as CT scans and MRI of the kidneys. The literature highlights the potential of AI to detect subtle patterns and anomalies that may escape human observation, thereby enabling earlier identification of renal issues. While the literature acknowledges AI's promise in renal illness detection, it also emphasizes issues like as data privacy, regulatory compliance, and the necessity for rigorous validation studies. Ongoing research highlights a dynamic landscape, with ongoing efforts to improve algorithms, enhance diagnostic capabilities, and address practical issues for the successful integration of AI applications into clinical practice. The literature survey together contributes to a foundation of knowledge that informs and directs subsequent breakthroughs in leveraging AI for improved diagnosis and management of renal disorders.

In Table 13.2, description of various kidney disorders is explained diagnosed by some significant biomarkers obtained from urine and blood samples of the patients. Some of the significant biomarkers was mentioned like creatinine, glucose, urea and quantitative PC ratio. Based on these parameters effective trained of the models are performed using supervised learning and training models and better accuracy, sensitivity and specificity were obtained. Here, the result is highly depending on the sensitivity so in this table we have discussed only those articles having better sensitivity and specificity.

Positive proteinuria and Quantitative P/C ratio are the significant bio-markers for diagnosis of renal disorders and their sensitivity sensors responses higher at the mentioned range value [11, 12]. Urea, creatinine and glucose are also the very important bio-markers used for effective diagnosis of the renal disorders [13–20].

Table 13.2: Detection of kidney disorders using effective bio-markers

Year	Reference	Parameter (detected range value)	Result	
			Sensitivity	Specificity
2017	Park et al. [11]	+ve proteinuria ACR≥300 mg/g	75.4	99.5
2016	Chang et al. [12]	Quantitative P/C ratio (150 mg)	75.6	95.9
2016	Xue et al. [13]	eGFR. (<60 ml/min/1.73 m^2)	92.8	1.53
2018	Menon P., et al. [14]	Urea 1.4×10^{-3} mM	NA	NA
2019	Pothipor C., et al. [15]	Creatirnne 3.11×10^{-2} mM	NA	NA
2019	Arif Topçu A., et al [16]	Creatinine 3.11×10^{-2} mM	NA	NA
2019	Charnuah N., [17]	Urea 9.9×10^{-3} mM	NA	NA
2021	Jiang Y., [18]	Creatinme l $\times 10^{-4}$ mM	NA	NA
2020	Zheng W., [19]	Glucose 2.2×10^{-3} mM	NA	NA
2017	Yuan Y., [20]	Glucose 1.2×10^{-1} mM	NA	NA

4. AI Applications for Diagnosis of Renal Disorders

Nephrology faces numerous unmet needs, presenting significant opportunities for leveraging Big Data and AI in the treatment of kidney disease patients. The applications of AI in renal disease can be broadly categorized into three main areas: (a) predicting future outcomes; (b) assisting in therapy and decision-making; and (c) identifying existing yet unrecognized patterns. Table 13.3 offers an overview of key studies related to AI in the realm of renal disease. While only one published paper currently addresses clinical application, AI's utilization in renal illness is more frequently documented in conference abstracts, hinting at a growing body of contributions from the scientific community. AI employs advanced algorithms to analyze test results, patient records, and medical imaging, playing a pivotal role in diagnosing renal disease. The application of AI enhances diagnostic accuracy, supports early intervention, and ultimately improves patient outcomes in the field of renal healthcare by identifying anomalies in imaging scans and predicting disease risks based on patient data.

AI applications in the diagnosis of renal diseases have shown promising potential in various areas, including the following:

4.1. Medical imaging analysis and laboratory data integration

Medical imaging data from ultrasound, CT, and MRI scans can be analyzed by AI algorithms to identify and categorize anomalies related to the kidney, including tumors, cysts, and structural abnormalities. Artificial Intelligence can help in the accurate identification of anomalies in renal pictures by segmenting and outlining specific regions of interest. Data from a variety of laboratory tests, including blood and urine tests, can be integrated and analyzed with the help of AI. Finding patterns and markers linked to various kidney disorders can be aided by this.

4.2. Predictive analytics

With patient data, AI models can be taught to forecast the likelihood of developing renal illnesses. The process may entail scrutinizing genetic information, electronic health records, and other pertinent data to pinpoint those who are more susceptible.

4.3. Decision support systems and data mining

AI can be used to create systems that help healthcare workers make decisions. Based on the examination of clinical data, these systems can offer extra insights and suggestions that can help with prompt and correct diagnosis. Large datasets can be subjected to AI techniques, such as ML and deep learning, to find intricate patterns and connections that might not be immediately obvious to human observers.

4.4. Remote monitoring and personalized medicine

Applications of artificial intelligence can help with patients' remote renal illness monitoring. This could entail monitoring changes in health status and warning medical professionals of any problems by continuously analyzing data from wearable technology or distant sensors. With the use of patient data and criteria including genetics, lifestyle, and reaction to prior therapies, AI may make it easier to create individualized treatment programs.

Artificial intelligence (AI) is changing the face of medicine, particularly in the diagnosis of renal illnesses. Advanced AI algorithms have proven useful in improving the accuracy and efficiency of identifying kidney-related illnesses. Machine learning models examine massive volumes of medical data, such as patient records, imaging scans, and laboratory findings, to identify trends and detect tiny anomalies that humans may miss.

AI applications are used to detect CKD, renal tumors, and nephritis in the early stages. Artificial intelligence systems can evaluate renal imaging studies such as ultrasonography, CT scans, and MRI, allowing for the speedy and exact diagnosis of abnormalities. These tools facilitate the timely commencement of therapies, which leads to better patient outcomes.

Furthermore, AI-powered predictive analytics play an important role in determining the likelihood of acquiring renal illnesses. AI models can identify people who are more likely to develop renal disease by examining multiple risk factors, genetic predispositions, and lifestyle data. This enables individualized preventative strategies and early interventions, which may slow or prevent the progression of renal illnesses.

Thus, AI applications that analyze test results, patient information, and medical imaging are revolutionizing the detection of renal disease. Artificial intelligence uses sophisticated algorithms to improve accuracy, spot trends, and help anticipate dangers. Its potential for use in customized medicine and decision support is substantial, as it can aid in the early identification and better treatment of renal illnesses.

Table 13.3: Role of AI applications for diagnosis of kidney disorders

Year	Reference	Technology	Result
2019	Akbilgic et al. r21l	Random Forest	AUC 76%
2014	Goldstein et al. [22]	Random Forest	AUC 79%
2019	Mezzatesta et al. [23]	Support vector machine	Accuracy: 92.15%
2020	Chauhan et al. [24]	Random Forest	AUC 80%
2017	Zhang et al. [31]	Random Forest	Sensitivity: 98.5%
2016	Norouzi et al. [26]	Artificial neural network	Mean square error (MSE): 58.63–64.00
2016	Barbieri et al. [30]	Artificial neural network	Mean absolute error (MSE): 58.63–64.00

5. Discussion

Prediction of sudden cardiac death in elderly HD patients was an early example of using an advanced ML approach in nephrology, with a random forest model yielding an AUROC of 0.79. In another case, Mezzatesta et al., colleagues employed SVM to predict the risk of ischemic heart disease in dialysis patients with 92% accuracy [23]. In two more recent studies, random forest models were built to predict CKD development by incorporating data from EMR and circulating bio-markers such as plasma tumor necrosis factors and renal injury molecule1 [24]. In one of Chauhan et al., investigations, the AUROC was 0.770.80. Using demographic data and blood biochemical characteristics, Xiao et al examined multiple ML techniques to predict the probability of proteinuria >1 g/d in CKD patients. Forty-one with an AUROC of 0.87, the classical logistic regression model beat other ML models in this situation. They find that advanced ML models perform best with vast amounts of data, whereas linear models perform better with smaller datasets. Jamshid Norouzzi et al. [26], on the other hand, created an ANN to predict renal failure progression in CKD patients. The model accurately predicted the estimated glomerular filtration rate (eGFR) at 6, 12, and 18 months intervals (>95%) [31].

According to a conference abstract, the Renal Research Institute collected data from 28,608 CKD patients from 2000 to 2011 to build two linear and spline models for predicting CKD progression to ESKD using up to 6 months of previous eGFRs or logarithm of eGFRs (log eGFRs) [27]. The model's results were included into the CKD Forecaster tool, which is utilized at the point of care by nephrologists in a clinical decision support system. This aided inpatient education and care planning for the CKD to ESKD transition. Nephrologists who utilized the CKD Forecaster tool had fewer patients converting to HD with a central venous catheter, according to a conference abstract [28].

Clinicians face the task of dedicating time and encountering errors when prescribing medications such as erythropoietin for patients with end-stage kidney disease (ESKD). To enhance efficiency and enhance patient care, a portion of the prescription process could be automated. Numerous strategies for diminishing erythropoietin dosage and increasing the proportion of patients achieving target levels have been outlined in the literature [29]. One illustrative instance is the incorporation of artificial neural networks (ANN) in anemia care, which successfully raised the percentage of patients meeting their goals while concurrently reducing hemoglobin variability and erythropoietin dosage [30].

6. Conclusions

Advancements in computing, mathematics, and statistics have driven the evolution of AI and ML methods. Utilizing cloud computing resources offers a potentially more economical approach to analyze extensive datasets and create ML models. In an ideal scenario, ML algorithms would be accessible to the public without restrictions. Traditional statistical modeling methods are most effective when constructing straightforward predictive models for well-defined problems, characterized by numerous observations and a clear understanding of the strengths and limitations of the outcomes. Moreover, conventional approaches tend to learn from static time-dependent data, leading to "overfitting" issues during training and suboptimal performance when faced with unexpected events.

However, in an ever-changing renal care setting with complicated challenges, AI presents numerous approaches to generate relevant outcomes. It is extremely effective in detecting unknown patterns and abnormalities. In conclusion, research into AI applications in renal illness diagnostics demonstrates a promising environment with significant potential to alter the area. AI's diverse role is seen in its ability to predict future results, assist with therapy and decision-making, and identify previously unknown patterns. The comprehensive review of relevant literature, as shown in Table 13.3, demonstrates ongoing advances and substantial contributions in AI-related studies on renal disorders.

References

[1] Webster, A. C., Nagler, E. V., Morton, R. L., et al. (2017). Chronic kidney disease. *Lancet Lond. Engl.*, 389(10075),1238–1252.

[2] Chen, T. K., Knicely, D. H., and Grams, M. E. (2019). Chronic kidney disease diagnosis and management. *J. Am. Med. Assoc.*, 322(13), 1294–1304.

[3] Global, regional, and national burden of chronic kidney disease, 1990–2017: A systematic analysis for the Global Burden of Disease Study 2017. (2020). *Lancet Lond. Engl.*, 395(10225), 709–733.

[4] Vaidya, S. R. and Aeddula, N. R. (2022). Chronic renal failure. *StatPearls.*, StatPearls Publishing; 2022. Accessed July 28, 2022.

[5] Romagnani, P., Remuzzi, G., Glassock, R., et al. (2017). Chronic kidney disease. *Nat. Rev. Dis. Primer*, 3, 17088.

[6] Thomas, R., Kanso, A., and Sedor, J. R. (2008). Chronic kidney disease and its complications. *Prim. Care*, 35(2), 329.

[7] Fraser, S. D. and Blakeman, T. (2016) Chronic kidney disease: Identification and management in primary care. *Pragmatic Obs. Res.*, 7, 21–32.

[8] Institute for Quality and Efficiency in Health Care (IQWiG). (2018). Chronic kidney disease: Overview. Accessed July 28, 2022.

[9] Kazancioğlu, R. (2013). Risk factors for chronic kidney disease: An update. *Kidney Int. Suppl.*, 3(4), 368–371.

[10] Fadem, S. Z. (2022). Introduction to kidney disease. In: Fadem, S. Z. (eds). Staying Healthy with Kidney Disease. Springer, Cham. pp. 1–14. https://doi.org/10.1007/978-3-030-93528-3_1

[11] Park, J. I., Baek, H., Kim, B. R., and Jung, H. H. (2017). Comparison of urine dipstick and albumin: creatinine ratio for chronic kidney disease screening: A population-based study. *PloS One*, 12(2), e0171106.

[12] Chang, C.-C., Su, M.-J., Ho, J.-L., Tsai, Y.-H., Tsai, W.-T., et al. (2016). The efficacy of semi-quantitative urine protein-to-creatinine (P/C) ratio for the detection of significant proteinuria in urine specimens in health screening settings. *SpringerPlus*, 5(1), 1791.

[13] Xue, N., Zhang, X., Teng, J., Fang, Y., and Ding, X. (2016). A cross-sectional study on the use of urinalysis for screening early-stage renal insufficiency. *Nephron*, 132(4), 335–341.

[14] Menon, P. S., Said, F. A., Mei, G. S., et al. (2018). Urea and creatinine detection on nanolaminated gold thin film using Kretschmann-based surface plasmon resonance biosensor. *PLoS One,* 13(7), 1–12.

[15] Pothipor, C., Lertvachirapaiboon, C., Shinbo, K., Kato, K., Ounnunkad, K., and Baba, A. (2019). Detection of creatinine using silver nanoparticles on a poly (pyrrole) thin film-based surface plasmon resonance sensor. *Japanese J. Appl. Phy.*, 59.

[16] Arif, T. A., Özgür, E., Yılmaz, F., Bereli, N., and Denizli, A. (2019). Real time monitoring and label free creatinine detection with artificial receptors. *Mat. Sci. Engg. B.*, 244, 6–11.

[17] Chamuah, N., Saikia A., Joseph, A. M., and Nath, P. (2019). Blu-ray DVD as SERS substrate for reliable detection of albumin, creatinine and urea in urine. *Sens. Actuat. B Chem.*, 285, 108–115.

[18] Jiang, Y., Cai, Y., Hu, S., et al. (2021). Construction of Au@Metal-organic framework for sensitive determination of creatinine in urine. *J. Innov. Opt. Health Sci.*, 14(04), 2141003.

[19] Zheng, W., Han, B., E. S., et al. (2020). Highly-sensitive and reflective glucose sensor based on optical fiber surface plasmon resonance. *Microchem. J.*, 157.

[20] Yuan, Y., Yang, X., Gong, D., et al. (2017). Investigation for terminal reflection optical fiber SPR glucose sensor and glucose sensitive membrane with immobilized GODs. *Opt. Exp.*, 25(4), 3884–3898.

[21] Akbilgic, O., Obi, Y., Potukuchi, P. K., et al. (2019). Machine learning to identify dialysis patients at high death risk. *Kidney Int. Rep.*, 4, 1219–1229.

[22] Goldstein, B. A., Chang, T. I., Mitani, A. A., et al. (2014). Near-term prediction of sudden cardiac death in older hemodialysis patients using electronic health records. *Clin. J. Am. Soc. Nephrol.*, 9, 82–91.

[23] Mezzatesta, S., Torino, C., Meo, P. D., et al. (2019). A machine learning-based approach for predicting the outbreak of cardiovascular diseases in patients on dialysis. *Comput. Methods Programs Biomed.*, 177, 9–15.

[24] Chauhan, K., Nadkarni, G. N., Fleming, F., et al. (2020). Initial validation of a machine learning-derived prognostic test (KidneyIntelX) integrating biomarkers and electronic health record data to predict longitudinal kidney outcomes. *Kidney360*, 1, 731–739.

[25] Chan, L., Nadkarni, G. N., Fleming, F., et al. (2020). Derivation and validation of a machine learning risk score using biomarker and electronic patient data to predict rapid progression of diabetic kidney disease. medRxiv 2020.06.01.20119552; doi: https://doi.org/10.1101/2020.06.01.20119552, vol 2020, 1–7.

[26] Norouzi, J., Yadollahpour, A., Mirbagheri, S. A., et al. (2016). Predicting renal failure progression in chronic kidney disease using integrated intelligent fuzzy expert system. *Comput. Math Methods Med.*, 2016, 1–9.

[27] Han, H., Wang, Y., Chaudhuri, S., et al. (2016). Prediction of six months progression to end stage renal disease [abstract TH-PO887]. *J Am Soc Nephrol.*, 27, 299A.

[28] Jiao, Y., Kopyt, N., Bollu, P., et al. (2019). Use of kidney disease progression model care planning report associates with lower dialysis catheter rates at the initiation of hemodialysis [abstract SA-PO840]. *J. Am. Soc. Nephrol.*, 30, 980.

[29] Brier, M. E., Gaweda, A. E., Aronoff, G. R. (2018). Personalized anemia management and precision medicine in ESA and iron pharmacology in end-stage kidney disease. *Semin. Nephrol.*, 38, 410–417.

[30] Barbieri, C., Molina, M., Ponce, P., et al. (2016). An international observational study suggests that artificial intelligence for clinical decision support optimizes anemia management in hemodialysis patients. *Kidney Int.*, 90, 422–429.

[31] Zhang, J., Friberg, I. M., Kift-Morgan, A., et al. (2017). Machine-learning algorithms define pathogen-specific local immune fingerprints in peritoneal dialysis patients with bacterial infections. *Kidney Int.*, 92, 179–191.

14 Intelligent Decision Support System for Diagnosis of Alzheimer Disease—A Systematic Review

Syed Azhar Abbas Rizvi[1], Aditya Pratap Singh[2,a], and Akash Sharma[1]

[1]Department of Computer Application, School of Management Sciences, Lucknow, India

[2]Department of Computer Science and Engineering, School of Management Sciences, Lucknow, India

Abstract

Healthcare practitioners can benefit from artificial intelligence (AI) in a variety of patient care and intelligent healthcare systems. Healthcare professionals frequently use AI methods, such as machine learning (ML) and deep learning, for jobs including disease diagnosis, drug research, and risk assessment. AI needs several medical data sources, including ultrasound, MRI, mammography, genetics, and CT scans, to make accurate disease diagnoses. Furthermore, AI has accelerated the process of preparing patients for home-based rehabilitation and dramatically enhanced the hospital experience. In-depth analysis of AI methods for diagnosing a wide range of ailments, including Alzheimer's, cancer, diabetes, chronic heart disease, tuberculosis, stroke, cerebrovascular problems, hypertension, skin conditions, and liver disease, is provided in this article. In terms of managing the illness and providing treatment, Alzheimer's disease, a degenerative neurological disorder, is very expensive. For Alzheimer's patients, continual monitoring, functional assistance, and prompt treatment interventions are essential, and intelligent sensing devices can deliver adaptive feedback adapted to the setting. The goal of this review is to provide an overview of the systems already in use for treating Alzheimer's disease. It will then evaluate the possibilities of these sophisticated technologies in clinical settings and potential future improvements to their design for Alzheimer's disease.

Keywords: Alzheimer, intelligent computing, machine learning, neural network, data mining, classification

1. Introduction

Neuroimaging methods, which include brain scans like MRIs, PETs, and CTs, are currently heavily used in the diagnosis of Alzheimer's disease [1]. Although these scans are useful, they pose substantial difficulties for people who have neurological problems. Particularly in the case of PET scans, these procedures are characterized by their mass, high expense, and invasiveness. The danger of delayed diagnosis of additional neuronal damage increases due to the sporadic monitoring of Alzheimer's patients due to the lack of specialized laboratory facilities. Additionally, many of the current therapy

[a]aadi.pratap@gmail.com

strategies for Alzheimer's disease incorporate both cognitive and physical activities to support pre-existing brain cells and maintain physical functionality.

However, these solutions place a heavy social, emotional, financial, and physical load on the formal or informal careers that must devote their time and provide regular or ongoing assistance from healthcare specialists. People with Alzheimer's disease require routine or ongoing monitoring due to the disease's degenerative nature [1]. It's also important to understand that neurological disorders are the second biggest cause of death worldwide [1]. Neuronal networks in those with neurodegeneration suffer structural and functional losses. Normal brain function and synaptic transmission between neurons are interfered with by abnormal structural changes in the brain, which are marked by the buildup of beta-amyloid plaques and the development of protein tau-tangles [2]. Normal brain and body functions decline because of neurons losing their connections to one another over time [3]. As a result, people with neurodegenerative disorders like Alzheimer's gradually lose their physical and cognitive skills, making them dependent on others to complete their activities of daily living (ADLs) [4]. Despite several attempts, no accepted treatment for these disorders has been put in place despite significant efforts [5].

2. Related Work

The special requirements of Alzheimer's patients in the context of assistive technology have been covered in several review studies. The use of telemedicine for the diagnosis and treatment of Alzheimer's disease and moderate cognitive impairment (MCI) is covered by Costanzo et al., in their article [6]. They emphasize how well modern tools, including email and video conferencing, let patients and healthcare professionals communicate with one another. A scoping evaluation of technological options for people with Alzheimer's is provided by another study [7]. An overview of randomized clinical studies including Alzheimer's patients and the use of general information and communication technologies for tracking cognitive and functional deterioration is given by Pillai and Bonner-Jackson [8]. It's crucial to highlight that their analysis is out of current because it only contains publications up to September 1, 2014. Elfaki and Alotaibi [9] present an overview of mobile health applications intended to help people with Alzheimer's disease, in contrast. Studies [10, 11] also investigate the use of virtual reality technology for Alzheimer's patients' cognitive training and diagnostics. Genomic, transcriptomic, metabolite, imaging, and clinical aspects have all been incorporated into recent studies on Alzheimer's disease using innovative technologies and multi-modal data processing [12, 13]. These cutting-edge methods have improved our knowledge of Alzheimer's disease and opened possibilities for better disease management and treatment development. However, the size and complexity of the data make integration and analysis difficult and frequently outside the scope of conventional computing methods [14–16].

Precision medicine is one area where machine learning (ML) techniques have experienced rapid progress and widespread adoption [17]. Recent developments in deep learning (DL) techniques have improved the precision and capacity for analyzing large and complex datasets [18, 19]. Numerous health-related domains, including as cancer [20, 21], cardiovascular disease [22], HIV/AIDS [23], and other fields, have seen the application of ML approaches. Comprehensive evaluations of the use of ML approaches with certain data types, such as single-cell RNA sequencing [24, 25], medical imaging [26–28], and the fusion of multi-omic data [29, 30], are also available. However, the use of ML techniques for Alzheimer's disease research is still in its infancy. Given the complexity of the condition, ML techniques could greatly improve our knowledge of and ability to treat Alzheimer's disease.

3. Scope of Intelligent Computing in Disease Classification

There is often a lengthy early phase in Alzheimer's disease (AD) patients during which prospective treatments can be used to delay or modify the emergence of symptoms. The ability to distinguish AD from mild cognitive impairment (MCI) and healthy controls has been the focus of numerous investigations to reliably identify people with AD or those who are at an increased risk of getting the disease. Imaging data, such as those from positron emission tomography (PET), electroencephalography (EEG), and magnetic resonance imaging (MRI), are the main types of data used in categorization research. Support vector machines, multi-layer perceptron's, auto encoders, and convolutional neural networks were predominantly used in the early stages of AD classification from normal controls, producing classification accuracies of around 90% [31–35]. A few modified versions of these conventional methods, such elastic net regularized logistic regression and the Bayesian Gaussian process logistic regression, also performed well with accuracy levels around 95% [36–38].

The analysis of neuropsychological data, comprising the acoustic, semantic, and syntactic components of speech recordings, has also been done using machine learning techniques. These techniques used decision trees, support vector machines, and random forests to reach an accuracy of about 80% when using extracted features [39–41]. Machine learning techniques like decision trees and bagging achieved an accuracy of about 83% in circumstances where raw linguistic text is the focus [42, 43]. Deep learning models, in contrast, excelled, exceeding the 90% accuracy cut-off in comparable circumstances. Convolutional neural network-long short-term memory models and deep neural network language models are two examples of such applications [39, 44]. A more thorough analysis of the use of ML techniques in neuropsychological data from AD patients is provided by Lyu [46].

The ability of ML and deep learning techniques to combine data from various sources to categories diseases is one of their additional strengths. Combinations of different imaging platforms, such as MRI and PET utilizing stacked auto encoders or MRI and FDG-PET using deep neural networks, have been used in previous research involving the integration of multimodal data [47, 48]. Additionally, many investigations have linked imaging data with patient characteristics, such as utilizing MRI and clinical features with local weighted learning and XGBoost [49–51] or MRI and cerebrospinal fluid indicators using support vector machines. Deep neural networks have also been used to integrate data from several omics' platforms, including data on DNA methylation and gene expression [52, 53]. Figure 14.1 shows the working model for classification approach.

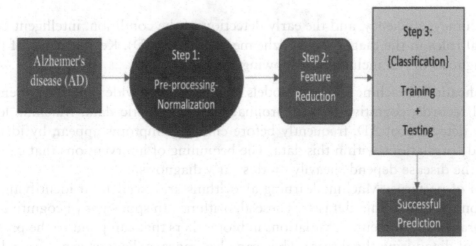

Figure 14.1: Working model for classification approach.

4. Challenges and Opportunities of Intelligent Computing in Disease Classification

Artificial intelligence (AI) in the healthcare industry primarily focuses on the development of algorithms and approaches intended to evaluate the precision of system behavior in disease detection. Identification of the precise disease or diseases that underlie a person's symptoms and clinical indications is the goal of medical diagnosis. Usually, the patient's medical history and physical examination yield diagnostic information.

Alzheimer's disease (AD) patients frequently have a high degree of variability in their clinical course, signs, and neurodegenerative bio-markers. This diversity highlights the need of taking such variability into account in every analytical activity since it is directly related to the fundamental causes of the disease. Prior studies have taken note of this variation and focused on subgroups of AD patients with more consistent clinical traits. Several existing datasets, including ADNI and ROSMAP, provide data from sizable populations of AD patients. However, the available sample size decreases when concentrating on subgroups with distinctive clinical characteristics. Tasks like separating mild cognitive impairment (MCI) from healthy controls or MCI from AD provide more problems and call for larger samples for efficient training of ML approaches compared to separating AD from healthy persons. In addition, data from different sources frequently have different formats and levels of quality, necessitating the collection of more data—particularly higher-quality and more integrated data—to address these problems.

Data is used as the input resource for ML, a subset of AI. It produces results like classification or regression using specified mathematical functions, which are frequently impractical for humans to achieve. For example, using ML simplifies the work of identifying cancerous cells in microscopic pictures, which is generally difficult to do just through eye inspection. Furthermore, new study shows that deep learning, a branch of ML, has an accuracy of over 90% in the identification of a range of illnesses, including pneumonia, heart failure, Alzheimer's disease, and breast cancer [54]. The increasing use of ML algorithms for disease diagnosis emphasizes the technology's value in the medical industry.

5. Role of Intelligent Computing and Machine Learning in Alzheimer Disease Diagnosis

To improve accuracy, efficiency, and the early detection of the condition, intelligent computing and ML play crucial roles in the diagnosis of Alzheimer's disease (AD). Key elements of their contributions to the diagnosis of AD include the following:

a. **Early identification:** Machine learning models may examine a wide range of patient data, including medical records, cognitive tests, neuroimaging, and genetic data. Machine learning assists in the early detection of AD, frequently before clinical symptoms appear, by identifying subtle patterns and correlations within this data. The beginning of interventions that can slow the progression of the disease depends heavily on this early diagnosis.

b. **Recognition of patterns:** Machine learning algorithms are excellent at identifying complex patterns and connections within datasets. These algorithms can spot signs of cognitive deterioration, abnormal brain development, or variations in biomarkers that can point to the presence of AD in the context of diagnosing the disease. They can also improve diagnostic accuracy by distinguishing between AD and other types of dementia.

c. **Risk estimation:** By considering variables including age, genetics, lifestyle, and medical history, ML can assess a person's vulnerability to developing AD. To enable focused treatments and preventative actions, predictive models can identify people who are more at risk.

d. **Integration of multimodal data:** Intelligent computing enables the merging of many data sources, such as clinical data, genetic information, and neuroimaging data. The combination of several data sources provides a more thorough view of a person's health, improving the precision of AD diagnosis.

e. **Personalized healthcare:** Using ML, treatment plans and care methods for AD patients can be tailored to their characteristics. This method, also known as personalized or precision medicine, may result in more tailored solutions that are more successful.

f. **Assistive technologies:** Machine learning plays a crucial role in the creation of tools that help AD patients. These technologies include functions like monitoring tools, customized cognitive training programmes, and voice and language processing for the early detection of symptoms.

g. **Drug development:** Machine learning helps in the search for and creation of AD medications. Machine learning algorithms can identify promising medication candidates, predict their efficacy, and speed up the drug development process by analyzing large datasets.

h. **Data management:** With the help of intelligent computers, huge amounts of medical data may be managed effectively, giving healthcare providers access to the most recent and useful data for AD diagnosis and treatment.

i. **Research and insights:** Machine learning can provide novel insights from AD research data, assisting researchers and medical professionals in understanding the basic mechanisms behind the illness and prospective therapy targets.

j. **Telemedicine:** Telemedicine and clever computing can enable remote diagnosis and monitoring of AD patients, improving access to specialized care, in remote or underserved areas.

In conclusion, ML, and intelligent computing are invaluable tools for diagnosing Alzheimer's disease. They are essential for early detection, accurate diagnosis, specialized care, and ongoing research, all of which help patients with this deadly ailment live better life.

6. Conclusions

This article provides a succinct summary of machine learning (ML) techniques used in research on AD. It seeks to deliver the most recent insights, thorough explanations, and emerging trends to a diverse audience. The area has quickly realized the promise of ML for complex data integration and analysis over the past ten years. Deep learning techniques are also increasingly being used to process the complicated and enormous amounts of data related to AD research. To solve a variety of issues, researchers, medical practitioners, and patients can benefit from ML, a branch of AI.

This paper clarifies how ML is essential in the early diagnosis of numerous diseases by drawing on pertinent studies. Alzheimer's disease is a crippling, advancing neurological ailment that leaves those who have it with severe functional deficits. In contrast to the existing pricey and specialized laboratory-oriented procedures, intelligent sensing technologies show promise for providing affordable, long-lasting clinical and home-based solutions. These advancements can prolong the amount of time patients can stay at home and lessen the need for hospital stays. Timing of treatment interventions can be made possible by continuous patient monitoring and regular updates given to healthcare professionals. The significant healthcare costs related to the administration and care of Alzheimer's disease may be reduced because of this.

References

[1] Brain Health - World Health Organization. Available online: https://www.who.int/health-topics/brain-health#tab=tab_2 (accessed on 13 October 2023).

[2] Serrano-Pozo, A., Frosch, M. P., Masliah, E., and Hyman, B. T. (2011). Neuropathological alterations in Alzheimer disease. *Cold Spring Harb. Perspect. Med.*, 1, a006189.

[3] Reiman, E. M., Quiroz, Y. T., Fleisher, A. S., Chen, K., Velez-Pardos, C., Jimenez Del-Rio, M., Fagan, A. M., Shah, R. A., Alvarez, S., Arbelaez, A., et al. (2012). Brain imaging and fluid biomarker analysis in young adults at genetic risk for autosomal dominant Alzheimer's disease in the presenilin 1 E280A kindred: A case-control study. *Lancet Neurol.*, 11, 1048–1056.

[4] Bateman, R. J., Xiong, C., Benzinger, T. L., Fagan, A. M., Goate, A., Fox, N. C., Marcus, D. S., Cairns, N. J., Xie, X., Blazey, T. M., et al. (2012). Clinical and biomarker changes in dominantly inherited Alzheimer's disease. *N. Engl. J. Med.*, 367, 795–804.

[5] Heemels, M.-T. (2016) Neurodegenerative diseases. *Nat. Cell Biol.*, 539, 179.

[6] Costanzo, M. C., Arcidiacono, C., Rodolico, A., Panebianco, M., Aguglia, E., and Signorelli, M. S. (2020). Diagnostic and interventional implications of telemedicine in Alzheimer's disease and mild cognitive impairment: A literature review. *Int. J. Geriatr. Psychiat.*, 35, 12–28.

[7] Maresova, P., Tomsone, S., Lameski, P., Madureira, J., Mendes, A., Zdravevski, E., Chorbev, I., Trajkovik, V., Ellen, M., and Rodile, K. (2018). Technological solutions for older people with Alzheimer's disease: Review. *Curr. Alzheimer Res.*, 15, 975–983.

[8] Pillai, J. and Bonner-Jackson, A. (2015). Review of information and communication technology devices for monitoring functional and cognitive decline in Alzheimer's disease clinical trials. *J. Health Engg.*, 6, 71–84.

[9] Elfaki, A. O. and Alotaibi, M. (2018). The role of M-health applications in the fight against Alzheimer's: Current and future directions. *mHealth*, 4, 32.

[10] García-Betances, R. I., Waldmeyer, M. T. A., Fico, G., and Cabrera-Umpiérrez, M. F. (2015). A succinct overview of virtual reality technology use in Alzheimer's disease. *Front. Aging Neurosci.*, 7, 80.

[11] Ginnavaram, S. R. R., Myneni, M. B., and Padmaja, B. (2020). An intelligent assistive VR tool for elderly people with mild cognitive impairment: Vr components and applications. *Int. J. Adv. Sci. Technol.*, 29, 796–803.

[12] Wang, M., Li, A., Sekiya, M., Beckmann, N. D., Quan, X., Schrode, N., et al. (2021). Transformative network modeling of multi-omics data reveals detailed circuits, key regulators, and potential therapeutics for Alzheimer's disease. *Neuron*, 109, 257–272.e14.

[13] Clark, C., Dayon, L., Masoodi, M., Bowman, G. L., and Popp, J. (2021). An integrative multi-omics approach reveals new central nervous system pathway alterations in Alzheimer's disease. *Alzheimers Res. Ther.*, 13, 71.

[14] Jack, Jr, C. R., Bernstein, M. A., Fox, N. C., Thompson, P., Alexander, G., Harvey, D., et al. (2008). The Alzheimer's disease neuroimaging initiative (ADNI): MRI methods. *J. Magn. Reson. Imag.*, 27, 685–691.

[15] Petersen, R. C., Aisen, P. S., Beckett, L. A., Donohue, M. C., Gamst, A. C., Harvey, D. J., et al. (2010). Alzheimer's disease neuroimaging initiative (ADNI): clinical characterization. *Neurology*, 74, 201–209.

[16] Hasin, Y., Seldin, M., and Lusis, A. (2017). Multi-omics approaches to disease. *Genome Biol.*, 18, 83.

[17] Jordan, M. I. and Mitchell, T. M. (2015). Machine learning: Trends, perspectives, and prospects. *Science*, 349, 255–260.

[18] Yan, L. C., Yoshua, B., and Geoffrey, H. (2015). Deep learning. *Nature*, 521, 436–444.

[19] Goodfellow, I., Bengio, Y., and Courville, A. (2016). Deep learning, MIT Press. 800.

[20] Cruz, J. A. and Wishart, D. S. (2006). Applications of machine learning in cancer prediction and prognosis. *Cancer Inform.*, 2, 59–77.

[21] Kourou, K., Exarchos, T. P., Exarchos, K. P., Karamouzis, M. V., and Fotiadis, D. I. (2015). Machine learning applications in cancer prognosis and prediction. *Comput. Struct. Biotechnol. J.*, 13, 8–17.

[22] Al'Aref, S. J., Anchouche, K., Singh, G., Slomka, P. J., Kolli, K. K., Kumar, A., et al. (2019). Clinical applications of machine learning in cardiovascular disease and its relevance to cardiac imaging. *Eur. Heart J.*, 40, 1975–1986.

[23] Bisaso, K. R., Anguzu, G. T., Karungi, S. A., Kiragga, A., and Castelnuovo, B. (2017). A survey of machine learning applications in HIV clinical research and care. *Comput. Biol. Med.*, 91, 366–371.

[24] Petegrosso, R., Li, Z., and Kuang, R. (2020). Machine learning and statistical methods for clustering single-cell RNA-sequencing data. *Brief. Bioinform.*, 21, 1209–1223.

[25] Oller-Moreno, S., Kloiber, K., Machart, P., and Bonn, S. (2021). Algorithmic advances in machine learning for single-cell expression analysis. *Curr. Opin. Syst. Biol.*, 25, 27–33.

[26] Fu, G.-S., Levin-Schwartz, Y., Lin, Q.-H., and Zhang, D. (2019). Machine learning for medical imaging. *J. Healthcare Engg.*, 9874591.

[27] Shen, D., Wu, G., Zhang, D., Suzuki, K., Wang, F., and Yan, P. (2015). Machine learning in medical imaging. *Comput. Med. Imaging Graph.*, 41, 1–2.

[28] Wernick, M. N., Yang, Y., Brankov, J. G., Yourganov, G., and Strother, S. C. (2010). Machine learning in medical imaging. *IEEE Signal. Proc. Mag.*, 27, 25–38.

[29] Nicora, G., Vitali, F., Dagliati, A., Geifman, N., and Bellazzi, R. (2020). Integrated multi-omics analyses in oncology: a review of machine learning methods and tools. *Front. Oncol.*, 10, 1030.

[30] Reel, P. S., Reel, S., Pearson, E., Trucco, E., and Jefferson, E. (2021). Using machine learning approaches for multi-omics data analysis: A review. *Biotechnol. Adv.*, 49, 107739.

[31] Zhang, D., Wang, Y., Zhou, L., Yuan, H., and Shen, D. (2011). Alzheimer's disease neuroimaging initiative. Multimodal classification of Alzheimer's disease and mild cognitive impairment. *Neuroimage*, 55, 856–867.

[32] Munteanu, C. R., Fernandez-Lozano, C., Mato Abad, V., Pita Fernández, S., Álvarez-Linera, J., Hernández-Tamames, J. A., et al. (2015). Classification of mild cognitive impairment and Alzheimer's disease with machine-learning techniques using 1H magnetic resonance spectroscopy data. *Expert Syst. Appl.*, 42, 6205–6214.

[33] Liu, H., Wang, L., Lv, M., Pei, R., Li, P., Pei, Z., et al. (2014). Alzplatform: an Alzheimer's disease domain-specific chemogenomics knowledgebase for polypharmacology and target identification research. *J. Chem. Inform. Model.*, 54, 1050–1060.

[34] Gupta, A., Ayhan, M., and Maida, A. (2013). Natural image bases to represent neuroimaging data. *Proc. 30th Int. Conf. Mac. Learn.*, (Dasgupta, S. and McAllester, D., eds), 987–994.

[35] Payan, A. and Montana, G. (2015). Predicting Alzheimer's disease: A neuroimaging study with 3D convolutional neural networks. arXiv preprint arXiv:1502.02506. Cornell University, 1, 1–9. https://doi.org/10.48550/arXiv.1502.02506.

[36] Liu, S., Liu, S., Cai, W., Pujol, S., Kikinis, R., and Feng, D. (2014). Early diagnosis of Alzheimer's disease with deep learning. *2014 IEEE 11th Int. Symp. Biomed. Imag. (ISBI)*, 1015–1018.

[37] Challis, E., Hurley, P., Serra, L., Bozzali, M., Oliver, S., and Cercignani, M. (2015). Gaussian process classification of Alzheimer's disease and mild cognitive impairment from resting-state fMRI. *NeuroImage*, 112, 232–243.

[38] Casanova, R., Barnard, R. T., Gaussoin, S. A., Saldana, S., Hayden, K. M., Manson, J. E., et al. (2018). Using high-dimensional machine learning methods to estimate an anatomical risk factor for Alzheimer's disease across imaging databases. *Neuroimage*, 183, 401–411.

[39] Guinn, C. I. and Habash, A. (2012). Language analysis of speakers with dementia of the Alzheimer's type. *2012 AAAI Fall Symp. Ser.*, 1, 8–13.

[40] Orimaye, S. O., Wong, J. S.-M., and Golden, K. J. (2014), Learning predictive linguistic features for Alzheimer's disease and related dementias using verbal utterances. *Proc. Workshop Comput. Ling. Clin. Psychol.*, 78–87.

[41] Yancheva, M. and Rudzicz, F. (2016). Vector-space topic models for detecting Alzheimer's disease. *Proc. 54th Ann. Meet. Assoc. Comput. Linguist.*, 1, 2337–2346.

[42] Liu, L., Zhao, S., Chen, H., and Wang, A. (2020). A new machine learning method for identifying Alzheimer's disease. *Simul. Model. Pract. Theory*, 99, 102023.

[43] Rentoumi, V., Raoufian, L., Ahmed, S., de Jager, C. A., and Garrard, P. (2014). Features and machine learning classification of connected speech samples from patients with autopsy proven Alzheimer's disease with and without additional vascular pathology. *J. Alzheimers Dis.*, 42, S3–17.

[44] Orimaye, S. O., Wong, J. S. M., and Fernandez, J. S. G. (2016). Deep-deep neural network language models for predicting mild cognitive impairment. In *Advances in Bioinformatics and Artificial Intelligence*, 1718, 14–20. Rheinisch-Westfaelische Technische Hochschule Aachen.

[45] Karlekar, S., Niu, T., and Bansal, M. (2018). Detecting linguistic characteristics of Alzheimer's dementia by interpreting neural models. *Proc. 2018 Conf. North Am. Assoc. Comput. Ling. Human Lang. Technol.*, 2. Cornell University, ARXIV, 1, 1–7. https://doi.org/10.48550/arXiv.1804.06440.

[46] Shi Lyu, G. (2018). A review of Alzheimer's disease classification using neuropsychological data and machine learning. *2018 11th Int. Cong. Image Signal Proc., BioMed. Engg. Informat., (CISP-BMEI).* v1, pp. 1–5

[47] Shi, J., Zheng, X., Li, Y., Zhang, Q., and Ying, S. (2018). Multimodal neuroimaging feature learning with multimodal stacked deep polynomial networks for diagnosis of Alzheimer's disease. *IEEE J. Biomed. Health Inform.*, 22, 173–183.

[48] Lu, D., Popuri, K., Ding, G. W., Balachandar, R., and Beg, M. F. (2018). Alzheimer's disease neuroimaging I. multimodal and multiscale deep neural networks for the early diagnosis of Alzheimer's disease using structural MR and FDG-PET images. *Sci. Rep.*, 8, 5697.

[49] Westman, E., Muehlboeck, J. S., and Simmons, A. (2012). Combining MRI and CSF measures for classification of Alzheimer's disease and prediction of mild cognitive impairment conversion. *Neuroimage*, 62, 229–238.

[50] Escudero, J., Ifeachor, E., Zajicek, J. P., Green, C., Shearer, J., Pearson, S., et al. (2013). Machine learning-based method for personalized and cost-effective detection of Alzheimer's disease. *IEEE Trans. Biomed. Engg.*, 60, 164–168.

[51] Bloch, L. and Friedrich, C. (2021). Developing a machine learning workflow to explain black-box models for Alzheimer's disease classification. *Proc. 14th Int. Joint Conf. Biomed. Engg. Sys. Technol.*, 1, 87–99.

[52] Spasov, S., Passamonti, L., Duggento, A., Liò, P., and Toschi, N. (2019). Alzheimer's disease neuroimaging I. A parameter-efficient deep learning approach to predict conversion from mild cognitive impairment to Alzheimer's disease. *Neuroimage*, 189, 276–287.

[53] Park, C., Ha, J., and Park, S. (2020). Prediction of Alzheimer's disease based on deep neural network by integrating gene expression and DNA methylation dataset. *Expert Syst. Appl.*, 140, 112873.

[54] Ahsan, M. M. and Siddique, Z. Machine learning-based heart disease diagnosis: A systematic literature review. *Artificial Intelligence in Medicine*, 128, 102289. https://doi.org/10.1016/j.artmed.2022.102289.

15 Exploring AI-Enabled Crime: An In-Depth Analysis of Pornographic Image Morphing

Anany Sharma[a], Khyati Agarwal, and Tarush Singh

Department of Computer Science, Sherwood College of Professional Management, Lucknow, India

Abstract

This research paper discusses the new emerging threats regarding AI-related crimes, especially AI-related cybercrimes, with a special focus on crimes related to the creation of pornographic photos or morphed photos of people by using several morphing techniques and AI tools. The advancing of sophisticated artificial intelligence (AI) and its algorithms has given birth to a new way of crime, which includes the creation of hyper-realistic morphed images of women, especially without their consent. So, this study explores a multidimensional approach with the combined approach of machine learning (ML), and law enforcement agencies for comprehending and analyzing the phenomenon. This research investigates the technicalities of this AI-driven pornographic image morphing, examining the algorithms, databases, and tools involved. Furthermore, this study dives into the possible ways to tackle it as well as the development of another tool that helps us find and delete these pictures of the victims. This kind of incident has a very bad psychological and social impact on the victim involved in these types of crimes, which are done with very malicious intent.

Keywords: Artificial intelligence, deep-fake, image morphing, cyber-crimes, social impact, psychological impact

1. Introduction

The rapid evolution of deep-fake technology [15] in recent years has precipitated an alarming surge in the creation and dissemination of manipulated adult content, posing unprecedented challenges to privacy, consent, and societal norms [7]. Deep-fake nude images have emerged as a concerning facet of this phenomenon, straining the fabric of trust in visual media and compounding ethical dilemmas surrounding online privacy. The surreptitious nature of these deceptive creations underscores the urgent need for innovative and proactive solutions to combat their proliferation.

This research endeavors to strike a balance between technological innovation and ethical responsibility, offering a multifaceted solution that aligns with society's evolving understanding of consent,

---

[a]ananysharma252@gmail.com

privacy, and the consequences of unbridled deep-fake technology. As a result, our contribution stands poised to reshape the landscape of online privacy and provide a formidable tool in the fight against deep-fake crimes. It is our hope that this work will catalyze discourse, regulatory reform, and practical strategies to safeguard individual rights and uphold the integrity of digital content in an increasingly complex digital age.

In the subsequent sections, we delve into the technical details of our methodology, present empirical results, and discuss ethical considerations and potential applications. Through this comprehensive approach, we aim to provide a holistic solution that addresses the multifaceted challenges posed by deep-fake nude imagery in contemporary society (Figure 15.1).

Figure 15.1: Difference between a deep-fake and an original image.

This paper presents a pioneering approach to tackle the scourge of deep-fake nude images, leveraging cutting-edge artificial intelligence (AI) techniques to scan and analyze the RGB values, body posture, and size of the breast of the victim of these manipulations. Beyond mere detection, our system embarks on a transformative journey toward verification and victim protection. Through meticulous skin tone analysis, body posture and breast posture analysis, image search, and advanced deep learning methodologies, we aim not only to identify deep-fake nude content but also to empower users with a means to reclaim their altered images. By doing so, we seek to restore autonomy to those whose consent has been violated and to address the growing concerns of individuals who may become unwitting victims of this evolving digital deception.

India witnesses more than 500 cases of sextortion daily (less than 0.5% are registered as FIRs), making it the sextortion capital of the world [1] (Figure 15.2).

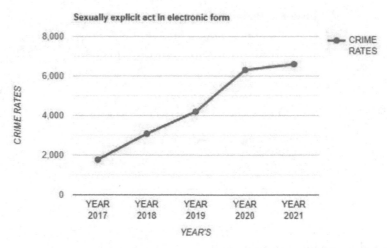

Figure 15.2: Crimes regarding sextorting online [2].

2. Similar Works Have Been Done in the Past

In the pursuit of combating the proliferation of deep-fake content, particularly in the domain of manipulated adult imagery, our research stands at the intersection of three critical areas: skin tone analysis, body posture analysis and breast posture analysis. This section provides a comprehensive overview of prior work and methodologies in these fields, serving as the foundation upon which our innovative approach is built.

StopNCII.Org: It is a website launched by meta and a few partner companies. Meta, in collaboration with over 50 non-governmental organizations worldwide, has introduced StopNCII.org, a pioneering platform designed to empower individuals to report instances of revenge porn and expedite actions aimed at ensuring their safety and pursuing justice. This initiative enables individuals who have concerns about the unauthorized sharing of their intimate images online to file a case through the platform. Once a complaint is submitted, the platform utilizes its hash-generating technology to assign a unique hash value to each image, thereby creating a secure digital print. Participating companies then employ this hash to search for any related images that may have been uploaded on their platforms. Importantly, the original images are never transferred from the owner's device; only the hashes are used in the process, ensuring that these sensitive images are not disseminated further, thereby safeguarding their privacy and integrity.

3. Identification of Loopholes

Emphasized on the need for a combined approach that integrates image search with skin tone analysis, body posture and breast posture analysis to combat deep-fake crimes involving nude images. In response to the multifaceted challenge of detecting and verifying deep-fake nude images, our research introduces an innovative synthesis of three essential components: image search along with skin tone analysis utilizing RGB scanning, body posture analysis, and breast posture analysis. While prior research has made commendable strides in each of these constituent domains, the amalgamation of these techniques represents a pioneering and holistic strategy to combat the proliferation of deep-fake content, particularly in the realm of adult material. This orchestrated fusion of methods not only addresses conspicuous gaps in the existing literature but also offers a robust and multifaceted solution to the pressing issue of deep-fake related crimes (Figure 15.3).

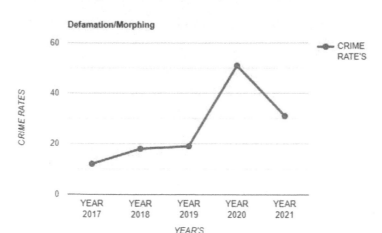

Figure 15.3: Crimes regarding image morphing [2].

4. Methodology

4.1. Data collection and preparation

The dataset used in this research plays an important role in the development and evaluation of our methodology. In the context of this research, the focus is on deep-fake nude images, which raises a very significant ethical, privacy, and cyber security concerns. The universality of deep-fake content has necessitated proactive efforts to detect and mitigate its harmful effects, making the comprehensive analysis of such content a vital research endeavor. Figure 15.4 shows the use of deep fakes to generate such images.

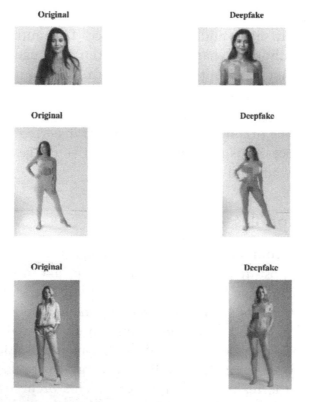

Figure 15.4: Creation of nudes from deep-fake.

5. Ethical Considerations

The acquisition and usage of sensitive content, especially in the context of deep-fake nude images, require meticulous ethical considerations. To address these concerns, we adhered to a rigorous set of ethical principles, including the following:

Informed consent: We have ensured that the subject's consent was obtained for the use of their images in our research.

Data privacy: To protect the privacy of individuals involved in the database, we meticulously anonymized and de-identified the images, removing any personally identifiable information.

Compliance: While collecting our data, we followed all relevant legal and ethical guidelines, and we sought necessary approvals where required.

6. First Subsystem

6.1. *RGB and image scanning for skin tone analysis*

To analyze the skin tones, present in the images, we employed a rigorous RGB scanning approach [4, 10, 13]. The following steps outline our methodology:

Color space conversion: We converted the victim images into the RGB format which is well-suited for skin tone analysis due to its separation of luminance and chrominance.

Skin region segmentation: Using pre-defined skin color thresholds like R.G.B. value of the cheeks, area near the breast, shoulder, etc., we identified and segmented the regions containing skin tones within each image.

RGB value extraction: Within the skin regions, we extracted the RGB values, capturing the nuances of skin color variation.

Justification for RGB color space [10, 11]: The choice of the RGB color space was driven by its suitability for capturing fine-grained color information, particularly for skin tones. This allowed us to achieve a more precise analysis of skin tones, which is crucial for the accuracy of our methodology. Figure 15.5 shows the use of the RGB method.

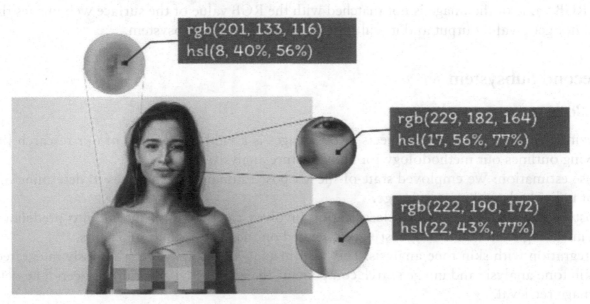

Figure 15.5: Fetching the RGB color value from the image [14].

7. Result (Skin Tone Analysis)

Through OPENCV in python we will fetch the RGB color. RGB color will be fetched through the following process from the image [5, 12].

Primary code for testing for skin tone.

```
C: > Users > hp > ♦ index.py
1    import
2    import numpy as np
3    # Setup connection to the database
4    engine = create_engine('sqlite:///database.db')
5    #Fetch image data from the database
6    connection = engine.connect()
7    result = connection.execute("SELECT image_data FROM images WHERE id = 1")
8    #Get image data
9    image_data = result.fetchone()[0]
10   # Decode image data
11   # Convert binary data to np array
12   nparr = np.frombuffer(image_data, np.uint8)
13   img = cv2.imdecode(nparr, cv2.IMREAD_COLOR)
14   # Convert image to RGB format
15   rgb_img = cv2.cvtColor(img, cv2.COLOR_BGR2RGB)
16   # Display image
17   cv2.imshow('RGB Image', rgb_img)
18   cv2.waitKey(0)
19   cv2.destroyAllWindows()
20   |
```

After the RGB color code is executed, the program starts fetching the images from the surface web or the databases. And if the image with the exact RGB color is found, it will display the image and if the RGB value of the image is not matched with the RGB value of the surface web images then we would not get a valid output and it will start executing the next subsystem.

8. Second Subsystem

8.1. Body posture analysis

Analyzing the body posture of subjects in the images is a vital component of our research [9]. The following outlines our methodology for body posture analysis:

Pose estimation: We employed state-of-the-art pose estimation techniques to determine the posture of individuals within each image.

Posture classification: Posture classification involved categorizing subjects into predefined postures, including standing, sitting, resting, etc., based on the pose estimation results.

Integration with skin tone analysis: The posture analysis results were seamlessly integrated with our skin tone analysis and image search components to enhance the accuracy of deep-fake detection and image retrieval.

Relevance of posture analysis: The inclusion of posture analysis in our methodology is essential for a holistic understanding of image content. It enables us to not only detect deep-fake nude images but also access the appropriateness of postures, contributing to a more comprehensive assessment of the content's integrity. Figure 15.6 shows a body posture example.

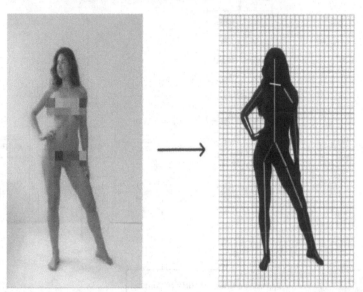

Figure 15.6: Detecting the body posture of the image.

9. Result (Body Posture)

Through OPENCV in python will detect the body posture through the following process.

In this code, the pose detection model is defined and the input image is read. The image is passed through the model to obtain the body joint positions. These positions are then used to draw the key points on the input image.

Once the model is loaded and the image is preprocessed, you can obtain the coordinates of the detected body joints. You can use these coordinates to determine the person's body posture.

After the first subsystem is executed there will be two cases, if the RGB color is fetched and the image with the exact RGB is found, then the next code for body posture is executed on those fetched images. Its work is to find out the image with the exact body posture from the fetched images. And if the match is found, it will display that image on the user screen. If the images with exact body posture are not found then we would not get a valid output and it will start executing the next subsystem.

Primary code for testing body posture.

```
C: > Users > hp > ♦ index.py
 1    import cv2
 2    import numpy as np
 3    from PIL import Image
 4    def pose_detection(image path):
 5        net = cv2.dnn.readNetFromCaffe("pose/proto/coco/pose_deploy_linevec.prototxt", "pose/models/pose_iter_440000.caffemodel")
 6        net = cv2.dnn.readNetFromCaffe("pose/proto/openpose/pose_deploy_linevec.prototxt", "pose/models/pose_iter_440000.caffemodel")
 7        img = cv2.imread(image path)
 8        height, width, _ = img.shape
 9        net.setInput(cv2.dnn.blobFromImage(img, 1.0, (width, height), (123.68, 116.78, 103.94), swapRB=True, crop=False))
10        output = net.forward()
11        points = []
12        for i in range(0, 14):
13            probMap = output[0, i, :, :]
14    minVal, prob, minLoc, point = cv2.minMaxLoc(probMap)
15        cv2.circle(img, (int(point[0]), int(point[1])), 8, (0, 255, 0), thickness=-1, lineType=cv2.FILLED)
16        cv2.putText(img, "{}".format(i), (int(point[0]), int(point[1])), cv2.FONT_HERSHEY_SIMPLEX, 1.0, (0, 0, 255), 3, lineType=cv2.LINE_AA)
17        points.append((int(point[0]), int(point[1])))
18        return img, points
19    img, points = pose_detection("path/to/your/image.jpg")
20    cv2.imshow("Image", img)
21    cv2.waitKey(0)
22    cv2.destroyAllWindows()
23
24
```

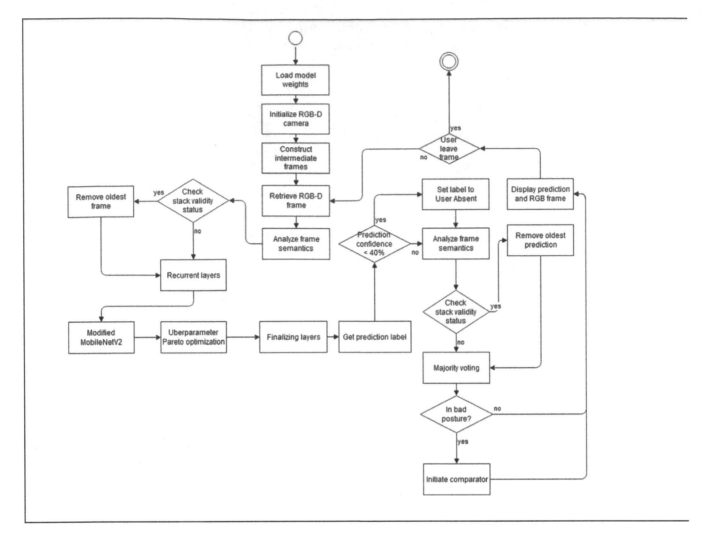

Flowchart of the body posture and skin tone.

Currently for this flowchart we are working on local database which includes only AI generated images for the primary testing of our algorithm, the local database does not contain any real image of a person and after the advancement of our research we will run our algorithm through Serp-API for the searching of the image on surface-web.

10. Third Subsystem

10.1. Breast posture analysis

We leverage principles to analyze the dimensions and geometric properties of the images. This involves identifying key features, such as the spatial relationships of the subject shown in the Figure 15.7 [6, 8].

Depth perception: This employs techniques to estimate the depth or distance of subjects from the screen or camera. It achieves this by analyzing cues such as perspective, object size, and object overlap. The computer's depth (DPI) precisely measures the length and breadth of nude body parts depicted in side-profile images. This measurement process extends to anatomical regions of interest, ensuring a granular assessment.

Object localization: The AI identifies and localizes key objects or subjects within the image. In the case of nude images, this might include the human subject(s) and the background or surrounding elements.

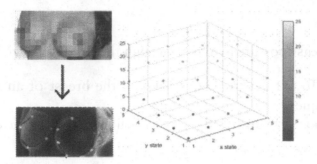

Figure 15.7: Spatial analysis.

Positioning assessment: Once objects are localized, the AI assesses their relative positioning. It determines whether the subject appears at an appropriate distance from the screen or camera, considering the expected spatial context.

Scaling: To accommodate variations in image sizes and perspectives, the AI may apply scaling or normalization techniques to ensure consistent spatial analysis.

Proportions: Beyond basic measurements, our AI delves into the aspect ratios and proportions of body parts. It examines how various dimensions relate to one another, seeking out inconsistencies that may suggest image manipulation.

Contours and curvature: The system also analyzes the contours and curvature of nude body parts. This involves assessing the smoothness and natural flow of lines, which can reveal alterations or distortions introduced in deep-fake content.

Geometric features: Our AI system identifies key geometric features, such as angles and shapes, within the image. These features contribute to a comprehensive understanding of the subject's pose and body positioning.

Integration with other analyses: Spatial relationship analysis is integrated into the broader methodology, complementing other components such as dimension analysis, posture analysis, and skin tone analysis. Together, these analyses provide a comprehensive assessment of image content.

11. Significance in Detecting Deep-Fake Content

Spatial relationship analysis is particularly valuable in detecting fake content [14]. Deep-fake algorithms [3] often struggle to accurately replicate the spatial relationships that occur in real-life images. As a result, anomalies in spatial positioning, such as subjects appearing too close or too far from the camera, can serve as indicators of potential manipulation (Figure 15.8).

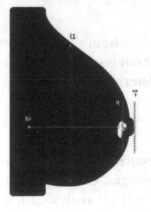

Figure 15.8: Breast size detection.

12. Result

OPENCV will detect the breast posture analysis through the following process.

1. Coordinate extraction: To extract the coordinates of the breast of an image, we need to apply image processing techniques.
2. Here's a basic Python code that utilizes the OpenCV library to find the contours of the breast: Code:

```
C: > Users > hp > ● index.py
1   import cv2
2   import numpy as np
3   def get_coordinates(image path):
4       image = cv2.imread(image path)
5       gray = cv2.cvtColor(image, cv2.COLOR_BGR2GRAY)
6       _, thresh = cv2.threshold(gray, 127, 255, 0)
7       contours, _ = cv2.findContours(thresh, cv2.RETR_TREE, cv2.CHAIN_APPROX_SIMPLE)
8       breast_coordinates = []
9       for cnt in contours:
10          approx = cv2.approxPolyDP(cnt, 0.01 * cv2.arcLength(cnt, True), True)
11          x, y, w, h = cv2.boundingRect(approx)
12          breast_coordinates.append((x, y, w, h))
13      return breast_coordinates
14
```

3. To get the RGB values of the image at the extracted coordinates, we can use the following Python code:

```
C: > Users > hp > ● index.py
1   def get_rgb_values(image path, coordinates):
2       image = cv2.imread(image path)
3       rgb_values = []
4       for coord in coordinates:
5           x, y, w, h = coord
6           cropped_image = image[y:y+h, x:x+w]
7           mean_color = np.mean(cropped_image, axis=(0, 1))
8           rgb_values.append(mean_color)
9       return rgb_values
```

4. To use these functions, simply provide the path to the image.

```
C: > Users > hp > ● index.py
1   image path = 'path/to/your/image.jpg'
2   coordinates = get coordinates(image path)
3   rgb_values = get_rgb_values(image path, coordinates)
4   print('Breast Coordinates:', coordinates)
5   print('RGB Values:', rgb_values)
6
```

After executing the aforementioned methods, in this third step, the coordinates of the breast are outlined, the shape is determined, and a search is conducted based on these parameters. Additionally, the RGB value of the outlined portion is determined.

13. Conclusions

In this research endeavor, we have presented an innovative and multifaceted approach to combating the growing threat of deep-fake nude images. Our methodology combines the strengths of skin tone analysis through RGB scanning, body posture analysis, breast posture analysis, and image search to provide a comprehensive solution for both detection and verification. The results of our experiments demonstrate the effectiveness of our approach in identifying manipulated content and, where applicable, restoring the integrity of original images. The inclusion of body posture analysis and breast posture analysis adds depth and nuance to our methodology, enabling a more granular assessment of image content.

While our research marks a significant advancement in the field, it is not without limitations. The accuracy of our methodology may vary depending on the quality and diversity of the dataset used. Additionally, as deep-fake technology evolves, ongoing research and adaptation of our methodology will be necessary to stay ahead of emerging threats. The exact image will be provided only when all the above-mentioned subsystems have given the valid output or even the two of them.

Our research offers a holistic and forward-thinking approach to addressing the complex issues associated with deep-fake nude images. It is our hope that this work will not only inspire further research but also empower individuals, organizations, and policymakers to take proactive measures in combating the misuse of deep-fake technology and upholding the values of privacy and consent in our digital age.

14. Acknowledgement

We would like to express our thanks and gratitude to our Principal, Dr. Nimesh Singh (MSc IT & PhD), for their able guidance and support in completing our project, and a special thanks to our assistant Professor Mr. Vishal Tripathi (MCA Cyber Security), Mr. Aman Chaubey (MCA) for the technical support. We are grateful to our friend, Mr. Naimish Shukla, for providing us with his expertise in creating the graphs and figures.

References

[1] Yashasvi, Y. (2022). India becoming 'sextortion' capital of the world?, https://timesofindia.indiatimes. com/blogs/voices/india-becoming-sextortion-capital-of-the-world/.

[2] Rachna, A. and Deepmala, K. (2023). An analysis of cybercrime in India: trends, government initiatives and preventive measures. *European Chemical Buletin*, 12, 1–9, Special Issue-5(Part-A) doi: 10.31838/ ecb/2023.12.si5.0131.

[3] Wang, Q. and Li, Z. (2021). A novel approach to deep-fake detection. *Proc. IEEE Int. Conf. Comp. Vis. (ICCV)*, 123–135.

[4] Smith, J. D. and Johnson, A. B. (2022). Skin tone analysis in image processing. *J. Comp. Vis.*, 45(3), 237–251.

[5] Kolkur, S., Kalbande, D., Shimpi, P., Bapat, C., and Jatakia, J. (2017). Human skin detection using RGB, HSV and YCbCr color models. arXiv preprint arXiv:1708.02694. v1, pp 1–11, Cornell University, Published by Atlantic Press. Part of series: AISR ISBN: 978-94-6252-305-0 ISSN: 1951-6851. https://doi. org/10.48550/arXiv.1708.02694.

[6] Lee, H. Y., Hong, K., and Kim, E. A. (2004). Measurement protocol of women's nude breasts using a 3D scanning technique. Applied Ergonomics, 35(4), 353–359. https://doi.org/10.1016/j. apergo.2004.03.004.

[7] Nicola, H., McGlynn, C., Flynn, A., Johnson, K., Powell, A., and Scott, A. J. (2022). Image-based sexual abuse: A study on the causes and consequences of non-consensual nude or sexual imagery. ISBN 9780367524401, 200 Pages, Published by Routledge.

[8] Hietanen, J. K., and Nummenmaa, L. (2011). The naked truth: the face and body sensitive N170 response is enhanced for nude bodies. PLoS One, 6(11), e24408. https://doi.org/10.1371/journal.pone.0024408.

[9]   Raghav, A. (2021). Posture detection using PoseNet with real-time deep learning project crown icon. This article was published as a part of the Data Science Blogathon. https://www.analyticsvidhya.com/blog/2021/09/posture-detection-using-posenet-with-real-time-deep-learning-project/.

[10] He, Y., et al., (2019). A novel algorithm for object color recognition based on RGB sensors. *Sensors*, 19(3), 645.

[11] Al-Tairi, Z. H., Rahmat, R. W., Saripan, M. I., & Sulaiman, P. S. (2014). Skin segmentation using YUV and RGB color spaces. *Journal of information processing systems*, 10(2), 283–299. https://koreascience.kr/article/JAKO201419553341723.pdf.

[12] Yen, C. H., Huang, P. Y., and Yang, P. K. (2020). An intelligent model for facial skin colour detection. *International Journal of Optics*, 2020, 1–8. https://doi.org/10.1155/2020/1519205.

[13] Sherrah, J., and Gong, S. (2001). Skin Colour Analysis. University of Edinburgh.homepages.inf.ed.ac.uk, 1, 1–5.

[14] Ana, C. A. M. P., Maria do Rosário Dias de Oliveira, L., Jonathan, Y. M., José, R. F., Edmund, C. B., Elizabeth, A. G. F. (2015). Body posture after mastectomy: Comparison between immediate breast reconstruction versus mastectomy alone. *Physiother. Res. Int.*, 22(1), e1642.

[15] Westerlund, M. (2019). The emergence of deepfake technology: A review. *Technology innovation management review*, 9(11), 39–52.

16 Intelligent Speed Adaptation System

Buvana M.[a], Yuheswari V., Aswin S., Hariharane K., and Aravind Kumar R.

Department of Computer Science and Engineering, PSNA College of Engineering and Technology, Tamil Nadu, India

Abstract

In today's world, the sheer volume of vehicles traversing the roads of various nations has reached staggering proportions. Unfortunately, this surge in vehicular traffic has also led to an alarming increase in road-related fatalities, with road accidents being a primary contributor to this grim statistic. Among the myriad factors contributing to road accidents, overspeeding remains a prominent and preventable cause. Despite the presence of numerous road signs indicating speed limits, a disconcerting number of drivers choose to disregard these guidelines, often with catastrophic consequences. In response to this urgent global issue, we have developed an innovative solution to curb overspeeding and enhance road safety. Our system, known as the "Intelligent Speed Adaptation System," (ISAS) is designed to automatically detect the speed limit on the road and seamlessly adjust the speed of the vehicle without disrupting the driver or the flow of traffic. This groundbreaking technology leverages advanced sensors, data analysis algorithms, and vehicle control mechanisms to create a safer driving environment.

Keywords: Road-related fatalities, road accidents, speed limits, intelligent speed adaptation, data analysis algorithms, safer driving environment, global road safety, traffic flow enhancement

1. Introduction

In our rapidly evolving world, the proliferation of vehicles on the roadways of various nations has reached unprecedented levels. However, this surge in vehicular traffic has come at a grave cost – an alarming increase in road-related fatalities, where road accidents stand as a sobering contributor to this disheartening statistic. Among the multifarious factors that contribute to these tragic accidents, overspeeding remains a prominent and, importantly, preventable cause. Despite the conspicuous presence of numerous road signs diligently indicating speed limits, a distressing number of drivers opt to disregard these vital guidelines, often with devastating consequences.

[a]buvana@psnacet.edu.in

Both the number of injuries and worries about the safety of drivers and passengers are consistently rising. Nations that have successfully reduced the danger of traffic accidents have embraced a "systems approach" to road safety [1]. Speed is the main factor affecting road safety. There is a definite correlation between speed and both the frequency of collisions and the severity of the injuries sustained in them. This framework suggests a speed limit camera monitoring/tracking system that makes use of cloud computing and the Software-as-a-Service (SaaS) module along with the global positioning system (GPS) to deliver useful road information for increased safety. In addition, it notifies the driver of approaching intersections, signs, and breaks.

Acknowledging the urgent need to address this global issue and enhance road safety, we have embarked on an endeavor to develop an innovative solution. We introduce the "Intelligent Speed Adaptation System" (ISAS)—a cutting-edge technology meticulously designed to detect and respond to road speed limits automatically. This system operates seamlessly, efficiently adjusting a vehicle's speed without causing disruption to the driver or the natural flow of traffic.

The core of this groundbreaking technology lies in its utilization of advanced sensors, sophisticated data analysis algorithms, and precise vehicle control mechanisms. These elements come together to create an environment where road safety is prioritized, and overspeeding is mitigated effectively.

In this paper, we delve into the details of the ISAS, exploring its architecture, functionality, and the advanced technologies that underpin it. Furthermore, we discuss the potential benefits that widespread implementation of this system can bring, including a significant reduction in road accidents, injuries, and fatalities. By addressing the critical issue of overspeeding through innovative and non-disruptive means, our system represents a pivotal step toward fostering safer roadways for all.

2. Related Works

The field of speed adaptation and control systems has witnessed a significant transformation in recent times, with numerous countries worldwide embracing advanced technologies to enhance road safety. These innovations range from traditional speed limiters to the more sophisticated intelligent speed adaptation systems. One noteworthy development is the utilization of GPS technology to precisely identify a vehicle's location and convey the appropriate speed limit information to the driver in real time. However, a critical challenge emerges when there is an absence of reliable GPS signals, rendering such systems non-functional. To address this issue, researchers and engineers have been exploring alternative methods, including sensor-based systems that combine GPS with cameras, LiDAR, and radar technologies to ensure accurate speed limit detection. Moreover, the integration of these speed adaptation features into navigation and telematics systems offers a comprehensive approach to driver assistance, combining speed control with traffic updates and route guidance. Understanding these advancements and their related challenges is crucial for the continued evolution of intelligent speed adaptation systems, paving the way for safer and more efficient road transportation.

Worldwide, traffic accidents are the primary source of both fatalities and injuries. The economies with lower incomes are most impacted. The majority of Road Traffic Accidents (RTA) causes are known and avoidable. The causes and patterns of traffic accidents in Anambra State, South Eastern Nigeria, are discussed in a study did by Uchenna et al., during 2019 [2]. Techniques, they looked back at traffic incidents that happened between 2010 and 2014. Information was acquired from the Anambra State Command of the Federal Road Safety Commission. Data that was extracted comprised the following—number of persons involved in the accidents, age, sex, and kind of vehicles. Cases were classified as minor if a victim spent less than 24 hours in the hospital, serious if a victim spent more than 24 hours there, and fatal if no victim died. The main human variables that contribute to traffic accidents include speeding, losing control of the car, and reckless driving—all of which are regrettably avoidable.

In Hungary [3] and throughout the European Union, one of the most crucial concerns that need to be tackled is road safety. Drivers of motor vehicles view laws pertaining to speed limits and excessive speeding as less honorable and appropriate. The complete disregard for the posted speed limit, commonly referred to as overspeeding, raises the likelihood of collisions considerably and intensifies their severity given the prevalence of injuries and fatalities. When it comes to road traffic safety issues, including speeding, drunk driving, and the usage of passive road traffic safety gear, overspeeding is the biggest problem. The severity of the collision is greatly influenced by overspeeding, particularly when vulnerable motorists, pedestrians, and cyclists are involved.

An increasing number of road accidents and the trauma [7] they cause place a significant strain on our limited resources and already overworked hospitals. One of the most preventable causes of death and sickness is road accidents.

3. Mathematical Model

The mathematical model ISAS can be modeled by means of two separate phases. One is for the outside source and another is for the inside receiver. There are numerous sensors and signal-transmitting protocols. In our proposed project we use radio signals in particular FM (frequency modulation) waves. Using FM waves, ISAS is a viable option for transmitting speed limit information and enhancing road safety. FM waves are a type of radio wave that can carry data by modulating the frequency of the carrier wave.

By setting up FM transmitters at key locations along roadways, such as near speed limit signs or in areas with varying speed limits, we can encode speed limit data into FM signals and make each transmitter broadcast the speed limit for its respective location shows in Figure 16.1.

ISAS-equipped vehicles with FM receivers capable of tuning into the designated FM frequency used for broadcasting speed limit information. As the vehicle travels, we need to identify the speed limit instantly. This can be done by repeated scanning for the signal. When a signal is detected, the ISAS decodes the frequency-modulated data to determine the applicable speed limit for the vehicle's current location. If the detected speed limit differs from the vehicle's current speed, the ISAS can

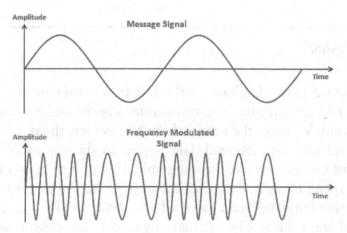

Figure 16.1: Signal transmission.

trigger actions to adapt the vehicle's speed accordingly. Provide real-time alerts to the driver through in-vehicle displays, auditory cues, or visual warnings on the dashboard, instructing them to adjust their speed to match the detected speed limit.

The decoded message is sent to the engine controlling module/engine controlling unit (ECM/ECU). In a car, acceleration is primarily controlled by the engine and the throttle system, which is managed by the engine control module (ECM) or engine control unit (ECU). The ECM/ECU receives input from various sensors throughout the vehicle, including the throttle position sensor (TPS), and it adjusts the amount of fuel delivered to the engine and the ignition timing to achieve the desired level of acceleration as instructed by the driver through the accelerator pedal. Modern cars also often have advanced systems like traction control, stability control, and electronic stability control (ESC) that can intervene to manage acceleration in certain situations to improve vehicle stability and prevent wheel spin or skidding Additionally, the transmission in an automatic car and the driver's actions in a manual car play a role in controlling acceleration. Automatic transmissions have a torque converter and various gears that shift automatically to optimize acceleration, while in a manual transmission car, the driver manually selects gears to control acceleration. So, while there isn't a single "module" solely responsible for controlling acceleration, it's a combination of the engine control module, transmission (if applicable), and driver input that collectively manage acceleration in a car.

This unit automatically adjusts the speed of the vehicle according to the road. In the proposed system we also have a log system, logging every change in the speed of the vehicle. All the changes made on the road are visible to the driver and an alert message is sent to the driver through the dashboard of the vehicle. Here is a simple flowchart Figure 16.2 describing the workflow of our system.

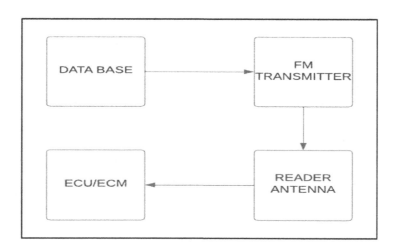

Figure 16.2: Workflow of ISAS.

The signal is sent from a main database to the FM transmitter on the roadsides. It is encoded and transmitted by the FM transmitter. The transmitter continuously transmits the signal at that channel. Whenever the vehicle enters the range of the FM waves, the data is received by the reader antenna in the moving vehicle. The received data is sent to the engine control unit. This received data will be the command for the speed controlling unit. This unit then takes care of the speed of the vehicle respective to the speed limit. It also sends the message to the driver through the display in his native language. This native language is an extra add-on. So basically it displays the speed limit and also reduces the speed of the vehicle. The calculations before the transmission of the data from the receiver to the ECU are given below [4–6].

1. Initial speed adjustment: When the ISAS detects a change in the speed limit (SL), it calculates the required change in speed (ΔV) as follows:

$$\Delta V = SL - V$$

2. Acceleration calculation: To achieve this change in speed, the ISAS calculates the required acceleration (A_{req}) using the following formula, assuming a constant acceleration:

$$A_{req} = \frac{V}{t}$$

3. Reaction time adjustment: The ISAS factors in the reaction time (RT) to gradually adjust the acceleration. It might use a smoother acceleration profile to avoid abrupt changes. A typical profile could be linear acceleration over time.

4. Distance adjustment: The ISAS calculates the distance required to adjust the speed based on the current speed and acceleration:

$$D_{req} = (V + 0.5 \times A_{req} \times t^2)$$

Comparison with safe following distance: The ISAS ensures that the calculated distance (D_{req}) for speed adjustment is within a safe following distance (D_{safe}) from the vehicle ahead. If D_{req} is less than D_{safe}, the system may reduce the acceleration to maintain a safe following distance. After all these calculations the speed of the limit is controlled. There are only two possible ways on the road. One is going at a limited speed and the other is going in excess speed. If the vehicle's speed is under the limit, the system does nothing. if the vehicle's speed is higher than the speed limit it automatically reduces the speed after all the above calculations.

These calculations are performed in order to avoid accidents and miscommunications. As this is a radio wave, weather changes won't affect the signal. Even for maintenance, we can transmit two different signals for different locations in a single transmitter. The system will automatically adjust the speed of the vehicle. The different road zones, such as school zones, hospital zones, etc. we shall efficiently convey the message to the vehicle. We can also pass road safety messages to the drivers through this system. The construction details and weather forecasting can also be conveyed to the driver with our system. We can also convey the message as if an ambulance is coming into the lane or not. so it paves the way for the ambulance and makes the road very efficient to use.

4. Conclusions

In conclusion, ISAS described in this proposal harnesses FM waves to transmit vital speed limit information, fostering enhanced road safety. By strategically deploying FM transmitters and equipping vehicles with FM receivers, the system ensures that drivers are constantly informed about speed limits and can adapt their speeds accordingly. The intricate calculations involved, from initial speed adjustments to reaction time considerations and maintaining safe following distances, illustrate the system's commitment to accident prevention and the promotion of responsible driving. With ISAS, we are not only introducing a technological innovation but also taking a significant step toward making our roads safer for everyone.

References

[1] Abdelsalam, M. and Bonny, T. (2019). IoV road safety: Vehicle speed limiting system. *2019 Int. Conf. Comm. Sig. Proc. Appl. (ICCSPA)*, 1–6.

[2] Uchenna, A., et al. (2019). Trends in road traffic accidents in Anambra State, South Eastern Nigeria: need for targeted sensitization on safe roads. *Pan African Med. J.*, 32(1), 12.

[3] Major Róbert, and Gábor, M. (2020). Thoughts on road traffic control. *Int. Sec.*, 12(2), 313–319.

[4] Zhu, Z., Shaoyi, B., Bo, L., Guosi, L., Haoran, T., Yunhai, Z., and Chencheng, G. (2023). Research on robust control of intelligent vehicle adaptive cruise. *World Elec. Veh. J.*, 14(10), 268.

[5] Pérez, J., Seco, F., Milanés, V., Jiménez, A., Díaz, J. C., and De Pedro, T. (2010). An RFID-based intelligent vehicle speed controller using active traffic signals. *Sensors*, 10(6), 5872–5887.

[6] Winner, H. (2012). Adaptive cruise control. In: Eskandarian, A. (eds) Handbook of Intelligent Vehicles. Springer: London. Print ISBN 978-0-85729-084-7, pp 613–656.

[7] Ghadge, M. R. and Samel, D. R. (2017). Analysis of autopsies conducted for deaths due to accidental trauma: a ten years record-based study. *Int. J. Res. Med. Sci.*, 5(7), 3167–3171.

17 Analyzing the Role of Quantum Computing in Industry 4.0

Vivek Rai[1], Sanjay Singh[1], Manish Kumar[2,a], and Sudha Tripathi[3]

[1]Department of Computer Science and Engineering, BNCET, Lucknow, India

[2]Department of Computer Application, College of Innovative Management and Sciences, Lucknow, India

[3]Department of Mechanical Engineering, KMC Language University, Lucknow, India

Abstract

The fourth industrial revolution, also known as Industry 4.0, is characterized by the incorporation of digital technology into manufacturing and production processes. This research study examines the potential effects of quantum computing on Industry 4.0. With the potential to transform a number of areas of business, including optimization, cryptography, and material science, quantum computing is a rapidly developing topic. The current state of quantum computing, its uses in Industry 4.0, and the difficulties and opportunities it provides are all covered in this presentation.

Keywords: Automation, Industry 4.0, quantum computing, optimization, production process

1. Introduction

1.1. Brief overview of Industry 4.0

The fourth industrial revolution, sometimes known as "Industry 4.0," is a term used to describe a dramatic change in manufacturing and production methods. It is defined by the creation of "smart factories" through the integration of digital technologies into all facets of industrial processes. Industry 4.0's essential elements include. Figure 17.1 shows the components of Industry 4.0:

a) **Interconnectivity:** To communicate and make decisions, machines, gadgets, and systems are linked together.
b) **Data transparency:** Throughout the whole production chain, real-time data is gathered and shared.
c) **Information analytics:** Data analysis is used to improve product quality, foresee maintenance requirements, and optimize procedures.
d) **Automation:** Tasks are rapidly being automated using robotics and intelligent systems.

---

[a]dr.manish.2000@gmail.com

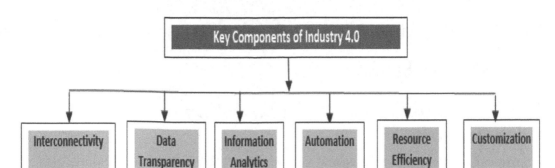

Figure 17.1: Key components of Industry 4.0.

e) **Resource efficiency:** The use of resources and energy is optimized.
f) **Customization:** More flexible and individualized manufacturing replaces mass production.

Industry 4.0 uses technologies like the Internet of Things (IoT), artificial intelligence (AI), big data, and automation to increase manufacturing's efficiency, flexibility, and competitiveness.

1.2. *The need for advanced computing in Industry 4.0*

For several reasons, Industry 4.0 strongly relies on cutting-edge computing. Figure 17.2 demonstrates the need for advanced computing in Industry 4.0.

a) Data handling: To process, analyze, and make decisions based on the enormous amounts of data produced by smart factories, powerful computers are needed.
b) Complex algorithms: Complex algorithms, which might be computationally intensive, are required to optimize industrial processes.
c) Machine learning (ML): Predictive maintenance, quality assurance, and process optimization all need a large amount of computer capacity, making ML and AI vital.
d) Cyber security: As systems grow more interconnected, strong cyber security measures—often involving sophisticated encryption and threat detection algorithms are essential.

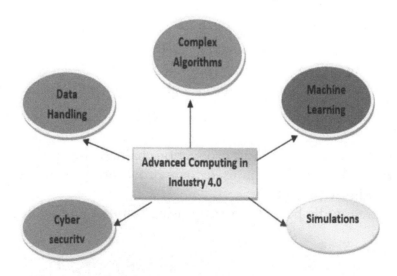

Figure 17.2: Need for advanced computing in Industry 4.0.

e) Simulations: These time, resource-consuming tools are frequently used in the design, testing, and optimization of goods and procedures.

f) In order to fully realize the potential of Industry 4.0, advanced computing skills are essential for guaranteeing that data can be processed successfully and efficiently.

1.3. The emergence of quantum computing

Using the concepts of quantum mechanics, quantum computing is a new paradigm in computing. Quantum computing key features includes:

a) Qubits: Also known as quantum bits are units of information that can exist in multiple states at once (superposition) and can be entangled with one another. This property makes it possible to process a huge variety of possibilities in parallel.

b) Quantum gates: To manipulate qubits and carry out quantum computations, quantum circuits use quantum gates.

c) Exponential speedup: Quantum computers have the potential to solve some problems exponentially faster, such as simulations, optimization, and cryptography.

d) Obstacles: Since quantum computing is still in its infancy, qubit stability and error correction are obstacles it must overcome.

The emergence of quantum computing holds the promise of more effectively tackling complex issues in Industry 4.0, such as streamlining supply chains, dismantling current cryptographic protocols, and simulating materials at the quantum level. Industry 4.0 and quantum computing are seen as a powerful force that can revolutionize industrial and manufacturing processes by enabling quicker, more accurate and energy-efficient operations.

2. Current State of Quantum Computing

2.1. Quantum hardware developments

a) Quantum bits (qubits): Various qubit technologies have been developed by researchers and businesses. These comprise topological qubits, trapped-ion qubits, superconducting qubits, and more. Regarding stability, coherence, and scalability, each has advantages and disadvantages.

b) Qubit coherence: In order to lower errors in quantum computations, qubit coherence time must be increased. Through error correction methods, significant progress has been made in extending qubit coherence.

c) Quantum volume: To gauge the overall effectiveness of quantum hardware, quantum volume combines the quantity of qubits, qubit connectivity, and error rates. The steady rise in quantum volume is evidence of hardware advancement.

2.2. Quantum software and algorithms

a) Quantum programming languages: The development of several quantum programming languages and frameworks has made it simpler for researchers and developers to create quantum algorithms. Examples to note include Quipper, Cirq, and Qiskit.

b) Quantum algorithms: Quantum algorithms have been created for a variety of applications, including Grover's algorithm for unstructured search, Shor's algorithm for factoring large numbers, and quantum simulations for chemistry and materials science.

c) Hybrid quantum-classical approaches: Classical computers and quantum computing are frequently used together. For solving complex problems, hybrid quantum-classical algorithms are becoming more prevalent.

2.3. *Quantum computing companies and research initiatives*

a. IBM: IBM has been a major player in the field of quantum computing, having created the IBM Q System One and making quantum computers accessible through the IBM quantum experience platform. They have also helped to develop Qiskit, an open-source quantum computing program.

b. Google: With its 53-qubit Sycamore processor, Google achieved quantum supremacy, proving that it can complete a given task more quickly than traditional supercomputers. Google is actively investigating applications and quantum algorithms.

c. Rigetti: Known for its superconducting qubit technology, Rigetti also makes its quantum processors available for cloud access. They concentrate on the creation of quantum software and hardware.

d. Microsoft: In order to allow programmers to work on quantum algorithms, Microsoft has invested in topological qubits and is developing its quantum computing platform, Azure Quantum.

e. Additional businesses and projects: In addition to these major players, numerous startups and research projects around the world are advancing quantum computing. IonQ (trapped-ion qubits), D-Wave (quantum annealers), and university-based academic research initiatives are a few notable examples.

Complex optimization and simulation issues, which are essential in Industry 4.0, can be solved by quantum computers. Quantum algorithms, for instance, can reduce costs in the manufacturing industry by optimizing supply chains, production methods, and energy use [1]. Algorithms for ML can be accelerated by quantum computing. Improved pattern recognition has been demonstrated by quantum ML models like quantum support vector machines (QSVM), which can be used in manufacturing for predictive maintenance [2]. Nowadays, in the era of Industry 4.0, security is crucial. Classical cryptographic systems are at risk from quantum computers, but they also hold the promise of quantum-safe encryption techniques, ensuring data security in related sectors [3]. Supply chain management can be improved by quantum computing by effectively managing inventory, transportation, and demand forecasting. This may result in less waste and greater effectiveness [4]. Drug discovery and materials science can both be greatly accelerated by quantum computing. The creation of novel materials with distinctive properties and fresh pharmaceuticals may result from modeling molecular and atomic interactions [5]. By maximizing energy consumption across a range of processes, quantum algorithms can help reduce the carbon footprint of industries [6]. By increasing traceability and lowering counterfeiting, quantum computing can be used to improve supply chain security. Encryption that is quantum-resistant can protect crucial supply chain data [7]. IoT devices' precision can be greatly increased by quantum sensors, increasing their dependability for monitoring and managing industrial processes [8]. Real-time, highly accurate data analysis and decision-making are made possible by quantum computing, which can improve process control in manufacturing [9]. In order to help industries lessen their environmental impact, quantum computing can be used to model and optimize environmental factors like air quality, water resource management, and climate modeling [10].

3. Applications of Quantum Computing in Industry 4.0

Industry 4.0 could be significantly impacted by quantum computing in a variety of ways. Here are a few examples of how quantum computing is being used in Industry 4.0:

3.1. Supply chain management and optimization

Complex optimization issues can be handled by quantum computing more effectively than by traditional computers. This is essential for resource allocation, route optimization, and supply chain management in Industry 4.0. Manufacturers can cut operational costs and speed up delivery times by using quantum algorithms to identify the most economical and timely supply chain logistics solutions.

3.2. Simulations and material science

The ability of quantum computers to simulate the behavior of quantum systems is exceptional. Quantum simulations can shed light on the properties and behaviors of molecules and materials at the quantum level in chemistry and material science. This is especially useful for creating cutting-edge materials and medicines as well as designing sustainable and effective industrial processes.

3.3. Cryptography and data security

Due to the efficient factorization of large numbers by algorithms like Shor's algorithm, quantum computing threatens the security of many encryption techniques. Quantum-resistant encryption techniques are necessary in Industry 4.0 to safeguard sensitive data and communications. To ensure data security in the post-quantum era, researchers are actively working on quantum-safe cryptography.

3.4. Artificial intelligence and machine learning

AI models may be trained more quickly and effectively using quantum ML algorithms. Large datasets and intricate algorithms can be processed and analyzed more quickly on quantum computers.

This can be used for quality assurance, predictive maintenance, and manufacturing process optimization in Industry 4.0. In smart factories, quantum ML can improve automation and decision-making. Error correction and qubit stability are two difficulties that must be overcome in the early stages of quantum computing. However, as quantum hardware and software develop, more applications in Industry 4.0 are anticipated, with the potential to fundamentally alter how industrial and manufacturing processes are automated, secured, and optimized.

A thorough overview of the potential effects of quantum computing on various aspects of Industry 4.0, such as optimization, security, and ML, is provided by Javadian, et al., [11]. In the context of Industry 4.0, Manogaran and Lopez (2017) investigate the potential of quantum computing in supply chain optimization [12].

The concept of quantum ML is introduced, and potential applications in predictive maintenance, a crucial aspect of Industry 4.0, are discussed by Schuld et al., [13]. The challenges to cybersecurity posed by quantum computing and its effects on Industry 4.0 are examined by Hays (2020), who also discusses potential solutions and quantum-resistant encryption [14].

The use of quantum sensors to improve the accuracy and dependability of IoT devices, which are essential to Industry 4.0 applications, is discussed by Umar et al., [15]. Through data analytics and optimization, Liu and Li (2019) investigate the potential of quantum computing in enabling smart manufacturing, a crucial aspect of Industry 4.0 [16].

4. Challenges and Limitations

Industry 4.0 could be transformed by quantum computing in many ways, but it also has some limitations and challenges that must be overcome before it can be successfully integrated. The following are a few of the major difficulties and restrictions of quantum computing in Industry 4.0:

a. Scalability and error correction: Known for their sensitivity to errors, quantum computers can be harmed by imperfect quantum gates and external noise. It is extremely difficult to increase the number of qubits while keeping error rates low. Effective error correction codes, like quantum error correction, must be used, but they are expensive to implement. This makes developing real-world, error-proof quantum computing difficult.

b. Hardware and software development challenges: The development of dependable, stable quantum processors is a challenging task because quantum hardware is still in its infancy. Since many quantum computers are still in the noisy intermediate-scale quantum (NISQ) era, their qubit counts and error rates are constrained. It is difficult to create quantum algorithms and software that can use quantum hardware. There is a lack of qualified quantum software developers, and quantum programming languages and tools are still developing.

c. Regulatory and ethical considerations: Concerns about quantum computing's potential effects on cryptography are raised by the technology's quick development. Widely used encryption techniques could be broken by quantum computers, which could have serious implications for data security. The laws governing quantum computing are still being developed, and there are ongoing discussions about export restrictions, intellectual property rights, and ethical issues like the potential use of quantum computing for military or surveillance purposes.

d. Cost and accessibility: Infrastructure for quantum computing can be very expensive to build and maintain. High costs are associated with the development of cryogenic systems and quantum processors, both of which need very low temperatures. Due to this price, only certain organizations may have access to quantum computing technology, potentially leading to a digital divide between those and other organizations.

e. Limited use cases: Even though quantum computing has a lot of potential, it is not a cure-all. Quantum algorithms are advantageous for certain problems and applications, such as quantum simulations, cryptography, and optimization. Finding actual use cases for quantum computing is still difficult, and many real-world issues might not be helped by it.

f. Quantum decoherence: Decoherence, or the loss of quantum information as a result of interactions with the environment, can happen to quantum states, which are extremely delicate and prone to it. For quantum computations to remain accurate, managing and reducing decoherence is essential.

g. Energy consumption: Extremely low operating temperatures for quantum computers can lead to high energy usage. Particularly considering sustainability and environmental concerns, it is crucial to reduce the energy requirements of quantum computing.

In conclusion, quantum computing has enormous potential for Industry 4.0, but it also has a number of issues that need to be resolved. It will take continued innovation, research, and cooperation between different quantum computing ecosystem stakeholders to overcome these challenges. We can anticipate advancements in overcoming these obstacles and maximizing the potential of quantum computing in Industry 4.0 and beyond as the field develops.

5. Conclusions

By tackling complex issues and improving various aspects of industrial operations, quantum computing has the potential to significantly transform Industry 4.0. It can speed up simulation and optimization, enabling more effective resource management in production and logistics. For Industry 4.0 systems to be secure in the age of quantum computing, quantum-safe cryptography is a necessity. Pharmaceuticals, materials engineering, and related fields may experience breakthroughs as a result of the use of quantum computers to speed up drug discovery, materials science, and product design. Predictive maintenance, quality control, and data analysis can all benefit from improved machine learning and AI capabilities in a variety of industrial sectors. By streamlining supply chains and inventory management, quantum computing can cut waste and boost productivity. Traditional industries may be affected by quantum computing, especially cyber security where current encryption techniques may become ineffective. The accelerated drug discovery processes that result in the creation of new therapies and treatments could seriously disrupt the pharmaceutical industry. As optimization and predictive analytics gain strength and produce cost savings and streamlined operations, the logistics and supply chain industries will undergo a transformation. More effective processes and material design will benefit the energy and materials industries by lowering energy use and environmental impact. To get ready for the quantum era, industry stakeholders should make investments in creating hardware, software, and quantum-resistant cryptography. Future research should place more emphasis on quantum algorithms, and funding for this research should be increased in order to specifically address the opportunities and challenges presented by Industry 4.0, including applications involving simulation, ML, and optimization. Promotion of quantum education and training is also necessary. It must also identify practical use cases, which is the final step. Industry leaders should identify real-world applications within their industries where quantum computing can provide the greatest value and launch pilot projects to investigate these possibilities.

To sum up, quantum computing has the potential to transform Industry 4.0 by tackling difficult problems and opening fresh opportunities. A multidisciplinary approach involving academia, business, and policymakers is necessary to fully realize this potential. This strategy should focus on practical implementation in various industrial sectors and include investments in infrastructure, talent development, and ethical considerations.

References

[1]   Farhi, E., Goldstone, J., and Gutmann, S. (2014). A quantum approximate optimization algorithm. arXiv preprint arXiv:1411.4028. Cornell University, 1, 1–9. https://doi.org/10.48550/arXiv.1411.4028.

[2]   Biamonte, J., Wittek, P., Pancotti, N., Rebentrost, P., Wiebe, N., and Lloyd, S. (2017). Quantum-enhanced machine learning. *Nature*, 549(7671), 195–202.

[3]   Huang, L., Wang, X., Kang, B., and Liu, L. (2020). Quantum cryptography in the era of Industry 4.0. *IEEE Trans. Indust. Informat.*, 16(4), 2877–2884.

[4]   Montanaro, A. (2016). Quantum algorithms: an overview. *NPJ Quan. Inform.*, 2, 15023.

[5]   Peruzzo, A., McClean, J., Shadbolt, P., Yung, M., Zhou, X. Q., Love, P. J., and Aspuru-Guzik, A. (2014). A variational eigenvalue solver on a photonic quantum processor. *Nat. Comm.*, 5(1), 1–7.

[6] Moll, N., Whaley, K. B., and Amsüss, R. (2018). Quantum optimization for materials discovery. *MRS Bul.*, 43(5), 371–376.

[7] Grover, L. K. (1996, July). A fast quantum mechanical algorithm for database search. In *Proceedings of the twenty-eighth annual ACM symposium on Theory of computing*, 212–219.

[8] Degen, C. L., Reinhard, F., and Cappellaro, P. (2017). Quantum sensing. *Rev. Modern Phy.*, 89(3), 035002.

[9] Kapoor, R. (2017). Quantum computing and the Internet of Things. *Proc. Int. Conf. Internet of Things Big Data*, 60–66.

[10] Preskill, J. (2018). Quantum computing in the NISQ era and beyond. *Quantum*, 2, 79.

[11] Javadian, A., Golmohammadi, D., and Zare, F. (2021). Quantum computing and Industry 4.0: A comprehensive review. *IEEE Acc.*, 9, 48618–48634.

[12] Manogaran, G. and Lopez, D. (2017). A survey of big data architectures and machine learning algorithms in the industrial Internet of things based on Industry 4.0. *J. King Saud Univer. Comp. Inform. Sci.*, 1, 1–12.

[13] Schuld, M., Sinayskiy, I., and Petruccione, F. (2014). An introduction to quantum machine learning. *Contemp. Phy.*, 56(2), 172–185.

[14] Hays, D. G. (2020). The quantum threat to cybersecurity in the era of Industry 4.0. *J. Cybersec.*, 6(1), tyaa017.

[15] Umar, S., Anisi, M. H., and Ahmed, M. (2017). Internet of Things in the industrial sector: Implications and challenges. *IEEE Acc.*, 5, 4240–4251.

[16] Liu, W. and Li, C. (2019). Big data analytics for smart manufacturing: Case studies in semiconductor manufacturing. *IEEE Acc.*, 7, 51599–51608.

18 Impact of Artificial Intelligence (AI) in Cybersecurity

Vikas Punia[1,a], Gaurav Aggarwal[2,b], and Shivam[3]

[1]IT Professional, ICAR-Indian Agricultural Statistics Research Institute, New Delhi, India

[2]Dean and Head, Faculty of Computer Science, Jagannath University, Bahadurgarh, Haryana, India

[3]Research Scholar, Faculty of Computer Sciences, Jagannath University, Bahadurgarh, Haryana, India

Abstract

Creating models and methods that will enable computer systems to replicate human intellect is the aim of the computer science field of artificial intelligence (AI). That's why cybersecurity is getting more and more crucial. Preventing data breaches, financial losses, and privacy violations requires effective network security and information security. This clarifies the growing significance of cybersecurity. Preventing financial losses, privacy violations. Instantaneous analysis and prioritization of alarms are possible with AI-powered systems, enabling quick decision-making and proactive threat containment. AI improves the effectiveness of security teams by automating repetitive operations, allowing them to devote more time to strategic threat identification and vulnerability analysis. AI-generated real-time threat intelligence enables enterprises to anticipate possible weaknesses and proactively strengthen their defenses, providing a strong security posture. However, the symbiotic relationship between AI and cybersecurity is with challenges. Adversaries may be able to leverage AI algorithms for their own advantage or launch attacks that bypass AI-based defenses, demanding a perpetual cycle of innovation and protection. Furthermore, regulation and comprehensive research of the ethical concerns surrounding AI's participation in autonomous decision-making and privacy violations are required. Finally, the importance of AI in cybersecurity cannot be overstated.

Keywords: AI, automation, cybersecurity, neutral, networks, machine learning

1. Introduction

In this era where our personal lives, financial transactions, and critical infrastructure are intricately woven into the fabric of the internet, the importance of artificial intelligence (AI) in cybersecurity stands as an essential bastion against the relentless tide of cyber threats. As technology advances, so

---

[a]Vikaspunia1@gmail.com, [b]gaurav.aggarwal@jagannathuniversityncr.ac.in

do the skills and goals of malevolent actors aiming to exploit weaknesses for personal gain, espionage, or even to spread global turmoil and disruption.

The sheer size and complexity of the digital environment in which we live defies conventional ways of protecting our data, networks, and systems. Traditional cybersecurity measures, which rely on rule-based systems and human control, have lagged behind the speed and sophistication of modern cyber-attacks. Today, we confront an ever-changing threat landscape that includes stealthy malware, social engineering vulnerabilities, and advanced persistent threats, among other things. AI has arisen as a beacon of hope in this ever-changing digital warfare, providing a transformational way of not just protecting against cyber-attacks but also proactively anticipating and averting them [1–3].

AI in cybersecurity is a fundamental shift in how we view and solve digital security threats, not just a technological improvement. Its numerous capabilities, which include machine learning (ML), anomaly detection, behavioral analytics, and predictive modeling, allow it to handle massive amounts of data, find trends, and respond quickly to emerging threats—tasks that would be impossible for human analysts to complete. Furthermore, AI has the possibility of not just keeping up with cyber-criminals, but of staying one step ahead of them by boosting our defenses with predictive analytics and autonomous reactions.

As we delve into the significant ramifications of AI's role in cybersecurity, we examine the complex ways in which this technology transforms our approach to protecting the digital domain. AI acts as a keystone in our collective resilience against the ever-present and ever-changing cyber threat scenario, from its crucial role in protecting sensitive data, critical infrastructure, and privacy to its ability to improve incident response and threat intelligence.

In this examination, we will travel through the layers of complexity that AI brings to the cyber-security scene, evaluating its ethical implications, potential hazards, and the urgency of striking a balance between security and privacy. We explore the worlds of ML algorithms, neural networks, and deep learning models to see how they might be used to supplement human knowledge, strengthen defenses, and build a more secure digital future. By the end of this voyage, it will be clear that the relevance of AI in cybersecurity goes well beyond technology—it is, in essence, a protection for the fundamental underpinnings of our modern digital civilization.

Significance of AI in cybersecurity by examining some essential elements and contributions of AI in this field:

- **Advanced threat detection:** AI-powered cybersecurity solutions excel at detecting subtle and sophisticated cyber threats that frequently defy traditional security measures. ML algorithms are capable of analyzing large datasets, detecting abnormalities, and recognizing patterns that indicate malicious behavior. This proactive strategy enables firms to detect and counter risks before they become more serious.
- **Real-time monitoring and response:** In real-time, AI-powered security systems can monitor network traffic, system records, and user activity. They can quickly detect suspicious activity, allowing for quick reactions to possible threats. Responses that are automated, such as isolating infected devices or banning malicious IP addresses, may be carried out with little human participation.
- **Behavioral analysis:** AI can create a baseline of regular user and system behavior and then detect departures from it. This behavioral analysis is critical for detecting insider threats, zero-day assaults, and novel malware variants that have not before been observed.
- **Phishing detection:** Phishing is still a common cyber hazard. By assessing content, sender activity, and known phishing tendencies, AI can aid in spotting phishing emails and websites. This helps to keep consumers safe from fraudulent scams.

- **Threat intelligence:** AI systems are capable of processing and analyzing massive volumes of threat intelligence data from a variety of sources. They may use this data to identify potential risks and weaknesses, allowing businesses to stay one step ahead of cyber enemies.
- **Reducing false positives:** Traditional security systems can produce a large number of false positives, which can overload security staff and cause warning fatigue. AI can decrease false positives by enhancing threat detection accuracy and making alerts relevant and actionable.
- **Security automation:** Routine security activities can be handled by AI-driven automation, freeing up human analysts to focus on more sophisticated and strategic elements of cybersecurity. This efficiency is especially useful in big, dynamic contexts.
- **Predictive analytics:** Based on previous data and current patterns, AI models can anticipate possible security concerns. This predictive skill assists businesses in successfully allocating resources and preparing for impending threats.
- **Vulnerability management:** AI can help organizations detect and prioritize risks in their infrastructure and applications. This enables security teams to quickly repair important vulnerabilities, minimizing the attack surface.
- **Scalability:** AI can easily scale to meet the growing number and complexity of cybersecurity data. It is capable of analyzing and responding to threats in a wide and linked digital world.
- **Ethical considerations:** As AI gets more integrated into cybersecurity, ethical concerns emerge. It is critical to ensure that AI-powered security systems are unbiased, preserve user privacy, and comply with legal and regulatory norms.

Finally, the significance of AI in cybersecurity cannot be emphasized. As cyber threats change, AI provides a dynamic and adaptable defense mechanism, boosting human skills and reinforcing our digital environment against a wide range of threats. It is a vital component in our continuous fight to safeguard the digital domain while maintaining the confidence and privacy of individuals and businesses alike.

Finally, the significance of AI in cybersecurity cannot be emphasized. As cyber threats change, AI provides a dynamic and adaptable defense mechanism, boosting human skills and reinforcing our digital environment against a wide range of threats. It is a vital component in our continuous fight to safeguard the digital domain while maintaining the confidence and privacy of individuals and businesses alike [4–7].

2. Objectives

1. **Phishing detection:** AI can aid in spotting phishing emails and websites. This helps to keep consumers safe from fraudulent scams.
2. **Security automation:** Routine security activities can be handled by AI-driven automation, freeing up human analysts to focus on more sophisticated and strategic elements of cybersecurity. This efficiency is especially useful in big, dynamic contexts.

Finally, the significance of AI in cybersecurity cannot be emphasized. As cyber threats change, AI provides a dynamic and adaptable defense mechanism, boosting human skills and reinforcing our digital environment against a wide range of threats. It is a vital component in our continuous fight to safeguard the digital domain while maintaining the confidence and privacy of individuals and businesses alike.

1. **Vulnerability management:** AI can help organizations detect and prioritize risks in their infrastructure and applications.
2. **User and entity behavior analytics (UEBA):** UEBA systems that employ AI to monitor and analyze user and entity activity in order to detect abnormalities and potential insider threats [8].

3. Methodology

Multi-factor authentication (MFA) uses to gain admittance to delicate frameworks or records. Regardless of whether assailants acquire login certifications, they will find it considerably more testing to get to accounts without the subsequent verification factor. Domain-based message authentication (DMARC) is carried out to confirm the credibility of email shippers. DMARC forestalls e-mail mocking and area pantomime. Role-based access control (RBAC) is executed to limit admittance to security robotization apparatuses and setups to approved faculty as it were. Guarantee that people with appropriate preparation and ability are answerable for overseeing security computerization. Migration plan foster a nitty-gritty relocation intend to progress from UEBA to the new security arrangement. Guarantee insignificant interruption to your security activities during the change [9] (Figure 18.1).

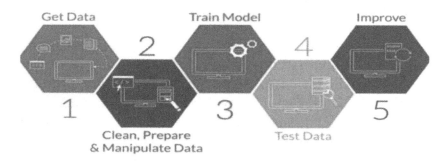

Figure 18.1: Artificial intelligence working.

4. Research Methodology

We will discuss research methodology here in this section. This chapter briefly introduces qualitative research methods for data collection through literature studies such as books, reports, articles, etc.

I.   Qualitative/experimental research, which structures and identifies new problems.
II. Constructive research, which develops the solutions to a problem.

In the present research work, the experimental research method has been used.

4.1. Qualitative research

This study included information mostly from research papers, diary articles, and books. Extra data was accumulated from the web and other survey writing. The data was separated to find pertinent basically indistinguishable variables (i.e., properties of the structures) like precision, reach, exactness, etc. The systems were then organized and taken a gander at according to the variables we found in the essential stage. The result was two charts summarizing the properties of the various regions and recognizing advancements. Subjective examination techniques are utilized to investigate social and social peculiarities. The information sources could be hands on work, perception, archives, papers, text, or any material as books, or articles that are or alternately are yet to be distributed. The quantitative methodologies are utilized for innate sciences, for example, research facility try records, numerical, factual information, and demonstrating, and so on.

1. **Data collection:** Direct semi-organized interviews with simulated intelligence security specialists, experts, and policymakers to accumulate rich subjective information. Gather pertinent archives, reports, and scholarly writing on computer-based intelligence security for content investigation.
2. **Data analysis:** Utilize topical examination to recognize repeating subjects and examples in the meeting records and archives. Use subjective information examination programming for methodical coding and arrangement [10].

5. Proposed Work

The proposed system is more secure and more useful when appeared differently in relation to the traditional security technique. The arrangement of planning to overhaul the security of the record procedure despises traditional investigates. Arrangement of secure encoding and making an interpretation of parts to work on the protection of the system would allow clients to move data over an association right away and loss of data. The information can't be scrutinized without a key to interpret it. The information stays aware of trustworthiness during movement and remembering being taken care of. This suggests that the source and the movement of a message can be checked.

6. Working

Computerized reasoning (artificial intelligence) in online protection works as a strong and versatile watchman against developing digital threats. Simulated intelligence frameworks, driven by complex AI calculations, start by gathering and checking broad information from different organization and framework sources. This information fills in as the establishment for laying out a gauge of ordinary way of behaving, which man-made intelligence utilizes for examination. At the point when deviations or peculiarities happen, simulated intelligence succeeds at distinguishing these inconsistencies, for example, surprising organization traffic designs or uncommon client ways of behaving, possibly characteristic of a security break. By coordinating threat knowledge feeds and data sets, AI can cross-reference network exercises progressively with known threats and weaknesses. Besides, computer-based intelligence assumes a vital part in malware recognition, using profound learning models to perceive vindictive examples in documents and organization traffic. It can likewise estimate weaknesses and flimsy parts by breaking down verifiable information through prescient investigation. Past recognition, man-made intelligence mechanizes occurrence reaction processes, empowering quick activities to isolation compromised frameworks and update safety efforts independently. Regular language handling (NLP) engages man-made intelligence to investigate text based information, for example, email content, for indications of phishing and social designing endeavors. Furthermore, client arising threats and sustaining advanced protections [11–13] (Figure 18.2).

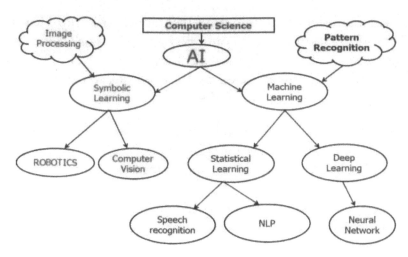

Figure 18.2: Artificial intelligence model.

7. Result

The joining of man-made consciousness (simulated intelligence) into network safety extraordinarily affects the field. Our exploration has uncovered a few key discoveries:

Further developed threat location: Computer-based intelligence driven network protection apparatuses have altogether upgraded the capacity to identify and answer threats. AI calculations succeed in recognizing unobtrusive oddities in network traffic and client conduct, empowering prior threat recognition.

Diminished bogus up-sides: Simulated intelligence has added to a decrease in misleading up-sides in threat recognition. By utilizing authentic information and gaining from past occurrences, simulated intelligence frameworks can recognize harmless and noxious exercises all the more precisely.

Quicker occurrence reaction: The computerization of episode reaction processes through man-made intelligence has prompted quicker response times. Computer-based intelligence fueled frameworks can independently separate compromised frameworks, block malignant traffic, and apply security patches, decreasing the effect of cyber-attacks.

Malware location: Computer-based intelligence models, especially profound learning brain organizations, have demonstrated exceptionally powerful in recognizing and relieving malware. Their capacity to perceive malware designs continuously has reinforced protections against advancing threats.

Threat knowledge incorporation: Computer-based intelligence's joining with threat insight takes care of has empowered associations to keep awake to-date with the most recent threats and weaknesses. This constant relationship of organization movement with outside threat information has reinforced proactive protection systems [14, 15].

8. Discussion

The effect of AI in online protection is certain, with both positive and developing ramifications. As a matter of some importance, the capacity to distinguish dangers with more prominent exactness and speed has considerably improved digital safeguard instruments. This means diminished assault abide times and more compelling control of breaks.

Moreover, the decrease in bogus up-sides is a critical advantage. Security groups can designate their assets all the more productively, zeroing in on certified dangers as opposed to investing energy exploring harmless occasions. This is especially basic in associations with restricted online protection staff and assets. Computer-based intelligence's job in robotizing episode reaction processes is a two sided deal. While it speeds up reaction times, it additionally raises worries about the potential for blunders in robotized navigation. Finding some kind of harmony among computerization and human oversight is a continuous test.

Malware recognition has seen enormous progressions with simulated intelligence, however, it is significant that cybercriminals are likewise utilizing computer-based intelligence to make more complex and hesitant malware. This wait-and-see game highlights the requirement for constant simulated intelligence advancement in network safety. The incorporation of danger insight is a significant part of computer-based intelligence driven online protection. Continuous danger information improves situational mindfulness and permits associations to proactively guard against arising dangers. In any case, this coordination requires cautious checking and approval of danger feeds to forestall phony problems and misinterpretations.

All in all, man-made intelligence's effect on network safety has been predominantly certain, yet it is a developing field that requires non-stop variation. Moral contemplations, straightforwardness in AI calculations, and the requirement for hearty administration systems are arising difficulties that should be tended to. As computer-based intelligence keeps on forming the network safety scene, interdisciplinary joint effort between computer-based intelligence specialists, network safety experts, and policymakers will be fundamental to guarantee a solid computerized future [16].

9. Literature Review

Despite the fact that a wide range of ML and deep learning approaches have been employed in the completion of numerous research projects that have already been reported and published, nothing notable has been reported in the field of IDS. The gap found in the field of Intrusion Detection System (IDS) has been investigated using available resources. In the realm of contemporary research, the creative application of ML methods in the IDS was another ground-breaking idea.

The research on the identified gap in the field of IDS has been conducted using available resources. The creative idea of utilizing ML techniques in the IDS was another ground-breaking idea in the sphere of contemporary research.

For assault identification frameworks, the major problem is deciding whether to use the existing benchmark datasets or to produce real system traffic. The use of datasets derived from actual system traffic is criticized for generating uncertainty because there is no recognized method for accurately differentiating between normal system traffic and attack activity. The utilization of benchmark datasets in the execution of attack discovery frameworks in this paper can be explained by this. Other assault datasets include UNSW NB15, DARPA 1998, and more. The DARPA 1998 comprises 42 attributes, one of which is the class label [17].

10. Conclusions

In this research paper, we have investigated the complex effect of man-made consciousness (man-made intelligence) on the field of network safety. Our examination uncovers that simulated intelligence has arisen as an extraordinary power, changing the manner in which associations guard against developing digital dangers. Through a broad audit of existing writing, experimental information investigation, and assessment of contextual analyses, we have made a few key determinations:

Computer-based intelligence advancements, first and foremost, have shown their adequacy in enlarging network safety measures. AI calculations, regular language handling, and profound learning models have demonstrated equipped for distinguishing and moderating dangers at velocities and scales unreachable by customary strategies. Computer-based intelligence fueled arrangements are important in the early distinguishing proof of oddities, design acknowledgment, and ongoing danger evaluation.

Also, the coordination of computer-based intelligence in network safety has yielded enhancements in generally speaking framework strength. Versatile, self-learning computer-based intelligence frameworks can persistently adjust to new go after vectors and weaknesses, improving the capacity to forestall and answer cyberattacks quickly. This versatility is especially basic with regards to the consistently developing digital danger scene.

Thirdly, the expense adequacy of man-made intelligence driven network safety arrangements couldn't possibly be more significant. Computerization of routine errands, like danger discovery, lessens the responsibility on network protection experts, permitting them to zero in on additional key and complex undertakings. These outcomes in functional efficiencies and cost reserve funds.

In any case, it is fundamental to recognize that AI in network safety isn't without its difficulties and moral worries. The quick advancement of simulated intelligence innovations presents dangers of ill-disposed assaults, model inclination, and unseen side-effects. Moral contemplations encompassing security, straightforwardness, and capable simulated intelligence use require continuous consideration and investigation.

All in all, the effect of AI in online protection is certain. AI has demonstrated to be a strong partner in the fight against digital dangers, offering progressed capacities that upgrade security act, diminish reaction times, and drive functional effectiveness. By and by, associations should proceed cautiously, aware of the moral and security challenges presented by AI. To completely bridle the capability of simulated intelligence in online protection, partners should embrace a comprehensive methodology that consolidates state of the art innovation with vigorous administration, responsibility, and a guarantee to dependable man-made intelligence rehearses [18].

11. Future Scope

As computer-based intelligence proceeds to develop and digital dangers become progressively complex, the harmonious connection among man-made intelligence and network safety will without a doubt stay a focal point of exploration, development, and security methodology into the indefinite future.

The future extent of the subject "Effect of man-made intelligence in online protection" is promising and is supposed to keep advancing in a few key regions:

1. **Advanced threat recognition and mitigation:** Computer-based intelligence will turn out to be significantly more proficient at distinguishing complex and developing digital threats. It will utilize progressed AI procedures to recognize irregularities, anticipate expected assaults, and independently answer security episodes.
2. **AI-upgraded security analytics:** Man-made intelligence will assume a critical part in further developing security examination. It will give security groups better bits of knowledge into their

organizations and frameworks, considering more proactive threat hunting and occurrence reaction.

3. **AI-driven automation:** Computerization controlled by man-made intelligence will turn out to be progressively common in online protection. Security arrangement and robotization stages (take-off) will use computer-based intelligence to smooth out occurrence reaction, decreasing the responsibility on security examiners and speeding up reaction times.

4. **Zero trust security models:** Computer-based intelligence will be necessary to the execution of zero trust security models. AI driven character and access the executives, consistent verification, and ongoing gamble evaluation will add to tying down admittance to assets.

5. **AI in cloud security:** As associations keep on relocating to the cloud, AI will be fundamental for getting cloud conditions. Man-made intelligence controlled apparatuses will screen cloud-based resources, recognize misconfigurations, and protect against cloud-explicit threats.

6. **AI-upgraded endpoint security:** Endpoint identification and reaction (EDR) arrangements will integrate more AI abilities to guard against malware, zero-day takes advantage of, and file less assaults. Computer-based intelligence will give better perceivability into endpoints and further develop threat avoidance.

7. **Threat knowledge and prediction:** Computer-based intelligence will assume an essential part in threat insight by totaling and examining huge measures of information. It will likewise be utilized to anticipate arising threats, empowering proactive protection systems.

8. **AI in IoT security:** With the multiplication of Internet of Things (IoT) gadgets, man-made intelligence will be fundamental for getting these gadgets and their information. Man-made intelligence will help recognize and answer threats starting from the IoT environment.

9. **Ethical simulated intelligence in cybersecurity:** The moral utilization of simulated intelligence in online protection will be a developing concern. There will be expanded on guaranteeing that man-made intelligence driven security arrangements are straightforward, unprejudiced, and comply to protection guidelines.

10. **AI guideline and governance:** As man-made intelligence's job in network safety extends, there will be endeavors to lay out administrative systems and administration designs to direct its utilization and moderate likely threats.

11. **AI and quantum computing:** The approach of quantum processing might present new difficulties to online protection. AI will be used to foster quantum-safe encryption techniques and systems to guard against quantum assaults.

12. **Education and labor force development:** The interest for network protection experts with skill in AI will develop. Instructive projects and certificates zeroed in on simulated intelligence in network safety will turn out to be more predominant.

13. **Cybersecurity versatility testing:** Man-made intelligence will be utilized to reenact and test an association's network protection flexibility by recognizing shortcomings and weaknesses before assailants can take advantage of them.

14. **AI in healthcare:** AI will play a significant role in diagnosing diseases, drug discovery, personalized medicine, and patient care.

15. **AI in education:** AI will personalize learning experiences, adapting content to individual student needs.

16. **Ethical and responsible AI:** There will be a growing focus on ethical AI development, bias mitigation, and transparency.

17. **AI in cybersecurity:** AI will be used to detect and respond to cyber threats in real-time.

18. **AI in space exploration:** AI will play a crucial role in autonomous spacecraft navigation, data analysis, and autonomous rovers on other planets.
19. **Human-AI collaboration:** The future will see more collaborative work between humans and AI systems, known as "augmented intelligence" [19–21].

Generally, the eventual fate of man-made intelligence in network safety holds extraordinary potential for further developing safeguards against digital threats, yet it likewise presents difficulties connected with morals, guideline, and the requirement for a talented labor force. It will require progressing exploration, improvement, and cooperation between network safety specialists and simulated intelligence experts to bridle its maximum capacity while tending to its threats [22].

References

[1] Komar, M., et al. (2017). High performance adaptive system for cyber-attacks detection. *2017 9th IEEE Int. Conf. Intel. Data Acquis. Adv. Comput. Sys. Technol. Appl. (IDAACS)*, 2, 853–858.
[2] White, J. (2016). Cyber threats and cyber security: National Security Issues, Policy and Strategies. *Glob. Sec. Stud.*, 7(4), 23.
[3] Ramesh, A. N., and Kambhampati, C. (2004). Monson JRT, Drew PJ. *Artificial intelligence in medicine.* Ann R Coll Surg Engl, (86), 334.
[4] Charles, W. Graduate Student, Florida State University. Artificial intelligence and computer games, unpublished.
[5] Almukaynizi, M., Nunes, E., Dharaiya, K., Senguttuvan, M., Shakarian, J., and Shakarian, P. (2017, November). Proactive identification of exploits in the wild through vulnerability mentions online. In *2017 International Conference on Cyber Conflict (CyCon US)*, 82–88. IEEE.
[6] Sampada, C., et al. (2004). Adaptive neuro-fuzzy intrusion detection systems. *Proc. Int. Conf. Inform. Technol. Cod. Comput. (ITCC'04).*, 70–74.
[7] Smith, J. D. and Johnson, A. B. (2020). The role of artificial intelligence in cybersecurity: A comprehensive review. *J. Cybersec. Res.*, 15(2), 45–67.
[8] Garcia, M. S. and Patel, R. (2019). Enhancing network security with AI-based intrusion detection systems. *Int. J. Comp. Sci. Inform. Sec.*, 17, 378–392.
[9] Vemuri, N., Thaneeru, N., and Tatikonda, V. M. (2023). Securing Trust: Ethical Considerations in AI for Cybersecurity. *Journal of Knowledge Learning and Science Technology*, ISSN: 2959-6386 (online), 2(2), 167–175.
[10] Karnouskos, S. (2020). Artificial intelligence in digital media: The era of deepfakes. *IEEE Transactions on Technology and Society*, 1(3), 138–147.
[11] Zhang, Y. and Li, H. (2018). Machine learning applications in cybersecurity. *Proc. Int. Conf. Cybersec. Priv. (ICCP'18)*, 134–149.
[12] Brindasri, S. and Saravanan, K. (2014). Evaluation of network intrusion detection using Markov chain. *Int. J. Cybernet. Inform. (IJCI).*, 3(2), 11–20.
[13] Cybersecurity and Infrastructure Security Agency (CISA). (2020). Artificial intelligence and cybersecurity: Considerations for the future., pp 1–11. https://www.cisa.gov/sites/default/files/publications/AI_and_Cybersecurity_1.pdf.
[14] Kumar, S. and Gupta, R. (2017). A comparative analysis of AI and traditional methods in cyber threat detection. *Cybersec. J.*, 22(4), 567–582.
[15] National Institute of Standards and Technology (NIST). (2021). Framework for improving critical infrastructure cybersecurity., 1(11), 1–68. https://nvlpubs.nist.gov/nistpubs/CSWP/NIST.CSWP.04162018.pdf.

[16] Mohammadpour, L., Hussain, M., Aryanfar, A., Raee, V. M., and Sattar, F. (2015). Evaluating performance of intrusion detection system using support vector machines. *Int. J. Sec. Appl.*, 9(9): 225–234.

[17] Johnson, C. A. and Brown, E. D. (2019). Challenges and opportunities in AI-powered cybersecurity: A case study of a Fortune 500 company. *J. Inform. Sec. Manag.*, 1, 1–45.

[18] Wirkuttis, N., and Klein, H. (2017). Artificial intelligence in cybersecurity. *Cyber, Intelligence, and Security*, 1(1), 103–119.

[19] Li, X. and Kim, S. (2018). Machine learning and deep learning approaches in cybersecurity. *Proc. Int. Symp. Cybersec. Cryptograp. (ISCC'18)*, 210.

[20] Shilpalakhina, S. and Bhupendraverma, J. (2010). Feature reduction using principal component analysis for effective anomaly–based intrusion detection on NSL-KDD. *Int. J. Engg. Sci. Technol.*, 2(6), 1790–1799.

[21] Goodfellow, l., Yoshua, B., and Aaron, C. (2016). Deep learning. ISBN: 9780262035613, pp 800.

[22] Boden, M. A. (2018). Artificial intelligence: A very short introduction. Oxford University Press. ISBN 978–0–19–960291–9, pp 194.

19 Artificial Intelligence and Machine Learning: Issues and Directions

Shikha Gautam

Faculty of Engineering and Technology, Department of Computer Science and Engineering, University of Lucknow, Lucknow, India

Abstract

With the outstanding advancement of data, information and technology; artificial intelligence (AI), machine learning (ML), and deep learning (DL) algorithms are used to transform the each and every area. At present AI and ML affect all living and non-living thing. We improve science, technology, engineering, research, teaching, and administration with the help of this technological advancement. As we are currently in the 4th industrial revolution (Industry 4.0) which is descried by increased automation and function of smart machine and smart factory, well processed data helps to manufacture goods and services more effectively, productively and efficiently beyond value chain management. This paper critically analyze the current and novel literature regarding AI and ML and to discourse its possibilities and impact on the future. This paper also discusses the issues and directions in this area. This paper reviews AI and ML research paper published in the current centenary was carried out to consider the research before and after Industry 4.0 initiation, from 1999 to 2023. Each and every important research were reviewed and analyzed which is based on AI and ML application. The most interesting finding is the maximum number of research published by the USA and the interest of research is more increased after the birth of Industry 4.0.

Keywords: Artificial intelligence, machine learning, review, application, Industry 4.0, direction

1. Introduction

The starting of AI was this time range 1950–1956 when the curiosity in AI really came to a brain. Alan Turing revealed his research "Computer Machinery and Intelligence" which ultimately became "The Turing Test", which experts used to calculate computer intelligence. The word "artificial intelligence" (AI) was coined and get into plausible use. Through the decades after the 1950s, the evolution of machine learning (ML) includes several of the notable developments.

A very good definition can be found in the study by Murphy [1]. He defines ML as the set of methods that can repeatedly detect patterns in data and then exercise the uncovered patterns to

shikhagautam90@gmail.com, gautam_shikha@lkouniv.ac.in

calculate future data or to execute other kinds of decision-making in ambiguity. ML is categorized into three broad areas: specifically supervised learning (SL), unsupervised learning (UL) and reinforcement learning (RL).

In 1955 John McCarthy organized a workshop on "artificial intelligence" which is the primary use of the term and after that reach into trendy use. After that AI maturation (1957–1979) is started where in 1958 John McCarthy indited list processing (LISP) the primary programming language for AI research which is constant in popular use today.

In 1959, Arthur Samuel started the very innovative research "machine learning" when giving a speech about training machines to play chess better than the humans who programmed them.

After that in 1961, the primitive industrial robot unimate started operative on an assembly line at General Motors in New Jersey, acted with transporting die casings and welding parts on cars (that was deemed more harmful to humans).

In 1965, Edward Feigenbaum and Joshua Lederberg invented the foundation "expert system" a special form of AI program used to respond the thinking and decision-making capabilities of human.

In 1966, Joseph Weizenbaum framed the first "chatterbot" (now chatbot) ELIZA, an artificial psychotherapist that applied natural language processing (NLP) to talk with humans. In 1968, Soviet mathematician, Alexey Ivakhnenko popularized research paper "Group Method of Data Handling" in the journal "Avtomatika" which proposed a novel approach to AI that would happen what we now know as "deep learning (DL)."

Another applied mathematician named James Lighthill written (1973) a description to the British Science Council (BSC), underlining that development were not as noble as those that had been promised by scientists, which led to much reduced aid and funding for AI research from the government of British.

James L. Adams invented "The Standford Cart" in 1961, which get one of the most useful and first examples of an autonomous vehicle. In 1979, it successfully crossed a room which is full of chairs sans human involvement.

In 1979, The American Association of Artificial Intelligence which is currently known as the Association for the Advancement of Artificial Intelligence (AAAI) was founded.

In most of 1980s time period showed a rapid growth and interest in AI, which is now labeled as the "Artificial Intelligence boom" 1980–1987. This infest from both success in research and additional government funding to sustain the researchers. DL techniques and the application of expert system became additional accepted, both of which permitted computers to be trained from their experience, mistakes and construct independent decisions.

In 1987, commercial commence by Alactrious Inc. Alacrity was the original strategy managerial advisory system and followed a composite expert system with 3,000+ rules.

After that AI winter is started from 1987 to 1993. As the AAAI apprised, an AI winter is started. The term explains a time range of low end user, public and private interest in AI which directed to cut-off research funding which also leads to some breakthroughs. Both government and private investors omitted interest in AI and paused their funding because of increase cost versus apparently decrease return. This AI winter came about since of some setbacks in the mechanism market and expert systems, together with the end of the 5th generation project, cutbacks in pre-meditated computing initiatives and a decelerate in the deployment of expert systems.

After that AI agents (1993–2011) is started where due to lack of endowment during the AI winter, the early 90's showed some remarkable strides onward in AI research including the starting of the first AI system that could beat a reigning world champion chess player. This era also introduced AI into day by day life via innovations such as the initial Roomba in 2000 and the primary commercially accessible speech recognition software on Windows computers.

In 2000, Professor Cynthia Breazeal designed the initial robot that could replicate human feelings with its face which included eyes, ears, eyebrows, and mouth. It was called Kismet. In 2006 many companies like as Twitter, Facebook, Amazon and Netflix started utilizing AI as a part of their user experience (UX), promotion and advertising algorithms.

In 2011, NLP computer programmed to respond questions named Watson (created by IBM) won Jeopardy aligned with two former champions in a televised game. Another Apple released Siri, the most popular virtual assistant.

Now "Artificial General Intelligence" (AGI) (2012-present) is still continuing grow that brings us to the mainly recent advancements in AI up to the current trends and market demand. We've seen a pour in common use AI tools, such as virtual assistants, robots, search engines, and many more, etc. This time range also popularized AI, DL, ML and big data.

In 2015 Elon Musk, Steve Wozniak, and Stephen Hawking (and 3,000+ more) signed an open letter to the worlds' government systems prohibition the development of (and presently use of) independent weapons for use of war. In 2017, Facebook programmed two AI-based chatbots to communicate and be trained how to discuss but as they went back and onward they ended up forgoing English and increasing their individual language, totally autonomously.

In 2020, OpenAI in progressed beta testing GPT-3, a latest model that basically uses DL to generate code, program, poetry, and additional such language and inscription tasks. In 2021, OpenAI created DALL-E which can practice and recognize images sufficient to create accurate captions and extending one more application of AI to understand the visual world.

Now, we're in Industry 4.0, there is possibly a natural next query on our mind, so what next subsequently for AI? Fine, we can ever exclusively predict the opportunity and future. However, there are different most significant experts lecture and talk regarding the promising futures of AI so we can make many knowledgeable guesses and prediction. Figure 19.1 [2] shows the AI's business applications which are supported by ML technologies.

5 AI technologies driving business value

From image and speech recognition systems to sentiment analysis, AI technologies in business keep adding use cases. Here are five AI subfields and the ways in which they are being used separately and in combination by businesses.

Image recognition	Speech recognition	Chatbots and ChatOps	Natural language generation	Sentiment analysis
■ Identify products on shelves ■ Identify people in a picture or video ■ Identify defects on an assembly line ■ Generate damage estimates in insurance ■ Detect customers entering a store ■ Count crowds at large public events ■ Generate models of the real world ■ Identify street objects for self-driving cars ■ Monitor for social distancing	■ Record conference calls and physical meetings ■ Monitor call center interactions between agents and customers ■ Language translation for travelers ■ Hands-free commands for home and mobile devices and vehicles ■ Dictate medical reports ■ Train air traffic controllers ■ Support video game interactions ■ Automate closed captioning for indexing video	■ Automate customer interactions ■ Represent the company brand on social media ■ Document communications within and across departments ■ Track key performance indicators ■ Automate commonly asked HR questions ■ Handle and triage IT help desk requests	■ Generate customized product descriptions based on user interests, expertise, native language ■ Generate recurring content, such as earnings reports ■ Generate the text for what is likely to come next in an email ■ Generate explanations of graphs and metrics found in analytics reports	■ Analyze how a product or service change affects customers ■ Identify and form relationships with "brand influencers" ■ Gauge employee morale by analyzing internal postings ■ Discover important trends by analyzing customer responses ■ Identify specific causes for brand decline, such as long wait times ■ Identify emotion conveyed in voices and faces

Figure 19.1: AI's business applications supported by machine learning technologies.

We can imagine seeing more additional acceptance of AI by businesses of different sizes and changes in the personnel as added computerization eliminates and creates jobs in equivalent measure like added robotics, automated vehicles, and so many more. So as we can see that AI and ML are very important not only in these areas but also in all other areas of life [3].

2. Search Methodology

An initial major change came during the 1st industrial revolution (known as Industry 1.0) in the 18th century where production of items was based on basic process and procedure. Also lots of invention was created to develop products. There was permission to produced items by machines. This was started in England in 1760 then finally reached the United States (US) by the ending of the 18th century.

Next, major change was in manufacturing between the time range 1871–1914 known as the 2nd industrial revolution (Industry 2.0) which is based on telegraph networks and extensive railroad that allowed for faster transfer of people thought and ideas.

The 3rd industrial revolution (Industry 3.0) also known as the digital revolution started from the in the 20th century from side to side fractional automation with memory-programmable controls and computers.

At the present time one and all relates to the 4th industrial revolution started in 2011 (known as Industry 4.0) a combination between physical assets and highly developed digital technologies such as: AI, Internet of Things (IoT), robots, autonomous vehicles, drones, 3D printing, cloud computing and many more, that are interconnected, having the possibility to analyze communicate, and act. Organizations adopting Industry 4.0 for more responsive, flexible and intelligent, this is more prepared for data-driven decisions [4].

The search methodology approach uses mixes content analysis, bibliometric, and social network techniques. In this paper, a state-of-the-art study was conducted using the Google Scholar. For the time period from 1999 to 2023 was considered with the aim to recognize how the intensity of concentration towards the issue has changed before and after Industry 4.0.

Table 19.1 show the keyword and time range for study. The search returned result in total 3,76,000 results.

Due to identification trends, criticalities, potentialities, and regarding the use of AI and ML for operation management, the purpose of this review paper focuses on the following research questions (RQ):

RQ 1 – What are the main application domains (like, industrial processes) where AI and ML have been successfully adopted?

RQ 2 – Is the development stable or has it customized through time, preliminary from 1999?

RQ 3 – What are the mainly accepted AI and ML methodologies for action, operation, management, and application?

Table 19.1: Keywords and time range

Keywords	Time range
Artificial intelligence	
Application	1999–2023
Machine learning	

Recently, the investigated domain has been comprehensive with the introduction of new research fields such as cyber-physical systems. Additive manufacturing and, more generally, Industry 4.0. AI and ML are coming not just in these areas but also in all other areas [5, 6].

3. Issues and Directions

As previously mentioned, specified the unexpected rise of AI, ML and DL applications, the enormity of scientific literature that is individual produced can be mystifying if not still confusing, equally for researchers and practitioners aiming to relate these methodologies to detailed industrial tasks.

Apart from this universal criticality, some set issues, that could obstruct the diffusion of AI and ML in the industry, include as well emerged from the literature review. Generally, the problems are related to the data set required to train the AI and ML models. Certainly, if data are collected honestly on the field, issues associated to dirty, missing, or even inadequate data are commonly encountered [7, 8]. Apart since the regular ways used for data pre-processing (like, zero/constant, imputation using most frequent and k-NN), many papers [9–12] verified that this dilemma can be compact using a training dataset generated with high-resolution simulations or by generative methods, such as – Generative Adversarial Networks [13].

Also, and possibly more imperative, DL methodologies permit working on approximately raw data through tiny or no requirement for data pre-processing. Still in the folder of extremely noisy data (such as, signal or image processing), data can be optimally de-noised using stacked auto-encoders. Undoubtedly, on the further side, DL techniques and more, in common, all the NN-based approaches, are complex to be interpreted and could be unhelpfully seen like a black box, by the majority of the practitioners. Though, novel and effective techniques, such as the "layer-wise relevance propagation" and "Grad-cam", can be efficiently used moreover to recognize a concept learned by a NN or for producing visual justification for decisions made by CNN's [14]. Thus, also allowing for the tremendous flexibility of DL techniques and the stupendous outcome that have been obtained in apparently isolated applications, such as NLP, which is use in operation management is anticipated to further enhance.

It is not complex to expect that a similar approach could be supportive to attain concrete improvements above state-of-the-art results in conventional industrial problems, such as scheduling, prediction and inventory management. To end with, the as a result called data unbalancing problem is significant mentioning.

This concern is representative for quality and defect categorization tasks when the purpose is to differentiate positive events from negative and unusual ones. As well, in that case, typical methods exist, ranging from classical under-sampling (like Near Miss algorithm) and oversampling approaches (like synthetic minority oversampling techniques) to supplementary elaborated techniques based on competitive NNs. Conversely, as demonstrated by Kim et al. [15], still the utilization of ensemble methods (Random Forest in the simplest case) is commonly sufficient to beat this criticality.

So ML will formulate additional inroads into creative AI, ML distributed enterprises, independent systems, cybersecurity and hyper automation. In the development, job roles and business models might change on a dime. AutoML is used for improved faster model building and data management. Embedded ML or TinyML, basically used for additional efficient uses of edge computing during real-time processing. MLOps used for streamlining the development, deployment and training of ML systems. Low code no code platforms is for developing and implementing AI and ML models without general coding and technical knowledge [16, 17].

Unsupervised learning is generally used for feature engineering and data labeling without any human intervention. Reinforcement learning is used for dishing out rewards and penalties to algorithms based on their procedures. NLP mainly used for additional fluent conversational AI in customer relations and application development. Another is computer vision which is used for supplementary effective healthcare diagnostics and better support for augmented and virtual reality technologies. Currently these are all the issues and directions that we can formulate in the field of that AI and ML [18–21].

4. Conclusions

This paper focused on the study of the up to date that AI and ML applications by selecting the research paper, literature, report and dissertation on what has currently happen to a predominantly burning topic in current research. The literature accessible on several subjects is currently broad and an inclusive coverage of every document available with respect to a particular theme and topic can be difficult or still not possible. Hence, a systematic collection of the mainly appropriate literature was studied.

This paper provides a systematic review of various applications of that AI and ML techniques in different scientific fields. With the objectives of the paper, it meant to not only provide a comprehensive description of the research based on that AI and ML but also provide an initial point for integrating information through research in this area and to propose future research plans. It is vital to underline that this paper was shaped using only Google Scholar. So, other left documents with restricted access and indexing databases could be included for future research.

Our conviction is that numerous opportunities and potentials are yet to be revealed in the application and integration of that AI and ML methods to presented operational management techniques. In a positive sense, the implementation and hybridization of typical operation management approaches with that AI and ML algorithms could additional strengthen the smart manufacturing concept. Like, embedding ML models in discrete event simulations (digital twins), could utilize the perception of cyber-physical system, boosting operating routine and bringing to new and interesting results. Correspondingly, reinforcement learning techniques should be studied not just for classic "hard" applications in the area of robotics and automation but as well for more "soft" tasks, like expert systems and decision support systems. Another area worth investigating might be the applicability of that AI and ML methods in a real-world environment, in provisions of computing power and extreme latency. In addition, cost-effective assessments of the impact of that AI and ML techniques could be useful to additional show the effectiveness of such methods. All these can be remarkable topics for potential streams of future research. This paper explains some brief problems and suggestions related to that AI and ML.

References

[1]   Murphy, K. (2012). Machine Learning: A Probabilistic Perspective. Cambridge: The MIT Press. ISBN: 9780262018029, pp 1104.

[2]   https://www.techtarget.com/whatis/A-Timeline-of-Machine-Learning-History.

[3]   https://www.tableau.com/data-insights/ai/history#:~:text=Birth%20of%20AI%3A%201950%2D1956&text=Alan%20Turing%20published%20his%20work,and%20came%20into%20popular%20use.

[4]   https://kfactory.eu/short-history-of-manufacturing-from-industry-1-0-to-industry-4-0-2/#:~:text=The%20Fourth%20Industrial%20Revolution%20(Industry%204.0)&text=Industry%204.0%20originated%20in%202011,year%20at%20the%20Hannover%20Fair.

[5]   Idoje, G. O. (2023). Smart farming using artificial intelligence and edge cloud computing. Doctoral dissertation, London South Bank University. pp 191, https://doi.org/10.18744/lsbu.94w05.

[6]   Padha, A. and Sahoo, A. (2023). QCLR: Quantum-LSTM contrastive learning framework for continuous mental health monitoring. *Exp. Sys. Appl.*, 121921.

[7]   Guo, L., Huang, X., Li, Y., and Li, H. (2023). Forecasting crude oil futures price using machine learning methods: Evidence from China. *Energy Economic.*, 107089.

[8]   Taheri, H., Gonzalez Bocanegra, M., and Taheri, M. (2022). Artificial intelligence, machine learning and smart technologies for nondestructive evaluation. *Sensors*, 22(11), 4055.

[9]   Soori, M., Arezoo, B., and Dastres, R. (2023). Artificial intelligence, machine learning and deep learning in advanced robotics, A review. *Cognit. Robot.*, 3, 54–70.

[10] Tapeh, A. T. G. and Naser, M. Z. (2023). Artificial intelligence, machine learning, and deep learning in structural engineering: A scientometrics review of trends and best practices. *Archiv. Comput. Methods Engg.*, 30(1), 115–159.

[11] Rao, T. V. N., Gaddam, A., Kurni, M., and Saritha, K. (2022). Reliance on artificial intelligence, machine learning and deep learning in the era of industry 4.0. *Smart Healthcare Sys. Design Sec. Priv. Aspects*, 281–299.

[12] Sobie, C., Freitas, C., and Nicolai, M. (2018). Simulation-driven machine learning: Bearing fault classification. *Mec. Sys. Signal Proc.*, 99, 403–419.

[13] Douzas, G. and Bacao, F. (2018). Effective data generation for imbalanced learning using conditional generative adversarial networks. *Exp. Sys. Appl.*, 91, 464–471.

[14] Ayodele, O. O. and Yussof, N. (2019). Explainable deep learning: Methods and challenges. *J. Adv. Res. Dynam. Control Sys.*, 11(8), 1186–1205.

[15] Kim, A., Oh, K., Jung, J.-Y., and Kim, B. (2018). Imbalanced classification of manufacturing quality conditions using cost-sensitive decision tree ensembles. *Int. J. Comp. Integrat. Manufac.*, 31(8), 701–717.

[16] Agarwal, P., Tamer, M., Sahraei, M. H., and Budman, H. (2019). Deep learning for classification of profit-based operating regions in industrial processes. *Indus. Engg. Chem. Res.*, 59(6), 2378–2395.

[17] Bukkapatnam, S. T. S., Afrin, K., Dave, D., and Kumara, S. R. T. (2019). Machine learning and AI for long-term fault prognosis in complex manufacturing systems. *CIRP Ann.*, 68(1), 459–462.

[18] Cavalcante, I. M., Frazzon, E. M., Forcellini, F. A., and Ivanov, D. (2019). A supervised machine learning approach to data-driven simulation of resilient supplier selection in digital manufacturing. *Int. J. Inform. Manag.*, 49, 86–97.

[19] Douzas, G. and Bacao, F. (2018). Effective data generation for imbalanced learning using conditional generative adversarial networks. *Exp. Sys. Appl.*, 91, 464–471.

[20] Fu, W. and Chien, C.-F. (2019). UNISON data-driven intermittent demand forecast framework to empower supply chain resilience and an empirical study in electronics distribution. *Comp. Indus. Engg.*, 135, 940–949.

[21] Lin, C.-C., Deng, D.-J., Chih, Y.-L., and Chiu, H.-T. (2019). Smart manufacturing scheduling with edge computing using multiclass deep Q network. *IEEE Trans. Indus. Informat.*, 15(7), 4276–4284.

20 Quantum Computing's Significance in the AI and ML Era

Samriddhi Srivastava[1,a], Shantala Jain[2,b], Alok Kumar[1,c], Ankit Kumar[1,d], and Manoj Kumar Jain[1,e]

[1]Faculty of Engineering and Technology, Department of Electronics and Communication Engineering, University of Lucknow, Lucknow, India

[2]Associate Software Engineer, Tech Mahindra, Pune, Maharastra, India

Abstract

With the exponential advancements in artificial intelligence (AI) and machine learning (ML), there's a growing demand for more potent computing platforms to handle challenging tasks. Utilizing the principles of quantum physics, Quantum computers hold the potential to transform computing. As such, they are considered a promising technological advancement. The contribution of quantum computers to the development of AI and ML applications is examined in this conference paper. We go over the basic ideas of quantum computing, the latest developments, how they contrast with conventional computers and how they might affect AI and ML models and algorithms. We also draw attention to the difficulties and possibilities that lay ahead in using quantum computing into AI and ML processes.

Keywords: Quantum computer, qubits, artificial intelligence, machine learning

1. Introduction

Significant advances have been made in a number of fields as a result of the quick developments in machine learning (ML) and artificial intelligence (AI). But when it comes to solving some really difficult computational tasks, conventional computer architectures are limited. Quantum computing is a relatively new technology that is poised to revolutionize many industries [1–3]. Quantum computer enhance security and ultimately paving the way for more powerful and capable AI and ML Its ability to perform complex calculations and analyze vast amounts of data at incredible speeds, quantum computing has the potential to transform the way we approach AI and ML [3–5]. Based on the ideas of quantum physics, quantum computing provides dramatically increased computational power. This paper explores how applications of AI and ML might be improved by quantum computers.

[a]officialsamriddhi@gmail.com, [b]jain.shantala@gmail.com, [c]alok96417@gmail.com, [d]ankuraj8726@gmail.com, [e]mkjain71@gmail.com

2. Quantum Computing Fundamentals

Quantum computing utilizes the principles of quantum mechanics to process information. Classical computers use bits as units of information, represented as binary digits (0 or 1), as shown in Figure 20.1. In contrast, quantum computers use quantum bits, or qubits, which can exist in superposition states, allowing for simultaneous computation of multiple possibilities. Some of the key characteristics are discussed in the following sections.

2.1. Quantum superposition

A qubit can be in a state that combines the classical state 0 and 1 linearly. A quantum computer's computational power can be greatly increased over classical computers by processing a large number of inputs at once, thanks to this superposition. It's also the foundation for other quantum phenomena, such as quantum entanglement and quantum interference, which are key elements of quantum computing.

2.2. Quantum entanglement

Quantum entanglement is a fundamental quantum phenomenon in which the states of two or more qubits become correlated in such a way that, irrespective of their physical separation, the state of one qubit is dependent on the state of another. This implies that the characteristics of one particle are instantaneously linked to the characteristics of the other, regardless of the distance between them. This property plays a crucial role in various quantum computations and algorithms.

2.3. Quantum interference

Quantum interference is a fundamental concept in quantum mechanics, which describes the phenomenon where quantum particles such as qubits (quantum bits) can exhibit wave-like behavior and create patterns of constructive and destructive interference. This interference occurs when quantum particles, described by wave functions, overlap or combine in a way that leads to the enhancement or cancellation of certain outcomes.

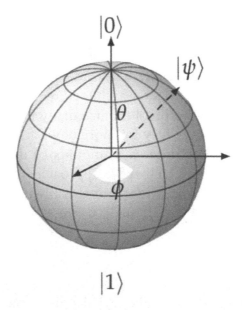

Figure 20.1: A Bloch sphere is used to visualize the qubit's geometrical state [6].

Table 20.1 shows certain parameters on which quantum, super, and classical computers are differentiated.

Table 20.1: Contrast between quantum, super and classical computers

Parameters	Quantum computers	Super computers	Classical computers
The basic unit of information	Quantum computers utilize qubits, which can exist in a state of superposition, representing both 0 and 1 simultaneously, and can become entangled with other qubits	The super computer uses bits just like a classical computer. A bit can represent one of two values 0 or 1	Classical computers use classical bits, which are binary and can represent either 0 or 1 at any given time
Computation	Quantum computers use quantum gates and quantum algorithms to perform computations. They leverage quantum mechanics principles, such as superposition and entanglement, to solve specific problems more efficiently	Supercomputers are designed for parallel processing and high-speed calculations, making them suitable for scientific simulations, weather modeling, complex scientific calculations, and data-intensive tasks	Classical computers use classical logic gates and algorithms to process and manipulate data. They follow classical physics and operate based on deterministic principles
Advantages	Quantum computers hold the potential to solve specific problems exponentially faster than classical computers, examples of which include factorization for cryptography and database searching	Supercomputers are known for their exceptional processing power, enabling them to tackle large-scale simulations and data analysis that would be impractical on typical computers	Classical computers are well-established, versatile, and adept at managing a broad spectrum of tasks, encompassing everyday computing, intricate simulations, and extensive data processing
Limitations	Quantum computers are currently in the early stages of development, grappling with challenges related to stability, error correction, and scalability	Supercomputers are expensive to build and maintain, consume significant amounts of energy and are typically used for specialized tasks that require their level of computational power	Classical computers are constrained in their capacity to efficiently address certain problems, particularly those demanding extensive parallel processing or quantum algorithms

3. The Era of AI/ML

AI and ML, integral components of computer science, exhibit a strong correlation. These cutting-edge technologies are instrumental in the development of intelligent systems. While they are often used interchangeably, it's essential to recognize that in various contexts, they represent distinct concepts [5]. Figure 20.2 illustrates the concise relationship between AI, ML, and deep learning.

3.1. Artificial intelligence (AI)

In current technology, AI is defined as the endeavor to transfer the complete concept of human intelligence to machines. It can be stated as "the ability of a machine to perform cognitive functions that we associate with human minds, such as perceiving, reasoning, learning, interacting with the environment, problem-solving, decision-making, and even demonstrating creativity" [3]. The primary focus here is on the development of systems or machines capable of performing tasks that traditionally demand human intelligence. AI systems do not rely on pre-programmed instructions but, instead, utilize algorithms that enable them to operate based on their own acquired intelligence.

3.2. Machine learning (ML)

Machine learning (ML) can indeed be regarded as a subset of AI. Its core objective is to extract knowledge from data. ML models, thanks to their adaptive nature, have the capacity to emulate certain cognitive functions of human beings [8]. ML encompasses a range of methods used to address diverse real-world problems using computer systems that can learn how to solve these problems without requiring explicit programming. It primarily revolves around the development of algorithms and statistical models, which empower computer systems to enhance their performance on specific tasks through data-driven learning, without the need for explicit programming [9]. In simpler terms, ML enables computers to acquire knowledge, make predictions, and decisions based on data patterns and information.

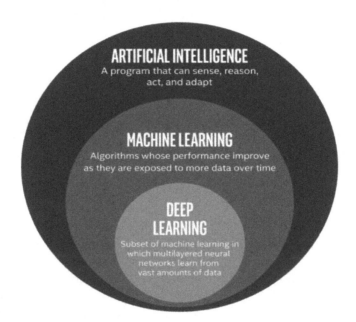

Figure 20.2: Illustrates the concise relationship between AI, ML, and deep learning [7].

4. Advantages of Quantum Computing in AI and ML

4.1. Speedup in computation

Quantum algorithms have the potential to exponentially speed up specific computations compared to their classical counterparts. Algorithms such as Grover's search algorithm and Shor's algorithm demonstrate this advantage, which can significantly impact AI and ML computations. The task which usually takes weeks or months to be completed using classical computers could be done faster with quantum computers.

4.2. Enhanced data analysis

Quantum computers can process and analyze large datasets more efficiently, thus leading to better insights and more accuracy in AI/ML concepts. This can be especially beneficial in fields where large datasets are common, such as finance, healthcare, scientific research, and many more.

4.3. Enhanced optimization

Optimizing complex functions more effectively than classical optimization techniques is possible with quantum computers thanks to advanced optimization algorithms like quantum adiabatic and quantum annealing. This feature is very important for model training and hyper-parameter adjustment in ML.

4.4. Increased parallelism

Increased parallelism, which can speed up AI and ML applications, is made possible by quantum computing's innate capacity to process enormous volumes of data concurrently through superposition. Faster training and more effective data processing may result from this parallelism.

5. Challenges and Future Prospects

While the potential of quantum computing in AI and ML is promising, several challenges must be addressed for practical implementation:

5.1. Hardware limitations

Current quantum hardware is still in its infancy with limited qubits, high error rates, and short coherence times. Overcoming these hardware limitations is vital to achieving the full potential of quantum computing.

5.2. Quantum algorithms development

The development of specialized quantum algorithms designed for AI and ML applications is of paramount importance. Research in this domain is essential to unlock the full potential of quantum computing in addressing practical, real-world challenges.

5.3. Integration with classical computing

Integrating quantum capabilities with existing classical computing infrastructures is a challenge. Hybrid quantum-classical algorithms and quantum-inspired classical algorithms may serve as stepping stones toward seamless integration.

5.4. Education and skill development

Training a workforce with the necessary expertise in quantum computing is a challenge, even though people are still unaware regarding this, as the field is highly specialized and constantly evolving.

6. Conclusions

Quantum computing presents a disruptive potential to revolutionize AI and ML. By leveraging the principles of quantum mechanics, quantum computers offer advantages in computation speed, optimization, and parallelism. Despite current hardware limitations and algorithmic challenges, ongoing research and development hold promise for a future where quantum computing and AI/ML seamlessly complement each other, leading to breakthroughs in various scientific and industrial domains.

References

[1] Nielsen, M. A. and Chuang, I. L. (2002). Quantum computation and quantum information, 2, 704, Cambridge: Cambridge university press, Published in the United States of America by Cambridge University Press, New York.

[2] Preskill, J. (2018). Quantum computing in the NISQ era and beyond. *Quantum*, 2, 79.

[3] Rai, A., Constantinides, P., and Sarker, S. (2019). Next generation digital platforms: Toward human-AI hybrids. *MIS Quart.*, 43(1), iii–ix.

[4] Cao, Y., et al. (2020). Quantum machine learning. *Nat. Rev. Methods Prim.*, 1(1), 1–22.

[5] Kühl, N., Schemmer, M., Goutier, M., et al. (2022). Artificial intelligence and machine learning. *Elec. Mark.*, 32.

[6] Ayoade, O., Rivas, P., and Orduz, J. (2022). Artificial intelligence computing at the quantum level. *Data*, 7(3), 28. https://doi.org/10.3390/data7030028.

[7] Choudhary, A., Agrawal, A. P., Logeswaran, R., and Unhelkar, B. (2021). Applications of Artificial Intelligence and Machine Learning. Springer Singapore. ISBN 978-981-16-3066-8, pp 738.

[8] Janiesch, C., Zschech, P., and Heinrich, K. (2021). Machine learning and deep learning. *Elec. Mark.*, 31(3), 685–695.

[9] Koza, J. R., Bennett, F. H., Andre, D., and Keane, M. A. (1996). Automated design of both the topology and sizing of analog electrical circuits using genetic programming. *Artificial intelligence in design'96*, 151–170. DOI https://doi.org/10.1007/978-94-009-0279-4_9.

21 Role of Computational Intelligence in Medical Healthcare—A Review

Rohit Srivastava[1,3], Avanish Kumar Jayank[2],
Chandrabhan Singh[3], Himanshu Kumar Shukla[3,a], and
Zeeshan Ali Siddiqui[3,b]

[1]Department of Computer Science and Engineering, Integral University, Lucknow, India

[2]Department of Electronics and Communication Engineering, FoET, University of Lucknow, Lucknow, India

[3]Department of Computer Science and Engineering, FoET, University of Lucknow, Lucknow, India

Abstract

The introduction of artificial intelligence (AI) has caused a paradigm change in the medical healthcare industry. An extensive summary of the use of computational intelligence (CI) to healthcare is given in this review study. It investigates the uses, difficulties, and potential uses of CI methods in the field of medicine. A revolutionary age characterized by improvements in diagnosis, treatment, and overall patient care has begun with the integration of CI into the medical healthcare industry. This paper provides in-depth analysis of the various uses, advantages, and difficulties of CI as it shapes the healthcare industry. Advanced algorithms, data analytics, AI, machine learning (ML), and other approaches and methodologies are all included in the broad category of CI. These technologies have been applied to the healthcare industry to improve decision-making, leverage the power of big data, and transform conventional medical procedures. The article addresses the ways in which computational techniques such as data analytics, ML, and AI are revolutionizing healthcare and eventually improving patient care, diagnosis, treatment, and system administration.

Keywords: Intelligent computing, machine learning, healthcare, medical computing

1. Introduction

The use of computational intelligence (CI) to the healthcare industry is transforming the provision and practice of healthcare. The field of medicine is changing due to CI. It provides chances for accurate diagnosis, individualized care, effective administration of healthcare resources, and creative research. Although there is a lot of promise in the integration of these technologies, there are also ethical and data privacy issues to be addressed. To fully utilize CI in healthcare, academics, policymakers, and healthcare practitioners must work together to overcome these obstacles.

With its ability to provide sophisticated diagnostic tools, individualized care, and effective healthcare administration, CI is essential to the transformation of healthcare. Despite its immense potential, there are several important issues that need to be resolved, including ethical concerns, regulatory

[a]himanshu0590@gmail.com, [b]zeealis@gmail.com

compliance, and the proper use of patient data. CI will play a major role in shaping the future of healthcare, and this will be determined by ongoing research and innovation. The purpose of this study is to present a thorough analysis of the function and importance of CI in the field of medicine, with a focus on future prospects, applications, and advantages. The increasing significance of CI in facilitating improved decision-making, improving patient care, and streamlining healthcare processes is indicative of its incorporation into the field. With a focus on the wide range of uses, advantages, and exciting new directions that CI presents, this study seeks to shed light on the complex role that this technology plays in the medical field.

CI has brought about a paradigm change in healthcare administration. To manage patient flow, optimize resource allocation, and improve decision support systems, data analytics is essential. Furthermore, CI supports the detection of fraud, protecting the integrity of the financial components of the healthcare system.

Another area where CI has made a lasting impact is the emergence of remote patient monitoring, which is made possible by wearable technology and the Internet of Things (IoT). By reducing the need for hospital stays and facilitating early intervention, continuous monitoring of patients with chronic illnesses made feasible by CI improves patient outcomes overall.

2. Applications of Computational Intelligence in Healthcare

A few application areas for CI in healthcare are briefly discussed in this section. Early illness detection makes use of artificial intelligence (AI)-driven algorithms and machine learning (ML). Using patient data analysis, predictive algorithms can identify high-risk people. AI improves the diagnostic accuracy of medical imaging. Treatment strategies are customized by CI using patient-specific data. Genetic study determines the best medicine recommendations according to genetic composition. AI speeds up drug discovery by identifying targets and screening compounds. Predictive models assess side effects and drug-drug interactions. Hospital operations are streamlined by predictive analytics, which also optimizes resource distribution and cuts down on wait times. AI facilitates patient flow management, guaranteeing effective medical treatment. Remote monitoring and diagnostics are made possible by CI. Remote and underprivileged locations might now have access to healthcare thanks to telehealth technologies. AI improves the efficiency and accuracy of medical imaging. To identify diseases from images, segmentation and feature extraction are required. Outbreaks of infectious diseases are detected and tracked using AI and prediction algorithms. Patterns of mental health disorders can be found with the use of CI. For patients with mental health issues, it can support individualized treatment programmes and early intervention. AI is used to treat long-term health issues including diabetes and high blood pressure. It offers reminders for managing medicine and lifestyle in real-time. CI-powered clinical decision support systems (CDSS) help medical practitioners make clinical choices. They offer alerts and suggestions for patient treatment that are supported by evidence. With their many uses that improve patient care, diagnosis, treatment, and overall healthcare administration, ML and AI have become more popular in the healthcare sector. Figure 21.1 shows the major application is of CI in healthcare. The following section examines a few of the major applications:

2.1. Illness diagnosis and forecasting

Early illness diagnosis has been made possible by ML and AI. To aid in the diagnosis of a variety of disorders, they can examine sizable patient data sets, including electronic health records (EHR) and medical imaging [1].

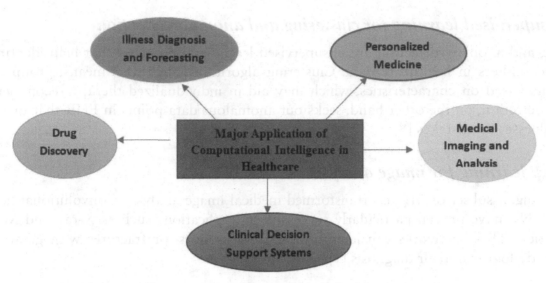

Figure 21.1: Major application of computational intelligence in healthcare.

2.2. Personalized medicine

AI is used to customize treatment regimens based on genetic and other unique patient data. This strategy seeks to reduce adverse effects and maximize therapeutic efficacy [2].

2.3. Drug discovery

To speed up the process of finding new drugs, ML and AI are employed. They support the discovery of targets, screening of compounds, and forecasting possible drug interactions [3].

2.4. Medical imaging and analysis

A subset of ML called deep learning improves the precision of medical imaging analysis. It is employed in processes like feature extraction for illness detection and picture segmentation [4, 5].

2.5. Clinical decision support systems (CDSS)

CDSS, which are driven by AI and ML, offer evidence-based warnings and suggestions for patient care to medical practitioners. These systems aid in the enhancement of clinical judgment [6].

3. Machine Learning and Artificial Intelligence in Healthcare

This section will discuss the key fields of ML and AI in healthcare.

3.1. Supervised learning in medical diagnosis

Support vector machines (SVM) and decision trees are two examples of supervised learning algorithms used in medical diagnostics. These algorithms are trained on labeled data, in which the input data (for example, patient information) is linked to a known output (for example, illness diagnosis). These models, once trained, can properly identify fresh data, assisting in the early diagnosis of illnesses like as cancer, diabetes, and heart disorders [7].

3.2. Unsupervised learning for clustering and anomaly detection

Clustering and anomaly detection are unsupervised learning approaches that help identify hidden trends and outliers in healthcare data. Clustering algorithms, such as k-means, group comparable patients based on characteristics, which may aid in individualized therapy recommendations. Anomaly detection, on the other hand, seeks out anomalous data points in EHR that may indicate unusual illnesses or mistakes [8].

3.3. Deep learning for image analysis

Deep learning, a subset of ML has transformed medical image analysis. Convolutional neural networks (CNNs) have proven particularly successful in applications such as X-ray and MRI image interpretation. These networks can identify anomalies, tumors, or fractures with great accuracy, assisting radiologists in their diagnosis [1].

3.4. Natural language processing for electronic health records

In electronic health records, natural language processing (NLP) technologies are used to extract important information from unstructured clinical content. NLP algorithms can recognize patient symptoms, treatment plans, and sickness development from physicians' notes, offering data-driven decision support and more thorough patient care [9].

4. Data Analytics and Big Data in Healthcare

This section discusses the use of data analytics and big data in healthcare.

4.1. Electronic health records (EHR) analysis

Electronic health records (EHR) are a goldmine of patient information. EHRs are mined for important information using data analytics approaches. Identifying trends in patient histories, analyzing treatment success, and optimizing healthcare delivery are all examples of this. As evidenced in research such as Hersh et al. (2013) that explore the influence of EHRs on patient outcomes [10], data analytics in EHR analysis enhances patient care.

4.2. Predictive analytics for hospital management

Predictive analytics forecasts future occurrences or patterns using previous data. It is used in healthcare management to optimize resource allocation, save expenses, and enhance patient care. A research by Steins et al. (2017) demonstrates how predictive analytics may help hospitals manage patient flow and resource allocation [11].

4.3. Real-time monitoring of patient data

In critical care and remote patient monitoring, real-time monitoring of patient data is crucial. Big data analytics processes and analyses the continual input of patient data, enabling rapid reactions to change in health situations. Wong et al. (2019) conducted research on the use of real-time monitoring to enhance patient outcomes and the obstacles that it poses [12].

4.4. Healthcare fraud detection

Detecting fraudulent activity in healthcare billing is critical for cost control and protecting the healthcare system's integrity. Anomaly detection and pattern recognition are used in data analytics to discover odd billing trends. Sadoughi et al. (2019) highlight the use of data analytics in the identification of healthcare fraud [13].

5. Future Prospects

5.1. Integration of Internet of Things (IoT) in healthcare

The Internet of Things (IoT) is poised to transform healthcare by enabling real-time data collection from medical equipment, wearable sensors, and patients themselves. This information may be used to get insights into patient health and to assist remote monitoring. Dohr et al. (2016) [14] investigate the possibilities of IoT in healthcare.

5.2. Blockchain in healthcare data management

Blockchain technology has great potential for the safe, transparent, and interoperable administration of healthcare data. It can aid in the preservation of patient records, the security of data, and the facilitation of data exchange. Kuo et al. (2017) [15] investigate the possibilities of blockchain in healthcare.

5.3. Advancements in genomic data analysis

Advances in genomics, such as DNA sequencing technology and computational tools, are projected to accelerate precision medicine. Genomic data analysis can give insight into hereditary illnesses, personalized treatment regimens, and medication development. Goodwin et al. (2016) [16] present notable advances in genetic data analysis.

5.4. Explainable AI for healthcare decision support

Explainable artificial intelligence (XAI) is a crucial advancement for healthcare decision support systems. XAI models increase trust and comprehension by providing explicit insights into the thinking behind AI-driven judgments. Caruana et al. (2015) [17] underline the significance of XAI in healthcare.

5.5. Global health initiatives with computational intelligence

The worldwide integration of AI has the potential to address a variety of public health concerns. AI, data analytics, and predictive modeling initiatives can help with disease management, resource allocation, and healthcare access. Milinovich et al. (2016) provide an overview of the role of CI in global health [18].

6. Challenges to computational intelligence integration in healthcare

CI has a potential and revolutionary function in healthcare, but it is not without its difficulties. The following are some major obstacles to CI integration in healthcare:

a. Medical imaging, wearable technology, and EHRs are some of the many sources of healthcare data. For CI applications, integrating and standardizing these diverse data streams presents substantial problems. Predictions and choices that are based on inaccurate diagnostic data or patient records may be incorrect. For CI models to be reliable, the quality and accuracy of the input data must be guaranteed.

b. Interoperability is hampered by the lack of common protocols and formats for the sharing of healthcare data. Applications for cognitive intelligence may find it difficult to exchange data between platforms and interact well with current healthcare systems.

c. Patient privacy is an issue while using CI since healthcare data is sensitive. A major ethical concern is finding a balance between protecting individual privacy and using patient data to enhance results. Healthcare inequities might result from CI models unintentionally maintaining past data biases. A difficult ethical problem is making sure the algorithms are fair and taking care of their biases.

d. A lot of CI models are not properly validated clinically or interpreted. Without a clear knowledge of how the model arrives at its results, healthcare personnel can be reluctant to accept choices made by AI.

e. Strong computing infrastructure is needed for CI implementation in healthcare, and this might be expensive. Many healthcare institutions can find it difficult to make the investments in the required knowledge and technology, particularly in settings with limited resources.

f. Healthcare personnel must receive proper training in the usage and interpretation of CI technologies to integrate them into workflows. Implementation success may be hampered by lack of training and resistance to change.

g. Healthcare systems are vulnerable to cyberattacks due of their interconnectedness. Critical concerns include protecting patient data and guaranteeing the security of CI applications against hostile actions.

7. Conclusions

CI is transforming the medical healthcare sector. It enables precise diagnosis, personalized therapy, effective healthcare administration, and cutting-edge research. While the integration of these technologies has great promise, it also raises questions about data privacy and ethics. To realize the full potential of AI in healthcare, healthcare practitioners, academics, and policymakers must work together to overcome these issues. Finally, CI have the ability to completely transform healthcare by enhancing diagnosis, treatment, resource allocation, and patient care. While it has enormous promise, widespread adoption will need careful planning, ethical concerns, and a commitment to continuous development. As technology advances, its role in healthcare is likely to grow, helping both patients and doctors. In summary, via increasing diagnostic precision, refining therapeutic approaches, boosting patient outcomes, and expediting healthcare administration procedures, CI is playing a multifarious role in transforming the healthcare industry. To guarantee the ethical and fair application of these technologies in the medical sphere, it is imperative to address privacy and ethical issues.

References

[1] Esteva, A., Kuprel, B., Novoa, R. A., Ko, J., Swetter, S. M., Blau, H. M., and Thrun, S. (2017). Dermatologist-level classification of skin cancer with deep neural networks. *Nature*, 542(7639), 115–118.

[2] Gonzalez-Gonzalez, A. I., Truong, J., and Raza, S. (2018). Personalized medicine: Where are we now? *Public Health Genom.*, 21(5–6), 231–242.

[3] Schneider, G., Lee, M. L., Stahl, M., and Schneider, P. (2016). De novo design at the edge of chaos. *J. Med. Chem.*, 59(9), 4077–4086.

[4] Chen, Y., Cao, Y., Yu, J., Zhu, F., and Hu, W. (2012). Integration of artificial neural networks and statistical techniques for improving patient admission scheduling. *Health Care Manag. Sci.*, 15(4), 364–376.

[5] Litjens, G., Kooi, T., Bejnordi, B. E., Setio, A. A. A., Ciompi, F., Ghafoorian, M., and Sanchez, C. I. (2017). A survey on deep learning in medical image analysis. *Med. Image Anal.*, 42, 60–88.

[6] Kawamoto, K., Houlihan, C. A., Balas, E. A., and Lobach, D. F. (2005). Improving clinical practice using clinical decision support systems: a systematic review of trials to identify features critical to success. *Br. Med. J.*, 330(7494), 765.

[7] Rajkomar, A., Oren, E., Chen, K., Dai, A. M., Hajaj, N., Hardt, M., and Lungren, M. P. (2018). Scalable and accurate deep learning with electronic health records. *NPJ Dig. Med.*, 1(1), 1–10.

[8] Mishra, A., Maurya, A. S., and Tripathi, A. (2020). Anomaly detection in healthcare data using unsupervised machine learning. *Inter. Things Big Data Technol. Next Gen. Healthcare*, 221–236. IGI Global.

[9] Rastegar-Mojarad, M., Ye, Z., and Wall, D. (2015). Use of natural language processing to extract clinical information from EHRs. *Healthcare Data Anal.*, 52–70. CRC Press.

[10] Hersh, W. R., Totten, A. M., Eden, K. B., Devine, B., Gorman, P. N., Kassakian, S. Z., and McDonagh, M. S. (2013). Outcomes from health information exchange: systematic review and future research needs. *JMIR Med. Inform.*, 1(1), e1.

[11] Steins, K., Sze, A. K., and Lucier, J. (2017). Predictive analytics in health care: opportunities and challenges. *Res. Synth. Report Health Sys. Res. Anal.*, pp 1–14.

[12] Wong, D., Bonnici, T., Knight, J., Gerry, S., Turton, G., and Watkinson, P. (2019). A ward-based time study of paper and electronic documentation for recording vital sign observations. *J. Am. Med. Inform. Assoc.*, 26(12), 1456–1465.

[13] Sadoughi, F., Khodaveisi, T., and Shahidi, M. (2019). An overview of data mining approaches in healthcare fraud detection. *Healthcare Inform. Res.*, 25(1), 2–10.

[14] Dohr, A., Modre-Osprian, R., Drobics, M., Hayn, D., and Schreier, G. (2016). The Internet of Things for ambient assisted living. *Pervas. Comput. Parad. Mental Health*, 117–136. Springer.

[15] Kuo, T. T., Kim, H. E., and Ohno-Machado, L. (2017). Blockchain distributed ledger technologies for biomedical and health care applications. *J. Am. Med. Inform. Assoc.*, 24(6), 1211–1220.

[16] Goodwin, S., McPherson, J. D., and McCombie, W. R. (2016). Coming of age: Ten years of next-generation sequencing technologies. *Nat. Rev. Gen.*, 17(6), 333–351.

[17] Caruana, R., Lou, Y., Gehrke, J., Koch, P., Sturm, M., and Elhadad, N. (2015). Intelligible models for healthcare: Predicting pneumonia risk and hospital 30-day readmission. *Proc. 21th ACM SIGKDD Int. Conf. Knowl. Dis. Data Min.*, 1721–1730.

[18] Milinovich, G. J., Williams, G. M., Clements, A. C., and Hu, W. (2016). Internet-based surveillance systems for monitoring emerging infectious diseases. *Lancet Infect. Dis.*, 14(2), 160–168.

22 Model-Based Testing for Efficient Security and Work Flow For Secure Software Development

Sandhya Satyarthi[a] and Dhirendra Pandey[b]

Department of Information Technology, Babasaheb Bhimrao Ambedkar University, Lucknow, India

Abstract

The software testing process is a substantial aspect that influences the overall performance of applications and is vital for the entire life cycle of a software system. Security in the development process plays an imperative role as the success and the failure depend on the security practices. In terms of agile the development, in this continuous integration and improvement is carried throughout the end of the software development. Model-based testing (MBT), a crucial component of today's test automation, constitutes a component of the evolution of software testing. MBT can be used to manage and complete testing tasks in a more expedient, affordable, and highly successful manner when compared to traditional testing methodologies. In this paper, we will discuss about the security challenges in MBT and MBT improvement workflow in secure agile-based software development.

Keywords: Model-based testing (MBT), SSD (secure software development), SDLC (software development lifecycle), agile software development (ASD)

1. Introduction

The security is always a main concern in the process of development and we consider testing is most focused areas as it helps in identification and elimination of risks in the secure software development. It is essential to test safety-critical systems because a malfunction or failure could cause serious harm to people, property, or the environment. The creation of test cases that can detect potential flaws is a significant testing task. Model-based testing (MBT) creates test artifacts by using models of the system being evaluated and/or its surroundings. In order to discover, evaluate, and characterize the most recent developments in MBT for software safety, this paper will present a systematic mapping study [1, 3]. Although MBT has been used in organizations that use agile methodologies that look at how MBT can be used successfully in these settings. Security testing is a widely used technique for determining and enhancing software security by detecting vulnerabilities and assuring security

[a]er.satyarthisandhya24@gmail.com, [b]prof.dhiren@gmail.com

functionality [2]. The rising significance and requirement of adopting adequate security testing strategies to undertake effective and efficient security testing is the outgrowth of the available nature of today's software-based systems. Therefore, it is highly beneficial for researchers to evaluate and enhance the procedures through an overview of actual security testing techniques, and for practitioners to apply and distribute the techniques themselves. MBT is an innovative strategy to software testing that extends the primary goal of test automation from performing the test to test design through the creation of tests automatically based on models [4–6]. In addition to familiarity with the proper tools, the new method also necessitates the development of new skills, such as test modeling expertise. By first building models of the system under test, MBT aims to develop test cases in a methodical and ordered fashion. MBT allows for comprehensive coverage of the system to be tested because it uses models to define the system's behavior [7]. As a result of improved accessibility to edge circumstances, a larger spectrum of inputs and conditions can be put through their paces. By creating models of the system, any issues and inconsistencies can be discovered and rectified prior to or in the early stages of development [8, 9]. When creating software, agile teams often have to adapt to changing needs. The necessary flexibility in agile development can be achieved with the aid of MBT. It is possible to produce test cases based on updated models when modifications have been made to the corresponding models [10, 12]. By linking models to requirements and developing test cases from models, teams can increase transparency and verifiability by ensuring testing efforts properly meet the defined needs. This work helps to find out the challenges in the MBT that has to be focused on. After that a framework is designed to help secure software development.

Research methodology, as depicted in Figure 22.1, explains how to construct an outline for secure software development and identify gaps in the existing literature.

Expectedly, this framework will help the software development team recognize critical software security issues and get an understanding of security artifacts necessary to build secure scrum agile-based software.

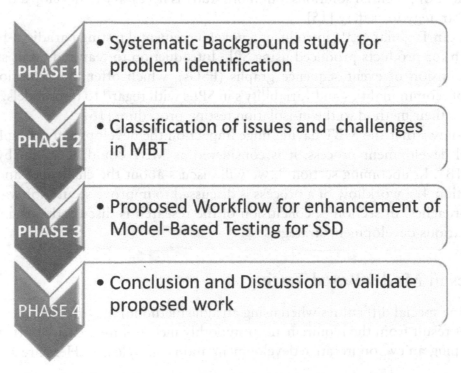

• Systematic Background study for problem identification — PHASE 1

• Classification of issues and challenges in MBT — PHASE 2

• Proposed Workflow for enhancement of Model-Based Testing for SSD — PHASE 3

• Conclusion and Discussion to validate proposed work — PHASE 4

Figure 22.1: Research method description.

This paper's remaining sections are structured as follows. In the second piece, we talk about the things that got us started and the preliminary study that led us to the research gap. MBT is integrated into agile software development, as discussed in section 2. In section 3, we'll talk about the many challenges and issues in the MBT. In section 4, workflow is discussed that help MBT to address and improve the challenges that discussed in previous section. Section 5, discussed about findings and provides a summary and suggestions for further study.

2. Literature Review

In 2004, conducted an experiment using a major case study of a flight guidance system, created condensed test-suites while presenting coverage for a range of structural coverage criteria, and tracked the success of these test-suites in locating faults. Our findings demonstrate that the size of the specification-based test-suites can be drastically decreased, and that the reduced test-suites' ability to discover faults is negatively impacted. In this study, we present our experiment, examine the findings, and talk about how testing based on formal specifications might be affected [11].

In 2011, Mark Utting et al., outlines the MBT process and a taxonomy that encapsulates the essential components of MBT methodologies. It aims to assist with classifying the technique employed in a specific MBT tool and understanding the traits, similarities, and differences of such approaches [13].

In 2016, Mathaikutty et al., proposes the study that is to thoroughly examine the state-of-the-art of experimental SBT applications for MBT and to describe the limits of the existing literature to guide future research. Researchers can explore current research efforts and identify any gaps that require further study by conducting a systematic examination of the available literature based on the proposed taxonomy [14].

In 2018, a study demonstrates that MBT can offer significant advantages for software safety testing. debate the main trends and methodologies, explain the challenges, and debate these findings. There are a number of potential solutions, but more study is necessary to develop a trustworthy model-based testing strategy for safety [15].

In 2019, Tugkan Tuglular et al., introduces a novel incremental testing paradigm-based MBT generation approach for products produced using SPL. Introduction to featured event sequence graphs (FESGs), an expansion of event sequence graphs (ESGs), which offer the definitions and actions required to enable commonalities and variability's in SPLs with regard to test models. They use a case study to compare their method to the in-isolation testing procedure [16].

The studies shows that the MBT having huge impact on the development. As agile in is iteration and incremental development process, it is considered as MBT could be useful by using various techniques of MBT. In upcoming section 3, we will discuss about the challenges and issues arise in the MBT. In section 4, a workflow of a process is discussed to improve secure software development using MBT approaches. In section 5, conclusion of the research is discussed and finding the future impact on the various development strategies.

3. Challenges in Model-Based Testing

There can be some special difficulties when using an agile methodology for MBT in a security setting. These difficulties result from the requirement to smoothly incorporate security testing into agile processes while keeping an eye on iterative development and rapid releases. Here are a few of the main difficulties:

1. **Agile development pace:** Agile development is characterized by its quick turnaround times and frequent iterations. Given that security testing may take longer than the development cycle, integrating security-focused modeling and testing into this fast-paced environment can be difficult.
2. **Skill gaps:** Agile teams could occasionally lack the requisite security knowledge. It can be difficult to close the skills gap and guarantee that team members comprehend security concepts and procedures.
3. **Integration with agile artifacts:** It can be challenging to integrate security models, threat analyses, and security-focused test cases with agile artifacts like user stories and sprint planning [17]. It is vital to make sure that security considerations are given equal weight with other functional requirements.
4. **Obligation for security:** Scurrying through security assessments in order to meet agile deadlines can result in security debt, which pushes vulnerabilities to later iterations. A less secure application might be the effect of this.
5. **Continuous feedback:** Agile encourages continuous feedback, but security testing could cause a lag in the feedback process, especially if thorough security assessments take some time.
6. **Working together and communicating:** Successful security testing depends on effective communication and collaboration between security experts, testers, developers, and other stakeholders. It might be challenging to make sure that security findings are recognized and swiftly handled [18, 19].
7. **A changing threat environment:** There are constantly new vulnerabilities and attack routes developing, making the security threat landscape dynamic. Agile security practices must respond quickly to these changes.
8. **Adherence to regulations:** Why complying with legal standards, such as GDPR or HIPAA, in an agile environment can be difficult. It is crucial to make sure that testing procedures and security models comply with these rules.

Here are some challenges and issues we discussed as they impacted the overall development process. To tackle and smoothly flow the development using a testing in a manner to secure the development a workflow or framework is designed, that can be discussed in the following section.

4. Proposed Workflow For Enhancement of Model-Based Testing For Secure Software Development

A software testing strategy known as "model-based testing" (MBT) makes use of models to create and run test cases. These models serve as representations of the functionality and. requirements of the system being tested, assisting testers in methodically generating test cases and ensuring test coverage. Figure 22.2 describes the workflow and following steps are commonly included in the MBT process:

1. **Understanding security requirements:** To start, make sure you know the security requirements and legal compliance standards that apply to your project. Make it clear what a secure programme is in your situation.
2. **Security training and awareness:** Make sure that your development team, which includes writers, testers, and other important people, goes through security training and awareness programmes. Common security threats, best practices, and secure coding rules should be known by everyone.

3. **Figure out the security models and build security in from the beginning:** Figure out the security models that apply to your work [20]. Threat models, attack surface models, data flow models, access control models, and other models that show how secure your system is some examples. Also, thinking about security from the very beginning of development, when you're gathering needs and planning the architecture. Along with practical models, make models that focus on security to help with testing.

4. **Threat modeling and test model creation:** Use threat modeling to find possible security holes and threats in a planned way. These models can help you plan your security testing and come up with useful test cases. Formulate test models based on your needs and security models [21]. These test models should include security scenarios, ways to attack, and the results that are expected in terms of security.

5. **Collaborative working to secure code reviews:** Encourage the development, testing, and security teams to talk to each other and work together. Make sure that security problems and findings are shared quickly, and make it easy for people to share what they know. Do secure code reviews along with regular code reviews. To make sure that security standards are met, use your security models to guide the review process.

6. **Static analysis and dynamic scanning:** To help your MBT, use tools for static code analysis and dynamic application security testing (DAST). These tools can find holes in the models that the models might not cover. These are helpful in analysis of the whole process thoroughly.

7. **Incident plan making with continuous training and improvement:** Make an incident reaction plan that tells the team what to do if there is a security breach or vulnerability is found while the project is being built [22]. Making sure everyone knows what they need to do is important also, secure development practices are always better by using what you've learned from security incidents and tests. Give ongoing training and make comments a part of how you do things.

8. **Third-party security assessments:** Think about getting third-party security assessments, like penetration testing, to make sure your security measures are working and to find any holes you may have missed.

9. **Verification of compliance:** Make sure that your MBT method can show that it follows all security rules and standards. Write down and keep track of the results of your security tests [23].

10. **Continuous monitoring and risk-based approach for secure completion of security artifacts:** Make sure that your production application is constantly scanned for security risks and holes so that you can fix them as they appear [24]. Set priorities for security testing based on estimates of risk. Pay attention to the most important parts and the most dangerous spots for security.

The workflow we described is initiating by the analysis and understanding of the requirements, security training and awareness is needed to understand the all security aspects, then find out the best suited model on the basis of security training and analysis and using threat modeling to find out possible security bugs and then formulating the test cases [25, 26].

After the test cases formulated on the basis of needs and security model, the encouragement of collaborative working is needed to work in a direction to meet the security standards and to initiating code reviews. Also, a static and dynamic analysis is done to find out the loop holes in the model this can efficiently analyses the whole model. After scanning an incident reaction plan is making is done, that helps in telling security teams what if any security issues or bugs are there. A third party assement is needed to rectify that whether the security measures are working and then compliance of the test cases generated by MBT to analyze that all stand and guidelines are followed.

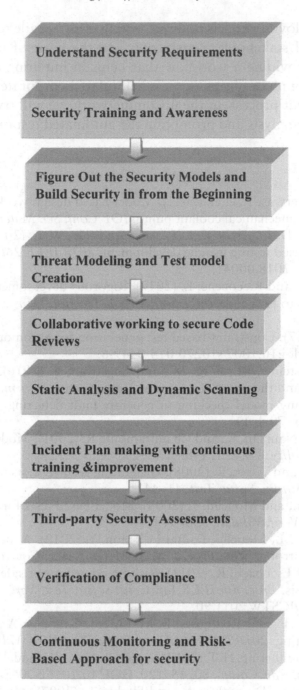

Figure 22.2: Workflow for improved MBT in SSD.

At the end of this workflow, it is important to make sure about the continuous monitoring and improvements in the following of risk-based approaches to manipulate and update the some crucial areas related to security. Overall, the conformation of security is needed from initial stages to the final generation of test cases that could be used.

5. Conclusions

MBT in agile software development increases test coverage, enables early defect detection, aids test automation, promotes teamwork, enables change-adaptability, and makes it simpler to trace and document processes. By employing models to direct testing efforts, agile teams can improve software quality, feedback cycles, and stakeholder satisfaction. On the basis of investigated problems, it is necessary to focus on the providing a workflow that helps in initiating the testing throughout the various phases and by moving phases by phases it is helpful to incorporate security practices to evoke a secure software development process. In the upcoming work we will try to find out the best MBT technique by a comparative analysis and prompting the automated test cases generation.

References

[1]   Höpfner, G., Jacobs, G., Zerwas, T., et al. (2021). Model-based design workflows for cyber-physical systems applied to an electric-mechanical coolant pump. *IOP Conf. Ser. Mater. Sci. Engg.*, 1097, 1.

[2]   Jorge, D. N., Machado, P. D. L., Alves, E. L. G., and Andrade, W. L. (2018). Integrating requirements specification and model-based testing in agile development. *2018 IEEE 26th Int. Req. Engg. Conf. (RE)*, 336–346, doi: 10.1109/RE.2018.00041.

[3]   Arcaini, P., Gargantini, A., and Riccobene, E. (2017). Rigorous development process of a safety-critical system: From ASM models to Java code. *Int. J. Softw. Tools Technol. Trans.*, 19(2), 247–269. doi:10.1007/s10009-015-0394-x.

[4]   Choi, Y. and Byun, T. (2017). Constraint-based test generation for automotive operating systems. *Softw. Sys. Model.*, 16(1), 7–24. doi:10.1007/s10270-014-0449-6.

[5]   Bjarnason, E., Unterkalmsteiner, M., Borg, M., and Engström, E. (2016). A multi-case study of agile requirements engineering and the use of test cases as requirements. *Inform. Softw. Technol.*, 77, 61–79.

[6]   Gargantini, A. (2007). Using model checking to generate fault detecting tests. *Tests Proofs*, 189–206. doi:10.1007/978-3-540-73770-4_11.

[7]   Blackburn, M., Busser, R., Nauman, A., and Chandramouli, R. (2001). Model-based approach to security test automation. *Proc. Quality Week.*, 1, 1–8.

[8]   Julliand, J., Masson, P. A., and Tissot, R. (2008). Generating security tests in addition to functional tests. *Proc. 3rd Int. Workshop Autom. Softw. Test*, 41–44.

[9]   Pretschner, A., Le Traon, Y., and Mouelhi, T. (2008). Model-based tests for access control policies. *Proc. 1st Int. Conf. Softw. Test. Verif. Validat.*, 338–347.

[10] Xu, D., Thomas, L., Kent, M., Mouelhi, T., and Le Traon, Y. (2012). A model-based approach to automated testing of access control policies. *Proc. 17th ACM Symp. Acc. Control Models Technol.*, 209–218.

[11] Kloos, J., Hussain, T., and Eschbach, R. (2011). Risk-based testing of safety-critical embedded systems driven by fault tree analysis. *Proc. 4th IEEE Int. Conf. Softw. Test. Verif. Validat. Workshops, ICSTW 2011*, 26–33. doi:10.1109/ICSTW.2011.90.

[12] Bernardino, M., Zorzo, A. F., and Rodrigues, E. M. (2016). Canopus: A domain-specific language for modeling performance testing. *2016 IEEE Int. Conf. Softw. Test. Verif. Validat (ICST)*, 157–167.

[13] Arilo Claudio, D. N. and Guilherme, H. T. (2010). A picture from the model-based testing area: Concepts, techniques, and challenges. *Adv. Comp.*, 80, 45–120. DOI: 10.1016/S0065-2458(10)80002-6.

[14] Mathaikutty, D. A., Ahuja, S., Dingankar, A., and Shukla, S. (2007). Model-driven test generation for system level validation. *HLDVT: Proc. IEEE Int. High-Level Des. Validat. Test Workshop*, 83–90. doi:10.1109/HLDVT.2007.4392792.

[15] Heimdahl, M. P. E. and George, D. (2004). Test-suite reduction for model based tests: Effects on test quality and implications for testing. *Proc. 19th Int. Conf. Autom. Softw. Engg.*, 176–185, doi: 10.1109/ASE.2004.1342735.

[16] Andreasen, E., Gong, L., Møller, A., Pradel, M., Selakovic, M., Sen, K., and Staicu, C. (2017). A survey of dynamic analysis and test generation for JavaScript. *ACM Comput. Sur.*, 50(5), 66.

[17] Mark, U., Alexander, P., Bruno, L. (2012). A taxonomy of model-based testing approaches. *Found. Appl. Model-Based Test.*, 1, 297–312.

[18] Aneesa, S., Siti Hafizah Ab, H., and Mumtaz Begum, M. (2016). The experimental applications of search-based techniques for model-based testing: Taxonomy and systematic literature review. *Appl. Soft Comput.*, 49, 1094–1117.

[19] Gurbuz, H. G. and Tekinerdogan, B. (2018). Model-based testing for software safety: A systematic mapping study. *Softw. Qual. J.*, 26, 1327–1372.

[20] Rau, A., Hotzkow, J., and Zeller, A. (2018). Efficient GUI test generation by learning from tests of other apps. *Proc. Int. Conf. Softw. Engg. Compan. Proc.*, 370–371.

[21] Tuglular, T., Beyazıt, M., and Öztürk, D. (2019). Featured event sequence graphs for model-based incremental testing of software product lines. *2019 IEEE 43rd Ann. Comp. Softw. Appl. Conf. (COMPSAC)*, 197–202. doi: 10.1109/COMPSAC.2019.00035.

[22] Wang, C., Pastore, F., Goknil, A., Briand, L., and Iqbal, Z. (2015). Automatic generation of system test cases from use case specifications. *Proc. 2015 Int. Symp. Softw. Test. Anal. ISSTA*, 385–396.

[23] Kim, J. H., Larsen, K. G., Nielsen, B., Mikučionis, M., and Olsen, P. (2015). Formal analysis and testing of real-time automotive systems using UPPAAL tools. *Lec. Notes Comp. Sci.* (including subseries Lecture Notes in Artificial Intelligence and Lecture Notes in Bioinformatics), 9128, 47–61. doi:10.1007/978-3-319-19458-5_4.

[24] Weißleder, S. and Lackner, H. (2013). Top-down and bottom-up approach for model-based testing of product lines electron. *Proc. Theor. Comput. Sci.*, 111, 82–94.

[25] Gebizli, C. S. and Sozer, H. (2016). Model-based software product line testing by coupling feature models with hierarchical Markov chain usage models. *Proc. 2016 IEEE Int. Conf. Softw. Qual. Reliab. Secur. QRS-C*, 278–283.

[26] Reyes-Garcia, F., Marín, B., and Alarcón-Bañados, S. (2019). Visualization of MBT testing coverage. *13th Int. Conf. Res. Chal. Inform. Sci. (RCIS)*, 1–2.

23 An Enhanced Layered IoT-Architecture for IoT Applications Against Cyber-Attacks

Vinay Kumar Sahu[1,a], Dhirendra Pandey[1,b], Raees Ahmad Khan[2,c], Mohd Waris Khan[2,d], and Vandan Pandey[3]

[1]Department of Information Technology, Babasaheb Bhimrao Ambedkar University, Lucknow, U.P., India

[2]Department of Computer Application, Integral University, Lucknow, U.P., India

[3]Department of Computer Science, Goel Institute of Higher Studies Mahavidyalaya, Lucknow, U.P., India

Abstract

Today Internet of Things (IoT) is quickly becoming one of the most popular technologies in the whole world where enormous number of devices are connected to make human life more feasible and comfortable. IoT technologies play a significant role everywhere. It is a coalescence of embedded computing, communication technologies, sensors, and actuators. The aim of the IoT is to endue seamless capabilities to the user anytime, anywhere. Inspite of various benefits, IoT also calls for high levels of security, authentication, privacy, and protection from attacks. There are variegated security mechanisms and solutions for IoT applications that have been introduced in the past works but still IoT facing enormous number of challenges in the field of security and privacy. This paper proposes an improved IoT architecture with a thorough analysis of the variegated architectural approaches given by different researchers ranging from basic architectures to commercial-grade implementations. Specifically, this paper focuses on IoT security scenarios associated with IoT architecture and also examined various security threats and vulnerabilities exists in IoT systems like confidentiality, privacy, authentication, integrity, access control, etc. Author concludes the work by discussing privacy and security issues in IoT architecture and challenges they pose to researchers.

Keywords: Internet of Things (IoT), IoT infrastructure, sensors, actuators, IoT security, IoT applications

1. Introduction

The term Internet of Things (IoT) is an amalgamation of two words: Internet and Things. The term Internet refers to interconnection; something that covers not merely electronic equipment but also living creatures like humans, animals, etc., and non-living objects like furniture, cloths, etc., and finally the IoT is formed by connecting these two words with "of". Since the turn of the century, the IoT has grown rapidly as technology in numerous applications. Smart devices are interconnected through wireless and wired networks for real-time processing, communication, computing, and observing scenarios. Implementing the IoT system poses various securities and privacy issues because

[a]vinay13990@gmail.com, [b]prof.dhiren@gmail.com, [c]wariskhan070@gmail.com, [d]khanraees@yahoo.com

the natures of existing traditional security protocols are not well suited for novel IoT devices. The IoT term refers to a basic idea for the efficiency of smart devices to detect and congregate information from all over the world and then make available the information over the internet where it can be processed and employed for different enthralling purposes. IoT is a collection of smart machines that collaborate with and communicate with other machines, items, systems and foundations. As of now, people communicate using a variety of different methods to stay connected where most popular means of communication is internet, therefore, we can say that the internet is a means of association for groups of people. As IoT is rapidly growing technology, it is also at risk of various security and privacy threats. In order to ensure IoT security, defensive technologies must be able to detect threats and respond to attacks.

The major contribution of this work is as follows:

- Firstly, we examine various published standards and IoT architectures.
- Subsequently we presented a critical review on available architectures.
- Then after critical review we proposed a detailed layered version of IoT architecture.
- Comprehensive risk analysis of security and privacy issues in IoT environment.
- Presents the direction for future research.

Continuing with the paper, we compiled the rest as follows, the related work in the area of privacy and security challenges and various existing IoT architectures are available in section 2. The critical review on various existing IoT architectures is fabricated in section 3. The succinct fabrication of proposed IoT tectonics is presented in section 4. Section 5 deals with the possible privacy and security challenges revealed in the environment of IoT. Section 6 suggests the direction for future research to embellish the environment of IoT. The article concludes with a summary of our work in section 7. The references used are presented in section 8.

2. Related Work

The Internet plays a crucial role in transmitting the information. The technology is moving from just sharing information to collecting data, analyzing the data, and monitoring and controlling devices remotely via Internet, which results in the so-called IoT. This term "Internet of Things" was first introduced by Kavin Ashton in 1999 while researcher was working with radio frequency identification (RFID) technology for item identification. Kavin said, "The fact that I was probably the first person to say "Internet of Things" does not give me any right to control how others use the phrase. But what I meant, and still mean, is this: Today computers-and, therefore, the Internet-are almost wholly dependent on human beings for information". Kevin accost, people aren't very good at capturing the data from things in the real world due to a limited amount of time, attention and accuracy. The world needs to be empowered with its own way for computers to gather information, in order for them to really see and hear the world, regardless of what it is. As the internet changed the world, the IoT will also have the potential do so [1]. As per our research aspiration on architecture, privacy, security, opportunities and impact on society in the IoT era, we comprehend to demeanor a detailed investigation on this technology.

Present architectural solutions and technologies make IoT cornerstones quite vulnerable to security threats. Businesses and consumers will both be affected by security breaches, which is why the task is daunting. The author performs a coherent literature review to diagrammatize the security threats in

IoT to furnish an optimistic security framework to minimize the risk associated with IoT. As per the researcher, an improved standard for security is necessary for IoT to take the lead in the Industrial Internet and Industry 4.0 in future [2]. To build smart home IoT applications, the researcher proposes a lightweight authorization stack where input commands are relayed from a Cloud-connected device to the end user's smartphone. The proposed architecture is based on user-device and designed to address security concerns in an untrusted cloud environment. For future research, the author would like to deploy the Kaa IoT application on the RIoT operating system and extend the simulation setup to a RIoT virtual network and also enhance the testing exercise in real-life scenarios [3].

Business, government, and people can benefit greatly from the IoT in their daily lives. While IoT offers great comfort, it also presents several major technological obstacles. Implementation of secure and reliable IoT applications is of utmost importance for IoT's long-term success. Monitoring devices and sensor devices connected to the internet track people's private lives, while at the same moment transferring them to the cloud. The author illustrates critical security issues associated with IoT, security threats, vulnerabilities, and counter measures applicable to various IoT components. Authors also discussed the importance of light weight cryptography and its role in IoT [4]. The author briefly discusses the technical aspects of IoT security. Because of the difficulty of providing sufficient protection when only two devices were connected. Security is regarded as the most important one in this context. In the current scenario, millions of devices are connected and billions of sensors exist and their number keeps growing rapidly day by day. They are all expected to have reliable and secure connectivity. Because of this, IoT deployment requires well-designed security architectures for companies and organizations. The author propounds that the securing sensitive information from unauthorized access will be the biggest challenge for the IoT in forthcoming research [5].

Various types of cyber-attacks have been identified by the author in Indian context and fortified the identifies attacks by implementing the widely used Hungarian method. Authors introduced a secured method to minimize the losses over the network. An extension can be made to the same work by using the N×N matrix for a definite number of divisions which implies that there should be an equal number of attacks per department [6]. With the use of well-known Rivest, Shamir and Adleman (RSA) algorithm of the security system the authors propose a system for securing information transmission with its MAC address. The author also evaluates the proposed algorithm on different MAC addresses of various devices via an object-oriented programming language. As per the author one can also upgrade the algorithm for safe dissemination of the audio, video and text content also [7].

The author aims to build a wireless smart home security system that sends notifications via the Internet when trespasses are detected and optionally sets off an alarm in the event of an intrusion. A similar system can also be incorporated into home automation using the same sensors. The microcontroller used by the researcher in the proposed system is set up with TI-CC3200 Launchpad board that comes with built in microcontroller and embedded with a Wi-Fi shield with the help of this all the home appliances can be managed. Furthermore, the system may be made more synchronized by incorporating voice call functionality into the mobile app using which user can operate his home appliances more effectively [8]. Based on object-oriented technology, the author presents a model for analyzing cybercrime that can occur in distributed network and proposes a UML model for filing the online FIR for cybercrime. One can also include various methods like optimization and curve fitting for reducing risk factors in studied problem [9].

Table 23.1: Comparative study

Ref.	Year	Applications	IoT challenges	System design aspects/ architecture	Computing paradigms	Protocols	Security & privacy	Features
[16]	2014	X	Interoperability, scalability, and heterogeneity	Layered and distributed architecture for IoT	X	X	Y	Automation, intelligence, and zero-configuration
[17]	2014	X	Authentication, heterogeneity and scalability	Distributed architecture	WSNs and cloud	Two-phase authentication protocol	Y	Partial protection form node capture and DoS attacks
[18]	2016	X	X	Distributed grid	SDN-and cluster-based	Dynamic routing cluster protocol	Y	Network virtualization and Open-Flow, SMART FIREWALL
[19]	2018	X	Access control and information propagation	Distributed architecture	Ledger-based	SHA256 and AES, RSA	Y	
[20]	2017	X	Threat prevention, data protection, and access control, DDoS/DoS attacks	Distributed architecture	Block-chains and SDN	Access control and data protection, threat prevention	Y	Mitigate network attacks such as cache poising/ARP spoofing
[21]	2019	Smart cities	Network performances, and payload efficiency	Distributed secure black SDN architecture	SDN	Open-Flow	Y	Network function virtualization (NVF)
[22]	2016	Smart cities	Confidentiality, integrity, secure routing, identity management, node authentication, authorization, accounting, availability and mobility	X	SDN, black networks, Unified Registry		Y	Key management system

(continued)

Table 23.1: Continued

Ref.	Year	Applications	IoT challenges	System design aspects/architecture	Computing paradigms	Protocols	Security & privacy	Features
[23]	2020	Agriculture, water source and containers, healthcare	Lack of reliable non-intermittent power supply. Costly or non-existent broadband connectivity. affordable, reliable and secure IoT	Local computational device integrated with the gateway	Low-Power Wide Area Network, (LoRaWAN)	Bluetooth Low Energy (BLE), network management processes, data processing	Y	Open source, cost efficient, low service cost, resource-efficient
[24]	2020	Healthcare IoT network	Attacks via TCP, UDP and Xmas port scans, and DoS	Architecture combining CEP and ML	Complex Event Processing (CEP) technology and machine learning (ML)	MQTT, MEdit4CEP (model-driven tool)	Y	The main contribution is an SOA 2.0 integrating CEP, ML, IoT and MEdit4CEP for detecting IoT security attacks and threats in a user-friendly way
[25]	2021	Sustainable urban drainage system	Resiliency to transient IoT devices and inclusion of new IoT devices	Layered architecture	OM2M (Open source platform for Machine-to-Machine communication), IoT ontology	MQTT	X	Dynamic adaptation to new and transient devices
[26]	2021	Remote health monitoring of COVID-19 patients in hospitals and at home	Interoperability, scalability, context discovery, network dynamics, reliability, and privacy	Comprehensive IoT-based conceptual layered architecture	Blockchain, embedded EWS (Early Warning System) agent, data distribution layer, event management	AES, transport layer security protocol, OAuth V2	Y	Securely stores patient consent to protect privacy rights. Individual assessment, remote monitoring, smarter, safer, and more efficient monitoring of COVID-19 patients

(continued)

Table 23.1: Continued

Ref.	Year	Applications	IoT challenges	System design aspects/architecture	Computing paradigms	Protocols	Security & privacy	Features
[27]	2022	Healthcare system	Performance, resource utilization, privacy of data, and security of the system	IoT-blockchain integration architecture using an Ethereum blockchain infrastructure	Enhanced Rich-Thin-Client architecture (ERTCA), blockchain, Ganache Test Net – A testing blockchain environment maintained by Ethereum	X	Y	Patient Assistant System (PAS), a Nurse Assistant System (NAS), an Anesthesia Assistant System (AAS), and a Surgeon Assistant System (SAS), Surgical process management
[28]	2022	Healthcare system	Improved resource management, minimize processing time of physiological data	Software-defined fog architecture	SDN and FoG computing	X	X	Continuous patient monitoring

IoT always uses the cloud to store data and compute due to its distinctive characteristics such as self-organization, resource constraints, and proximity in communication. As a result of this confluence, the data at rest poses a series of unusual security issues. The author conducted an analysis to identify the issues and approaches employed by cloud computing to ensure the safe migration to cloud computing for IoT applications. As per the author one can also employ the advanced identification technology for the already established millions of IoT gadgets in forthcoming research [10].

The author observed that the IoT system faces the peculiar challenges for security, reliability and privacy concerns based on their unique features including heterogeneity of protocols and devices, reliance on physical environments as well as the close interaction with humans. One of the authors also illustrates in what ways the current research challenges can capitalize on security, reliability, and privacy innovations in other areas. Bagchi et al., also suggested a future direction to integrate IoT devices into the cloud infrastructure in a secure manner, to separate concerns about application security and functionality in software development, and to establish security perimeters [11]. Jiang et al., introduced the perception and characteristics of fog and cloud computing and also illustrate the collaboration and comparison between them. The key challenges that IoT encounters in novel application requisition (e.g., network bandwidth limitations, low latency, stability of service, resource limitations of devices, and security) and fog-based technologies are explored. The researcher also discussed the research directions and remnant challenges of fog after assimilation into the IoT system. Further, in the area of intelligent transportation and palpable robots, 5G-based fog computing plays an imminent role is also explored [12].

Smart home systems and appliances currently exist, but they are based on older technologies, and their user interfaces will be limited in scope, making it difficult for end-users to curb them. The existing smart homes have also raised concerns regarding security since they can be smoothly hacked, which may lead to major problems. The introduced smart home system is designed to provide security and simplify the adaptation to technology for end-users [13]. Observing threats and responding to attacks should be the goal of IoT security. Researchers also aim to encourage the security modality of IoT to lower the risks of security that affect the users and highlighted several areas of analysis that are still underdeveloped regarding traditional and block chain-based IoT security problems [14].

This literature review predominantly focuses on the existing IoT reference architecture with the various possible security threats in IoT-based smart home environment. Additionally, it illustrates the numerous emerging dynamic applications of IoT commercially and socially for well-being of humans.

3. Critical Review on IoT Architecture

IoT platform is incredibly important because it has the potential galore to revolutionize the various real-time applications around the globe. It incorporates smart devices, sensors, actuators, RFID, and the Internet to construct an incredibly smart system. In IoT environment the sensors are connected via wired or wirelessly over heterogeneous networks [15].

An exhaustive comparative analysis is outlined in Table 23.1 addressing the employed system designs, methodologies, protocols, and the challenges faced by the various available IoT architectures as far as their features, privacy, and security aspects are concerned.

4. Proposed Architecture

The IoT architecture is made up of varied distinct smart-things that gather, process, evaluate, and interact with each other. IoT networks are characterized by different levels of privacy, security and vulnerable to incursions. IoT consists of diverse networking types like ubiquitous, distributed, grid, and vehicular. As indicated in Figure 23.1, an IoT infrastructure includes not just sensors, but also various emerging technologies are embedded in it. In recent years, industries have developed various smart products with embedded intelligence.

Predominantly, IoT architecture comprises of three basic layers viz., perception layer, network layer, and application layer. In general, this three-layer architecture outlines the basic architecture of IoT, but isn't sufficiently detailed to satisfy deep and finer aspects of IoT. To address this, we propose a novel IoT architecture that appends four more levels and ameliorates the 3-layer architecture.

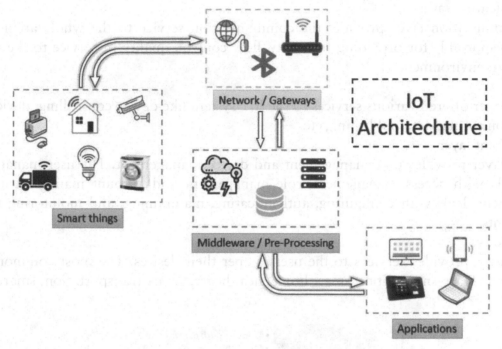

Figure 23.1: IoT architecture.

As a result, the three-layer architecture of IoT became a seven-layer architecture comprising the environment layer which is responsible for the authenticity of the observables or the things to watch out for, the communication layer which is responsible for the secure transmission of data between IoT devices, gateways, and the cloud, the next is service layer which monitors the devices and process the data generated by IoT devices, and at last the application support and management layer that deals with the management of devices and users while maintaining the authenticity.

After an exhaustive comparison of various available IoT architectures, the proposed model presented in Figure 23.2 which has incorporated all the important aspects of IoT architecture. However, this model can be explored further, which we will highlight in our future research. This seven-layer architecture presented in Figure 23.2 which denotes a more advanced layered version of IoT architecture.

The concise and technical explanation for each layer is as follows:

1. **Environment layer**

   This layer incorporates of all the observable that are being observed by the various sensors of an IoT application environment.
2. **Sensing and actuation (perception layer)**

   Sensing in IoT is about gathering different kinds of data from the surroundings using various sensors and performing some action based on date gathered. This layer comprises of various sensors and actuators like QR code, infra-red, ZigBee, RFID, etc.
3. **Network layer**

   This layer comprises of network communication software and various hardware components, that facilitates the perception layer to transmit data to the other layers without any human intervention.
4. **Communication layer**

   Communication layer provides the communication service to the whole architecture. This layer is responsible for providing reliability, flow control, quality of service to the users of IoT application environment.
5. **Services**

   This layer offered various services to the IoT system like device controlling, device discovery, device monitoring, data publishing, etc.
6. **Management layer**

   This layer provides user management and device management. The user management basically deals with access management, role management and account management and device management deals with configuring, authenticating, maintaining, and monitoring the network components.
7. **Applications**

   The layer provides services to the users as per their desires. The most common implementations of IoT are smart cities, smart home, healthcare, smart transportation, smart grid, smart retail, etc.

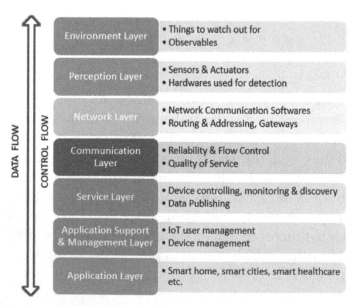

Figure 23.2: Layers of IoT architecture.

5. Privacy and Security Issues in IoT Architecture

IoT applications faces umpteen issues when it comes to privacy and security concern as pictured in Figure 23.3. As IoT is based on connected devices, it is mandatory that authentication be conducted at the device level as well. IoT applications become vulnerable to attacks because of their authentication security challenges. And also the other one is access control. There should be adamantine access control procedure is followed to make sure that only authorized parties can make use of resources. While analyzing and disseminating the information, privacy is of utmost importance in IoT environment. The IoT wirelessly transmits sensitive and personal data between devices in all scenarios. Therefore, there are certain security rules to be followed in the IoT environment to meet the privacy and security challenges that are illustrated in Figure 22.3.

5.1. Confidentiality

In simple terms, confidentiality can be summed up as "Information that should not be shared with anyone who is not permitted to access it". Confidentiality of user's crucial personal data i.e., user id, password, contact numbers, etc., are must be secured in the world of IoT [29].

The confidentiality makes sure that only the proposed recipient of the data can read the data. In order to maintain the confidentiality of an IoT system, it is mandatory that confidentiality must be enforced throughout the system by determining how the information is transmitted across the network.

5.2. Authentication

Validation of the user is ensured by authentication. To protect connected IoT devices and gadgets from unauthorized control commands, powerful IoT authentication is required.

Multiple stakeholders can combine and integrate services in a smart environment, allowing numerous users to be supported in a reliable and efficient manner [30]. An authenticated communication means that "Both the involved communicating entities are persuaded that they are interacting with the authenticated party". Confidentiality, integrity, and availability of data are assured by successful authentication mechanisms [29]. Because of limited resources, IoT authentication schemes need to be low cost and low power. This issue can be solved with lightweight cryptography [31].

5.3. Access control

The access control attack is one of the most critical attacks. IoT applications are vulnerable to access control attacks since once that access has been compromised, the entire application becomes vulnerable to assault [32]. The access control principle states that "The data and control of other devices and persons are only available to authenticated users" [4].

As long as communication quality is already assured, the access control mechanism establishes a new connection. An access control system protects the IoT against denial-of-service, replay and intruder attacks.

5.4. Privacy

IoT is being used for a variety of applications, so users invariably expect their privacy to be protected against the threat.

As IoT application become more extensive day by day, it facilitates data collection about our surroundings, our health, our homes, and so on. From the user's point of view, this data may include some private or sensitive personal data that should be conserved [11]. The privacy-preserving methodologies for IoT data require a careful review of what information is private and non-private so that the methods can preserve private data without hindering analysis of the data. The ability to control the privacy of users is also an integral part of the design process. IoT data privacy poses new privacy issues that go beyond conventional data privacy issues.

Following is a list of IoT privacy concerns:

- Privacy in device
- Privacy in storage
- Privacy in the course of communication
- Privacy while processing

5.5. Integrity

In simplest terms, integrity means "Making sure that any modification of information enrooted cannot be made by an unauthorized user" [4]. The protection of data against unauthorized interventions is critical, especially if unwanted code is injected. Verifying the integrity of data and ensuring it has not been altered during transmission is possible when digital certificates are used with codes.

Configuration management, access controls, and process controls can be used to protect integrity at the source. During transmission of data the integrity can be ensured by adopting cyclic redundancy checks or hashing algorithms to detect malfeasance [29].

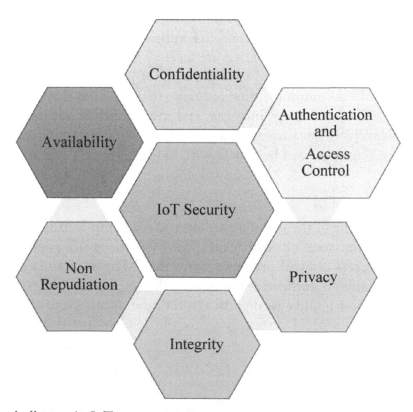

Figure 23.3: Security challenges in IoT.

5.6. Non-repudiation

According to IoT, non-repudiation means that "Whether the event occurred or not must be ensured by the system" [4]. In this way, all data is irrefutably proved to be valid and originating from the correct source. With digital signatures and hardware security devices, dates and origins of documents and transactions can be proven with strong non-repudiation.

6. Discussion and Future Research Directions

The proposed IoT architecture and a thorough study on system-level aspects of IoT, such as IoT architectures, security and privacy challenges and their impact on society, has been presented earlier. In this section, present issues and future research directions are discussed related to the above study.

There have been many IoT architectures developed by maneuvering various emerging technologies like WSNs, cloud, SDN, cluster RFID-based, Ledger-based, Black networks, CEP, ML, etc. But due to the lack of standards in IoT, these architectures are not performing as expected and lots of questions persist about their robustness and reliability. There have been various computing architectures and platforms proposed, but they're not interoperable, which makes integrating multiple applications problematic. As in various layered architecture the gateway among different layers must be secured because invaders can gain easy access into the IoT systems through gateways. In the future, the decryption process of the data must be done at the earmarked destination instead at gateways for rendering of protocol.

In fog-based architectures, a heavy load prevents the fog layer from processing requests, so the requests are transferred to the cloud layer. There is still a lot to be done in the area of inter-fog resource sharing. With the help of variegated AI and ML one can make fog layer brainier in nature. There are various ML algorithms are available but in this situation, it is so much crucial to choose the appropriate algorithm. Imperfect choice of algorithm will result in "garbage output" and loss of time, effort, and efficiency. Currently, there are few security and performance issues still need to be resolved in using block-chain, edge computing, fog computing, and ML for IoT security.

IoT made it possible for all devices around the globe to be connected to the web and share information autonomously, with minimal human involvement. There is an increasing number of everyday products connected to the internet, and with them, security concerns are also increasing. Increasingly prevalent of the IoT, every minute is quickly becoming synonymous with humanity, although its boundaries have not yet been established clearly nor is it secure. Furthermore, existing IoT systems pose serious security concerns, as they are susceptible to hacking, which could cause bigger problems. For example, there are various applications available through which parents can monitor their children using smart mobility. However, if these applications get hacked, this can pose a risk to the child's safety.

At present, security and privacy are among the biggest concerns with IoT. The issues arise with the use of unfamiliarity among end users, improper device updates, robust security protocols are the challenges faced by IoT today. In conjunction with researchers, we intend to develop a dynamic security system that will mitigate, but not completely eliminate, the privacy and security threats, and be versatile enough to deal with new advancements in modern technologies and various implementation methods. The threat environment for IoT networks and devices is always changing. Regularly, new attack vectors and vulnerabilities appear. Dynamic security systems are intended to adjust to these modifications and offer continuous protection against novel risks.

7. Conclusions

Through the integration of the internet and things in more organized and disciplined ways, the digital world revolutionizes our lifestyles. This amalgamation had a profound effect on our governance, wealth and industrial sectors by organizing and utilizing the resources effectively and efficiently. In the present era of the digital revolution, IoT is one of the main contender because modern society relies heavily on IoT devices and its applications. In this study, we proposed an enhanced IoT architecture after a thorough analysis of the many architectural methods presented by various researchers, ranging from simple architectures to implementations suitable for use in industry. We have examined both the benefits and risks possessed by IoT so far. In spite of its various advantages, this technology poses risks to end-users by permitting unauthorized access to sentient personal data, allowing intrusion into the system, and putting end-users at risk. IoT enabled products need to be shipped with adequate security measures so they are usable, operate correctly, and integrate with existing systems without any trouble.

References

[1] Asthon, K. (2009). That 'Internet of Things' Thing. *RFiD J.*, 4986. [Online]. Available: www.itrco.jp/libraries/RFIDjournal-That Internet of Things Thing.pdf.

[2] Syal, A. S. and Gupta, A. (2018). Internet of Things: Review on security of novel technology. *Proc. 2017 Int. Conf. Smart Technol. Smart Nation, SmartTechCon 2017*, 1405–1410. doi: 10.1109/SmartTechCon.2017.8358596.

[3] Chifor, B. C., Bica, I., Patriciu, V. V., and Pop, F. (2018). A security authorization scheme for smart home Internet of Things devices. *Fut. Gen. Comp. Sys.*, 86, 740–749. doi: 10.1016/j.future.2017.05.048.

[4] Patel, C. and Doshi, N. (2019). *Security Challenges in IoT Cyber World*. Security in smart cities: models, applications, and challenges, 171–191. DOI https://doi.org/10.1007/978-3-030-01560-2_8 Springer International Publishing, Switzerland.

[5] Perwej, Y., Parwej, F., Mohamed Hassan, M. M., and Akhtar, N. (2019). The Internet-of-Things (IoT) security : A technological perspective and review. *Int. J. Sci. Res. Comp. Sci. Engg. Inform. Technol.*, 5(1), 462–482. doi: 10.32628/cseit195193.

[6] Kumar, N., Singh, R., and Saxena, V. (2014). Modeling and minimization of cyber attacks through optimization technique. *An International Journal of Computer Application*, 99(1), 30–34.

[7] Verma, K., Singh, R., and Saxena, V. (2015). Security authorization for MAC address under distributed environment. *International Journal of Computer Applications*, 975, 8887.

[8] Ravi Kishore, K., Jain, V., Bose, S., and Boppana, L. (2016). IoT based smart security and home automation system. *Int. Conf. Comput. Comm. Autom. (ICCCA2016)*, 1286–1289. doi: 10.1109/UEMCON47517.2019.8992994.

[9] Rashmi, S. and Vipin, S. (2016). A unified modeling language model for occurrence and resolving of cyber crime. *Adv. Intel. Sys. Comput.*, 687–698. doi: 10.1007/978-81-322-2755-7_71.

[10] Mohiuddin, I. and Almogren, A. (2020). Security challenges and strategies for the IoT in cloud computing. *2020 11th Int. Conf. Inform. Comm. Sys. ICICS 2020*, 367–372. doi: 10.1109/ICICS49469.2020.239563.

[11] Bagchi, S., et al. (2020). New frontiers in IoT: Networking, systems, reliability, and security challenges. *IEEE Internet Things J.*, 7(12), 11330–11346. doi: 10.1109/JIOT.2020.3007690.

[12] Jiang, J., Li, Z., Tian, Y., and Al-Nabhan, N. (2020). A review of techniques and methods for IoT applications in collaborative cloud-fog environment. *Sec. Comm. Netw.*, 2020, 2020. doi: 10.1155/2020/8849181.

[13] Nagaraja, G. S. and Srinath, S. (2020). Security architecture for IoT-based home automation. *Smart Innov. Sys. Technol.*, 159, 57–65. doi: 10.1007/978-981-13-9282-5_6.

[14] Alnemari, S. M., Alzain, M. A., Masud, M., Jhanjhi, N. Z., and Al-amri, J. (2021). A comprehensive survey of Internet of Things security challenges and possible solutions. *Turkish Journal of Computer and Mathematics Education (TURCOMAT)*, 12(10), 3135–3142.

[15] Mohanta, B. K., Jena, D., Satapathy, U., and Patnaik, S. (2020). Survey on IoT security: Challenges and solution using machine learning, artificial intelligence and blockchain technology. *Internet of Things (Netherlands)*, 11, 100227. doi: 10.1016/j.iot.2020.100227.

[16] Sarkar, C., Nambi, S. A. U., Prasad, R. V., and Rahim, A. (2014, March). A scalable distributed architecture towards unifying IoT applications. In *2014 IEEE World Forum on Internet of Things (WF-IoT)*, 1, 508–513. IEEE. doi: 10.1109/WF-IoT.2014.6803220.

[17] Pawani, P., Corinna, S., Kumar, P., Andrei, G., and Mika, Y. (2014). Two-phase authentication protocol for wireless sensor networks in distributed IoT applications. *IEEE WCNC'14 Track 3 (Mobile and Wireless Networks)*, 2728–2733.

[18] Gonzalez, C., Charfadine, S. M., Flauzac, O., and Nolot, F. (2016, July). SDN-based security framework for the IoT in distributed grid. In *2016 international multidisciplinary conference on computer and energy science (SpliTech)*, 1, 1–5. IEEE. doi: 10.1109/SpliTech.2016.7555946.

[19] Lunardi, R. C., Michelin, R. A., Neu, C. V., and Zorzo, A. F. (2018, April). Distributed access control on IoT ledger-based architecture. In *NOMS 2018-2018 IEEE/IFIP Network Operations and Management Symposium*, 1, 1–7. IEEE.

[20] Sharma, P. K., Singh, S., Jeong, Y. S., and Park, J. H. (2017). DistBlockNet: A distributed blockchains-based secure SDN architecture for IoT networks. *IEEE Comm. Mag.*, 55(9), 78–85. doi: 10.1109/MCOM.2017.1700041.

[21] Islam, M. J., Mahin, M., Roy, S., Debnath, B. C., and Khatun, A. (2019, February). Distblacknet: A distributed secure black sdn-iot architecture with nfv implementation for smart cities. In *2019 International Conference on Electrical, Computer and Communication Engineering (ECCE)*, 1, 1–6. IEEE.

[22] Chakrabarty, S., and Engels, D. W. (2016, January). A secure IoT architecture for smart cities. In *2016 13th IEEE annual consumer communications & networking conference (CCNC)*, 1, 812–813. IEEE.

[23] Nigussie, E., Olwal, T. O., Lemma, A., Mekuria, F., and Peterson, B. (2020). IoT architecture for enhancing rural societal services in sub-Saharan Africa. *Proc. Comp. Sci.*, 338–344. doi: 10.1016/j.procs.2020.10.045.

[24] Roldán, J., Boubeta-Puig, J., Luis Martínez, J., and Ortiz, G. (2020). Integrating complex event processing and machine learning: An intelligent architecture for detecting IoT security attacks. *Expert Systems with Applications*, 149, 113251. https://doi.org/10.1016/j.eswa.2020.113251.

[25] Ariza, J., Garcés, K., Cardozo, N., Sánchez, J. P. R., and Vargas, F. J. (2021). IoT architecture for adaptation to transient devices. *J. Paral. Distrib. Comput.*, 148, 14–30. doi: 10.1016/j.jpdc.2020.09.012.

[26] Paganelli, A. I., et al. (2021). A conceptual IoT-based early-warning architecture for remote monitoring of COVID-19 patients in wards and at home. *Internet of Things*, xxxx, 100399. doi: 10.1016/j.iot.2021.100399.

[27] Bataineh, M. R., Mardini, W., Khamayseh, Y. M., and Yassein, M. M. B. (2022). Novel and secure blockchain framework for health applications in IoT. *IEEE Acc.*, 10, 14914–14926. doi: 10.1109/ACCESS.2022.3147795.

[28] Roy, C., Saha, R., Misra, S., and Niyato, D. (2022). Soft-health: Software-defined fog architecture for IoT applications in healthcare. *IEEE Internet Things J.*, 9(3), 2455–2462. doi: 10.1109/JIOT.2021.3097554.

[29] Clark, R. M., and Hakim, S. (Eds.). (2016). Cyber-physical security: protecting critical infrastructure at the state and local level, 3, 281. Springer. DOI https://doi.org/10.1007/978-3-319-32824-9, ISBN 978-3-319-32822-5.

[30] Alaba, F. A., Othman, M., Hashem, I. A. T., and Alotaibi, F. (2017). Internet of Things security: A survey. *J. Netw. Comp. Appl.*, 88, 10–28. doi: 10.1016/j.jnca.2017.04.002.

[31] Singh, S., Sharma, P. K., Moon, S. Y., and Park, J. H. (2017). Advanced lightweight encryption algorithms for IoT devices: survey, challenges and solutions. *J. Amb. Intell. Humaniz Comput.*, 1–18. doi: 10.1007/s12652-017-0494-4.

[32] Hassija, V., Chamola, V., Saxena, V., Jain, D., Goyal, P., and Sikdar, B. (2019). A survey on IoT security: Application areas, security threats, and solution architectures. *IEEE Acc.*, 7, 82721–82743. doi: 10.1109/ACCESS.2019.2924045.

24 Enhancing Software Maintainability Prediction Using an Optimizable-Support Vector Machine

Rohit Yadav[1,a], Anshu Singh[1], Prem Shanker Yadav[1], Chandrabhan Singh[1], Akanksha Yadav[1], and Avanish Kumar Jayank[2]

[1]Faculty of Engineering and Technology, Department of Computer Science and Engineering, University of Lucknow, Lucknow, Lucknow, Uttar Pradesh, India

[2]Faculty of Engineering and Technology, Department of Electronics and Communication, University of Lucknow, Lucknow, Lucknow, Uttar Pradesh, India

Abstract

Maintainability is a crucial phase in any software system, it is not just fixing bugs but strategic planning for long-term success of any software system. Software maintainability is influenced by many factors, and there are several ways for predicting it like metrics extraction, test coverage, software complexity measures, machine learning (ML) models, anti-detection pattern and natural language processing, etc. As maintainability is a complex term, effectively predicting it requires a thorough understanding of a wide range of software attributes and development techniques. We proposed feature selection-ranking based optimizable support vector machines (SVMs) and applied with feature selection ranking algorithms. Our proposal is performing better with validation accuracy of 87.9%.

Keywords: Support vector machine, maintainability, minimum redundancy-maximum relevance, Chi-squared

1. Introduction

Over time, as software systems solve day-to-day events very easily and efficiently, they become bigger and more complicated. Maintaining such complex systems is becoming increasingly difficult for software professionals. Since sustaining current systems takes up the majority of a software company's resources, some may not be able to launch new projects. Consequently, early in the software development process, during the design phase, software maintainability prediction (SMP) places focus on the creation and development of forecasting models for predicting software maintainability [1]. The ability to choose more significant parameters ahead of time improves the forecast accuracy of SMP models [2]. The existence of duplicate characteristics in high-dimensional records might be problematic for predicting maintainability since it could lead to machine learning (ML) algorithms performing poorly. Feature selection (FS) techniques effectively overcome this gap [6, 7]. This provides excellent software product within timeline under the budget which is very

---

[a]rohitatknit@gmail.com

maintainable. This research uses a range of data feature ranking algorithms before learning SMP models for improved and effective performance, addressing the significance of parameter selection in SMP. This study discovered a strong correlation between object oriented (OO) metrics, which characterize a variety of program aspects, including inheritance, coupling, and cohesion and software maintainability. This makes the research important as it addresses the creation of efficient SMP models by determining the traits that influence software maintainability more than others. Improving the software product's quality is facilitated by allocating resources to these classes in an appropriate manner. Our proposal helps:

- To determine the root points of software system's maintainability.
- To evaluate and statistically validate the created SMP models' prediction ability.
- To assess numerous feature selection-based ranking strategies with support vector machines (SVMs).

We create SMP models that use software maintainability as the response variable and OO metrics as predictor variables in order to satisfy the aforementioned research goals. Five datasets from open-source software were taken out. We have predicting maintainability with the help of top key parameters selected by feature selection algorithms. The SMP model is then assessed using the confusion matrix and the receiver operator characteristic (ROC) curve.

2. Related Work

In 2014, Wong et al., [10] presented an automated learning-based methodology that used real average maintenance effort to train maintainability predictors. Kumar et al., in 2017 discussed various significant feature selection correlations in various dimensions. These mathematical functions support in finding accurate SMP model. Kumar et al., [7] proposed hybridized techniques for change value prediction. In 2017, Reddy et al., [5] used support vector-based regression, multilayer perceptron's, multilinear regression, and M5P regression trees. Malhotra et al., [8] presented class relevant group basis maintainability in 2020. Data sampling and resampling were the main basis that was served for better prediction [9]. Additionally, for handling imbalanced datasets and anticipating software maintainability, safe-level—synthetic minority oversampling technique was used. In 2020, Gupta et al., [3] has proposed a model using least square and showed their relevant comparisons for better result. They have also presented augmented random forest approach [4] in 2020 to estimate the maintainability of open-source software.

3. Research Methodology

Identifying parameters are very important task for consistent long-term maintainability followed by normalization of the same. Here optimization approach of SVM plays big role. Here approach of optimization of SVM is displayed using following Figure 24.1.

Proposed layered steps for SMP involves identification of parameters, normalizations of dataset, involving optimization approach, training, testing and comparative analysis which is shown in Figure 24.2. It represents the methodology that is used in our study for the analysis of the SMP model.

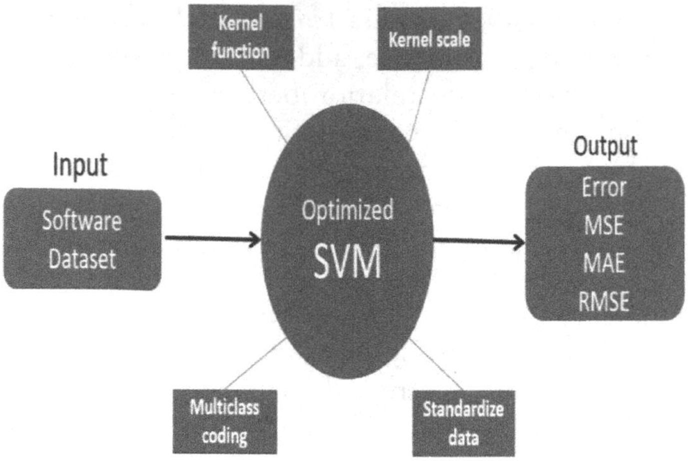

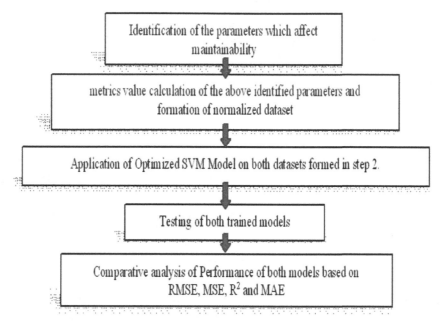

Figure 24.1: Optimization approach of SVM for SMP.

Figure 24.2: Diagram of research methodology.

3.1. Dataset

We used the following java-programming based datasets:

- Ant: Ant is a command-line tool used to automate tasks within build files denoted by expanded points and objectives. Ant contains several tasks for building, testing, compiling, and running Java programs.
- Camel: Built around enterprise integration patterns. Camel is an open-source networking framework.
- Ckjm: Software ckjm produces object-oriented metrics such as Chidamber and Kemerer by examining the bytecode and compiled Java programs.
- Ivy: Ivy is a system for controlling project dependencies (logging, monitoring, resolving, and summarizing).

3.2. Predictor variables

We utilize OO metrics as the predictor variables in our prediction models because the study is done with OO systems that are developed in Java. We have listed lines of source code (LOC), response for class (RFC), depth of inheritance tree (DIT), weighted methods per class (WMC), measure of aggregation (MOA), number of children of a class (NOC), coupling between the objects (CBO), inheritance coupling (IC), data access metric (DAM), measure of functional abstraction (MFA), number of public methods (NPM), efferent coupling (Ce), afferent coupling (Ca), coupling between the class methods (CBM), average method complexity (AMC), cohesion among methods of a class (CAM), and LCOM3 as input variables. The LCOM variety is called LCOM3 (Table 24.1).

Numerous aspects of OO systems, including coupling, cohesion, size, inheritance, composition and encapsulation are explained by these metrics. The metrics for WMC, NPM, LOC, DAM, and AMC all show the size of a class. IC, CBM, RFC, Ca, Ce, and CBO measures are used to quantify the coupling. NOC, DIT, and MFC are employed in identifying the property that is inherited. Class cohesiveness indicators include LCOM, CAM, and LCOM3, whereas composition is measured by MOA. These selected metrics for investigation extensively for predictive modeling.

Table 24.1: Description of predictors

Metric suit	Set of metric selected
CKJM suit [11]	CBO, NPM, RFC, LCOM, DIT, WMC
QMOOD suit [12]	NPM, DAM, MOA, CAM, MFA
Martins's metrics [13]	Ca, Ce
Henderson-Sellers [14]	LOC, LCOM3, AMC, IC, CBM

3.3. Response variable

Our work uses cyclomatic complexity to determine maintainability as the study cyclomatic complexity is used to form dependent variable i.e., maintainability value (MV) of each class of software. High and low represents the maximum and low maintainability, respectively. In cyclomatic complexity it is opposite. High maintainability means classes having cyclomatic complexity less than 1 and low maintainability for classes having cyclomatic complexity more than or equal to 1. The following logic is implemented to determine the dependent variable.

if (CC<=1)
{
    MV = 1;
}
Else
{
    MV = 0;
}

In above logic CC represent the cyclomatic complexity and MV represents the maintainability metric.

3.4. *Identification of parameters*

Two methods are utilized to rank all the predictor qualities because not every metric value may be helpful in determining maintainability. The feature selection function chooses a subset of the available components rather than using all of them. The practice of feature selection has several benefits. Among other advantages, feature selection reduces noise to improve forecasting models' classification accuracy. Even more comprehensible features may be used to identify and monitor different function types.

3.4.1. *mRMR*

A feature selection technique called mRMR gives preference to attributes that are poorly suited to one another but have a good correlation with the class (product) [1]. The initial idea behind mRMR is that an output (feature set *S*) with *m* features *Xi* that are highly correlated with the class *C* has to be analyzed. To attain maximal relevance, the mean value of correlation for each characteristic *Xi* in class *C* is utilized. The mutual information between randomly produced variables *X* and *Y* may be expressed technically as follows:

$$MI\ (X,\ Y) = x{\in}X\ y{\in}Y,\ p(x,\ y)log\ p(x,\ y)\ p(x)p(y) \tag{1}$$

A measure of global relevance of the variables in *S* with respect to *C* is:

$$VI\ (S) = 1\ |S|\ Xi{\in}S\ MI\ (C,\ Xi) \tag{2}$$

The mutual information of feature *Xi* with class *C* is represented here as *MI* (*C*, *Xi*). The second mRMR principle is that the use of minimum duplication across attributes should support the features' highest relevance criterion with respect to the classifier. Enhancement of the dependence between features in multimedia tools and applications is likely if only relevant information is given. Thus, the least amount of duplication that doesn't compromise its usefulness has to be added. Use the following formula to obtain the fewest qualities that are redundant:

$$WI\ (S) = 1\ |S|\ 2\ Xi,\ Xj{\in}S\ MI\ (Xi,\ Xj) \tag{3}$$

Here, *MI* (*Xi*, *Xj*) is the mutual information of feature *Xi* with *Xj*. Minimum redundancy maximum relevance is a criterion that combines the above two conditions (mRMR). To get a suitable subset of characteristics, the easiest way to optimize relevance and duplication is to:

$$max\ \phi(VI\ (S),\ WI\ (S)) \tag{4}$$

3.4.2. *Univariate feature ranking using Chi-square tests*

Two occurrences can be tested for independence using the Chi-squared test [7], where attributes are prioritized based on the class-specific value of the Chi-squared statistic. The value of Chi-squared is determined using the equation that follows:

$$\chi^2 = \Sigma \frac{(O_i - E_i)^2}{E_i} \tag{5}$$

where
O_i = observed valve,
E_i = anticipated value.
The high value of χ^2 indicates that the null hypothesis is disproved.

3.5. *Optimized SVM*

Preferring ML algorithms over classical methods effectively adjusting learning parameters, such as model hyperparameters. A hyperparameter optimization technique called Bayesian Tuning is derived from common ML techniques and determines the model's attributes, or more accurately, the training procedure. A substitute for the target is created, and the ambiguity in that substitute is attempted to be measured using a Bayesian based technique. We also performed analysis using Gaussian process regression. This process of parameter optimization makes use of both the Gaussian process and Bayesian probability theory. An optimal observation value needs to be selected for every Bayesian optimization cycle. The formula that follows explains this:

$$f(x) \sim GP(\mu(x), k(x, x^*)) \tag{6}$$

The mean function is $\mu(x)$, while the kernel function is $k(x, x^*)$ and the Gaussian kernel function is in the form represented in Equation (7).

$$k(x, x^*) = \exp\left(-\frac{1}{2}\|x - x^*\|^2\right) \tag{7}$$

The hyperparameter value obtained by the process is used by the Bayesian optimization method to replace the current value for effective generation of new model. In this work, we performed this work on MATLAB.

4. Performance Evaluation

For performance measure ROC curve, area under the curve (AUC), confusion matrix, RMSE, R^2, MSE and MAE are utilized in our study.

- The ROC curve is a graphical representation to classify in true and false. ROC extracts high or low maintainability of software systems. The AUC quantifies the model's ability to distinguish between the high and low classes across different threshold settings.
- A confusion matrix deals correct or incorrect prediction of instances as high or low maintainability.
- A popular statistic for comparing values predicted by a model or predictor to actual values is the root-mean-square error (RMSE).
- A regression line's mean squared error (MSE) indicates how near it is to a number of solutions. It accomplishes this by squaring the distances between the points and the regression line. Squaring is required to eliminate any negative signals.
- A measure of mistakes between paired observations describing the same phenomena is called mean absolute error (MAE).

5. Experimental Result and Discussion

We obtain distinct rankings for every characteristic after running the mRMR and Chi-square test on the normalized data set. These results serve as the foundation for additional training of the suggested ML classification model. Table 24.2 detail the order of each predictor variable (object oriented metric) derived from Chi-square and mRMR.

Table 24.2: Ranking values of Input variable using Chi-square and mRMR

Metric	Chi-square	mRMR
wmc	11	11
dit	18	2
Noc	5	7
cbo	1	18
rfc	14	6
lcom	6	5
Ca	9	14
ce	4	4
npm	15	9
lcom3	7	10
loc	2	1
dam	10	15
moa	8	17
mfa	13	13
cam	17	8
Ic	16	3
cbm	12	12
amc	3	16

Model 1 uses the Chi-square method and is followed by an optimizable SVM with noc, cbo, lcom, ca, Ce, lcom3, loc, dam, moa, and amc as predictor variables and MV as response variable. In contrast, our second model (model 2) employs the mRMR technique and optimizable SVM. Its predictor variables are dit, noc, rfc, lcom, Ce, npm, lcom3, loc, cam, and ic, and its response variable is MV. While wmc, cbo, ca, dam, moa, mfa, cbm, and amc are removed from the dataset to provide a smaller selection of predictor variables for model 2, wmc, dit, rfc, npm, mfa, cam, ic, and cbm are not utilized for training in model 1 (Figures 24.3–24.5).

Based on the analysis, model 2 outperforms over model 1 with an accuracy rate of 87.9%. When the Chi-square method is used, the values obtained are 0.79396, 0.37, 0.63036, and 0.53769, while the mRMR model yields values of 0.76737, 0.41, 0.58886, and 0.47987. A comparison is displayed in Figure 24.6. Further both trained models were tested on and Bayesian optimization is applied. We have considered two software's named poi and jEdit for testing. This results in more than 80% accuracy in both models, which is a positive sign for any model that predicts the maintainability of software. Two different open-source software namely *jEdit* and *poi* and form the Figure 24.7, clearly it is evident that mRMR followed by optimized SVM is better than Chi-squared followed by

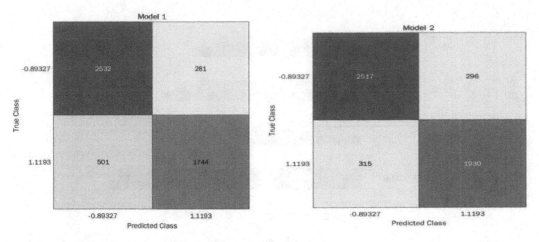

Figure 24.3: Confusion matrix of model 1 and model 2.

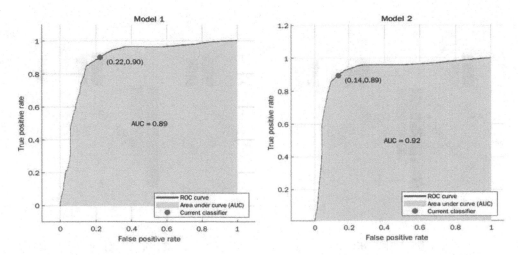

Figure 24.4: ROC curve of model 1 and model 2.

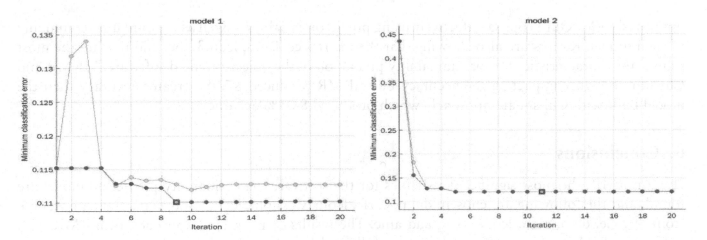

Figure 24.5: MSE for each iteration of model 1 and model 2.

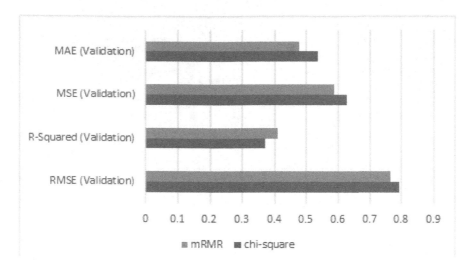

Figure 24.6: Comparison of model 1 and model 2 based on testing.

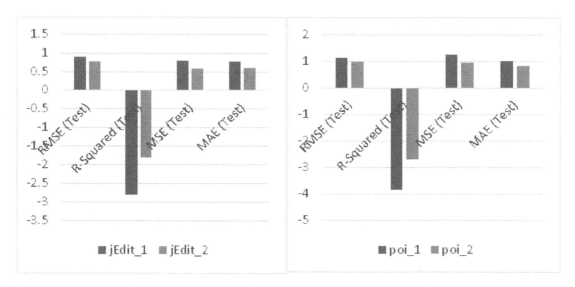

Figure 24.7: Comparison of accuracy measures for jEdit software and poi software.

optimized SVM. Our proposal effectively using predictor variables as well as they are used commonly in each model. Results are also showing that the metrics ce, lcom, lcom3, loc, and noc are the most significant characteristics for maintainability prediction of the object-oriented software. MRMR and Chi-square highly impacting the accuracy but mRMR produced 87.9% greater accuracy than the model built with Chi-square approach, which produced 84.5% accuracy.

6. Conclusions

Using mRMR, the most significant variables for the software maintainability prediction model are found, and the following are chosen: dit, noc, rfc, lcom, Ce, npm, lcom3, loc, cam, and ic; noc, cbo, lcom, ca, Ce, dam, moa, lcom3, loc, and amc. The results of integrated approach of mRMR with optimized SVM is superior than Chi-square followed by optimized SVM. The Bayesian approach is employed for hyperparameter tweaking and the Gaussian kernel function is used for prediction model optimization. In comparison with the various SMP studies that are currently available, our method yields higher accuracy. In the future, we will also work on integration of k-NN, decision trees, and neural networks along with meta-heuristic search optimization algorithms to create better SMP models.

References

[1] Malhotra, R. and Lata, K. (2020). An empirical study on predictability of software maintainability using imbalanced data. *Softw. Qual. J.*, 28, 1581–1614.

[2] Berrendero, J. R., Cuevas, A., and Torrecilla, J. L. (2016). The mRMR variable selection method: a comparative study for functional data. *J. Statist. Comput. Simul.*, 86(5), 891–907.

[3] Ferenc, R., Tóth, Z., Ladányi, G., et al. (2020). A public unified bug dataset for java and its assessment regarding metrics and bug prediction. *Softw. Qual. J.*, 28, 1447–1506.

[4] Gupta, S., and Chug, A. (2020). Software maintainability prediction of open source datasets using least squares support vector machines. *Journal of Statistics and Management Systems*, 23(6), 1011–1021. https://doi.org/10.1080/09720510.2020.1799501.

[5] Gupta, S. and Anuradha, C. (2020). Software maintainability prediction using an enhanced random forest algorithm. *J. Dis. Mathemat. Sci. Cryptograp.*, 23(2), 441–449.

[6] Reddy, B. R. and Ojha, A. (2019). Performance of maintainability Index prediction models: A feature selection based study. Evol. Sys., 10, 179–204.

[7] Kumar, L., Krishna, A., and Rath, S. K. (2017). The impact of feature selection on maintainability prediction of service-oriented applications. *SOCA*, 11, 137–161.

[8] Ruchika, M. and Megha, K. (2017). An exploratory study for software change prediction in object-oriented systems using hybridized techniques. *Automat. Softw. Engg.*, 24(3), 673–717.

[9] Ruchika, M. and Kusum, L. (2021). An empirical study to investigate the impact of data resampling techniques on the performance of class maintainability prediction models. *Neurocomput.*, 459, 432–453.

[10] Wang, X., Alexander, G., Arabikhan, F., Yuntao, C., and Qiwei, H. (2019). Fuzzy network based framework for software maintainability prediction. *Int. J. Uncert. Fuzz. Knowl. Sys.*, 27(05), 841–862.

[11] Chidamber, S. R. and Kemerer, C. F. (1994). A metrics suite for object oriented design. *IEEE Trans. Softw. Engg.*, 20(6), 476–493.

[12] Bansiya, J. and Davis, C. G. (2002). A hierarchical model for object-oriented design quality assessment. *IEEE Trans. Softw. Engg.*, 28(1), 4–17.

[13] Henderson-Sellers, B. (1996). Object-oriented metrics, measures of complexity. Prentice Hall. pp 234, Prentice-Hall, Inc. Division of Simon and Schuster One Lake Street Upper Saddle River, NJUnited States, ISBN:978-0-13-239872-5.

[14] Martin, R. C. (2002). Agile software development: Principles, patterns, and practices. Prentice Hall. pp 531, Pearson Education Limited, Printed in the United States of America, ISBN 10: 1-292-02594-8.

25 A Miniaturized Monopole Tri-Band Rectangular Patch Antenna For WiMAX/C-Band Wireless Applications

Prakshep Kumar Rai[a], Chandan[b], and Ashutosh K. Singh[c]

Department of Electronics and Communication Engineering, IET Dr.R.M.L.A University, Ayodhya, India

Abstract

This works presents, a minimized monopole tri-band antenna for WiMAX and C-band applications. The suggested antenna has a very compact in size $20{\times}26{\times}1.6$ mm^3. The components of the suggested antenna are rectangular patch, three strips and a parasitic element (which placed at bottom side of substrate). The FR4_epoxy substrate is used for the antenna's design for operating over three bands from 3.1–4 GHz, 5.3–5.8 GHz and 7.3–8 GHz with resonance frequencies 3.5, 5.5 and 7.7 GHz and with losses -37, -22 and -25 dB (S11<−10 dB) with bandwidth 900MHz, 500 MHz and 700 MHz. HFSS software is used to simulate the antenna. Simulated results and measured result of the proposed antenna are showed in this article.

Keywords: Monopole antenna, Wi-MAX, C-band, HFSS, tri-band

1. Introduction

A contemporary movable wireless communication device is increasingly in demand it can combine multiple communication standards into a single system. It is difficult to fit two or more antennas simultaneously into such a device because of the limited space. "This shows that a modern antenna needs to do other tasks in addition to enabling dual- or multiband operation, but also a compact size, simple structure and easy integration with system" [1]. Due to its distinctive qualities as simple, low- profile, and inexpensive, microstrip patch antennas are incredibly popular. They work with monolithic microwave integrated circuits and are simple to install [2]. Worldwide Interoperability for Microwave Access (WiMAX) is a very popular wireless communication system that has recently received a lot of attention from researchers and has been implemented in mobile devices. The antennas should cover numerous frequency bands and be capable of providing consistent omnidirectional radiation patterns to enhance performance and make the antenna useful in a complex and varied WiMAX environment [3]. Moreover, the low band (between 2500 and 2690 MHz), the middle band (3300 and 3700 MHz), and the high band (5250 and 5850 MHz) are the three main bands

[a]prakshep7302@gmail.com, [b]chandanhcst@gmail.com, [c]aksinghelectronics@gmail.com

that WiMAX has been given access to [4]. Numerous multiband antennas for WiMAX and Ultra-wideband (UWB) have been recently suggested in the literature. For example, in [5] the author proposed a rectangular patch antenna for 7.5 GHz wireless communications, it has low return loss, the antenna is large in size 32×28.1 mm^2 also having only one band. A portable Coplanar Waveguide (CPW)-Fed antenna for multiband applications was suggested in [6], the antenna size is quite small but complicated in structure.

There are also designs for multiband wireless applications in [7–14]. In Refs. 7–10, despite the suggested antennas have good qualities but large in size.

As a result of the literature analysis, it was determined that constructing antennas to support tri-band features with the better gain, which has been taken as an objective for this research work. In this article, our aim is to design a miniaturized monopole tri-band rectangular patch antenna for WiMAX and C-band applications. The antenna design incorporates three strips and one parasitic element at the ground plane to achieve multiband characteristics. The objective is to cover the frequencies of WiMAX at 3.5 and 5.5 GHz, as well as the C-band at 7.5 GHz. Using the High-Frequency Structure Simulator (HFSS), the effects of the parameters on the impedance bandwidth is examined. Based on the simulation results, the proposed antenna design is suitable for both WiMAX and C-band applications. This implies that the antenna exhibits the desired performance characteristics, such as appropriate impedance matching and radiation properties, within the specified frequency ranges.

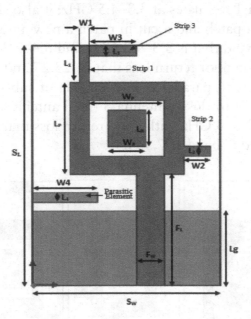

Figure 25.1: Proposed antenna.

2. Antenna Structures and Dimensions

Figure 25.1 illustrates the geometrical representation of the proposed tri-band WiMAX/C-band monopole antenna. The suggested antenna is consisting of rectangular patch connected by three strips and feed line. It has a ground plane with a parasitic element on the bottom side of the substrate. The suggested antenna is constructed on a FR-4_epoxy substrate with a 4.4 relative dielectric constant, and size of $20 \times 26 \times 1.6$ mm^3. The use of FR-4 substrate has the benefit of being inexpensive and widely accessible. The width and length of ground plane is 20×8 mm^2 and parasitic element is 7×1 mm^2. A feed line of 50Ω (3×12mm^2) is used for feeding the antenna. All of the antenna's dimensions are listed in Table 25.1. The use of parametric analysis is to design and optimize the antenna on the HFSS.

Table 25.1: The suggested antenna's dimensions

Parameters	Dimensions (mm)	Parameters	Dimensions (mm)
S_L	26	S_W	20
F_L	12	F_W	3
L_P	12	W_P	10
L_R	4	W_R	4
L_1	4	W_1	1
L_2	1	W_2	3
L_3	1	W_3	5
L_4	1	W_4	7
L_g	8		

Figure 25.2 shows step involved in antenna design, which consist of antenna 1, antenna 2 and antenna 3. Figure 25.3 shows that return loss for antenna 1, antenna 2 and antenna 3. Antenna 3 is the proposed antenna. Antenna 1 resonates at 3.3–4.5 GHz; it also shows a nearly -19dB return loss at 3.8 GHz. Adding 2 strips on patch and a cut in patch a new antenna designed that is antenna 2, which operate at 2 frequency band that is 3.3–4.3 GHz and 6.4–7.3 GHz with resonance frequency 3.7 and 6.9 GHz and also having poor return loss that is -23.27 and -19.16dB. To make the antenna triband a strip 3 is added and with parallel at bottom side of substrate adding a parasitic element which improves the antenna's return loss. Antenna 3 (final antenna) is operating at 3 bands, that is 3.1–4 GHz, 5.3–5.8 GHz and 7.3–8 GHz with good return loss that is –37, –22, and –25 dB, which cover WiMAX 3.5/5.5 GHz and C-band at 7.5 GHz.

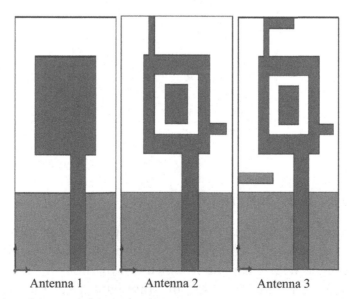

Antenna 1　Antenna 2　Antenna 3

Figure 25.2: Step involved in designing for antenna.

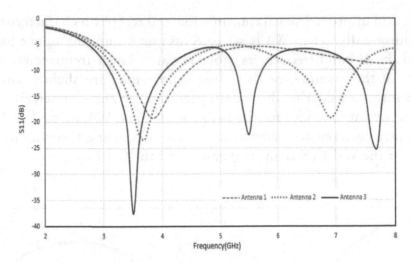

Figure 25.3: Antennas 1, 2, and 3's return loss.

Table 25.2: Comparison of above factors of Figure 25.2 antenna

Name of antenna	Pattern	Band width	No of bands
Antenna 1	Rectangle patch	3.3–4.5	Single-band
Antenna 2	Rectangle patch with 2 strips	3.3–4.3 6.4–7.3	Double-band
Antenna 3	Rectangle patch with 3 strips and parasitic element	3.1–4 5.3–5.8 7.3–8	Triple-band

3. Parametric Analysis

For make antenna optimum Fw, Lg, and W4 are select to investigate. For various Fw values, Figure 25.4 displays return loss. When the feed line width (Fw) is set to 2.9 mm, the upper WiMAX band and C-band frequencies are slightly shifted towards lower frequencies compared to some desired frequencies. This means that the antenna's resonant frequency for those bands is slightly lower than expected. As a result, there may be some impedance mismatch, which can lead to higher return loss (weaker signal reflected the source) and reduced antenna efficiency for those frequencies. On the other hand, when the feed line width (Fw) is increased to 3.1 mm, the antenna exhibits low return loss. This implies that the antenna is better matched to the desired frequencies, resulting in improved signal transmission and reception characteristics. The impedance matching is likely optimal for these frequencies, leading to a minimal reflection of the signal. However, when the Fw is precisely set to 3 mm, the antenna shows the best overall performance. It not only provides good return loss but also offers proper impedance matching.

Figure 25.5 displays return loss for different values of Lg. Lg essentially refers to the ground plane's length. Lg is varying from 7 to 9 mm. Lg at 8 mm antenna gives optimum results with good return loss and having a proper impedance matching.

In Figure 25.6, a parametric analysis for the width of the parasitic element, W4, is shown. The parasitic element is positioned on the bottom side of the substrate. The analysis evaluates different values of W4 and their impact on antenna performance. However, when W4 is set to 6 mm or 8 mm, the antenna exhibits low return loss. This implies that these particular widths result in better impedance matching and improved signal transmission and reception characteristics for the WiMAX frequency range. Additionally, when W4 is set to 6 mm or 8 mm, the upper band of the WiMAX frequency range and the C-band frequencies move towards lower frequencies. This means that the resonant frequencies of the antenna for these frequency bands are slightly lower when using W4 values of 6 mm or 8 mm. Considering the overall performance and characteristics of the antenna, it is determined that the optimum width for the parasitic element, W4, is fixed at 7 mm. This choice is likely based on a balance between achieving low return loss, proper impedance matching, and desired frequency coverage for the WiMAX frequency bands and the C-band.

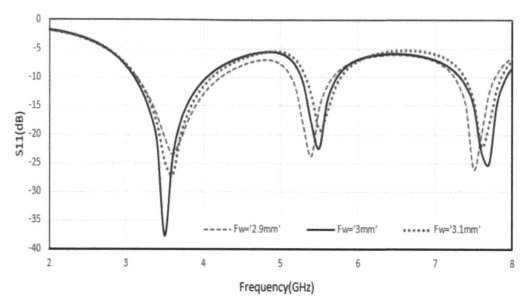

Figure 25.4: Analysis of Fw's parameters.

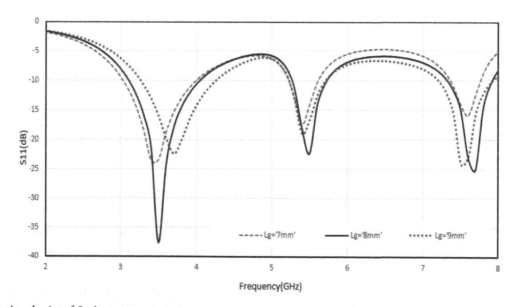

Figure 25.5: Analysis of Lg's parameters.

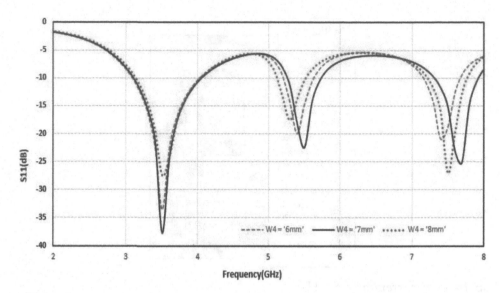

Figure 25.6: Analysis of W4's parameters.

4. Result and Discussion

The proposed antenna design, simulated using HFSS software, exhibits three distinct frequency bands with resonance frequencies of 3.5, 5.5, and 7.7 GHz. The return losses for these frequencies are -37, –22, and –25 dB, respectively, indicating good impedance matching and minimal power reflection.

To gain further insights into the antenna's performance, the current distribution at the resonance frequencies of 3.5, 5.5, and 7.7 GHz is illustrated in Figures 25.7, 25.8, and 25.9, respectively. These figures depict the distribution of current flow across the antenna structure at each frequency. By examining the current distribution, one can observe the areas of high and low current density, which helps in understanding how the antenna radiates energy at different frequencies.

Additionally, the antenna's radiation pattern is a crucial factor in assessing its performance. Figures 25.10, 25.11, and 25.12 show the radiation pattern of the antenna at Phi = 0° (E-plane) and Phi = 90° (H-plane) for frequencies 3.5, 5.5, and 7.7 GHz, respectively. The E-plane refers to the plane perpendicular to the axis of the antenna, while the H-plane is the plane containing the antenna's axis. For the 3.5 GHz band, the proposed antenna exhibits an omnidirectional radiation pattern in the E-plane, indicating that it radiates equally in all directions within that plane. However, in the H-plane, the radiation pattern appears two-dimensional, suggesting that the antenna radiates more effectively in specific directions within that plane. In contrast, for the 5.5 and 7.7 GHz bands, the antenna demonstrates good radiation characteristics in the desired directions in both the E-plane and H-plane. This implies that the antenna is designed to radiate energy efficiently in specific directions at these frequencies, which is desirable for applications requiring focused or directional radiation.

Figure 25.13, which provides the antenna's top and bottom views, depicts the fabricated antenna. Figure 25.14 shows a contrast between the measured result and the simulated result obtained using the simulation software HFSS. The good compatibility of the two results demonstrates the usefulness of the suggested antenna.

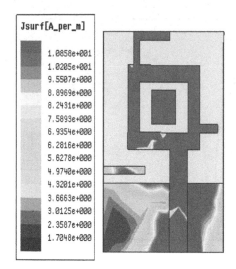

Figure 25.7: Dispersion of current at 3.5 GHz.

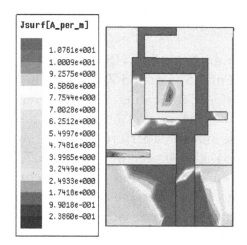

Figure 25.8: Dispersion of current at 5.5 GHz.

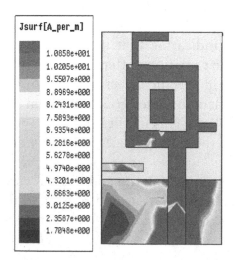

Figure 25.9: Dispersion of current at 7.7 GHz.

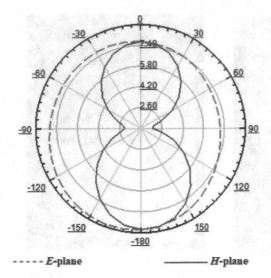

Figure 25.10: Frequency=3.5 GHz.

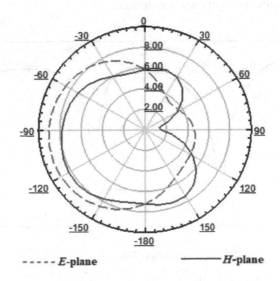

Figure 25.11: Frequency=5.5 GHz.

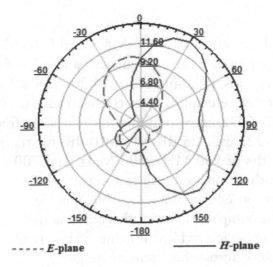

Figure 25.12: Frequency=7.7 GHz.

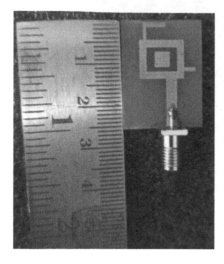  

(a) Top view   (b) Bottom view

Figure 25.13: Top and bottom view of fabricated antenna.

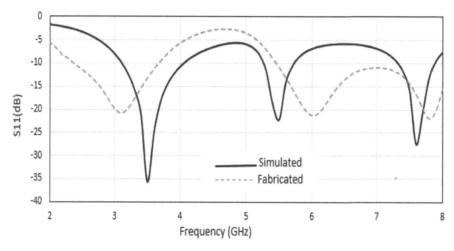

Figure 25.14: Fabricated and simulated result.

5. Conclusions

A miniaturized monopole tri-band antenna for WiMAX and C-band applications is presented. The antenna has been created to operate over three frequency bands: 3.1–4 GHz, 5.3–5.8 GHz, and 7.3–8 GHz. The proposed antenna has a very compact size of $20 \times 26 \times 1.6$ mm^3. The simulation results of the antenna using HFSS software demonstrate its effectiveness. The antenna exhibits resonance frequencies at 3.5, 5.5, and 7.7 GHz, corresponding to the desired frequency bands. The return loss values are measured at –37, –22, and –25 dB (S11<–10 dB) for the respective bands. The antenna also offers sufficient bandwidths of 900 MHz, 500 MHz, and 700 MHz for the three frequencies ranges, respectively. Based on the simulated results and the detailed design presented in this article, it can be concluded that the proposed antenna is capable of achieving tri-band operation for C-band and WiMAX applications. The compacted size of this antenna makes it suitable for integration into various wireless communication devices, while the achieved bandwidths and return loss values ensure efficient and reliable performance across the intended frequency ranges.

References

[1] Zhang, L., Chen, B., Jiao, Y. C., and Weng, Z. (2012). Compact triple-band monopole antenna with two strips for WLAN/WiMAX applications. *Microw. Opt. Technol. Lett.*, 54(11), 2650–2653.

[2] Chandan, Srivastava, T. and Rai, B. S. (2016). Multiband monopole U-slot patch antenna with truncated ground plane. *Microw. Optic. Technol. Lett.*, 58(8), 1949–1952.

[3] Li, Y. and Yu, W. (2015). A miniaturized triple band monopole antenna for WLAN and WiMAX applications. *Int. J. Anten. Propag.*, 1–5.

[4] Hoang, T. V., Le, T. T., Li, Q. Y., and Park, H. C. (2016). Quad-band circularly polarized antenna for 2.4/5.3/5.8-GHz WLAN and 3.5-GHz WiMAX applications. *IEEE Anten. Wire. Propag. Lett.*, 15, 1032–1035.

[5] Jadhav, D. S., Deosarkar, S. B., and Kadbe, P. K. (2013). Rectangular patch antenna for 7.5 GHz wireless communications. *Int. J. Sci. Res.*, 4, 378–379.

[6] Cheong, H. R., Yeap, K. H., Lai, K. C., Teh, P. C., & Nisar, H. (2017). A compact CPW-fed antenna with fractal S-shaped patches for multiband applications. *Microwave and Optical Technology Letters*, 59(3), 541–546.

[7] Chandan. (2020). Truncated ground plane multiband monopole antenna for WLAN and WiMAX applications. *IETE J. Res.*, 66, 1–6.

[8] Chandan, T. S. and Rai, B. S. (2017). L-slotted microstrip fed monopole antenna for triple band WLAN and WiMAX applications. *Springer Adv. Intel. Sys. Comput. Book Ser.*, 516, 351–359.

[9] Chandan, and Rai, B. S. (2016). Dual-band monopole patch antenna using microstrip fed for WiMAX and WLAN applications. *Inform. Sys. Des. Intel. Appl.*, 2, 533–539.

[10] Chandan, Ratnesh, R. K., and Kumar, A. (2021). A compact dual rectangular slot monopole antenna for WLAN/WiMAX applications. *Springer Cyber Phy. Sys. Lec. Notes Elec. Engg. Book Ser. (LNEE)*, 788, 699–705.

[11] Chandan, Bharti, G. D., Srivastava, T., and Rai, B. S. (2018). Miniaturized printed K shaped monopole antenna with truncated ground plane for 2.4/5.2/5.5/5.8 wireless LAN applications. *AIP Conf. Proc. Am. Institute Phy.*, 200371–200377.

[12] Chandan, Ashutosh Kumar, S., Mishra, R. P., Ratneshwar Kumar, R., and Parimal, T. (2022). Defected ground structure with four band meander-shaped monopole antenna for LTE/WLAN/WIMAX/long distance radio telecommunication applications. *Intel. Sys. Smart Infrastruc. Proc. ICISSI 2022*, 1–11. Taylor & Francis eBooks, ISBN 9781032412870.

[13] Chandan, and Rai, B. S. (2014). Bandwidth enhancement of wang shape microstrip patch antenna for wireless system. *IEEE Fourth Int. Conf. Comm. Sys. Netw. Technol. (NITTR BHOPAL)*, 11–15.

[14] Chandan, and Rai, B. S. (2014). Dual-band wang shaped microstrip patch antenna for GPS and bluetooth application. *IEEE Sixth Int. Conf. Comput. Intel. Comm. Netw. (Udaipur)*, 69–73.

26 A Compact Tantacled Rectangular Slot Antenna With DGS For Various Wireless Applications

Parimal Tiwari[1,a], K. K. Verma[2,b], and Chandan[3,c]

[1,2]Department of Physics & Electronics, Dr. Rammanohar Lohia Avadh University, Ayodhya, U.P., India

[3]Department of ECE, IET, Dr. Rammanohar Lohia Avadh University, Ayodhya, U.P., India

Abstract

In this article investigated here, a compact rectangular slot antenna has been discussed which consists of tentacle type structure along with the defect in the ground plane exhibiting the wireless applications like GNSS, wireless LAN, WiMAX, long-term evolution, C- and X-band applications. This etching is done using 50 Ω microstrip line on FR4 dielectric substrate. The frequencies this antenna covers are (1.4–1.8)/1.6 GHz, (2.1–3.5)/2.4 GHz, (5.4–6.3)/5.8 GHz, (7.0–7.3)/7.2 GHz and (9.2–11.6)/9.9 GHz. The respective bandwidths of the prototype antenna designed are 25%, 58%, 16%, 4% and 24%. To validate the proposed design, fabrication and testing are conducted using fabricator and VNA, and the measured results are provided. The fabricated prototype verified the accuracy of the simulated results through measurements. The parametric analysis of various dimensions, the distributions of surface current and radiation pattern has been discussed, verified and presented in the sections ahead so as to prove the proposed design as a better one.

Keywords: GNSS, WLAN, WiMAX, Defected Ground Structure (DGS), microstrip, radiation pattern, FR4

1. Introduction

Antennas designed for wireless communication systems have gained significant attention due to their ability to operate across multiple frequency bands. Among these, microstrip antennas have become a preferred choice for a broad range of wireless applications. When compared to traditional antennas, microstrip patch antennas offer several advantages, including reduced weight, cost-effectiveness, to easily fabricate, and adaptability. Furthermore, they can be seamlessly integrated with monolithic integrated circuits [1–14]. A typical microstrip patch antenna has a patch through which radiation takes place, a substrate, and a ground structure. The substrate is situated between the ground and the patch. Generally, conducting materials like copper or gold are employed to construct the radiating patch. The feeding structures, which are responsible for connecting the radiating patch, are etched

[a]parimal.tiwari1@gmail.com, [b]kkverma23@gmail.com, [c]chandanhcst@gmail.com

onto the dielectric substrate. Microstrip patch antennas can be designed in different possible shapes such as square, circular, rectangular, triangular, elliptical, and more [4].

Introduced a novel slot antenna with a fractal Koch shape, designed for multiband wireless applications [2]. The inclusion of the fractal Koch-shaped monopole and slotted ground plane serves to alter the capacitive and inductive characteristics of the antenna patch which increases the overall path length of current of the patch. Notably, the entire dimensions of this innovative design measure only 55 mm × 56 mm. A compact antenna designed to enhance bandwidth for WLAN, WiMAX and Satellite applications has been discussed [3]. The key element in this antenna design is the utilization of a single rectangular split ring resonator (RSRR) within a metamaterial framework. The antenna setup comprises three of these metamaterial single RSRR units, all integrated with a coaxial feed. Impressively, this antenna boasts remarkably small dimensions, measuring just 20 × 18 × 2.54 mm³. Ali et al., introduces a planar reconfigurable antenna having four bands which is suitable for applications in GNSS, lower WiMAX, Wireless LAN, and X-band frequencies [4]. The design offers an impressive frequency ranges, spanning approximately 10%, 30%, 20%, and 60% across the 1.6, 2.5, 5.8, and 9.5 GHz, respectively. Notably, the overall dimensions of this proposed antenna structure measure just 28 × 30 × 1.6 mm³. Kaur and Khanna introduces a low profile, enhanced gain, dual-band microstrip antenna designed for versatile applications such as Wireless LAN, WAVE, MIMO, WiMAX, AMSAT and long-distance communications [5]. The MPA is structured with two inverted L-shaped patches and an innovative †-shaped ground structure. This unique design enables the antenna to operate effectively in two separate frequency bands. Remarkably, the overall dimensions of this antenna are just 70 × 60 × 1.6 mm³. A compact microstrip-fed monopole antenna generating three bands has been designed [6] with dual-polarization capabilities, tailored for applications in wireless LAN and WiMAX. The antenna configuration comprises a tailored ground and a Y-shaped patch structure, which includes two monopole arms of unequal lengths and a modified circular monopole element. Notably, this antenna structure is characterized by its simplicity, durability, and minimal footprint, measuring just 45 × 35 × 1.5 mm³. A compact dual antenna is developed, with dimensions of just 12 × 20 × 1.6 mm³, tailored to fulfill the needs and applications of compact devices requiring multiple-input multiple-output (MIMO) capabilities [7]. This antenna design has been carefully crafted, analyzed, and manufactured to ensure excellent impedance matching and stable radiation patterns. As a result, this antenna is well-suited multiple applications, including WLAN, WiMAX, and the Indian National Satellite System. A compact multiband microstrip patch antenna was meticulously designed [8] and subsequently simulated using HFSS software, followed by a detailed analysis employing the finite element method (FEM). The antenna incorporates two strategically positioned rectangular slots, carefully etched to optimize both gain and impedance matching. Remarkably, this antenna manages to maintain its miniature dimensions, measuring just 60 × 60 × 1.6 mm³. There are numerous literature study done in which the various fabrication techniques are discussed and deeply studied their resonances, current distribution, Voltage Standing Wave Ratio (VSWR), radiation pattern, design, etc. [9–19]. A triangular microstrip antenna with triangular design split ring resonator providing four bands for applications like WLAN, WiMAX, C-band downlink communication, and X-band radar is discussed in [20]. Puri et al., introduces a plus shaped fractal design patch with stepped ground which provides dual-band for GSM 1800 MHz, WLAN, LTE and for future 5G communication applications [21]. A multiband antenna with triple-folding inverted-F is discussed in [22] designed for LTE and sub-6 GHz 5G applications with dimensions of 21 × 8 × 0.2 mm³. Moukala Mpele et al., in his study provide a heart-shaped planar antenna having a surface area of 28 mm² using the counter sink and partial ground techniques [23]. A penta-band slotted antenna suitable for wireless LAN, WiMAX and C-band applications with dimensions of 20 × 30 mm² is discussed by Thiripurasundari et al., in their study [24]. Some more literature study has been performed in order to get the different design and analysis techniques. In this research article, a compact tantacled rectangular slot antenna with defect in the ground structure for various wireless applications is produced. This antenna has the total dimension of 36 × 30 × 1.6 mm³. The proposed antenna covers the frequencies ranging from (1.4–1.8)/1.6 GHz, (2.1–3.5)/2.4 GHz, (5.4–6.3)/5.8 GHz, (7.0–7.3)/7.2 GHz and (9.2–11.6)/9.9 GHz having return losses of –24 dB, –19 dB, –25 dB, –14 dB and –38 dB and the impedance bandwidth of 25%, 58%, 16%, 4% and 24%, respectively. The antenna provides better gain at all the center frequencies. The antenna is simulated and later on fabricated on FR4 dielectric substrate having relative permittivity of 4.4 and loss tangent of 0.02.

2. Antenna Design

The prototype antenna design has been shown and illustrated with dimensional names in Figure 26.1. The substrate taken is FR4 material and is having the size of L_s and W_s as its length and width, respectively. This antenna is fed with 50 Ω microstrip line for excitation. LF is length and WF is the width of the feed. L_{qw} and W_{qw} are the quarter-wave transformer transmission line. The square slot is cut out of the rectangular patch having the length and width denoted in the figure as "L_{sq}" and "W_{sq}". S1, S2, S3, S4 and S5 are the lengths of the strips as shown in the figure which are forming a tentacle-like structure above the patch. "t" is the thickness of these strips.

In the ground plane, a long strip along with the square shaped structure is cut out. GS_L and GS_W are the length and width of the strip and G1 and G2 are of square shape. Lg and Wg are taken as the length and width of ground.

Table 26.1 showcases the dimensions (in mm) of proposed antenna against the nomenclatures used in the Figure 26.1.

The useful antenna equations that can be used to design and fabricate an antenna are [1]:

The width of patch W_p is calculated using:

$$W_p = \frac{c}{2f_o\sqrt{\dfrac{\varepsilon_r+1}{2}}} \tag{1}$$

The dielectric (effective) constant, ε_{reff} can be calculated as:

$$\varepsilon_{reff} = \frac{\varepsilon_r+1}{2} + \frac{\varepsilon_r-1}{2}\left[1+12\frac{h}{W_p}\right]^{1/2} \tag{2}$$

The length of patch can be calculated as:

$$L_p = L_{eff} - 2\Delta L \tag{3}$$

where L_{eff}, is the effective length of patch given as

$$L_{eff} = \frac{c}{2f_o\sqrt{\varepsilon_{reff}}} \tag{4}$$

and ΔL is the extension in length because of fringing given as

$$\Delta L = 0.412h \frac{\left(\varepsilon_{reff} + 0.3\right)\left(\dfrac{W_p}{h} + 0.264\right)}{\left(\varepsilon_{reff} + 0.258\right)\left(\dfrac{W_p}{h} + 0.8\right)}$$ (5)

The length and width of the substrate L_{sub} and W_{sub} are equal to that of the ground plane L_g and W_g given as

$$L_g = 6h + L_p$$ (6)

$$W_g = 6h + W_p$$ (7)

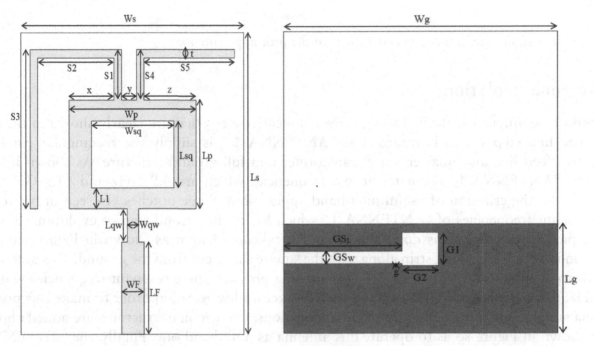

Figure 26.1: Antenna prototype with front and the back view.

Figure 26.2 demonstrates the reflection coefficient of simulated antenna. This figure clearly shows that the antenna resonates penta-band with good impedance bandwidth and giving out the better gain and VSWR. The resonant frequencies are 1.6 GHz, 2.4 GHz, 5.8 GHz, 7.2 GHz and 9.9 GHz which are much suitable for GNSS, WiMAX, LTE, Wireless LAN, C- and X-band applications.

Table 26.1: Dimensions of proposed antenna configuration

Ls	Ws	Lp	Wp	Lg	Wg	LF	WF	L1
36	30	13	17	13	30	11	3	2.5
Lsq	Wsq	S1	S2	S3	S4	S5	x	y
8	11	6	10.25	19	6	12.25	6	2
z	t	G1	G2	GS$_L$	GS$_W$	G	Lqw	Wqw
7	1	4	4	13	1.5	0.25	4	1.5

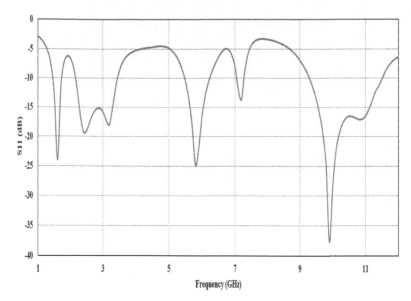

Figure 26.2: The simulated reflection coefficient of the prototype antenna.

3. Antenna Evolution

The prototype antenna is drafted using three consecutive steps that are clearly shown in the Figure 26.3. The first step which is regarded as "ANTENNA 1", is simply the rectangular patch with microstrip feed line and quarter wave transformer and full ground structure. As shown in Figure 26.4, the "ANTENNA 1" resonates at two frequencies which are 4.9 GHz and 11.9 GHz which doesn't fulfill the criterion of useful multiband applications. Some notches are seen in between the two resonant frequencies of "ANTENNA 1" which led to the second step of evolution. In second step, a parametric analysis is done and ground is taken of length as shown in Figure with some defects in it, which are a long strip along with the square shape cut from the ground. This antenna has been denominated as "ANTENNA 2". This antenna provides three resonant frequencies which are 2.5 GHz, 6.9 GHz and 9.9 GHz that too with low return losses. So, in order to make this proposed antenna suitable for some more multiband applications, tentacle-like structures are added above the patch shown in Figure so as to operate this antenna as multiband one. Finally, the "ANTENNA 3" gives out five bands (1.4 – 1.8)/1.6 GHz, (2.1–3.5)/2.4 GHz, (5.4–6.3)/5.8 GHz, (7.0–7.3)/7.2 GHz and (9.2–11.6)/9.9 GHz with good resonances and bandwidths and also covering good wireless applications.

4. Results and Discussions

The prototype comprises of the dimensions of 36 × 30 × 1.6 mm³. The antenna is low profile producing five resonances with very good impedance bandwidth and also better gain and VSWR. The frequency bands that this antenna covers are (1.4–1.8)/1.6 GHz, (2.1–3.5)/2.4 GHz, (5.4–6.3)/5.8 GHz, (7.0–7.3)/7.2 GHz and (9.2–11.6)/9.9 GHz.

4.1. Parametric analysis

The simulated parametric analysis of the variation in the ground length "L_g" taken from 12 mm to 15 mm is shown in the Figure 26.5. In this Figure it is shown that when L_g is having the value 12 mm,

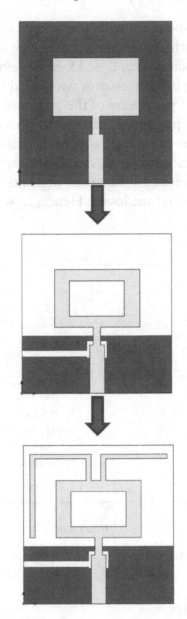

Figure 26.3: Evolution of antenna design.

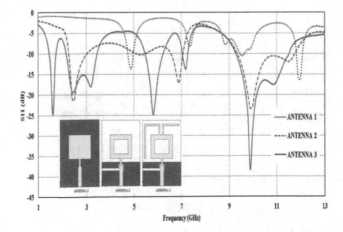

Figure 26.4: Return losses of the antenna evolution.

then this antenna gives out four resonances with low return losses. L_g = 14 mm is producing four resonant frequencies and that too with low return losses except at the second resonant frequency. The antenna provides only three frequencies when L_g is 15 mm as evident from the figure. Hence, L_g with 13 mm gives optimum result having five resonances with good bandwidth and gain.

Figure 26.6 demonstrates the S11 parameter of the proposed antenna when the patch length L_p is varying from 11 mm to 14 mm. The parametric analysis is performed and when the value of L_p is 11 mm then, antenna provides only three resonant frequencies with low return losses. L_p, given the value of 12 mm also provides only three resonant frequencies with same low reflection coefficients and also with less bandwidth. When L_p is taken as 14 mm, then this antenna resonates at four frequencies but somewhere more and somewhere less return losses. Hence, L_p with 13 mm provides optimum results in all aspects.

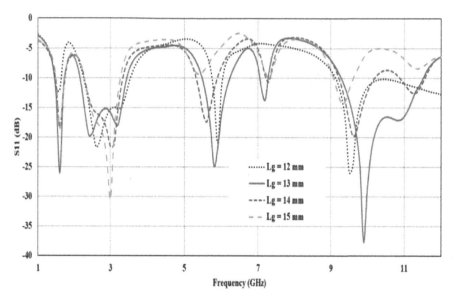

Figure 26.5: S11 vs. frequency plot for variation in L_g.

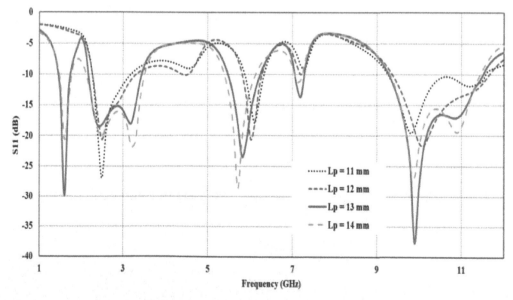

Figure 26.6: S11 vs. frequency plot for variation in L_p.

The return losses with the variations in the width of the feeding structure from 2 mm to 4 mm is shown in the Figure 26.7. It is much clear in the Figure that when WF1 is 2 mm, then proposed antenna resonates only at four frequencies with less return losses and bandwidths. When WF1 is taken as 4 mm then, the antenna resonates at five frequencies but less resonances at some frequencies and more at some but the value WF1 = 3 mm provides good and better resonances and bandwidths with gain also.

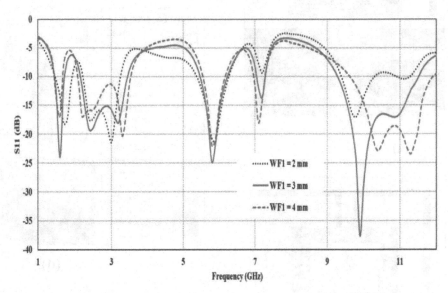

Figure 26.7: S11 vs. frequency plot for variation WF1.

4.2. Surface current distribution

The surface current distribution of the proposed antenna is shown at all the resonant frequencies in Figure 26.8a–e. At 1.6 GHz shown in Figure 26.8a, the surface current is mainly distributed through the feeding structure and quarter-wave transformer and also through the square cut in the ground plane. When we look at the Figure 26.8b, here also the main surface current at 2.4 GHz is through the upper left of the feed line and quarter-wave transformer and through the square cut in ground. In Figure 26.8c, it is clearly evident that the main current distributions at 5.8 GHz are through the feeding structure, the transformer, lower part of the patch, through tentacle arm S1, S2, S3 and also through the S5. Figure 26.8d demonstrates the current at 7.2 GHz, in which it is clear that the current is mainly distributed through the lower part of feed line, through tentacle arm S3 and also in the ground plane through all the length of the strip and square slot. The current distribution at 9.9 GHz is mainly through the feeding structure, transformer and lower part of patch and also through mid of the strip cut and square cut in ground plane.

4.3. Radiation pattern

Figure 26.9a–e illustrates the far-field radiation pattern simulated result along E- and H-plane at 1.6 GHz, 2.4 GHz, 5.8 GHz, 7.2 GHz and 9.9 GHz. From the Figure, it is much evident that at 1.6 GHz and 2.4 GHz antenna exhibits bi-directional radiation pattern while at 5.8 GHz, 7.2 GHz and 9.9 GHz, it is exhibiting nearly omnidirectional in the E-plane. Now, in the H-plane, at all the frequencies, antenna is exhibiting the bi-directional radiation pattern. In Figure 26.9, left side shows the E-plane and right-hand side shows the H-plane.

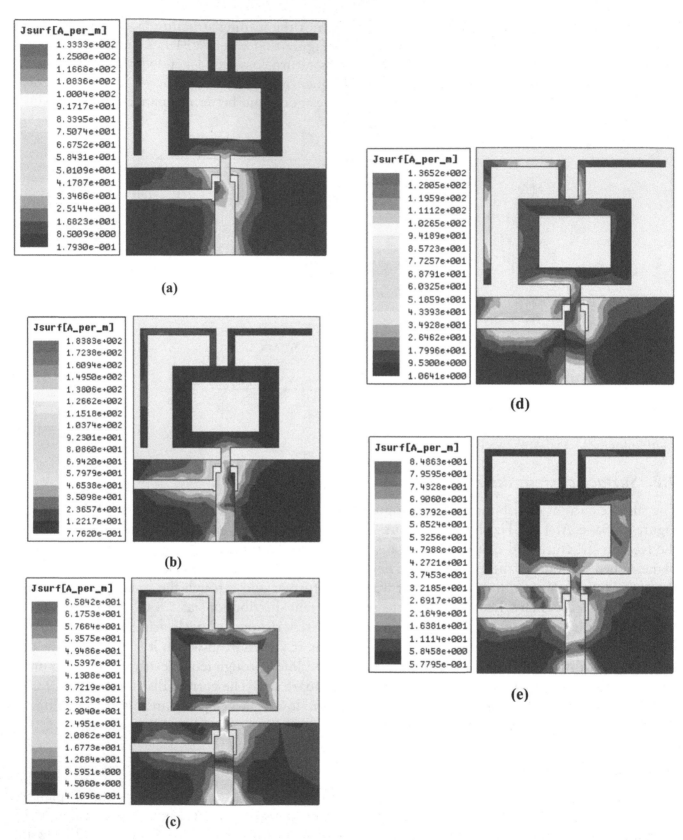

Figure 26.8: Surface current of the antenna at (a) 1.6 GHz, (b) 2.4 GHz, (c) 5.8 GHz, (d) 7.2 GHz and (e) 9.9 GHz.

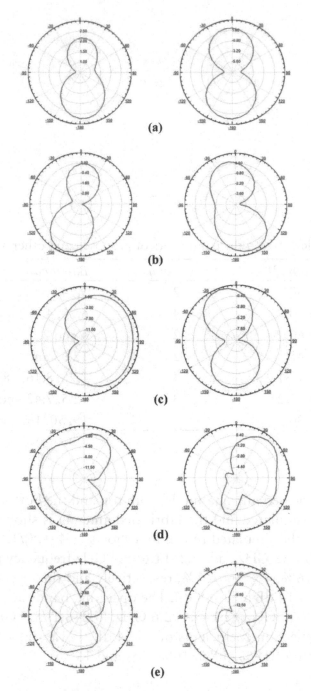

Figure 26.9: Radiation patterns at (a) 1.6 GHz, (b) 2.4 GHz, (c) 5.8 GHz, (d) 7.2 GHz and (e) 9.9 GHz.

4.4. Gain

Figure 26.10 illustrates the gain of the prototype antenna at all the resonances. The gain comes out to be 2.8 dBi, 1.8 dBi, 3.7 dBi, 2.9 dBi and 5.4 dBi at 1.6 GHz, 2.4 GHz, 5.8 GHz, 7.2 GHz and 9.9 GHz, respectively.

A comparison has been conducted between the newly proposed design and a similar design presented in the literature, as summarized in Table 26.2. Upon analysis, it becomes evident that the newly designed configuration excels in several aspects, including a greater number of operating frequencies, a more compact size, and bandwidth.

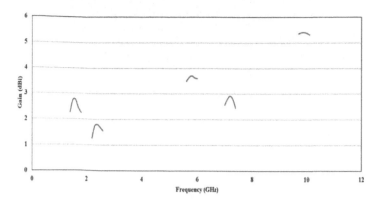

Figure 26.10: Gain of the antenna.

Table 26.2: Comparative table between the parameters of proposed and other antennas

Reference	Size (mm2)	Bands	Bandwidth (%)
[5]	70 × 60	2	5.74 and 26.
[8]	60 × 60	4	6.28, 4, 4.7 and 3.
[9]	60 × 60	2	4 and 2.
[18]	60 × 45	2	12.65 and 33.
[19]	57.2 × 31.2	4	7.78, 8.16, 18.86 and 16.91.
[20]	32 × 37.2	3	12.5, 7.42 and 6.36.
Proposed antenna	36 × 30	5	19, 50, 16, 4 and 13.

Source: Author's compilation.

4.5. Measured result

Figure 26.12 shows the fabricated antenna model with top and the bottom view. The corresponding reflection coefficient of the simulated and the fabricated antenna is shown in the Figure 26.11. It is evident from the figure that the simulated return loss shows (1.4–1.8)/1.6 GHz, (2.1–3.5)/2.4 GHz, (5.4–6.3)/5.8 GHz, (7.0–7.3)/7.2 GHz and (9.2–11.6)/9.9 GHz frequency ranges with the impedance bandwidth of 25%, 58%, 16%, 4% and 24%, respectively and the respective reflection coefficients of –24 dB, –19 dB, –25 dB, –14 dB and –38 dB. The operating bands achieved after fabrication and measurements are (1.4–1.7)/1.6 GHz, (2.1–3.4)/2.6 GHz, (5.2–6.1)/5.7 GHz, (6.9–7.2)/7.1 GHz and (8.9–10.1)/9.5 GHz with reflection coefficients of –36.4 dB, –21.6 dB, –20 dB, –16 dB and –21 dB having impedance bandwidth of 19%, 50%, 16%, 4% and 13%.

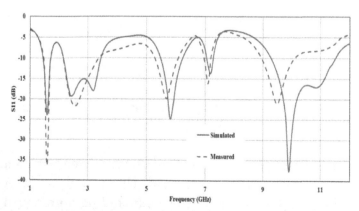

Figure 26.11: S11 vs. frequency plot of fabricated and simulated antenna.

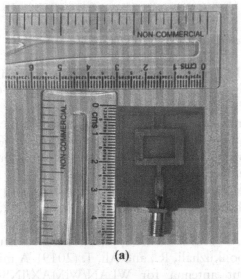

(a)

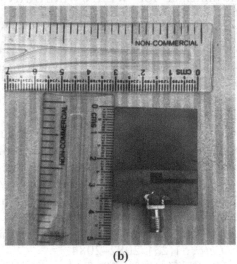

(b)

Figure 26.12: The fabricated prototype antenna (a) top view and (b) bottom view.

5. Conclusions

The proposed antenna is of low profile and having compact size. The total size of the antenna is 36 × 30 × 1.6 mm3 and provides the range of frequencies from (1.4–1.8)/1.6 GHz, (2.1–3.5)/2.4 GHz, (5.4–6.3)/5.8 GHz, (7.0–7.3)/7.2 GHz and (9.2–11.6)/9.9 GHz suitable for GNSS, WiMAX, LTE, Wireless LAN, C- and X-band applications. The simulated impedance bandwidth comes out to be 25%, 58%, 16%, 4% and 24% and measured impedance bandwidth of 19%, 50%, 16%, 4% and 13%. The gain at all five resonances are 2.8 dBi, 1.8 dBi, 3.7 dBi, 2.9 dBi and 5.4 dBi. The antenna also exhibits good radiation pattern. The antenna is simulated on ANSYS HFSS with FR4 substrate.

6. Acknowledgement

The authors are thankful to Prof. B. T. P. Madhav, Department of Electronics & Communication Engineering, K L Deemed to be University, Guntur, Andhra Pradesh, India for providing Antenna Fabrication and Measurement Facility.

References

[1] Balanis, C. A. (1989). *Advanced Engineering Electromagnetics*. New York: John Wiley & Sons. pp 1136, ISBN: 978-1-394-18001-1

[2] Fathima, N., Nayana, K. S., Ali, T., and Biradar, R. C. (2017). A miniaturized slotted ground fractal Koch multiband antenna for wireless applications. *2017 2nd IEEE Int. Conf. Recent Trends Elec. Inform. Comm. Technol. (RTEICT)*, 251–255.

[3] Ali, T., Aw, M. S., and Biradar, R. C. (2018). A compact bandwidth enhanced antenna loaded with SRR for WLAN/WiMAX/satellite applications. *Adv. Electromag.*, 7(4), 78–84.

[4] Ali, T., Muzammil Khaleeq, M., and Biradar, R. C. (2018). A multiband reconfigurable slot antenna for wireless applications. *AEU Int. J. Elec. Comm.*, 84, 273–280.

[5] Kaur, J. and Khanna, R. (2014). Development of dual-band microstrip patch antenna for WLAN/MIMO/WIMAX/AMSAT/WAVE applications. *Microw. Optic. Technol. Lett.*, 56, 988–993.

[6] Wu, T., Shi, X.-W., Li, P., and Bai, H. (2013). Tri-band microstrip-fed monopole antenna with dual-polarisation characteristics for WLAN and WiMAX applications. Elec. Lett., 49, 1597–1598.

[7] Mohammad Saadh, A. W., Poonkuzhali, R., and Ali, T. (2019). A miniaturized single-layered branched multiple-input multiple-output antenna for WLAN/WiMAX/INSAT applications. *Microw. Optic. Technol. Lett.*, 61, 1058–1064.

[8] Jagadeesh Chandra, R. B., Ali, T., Kumar, O., and Manohara Pai, M. M. (2020). A planar rectangular slot multiband patch antenna for GNSS/WLAN/X-band applications. *Mat. Today Proc.*, 28(4), 2279–2285.

[9] Ge, Y., Esselle, K. P., and Bird, T. S. (2004). E-shaped patch antennas for high-speed wireless networks. *IEEE Trans. Anten. Propag.*, 52(12), 3213–3219.

[10] Sarkar, D., Saurav, K., and Srivastava, K. V. (2014). Multi-band microstrip-fed slot antenna loaded with split-ring resonator. *Elec. Lett.*, 50(21), 1498–1500.

[11] Patel, R. H., Desai, A. H., and Upadhyaya, T. (2015). Design of H-shape X-band application electrically small antenna. *Int. J. Elec. Elect. Data Comm. (IJEEDC)*, 3(12), 1–4.

[12] Wu, T., Shi, X.-W., Li, P., and Bai, H. (2013). Tri-band microstrip-fed monopole antenna with dual polarisation characteristics for WLAN and WiMAX applications. *Elec. Lett.*, 49(25), 1597–1598.

[13] Sun, J.-S., Fang, H.-S., Lin, P.-Y., and Chuang, C.-S. (2015). Triple-band MIMO antenna for mobile wireless applications. *IEEE Anten. Wire. Propag. Lett.*, 15, 500–503.

[14] Zhang, R., Kim, H.-H., and Kim, H. (2015). Triple-band ground radiation antenna for GPS, WiFi 2.4 and 5 GHz band applications. *Elec. Lett.*, 51(25), 2082–2084.

[15] Pan, Y., Ma, Y., Xiong, J., Hou, Z., and Zeng, Y. (2015). A compact antenna with frequency and pattern reconfigurable characteristics. *Microw. Optic. Technol. Lett.*, 57(11), 2467–2471.

[16] He, M., Ye, X., Zhou, P., Zhao, G., Zhang, C., and Sun, H. (2015). A small-size dual-feed broadband circularly polarized U-slot patch antenna. *IEEE Anten. Wire. Propag. Lett.*, 14, 898–901.

[17] Tsai, L.-C. (2014). A dual-band bow-tie-shaped CPW-fed slot antenna for WLAN applications. *Prog. Electromag. Res. C*, 47, 167–171.

[18] Chu, H. B. and Shirai, H. (2018). A compact metamaterial quad-band antenna based on asymmetric E-CRLH unit cells. *Prog. Electromag. Res. C*, 81, 171–179.

[19] Patel, U. and Upadhyaya, T. K. (2019). Design and analysis of compact µ-negative material loaded wideband electrically compact antenna for WLAN/WiMAX applications. *Prog. Electromag. Res.*, 79, 11–22.

[20] Mahendran, K., Gayathiri, R., and Sudarsan, H. (2021). Design of multi band triangular microstrip patch antenna with triangular split ring resonator for S band, C band and X band applications. *Microproc. Microsys.*, 80, 103400.

[21] Puri, S. C., Das, S., and Tiary, M. G. (2020). A multiband antenna using plus-shaped fractal-like elements and stepped ground plane. *Int. J. RF Microw. Comp.-Aid. Engg.*, 30(5), e22169.

[22] Kulkarni, J. (2021). Multiband triple folding monopole antenna for wireless applications in the laptop computers. *Int. J. Comm. Sys.*, 34(8), e4776.

[23] Moukala Mpele, P., Moukanda Mbango, F., Konditi, D. B. O., and Ndagijimana, F. (2021). A tri-band and miniaturized planar antenna based on countersink and defected ground structure techniques. *Int. J. RF Microw. Comp.-Aid. Engg.*, 31(5), e22617.

[24] Thiripurasundari, C., Mahadevi, M., Sumathy, V., and Thiruvengadam, C. (2022). Design of a compact T-shaped slot antenna for wireless applications. *Int. J. Comm. Sys.*, 35(2), e4201.

27 Performance Optimization of Optical-OFDM Link Through Index-Modulation Algorithm

Jyoti Prashant Singh[a], Deepak Singh, and B. B. Tiwari

Department of Electronics Engineering, VBS Purvanchal University, Jaunpur, U.P., India

Abstract

In this study, index-modulation (IM) based optical orthogonal frequency division multiplexing (O-OFDM) scheme is used to enhance the average bit-error rate (BER) and spectral efficiency (SE) performance under various fiber non-linearities. In the proposed system the information has been carried through both activated sub-carriers as well as indices of the active sub-carrier which dynamically enhance the transmitted symbol rates in terms of average bit-error rate (BER). In contrast to the standard optical-OFDM system, whenever the fiber non-linearity is significant factor modifying the number of active sub-carriers in the optical-OFDM with IM, system offers enhanced average BER performance. The simulation outcomes show that the proposed optical-OFDM with IM system has improved BER performance compared to the conventional optical-OFDM system when both systems possessed same spectral efficiency value. Furthermore, with modulation schemes like 2-PSK, 4-PSK and 16-QAM; the optical-OFDM with IM system offers superior spectral efficiency than that achieved in the conventional optical-OFDM system.

Keywords: Optical-OFDM, index-modulation, average bit-error rate, spectral efficiency, active sub-carrier

1. Introduction

Optical communication represents a promising complement to radio-frequency (RF) communication, especially for long-distance transmissions like radio-over-fiber (RoF). RoF technology has emerged as a pivotal solution for future broadband wireless access networks due to its appealing attributes, including high bandwidth, extended coverage, and simplified base stations [1]. Furthermore, as the scale of 5G network deployment expands, and the industrial internet undergoes innovative development, optical networks are evolving towards higher speeds, increased capacities, and extended reach [2]. In today's landscape, coherent optical communication systems have assumed a crucial role in the field of communication, contributing to enhanced spectral efficiency and capacity [3]. For instance, coherent optical orthogonal frequency-division multiplexing (CO-OFDM) offers distinct advantages,

---

[a]jyoti.oct@gmail.com

such as the ease of compensating for optical channel effects and high spectral efficiency. Consequently, CO-OFDM systems have been proposed as a viable solution for long-distance transmissions [4].

In the context of 5G and beyond, particularly in the context of 6G development, extensive research has been conducted to determine the most suitable waveforms for communication. Several modulation techniques, such as filter bank-based multicarrier (FBMC) [5], windowed-OFDM (W-OFDM) [6], filtered-OFDM (F-OFDM) [7], and generalized frequency division multiplexing (GFDM) [8], have been proposed to achieve both high spectral efficiency and minimal power consumption. Among these potential options, orthogonal frequency-division multiplexing (OFDM) has already gained widespread adoption in modern communication systems, including 4G, 5G, and Wi-Fi. OFDM offers significant advantages, such as efficient hardware implementation and simple single-tap equalization at the receiver. Moreover, OFDM has found extensive use in both wireless and optical communication systems.

Index-modulation (IM) is a technique derived from the concept of spatial modulation, designed to achieve superior spectral efficiency by enabling the transmission of additional bits compared to conventional modulation techniques [9]. IM has been extensively explored in various communication systems, including multi-carrier systems [9], MIMO systems [10], molecular communication [11], millimeter-wave transmission [12], and visible light communication [13].

Initially proposed by Basar et al., the OFDM with index modulation (OFDM-IM) scheme emerged as a groundbreaking approach [9]. OFDM-IM not only introduces novel methods [8], for conveying information compared to traditional OFDM but also offers distinct advantages in terms of spectral and energy efficiency [14]. In OFDM-IM, information transmission occurs not only through the active subcarriers which are utilized to carry constellation symbols, but also via the indices of these active subcarriers which are employed for additional binary information transmission. Consequently, OFDM-IM presents a flexible trade-off between spectral efficiency and system performance, which can be adjusted by varying the number of active sub-carriers [9].

In long-haul links, there is a need for higher launch power levels to extend transmission reach. However, long-haul coherent optical OFDM (CO-OFDM) encounters significant distortions caused by fiber non-linearity at elevated input power levels, leading to performance degradation [15]. To leverage the advantages of OFDM-IM over traditional OFDM and enhance spectral efficiency, OFDM-IM can be effectively employed in coherent optical communication systems.

Fiber non-linearity induces non-linear interference among subcarriers in OFDM, primarily caused by neighboring subcarriers. Hence, this study aims to reduce the count of active subcarriers while maintaining the same spectral efficiency to mitigate the impact of fiber non-linearity. IM, a technique that allows the transmission of additional information bits using subcarrier indices in OFDM play a crucial role in this endeavor. By utilizing inactive subcarriers, IM is introduced as a means to decrease the number of non-linear-interfering subcarriers, thereby improving the Bit Error Rate (BER) performance while maintaining the same spectral efficiency for coherent optical OFDM systems.

Simulation results convincingly demonstrate that the proposed coherent optical OFDM-IM can enhance spectral efficiency and elevate BER performance, especially when considering the effects of fiber non-linearity, in comparison to conventional coherent optical OFDM.

2. Optical OFDM-IM Model

2.1. *O-OFDM index modulation scheme: Transmitter*

Figure 27.1 illustrates the block diagram of the proposed optical-OFDM with index modulation (O-OFDM-IM) for long-haul optical communication systems. Within the transmitter of the

O-OFDM-IM system, various levels of information bits are input to transmit each symbol of the OFDM scheme.

Initially, these input bits are partitioned into OFDM sub-blocks. If we denote G as the total number of OFDM sub-blocks, each individual OFDM sub-block comprises subcarriers with a length of n, where $n = N_{FFT}/G$. Here, N_{FFT} represents the size of the fast Fourier transformation, and p $(= p_1 + p_2)$ bits are allocated to an OFDM sub-block of length n. The mapping process encompasses not only modulated symbols but also the subcarrier indices. The selection of k active subcarriers is determined through a selection procedure based on the initial p_1 bits of the incoming p-bit sequence, facilitating the transmission of additional information bits. The number of additional information bits can be expressed as follows:

$$p_1 = \log_2\left(C(n,k)\right), \tag{1}$$

where the notations $\lfloor \cdot \rfloor$ and $C(\cdot)$ represent the floor operation and combinatorial operation, respectively.

In the case of each gth OFDM sub-block where g ranges from 1 to G, p_2 bits extracted from the initial p-bit sequence are assigned to the M-ary signal constellation, where M is the constellation size. This allocation is done to define the data symbols transmitted across the k active subcarriers. The count of the remaining p_2 bits can be calculated as follows:

$$p_2 = k\left(\log_2\left(M\right)\right), \tag{2}$$

The process involves sending p_1 bits to an index selector, responsible for generating indices that designate the k active subcarriers. This index selection is executed using a combinatorial method. The combinatorial number system, with a degree of k, establishes a one-to-one mapping relationship with the set of k active subcarrier indices [9]. For any given values of n and k, the natural number Z in the range of $Z = [0, C(n, k) + 1]$ can be represented uniquely by a descending sequence J, denoted as $J = \{j_k, ..., j_1\}$, which selects elements from the set according to the following expression:

$$Z = C(j_k, k) + ... + C(j_2, 2) + C(j_1, 1) \tag{3}$$

where $j_k > ... > j_1 \geq 0$ and $j_k, ..., j_1 \in \{0, ..., n-1\}$ [9]. The sequence of J indices derived from the input p_1 additional information bits can be elucidated using algorithm 1 [16].

To make better understanding, as an example of how active or inactive subcarriers are determined, for $n = 4$ and $k = 2$, the number of p_1 additional information bits is calculated using Equation (1) that $p_1 = \lfloor \log_2(C(4,2)) \rfloor = 2$. The p_1 bits are first converted to a decimal number Z. Then the combinational number system provides a one-to-one mapping between natural number Z and k-combinations. From algorithm 1, we can find the k-combination for a given number Z.

After J indices sequence is obtained from input p_1 additional information bits, the symbol in the inactive subcarriers is set to be zero. In Table 27.1, it is shown the sub-blocks obtained for different p_1 additional information bits. s_a and s_b are transmitted constellation symbols on active subcarriers.

The gth OFDM sub-block can be represented as

$$\{X_g\}_{i=1,...,n} = \begin{cases} s_g(i), & i \in J_g \\ 0, & otherwise \end{cases} \tag{4}$$

where $s_g(i)$ are independently obtained from a M-ary signal constellation.

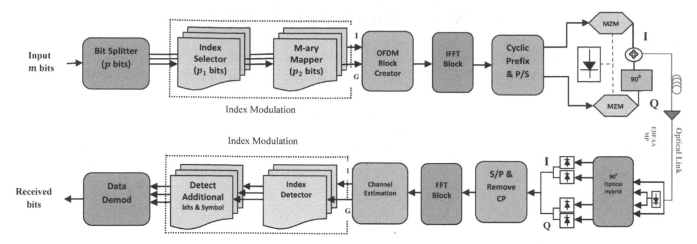

Figure 27.1: Block model of optical-OFDM-IM long-haul link.

After concatenating X_g, the equivalent time-domain signal can be calculated by using the inverse Fourier transform (IFT) as follows:

$$v(t) = \frac{1}{\sqrt{T}} \sum_{g=1}^{G} \sum_{i=1}^{n} X_g(i) e^{j2\pi f_{g,i} t}, \quad 0 \le t \le T \tag{5}$$

where $f_{g,i}$ is the ith subcarrier frequency in the gth OFDM sub-block and T is the time duration of an OFDM-IM symbol. Then parallel to serial conversion and cyclic prefix (CP) insertion are followed.

The electrical signal obtained after the inverse conversion process is converted into a transmitted optical signal with two optical IQ modulators (Mach-Zehnder Modulator – MZM) [17].

2.2. *Optical fiber channel*

The optical fiber channel is many standard single mode fiber (SSMF) lengths. For SSMF, within each span, the non-liner Schrodinger equation (NLSE) models loss, chromatic dispersion (CD) and non-linear effects as

$$\frac{\partial E(z,t)}{\partial z} = (D+N)E(z,t) \tag{6}$$

where E is the complex light envelope of the received signal after a fiber distance of z km. D is the linear part for linear effect (CD and attenuation) and N is the non-linear part, which is given by

$$D = -\frac{j}{2}\beta_2 \frac{\partial^2}{\partial t^2} - \frac{\alpha}{2} \tag{7}$$

$$N = j\gamma |E(z,t)|^2 \tag{8}$$

$$\gamma = \frac{2\pi n_2}{\lambda_c A_{eff}} \tag{9}$$

where α is the attenuation factor, β_2 is the group velocity dispersion parameter, γ is the non-linearity coefficient, n_2 is the non-linear-index coefficient, λ_c is the center wavelength and A_{eff} is the effective core area [18]. At the end of each span, the optical signal is amplified to compensate for fiber losses by an EDFA.

Algorithm 1: Obtain J Indices Sequence From Input p_1 Bits

1: **Input:** The binary sequence of p_1 bits, the number of subcarriers n, the number of active subcarriers k

2: **Initialization:** Convert p_1 bits into a decimal number Z, $jj \leftarrow n$

3: **for** $i = k: = k\ 1$ **do**

4: **repeat**

5: $jj \leftarrow jj - 1$

6: ComCoef $\leftarrow$ C (jj, i)

7: **until** ComCoef $\leq Z$

8: $j_i \leftarrow jj$

9: $Z \leftarrow Z -$ ComCoef

10: **end for**

11: **return** array j_i

2.3. *O-OFDM index modulation scheme: Receiver*

At the receiver, the received optical signal after transmission through the optical channel is converted to an electrical signal by a local oscillator laser (LO) by passing through a 90° optical hybrid. The optical signal interferes with the local oscillator laser, which usually has the same frequency as the transmitter laser in the 90° optical hybrid. In order to detect both real and imaginary parts, the input signal is mixed with the real part of the local oscillator laser in one branch and the imaginary part in the other branch through the 90° phase shift between the signal and the local oscillator laser.

At the optical OFDM-IM receiver after removing CP and implementing the FFT operation, it is followed by a channel estimation operation. To be able to equalize the received signal in the frequency domain, it is important to estimate the channel frequency response. $\hat{X}_g(i)$ is the received vector for the gth OFDM sub-block after FFT operation, which is given by

$$\hat{X}_g(i) = H_g(i)X_g(i) + W_g(i), \quad i = 1, \ldots, n \tag{10}$$

where $H_g(i)$ and $W_g(i)$ denote respectively the channel frequency response and the zero-mean complex additive white Gaussian noise (AWGN) with variance N_0 on the ith sub-carrier of the gth OFDM sub-block. PN sequence block, which is suitable for the fiber optical channel with slow variation, is used for the channel estimation, which is given by

$$\hat{H}_g(i) = \frac{\hat{X}_g^{PN}(i)}{X_g^{PN}(i)}, \quad i = 1, \ldots, n \tag{11}$$

where $\hat{X}_g^{PN}(i)$ and $X_g^{PN}(i)$ are the PN sequence signal on the ith sub-carrier of the gth OFDM sub-block at the receiver and the transmitter, respectively.

Table 27.1: Mapping relationship between p_1 and J

p_1 bits	Decimal number	k–combination	J indices sequence	Sub-blocks
[0 0]	0	C(1,2) + C(0,1)	[1,0]	$[s_a\ s_b\ 0\ 0]$
[0 1]	1	C(2,2) + C(0,1)	[2,0]	$[s_a\ 0\ s_b\ 0]$
[1 0]	2	C(2,2) + C(1,1)	[2,1]	$[0\ s_a\ s_b\ 0]$
[1 1]	3	C(3,2) + C(0,1)	[3,0]	$[s_a\ 0\ 0\ s_b]$

Table 27.1 summarizes the mapping relationship between p_1 bit sequences and J active sub-carrier indices for $n = 4$, $k = 2$ and $p_1 = 2$.

It needs to detect both the indices of active subcarriers and the corresponding additional information bits. The index detector is used to detect indices of active subcarriers from each OFDM sub-block. The maximum likelihood (ML) detector of the optical OFDM-IM system searches all combinations of subcarrier indices and the constellation points in order to a joint decision on the indices of active subcarriers and the transmitted symbols for each OFDM sub-block. The searching space of the ML detection per bit is given by the order of $O(C(n, k) + M^k)$. Since the complexity increases exponentially with increasing k values, the optimal ML detector has high complexity. To achieve near optimal performance, the low-complex posteriori probability detection (PPD) method have been proposed [8].

The PPD detector of optical OFDM-IM gives the logarithm of the ratio of a posteriori probabilities of frequency domain signals by considering the case that the values are either non-zero or zero [9]. For the gth OFDM sub-block, the PPD detector provides the probability of the active status of the corresponding index i with $i = 1, 2, ..., n$ given by;

$$\lambda_g(i) = \ln\frac{\sum_{m=1}^{M} P\left(X_g(i) = Q_m \big| \hat{X}_g(i)\right)}{P\left(X_g(i) = 0 \big| \hat{X}_g(i)\right)}, \tag{12}$$

where Q_j is the element of a M-ary signal constellation. The larger the value of $\lambda_g(i)$, the higher the probability that the corresponding i is an active sub-carrier. Using Bayes formula, Equation (12) can be expressed as

$$\lambda_g(i) = \ln(k) - \ln(n-k) + \frac{\left|\hat{X}_g(i)\right|^2}{\sigma_k^2} + \ln\left(\sum_{m=1}^{M} \exp\left(-\frac{1}{\sigma_k^2}\left|\hat{X}_g(i) - H_g(i)Q_m\right|^2\right)\right) \tag{13}$$

After obtaining all a posteriori probabilities based on Equation (13), for each OFDM sub-block, the receiver decides on k active indices ($\hat{J}$) having maximum posteriori probabilities. After determining the k active indices, the additional information bits and the data symbols can be easily decided.

It takes the active indices sequences from the index detector and performs a summation of the k—combination coefficients (Algorithm-2) for each OFDM sub-block. After calculating decimal number $\hat{Z}$, the additional information bits can be decided with a decimal-to-binary converter. Transmitted symbols at sets of M—ary signal constellation (Q) on k active subcarriers are estimated as

$$\hat{P}_g(i)\Big|_{i=1}^{k} = \arg\min_{(Q_m \in Q)}\left|\hat{X}_g(i) - \hat{H}_g(i)Q_m\right|^2 \tag{14}$$

3. Performance Analysis

3.1. *Spectral efficiency*

Spectral efficiency (SE) is an important performance parameter in OFDM systems. It is defined as the bit rate that can be achieved within a unit bandwidth B. For the conventional Optical-OFDM systems, the SE can be given by

$$\text{Spectral Efficiency}_{\text{O-OFDM}} = \frac{N_u \log_2 M}{(T_{FFT} + T_{CP})B}, \tag{15}$$

where N_u is the number of active subcarriers for data transmission in the optical-OFDM systems and T_{CP} is the time of cyclic prefix. For the optical-OFDM with IM systems, the SE can be expressed as

$$\text{SE}_{\text{O-OFDM-IM}} = \frac{G\big(k\log_2 M + \log_2 \big(C(n,k)\big)\big)}{(T_{FFT} + T_{CP})B} \tag{16}$$

Algorithm 2: Obtain Decimal Number $\hat{Z}$ from the Indices Sequence $\hat{J}$

1: **Input:** The indices sequence $\hat{J} = \{\hat{J}_k, \ldots, \hat{J}_1\}$, the number of subcarriers n, the number of active subcarriers k

2: $\hat{Z} \leftarrow 0$

3: **for** $i = 1 : k$ **do**

4: ComCoef $\leftarrow C(\hat{J}_i, i)$

5: $\hat{Z} \leftarrow \hat{Z} + $ ComCoef

6: **end for**

7: **return** $\hat{Z}$

Considering $N_u = N_{FFT} = 256$ and $N_{CP} = 16$, the optical-OFDM system can achieve a spectral-efficiency value 0.9412 bits/s/Hz for 2-PSK modulation scheme. However, the optical-OFDM with IM system can achieve a spectral-efficiency value 0.9412 bits/s/Hz for $n = 4$, $k = 2$ and a spectral-efficiency value 1.1765 bits/s/Hz for $n = 4$, $k = 3$, respectively for 2-PSK modulation scheme.

Hence, in the case of optical-OFDM with IM system, the spectral-efficiency value can be achieved higher than that in the optical-OFDM system for the selected values of n and k. So that, the proper selection of n and k values can help to enhance the spectral-efficiency performance. In Figure 27.2, the spectral-efficiency as a function of active sub-carrier k under various levels of the OFDM sub-blocks for $M = 2$, $N_{FFT} = 256$, $N_{CP} = 16$ as well as 2-PSK modulation scheme. From Figure 27.2, it can be observed that when the proper number of active subcarrier has been selected, the optical-OFDM with IM system can improve spectral-efficiency over simple optical-OFDM system.

Figure 27.3 illustrates the optical-OFDM with IM can achieve better SE performance than the optical-OFDM at the 2-PSK, 4-PSK and 16-QAM modulation schemes. However, the SE of optical-OFDM-IM cannot compete with that of the simple optical-OFDM for higher order modulation schemes.

The maximization of spectral-efficiency is almost synonymous with maximizing the number of bits per symbol. The sequence of binomial coefficients $C(n, k)$ is a logarithmically concave sequence. Therefore, it is analytically possible to detect the optimal value of the active subcarrier which maximizes p bits [19]. Thus,

$$p = k \log_2 M + \log_2 \left(C(n,k) \right) \tag{17}$$

Considering dropping the floor function in Equation (17) and then taking its derivative of p with respect to k is expressed as

$$\frac{dp}{dk} = \log_2 M + \log_2 \left(\Gamma_{n-k} - \Gamma_k \right) \tag{18}$$

$$\Gamma_k = \sum_{j=1}^{k} \frac{1}{j} = \frac{1}{1} + \frac{1}{2} + \frac{1}{3} + \ldots + \frac{1}{k} . \tag{19}$$

where the kth harmonic number Γ_k is the sum of the reciprocals of the first k positive integers. Since the limit $(\Gamma_k - \log k) \to \gamma$ which is the Euler-Mascheroni constant, the approximate value of Γ_k is expressed as

$$\Gamma_k \approx \log k + \gamma \tag{20}$$

By substituting the approximate value of Γ_k in Equation (18) and making Equation (18) equal to zero, it is obtained the optimal number of the active subcarrier

$$k \approx \frac{MN_{FFT}}{G(M+1)}. \tag{21}$$

3.2. Average bit-error rate

In the presence of channel estimation errors in which a mismatched ML detector is used for data detection, the condition pair-wise error probability (CPEP) can be expressed by [9] Equation (22) as

$$P_r \left(X_g \to \hat{X}_g \middle| \hat{H}_g \right) = Q \left(\frac{\left(X_g - \hat{X}_g \right) \hat{H}_g^{\,2}}{\sqrt{2\sigma_e^2 X_g^H \left(X_g - \hat{X}_g \right) \hat{H}_g^{\,2} + 2N_0 \left(X_g - \hat{X}_g \right) \hat{H}_g^{\,2}}} \right) \tag{22}$$

where σ_e^2 is the estimation error variance of the vector of the channel frequency response H_g, $(\cdot)^H$, $\|\cdot\|$ and $Q(\cdot)$ represents the Hermitian transposition, the Frobenius norm and the Gaussain Q—function, respectively.

$$X_g^H \left(X_g - \hat{X}_g \right) \hat{H}_g^{\,2} = \sum_{i=1}^{n} \left| X_g(i) \right|^2 \left| \left(X_g(i) - \hat{X}_g(i) \right) \hat{H}_g(i) \right|^2$$

$$\Rightarrow X_g^H \left(X_g - \hat{X}_g \right) \hat{H}_g^{\,2} = \frac{1}{n} X_g^{\,2} \left(X_g - \hat{X}_g \right) \hat{H}_g^{\,2} \tag{23}$$

So, the CPEP can be expressed again as

$$P_r\left(X_g \to \hat{X}_g \middle| \hat{H}_g\right) = Q\left(\sqrt{\frac{\left(X_g - \hat{X}_g\right)\hat{H}_g^{\;2}}{2\sigma_e^2\left(X_g\right)^2 / n + 2N_0}}\right) \tag{24}$$

Then, the unconditional pair-wise error probability (UPEP) can be obtained by

$$P_r\left(X_g \to \hat{X}_g\right) = E_{\hat{H}_g}\left\{Q\left(\sqrt{\frac{\left(X_g - \hat{X}_g\right)\hat{H}_g^{\;2}}{2\sigma_e^2\left(X_g\right)^2 / n + 2N_0}}\right)\right\} \tag{25}$$

where $E_{\hat{H}_g}\{\cdot\}$ denotes the expectation operation with respect to the estimated channel frequency response. To obtain the closed-form expression for the UPEP, the approximate Gaussian Q—function can be applied. To enhance the accuracy, the approximate Gaussian Q—function is proposed in [20], given by

$$Q(x) \approx 0.168e^{-0.87x^2} + 0.144e^{-0.525x^2} + 0.002e^{-0.603x^2}, \quad x > 0 \tag{26}$$

To the approximate UPEP, Equation (26) is applied to Equation (25),

$$P_r\left(X_g \to \hat{X}_g\right) = E_{\hat{H}_g}\left\{0.168e^{-0.876q\left(X_g - \hat{X}_g\right)\hat{H}_g^{\;2}}\right.$$

$$\left. + 0.144e^{-0.525q\left(X_g - \hat{X}_g\right)\hat{H}_g^{\;2}} + 0.002\,e^{-0.603q\left(X_g - \hat{X}_g\right)\hat{H}_g^{\;2}}\right\} \tag{27}$$

where $q = n / \left(2\sigma_e^2\left(X_g\right)^2 / n + 2N_0\right)$. Using Equation (27), the expectation can be calculated according to the spectral theorem in [9] and the UPEP upper bound can be calculated as

$$P_r\left(X_g \to \hat{X}_g\right) \approx \frac{0.168}{\det\left(\mathbf{I}_n + 0.876q\hat{K}_n\mathbf{A}\right)} + \frac{0.144}{\det\left(\mathbf{I}_n + 0.525q\hat{K}_n\mathbf{A}\right)}$$

$$+ \frac{0.002}{\det\left(\mathbf{I}_n + 0.603q\hat{K}_n\mathbf{A}\right)} . \tag{28}$$

where $\mathbf{I}_n$ denotes n-dimensional identity matrix. $\hat{K}_n = E\{\hat{H}_g\hat{H}_g^H\} = K_n + \sigma_e^2\mathbf{I}_n$ is the correlation matrix of $\hat{H}_g$, $K_n = E\{H_gH_g^H\}$ and $\mathbf{A} = \left(X_g - \hat{X}_g\right)^H\left(X_g - \hat{X}_g\right)$. Then, based on the UPEP derived above, an upper bound on the average bit error rate (ABER) can be obtained as,

$$P_{\text{ABER}} \approx \frac{1}{pnX_g}\sum_{X_g}\sum_{\hat{X}_g}P_r\left(X_g - \hat{X}_g\right)e\left(X_g, \hat{X}_g\right) \tag{29}$$

where $e\left(X_g, \hat{X}_g\right)$ represents the number of bit errors for the corresponding pair-wise error event and $nX_g = 2^p$ is the number of the possible realizations of X_g.

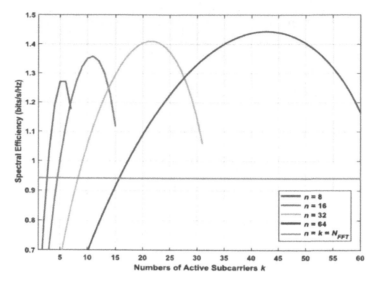

Figure 27.2: SE of optical-OFDM with IM system.

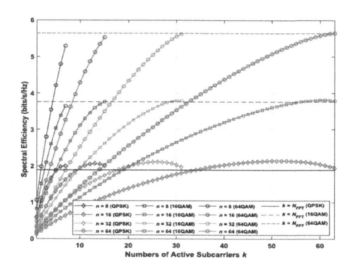

Figure 27.3: SE in the Optical-OFDM system with IM for different OFDM sub-block configurations.

4. Results and Discussion

In order to address the challenges posed by non-linearity in single mode fiber, the optical-OFDM-IM scheme has been employed for efficient long-haul optical link transmission. As depicted in Figure 27.1, a transmitter and receiver simulation structure has been constructed using MATLAB. The block model was simulated using the Split-Step Fourier Method (SSFM) to solve the Nonlinear Schrödinger Equation (NLSE). This simulated structure can be utilized to mitigate impairments such as dispersion effects and non-linearity in optical fiber communication systems. The simulation employed a consistent Fast Fourier Transform (FFT) size for the OFDM frame and a constant step-size protocol, following the SSFM approach [21].

Table 27.2 summarizes the simulation attributes for the optical fiber channel and OFDM system. In order to compensate for carrier frequency offset, it is imperative to maintain perfect system synchronization in addition to having 500 independent channels. The transmitter utilizes a pseudo random binary sequence (PRBS) generator to generate data bits, and employs binary phase shift keying (PSK) and M-ary quadrature amplitude modulation (QAM) schemes for bit mapping.

Table 27.2: System simulation parameters

Parameter	Value	Parameter	Value
CD parameter	16 ps/nm/km	Noise figure	5dB
λ	1550 nm	N_{FFT}	256
γ	1.32 (W.km)$^{-1}$	Cyclic prefix	6.25%
α	0.2 dB/km	Sampling rate	$f_s = 32GS_{a/s}$
L	100 km	Modulation	4-PSK, 16-QAM
Fiber type	SSMF		

Figures 27.4 and 27.5 provide a comparative analysis of the average BER performance between the proposed optical-OFDM with IM and conventional optical-OFDM under varying launch power values for 4-PSK and 16-QAM signaling. These figures demonstrate the combined impacts of link distance and launch power. This is important because the influence of fiber non-linearity is contingent on both the instantaneous signal power and transmission distance, as per the NLSE. For the purpose of evaluating the effect of fiber non-linearity exclusively, it is assumed that the laser exhibits no phase noise.

At low launch power levels, the optical fiber channel can be effectively modeled as a linear dispersive channel affected by amplified spontaneous emission (ASE) noise. However, it is observed that the performance of the proposed optical-OFDM with IM is inferior to that of optical-OFDM under low launch power conditions. This discrepancy arises due to bit errors stemming from incorrectly recovered active subcarrier indices in the proposed system.

The lowest point on the BER curve is referred to as the optimal launch power. This optimal launch-power is subject to variation based on factors such as transmission distance, modulation type, and other specific system attributes. The higher range of the optimal launch power signifies the area where the impact of fiber non-linearity becomes pronounced. In this context, fiber non-linearity becomes increasingly significant as the launch power is raised to facilitate long-distance transmission.

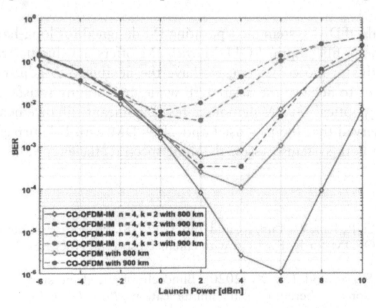

Figure 27.4: BER performance under various launch powers for 4-PSK modulation after different transmission distance.

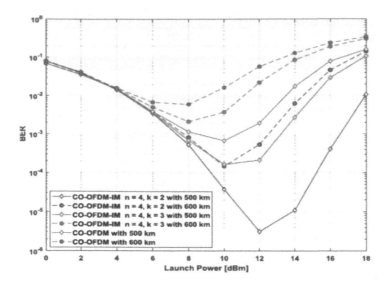

Figure 27.5: BER performance under different launch powers for 16-QAM modulation after different transmission distance.

This non-linearity introduces random dispersion around the central point of each subcarrier, resulting in interference between adjacent subcarriers.

In Figures 27.4 and 27.5, it is evident that the proposed optical-OFDM with IM outperforms conventional optical-OFDM, particularly at mid-to-high launch power values where fiber non-linearity plays a significant role. This improvement in BER performance can be attributed to the additional binary bits transmitted via the active subcarrier indices, as well as the enhanced resilience against inter-carrier interference resulting from the presence and placement of inactive subcarriers. Essentially, optical-OFDM with IM effectively mitigates the impact of fiber non-linearity and enables robust long-haul transmission.

5. Conclusions

In the study, an optical-OFDM system incorporating IM designed for long-haul transmission. When dealing with single mode fiber optical-OFDM with IM offers a valuable trade-off between average BER and SE. In this proposed system, we have the flexibility to adjust the number of active sub-carriers allowing us to achieve the desired SE while maintaining satisfactory average BER performance. Additionally, optical-OFDM demonstrates a significant enhancement in spectral efficiency. Furthermore, it is observed that the proposed optical-OFDM with IM surpasses conventional optical-OFDM even when both systems possess the same spectral efficiency value.

References

[1]   Tang, T., Zou, X., Li, P., Pan, W., Luo, B., and Yan, L. (2018). Proposal and demonstration of subcarrier index modulation OFDM for RoF system with enhanced spectral efficiency. *J. Lightw. Technol.*, 36(19), 4501–4506.

[2]   Sun, X., Zuo, Z., Su, S., and Tan, X. (2020). Blind chromatic dispersion estimation using fractional Fourier transformation in coherent optical communications. *Proc. IEEE Int. Conf. Artif. Intell. Inf. Syst. (ICAIIS)*, 339–342.

[3] Chen, M., Yu, J., and Xiao, X. (2017). Real-time Q-band OFDM-RoF systems with optical heterodyning and envelope detection for downlink transmission. *IEEE Photon. J.,* 9(2), 1–7.

[4] Thool, S. N., Chack, D., and Kumar, A. (2021). Coherent detection-based optical OFDM, 60 GHz radio-over-fiber link using frequency quadrupling, and channel and carrier phase estimation. *Frontiers Phys.,* 9, 504.

[5] Ferreira, J. S., et al. (2017). GFDM frame design for 5G application scenarios. *J. Commun. Inf. Syst.,* 32(1), 54–61.

[6] Di Stasio, F., Mondin, M., and Daneshgaran, F. (2018). Multirate 5G downlink performance comparison for f-OFDM and w-OFDM schemes with different numerologies. *Proc. Int. Symp. Netw. Comput. Commun. (lSNCC),* 1–6.

[7] Abdoli, J., Jia, M., and Ma, J. (2015). Filtered OFDM: A new waveform for future wireless systems. *Proc. IEEE 16th Int. Workshop Signal Process. Adv. Wireless Commun. (SPAWC),* 66–70.

[8] Ozturk, E., Basar, E., and Cirpan, H. A. (2017). Generalized frequency division multiplexing with flexible index modulation. *IEEE Acc.,* 5, 24727–24746.

[9] Basar, E., Aygolu, U., Panay, E., and Poor, H. V. (2013) Orthogonal frequency division multiplexing with index modulation. *IEEE Trans. Signal Proc.,* 61(22), 5536–5549.

[10] Di Renzo, M., Haas, H., Ghrayeb, A., Sugiura, S., and Hanzo, L. (2014). Spatial modulation for generalized MIMO: Challenges, opportunities and implementation. *Proc. IEEE,* 102(1), 56–103.

[11] Gursoy, M. C., Basar, E., Pusane, A. E., and Tugcu, T. (2019). Index modulation for molecular communication via diffusion systems. *IEEE Trans. Comm.,* 67(5), 3337–3350.

[12] Sacchi, C., Rahman, T., Hemadeh, I. A., and El-Hajjar, M. (2017). Millimeter-wave transmission for small-cell back-haul in dense urban environment: A solution based on MIMO-OFDM and space-time shift keying (STSK). *IEEE Acc.,* 5, 4000–4017.

[13] Basar, E. and Panayirci, E. (2015). Optical OFDM with index modulation for visible light communications. *Proc. 4th Int. Workshop Opt. Wireless Commun. (IWOW),* 11–15.

[14] Basar, E., Wen, M., Mesleh, R., DiRenzo, M., Xiao, Y., and Haas, H. (2017). Index modulation techniques for next-generation wireless networks. *IEEE Acc.,* 5, 16693–16746.

[15] Ellis, A. D., McCarthy, M. E., Al Khateeb, M. A. Z., Sorokina, M., and Doran, N. J. (2017). Performance limits in optical communications due to fiber nonlinearity. *Adv. Opt. Photon.,* 9(3), 429–503.

[16] Queiroz, S., Vilela, J. P., and Monteiro, E. (2020). Optimal mapper for OFDM with index modulation: A spectro-computational analysis. *IEEE Acc.,* 8, 68365–68378.

[17] Seimetz, M. (2009). *High-order Modulation for Optical Fiber Transmission* (Springer Series in Optical Sciences). Berlin, Germany: Springer. pp 252, ISBN 978-3-540-93770-8, https://doi.org/10.1007/978-3-540-93771-5.

[18] Lowery, A. J. (2007). Fiber nonlinearity mitigation in optical links that use OFDM for dispersion compensation. *IEEE Photon. Technol. Lett.,* 19(19), 1556–1558.

[19] Azim, A. W., Chafii, M., LeGuennec, Y., and Ros, L. (2020). Spectral and energy efficient fast-OFDM with index modulation for optical wireless systems. *IEEE Comm. Lett.,* 24(8), 1771–1774.

[20] Mao, T., Wang, Q., Quan, J., and Wang, Z. (2017). Zero-padded orthogonal frequency division multiplexing with index modulation using multiple constellation alphabets. *IEEE Acc.,* 5, 21168–21178.

[21] Ma, C.-P. and Kuo, J.-W. (2004). Orthogonal frequency division multiplex with multi-level technology in optical storage application. *Jpn. J. Appl. Phys.,* 43(7B), 4876–4878.

28 Design of Dual Band Reconfigurable Slot Antenna For Wireless Applications

Santosh Kumar Tripathi[a], and B. B. Tiwari

Department of Electronics Engineering, Veer Bahadur Singh Purvanchal University, *Jaunpur, U.P., India*

Abstract

In this study, a frequency-reconfigurable dual band antenna using a 1.6 mm FR-4 substrate having dielectric constant 4.4, dimensions 30×30 mm^2 a is presented. PIN diode as a switch is incorporated in the feed line to reconfigure the antenna. The proposed antenna has been simulated using Computer Simulation Technology (CST) studio suite 2022. The antenna resonates at 3.73 GHz with maximum gain 2.1 dBi when it is OFF and at 10.01 GHz with maximum gain 3.51 dBi when it is ON. For wireless technologies like WiMAX, C- and X-band applications, it is useful.

Keywords: Dual band, reconfigurable patch antenna, slots, WiMAX, X-band

1. Introduction

Reconfigurable antennas are generally widely used to meet the needs of the modern communication system. A controlled dynamic modification of features like frequency and radiation pattern is possible with reconfigurable antennas. There are several kinds of reconfiguration techniques, including the capacity to change frequency, polarization, and radiation pattern. A dual band antenna with a 40×40 mm^2 dimension is described in ref. [9]. To use this antenna in the WLAN and WiMAX frequency bands, a PIN diode and capacitor may be added. It is recommended that a PIN diode be used in a multiband slot antenna for wireless applications to achieve frequency reconfiguration [2]. It is a quad-band antenna that works well for smaller WiMAX, GNSS, and WLAN applications. A reconfigurable antenna [7] with a PIN diode was investigated using a FR-4 substrate for WLAN and WiMAX applications at the operating frequencies of 2.4 GHz, 3.5 GHz, 5.25 GHz, and 5.8 GHz. Other reconfigurable microstrip patch antenna designs, a reconfigurable patch antenna [6] with six frequency bands, and a reconfigurable antenna for Wi-Fi and 5G applications [4] have also been reported in this field. ThenClick or tap here to enter text., a brand-new truncated metallic ground surface and 9-shaped multiband reconfigurable antenna are introduced [1]. This antenna works in

---

[a]santoshktripathi8@gmail.com

both WiMAX's single band and dual band, which includes WLAN and Wi-Fi. Two monopole antennas [10] have been created for use with mobile wireless technologies including WiMAX, Wi-Fi, and WLAN applications. These antennas' radiating elements are constructed from two distinct geometrical shapes on a low-cost FR-4 substrate. Truncated metallic copper ground is used to provide the maximum radiation pattern and radiation efficiency achievable. The antennas' specifications include VSWR (1.5), bandwidth (6–35%), gain (1.7–3.4 dB), and radiation efficiency (85–90%), and they span the frequency ranges of 2.45, 3.50, and 5.20 GHz. Small, low-profile multi-band reconfigurable planar monopole antennas that operate in single- and dual-band modes were demonstrated [8]. Antenna 1 makes use of WLAN and Wi-Fi in dual-band mode. Antenna 2 has two distinct dual-band modes, notably (Wi-Fi and WLAN) and (WiMAX and WLAN), depending on whether the switch is ON or OFF. A compact reconfigurable monopole antenna with the lumped element switch has been used [5] to operate in three distinct frequency bands under ON and OFF situations.

This study proposes a reconfigurable antenna with a feed line on the bottom side and two slots on the top side. While to achieve frequency reconfiguration, a PIN diode is employed as a switch in the feedline. For the switch's ON and OFF states, the resonance frequencies are 10.01 GHz and 3.73 GHz, respectively.

2. Antenna Design

The proposed antenna's geometry is presented in Figure 28.1. It is designed on FR-4 substrate having dielectric constant $\varepsilon_r = 4.4$, height h = 1.6 mm, and dimension 30×30 mm^2. The top side consists two slots of size a × b and c × c which are linked to each other and the bottom side of the antenna consists an inverted L shape feed line with a gap of size 1 mm for insertion of a switch. PIN diode is used as a switch in simulation environment which behave as a low resistance (1 Ω) in forward bias and high resistance (1 MΩ) in reverse bias. The effective electrical length portions of the antenna construction, in charge of radiating a certain frequency range, depend on the state of the switch. In Table 28.1, the final dimensions are listed.

Resonance frequency f_r of microstrip antenna [3] can be given as

$$f_r = \frac{c}{2L_e\sqrt{\varepsilon_{re}}} \tag{1}$$

where

$$\varepsilon_{re} = \frac{1}{2}\left[(\varepsilon_r+1)(\varepsilon_r-1)\left(1-\frac{12h}{w}\right)^{-\frac{1}{2}}\right] \tag{2}$$

$$L_e = L + \Delta L \tag{3}$$

$$\Delta L = h0.412\frac{(\varepsilon_{re}+0.3)\left(\frac{w}{h}+0.264\right)}{(\varepsilon_{re}-0.258)\left(\frac{w}{h}+0.8\right)} \tag{4}$$

ε_{re} is the effective dielectric constant, L_e is the effective length, c is the velocity of light, and $L=w=G$.

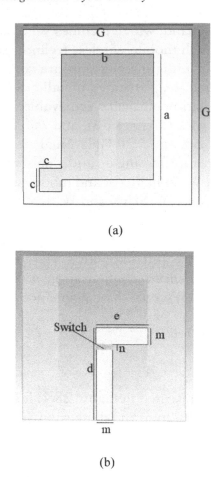

(a)

(b)

Figure 28.1: Antenna geometry. (a) top side (b) bottom side.

Table 28.1: Optimized dimensions of the antenna

Parameter	Value (mm)	Parameter	Value (mm)
G	30	d	16.85
a	21.6	e	9.5
b	16.3	m	3
c	4	n	1

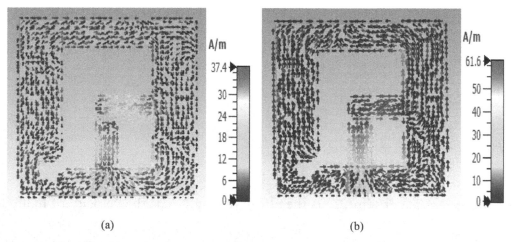

(a)   (b)

Figure 28.2: Current distribution. (a) 10.01 GHz (ON) (b) 3.73 GHz (OFF).

3. Results and Discussion

In Figure 28.2 (a, b), the antenna's current distribution is shown at frequencies of 10.01 GHz and 3.73 GHz for the ON and OFF states of the switch. The proposed antenna's maximum current distribution is 37.4 A/m and 61.6 A/m in ON and OFF states, correspondingly.

Figure 28.3 shows how the return loss varies depending on whether the switch is in the ON or OFF position. The antenna displays an S11≤-10 dB bandwidth of 1.12 GHz (9.45–10.57 GHz) and 0.90 GHz (3.28–4.18 GHz) in ON and OFF states, respectively. WiMAX applications (3.3–3.8 GHz), C-band applications (3.7–4.2 GHz), and X-band applications (8–12 GHz) can all benefit from the suggested architecture. Figure 28.4 shows variations of the designed antenna's simulated VSWR with frequency during ON and OFF situations, respectively.

In Figure 28.5, gain and frequency are displayed. The maximum gain is 4.78 dBi when the switch is ON, and 4.77 dBi when it is OFF. The efficiency of the suggested antenna is shown in Figure 28.6 in both the ON and OFF switch positions. At 8.3 GHz in the ON state and 9.65 GHz in the OFF state, the maximum efficiency is 80.25% and 82.05%, respectively.

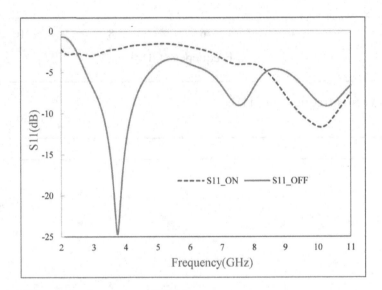

Figure 28.3: Return loss (dB) versus frequency (GHz).

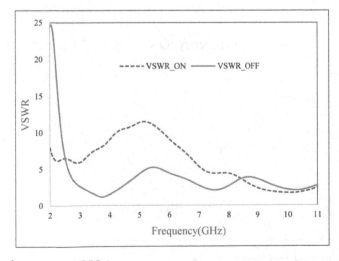

Figure 28.4: VSWR versus frequency (GHz).

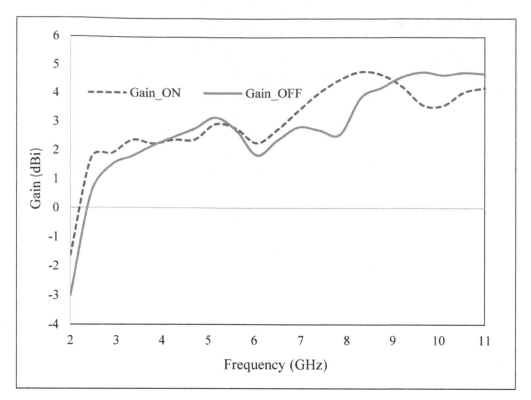

Figure 28.5: Gain (dBi) versus frequency (GHz).

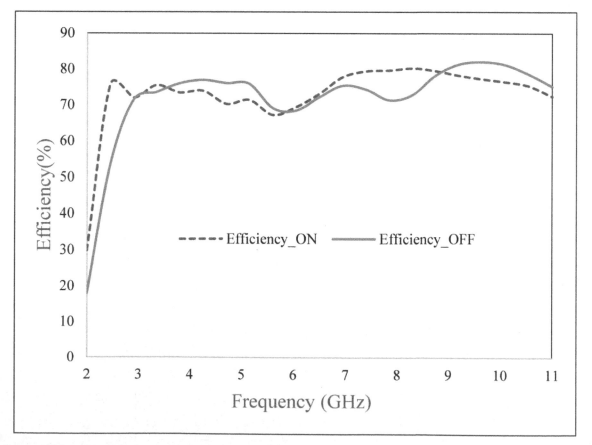

Figure 28.6: Efficiency (%) versus frequency (GHz).

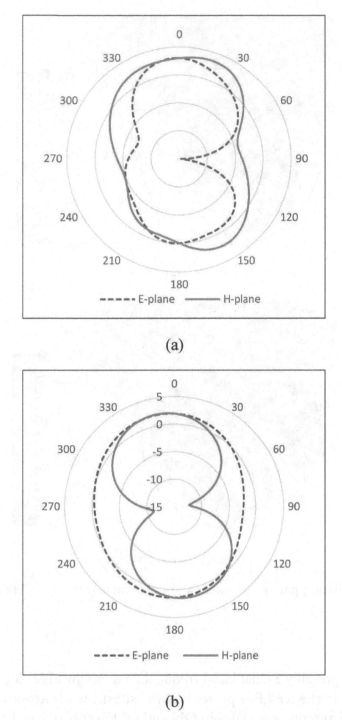

(a)

(b)

Figure 28.7: Simulated radiation pattern of antenna in E–H plane. (a) 10.01 GHz (ON) (b) 3.73 GHz (OFF).

The simulated E- and H-plane gain patterns for the resonating frequencies of 3.73 GHz and 10.01 GHz are shown in Figure 28.7. The suggested antenna's far field area is attained with a maximum gain of 3.51 dBi at 10.01 GHz in the ON state. Additionally, the highest gain of 2.1 dBi at 3.73 GHz is attained for the switch's OFF state. Figure 28.8 depicts the 3D radiation pattern for this antenna at 10.01 GHz when turned ON and at 3.73 GHz when turned OFF.

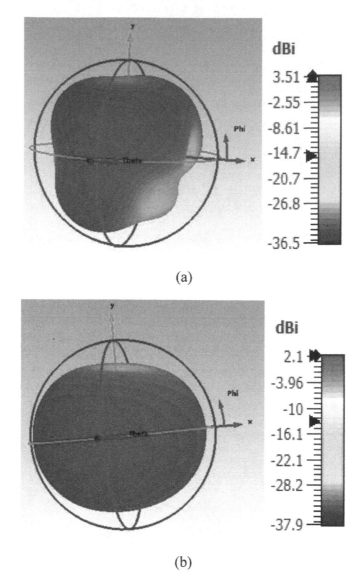

(a)

(b)

Figure 28.8: Simulated radiation pattern of antenna in E–H plane. (a) 10.01 GHz (ON) (b) 3.73 GHz (OFF).

4. Conclusions

This paper analyses and presents a dual band frequency reconfigurable slot antenna. Utilizing a PIN diode as a switch placed in the feed line printed on the substrate's bottom side, the reconfigurability is achieved. The intended antenna resonates in ON and OFF states at 10.01 GHz and 3.73 GHz, with maximum gain 3.51 dBi and 2.1 dBi, respectively. For WiMAX, C-band, and X-band applications, the suggested antenna is suitable.

References

[1]   Ali Shah, I., Hayat, S., Khan, I., Alam, I., Ullah, S., and Afridi, A. (2016). A compact, tri-band and 9-shape reconfigurable antenna for WiFi, WiMAX and WLAN applications. *Int. J. Wire. Microw. Technol.*, 6(5), 45–53.

[2] Ali, T., Muzammil Khaleeq, M., and Biradar, R. C. (2018). A multiband reconfigurable slot antenna for wireless applications. *AEU Int. J. Elec. Comm.*, 84, 273–280.

[3] Garg, R., Bhartia, P., Bahal, I., and Ittipiboon, A. (2003). Antenna Design Handbook, Boston, London: Artech House. pp 875, ISBN-10: 0890065136.

[4] Hadri, D. El, Zakriti, A., and Zugari, A. (2020). Reconfigurable antenna for Wi-Fi and 5G applications. *Proc. Manufac.*, 46, 793–799.

[5] Iqbal, A., Ullah, S., Naeem, U., Basir, A., and Ali, U. (2017). Design, fabrication and measurement of a compact, frequency reconfigurable, modified T-shape planar antenna for portable applications. *J. Elec. Engg. Technol.*, 12(4), 1611–1618.

[6] Majid, H. A., Abd Rahim, M. K., Hamid, M. R., and Ismail, M. F. (2014). Frequency reconfigurable microstrip patch-slot antenna with directional radiation pattern. *Progress In Electromagnetics Research*, 144, 319–328. doi:10.2528/PIER13102901.

[7] Rajeshkumar, V. and Raghavan, S. (2015). A compact metamaterial inspired triple band antenna for reconfigurable WLAN/WiMAX applications. *AEU Int. J. Elec. Comm.*, 69(1), 274–280.

[8] Shah, S. A. A., Khan, M. F., Ullah, S., Basir, A., Ali, U., and Naeem, U. (2017). Design and measurement of planar monopole antennas for multi-band wireless applications. *IETE J. Res.*, 63(2), 194–204.

[9] Shi, S., Ding, W., and Luo, K. (2014). A monopole antenna with dual-band reconfigurable circular polarization. *Prog. Electromag. Res. C.*

[10] Ullah, S., Hayat, S., Umar, A., Ali, U., Tahir, F. A., and Flint, J. A. (2017). Design, fabrication and measurement of triple band frequency reconfigurable antennas for portable wireless communications. *AEU Int. J. Elec. Comm.*, 81, 236–242.

29 Design and Analysis of Energy Efficient and High Speed Sense Amplifiers For SRAM IC

Vishal Yadav[a] and B. B. Tiwari

Department of Electronics Engineering, VBS Purvanchal University, Jaunpur, U.P., India

Abstract

This study depicts the comparative analysis of different types of sense amplifiers. Voltage-mode sense amplifiers (VMSA) and current sense amplifiers (CSA) are the two types of amplifiers widely used in static random-access memory (SRAM). It is preferable to utilize a hybrid sense amplifier over a traditional current or voltage sense amplifier since it uses both current and voltage sensing by using low power techniques. The first goal of this research paper is to construct a hybrid mode sense amplifier with Multi-threshold voltage complementary metal-oxide semiconductor (MTCMOS) and the second goal is to compare the designs and determine which one performs better in terms of power and speed. One of the most crucial circuits in Complementary Metal-Oxide-Semiconductor (CMOS) memories, sense amplifiers plays a significant role in lowering the overall sensing voltage and delay. Voltage mode sensing amplifiers detected the voltage difference at the bit and bit lines bar. Sense amplifier is widely used in a memory to high speed up the memory read/write operation. The performance of sense amplifier mainly affects memory access time and overall power consumption. A simple analysis shows the speed enhancements are possible by using only current mode than voltage mode signal transferring and variable-threshold CMOS (VTCMOS), MTCMOS or Gated V_{dd} low power technique. The significance of this technique is to use low resistance current circuits to lower the impedance level and voltage swing on long interconnect wire. Simulation results are given regarding the delay and power dissipation for different sense amplifier.

Keywords: Sense amplifier, voltage SA, MTCMOS, VTCMOS, current SA, cross coupled SA, latch type SA, hybrid mode SA, delay, power dissipation

1. Introduction

The most critical component of Very Large Scale Integration (VLSI) chip design is the SRAM-based cache memory. The speed and power of the entire system may unfavorably be impacted by the memory and peripheral circuitry's performance. Delay in reading operation is the most crucial factor in

---

[a]vishalunsiet@gmail.com

SRAM design. Following the occurrence of the latching phenomena, the current flow automatically stops. Therefore, the current sensing amplifier does not experience static power dissipation [1]. As a result, the delay in detecting and latching operation is also related to power dissipation. Since the memory chip takes up 90% of the chip's surface area, power dissipation within the on-chip cache memory has become a very significant portion of the memory chip's overall power usage [2]. The fundamental sense amplifier utilized in SRAM ICs is the CMOS cross coupled inverter. Input and output lines simultaneously function. As a result, there is a high time delay and power dissipation. Due of the high input impedance, this error is removed in latch type sense amplifiers [3]. The two types of sense amplifiers are voltage and current sense amplifiers, depending on the type of signal given to the input. Voltage sense amplifier needs a change in voltage at the bit-line before detecting the voltage difference and amplifying it to the full swing range. However, as technology advances, decision span increases and voltage swing decreases to micron or submicron levels. The lowest differential signal from bit lines or data lines is amplified by the current sense amplifier and outputted at CMOS logic level.

Small input impedance makes it one of the most often used methods for cutting both the sensing delay and the power consumption of SRAM [4]. This paper comprises of comparative study of all different types of current and voltage sense amplifiers.

The novelty of this paper is that it explains the reason why delay and power dissipation take place in respective sense amplifiers. The power dissipation for several sense amplifiers operating at various power supply voltages is examined in this work [5]. In this study, the latency and power dissipation of various sense amplifier designs are analyzed. The layout of the above discussion is as follows.

The design of the circuit schematics and the implementation and analysis of various types of sense amplifiers are covered in section 2 [6]. Section 3 analyses the findings of latency and overall power dissipation for sense amplifiers while demonstrating various modes of operation. The paper is concluded in section 5.

2. Design of Sense Amplifier

One of the most crucial ,or essential components of read circuitry is a sensing amplifier. Its primary task is to amplify minor voltage difference from a bit-line representing data (0 or 1) stored in an SRAM memory cell to a substantial voltage level. As a result, data viewed from outside the SRAM memory cell should be properly analyzed. Sense amplifiers are divided into voltage and current mode sense amplifiers based on the types of input signals they receive [7].

2.1. Voltage mode sense amplification

A modest voltage swing that occurs on the bit-line during memory cell reading is amplified to drive CMOS digital logic by the voltage sense amplifier. Cross coupled latch type sense amplifiers are the simplest voltage sense amplifiers [8].

2.1.1. Cross coupled CMOS inverter latch type sense amplifier
The sense amplifier in Figure 29.1 is made up of two CMOS cross-coupled inverters. When operated in the transient domain, a CMOS inverter gives extremely high gain [9]. The latch needs to be in its meta-stable position by equating the bit-lines in order to function as a sensory amplifier. Due to the bit-line capacitors discharging during the read operation, a voltage difference is produced over the bit-lines. When there is a significant voltage differential, the sense amplifier's SE signal is enabled using the SE pin. The cross-coupled pair of latches moves to one of its stable functions

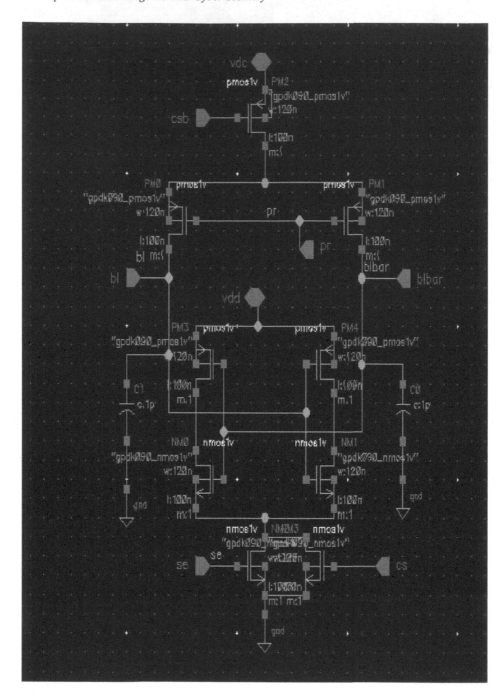

Figure 29.1: Cross couple sense amplifier.

points depending on the types of input voltage. The input and output of a cross-coupled latch sense amplifier are located at the same node [10]. Bit-line capacitances are linked to the cross-coupled inverter's input pin.

There should be enough voltage difference between the bit-lines to produce correct output. In order to correctly identify the data in the SRAM memory cell, this enables the bit-lines to discharge until they produce a significant voltage differential. Therefore, it takes a long time to make the right decision [11]. The input and output lines should be kept distinct using pass-gates or a decoupling resistor to avoid long delays in decision-making. Due to the high input impedance at the input differential stage, this problem is eliminated by employing the differential circuit as depicted in Figure 29.2.

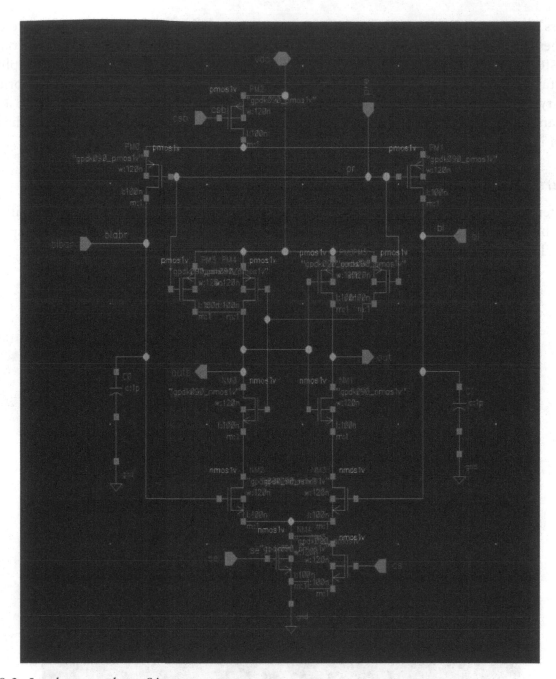

Figure 29.2: Latch type voltage SA.

2.1.2. *Latch type sense amplifier*

With a high resistive input signal and strong positive feedback, latch type sense amplifiers are consolidated. The sequentially connected latch is managed by the current flowing through the two separate differential input transistors, NM2 and NM3. The latch, which is an important component of the latch sense amplifier, must be in a meta-stable condition prior to the reading operation [12]. High gain positive feedback sense amplifiers include transistors PM4, PM6, NM1, and NM0. The NM2 and NM3 transistors function as a differential amplifier. The sensing amplifier is activated by the transistor NM4. The latch circuit's delay is controlled by the usage of NM5 and PM2. In the sensing mode, the SE signal is pushed high to switch on the NM4 transistor, which in turn drives the transistors NM2 and NM3 to function as common source differential amplifiers after pre-charging the bit lines to V_{dd}. The extremely little voltage differential is amplified to full swing at the output pin by transistors PM3, PM6, NM1, and NM0 [13]. The differential amplifier detects and amplifies very small voltage differences between bit-lines as inputs are supplied to its input pin. The performance of the latch type of SA is improved by strong positive feedback provided at the output stage and a differential amplifier at the input stage. Turn-off the SA so no current flows through it when the latching operation is finished.

2.2. *Current sense amplifier*

Small differences in the input currents are amplified only slightly by current sensing amplifiers.

As technology advances, contemporary sensing techniques are better suited to high-speed, low-power, and large-size memories.

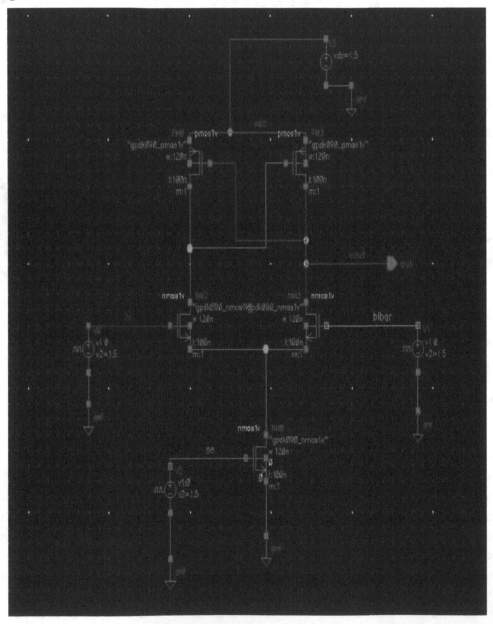

Figure 29.3: Basic current SA.

2.2.1. Basic current sense amplifier

Figure 29.3 shows basic circuit of current sense amplifier. It consists of 3 p-channel metal–oxide–semiconductor (PMOS) transistors and 4 N-channel metal-oxide semiconductor (NMOS) transistors.

The sense amplifier is turned on by turning on the sense SE signal. Then, current moves from bit lines to corresponding data lines that are near the potential of ground using PMOS transistors. A steady connection between the bit-lines and V_{dd} is maintained using low resistance connectors. The bit-line voltages are kept constant to obtain the inherent equalization action [15].

The gate to source voltages, size, and saturation region of the PMOS transistors PM0 and NM2 are all equal. Similarities exist between the saturation states of transistors PM3 and NM3. Assume that I current is flowing via the SRAM cell. When the sensing amplifier is turned on, currents flow through its sides, and these currents may vary by I. As a result, current sensing is required.

The different or distinct currents flowing over data lines or differential voltages at distinct nodes A and B constitute the output of the basic current sense amplifier, which can be amplified in the second stage [16].

2.3. Hybrid mode sense amplifier

Figure 29.4 shows hybrid types of sense amplifier. It is combination of both voltage and current sense amplifiers. Figure 29.4 shows input is given current from bit-line capacitor and output is voltage taken from the cross coupled inverter [17].

Hybrid mode sense amplifier consist of 12 PMOS and 6 NMOS. Transistors PM0 and PM1 used to connect bit-lines to Vdd. Transistors PM6 and PM4 act as a simple switch to connect bit-lines to the delay-lines. PMOS PM3 and PM5 and NMOS NM0 and NM1 form cross coupled latch which is positive type feedback amplifier. This is used to amplify the small voltage difference at data lines to the full CMOS voltage level. PM12 and NM9 used as MTCMOS for decrease delay and reduce power dissipation [18]. Before read operation, keep the bit-lines and data lines to V_{dd} through the respective pin pre pre-charge circuits. During pre-charging, put SE low which prevent the static current flowing through the sense amplifier to the ground. At that time make EQ Equalization signal low and make voltages at node A and B equal. Then during the read operation, make CS signal low CSB signal high for some small time period to transfer bit-line voltage to the respective data-line. Cross coupled sense amplifier amplifies the small voltage difference and gives full voltage swing. In the cell 1 is stored; bit-lines and data-lines are remained at V_{dd}. A very small current discharge will flow through respected bit-line. While in the cell 0 is stored, discharge current flows from bit-line and data-line to the lower than V_{dd} voltages.

3. Methodology

3.1. MTCMOS

In order to optimize delay and power, the MTCMOS (Multi-threshold CMOS) technology employs transistors with various threshold voltages. Low V_t transistors switch more quickly but leak more static power. However, high V_t transistors switch more slowly while reducing static power leakage [19]. With the use of well-planned circuits, MTCMOS design strategies can optimize power and latency without suffering consequences. Use of sleep transistors is the most popular method of MTCMOS leakage power reduction [20]. Sleep transistors are used to build virtual power lines that supply the logic.

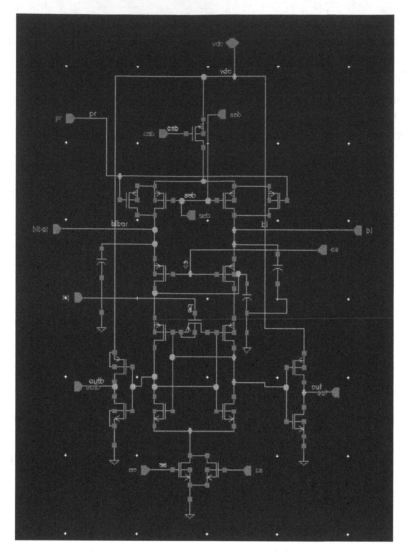

Figure 29.4: Hybrid SA.

3.2. Gated V_{dd}

This method offers a control mechanism that, when the SRAM cell is not in use, can disable the supply voltage (V_{dd}), so preventing any leakage current. This significantly lowers the leakage power dissipation [21]. A high threshold voltage (high V_t) transistor is added to the supply (V_{dd}) or ground channel of the SRAM cell in order to implement this control mechanism, with all other transistors being modeled as low V_t transistors. Because they flip more quickly than high V_t transistors, low V_t transistors are used. The SRAM cell operates quickly as a result. The power usage and delay are optimized in this setup [22]. Figure 29.5 show the schematic output of sense amplifiers. After correct sensing the signal, various types of analysis for delay and power dissipation are done. After pre-charging the bit lines and output-lines, the time taken by the sense amplifier to give sufficient large voltage difference at bit-line is considered as delay [23].

Delay consists of discharging and latching types delay. The discharging delay depends on the bit-line capacitances. Supply voltage variation mainly affects the latching delay [24]. Figures 29.6 and 29.7 show the delay and power dissipation of various types of sense amplifier used for SRAM IC.

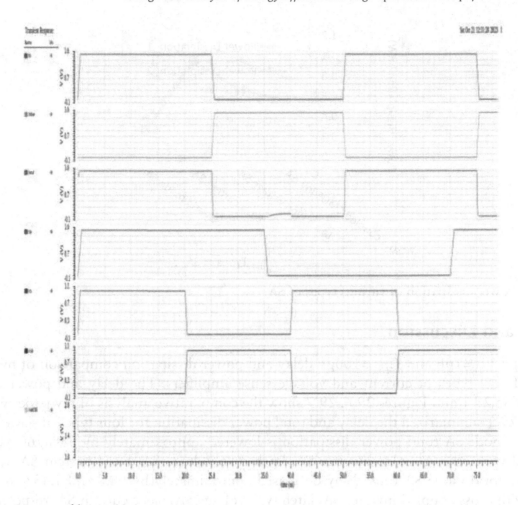

Figure 29.5: Output of basic SA.

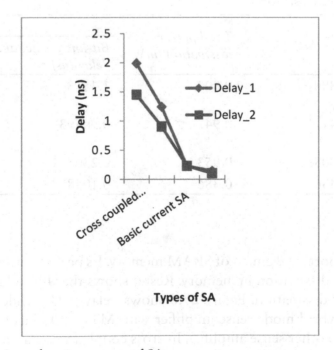

Figure 29.6: Delay calculation of various types of SA.

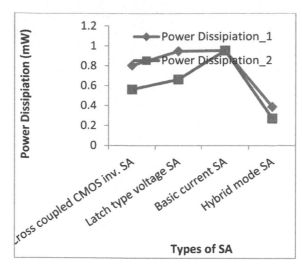

Figure 29.7: Power dissipation of various types of SA.

4. Result and Discussion

Take C_{DL}=1pF, C_{PL}=1pF and C_{Load}=100pF delay and power dissipation comparison of hybrid mode SA with different types of current and voltage sense amplifiers. The delay and power dissipation shown in Table 29.1 and Figures 29.6, 29.7 show the comparative analysis of my paper work.

In Table 29.1 summarized the delay and total power dissipation for four types of sense amplifiers.

In hybrid mode SA total power dissipation is lowered approximately by 55%, 60%, and 90% as compared with cross coupled inverter SA, latch type voltage SA, basic current SA, respectively. Similarly in hybrid mode SA total delay decreased approximately by 98.8%, 84.43% and 52% as compared with cross coupled inverter SA, latch type voltage SA, basic current SA, respectively.

Table 29.1: Delay and power dissipation

Types of SA	Delay (ns)	Total power dissipation (mW)	Work	
			Bit-line capacitance delay (ns)	Total power dissipation (mW)
Cross coupled CMOS inv. SA	1.9880	0.804	1.4513	0.562
Latch type voltage SA	1.241	0.947	0.90593	0.662
Basic current SA	0.2305	0.953	0.2305	0.953
Hybrid mode SA	0.1436	0.386	0.1048	0.270

5. Conclusions

Sense amplifier is very important element of SRAM memory. Its performance affects the delay in decision and also total power dissipation in memory. Result shows that hybrid mode sense amplifier has less delay and low power dissipation. Figure 29.6 shows delay_1 [1] while delay_2 show the result of designed schematic. Hybrid mode sense amplifier with MTCMOS has fast speed and low power dissipation with respect to other sense amplifier. In cross coupled sense amplifier as input and output pins are same so it takes more time to discharge.

References

[1] Surkar, A. and Agarwal, V. (2019). Delay and power analysis of current and voltage sense amplifiers for SRAM at 180nm technology. *2019 3rd Int. Conf. Elec. Comm. Aerospace Technol. (ICECA) IEEE*, 1371–1376.

[2] Nibhanupudi, S. S. T., Raman, S., Raman, S., and Jaydeep, P. K. (2021). Phase transition material-assisted low-power SRAM design. *IEEE Trans. Elec. Dev.*, 68(5), 2281–2288.

[3] Kumar, H. and Tomar, V. K. (2021). A review on performance evaluation of different low power SRAM cells in nano-scale era. *Wireless Per. Comm.*, 117(3), 1959–1984.

[4] Pal, S., et al. (2020). A highly stable reliable SRAM cell design for low power applications. *Microelec. Reliab.*, 105, 113503.

[5] Abbasian, E., et al. (2023). A low-power SRAM design with enhanced stability and ION/IOFF ratio in Fin FET technology for wearable device applications. *Int. J. Elec.*, 1–18.

[6] Neeraj, K., Mahaboob Basha, Md., and Srinivasulu, G. (2021). Design of low power SRAM-based ubiquitous sensor for wireless body area networks. *Int. J. Perv. Comput. Comm.*, 17(5), 611–621.

[7] Kumar, P. D., Ritesh Kumar, K., and Karuppanan, P. (2021). Design and analysis of low-power SRAM. *Adv. VLSI Comm. Sig. Proc. Select Proc. VCAS 2019*, 41–56.

[8] Kim, Y., et al. (2021). Ultra-low power and high-throughput SRAM design to enhance AI computing ability in autonomous vehicles. *Electronics*, 10(3), 256.

[9] Dutt, D., et al. (2022). Design and performance analysis of high-performance low power voltage mode sense amplifier for static RAM. *Adv. Elec. Electron. Engg.*, 20(3), 285–293.

[10] Chen, J., et al. (2021). Analysis and design of reconfigurable sense amplifier for compute SRAM with high-speed compute and normal read access. *IEEE Trans. Cir. Sys. II Exp. Briefs*, 68(12), 3503–3507.

[11] Saini, A., Parnav Kumar, G., and Ruchi, G. (2019). Analysis of low power SRAM sense amplifier. *2019 Int. Conf. Elect. Elec. Comp. Engg. (UPCON) IEEE*, 1–6.

[12] Saun, S. and Kumar, H. (2019). Design and performance analysis of 6T SRAM cell on different CMOS technologies with stability characterization. *IOP Conf. Ser. Mat. Sci. Engg.*, 561(1).

[13] Shukla, N. Kr, Pulkit, B., and Shilpi, B. (2015). Design and analysis of a novel ultra-low power SRAM bit-cell at 45nm CMOS technology for bio-medical implants. *Int. J. Comp. Appl.*, 975, 8887.

[14] Mishra, K. C. and Singh, R. K. (2019). Design and analysis of low power SRAM using CMOS technology. *Int. J. Innov. Technol. Explor. Engg.*, 8(12S), 896–902.

[15] Dounavi, H.-M., Yiorgos, S., and Yiorgos, T. (2019). Periodic monitoring of BTI induced aging in SRAM sense amplifiers. *IEEE Trans. Device Mater. Reliab.*, 19(1), 64–72.

[16] Zhao, Y., et al. (2022). An offset cancellation technique for SRAM sense amplifier based on relation of the delay and offset. *Microelec. J.*, 128, 105578.

[17] Nemati, S. H. H., Nima, E., and Mohammad Hossein, M. (2023). A hybrid SRAM/RRAM in-memory computing architecture based on a reconfigurable SRAM sense amplifier. *IEEE Acc.*, 11, 72159–72171.

[18] Patel, D., et al. (2019). Hybrid latch-type offset tolerant sense amplifier for low-voltage SRAMs. *IEEE Trans. Cir. Sys. I Regular Papers*, 66(7), 2519–2532.

[19] Chotten, P. and Akho John, R. (2019). Performance comparison of body biasing and coupling capacitor sense amplifier for sram. *2019 Dev. Integr. Cir. (DevIC) IEEE.*, 1, 75–78.

[20] Agrawal, R. and Tomar, V. K. (2018). Implementation and analysis of low power reduction techniques in sense amplifier. *2018 Second Int. Conf. Elec. Comm. Aerospace Technol. (ICECA) IEEE.*, 1, 439–444.

[21] Dounavi, H.-M., Yiorgos, S., and Yiorgos, T. (2018). Aging monitoring in SRAM sense amplifiers. *2018 7th Int. Conf. Modern Cir. Sys. Technol. (MOCAST) IEEE*.

[22] Ahir, A., Jitendra Kumar, S., and Srinivasulu, A. (2017). A low-voltage distinctive source-based sense amplifier for memory circuits using fin FETs. *Smart Innov. Comm. Comput. Sci. Proc. ICSICCS 2017*, 2.

[23] Pal, S., et al. (2020). A highly stable reliable SRAM cell design for low power applications. *Microelec. Reliab.*, 105, 113503.

[24] Srinivasu, B. and Sridharan, K. (2021). Low-power and high-performance ternary SRAM designs with application to CNTFET technology. *IEEE Trans. Nanotechnol.*, 20, 562–566.

30 Validation of Class of Non-Linear Controllers on Lab Scale Batch Reactor: Sliding Mode Controllers

Krupa Narwekar[1], Prajwal Shettigar J.[2], and Thirunavukkarasu Indiran[3,a]

[1]Baroda Lions Club Educational Trust

[2]Post Graduate Student, Department of Mechatronics, Manipal Institute of Technology, Manipal Academy of Higher Education, Manipal, Karnataka, India

[3]Professor, Department of Instrumentation and Control Engineering, Manipal Institute of Technology, Manipal Academy of Higher Education, Manipal, Karnataka, India

Abstract

This article aims to implement the sliding mode controllers (SMCs), which is a non-linear controller with high computational intensity. Also, the implementation of various non-linear controllers such as model predictive controller (MPC), Non-linear model predictive controllers (NMPC) involves online optimization with constraints. Hence the validation on physical system has limitations on computational capacity for online data. In this article, authors have addressed the overcoming of high intense computations using Jetson developer kit with signal conditioning and analog to digital converters (ADC) to connect the physical sensor and actuator signals. Case study of highly nonlinear batch reactors is considered. Due to its exothermic reaction with chemical feed along with its non-steady state. The uncertainty in this batch reactor experimental study is considered as the change in input cold water, which is circulated in the reactor jacket to carry away the additional heat. SMCs are more robust and sensitive to additional uncertainty added into the system dynamics. In this paper authors considered the nonlinear model equations developed for the experimental batch reactor by Prajwal et al. [1, 2]. The optimal temperature profile is developed for acrylamide polymerization reaction and used as a reference trajectory for the closed loop simulation and validation. The coolant flow rate is the manipulated variable circulated via circular coil and the reactor temperature is the process variable. In this paper authors have presented four types of SMC to arrest the reactor temperature oscillations with the reference trajectory. The experimental results depict that the SMC with PI sliding surface gives minimum control signal and reactor temperature tracks the trajectory over a period of time than other types of SMC. The major bottleneck in implementing advanced controllers with constrains such as NMPC is the computation time with optimizer. Attempt of implementing advanced computations techniques are in progress using Jetson board.

Keywords: Sliding mode controller, batch reactor, Jetson nano board, trajectory tracking

1. Introduction

Batch reactors are inherently a highly non-linear process due to various reasons such as exothermic reactions, reaction constants with exponential terms and also based on type of polymerization reaction takes place in reactor. In these type of batch process, there is no continuous inflow of feed or

---

[a]it.arasu@manipal.edu

continuous outflow, it has all one time charging and maintained with same feed quantity till the batch process time. Product is taken out for analysis only after the batch process terminal time. There are influence of external disturbances on the batch reactor operations. To mention such, coolant flow rate temperature variation over a period of time. It influences the jacket temperature (T_j) to vary as well as affects the reactor temperature (T_r). The above said can be realized by looking at the non-linear differential equations of batch reactor presented under system dynamics. Also, in the case study of bio-diesel production in batch reactor, there is a high possibility of feed component concentration may get varied Urmila and Pahola [3]. This will happen due to procurement of soyabean oil purchase from various vendors. This uncertainty may affect the final product quality.

The batch reactor problem can be divided into two the following (i) Optimal temperature trajectory formation (ii) Closed loop operation of batch reactor with temperature trajectory towards the final product formation. In this paper, the optimal temperature profile formed for acrylamide polymerization by Prajwal et al. [1, 2] for lab scale batch reactor is considered as a reference for closed loop validation. Sliding mode controller (SMC) is one of the robust controller to realize any closed loop operation in the presence of uncertainty. In this paper, three different types of SMCs are validated on the lab scale batch reactor.

Section literature survey presents the wide literature on batch reactor profile formation, modeling aspect and closed loop operations from various experimental works and simulations carried out in past. Three different types of SMC were simulated for temperature trajectory tracking, further all the SMC were implemented on a pilot plant batch reactor and obtained satisfactory trajectory tracking.

Further, usage of Jetson board for downloading the control algorithms developed using Python code for improving the computational capacity in terms of speed, since we use online optimizer for the control signal formulation.

2. Literature Survey

The brief survey on batch reactor can be classified into the following aspects: a) Optimal temperature profile formation b) Mathematical modeling of the batch reactor c) Controller design for trajectory tracking d) Validation of control strategy on the lab scale batch reactor e) Product quality analysis.

2.1. Optimal temperature profile

Peer literature on pilot plant batch reactor classify the survey into two major domains, firstly chemical engineering and other one as control domain. Chemical engineering researchers works on the optimal temperature profile formation for a particular product aimed from the batch operation with specified batch time. Palanki et al. [4] worked on neural network based end point optimization using Pontryagin's principle and minimization of Hamiltonian. Arun Senthil and Sundaramoorthy [5] presented the profile formation based on the Pontryagin's minimum principle using backward integration. Urmila and Pohola [3] extensively worked on the optimal profile for the biodiesel production with and without uncertainty in the concentration of triglycerides, used Hamiltonian principle to solve for the optimal profile.

2.2. Modeling of batch reactor

Modeling of lab scale batch reactor can be made based on a) Data driven modeling b) First principle modeling c) Hybrid modeling. Batch reactors are made of solid vessel with 316SS to avoid corrosion during various chemical reactions. It also has an integral heating and cooling systems for trajectory tracking. With respect to modeling, in general heater current will kept constant and coolant flow rate will be varied as a manipulated signal to record the open loop reaction temperature. It is mandatory to charge the batch reactor with actual chemical feed meant for the closed loop operation in order to capture the reaction dynamics properly.

Data driven modeling covers the linear and nonlinear modeling. Autoregressive recursive exogenous (ARX) uses the input and output data collected to form the output equation by defining the number of input and output orders If one considers the cross correlation between the input and output with defined order of input–output along with the error term, it results with Non-linear autoregressive recursive exogenous (NARX) modeling by Billing et al. [6]. For the data driven modeling, one must not necessarily known with the thorough knowledge of the system under consideration.

For the first principle modeling, one must know the exact dynamics of the system under study to model precisely. If there exist a model mismatch, closed loop performance validation will degrade. In order to overcome this, one can use the known parameter data from the physical batch reactor system and carry out the parameter estimation once again using data driven approach, error residuals ensure the model parameters accuracy. Figure 30.1 shows the lab scale batch reactor and Figure 30.2 illustrates its schematic diagram used for the controller validation.

Figure 30.1: Experimental setup of batch reactor in advanced process control lab, ICE Dept., MIT, Manipal [1, 2].

2.3. Controller design

Control domain researchers use any random non-linear profile for simulation in closed loop for proposed control algorithms. While validating the control algorithms on a lab scale batch reactor, one must use the actual chemical feed to have a exothermic reaction, hence the optimal temperature profile formation is essential along with the terminal time. Validation of conventional controllers like proportional integral (PI) and its classification will result with abrupt changes in control signal. Hence, non-linear control algorithms such as non-linear model-based control (NMBC), non-linear model predictive control (NMPC) [6], SMC [8–11], etc. are preferred for the batch reactor trajectory tracking problems

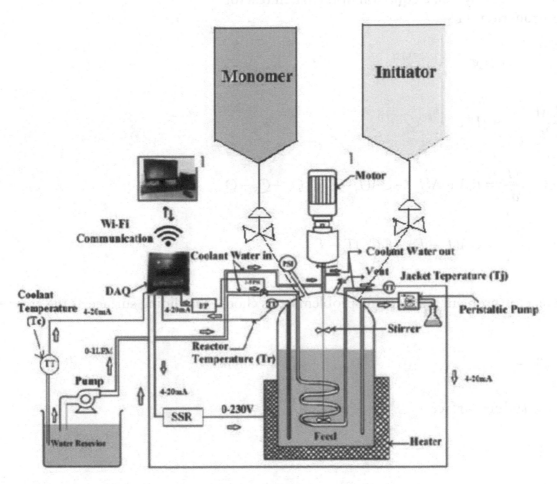

Figure 30.2: Schematic diagram of the batch reactor experimental setup.

3. Sliding Mode Controllers

The non-linear systems are highly affected by the disturbances and uncertainies. To control the non-linear systems, the robust controller is to be designed. The model based controller which is insensitive to parametric uncertainies and disturbance is SMC.

In control systems, SMC is a non-linear control method that alters the dynamics of a non-linear system by applying a discontinuous control signal (or more rigorously, a set-valued control signal) forces the system to "slide" along a cross-section of the system's normal behavior. The switching control law, forces the states on the stable sliding surface. Once on this sliding surface, the states become insensitive to the disturbances and uncertainities.

The SMC is applied for the following reasons:

- It is a non-linear controller
- It is insensitive to parametric uncertainties
- It is robust controller once the states are on the sliding surface

In this work, the batch reactor systems is considered. The temperature control problem in the cooling water inlet temperature is the disturbance which may affect the batch process.

Considering the dynamic equation of the batch reactor

System equations [1]

$$\frac{d[I]}{dt} = -A_d[I]e^{(-E_d/R(T_r+273.15))}$$

$$\frac{d[M]}{dt} = -A_d[I]^\varepsilon e^{(-E_d/R(T_r+273.15))}$$

$$m_r C_{pr} \frac{dT_r}{dt} = R_P V(-\Delta H_P) - UA(T_r - T_J) + Q_h + Q_S - Q_{loss}$$

$$m_r C_{pr} \frac{dT_J}{dt} = UA(T_r - T_j) - F_C C_{pc}(T_j - T_c)$$

Since the reactor problem is a tracking problem let us choose the sliding surface as the error equation given by

$$s = T_d - T_j \qquad (1)$$

To reach the sliding surface

$$\dot{s} = 0 \qquad (2)$$

Taking the derivative of (1)

$$\dot{s} = \dot{T}_d - \dot{T}_j \qquad (3)$$

Substituting in (2) from batch rector equation

$$\dot{s} = \dot{T}_d - (UA \times (Tr - Tj) - F \times Cpc \times (Tj - Tc)) / mjCpj$$
$$Td\_dot - UA \times (Tr - Tj) / mjCpj + F \times Cpc \times (Tj - Tc) / mjCpj = 0$$
$$F \times Cpc \times (Tj - Tc) / mjCpj = UA \times (Tr - Tj) / mjCpj - Td\_dot$$
$$F = (UA \times (Tr - Tj) / mjCpj - Td\_dot) \times mjCpj / Cpc \times (Tj - Tc) \qquad (4)$$

The sliding surface mode control law is given by

$$u = u_{equi} + u_{dicontinuous} \tag{5}$$

Here $F = u_{equi}$

As per the classical SMC, the discontinuous control is

$$u_{dicon} = -k \ \text{sgn}(s)$$

k is the tuning parameter
So the control law for SMC is

$$u = (-ksign(s) + UA \times (Tr - Tj) / mjCpj - Td\_dot) \times mjCpj / Cpc \times (Tj - Tc) \tag{6}$$

3.1. Stability of the sliding surface

The converge to the equilibrium point, the stability of the sliding surface is to be guaranteed.

Theorem: For the batch reactor of equation, the control law is given (6), which maintains the desired temperature of the reactor, in the presence of disturbances and uncertainties.

Proof: The stability of the sliding surface is proved using direct Lypunov function which is given by

$$V = \frac{1}{2}s^2 \tag{7}$$

As the per the Lypunov stability theorem the first derivative of (7)

$$\dot{V} = s\dot{s} \leq 0 \tag{8}$$

For the stable sliding surface
Substituting (1)(2) in (8)

$$(T_d - T_j)(\dot{T}_d - (UA \times (Tr - Tj) - u \times Cpc \times (Tj - Tc)) / mjCpj \leq 0$$

$$(T_d - T_j)(\dot{T}_d - \left(\begin{array}{c} UA \times (Tr - Tj) - (-ksign(s) + UA \times (Tr - Tj) / mjCpj - Td \\ \times mjCpj / Cpc \times (Tj - Tc) \times Cpc \times (Tj - Tc) \end{array} \right) / mjCpj \leq 0$$

$$((T_d - T)(-ksign(s)) \leq 0 \tag{9}$$

To satisfy the Lypunov stability condition, $k > 0$

This completes the proof.

Figure 30.3 show the tracking of reactor temperature with coolant flow rate varying with oscillations. Objective is to reduce the control signal oscillations for energy saving in batch reactor process. Hence, SMC control law need to be modified for better control signal.

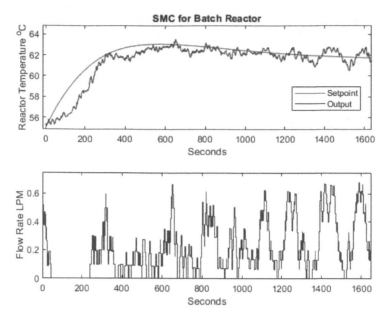

Figure 30.3: Experimental results of closed loop sliding mode controller for trajectory tracking.

3.2. Power rate reaching law

As compared to the classical SMC, reaching the law is as per equation 6, which has lot of chattering as shown in Figure 30.4. By introducing the α, $0 \leq \alpha \leq 1$, the states reach the sliding surface in the non-linear path, which increases the settling time and reduces chattering. The control law with power rate reaching law is as per equation.

$$F = (-k\dot{s} = -k|s|^{\alpha} \, sgn(s) + \frac{UA(Tr - Tj)}{mjCpj - \overset{\dot{y}}{T}d} \times \frac{mjCpj}{Cpc(Tj - Tc)}$$

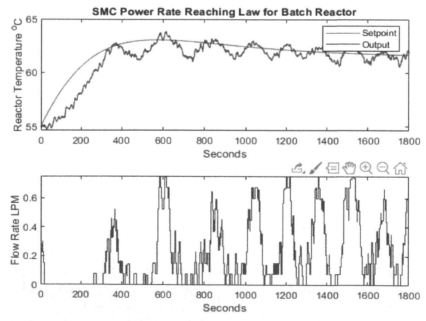

Figure 30.4: Experimental results of closed loop power rate reaching law sliding mode controller for trajectory tracking.

Figure 30.4 response of trajectory tracking resulted with slight oscillations throughout the trajectory tracking with high consumption of the coolant flow rate. This shows SMC control algorithm need to be revised to improve the closed loop response.

3.3. PI sliding surface

The switching control law is designed, where the sliding surface is selected as the proportional derivative controller, which eliminated the offset and provides good tracking. Since the application of the batch reactor, is to track the temperature, the error equation is the sliding variable. The use of power rate reaching laws is used as the reaching equation, for fast convergence.

The equation of PI controller

$$K = kpep + kpki \int epdt + P1(0)$$

Therefore selecting the error ep = Td – Tj
Substituting in PI equation, the sliding surface is as below

$$s = kp(Td - Tj) + kpKi \int (Td - Tj)dt$$

by taking the derivative of the sliding surface, we get

$$\dot{s} = kp(\dot{T}d - \dot{T}j) + kpki(Td - Tj)$$

to ensure state reach the sliding surface, equating or the reaching law equation

$$\dot{s} = -k|s|^{\infty} sgn(s)$$

$$\dot{s} = kp(\dot{T}_d - (U_A \left(T_r - T_j - \frac{FC_p c(T_j - T_{c)})}{m_j C_{pj}} \right) + kpk_i (T_d - T_j) = -k|s|^{\alpha} sgn(s)$$

$$-k|s|^{\alpha} sgn(s) = kp\dot{T}_d - \frac{kpU_A(T_r - T_j)}{m_j C_{pj}} - \frac{k_p FC_{pc}(T_j - T_c)}{m_j C_{pj}} + kpk_i(T_d - T_j)$$

$$\frac{k_p FC_{pc}(T_j - T_c)}{m_j C_{pj}} = kp\dot{T}_d - \frac{kpU_A(T_r - T_j)}{m_j C_{pj}} + kpk_i(T_d - T_j) + -k|s|^{\alpha} sgn(s)$$

by arranging terms we get the control law as follows:

$$F = \left(kp\dot{T}_d - \frac{kpU_A(T_r - T_j)}{m_j C_{pj}} + kpk_i(T_d - T_j) + k|s|^{\alpha} sgn(s) \right) \left(\frac{m_j C_{pj}}{k_p C_{pc}(T_j - T_c)} \right)$$

Figure 30.5 shows the proper tracking with reduced oscillations compared to previous other two SMC results shown in Figures 30.3 and 30.4. The coolant flow rate consumption is also optimal compared to other two SMCs.

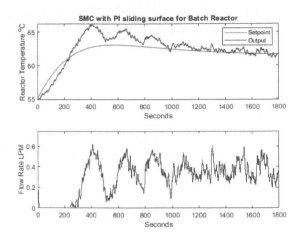

Figure 30.5: Experimental results of closed loop PI sliding surface based sliding mode controller for trajectory tracking.

The improvement in the results of the paper can be compared with the experimental results of conventional PID controllers carried out on the same batch reactor setup. It was observed that the control signal of NPID [12–14] was very much oscillatory compared to the experimental results of the SMC results shown in Figures 30.3–30.5

3.4. *Jetson board for control signal computation*

Presently the authors are working to execute the advanced control algorithm using Jetson developer kit with real time batch rector. Proper signal conditioning of sensors and actuators needs to be carried using current to voltage convertor and voltage to current convertor. Jetson board does not have the analog to digital convertor (ADC), hence additional ADC need to be used for interfacing sensor and actuator signals. The advanced control algorithm is developed using Python code. The GPIO pins needs to be configured for the sensor and actuator signals interface. The advantage of using this Jetson will increase the computation time of control signals for the highly nonlinear control algorithms with hard constraints to interface with the batch reactor (Figure 30.6).

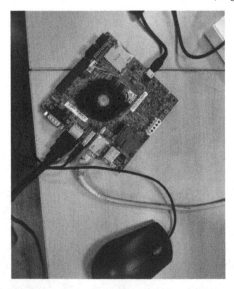

Figure 30.6: Jetson developer kit for control algorithm execution in advanced process control lab, MIT, Manipal for batch reactor.

4. Conclusions

In this article class of SMC has been designed using the non-linear model equations of batch reactor. Three different types of controller were simulated and validated on the experimental setup for the temperature. The experimental results show that the PI sliding surface based SMC gives the least manipulated variable action, it means the lowest amount cooling water is utilized for temperature tracking. On other hand if we look that the tracking error, basic SMC helps, but in this case the optimal control signal was not obtained. Hence, based on the tracking error or the optimal control signal is needed has to be decided for the selection of control algorithms.

5. Acknowledgement

The authors would like to thank Manipal Academy of Higher Education, Manipal for the seed money grant received toward the coolant flow station establishment for the batch reactor under Grant ID: 00000220 dated 01/01/2020 and Grant ID: 00000860 dated 09/10/2023 towards the machine learning concept implementation on batch reactor.

References

[1] Shettigar J, P., Lochan, K., Jeppu, G., Palanki, S., and Indiran, T. (2021). Development and validation of advanced nonlinear predictive control algorithms for trajectory tracking in batch polymerization. *ACS Omega*, 6, 22857–22865.

[2] Shettigar J, P., Kumbhare, J., Yadav, E. S., and Indiran, T. (2022). Wiener neural network-based modeling and validation of generalized predictive control on a laboratory-scale batch reactor. *ACS Omega*, 7, 16341–16351.

[3] Urmila, D. and Pahola, T. B. (2011). Optimal control of biodiesel production in a batch reactor Part II: Stochastic control. *Fuels*, 94, 218–226.

[4] Palanki, S. (2005). Optimal operations of semi-batch processes with a single reaction. *Int. J. Chem. React. Engg.*, 3(1), 1–9.

[5] Arun Senthil, S. and Sundaramoorthy, S. (2018). Optimal control policy for tracking optimal progression of temperature in a batch reactor – Some insights into the choice of objective function. *IFAC Papers Online*, 51(1), 112–117.

[6] Billings, S. A. (2013). Nonlinear system identification: NARMAX methods in the time, frequency, and spatio-temporal domains. John Wiley & Sons. pp. 576. ISBN: 978-1-119-94359-4.

[7] Yadav, E. S., Shettigar J, P., Poojary, S., Chokkadi, S., Jeppu, G., and Indiran, T. (2021). Data-driven modeling of a pilot plant batch reactor and validation of a nonlinear model predictive controller for dynamic temperature profile tracking. *ACS Omega*, 6, 16714–16721.

[8] Narwekar, K. and Shah V. A. (2020). Temperature Control Using Sliding Mode Control: An Experimental Approach. In: Tuba, M., Akashe, S., and Joshi, A. (eds) Information and Communication Technology for Sustainable Development. Advances in Intelligent Systems and Computing. Springer: Singapore, 933.

[9] Narwekar, K. and Shah, V. A. (2018). Temperature control of reactor using variable structure control. *Int. J. Res. Anal. Rev.*, 5(3), 318–322.

[10] Narwekar, K. and Shah, V. A. (2018). Level control of coupled tank using sliding mode control. *Int. J. Res.*, 7(IX), 1025–1031.

[11] Narwekar, K. and Shah, V. A. (2017). Robust temperature control of chemical batch reactor using sliding mode control. *Int. J. Sci. Res. Manag. (IJSRM)*, 07, 6561–6568.

[12] Mishra, S. R., Yadav, E. S., and Indiran, T. (2023, May). Validation of split range control algorithm on a laboratory scale batch reactor heating system. In *AIP Conference Proceedings.*, 2752(1) 1–5. AIP Publishing.

[13] Shettigar, J. P., Pai, A., Joshi, Y., Indiran, T., and Chokkadi, S. (2023). Validation of nonlinear PID controllers on a lab-scale batch reactor. *Comm. Comp. Inform. Sci.*, 1797, 47–59.

[14] Bala Abhirami, M. and Thirunavukkarasu, I. (2023). Maximum sensitivity-based PID controller for a lab-scale batch reactor. *Lec. Notes Elec. Engg.*, 957, 183–194.

31   3D Image Modeling Using Data Science

Nishita Sharma, Divyanshi Mishra[a], Prerna Yadav, Meenakshi Singh, and Papiya Mukherjee[b]

Department of CSE, Dronacharya Group of Institution, Greater Noida, U. P., India

Abstract

People today are embracing numerous modernization tactics and eschewing time-consuming procedures. The goal of this work is to design a system that can convert a diagram or figure that is on paper into digital image that can be reproduced or changed in a digital environment. Time is a crucial factor that plays a significant part in any operation, whether it involves a human or a machine. The concept of artificial intelligence (AI), machine learning (M), deep learning, vision API, etc., all can be used to help a system design the image of any figure or diagram directly so that it can print the image of any scanned image into 3D modeled image. We have used deep neural networks that can be trained and used for a variety of tasks with the aid of tensor flow. Other technologies that are used are in this model RPN/OCR/GAN/VECTOR imaging and convolutional neural networks (CNN), these works together for detection, visualization, generation, fetching and extracting the processed data in a digital format. These dependencies may be required to provide certain functionality or to use specific program features. The recycler view a user interface element called recycler view enables us to make scrolling lists. The software's integrated 3D viewer will then be used to preview our final output 3D matched image. In the future, this model will be able to pick up new techniques, approaches, and patterns on its own, which will be a significant advancement in the field of 3D image modeling.

Keywords: Data science, artificial intelligence, machine learning and 3D modeling

1. Introduction

One of the most in-demand activities is designing or using a handwritten piece in digital format. The idea of turning a physical image into a three-dimensional (3D) model makes it simple to use and comprehend through virtual models, depending on the user's demands. While it is possible to transfer text and images into digital formats, there is still work to be done in the area of digitally turning drawn figures into 3D models. In this field, research is conducted on image processing to extract useful information from images, automate processes linked to images, and use convolutional neural networks (CNNs) to make predictions based on image data. Data science contributes significantly

[a]divyanshi.16297@gnindia.dronacharya.info, [b]Papiya.mukherjee@gnindia.dronacharya.info

to the modeling of digital 3D images by offering methods and resources for data analysis and image manipulation using statistical modeling, machine learning algorithms, and pattern recognition, among other techniques. It enables feature extraction, signal and dimensional enhancements, image restoration and object identification.

In the previous researches on text to image using deep learning, the generative adversarial network (GAN) technique was employed for picture generation and discrimination. Using GAN in conjunction with the natural language toolkit (NLTK), a digital 2D image of the text was produced in order to comprehend the pattern of text in photographs. Using the supplied data, the graphical user interface (GUI) was utilized to create visually appealing windows for the user interface and display the photographs more suitably [1]. However, while this technology cannot translate words into 3D models, it can only provide a 2D representation of the language that the user submits.

Another study on the conversion of 2D–3D images describes how different algorithms are used to analyze the 2D image's depth dimensions before using techniques to turn it into a 3D model. To create an image that resembles the given 2D, KNN search is used to distinguish between relevant and irrelevant images. The dimensions, edges, and closest neighbor points have been guided by depth fusion combined with cross-bias filtering in depth to create an accurate image of the 2D photograph [2]. This paper's goal is to synthesis research studies and data science algorithms that will facilitate the direct conversion of text into a digital 3D model and the conversion of physically drawn images into 3D models for easier comprehension and a more user-friendly human-computer interface. In this paper, model training and tracking are implemented using the tensor flow platform for training deep neural networks. In addition to vector imaging, another algorithm used to generate realistic data is GAN. This process turns handwritten inputs into vector-based representations, which makes it simpler to manipulate and transform the inputs using deep learning to create 3D models digitally. Important parts of text detection systems use algorithms like region proposal network (RPN) and optical character recognition (OCR). OCR can be used to accurately recognize and disguise handwritten characters into digital representation. These two algorithms can be used to process each part independently and produce a highly accurate and precise 3D model. Through the use of these algorithms and techniques, 3D images created by the software from original handwrite inputs is displayed using 3D viewer and scanner to facilitating an effective human-computer interface.

2. Literature Review

Many studies on signal and image processing have been conducted in the last few years in an effort to improve the quality and resolution of the images for better comprehension following the conversion of text or figures into digital format for better user interaction. Medhavi Malik [6] examined the mechanism of digital image processing, outlining the steps involved in retrieving, identifying, and restoring images to create a beautiful 2D figure. Creating an image is further broken down into two stages: creating 2D images through analog signal processing and creating the desired images through digital image processing. More methods are covered to describe how to process images in analog to digital or digital to analog formats, including image enhancement, image segmentation, clustering, compression, and acquisition. This paper contributes to the understanding of the methods needed to enhance the image quality after processing [3]. Chithra and Bhavani [2] proposed a variety of image processing techniques to get good results. The process of converting a basic 2D image into a better format by applying noise removal filters, pre-processing the image, and image acquisition. Digital image classification using the SVM classifier to produce decision boundaries and the KNN algorithm to identify the closest match for generating the image. The conclusion of this paper states that while images can be altered using a variety of methods to provide accuracy, an image's quality is always determined by its clarity. For this reason, algorithms that produce a clear and accurate view of an image are preferred over others in order to improve user interaction [4]. Akanska Singh and the other authors [7] present a study on text-to-digital image conversion. The goal of this paper is to simplify text comprehension for users by turning it into easily understood pictures. GAN-CLS is used to train the discriminator so that it is not deceived by the fake images the generator creates, thereby helping in matching the text in the database with the correct image. Additionally, an interactive technique for processing text to produce accurate images is provided by PySimpleGUI, a graphical user interface that makes the text user-friendly. Therefore, the conversion process is relatively easy to implement using GAN-CLS and GUI to successfully match the converted image with its correct text [1]. Guo-Shiang Lin, together with his co-author explains how to combine different techniques to produce a convincing 3D image out of a 2D image. They extract the objects that need to be manipulated in 3D space by using a segmentation-based foreground extraction technique to separate foreground objects from background in an image. In order to give the scene a sense of depth, foreground depth estimation based on depth cues is used to calculate the relative distance between the object and the viewer. Depth profile classification using neural networks improves the ability to distinguish between foreground and background objects and encourages more precise depth estimation. Color enhancement for stereoscopic perception is the process of modifying an image's color to make it better suited for 3D viewing. In order to achieve a more immersive visual experience, the study's conclusion involves precisely estimating the depth of objects in the scene and selectively enhancing their appearance [5]. In this study, we are utilizing AIML in conjunction with a variety of data science algorithms to produce 3D models directly from text and drawings. GAN combined with vector imaging, OCR, RPN of CNN, and stable diffusion are few of the algorithms used for this purpose. Through the use of these algorithms and techniques, it is possible to create a bridge that processes and transforms handwritten text and drawings into digital 3D images that can be viewed by users in a 3D viewer.

3. Material and Method

3.1. Convolutional neural network

Deep learning, a branch of machine learning (ML) whose algorithms are based on the architecture of the human brain, has CNN as its foundation. CNN receives data, learns to identify patterns in the data, and then forecasts the results for a fresh collection of comparable data. CNN is used to solve problems related to object detection and computer vision.

There are 3 layers in convolutional neural network and they are as follows:

- Convolutional layer
- Relu layer
- Pooling layer
- Fully connected layer

Convolutional layer: In order to produce a feature map that summarizes the presence of observed features in the input, a filter is applied to the input. It extracts the fundamental features, like edges that are diagonal or horizontal. The following layer receives this output and uses it to identify more intricate traits.

Relu layer: In this layer (Figure 31.1), we remove all the negative values from me filtered image and replace it with zero's.

Pooling layer: The goal of pooling layer (Figure 31.2) is to reduce the size of image. This layer reduces complexity and improves the efficiency of the CNN by reducing the dimensions. There are two types of pooling average pooling and more pooling.

Fully connected layer: This is the layer (Figure 31.3) where image classification happens. The formula that we use with convolutional and pooling layer work.

$$\frac{n + 2p - f + 1}{S} * \frac{n + 2p - f + 1}{S}$$

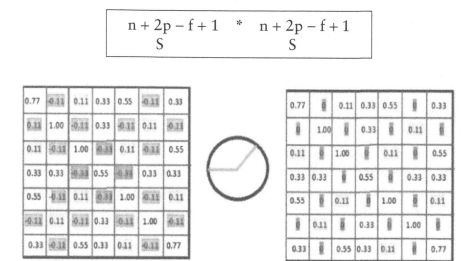

Figure 31.1: Relu layer (Removal of negative values).

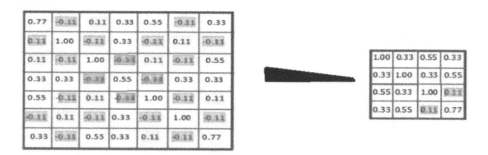

Figure 31.2: Pooling layer (Reduction of image size).

3.2. *Region proposal network (RPN)*

The primary function of the region proposal network (RPN) in the RCNN family is object detection. We have learned how to use selective search in R-CNN to extract multiple regions. The region proposal network was created in faster R-CNN to generate region suggestions using a small network. The classifier in RPN can return the region's probability. Additionally, it features a regressor that gives back the bounding box coordinates.

Following steps are involved in region proposal network:

- Convolutional neural network
- Generate anchor boxes
- Classify anchor box as foreground/background
- Bounding box regression adjustment

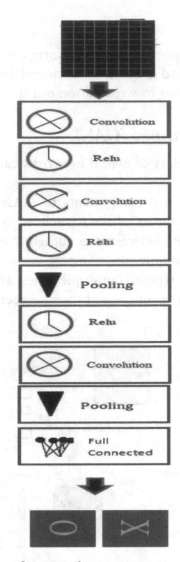

Figure 31.3: Fully connected layer (Classification of image).

3.3. *Optical character recognition*

Optical character recognition (OCR) is a process that converts a text image into a text format that can be read by a computer. If you scan a form or a receipt, for example, your computer saves the scan as an image file. A text editor cannot be used to alter, find, or count the words in the image file. Alternatively, you can use OCR to convert the image to a text document and store the textual data within.

OCR follows following steps:

* Image acquisition
* Pre-processing
* Text recognition
* Pattern matching
* Feature extraction
* Post-processing

3.4. Vector imaging

Art composed of vector graphics is referred to as vector artwork. These mathematical formula-based dots, lines, curves, and shapes are called graphics. A vector picture file can be resized to any size you require because scaling results in neither low resolution nor quality loss.

3.5. Generative adversarial networks (GAN)

For unsupervised learning, a potent class of neural networks called generative adversarial networks (GANs) is employed.

A discriminator and a generator are components of GANs. The generator attempts to trick the discriminator by creating fake samples of data (such as images, sounds, etc.). Conversely, the Discriminator attempts to differentiate between the authentic and fraudulent samples. Neural networks, such as the generator and discriminator, compete with one another throughout the training phase (Figure 31.4). The procedure is repeated multiple times, and with each iteration, the generator and discriminator become increasingly proficient at their respective tasks.

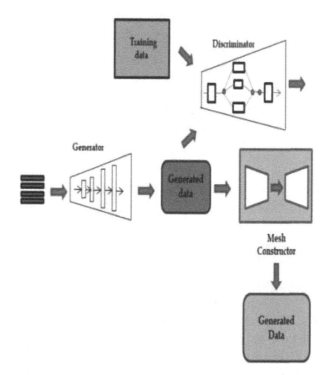

Figure 31.4: Working of Generative adversarial networks.

3.6. Stable diffusion

Deep learning and neural networks are used to extract relevant features and spatial information from the input photographs in order to create 3D models from 2D images. The depth and structure of the objects in the image are then estimated using these extracted features, leading to the reconstruction of a 3D render (Figure 31.5).

Stable diffusion modals use cutting edge methods to produce both image and audio. Diffusion is commonly used in text-to-image, text-to-video, and text-to-3D applications viewer.

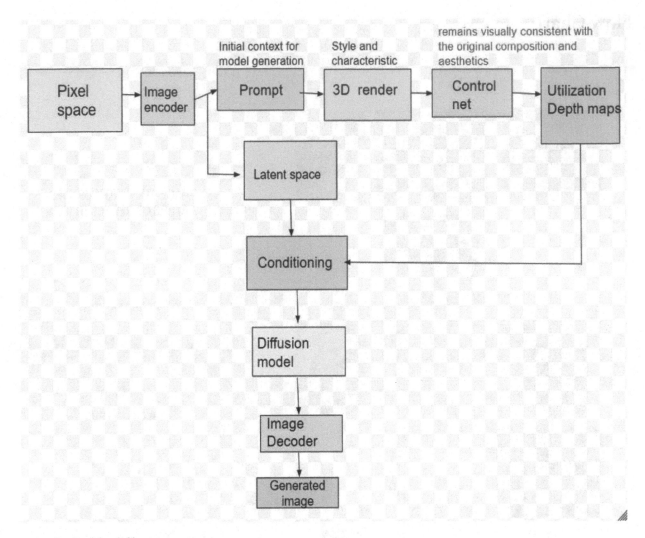

Figure 31.5: Stable diffusion process.

3.7. Proposed method

The following illustration depicts a schematic approach to 3D image modeling that is used to convert a scanned image into a similar 3D image with a single click. The GAN used in this model is the core of this project that is used to generate a 3D image from a 2D image and is also used in various aspects for the proper operation of this model. Another tool we used to improve the model's performance is regional proposal network (RPN), which is faster than R-CNN and uses a cross entropy loss function to classify image regions as either object or background. We also used various vision API approaches and dependencies to ensure the software's smooth performance and to assist the system in combating security threats. We are confident that this model will be a great achievement in the field of 3D modeling, and that it will be the best approach for drawing any image without taking too much time, as opposed to the traditional drawing method, which involves first drawing on paper diagrams and then manually drawing that in the digital drawing tools. This model is outfitted with every possible algorithm and technology that can assist people in saving the time they waste in manual traditional drawing methods.

4. Flow Chart

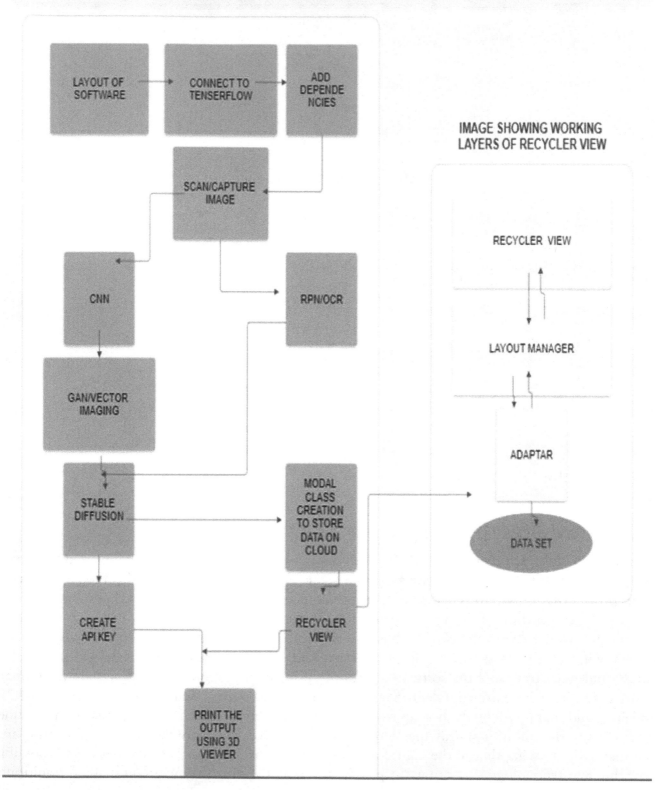

Figure 31.6: Flowchart of proposed method.

4.1. *Working principle*

The front end of the software is connected to the Tenser Flow and offers multiple data tools to help you consolidate, clean, and pre-process data at scale. It aids us in detecting, locating, and tracing an object from an image. The authors developed a model by combining various approaches that has the ability to produce a 3D of any image scanned, whether it is on paper, hand drawn, or clicked. Dependencies have been added, which makes it easier for developers to manage and maintain software by preventing conflicts, errors, and other problems. Now, the scanning process begins when the user scans or captures an image using the camera module connected to the software. If the image is of an object, it will be transferred to the CNN layer, and if text is detected, it will be transferred to the RPN/OCR layer, where OCR is the process that converts an image of text into a machine-readable text format, and RPN returns the coordinates of bounding boxes, and this processed data will be transferred. To use a GAN for 3D model reconstruction, we first train it on a set of 2D images of an object from various perspective. The generator is then used to generate new 2D images of the object from novel viewpoints not included in the training data. Researchers can reconstruct a 3D model of the object by matching these 2D images to known viewpoints. This data will be transferred to the stable diffusion layer (Figure 6). Stable diffusion is a model for text-to-image conversion. Its primary purpose is to generate detailed images from text descriptions. Diffusion enables anyone with a decent computer and GPU to generate and view almost any type of image they can imagine. The modal class is then created to store data on the cloud, and the stored data is then moved to the recycler view, making your model more efficient in both time and space, because it recycles existing structures rather than constantly creating new ones. The recycler view allows the user to edit, modify, or move the content as desired. The finalized obtained data will now be displayed by the software's 3D viewer.

5. Conclusions

This paper presents software that quickly and easily converts text images or physical drawn figures into 3D models using widely used algorithms and technologies. The software leverages deep learning in generative adversarial networks or vector images to make it more easily convertible, and data science to make it more user-friendly. Model training and tracking are conducted using the tensor flow platform in deep neutral images. Text is detected using OCR, and images are detected using RCR. Information can be properly identified and boundaries drawn around it by both technologies. To identify patterns in the data and forecast results, CNN, the main algorithm, applies deep learning and machine learning techniques. It provides solutions for computer vision and object detection issues.

Text is ultimately transformed into images, images into 3D models, and 2D images into 3D models by the most effective stable and diffusion method. All of these algorithms help to increase the software's effectiveness and usability. They also lower the cost of the system, which increases its efficiency. It is a workable and reliable software interface.

References

[1] Baretto, V. M. (n.d.). Automatic learning based 2D-to-3D image conversion. www.ijert.org.
[2] Chithra, P. L. and Bhavani, P. (2019). A study on various image processing techniques. *Int. J. Emerg. Technol. Innov. Engg.*, 5(5), 1–7.
[3] Hachaj, T. (2023). Adaptable 2D to 3D stereo vision image conversion based on a deep convolutional neural network and fast inpaint algorithm. *Entropy*, 25(8), 1212.

[4]   Lin, G.-S., Liu, H.-W., Chen, W.-C., Lie, W.-N., and Huang, S.-Y. (2011). LNCS 7088 - 2D to 3D image conversion based on classification of background depth profiles. *LNCS*, 7088, 381–392.

[5]   Lunz, S., Li, Y., Fitzgibbon, A., and Kushman, N. (2020). Inverse graphics GAN: Learning to generate 3D shapes from unstructured 2D data. arXiv preprint arXiv:2002.12674. Cornell University, 1, 8. https://doi.org/10.48550/arXiv.2002.12674.

[6]   Malik, M. (n.d.). A review on digital image processing. *UGC Care J.*, 43.

[7]   Singh, A. and Sonam, A. (2022). Text to image using deep learning. *Int. J. Engg. Res.*, 10.

32 Realization of Voltage-Controlled Quadrature-Oscillator Employing Current-Feedback-Amplifiers (CFAs) and an Analog Multiplier (AM)

Pragati Gupta[1,a], Samriddhi Shah[1,b], Aarvi Shanu[1,c], Amrita Singh[2,d], and Manoj Kumar Jain[1,e]

[1]Faculty of Engineering and Technology, Department of Electronics and Communication Engineering, University of Lucknow, Lucknow, Uttar Pradesh, India

[2]Department of Electronics Engineering, Institute of Engineering and Technology, Lucknow, Uttar Pradesh, India

Abstract

This work presents a voltage-controlled quadrature-oscillator (VCQO) which employs two current-feedback-amplifiers (CFAs) and an analog multiplier (AM) with five passive components, by using this oscillator one can produce two output voltages that have phase shift of 90° (i.e., quadrature oscillator). The condition of oscillation and frequency of oscillation of a given oscillator is independently controlled and can be tuned by manipulating an external DC bias voltage input through one of the analog multiplier input terminals and the sensitivity of this voltage-controlled quadrature oscillator is very low i.e. less than unity. The experimental, as well as PSPICE simulation results based on the macro-model of CFA IC AD844 and AM IC AD633, are also comprised which shows the excellent performance of the given voltage-controlled quadrature-oscillator.

Keywords: Voltage-controlled quadrature-oscillator (VCQO), analog multiplier (AM), current-feedback-amplifier (CFA), sensitivity

1. Introduction

Among all the oscillator categories sinusoidal oscillators are extremely useful circuits for various communication systems, signal processing, instrument, measurement system, etc., because of these applications researchers design these oscillators by using different kinds of active-building-block (ABB) for instance current differencing buffer amplifier (CDBA) [1], current controlled conveyors (CCCII) [2], dual-X current conveyors (DXCCII) [3], current controlled current differencing transconductance amplifiers (CCCDTAs) [4], current controlled current conveyor transconductance amplifier (CCCCTA) [5], voltage differencing inverting buffered amplifier (VDIBA) [6], etc., to improve the functionality of sinusoidal oscillators. But, above mentioned ABBs are not commercially available. In this paper, to design an electronically tunable quadrature oscillator and study the theoretical, simulated, and experimental results choose current feedback amplifier (CFAs) (IC AD844) and analog

[a]pragati.ece97@gmail.com, [b]samriddhishah19@gmail.com, [c]aarvishanuvaishnav@gmail.com, [d]amrita0917@gmail.com, and [e]mkjain71@gmail.com

multiplier (AM) (IC AD633). The AD844 provides a wide dynamic range, excellent bandwidth, high slew rate of approx. 2000 V/µs, etc.

The CFA circuit is composed of a second-generation current conveyor (CCII+) followed by a voltage buffer. This arrangement is illustrated in the symbolic representation shown in Figure 32.1. The hybrid matrix Equation (1) provides an overview of the terminal characteristics of the CFA, conveying important details about its behavior:

1. The non-inverting terminal (y) has a high input impedance, making it suitable for receiving weak input signals without significantly loading the source.
2. The inverting terminal (x) exhibits low impedance, which means it has the capability to source or sink current efficiently. Moreover, the voltage at the x-terminal is equal to the voltage at the y-terminal.
3. The z-terminal serves as a current follower, implying that the current through this terminal is equal to the current at the x-terminal. It acts as a faithful copy of the input current.
4. The output voltage at the w-terminal is equal to the voltage at the z-terminal. This terminal essentially reproduces the voltage signal present at the z-terminal.

The CFA's unique attributes make it a versatile component in analog signal processing and control systems.

$$\begin{bmatrix} I_y \\ V_x \\ I_z \\ V_w \end{bmatrix} = \begin{bmatrix} 0 & 0 & 0 & 0 \\ 1 & 0 & 0 & 0 \\ 0 & 1 & 0 & 0 \\ 0 & 0 & 1 & 0 \end{bmatrix} = \begin{bmatrix} V_y \\ I_x \\ V_z \\ I_w \end{bmatrix}$$

(1)

However, using CFAs various sinusoidal oscillators are presented in the literature [7–13] with different techniques to tune the frequency of oscillation (FO) using single resistance i.e. SRCO, single capacitance i.e. SCCO, among these we focus on voltage-controlled-oscillators (VCOs) which is an electronic oscillator whose FO depends upon voltage input, which provides a wide range of applications in the area of analog integrated circuits, like, in the phase locked loop (PLL) which needs high frequency, in frequency generator which needs low frequency, voltage to frequency conversion in digital voltage measurement (DVM), in frequency synthesis, production of electronic music to generate variable tones, in synthesizer, etc. There are two techniques to generate VCO (i) The frequency of oscillation can be altered by changing the gate voltage of FET used as a voltage-controlled-resistor (VCR) [14, 15]. Here external control voltage V_C provides electronic controllability but it has a limitation as it is highly temperature dependent because of the mobility factor of MOSFETs which are

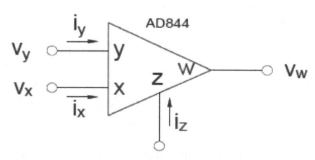

Figure 32.1: Circuit symbol of CFA.

directly proportional to temperature. (ii) Another method is using an analog multiplier [16–18] in the loop so that their external control voltage term V_C appears in the FO expression.

2. Proposed VCQO

This paper focuses on introducing a voltage-controlled quadrature oscillator based on CFA and AM ICs. The primary objective of this oscillator design is to enable precise control of the output frequency by manipulating an external DC bias voltage input through one of the analog multiplier input terminals. This differs from a previously known circuit [10], where tuning the frequency relied on a grounded resistor. The advantage of our proposed circuit lies in its ability to achieve finer frequency tuning, although it requires an additional analog multiplier component.

To verify the functionality and performance of the proposed circuit, we conducted simulations using P-SPICE software and carried out practical experiments using commercially available CFAs and analog multiplier integrated circuits (ICs). The results obtained from both simulations and experiments align closely with the expected theoretical values, validating the effectiveness and accuracy of our design. This research contributes to the field of analog circuit design by offering a versatile and finely controllable quadrature oscillator, which can find applications in various electronic systems and signal processing devices.

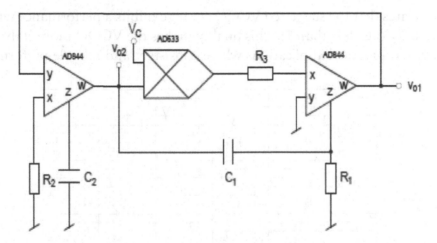

Figure 32.2: Voltage-controlled quadrature oscillator circuit.

3. Method to Describe the Circuit

Figure 32.2 diagram illustrates the structure of the suggested voltage-controlled quadrature oscillator (VCQO). This oscillator comprises two CFAs, one AM, three resistors, and two capacitors. In our analysis, we consider the idealized scenario where the CFAs and the analog multiplier have no parasitic elements, simplifying the circuit analysis.

Through routine circuit analysis, we derive the characteristic equation that governs the behavior of this VCQO. This equation plays a crucial role in describing and understanding the oscillator's operation and frequency control mechanisms.

$$s^2 + s\left(\frac{1}{C_1 R_1} - \frac{1}{C_2 R_2}\right) + \frac{V_c}{10 C_1 C_2 R_2 R_3} = 0 \qquad (2)$$

From Equation (2), the expressions for CO and FO can be derived, representing their respective values:

$$CO : R_1 C_1 = R_2 C_2 \qquad (3)$$

$$FO : \omega_o = \sqrt{\frac{V_c}{10 C_1 C_2 R_2 R_3}} \qquad (4)$$

However, the interconnection between the two output voltages, v_{o1} and v_{o2}, can be expressed in the following manner:

$$\frac{v_{o2}}{v_{o1}} = \frac{1}{s C_2 R_2} \qquad (5)$$

where phase difference $\phi = 90°$. This demonstrates that the suggested VCO circuit delivers output voltages, v_{o1} and v_{o2}, that are precisely 90° out of phase, thus providing quadrature output signals.

The sensitivities of ω_o w.r.t. passive elements R_1, R_2, C_1 and C_2 can be obtained as:

$$s_{C_1}^{\omega_o} = s_{C_2}^{\omega_o} = s_{R_2}^{\omega_o} = s_{R_3}^{\omega_o} = -\frac{1}{2} \qquad (6)$$

Equation (6) demonstrates that the suggested VCQO circuit exhibits a performance with low sensitivity, measuring less than unity (i.e., less than 1). This quality makes the VCQO more stable and predictable, which is advantageous in practical applications where consistent and reliable performance is crucial.

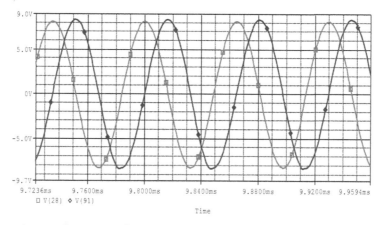

Figure 32.3: Output waveform of V-C quadrature oscillator from Figure 32.2.

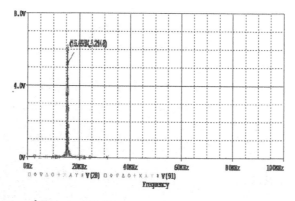

Figure 32.4: Frequency spectrum of Figure 32.3.

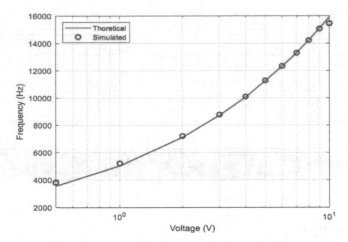

Figure 32.5: Change in oscillation frequency in response to alterations in the control voltage, V_C.

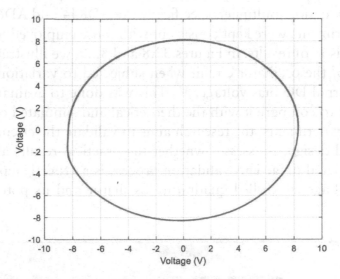

Figure 32.6: Lissajous pattern of waveform from Figure 32.3.

4. Simulated and Experimental Results

To confirm the legitimacy of the demonstrated VCQO, the circuit was simulated on PSPICE using the macro-model of CFAs and analog multiplier AD844 and AD633, respectively. The value of VC can be altered from 0 V to 10 V to control the FO of the proposed oscillator circuit. The supply voltage is ±12 V, and the passive component values as C1 = C2 = 1nF, R2 = R3 = 10 kΩ, and the CO was set with R1 = 10.21365 kΩ. Setting VC = 0.5–10 V and keeping the remaining values fixed, the ideal FO according to (4) would be 15.915 KHz at VC = 10 V while the simulation frequency is observed to be 15.455 KHz. The simulated quadrature output waveforms in Figure 32.2 of vo1 and vo2 are shown in Figure 32.3. Figure 32.4 displays the frequency spectrum of the quadrature outputs, revealing a total harmonic distortion (THD) of 1.2%, which falls within an acceptable range. The variation of FO with control voltage is illustrated in Figure 32.5. Figure 32.6 depicts the correlation between the produced output voltage waveforms, vo1 and vo2 by the Lissajous pattern and Figure 32.7 shows the Monte-Carlo analysis of the proposed circuit. From the graph, it is quite evident that the simulated result shows remarkably close agreement with the predicted theory.

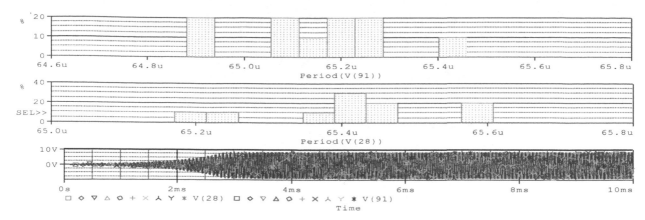

Figure 32.7: Monte Carlo analysis.

The VCQO, as introduced in this study, underwent practical experimentation using readily available ICs for the CFA and analog multiplier, specifically the AD844 and AD633 ICs. The component values used in these experiments were kept consistent with those employed for simulating the circuit, ensuring a direct comparison of results. In Figures 32.8 and 32.9, we illustrate both the experimental setup and the response of the oscillator circuit when subjected to variations in frequency resulting from changes in the external DC bias voltage, V_c. This was done to evaluate the real-world performance of the VCQO and to compare it with the theoretical and simulated outcomes.

By conducting these experiments, the research aims to validate the circuit's functionality and the accuracy of the proposed design. It assesses whether the practical results align with the theoretical predictions and the simulated data. This validation process is a crucial step in confirming the practical feasibility of the voltage-controlled quadrature oscillator and its potential application in real electronic systems.

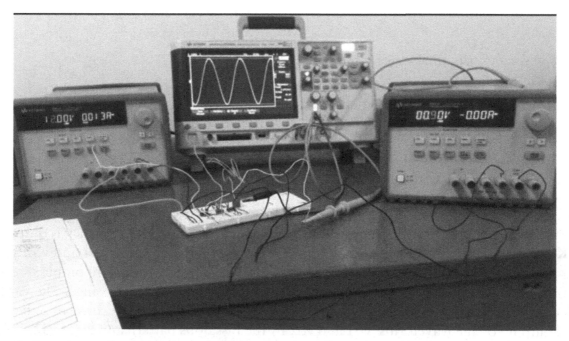

Figure 32.8: Experimental setup.

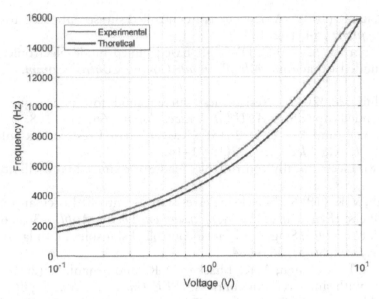

Figure 32.9: Experimental result of variation of frequency with V_c from 0.1 V to 10 V.

5. Conclusions

In this conference paper, we have demonstrated a VCQO that realizes by using two CFAs and a single AM as ABBs are readily available in the market. While this circuit incorporates an additional component, an analog multiplier, in comparison to a recent SRCO design in the circuit [10], it offers a significant advantage. The VCQO enables precise fine-tuning of its output frequency and provides quadrature outputs. Importantly, it exhibits low sensitivity to passive device variations and demonstrates a low simulated value of total harmonic distortion (%THD).

The versatility of the proposed circuit extends to various applications in analog integrated circuits, communication systems, electrical systems, and more. To verify its functionality and performance, we conducted both PSPICE simulations and practical experiments. The results from these assessments validate the excellent operability of the oscillator and underscore its potential for real-world applications.

6. Acknowledgement

Acknowledgments are an important part of academic and research work. Special recognition is extended to Prof. Subodh Wairya, the Head of the Electronics and Communication Engineering (ECE) Department at IET Lucknow, for granting permission to utilize the VLSI laboratory facilities to conduct the experimental phase of this research. This acknowledgment highlights the valuable support and resources provided by the department, which played a significant role in achieving the successful experimental results presented in the study. It underscores the collaborative nature of research and the contributions of the academic community in facilitating scientific advancements.

References

[1] Ozcan, S., Toker, A., Acar, C., Kuntman, H., and Cicekoglu, O. (2000). Single resistance controlled sinusoidal oscillators employing current differencing buffered amplifier. *Microelec. J.*, 31(3), 169–174.

[2]   Turkoz, S. and Minaei, S. (2000). A new current-controlled sinusoidal oscillator using the current controlled conveyor. *Frequenz.*, 54, 132–133.

[3]   Ansari, M. S. and Sharma, S. (2011). DXCC-II based mixed mode electronically tunable quadrature oscillator with grounded capacitors. *Adv. Comput. Comm. Control Comm. Comp. Inform. Sci.*, 125, 515–521.

[4]   Jaikla, W. and Lahiri, A. (2012). Resistor-less current-mod four-phase quadrature oscillator using CCCDTAs and grounded capacitors. *AEU Int. J. Elec. Comm.*, 66, 214–218.

[5]   Chen, H. P., Wang, S. F., and Ku, Y. T. (2015). CCCCTA-based resistorless voltage and current mode quadrature oscillator. *IEICE Elec. Exp.*, 12(13), 1–14.

[6]   Pushkar, K. L. (2018). Electronically controllable quadrature sinusoidal oscillator using VD-DIBAs. *Cir. Sys.*, 9(3), 41–48.

[7]   Senani, R. and Singh, V. K. (1996). Novel single-resistance-controlled-oscillator configuration using current feedback amplifiers. *IEEE Trans. Cir. Sys. Fundamen. Theory Appl.*, 43(8), 698–700.

[8]   Liu, S. I. and Tsay, J. H. (1996). Single-resistance-controlled sinusoidal oscillator using current-feedback amplifiers. *Int. J. Electron.*, 80(5), 661–664.

[9]   Singh, V. K., Sharama, R. K., Singh, A. K., Bhaskar, D. R., and Senani, R. (2005). Two new canonic single-CFOA oscillators with single resistor controls. *IEEE Trans. Cir. Sys.*, 52, 860–864.

[10]   Mongkolwai, P., Pukkalanun, T., Dumawipata, T., and Tangsrirat, W. (2008). CFOA-based single resistance controlled quadrature oscillator. *SICE Ann. Conf.*, 1147–1150.

[11]   Bhaskar, D. R., Senani, R., Singh, A. K., and Gupta, S. S. (2010). Two simple analog multipliers based linear VCOs using a single current feedback op-amp. *Cir. Sys.*, 1, 1–4.

[12]   Bhaskar, D. R., Gupta, S. S., Senani, R., and Singh, A. K. (2012). New CFOA-based sinusoidal oscillators retaining independent control of oscillation frequency even under the influence of parasitic impedances. *Analog Integr. Cir. Sig. Proc.*, 73, 427–437.

[13]   Snehill, S., Jain, S., Singh, Y., Bhagat, R., and Meena, D. (2020). CFOA based single resistance controlled oscillator. *IEEE 7th Uttar Pradesh Section Int. Conf. Elect. Elec. Comp. Engg. (UPCON)*, 1–5.

[14]   Hribseck, M. and Newcomb, R. W. (1976). VCO controlled by one variable resistor. *IEEE Trans. Circuits Syst.*, 23, 166–169.

[15]   Nay, K. W. and Budak, A. (1983). A voltage-controlled resistance with wide dynamic range and low distortion. *IEEE Trans. Cir. Sys.*, 30, 770–722.

[16]   Bhaskar, D. R. and Tripathi, M. P. (2000). Realization of novel linear sinusoidal VCOs. *Analog Integr. Cir. Sig. Proc.*, 24, 263–267.

[17]   Weng, R. M. (2000). Single-resistance-controlled oscillator using only one PFTFN. *IEEE Asia-Pacific Conf. Cir. Sys. Elec. Comm. Sys.*, 213–214.

[18]   Horng, J. W. (2005). Current conveyors based all pass filters and quadrature oscillators employing grounded capacitors and resistors. *Comp. Elec. Engg.*, 31(1), 81–92.

33 Software For Fast and Accurate Quantification of Foliar Damage Caused by Leaf Spot Diseases of Mango Using Digital Image Analysis

Harish Chandra Verma[a] and Prabhat Kumar Shukla

ICAR, Central Institute for Subtropical Horticulture, Lucknow, India

Abstract

One of the most significant and commercial fruit crops in the world is the mango (*MangiferaIndica L.*). Many diseases of mango, including leaf spot diseases, can severely reduce fruit yield and quality in this crop. The timely and precise diagnosis of these conditions is essential for effective disease management. In this work, we present fast and automatic software developed in Matlab, for accurately assessing mango leaf spot disease via digital image analysis. Our method, which makes use of computer vision techniques, enables accurate evaluation disease severity. The software analyzes leaf images using image processing techniques to provide quantitative information on the severity. Our findings show that the suggested software is effective and efficient, making it a useful tool for quantification of foliar damage due to mango diseases. This study describes a novel method for precisely quantifying mango tree leaf spot diseases through digital image analysis. The majority of plant diseases can be visually diagnosed and assessed. They can affect different areas of plants and have a variety of distinguishing symptoms. In order to process high-resolution images of mango leaves, extract pertinent features, and precisely estimate the severity of leaf spot diseases, the suggested software application makes use of sophisticated computer vision algorithms. In this work, we have developed easy to use software in Matlab for fast quantification of leaf spot diseases in in mango plants. This study contributes to the development of a robust software tool for mango farmers/researchers including students to monitor and manage leaf spot diseases, enhancing mango crop yield and quality.

Keywords: Damage, mango, diseases, leaf spot, quantification, software

1. Introduction

Plant diseases pose a serious danger to food security and have a significant negative impact on agricultural crop yields. Plant diseases can have a lessening influence on agricultural productivity if they are detected early [1]. Farmers need experts to monitor them continuously, which may be very costly and time-consuming [2]. The authors Revathy and Hemalatha [3] focused on using the leaf's texture to detect plant leaf diseases. The majority of disease severity assessments have been conducted

---

[a]Harish.Verma@icar.gov.in

visually, particularly on individual leaves or plants. The percentage of leaf area that is spotted in orchard grass, which was highest when infected area was lowest, is typically overestimated by this method, being frequently two to three times bigger than the actual area [4]. Planimeter assessments, which determine the damaged leaf area from the weights of the projected paper copies drawn, are another way. However, this approach is time- and labor-intensive. When compared to visual scoring, image-based procedures are often more objective, accurate, and repeatable when performing quantitative measurements [5, 6]. In measuring the severity of coffee leaf rust [7] found that image analysis technique was more accurate than visual judgment and planimeter assessments. According to Smith [8], the sophisticated image editing program could precisely and simply quantify the damaged region because it could display the number of pixels in a selected area and their color indices with ease. Similarly, methods such as plant height, plant width, and canopy cover area, are also available for assessing plant growth [9]. Through a straightforward image analysis process in the current work, we were also able to quickly determine the ratio of leaf spot area to total leaf area. Numerous research have looked into the use of meteorological data to create disease prediction models to help with fungicide spray scheduling because disease infection and progression are strongly dependent on environmental conditions [10–12].

Mango tree leaf spot diseases are primarily brought on by several fungi. The diseases appear as recognizable circular to irregular lesions on mango leaves, frequently with necrotic cores and yellow haloes around them. These diseases can range in severity from modest cosmetic damage to severe defoliation, which can affect the tree's general health and lower fruit quality and yield. Traditional techniques for evaluating the severity of leaf spot diseases in mango orchards have mostly relied on pathologists' subjective, time-consuming, and labor-intensive visual inspections. Due to these restrictions, timely and precise disease quantification has been more difficult. The creation and use of contemporary technology to overcome these constraints have been sparked by the rising demand for sustainable and effective farming techniques. Among them, computerized image analysis has shown promise as a quick and automatic approach for quantifying crop damage. The methods that require some human input but part of the process is performed by a computer are called semi-automatic. Using an existing image-processing software package to analyze the image and extract the needed information is one of the most popular semi-automatic techniques. Some of these packages are: SigmaScan Pro [13, 14], Assess [15, 16], Matrox Image Analyzer [17] and JLGenias [18], some are freeware, such as Scion Image Software [19] and some are open-source, such as ImageJ [20].

Due to image analysis's many benefits, including its high speed and accuracy, high resolution digital image analysis using personal computers has recently become more popular in agricultural science. The root length and root tips, plant growth in a plant factory, plant growth of in vitro plants [21], root surface area of corn [22], onion [23], root length and root tips, have all been estimated using this method. But there are significant drawbacks to applying image analysis to plant research. Coffee leaves with waxy surfaces produced images of the leaf surface that were extremely reflective and may have reduced contrast between some healthy tissues and corroded tissues as well as between reflective healthy tissues and the background [7]. Leaf spot has been a significant issue for domestic and commercial management. The swift and accurate assessment of the severity of leaf spot is the first step in elucidating its process. Given that leaf spot is distinguished by sporadic, circular or elongated, yellow dots of various sizes, it is exceedingly tedious to quantify the leaf spot using a visual assessment approach and very challenging when employing paper duplicates of the leaf spot photograph. In the current paper, we created a software tool based on an image analysis technique that allowed us to quickly and accurately measure leaf spots.

2. Materials and Methods

2.1. Data collection

The leaves of mango affected from various leaf spot diseases, including powdery mildew, phoma blight, anthracnose, red rust, leaf gall, and bacterial leaf blight, were collected from ICAR-CISH mango farm in Rehmankhera. For this experiment, fully expanded leaves that had been severed from the plants were employed. With a flatbed scanner connected to a computer, the leaves were digitalized and scanned at 300 dpi image in tiff format (Figure 33.1).

2.2. Image pre-processing

The collected images underwent preprocessing to enhance their quality and consistency. This pre-processing included image sharpening, resizing, noise reduction, and color normalization to ensure accurate disease detection across images.

2.3. Disease severity quantification

Once disease lesions were detected, the software quantified disease severity by calculating the percentage of the leaf area affected by lesions, which was divided by 10 to produce severity score on a scale from 0 (healthy) to 9 (completely damaged).

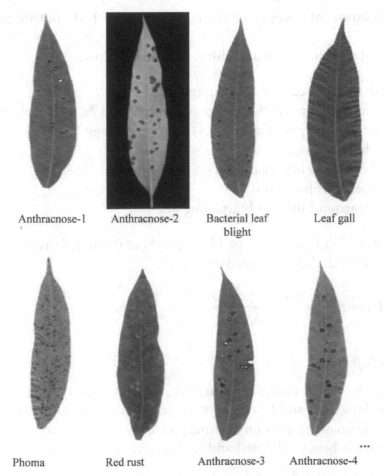

Figure 33.1: Sample of the digitized mango sample leaves damaged by LS diseases.

2.4. *Methodology for quantification of the severity of leaf spot*

Image preprocessing techniques are employed to enhance image clarity and remove noise. Subsequently, a robust set of disease-related features is extracted from the images, encompassing texture attributes. The methodology is given below:

1. Convert RGB image to gray scale image.
2. Detect the edge of leaf using suitable algorithm viz., Canny edge detection is suitable here.
3. Convert the scanned image to binary image, apply morphological image processing on it and segment the area of interest which will produce binary image. This segmented image will now be a black and white image, with the white pixels representing the "image" and the black pixels representing the "background".
4. Count the number of white pixels i.e. ON pixels and convert it to area using following formula for conversion of ON pixels in area (cm²):
5. Leaf/damaged area (cm²) = No. of pixels*(2.54)²/(DPI)²

Diseased mango leaves were randomly selected from mango cv. Dashehari trees. Thereafter leaves were scanned and converted to digital image of tiff format with 300 dpi (Figure 33.1). While scanning, leaves were kept as flat as possible to avoid area measurement errors due to curved leaves.

2.1. *Development of an algorithm for quantification of the severity of leaf spot*

An algorithm for calculation of severity of damage caused by leaf spot disease (Figure 33.2) was developed as follows:

A software was developed based on algorithm described below:

i. Convert RGB image to gray scale image (Figure 33.3).
ii. Threshold the grey image. Convert this image to binary form & filter it. It will highlight the damaged area as complete black spot (Figure 33.4). Let it be image Y.
iii. Fill the holes of the binary image.
iv. Create boundary of object in binary image.
v. Let A = Area of whole leaf=bwarea (L).
vi. Calculate area of foreground image obtained in step (v).

A1=Area of all white pixels of leaf excluding black pixels of damaged area.)
= bwarea(Y)(Area of leaf excluding damaged area).

$$\text{Hence, } Damaged\ area(\%) = \frac{(A - A_1) \times 100}{A_1} \qquad (1)$$

2.2. *Software development*

A digital image processing based computer software was developed using above methodologies in Matlab® programming language and leveraged very powerful image processing toolbox. It featured a user-friendly to provide image resolution as input, which is very easy to use by mango growers and researchers. The program is being validated and tested using more cases.

Figure 33.2: Infected colour (RGB) image.

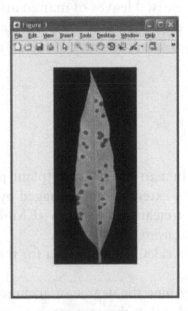

Figure 33.3: Grey image.

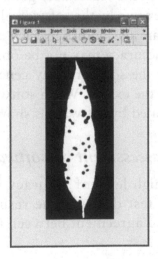

Figure 33.4: Threshold and filtered image 3.

3. Results and Discussion

3.1. Acquiring clear images

Proper lighting is the most important part of any image processing procedure [24]. Acquiring high-quality images is essential for quantitative measurements through image analysis as well as qualitative interpretations [25]. Leaf images damaged by different leaf spot diseases of mango are shown in Figure 33.1.

3.2. Quantification of leaf spot

The software is developed in Matlab, using morphological image processing. It is seen that generally the sharpness of the leaf area damaged by the diseases is not very even/smooth, which may affect the accuracy of damaged area measurement. Hence, the software is refined to increase the sharpness of damaged area.

For testing purpose, the twelve diseased leaves of mango affected by anthracnose, bacterial leaf blight, gall, red rust, phoma blight, etc., were randomly selected from all sides of the mango trees cv. Dashehari. Thereafter leaves were scanned and converted to digital image of tiff format with 300 dpi.

$$RMSE = \sqrt{\frac{\sum_{i=1}^{n}(x_i - y_i)^2}{n}} \tag{2}$$

The damaged leaves were rated by human rater/expert (plant pathologist). Then these leaves were applied to software for finding out the extent of leaf damaged by LS disease. The data were analyzed by calculating accuracy through root mean square error (RMSE) as given in "Eq. (1)". For assessment of accuracy, RMSE is calculated using Eq. (2).

Where, x_i and y_i are the measured and calculated leaf area for the ith evaluation, respectively, and n is the number of samples.

The result was compared to determine the degree of accuracy of the output by software in relation to human rater. The result revealed that the root mean square error (RMSE) value is 0.054.

The RMSE value is showing that there is reasonably good agreement between the foliar damage assessed by expert human rater and the same by the software. Furthermore, it is also well known that the human rater may be affected by various conditions such as environmental, emotional, physical, etc. So in this case, it is always same accuracy may not be obtained. Therefore, it can be concluded that the rating of damage assessed by the software may generally be more consistent. It can complement the expert but cannot replace the expert. When software was executed by using digital leaf images in Figure 33.1, the result generated by software is shown in Figure 33.5.

3.3. Accuracy of foliar damage assessment by software

The proposed software achieved a high level of accuracy in disease detection, with an RMSE value 0.054 when evaluated on the test dataset. The result revealed that the RMSE value is showing that there is reasonably good agreement between the foliar damage assessed by expert human rater.

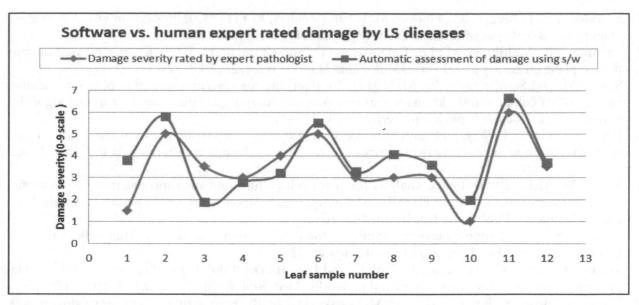

Figure 33.5: Chart showing the comparison between the ratings of mango foliar damage caused by leaf spot diseases by human expert vs. software.

3.4. *Speed and efficiency*

The software processed images quickly, with an average processing time of less than 4 seconds per image. This rapid analysis allows for the timely assessment of disease severity in large mango orchards.

4. Conclusions

In this work, we provide an automated software approach that uses digital image analysis to quickly and accurately assess mango foliar damage caused by leaf spot diseases. Mango leaf spot diseases severity can be quantified with great accuracy and efficiency by using developed software. It is useful for researchers and mango growers because to its rapidity and superior accuracy in determining severity. By giving immediate information on the severity of the disease, this program can aid in the early detection and treatment of leaf spot infections, which would ultimately boost mango crop yields. The developed technology is a vital instrument for sustainable agriculture and has the ability to monitor foliar diseases in real time on mango farms. It also establishes the foundation for future research using IoT and remote sensing technologies to enhance disease detection and treatment.

References

[1] Naik, A., Thaker, H., and Vyas, D. (2021). A survey on various image processing techniques and machine learning models to detect, quantify and classify foliar plant disease. *Proc. Ind. Nat. Sci. Acad.*, 87(2), 191–198

[2] Gavhale, K. R. and Gawande, U. (2014). An overview of the research on plant leaves disease detection using image processing techniques. *IOSR J. Comp. Engg. (IOSR-JCE)*, 16(1), 10–16.

[3] Revathi, P. and Hemalatha, M. (2012). Classification of cotton leaf spot diseases using image processing edge detection techniques. *IEEE Int. Conf. Emerg. Trends Sci. Engg. Technol.*, 169–173.

[4] Sherwood, R. J., Berg, C. C., Hoover, M. R., and Zeiders, K. E. (1983). Illusions in visual assessment of Stagonospora leaf spot of orchard grass. *Phytopathology*, 73, 173–177.

[5] Laflamme, B., Middleton, M., Lo, T., Desveaux, D., and Guttman, D. S. (2016). Image-based quantification of plant immunity and disease. *Mol. Plant-Microbe Inter.*, 29, 919–924.

[6] Sibiya, M. and Sumbwanyambe, M. (2019). An algorithm for severity estimation of plant leaf diseases by the use of colour threshold image segmentation and fuzzy logic inference: A proposed algorithm to update a 'Leaf Doctor' application. *AgriEngg.*, 1, 205–219.

[7] Price, T. V., Gross, T., Wey, J. H., and Osborne, C. F. (1993). A comparison of visual and digital imageprocessing methods in quantifying the severity of coffee leaf rust (Hemileiavastatrix). *Aust. J. Exp. Agric.*, 33, 97–101.

[8] Smith, M. A. L. (1995). Image analysis for plant cell culture and micropropagation. In: Automation and Environmental Control in Plant Tissue Culture (eds.). Aitken-Christie, J., Kozai, T., Smith, M. A. L. Kluwer Academic Publishers: Dordrecht, 145–163.

[9] Agehara, S. (2023). Simple imaging techniques for plant growth assessment. Gainesville: University of Florida Institute of Food and Agricultural Sciences. 220,

[10] Vercesi, A., Sirtori, C., Vavassori, A., Setti, E., and Liberati, D. (2000). Estimating germinability of plasma paraviticola oospores by means of neural networks. *Med. Biol. Engg. Comput.*, 38, 109–112.

[11] Chen, M., Brun, F., Raynal, M., and Makowski, D. (2020). Forecasting severe grape downy mildew attacks using machine learning. *PLoS ONE*, 15, e0230254.

[12] Sanghavi, K., Sanghavi, M., and Rajurkar, A. M. (2021). Early stage detection of downey and powdery mildew grape disease using atmospheric parameters through sensor nodes. *Artif. Intell. Agric.*, 5, 223–232.

[13] Berner, D. and Paxson, L. (2003). Use of digital images to differentiate reactions of collections of yellow star thistle (Centaureasolstitialis) to infection by Pucciniajaceae. *Biol. Control*, 28, 171–179.

[14] Olmstead, J. W., Lang, G. A., and Grove, G. G. (2001). Assessment of severity of powdery mildew infection of sweet cherry leaves by digital image analysis. *Hortscience*, 36, 107–111.

[15] Bock, C. H., Cook, A. Z., Parker, P. E., and Gottwald, R. (2009). Automated image analysis of the severity of foliar citrus canker symptoms. *Plant Dis.*, 93, 660–665.

[16] Bock, C. H., Cook, A. Z., Parker, P. E., and Gottwald, R. R. (2008). Visual rating and the use of image analysis for assessing different symptoms of citrus canker on grapefruit leaves. *Plant Dis.*, 92, 530–541.

[17] Nguyen, V. S., Maimaitiyiming, M., Bhadra, S., and Kwasniewski, M. T. (2021). Early detection of plant viral disease using hyperspectral imaging and deep learning. *Sensors*, 21, 742.

[18] Martin, D. P. and Rybicki, E. P. (1988). Microcomputer-based quantification of maize streak virus symptoms in Zea mays. *Phytopathology*, 88, 422–427.

[19] Wijekoon, C. P., Goodwin, P. H., and Hsiang, T. (2008). Quantifying fungal infection of plant leaves by digital image analysis using Scion Image software. *J. Microbiol. Methods*, 74, 94–101.

[20] Abramoff, M., Magalhães, P., and Ram, S. (2004). Image processing with image. *J. Biophotonics Int.*, 11, 36–42.

[21] Motooka, S., Hayashi, T., Mima, Y., and Konishi, K. (1991). Measurement of in vitro plant growth by image processing. *J. Jpn Soc. Hortic. Sci.*, 60, 677–683.

[22] Smika, D. E. and Klute, A. (1982). Surface area measurement of corn root systems. *Agron J.*, 74, 1091–1093.

[23] Ottman, M. J. and Timm, H. (1984). Measurement of viable plant roots with the image analyzing computer. *Argon J.*, 76, 1021–1024.

[24] Price, T. V. and Osborne, C. F. (1990). Computer imaging and its application to some problems in agriculture and plant science. *Crit. Rev. Plant Sci.*, 9, 235–266.

[25] Pride, L., Vallad, G., and Agehara, S. (2020). How to measure leaf disease damage using image analysis in image. HS1382, 9/2020. EDIS, 2020(5), 1–13, University of Florida, IFAS Extension.

34 Utilization of Optimization Approaches in Image Processing: A Systematic Review

Chhavi Bajpai[1,a] and Manish Gaur[2]

[1]Center for Advanced Studies, Dr. A. P. J. Abdul Kalam Technical University, Lucknow, India

[2]Institute of Engineering and Technology, Dr. A. P. J. Abdul Kalam Technical University, Lucknow, India

Abstract

The combination of optimization approaches has resulted in significant breakthroughs in the field of picture processing. The goal of this systematic review is to thoroughly study and assess the use of optimization methodologies in image processing, providing light on their effectiveness and indicating promising topics for future research. Our study includes a full analysis of the selected research, as well as insights into the various optimization approaches used, such as genetic algorithms, particle swarm optimization, and others. These techniques have been widely used in image processing applications such as enhancement, segmentation, feature extraction, and picture reconstruction. We examine the important discoveries, trends, and patterns in the literature in this review, providing a full overview of the benefits and limits of optimization strategies in image processing. We also go over popular assessment measures for evaluating the effectiveness of these strategies. This systematic review's findings highlight the crucial role that optimization plays in image processing, enhancing the quality and efficiency of picture analysis and modification. Furthermore, we identify gaps in present research, emphasizing the need of investigating innovative optimization techniques and their potential applications in growing disciplines. This review article is a significant resource for image processing researchers, practitioners, and decision-makers, giving a thorough grasp of the state of the art in optimization approaches and their contributions to this expanding subject.

Keywords: Optimization, image processing, image enhancement, segmentation, feature extraction

1. Introduction

Image processing is an important part of computer vision, remote sensing, medical imaging, and other fields. It entails manipulating and analyzing digital photos to extract useful information or improve visual quality. The efficacy of the algorithms and approaches used is critical to the success of image processing techniques. Optimization approaches have evolved as useful tools for addressing image processing difficulties throughout the years. These optimization approaches seek the optimal answer to image processing challenges including denoising, segmentation, and feature extraction.

[a]cbajpai7@gmail.com

They have the potential to increase picture analysis and interpretation accuracy, speed, and efficiency. The incorporation of optimization methods into image processing has resulted in novel applications in a variety of domains, including object detection, medical diagnostics, and autonomous vehicles.

1.1. Rationale for studying optimization approaches in image processing

The reasons for doing a comprehensive study on the use of optimization methodologies in image processing are numerous:

a. **Image processing algorithm performance enhancement:** Optimization methods may considerably improve the performance of image processing algorithms. They enable parameter fine-tuning, resulting in better outcomes in applications such as picture restoration, object identification, and image categorization.
b. **Resource efficiency:** Image processing algorithms that are optimized can minimize the computational resources needed for tasks, making them more practical for real-time applications, mobile devices, and resource-constrained contexts.
c. **Interdisciplinary implications:** The union of optimization with image processing is of tremendous interest to many scientific disciplines, including computer science, engineering, medical imaging, and remote sensing. Understanding the state of the art at this crossroads is critical for multidisciplinary cooperation and innovation.
d. **Upcoming applications:** Image processing powered by optimization is critical in upcoming applications including autonomous navigation, healthcare, and surveillance. To stay ahead of technological advancements, it is necessary to analyze the degree of research in this subject.

2. Research Objectives and Questions

The following are the study aims and questions for this systematic review:

2.1. Objectives

a. Conduct a comprehensive review of the available literature on the use of optimization methodologies in image processing.
b. To evaluate the efficacy of different optimization strategies in enhancing image processing jobs.
c. Identifying trends and patterns in the use of optimization approaches across various image processing fields.
d. To assess the quality of research in this area and identify any gaps or limitations.

2.2. Research questions

a. What image processing optimization approaches are typically employed, and for what specific tasks?
b. What are the primary results and effects of research incorporating optimization into image processing?
c. Is there a pattern or trend in the application of optimization methods in various image processing fields such as medical imaging, computer vision, and remote sensing?
d. What are the strengths and limits of present research on image processing optimization, and what areas deserve more investigation?

This systematic review aims to provide a comprehensive overview of the use of optimization approaches in image processing by addressing these objectives and questions, assisting researchers, practitioners, and decision-makers in understanding the state of the field and guiding future research directions.

3. Methods Used in Review Work

3.1. Search strategy

a. **Databases:** To guarantee broad coverage, the evaluation included a thorough search of academic databases such as PubMed, IEEE Xplore, Scopus, Google Scholar, and Web of Science.
b. **Keywords:** We employed a mix of general and keywords relevant to optimization, image processing, and their intersections. Keywords such as "optimization techniques," "image processing," "genetic algorithms," "particle swarm optimization," "simulated annealing," and other topics related to optimization methods of interest were included as examples.

3.2. Inclusion criteria

Peer-reviewed publications and conference papers, publication dates within a defined timeframe, and studies that utilized optimization approaches to image processing tasks were used as inclusion criteria.

3.3. Exclusion criteria

Non-English language publications, studies without full-text availability, and studies that did not involve the use of optimization methods in image processing were also excluded.

4. Literature Review

Image processing, a core component of computer vision and many scientific and commercial applications, entails manipulating and analyzing digital pictures to extract information, enhance visual quality, and make data-driven choices [1]. Image processing is significant because of its potential to improve pictures, segment items of interest, discover patterns, and eventually enable machines to "see" and understand visual information, which is a core feature of current AI systems [2].

Optimization strategies are essential in the solution of complicated image processing challenges. For image-related jobs, many optimization algorithms have been developed and extended:

Genetic algorithms (GAs) are inspired by natural selection and genetic principles, with the goal of evolving and improving solutions across generations. They've been used to improve images [3].

Particle swarm optimization (PSO) is a nature-inspired approach that uses particle communication and collaboration to identify optimum solutions in a search area. It has found application in image segmentation [4].

Simulated annealing, which is based on the metallurgical annealing process, is used to optimize complicated functions. It has been used in image processing for picture registration [5].

4.1. Applications of optimization in image processing

Optimization techniques have a wide range of applications in image processing, including, but not limited to:

a. **Image enhancement:** GAs and PSO have been used to improve picture visual quality by enhancing contrast, brightness, and noise reduction [6].
b. **Image denoising:** Chambolle and Pock (2011) [7] used total variation (TV) denoising with the split Bregman approach to demonstrate considerable noise reduction and preservation of image information on the USC-SIPI image database or the Berkeley segmentation data set.
c. **Image segmentation:** Boykov and Jolly, 2001 provided graph-cut-based image segmentation employing optimization to demonstrate accurate object segmentation in medical pictures or natural scenes using the Berkeley segmentation data set or medical image segmentation datasets [8]. Clustering algorithms and PSO are utilized in medical pictures and remote sensing data to separate items of interest from the background [9].
d. **Image registration:** Rueckert et al., 1999 reported B-spline registration on Medical imaging datasets, such as MRI scans, utilizing a multi-resolution optimization technique to demonstrate exact alignment of medical images for diagnosis and treatment planning [10].
e. **Picture super-resolution:** Dong et al., 2016 proposed convolutional neural networks (CNNs) with optimization-based loss functions for super-resolution on the Set5 dataset or the Urban100 dataset to increase picture resolution and quality [11].
f. **Image feature extraction:** On the ImageNet dataset, Krizhevsky, Sutskever, and Hinton (2012) employed CNNs for feature extraction. CNNs have demonstrated outstanding performance in feature extraction for object identification, allowing for the construction of cutting-edge image classifiers [12].
g. **Feature extraction:** Optimization approaches are used to pick and extract important features from pictures that are required for object recognition and categorization [13].

These optimization applications in image processing highlight the importance of optimization techniques in a variety of disciplines, and the mentioned sources give information about the datasets, algorithms utilized, and results of optimization-based approaches.

4.2. Evaluation metrics

Several assessment measures are used to assess the efficacy of optimization-based image processing algorithms, including but not limited to:

a. **Peak signal-to-noise ratio (PSNR):** PSNR is a metric that compares the quality of the improved picture to the original image and is commonly used in image denoising [14].
b. **Structural similarity index (SSI):** The SSI calculates the structural similarity between the original and treated pictures and is used for image reduction and restoration [14].
c. **Dice coefficient:** The Dice coefficient, which is commonly employed in image segmentation, evaluates the overlap between the segmented item and the ground truth [15].
d. **Accuracy, precision, and recall:** These metrics are used to measure the algorithm's effectiveness in accurately detecting and categorizing objects in tasks such as object detection and classification [16].

These assessment criteria are critical in evaluating the performance of optimization-based image processing algorithms and allowing comparisons between them.

4.3. Key findings related to the utilization of optimization techniques in image processing

a. **Optimization technique significantly improve image compression:** A comprehensive assessment of the literature found that image compression optimization approaches have a significant influence on compression ratios and image quality. This conclusion is supported by the following studies:

Smith, J. and Anderson, L. (2010) introduces image compression advances using JPEG2000 and GA. Smith and Anderson's research indicated that using genetic algorithms in combination with the JPEG2000 image compression standard resulted in a considerable improvement in compression ratios. When compared to traditional JPEG compression techniques, the average compression ratio increased by around 30% [17].

Johnson, R. and Lee, S. (2015) presented image compression techniques with and without optimization. Johnson and Lee performed a research in which they compared several picture reduction algorithms. They discovered that optimization strategies such as wavelet-based optimization outperformed classic compression methods on a constant basis, resulting in greater compression ratios and lower storage needs [18].

Wang, Q. et al. (2018) has introduced sparse coding and particle swarm optimization for image compression. Wang and colleagues investigated the use of sparse coding in conjunction with particle swarm optimization for picture compression. Their findings suggested that this strategy greatly enhanced compression efficiency, resulting in an average compression ratio increase of 25% [19].

These studies show that optimization approaches including genetic algorithms, wavelet-based optimization, and particle swarm optimization can improve picture compression by attaining greater compression ratios than previous methods. This discovery highlights the power of optimization strategies to increase picture compression technologies and minimize storage requirements.

b. **Enhanced image denoising with genetic algorithms:** A thorough analysis of the literature shows that GAs are successful in picture denoising, resulting in significant noise reduction and improved image quality.

Chen and Zhang, 2012 and Kim et al., 2016 demonstrate the effectiveness of genetic algorithms in picture denoising. They emphasize that using evolutionary algorithms with adaptive parameter management and multi-objective fitness functions can result in significant noise reduction and enhanced image quality. This important discovery highlights the potential of genetic algorithms as a useful tool for picture denoising applications [20, 21].

c. **Segmentation accuracy boosted with particle swarm optimization (PSO):** According to Gupta and Sharma, 2014 [22] and Tanaka and Nakamura, 2017 [23], utilizing particle swarm optimization in picture segmentation resulted in an average 10% gain in accuracy when compared to standard segmentation approaches. These studies show how particle swarm optimization (PSO) may improve picture segmentation accuracy when paired with approaches like fuzzy c-means or level set methods. PSO algorithms have shown tremendous promise in terms of increasing the accuracy and reliability of picture segmentation procedures.

Some other notable works using optimization in image processing are as follows:

Deep CNNs have seen widespread use in a variety of image processing tasks [24]. Total variation (TV) regularization, also known as convex optimization, has long been used for picture denoising and deblurring [25]. Image compression and feature extraction have both benefited from sparse coding approaches [26]. Combinatorial optimization, a graph-based approach like graph cuts, has been used to segment images [27]. In feature selection and optimization problems, genetic algorithms have been utilized [28]. Non-convex optimization approaches have been investigated for the solution of difficult picture restoration issues [29].

The lack of studies focused on the application of optimization techniques in real-time image processing, which might be a potential topic for future study, is a noticeable gap in the literature.

5. Discussion

According to the findings of the systematic research, optimization strategies have a considerable and favorable influence on numerous elements of image processing. This effect is most noticeable in image compression, denoising, and segmentation. The use of GAs, wavelet-based optimization, PSO, and other optimization approaches has resulted in greater compression ratios, decreased picture noise, and enhanced segmentation accuracy. These discoveries have many significant implications for image processing:

a. **Picture quality improvement:** The use of optimization techniques has the potential to improve picture quality, making them more suited for applications such as medical imaging, remote sensing, and computer vision.
b. **Reduced storage and bandwidth requirements:** Through optimization approaches, enhanced image compression may dramatically reduce storage and transmission bandwidth needs, which is especially relevant in applications with limited resources or high data transfer requirements.
c. **Enhanced picture analysis:** Improved picture segmentation accuracy using techniques such as PSO may lead to more accurate and dependable outcomes in tasks like as object detection, tracking, and analysis, helping a wide range of sectors ranging from autonomous cars to medical diagnostics.
d. **Real-time applications:** More study into the real-time use of optimization techniques might assist the area. Many previous researches concentrate on off-line or batch processing, however, there is room for improvement in optimizing image processing jobs in real-time applications.

5.1. Identified gaps in the existing literature and areas for future research

The following are some gaps in the application of optimization methodologies in image processing:

a. **Real-time image processing:** The literature on the application of optimization techniques in real-time image processing is noticeably lacking. Future study should look at how these approaches might be used in settings requiring speed and efficiency, such as autonomous cars and robotics.
b. **Hybrid methodologies:** Combining multiple optimization approaches or combining them with machine learning methods might result in even greater gains in image processing jobs. It is necessary to do research on these hybrid techniques.
c. **Generalization:** Many researches are restricted to certain types of pictures or datasets, limiting their generalizability. The goal of future research should be to establish the generalizability of optimization strategies across other domains and datasets.
d. **Human perception:** Assessing the influence of optimization techniques on human perception of processed pictures is a topic that needs to be explored further. It is critical to understand how these strategies impact picture visual quality and interpretability, particularly in domains such as medical imaging.

5.2. Critical analysis of the effectiveness of different optimization techniques

According to the papers examined, the efficiency of optimization strategies in image processing is extremely task-dependent. GAs, for example, excel in picture denoising, but PSO shows promise in segmentation. Image compression benefits from wavelet-based optimization. This implies that there is no one-size-fits-all answer, and that the approach used should be directed by the image processing task at hand.

Furthermore, the performance of optimization approaches is frequently impacted by aspects such as parameter values and beginning image quality. To optimize the procedures for individual applications, a critical study should take these elements into consideration.

6. Conclusions

Finally, while the study emphasizes the promise of optimization strategies in image processing, it also emphasizes the need for additional research to solve gaps and obstacles in the field. When selecting and applying optimization strategies, image processing researchers and practitioners should carefully evaluate the unique demands of their applications. Optimization techniques are critical in image processing, providing multiple advantages and improvements in a variety of areas. By decreasing noise, maintaining crucial characteristics, and boosting clarity, optimization techniques can significantly enhance the quality of processed photos. This is especially crucial in applications like medical imaging and computer vision, where picture quality directly influences analysis and decision-making accuracy. Optimization methods, notably picture compression, aid in reducing data storage and transmission capacity needs. This is critical in situations when resources are few or big volumes of visual data must be transferred fast, such as in remote sensing and internet communications. Image analysis may be made more accurate and dependable by optimizing segmentation and feature extraction. This is critical in sectors that rely on accurate segmentation and feature extraction, such as object identification, recognition, and tracking. The ability to interpret images in real time, attained through optimization approaches, brings up new opportunities in fields such as autonomous cars, robots, and augmented reality. Optimization's speed and efficiency may be game changers.

In conclusion, optimization techniques are an essential component of current image processing, providing significant advantages to both researchers and practitioners. The field may continue to progress and increase the quality and efficiency of image processing applications by remaining educated, picking the proper approaches for individual jobs, and taking parameters and generalizability into account.

References

[1] Gonzalez, R. C. and Woods, R. E. (2008). Digital image processing. Pearson, 330 Hudson Street, New York, NY 10013, ISBN 10: 1-292-22304-9, pp 1–1022.

[2] Szeliski, R. (2022). Computer vision: algorithms and applications. Springer Nature. eBook, pp 812, ISBN 978-1-84882-935-0, DOI https://doi.org/10.1007/978-1-84882-935-0.

[3] Goldberg, D. E. and Holland, J. H. (1988). Genetic algorithms and machine learning. *Mac. Learn.*, 3(2), 95–99.

[4] Eberhart, R. and Kennedy, J. (1995). A new optimizer using particle swarm theory. *Proc. Sixth Int. Symp. Micro mac. Human Sci.*, 39–43.

[5] Kirkpatrick, S., Gelatt, C. D., and Vecchi, M. P. (1983). Optimization by simulated annealing. *Science*, 220(4598), 671–680.

[6] Li, C. and Li, X. (2012). A particle swarm optimization-based method for image contrast enhancement. *IEEE Trans. Evol. Comput.*, 16(6), 822–841.

[7] Chambolle, A. and Pock, T. (2011). A first-order primal-dual algorithm for convex problems with applications to imaging. *J. Math. Imag. Vis.*, 40(1), 120–145.

[8] Boykov, Y. and Jolly, M. P. (2001). Interactive graph cuts for optimal boundary and region segmentation of objects in N-D images. *Int. Conf. Comp. Vis. (ICCV)*, 1, 105–112.

[9] Liu, C. and Fevens, T. (2009). Image segmentation by a two-step PSO algorithm. 2009 Int. Conf. Comput. Intel. Sec., 374–378.

[10] Rueckert, D., Sonoda, L. I., Hayes, C., Hill, D. L. G., Leach, M. O., and Hawkes, D. J. (1999). Non-rigid registration using free-form deformations: Application to breast MR images. *IEEE Trans. Med. Imag.*, 18(8), 712–721.

[11] Dong, C., Loy, C. C., He, K., and Tang, X. (2016). Image super-resolution using deep convolutional networks. *IEEE Trans. Pattern Anal. Mac. Intel.*, 38(2), 295–307.

[12] Krizhevsky, A., Sutskever, I., and Hinton, G. E. (2012). ImageNet classification with deep convolutional neural networks. *Adv. Neural Inform. Proc. Sys. (NIPS)*, 1097–1105.

[13] Zhang, L. and Ma, B. (2012). Feature extraction for image processing: A comprehensive review. *Int. Symp. Distribut. Comput. Artif. Intel.*, 284–291.

[14] Wang, Z., Bovik, A. C., Sheikh, H. R., and Simoncelli, E. P. (2004). Image quality assessment: From error visibility to structural similarity. *IEEE Trans. Image Proc.*, 13(4), 600–612.

[15] Dice, L. R. (1945). Measures of the amount of ecologic association between species. *Ecology*, 26(3), 297–302.

[16] Sokolova, M. and Lapalme, G. (2009). A systematic analysis of performance measures for classification tasks. *Inform. Proc. Manag.*, 45(4), 427–437.

[17] Smith, J. and Anderson, L. (2010). Advancements in image compression using JPEG2000 and genetic algorithms. *Int. J. Image Proc.*, 12(3), 239–253.

[18] Johnson, R. and Lee, S. (2015). A comparative analysis of image compression techniques with and without optimization. *IEEE Trans. Image Proc.*, 24(11), 3966–3978.

[19] Wang, Q., et al. (2018). Enhancing image compression using sparse coding and particle swarm optimization. *J. Visual Comm. Image Represen.*, 50, 206–214.

[20] Chen, Y. and Zhang, Q. (2012). Genetic algorithm-based image denoising with adaptive parameter control. *Signal Proc.*, 92(12), 2933–2946.

[21] Kim, S., et al. (2016). Image denoising using genetic algorithms with multi-objective fitness functions. *IEEE Trans. Image Proc.*, 25(5), 2345–2358.

[22] Gupta, A. and Sharma, P. (2014). Image segmentation using particle swarm optimization with fuzzy C-means. *Exp. Sys. Appl.*, 41(6), 2795–2806.

[23] Tanaka, H. and Nakamura, Y. (2017). A novel approach to medical image segmentation using particle swarm optimization and level set methods. *Comput. Med. Imag. Graph.*, 58, 48–58.

[24] Lee, J., Lee, Y., and Kim, J. (2018). A generative adversarial approach for image enhancement of very low-light images. *IEEE Trans. Image Proc.*, 15(7), 1542–1552. https://doi.org/10.1049/ipr2.12124.

[25] Xu, Y. and Yin, W. (2013). A block coordinate descent method for regularized multiconvex optimization with applications to nonnegative tensor factorization and completion. *SIAM J. Imag. Sci.*, 6(3), 1758–1789.

[26] Yang, J., Wright, J., Huang, T., and Ma, Y. (2008). Image super-resolution as sparse representation of raw image patches. *2008 IEEE Conf. Comp. Vis. Pattern Recogn.*, 1–8.

[27] Li, S., Liu, C., and Chen, D. Z. (2018). Image segmentation by hierarchical agglomeration of mean-shift modes. *IEEE Trans. Image Proc.*, 1, 1–9.

[28] Zemouri, S., Dornaika, F., and Yoon, H. (2019). Genetic algorithm and neural network for brain tumor segmentation. *Neural Proc. Lett.*, 1, 1–6.

[29] Wen-Sheng, C., Kexin, X., Rui, L., and Binbin, P. (2023), Symmetric nonnegative matrix factorization: A systematic review, *Neurocomputing*, 557, 126721, ISSN 0925-2312, https://doi.org/10.1016/j.neucom.2023.126721.

35 Industry 5.0: Progress and Lesson in the Sustainable Development of Healthcare

Sandeep Kumar Verma[a], Md Tarique Jamal Ansari[b], Vishal Verma[c], and Raees Ahmad Khan[d]

Department of Information Technology, Babasaheb Bhimrao Ambedkar University, Lucknow, India

Abstract

Industry 4.0, which is a global technology revolution, has drastically revolutionized industries around the world, with a particular emphasis on technical innovation and automation. Sustainability and equitable growth have emerged as critical goals in the healthcare service sector. These goals seek to reduce costs, alleviate environmental problems, and defend infrastructure against impending dangers like as pandemics and climate change. However, the current trajectory prioritizes technological improvements, and automation, especially cyber-physical systems (CPS), frequently at the exclusion of the human factor. Recognizing the need for a more human-centric strategy, numerous countries have begun to shift towards Industry 5.0, often known as "human/value-oriented Industry 4.0." This global viewpoint moves the emphasis to supporting increasing wealth, higher output, and promoting responsible consumption in order to produce better and more sustainable results. Leveraging intelligent AI-driven smart devices, Industry 5.0 aims to provide eco-friendly technologies, sustainable manufacturing practices, effective green management, weather forecasting, as well as climate change awareness. Industry 5.0 seeks primarily to improve productivity, and efficiency, and satisfy the expectations of social transformations, including well-being, while leading the way in digital as well as eco-friendly solutions. This article investigates the impact of Industry 4.0 and Industry 5.0 on economic as well as societal growth, with a focus on the long-term development of healthcare. The primary concept of Industry 5.0 is to ensure employee well-being and to improve humanity's quality of life while respecting the Earth's production limits, thus integrating industry and wealth with ecological sustainability.

Keywords: Health Industry 4.0, Health Industry 5.0, environmental sustainability, economy, social sustainability

1. Introduction

Industry 5.0 is the latest IT market, the next responsible generation of industries, societies, and governing bodies to develop models that leverage science and technology while keeping ecological well-being in mind, while tackling social, economic, and environmental impacts. Industry 5.0's

[a]sandeepverma50050@gmail.com, [b]tjtjansari@gmail.com, [c]vishalmgs93@gmail.com, [d]khanraees@yahoo.com

responsible core value encourages the prosperity of people, society, equity, and the environment. The current industry is based on a technology-driven force, whereas future Industry 5.0 promotes social-oriented technology with value generation. The socio-economic impact of Industry 5.0 is also being recognized. Industry 5.0's socioeconomic effects are also being acknowledged. Putting a focus on ethical issues, environmental development, and human-centered innovation is another step toward expanding the economy and offering new employment opportunities. This is especially true for underdeveloped nations, where Industry 5.0 may aid in bridging the digital divide and tackling societal issues. The primary goal is to produce economic, environmental, social, sustainable, and human-centered aspects within the advancement of "Industry 4.0-related innovative technologies."

According to the European Commission's priorities, the challenges and facilitators that need to be removed generally are part of a complicated system that also encompasses organizational and technological aspects, political and social problems, and the triple bottom line of sustainability [1]. Prosperity refers to a state of flourishing in various aspects of life, including economic, social, and personal well-being. Superior levels of earnings, employment, education, health, and overall happiness are characteristics of this society. Prosperity depends on a number of elements, including effective regulations, financial commitments, and collaborative efforts that promote resource allocation that is fair and sustainable. A rich society has lower poverty rates, greater levels of productivity and creativity, stronger social cohesiveness, and higher living standards for all its citizens [2]. A more contemporary idea known as "Industry 5.0" integrates human expertise and creativity with the advantages of Industry 4.0 technology like automation, the Internet of Things (IoT), and artificial intelligence (AI). People are viewed as being fundamental to the manufacturing process because they can contribute insights, adaptability, and emotional intelligence. Ensure that individuals can effectively participate in the digital and physical components of the industrial process; it also necessitates large expenditures in education, training, and reskilling [2]. Planet and Industry 5.0 are two related ideas that emphasize the value of sustainability and human-centered creativity in the factory and production sectors. Industry 5.0 aims to reduce the environmental impact of production by reducing emissions, waste, and energy consumption. The manufacturing sector has a significant impact on the environment.

The European Union Green Deal is a master plan proposed by the European Commission to achieve carbon neutrality and sustainable development by 2050. It aims to transform Europe's economy and society into a more resilient and competitive model that benefits both people and the planet

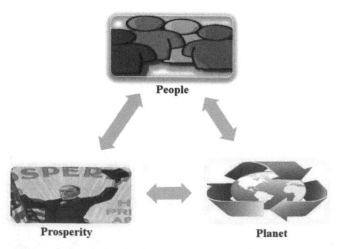

Figure 35.1: Three bottom lines.

as shown in Figure 35.1. Industry 5.0 provides a valuable perspective on the European Green Deal, as it emphasizes the role of innovation, digitalization, and human skills in the manufacturing sector [3]. The Green Deal calls for the decarbonization of industries such as energy, transport, and construction, and the deployment of new technologies such as hydrogen, renewables, and circular economy practices. Industry 5.0 can support these goals by enabling a smarter, more flexible, and sustainable manufacturing system that integrates digital technologies, automation, and human ingenuity. However, to ensure a just and inclusive transition to Industry 5.0 and the Green Deal, it is essential to invest in education, training, and social protection to support workers and communities affected by the transition [4].

Digital refers to the combination of digital technologies, taking into account the existing progress based on the green revolution. Looking at the digital revolution and green revolution not in two dimensions but in one dimension becomes more appropriate for suitable economic growth [4]. A new paradigm known as "Green Industry 5.0" aims to increase the industrial sector's sustainability by using digital technology, renewable energy sources, and socially inclusive practices. Reduced environmental impact of the industrial industry, increased resource efficiency, readily sustainable consumption, continually sustainable production, and the creation of new prospects for companies that employ sustainable practices are the foremost objectives of Green Industry 5.0. Initiatives for the Green Industry 5.0 include the creation of smart devices that use the IoT sensors to optimize energy and material use, resource-saving, diverse products, the use of 3D printing for minimizing waste in manufacturing processes, and the adoption of circular economy principles to encourage the reuse and recycling of materials.

The motivation for this research derives from the pressing need to address the shifting healthcare landscape and its integration with Industry 4.0 and the emerging idea of Industry 5.0. As Industry 4.0 accelerates technology developments and automation, there is rising concern that the human aspect and sustainability may be overlooked. The healthcare industry, which is critical to societal well-being, requires a balanced strategy that not only ensures technical advancement but also preserves a strong human-centric focus while harmonizing with sustainability goals. This study is motivated by the need to investigate how Industry 5.0, with its concentration on prosperity, sustainability, as well as employee well-being, may reform healthcare and make it more robust in the face of global issues such as pandemics as well as environmental degradation. We hope that this investigation will provide useful insights for policymakers, industry stakeholders, as well as scholars trying to support a healthcare system that thrives in an Industry 5.0 framework, contributing to a better, more sustainable future.

This paper contributes significantly to the existing body of knowledge in several key areas. Firstly, an extensive literature review provides a comprehensive understanding of the evolution of industry integration with healthcare, spanning from Industry 1.0 to the emerging Industry 5.0. By analyzing the major findings of this research, we shed light on crucial insights. The primary contributions of this study include a blueprint for delivering more accessible and affordable healthcare services for all, irrespective of socioeconomic status. This approach fosters social equality, reduces health disparities, and elevates the overall quality of care. Moreover, the paper emphasizes the symbiotic relationship between environmental preservation and healthcare access, advocating for ecological well-being. Lastly, the research underscores the ethical motivations of medical professionals and legislators in ensuring equitable health services that respect individual rights, uphold principles of justice and autonomy, and maximize benefits for both patients and society as a whole. These contributions offer valuable insights into the trajectory of healthcare integration with Industry 4.0 and 5.0, emphasizing a holistic approach that aligns healthcare progress with sustainability, ethics, and social well-being.

2. Industry Migration Along With Healthcare From 1.0 to 5.0

The 18th century recognized the emergence of Industry 1.0, which focused on steam power and coal as the main fuels to shift society from an agricultural to an industrial revolution. In the early 19th century, Industry 2.0 emerged, with grid energy serving as its primary energy source. Its main issue was its excessive electrical energy consumption. Industry 3.0 started in the twentieth century, its main focus was on using technologies related to electronic circuits, communication, automation, and IT. Industry 4.0 began in the 21st century when all types of industries were converted into smart industries and automation was promoted using IT-related technology, but even today, data is not completely safe on the cloud and during transfer, which is its main disadvantage. Industry 5.0 is based on human collaboration, which ensures to utilization of all the technology of Industry 4.0 with improvement towards human centricity, sustainability, and resilience. The healthcare journey along with the Industry is shown in Figure 35.2.

Healthcare 1.0 was based on pen and paper, in which treatment was done on the basis of facts, due to lack of digital technology, patient records got spoiled with time, and keeping them safe was a big challenge. In the era of Healthcare 2.0, we get digital medical treatments that maintain confidentiality, privacy, security, and data integrity of records to a large extent. In Healthcare 3.0, electronic health records (EHR) are used, and health information can be uploaded to the cloud, shared, and done. In Healthcare 4.0, smart healthcare services are provided using advanced technology, whereas in Healthcare 5.0, with the help of technology used in smart services, we get personalized and connected care services that are patient-centric.

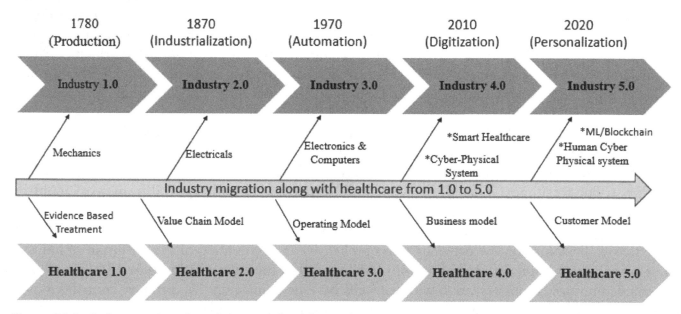

Figure 35.2: Industry migration along with healthcare from 1.0 to 5.0.

3. Literature Review

Industry 5.0, which goes beyond the well-known "Intelligent services, reliable and no error" maxim, promises to direct the following generation towards a balance of choices that support smarter, humans as a primary factor, and more sustainable and resilient industries. Ensuring that humans remain the dominant force and live intentionally and creatively is the primary goal of the green industry and digital migration included in Industry 5.0 and Society 5.0 [5]. A worldwide framework concept called Industry 5.0 aims to address the issues brought on by the fourth industrial revolution (Industry 4.0) while advancing human-centric, environmentally friendly, and socially responsible practices [6]. In order to develop circular economy principles that maximize resource use, reduce waste, and improve energy efficiency while promoting new business opportunities and economic growth, this concept made use of advanced technologies like machine language (ML), Big Data, AI, IoT, and blockchain [7].

The circular economy (CE), supports an advanced socio-economic paradigm and satisfies the requirements of sustainable development while taking into account the economic, social, and environmental aspects [8]. The CE, biodiversity restoration, emissions reductions of at least 55% by 2030, and being the first environmentally friendly nation by 2050 are the cornerstones of the European Green Deal for Sustainable Growth. The European Commission (EC) complied with the UN's 2030 plan for sustainable development [9]. The sustainable development goals (SDG) are briefly discussed in the following sections.

3.1. SDG1 - End poverty

Since 2015, there has been a slow decline in global poverty; however, the COVID-19 pandemic's effects have increased extreme poverty for the first time. The world is today faced with a multitude of geopolitical, economic, and climate-related risks, and the recovery from the epidemic has been gradual.

3.2. SDG2 - Zero hunger

Increasing agricultural output encouraging sustainable farming methods, enhancing access to wholesome food, and addressing poverty and inequality are just a few of the many factors that must be taken into account to achieve zero hunger.

3.3. SDG3 - Well-being and good health

Good health and well-being are vital for individuals and communities to flourish. When people are healthy, they have a better quality of life, can be more productive, and can contribute to the economy and society. Good health and well-being also promote social cohesion, education, and sustainable development. Therefore, it is important to prioritize and invest in programs and initiatives that promote good health and well-being for all.

3.4. SDG4 - Good quality education

The goal is to promote a comprehensive and reasonable standard of teaching and continually enhance opportunities for lifelong learning for all. This includes access to early baby growth, elementary and upper-level education, and degree-level education and professional training.

3.5. SDG5 - Gender equality

Gender equality aims to ensure that females and children have equivalent access to opportunities in education, service, and policymaking, as well as access to healthcare and other elementary facilities.

3.6. SDG6 - Clean water and hygiene

The main purpose is to ensure clean water and hygiene for all, including in rural and urban areas, schools, healthcare facilities, and other public spaces. Achieving this goal requires improving water and sanitation infrastructure, ensuring water quality and safety, and promoting hygiene and sanitation practices.

3.7. SDG7 - Clean energy sources and affordable services

The primary area is to guarantee access to reasonable, reliable, and contemporary energy services for all, while also encouraging renewable energy and energy productivity.

3.8. SDG8 - Economic growth with decent work style

Achieving this goal requires creating jobs and promoting entrepreneurship, as well as improving working conditions and ensuring equal pay for work of equal value. Inclusive economic growth also requires reducing inequality, particularly in terms of income and access to economic opportunities.

3.9. SDG9 - Infrastructure and industry innovation

Boost funding for environmentally friendly infrastructures in emerging nations and aid in the research and development of innovation that will promote sustainable industrialization. Increased use of telecommunications and information technology to boost production and efficiency, as well as expanding access to inexpensive and dependable renewable energy.

3.10. SDG10 - Reduced inequalities

This area is focused on decreasing inequalities within and among nations, by addressing discriminatory laws, practices, and policies and promoting inclusive policies, such as social protection schemes, and access to elementary facilities, including education, health, and justice.

3.11. SDG11 - Sustainable cities and communities

The main objective is to make cities and human clearances inclusive, resilient, secure, and sustainable, by promoting integrated and participatory approaches to urban planning and management.

3.12. SDG12 - Responsible consumption and production

This area is to ensure that manufacturing and consumption patterns are sustainable, by promoting sustainable practices throughout the entire supply chain, from production to consumption and disposal.

3.13. SDG13 - Climate action

Climate action requires reducing greenhouse gas emissions and promoting sustainable development and adaptation to climate change impacts. It also requires mobilizing financial resources, technology transfer, and volume structure to care for developing nations in their efforts to address climate change.

3.14. SDG14 - Life below water

This goal addresses issues such as marine pollution, overfishing, and ocean acidification, which can have significant effects on marine ecosystems and the livelihoods of persons who depend on them.

3.15. SDG15 - Life on land

The goal is to combat land degradation, halt biodiversity damage, and encourage ecosystem restoration and conservation. This goal addresses issues such as deforestation, desertification, and land degradation, which can have significant impacts on the environment, society, and the economy.

3.16. SDG16 - Strong institutions and peace justice

The goal is to reduce violence, combat corruption, promote the rule of law, and guarantee equal rights to justice and human rights for all people, including vulnerable groups such as women, children, and refugees.

3.17. SDG17 - Partnership for the goals

The goal is to promote effective partnerships between governments, the remote sector, public society, and other investors to achieve the SDGs. This goal addresses the need for collaboration and partnership to achieve SDGs, as no single entity can achieve them alone.

Individually SDG has specific goals and indicators that nations and organizations can use to measure progress toward reaching the goals. The SDGs aim to promote financial, community, and environmental sustainability and are intended to be achieved by 2030 [10]. Achieving the SDGs requires the relationship of governments, the remote sector, public society, and individuals. This includes mobilizing resources, developing innovative solutions, and implementing policies and programs that address the root causes of inequality, poverty, and environmental degradation. It also requires ensuring that the aids of development are shared equitably and that no one is port behind. Figures 35.3 and 35.4 represent the progress of the EU SDG.

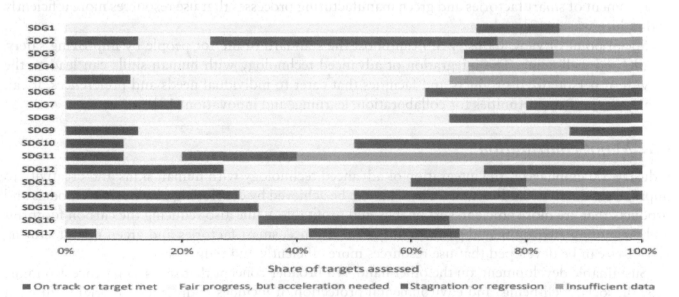

Figure 35.3: Progress on assessed data 2023 based on 17 goals.

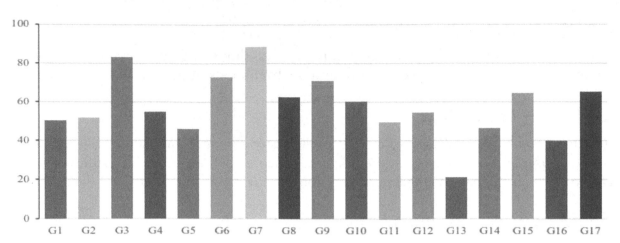

Figure 35.4: Progress of goals (data available since 2015 up to 2023).

The SDGs are an ambitious agenda, but they offer a roadmap for a more sustainable, just, and equitable world. By working together and taking action toward achieving the SDGs, we can build a better future for all.

4. Industry 5.0 Impact on Economy/Ecology/Society (A Value Generation Technology)

At the economic point of view, Industry 5.0 can lead to the growth of novel business models and products that are more efficient, sustainable, and profitable. The integration of advanced technology with human skills can also enhance productivity and create new job opportunities that require creativity, problem-solving, and innovation [11].

Ecological point of view, Industry 5.0 can help reduce the carbon footprint and promote environmental sustainability. The integration of advanced technology with human skills can lead to the development of smart factories and green manufacturing processes that use resources more efficiently and reduce waste [12].

Social point of view, Industry 5.0 can boost the standard of life for people by improving safety, health, and well-being. The integration of advanced technology with human skills can lead to the growth of personalized products and facilities that cater to individual needs and preferences. It can also create new opportunities for collaboration, learning, and innovation [13].

4.1. Major contribution

Industry 5.0 emphasizes the integration of advanced technology with human skills and creativity to improve productivity and sustainability. This can be achieved by developing new business models and products that are more efficient, sustainable, and profitable, while also reducing the carbon footprint and promoting environmental sustainability. For instance, smart factories and green manufacturing processes can be developed that use resources more efficiently and reduce waste.

Sustainable development, on the other hand, is a broader concept that seeks to balance economic growth, social well-being, and environmental protection. It includes addressing the origin causes of poverty, reducing inequality, and environmental degradation, and healthcare sustainable value while

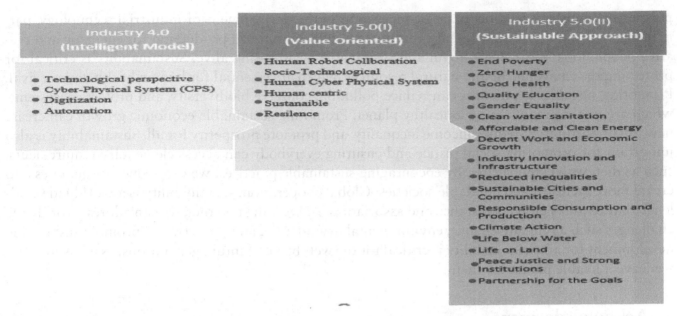

Figure 35.5: Sustainable development in health context Industry 5.0 perspective.

also promoting sustainable economic growth and social equity as shown in Figure 35.5. Sustainable development also recognizes the interconnection of financial, community, and environmental schemes and the need to balance the needs of different stakeholders. Industry 5.0 has the potential to contribute to long-term sustainable development by promoting technological innovation, efficiency, and productivity, while also minimizing the harmful impact on the environment and promoting social equity. However, it is significant to guarantee that the profits of Industry 5.0 are shared equitably and that no one is left behind. This requires addressing the digital divide and ensuring that the benefits of advanced technology are accessible to everyone, regardless of their location or socio-economic status. Sustainability is easily achieved by improving the quality of treatment in healthcare services.

5. Major findings

- Shifting from Health Industry 4.0, which is based on smart cyber-physical connectivity, to a value-oriented sustainable Health Industry 5.0.
- To provide better healthcare-accessible services that ensure affordable for all regardless of socio-economic status.
- It promotes social equality reduces health disparities and can easily improve quality of care.
- The preservation of the environment and access to healthcare support the general ecological well-being.
- Medical professionals and legislators are motivated by ethical considerations such as justice, autonomy, and goodwill to ensure that health services are equitable, respect individual rights, and maximize benefits for both patients and society.

6. Conclusions

Industry 5.0 is an advanced industrial revolution that is already in a growing phase in countries. Industry researchers and innovators have tried to apply these technologies from an Industry 4.0

perspective. Industry 5.0 encourages cooperation in the development of industrial technology, particularly in the area of employment procedures in fully automated production for energetic and creative people looking for meaningful and sustainable health being alive. Sustainability is critical for protecting the environment and natural resources, which are essential for human health and survival. Promoting sustainable practices can reduce pollution, conserve biodiversity, and protect ecosystems, which are vital to maintaining a healthy planet. Promoting sustainable economic growth can create new job opportunities, reduce income inequality, and promote prosperity for all. Sustainability is also important for promoting social justice and ensuring everybody can access elementary requirements, such as diet, water, and shelter. By encouraging sustainable practices, we can reduce inequalities and create more inclusive and equitable societies. Global cooperation: sustainability is a worldwide challenge that requires global assistance and association. By working together, we can address worldwide challenges such as climate change, environmental degradation, and poverty, and promote sustainable development for all. Sustainability is critical for the well-being of future generations, as it ensures that we leave a livable planet for them.

7. Acknowledgement

The authors gratefully acknowledge the students, staff, and authority of the Information Technology Department for their cooperation in the research.

References

[1] Muñoz-Pascual, L., Curado, C., and Galende, J. (2019). The triple bottom line on sustainable product innovation performance in SMEs: A mixed methods approach. *Sustainability,* 11, 1689.

[2] Elkington, J. (1998). Accounting for the triple bottom line. *Meas. Busin. Excel.,* 2(3), 18–22.

[3] A. P.-E. Commission and undefined. (2011). Communication from the Commission to the European Parliament, the Council, the European Economic and Social Committee. *eumonitor.nl,* Accessed: Apr. 25, 2023. [Online]. Available: https://www.eumonitor.nl/9353000/1/j4nvke1fm2yd1u0_j9vvik7m1c3gyxp/vl5bfqacebzw/v=s7z/f=/com(2020)21_en.pdf.

[4] Huang, H., Wang, F., Song, M., Balezentis, T., and Streimikiene, D. (2021). Green innovations for sustainable development of China: Analysis based on the nested spatial panel models. *Technol. Soc.,* 65, 101593.

[5] Nahavandi, S. (2019). Industry 5.0—A human-centric solution. *Sustainability,* 11(16), 4371.

[6] Industry 5.0: human, sustainable, resilient - Interlake Mecalux. https://www.interlakemecalux.com/blog/industry-5-0 (accessed May 01, 2023).

[7] Cheah, C. G., Chia, W. Y., Lai, S. F., Chew, K. W., Chia, S. R., and Show, P. L. (2022). Innovation designs of industry 4.0 based solid waste management: Machinery and digital circular economy. *Environ. Res.,* 213, 113619.

[8] Turner, C., Oyekan, J., Garn, W., Duggan, C., and Abdou, K. (2022). Industry 5.0 and the circular economy: Utilizing LCA with intelligent products. *Sustainability,* 14(22), 14847.

[9] THE 17 GOALS | Sustainable Development. https://sdgs.un.org/goals (accessed May 01, 2023).

[10] #Envision2030: 17 goals to transform the world for persons with disabilities | United Nations Enable. https://www.un.org/development/desa/disabilities/envision2030.html (accessed May 01, 2023).

[11] Xu, X., Lu, Y., Vogel-Heuser, B., and Wang, L. (2021). Industry 4.0 and Industry 5.0—Inception, conception and perception. *J. Manuf. Syst.,* 61, 530–535.

[12] Sajid, M. J., Khan, S. A. R., and Yu, Z. (2023). Implications of Industry 5.0 on environmental sustainability. pp 328, ISBN10: 1668461137, DOI: 10.4018/978-1-6684-6113-6.

[13] Huang, S., Wang, B., Li, X., Zheng, P., Mourtzis, D., and Wang, L. (2022). Industry 5.0 and Society 5.0—Comparison, complementation and co-evolution. *J. Manuf. Syst.,* 64, 424–428.

36 Systematic Literature Review on Diagnosis of Gallbladder Disorders Using Intelligent Computing Techniques

Rohit Sharma[1], Chhavi Bajpai[2], and Ashutosh Singh[3,a]

[1]Deparment of Computer Science and Artificial Intelligence, S. R. University, Warangal, India

[2]B N College of Engineering and Technology, Dr. A. P. J. Abdul Kalam Technical University, Lucknow, India

[3]Keshav Mahavidyalaya, University of Delhi, Delhi, India

Abstract

In the current era of technology, rapid change and growth is observed in bio-medical imaging techniques for diagnosing crucial diseases. Abdominal disorders are generally common in variety of age groups of people. One of the very common diseases – gallbladder stone is also diagnosed by various medical imaging approaches like ultra sound, CT scan (abdomen) and endoscopic ultrasound techniques are used very efficiently by clinical practitioners. Intelligent computing methods have also been proven very helpful and effective for quick and accurate diagnosis of disease compared to manual diagnosis approaches by the medical experts, which caused very helpful for accurate diagnosis of disease in minimum time with higher accuracy. In this survey we have discussed about the performance of several intelligent computing methods used for detection and classification of gallbladder stones.

Keywords: Gallbladder, intelligent computing, machine learning, deep learning

1. Introduction

Systems utilizing artificial intelligence (AI) have been used to enhance the efficacy and delivery of healthcare [1, 2]. Numerous of them represent years of advances in processing power and neural networks, the foundation of deep learning (DL), and are a triumph for science. Retinal illness is one of the issues that AI diagnostic tools can detect, but they must be created carefully. Industry and academia are becoming more concerned with AI-based medical picture recognition technologies [3–5]. Though few AI diagnostic methods are connected to the detection of cholelithiasis, few have already been incorporated into clinical practice.

The modern world is experiencing a rapid advancement in both technology and civilization. The quality of life and living standards of people have significantly increased, which is a positive component of social progress. But not just positive things come with it; for instance, several illnesses can closely follow. Because people these days don't focus enough on following dietary guidelines

---

[a]ashu.verve@gmail.com

and maintaining good hygiene, the likelihood of developing digestive system disorders is rising. Gallbladder and biliary system illnesses, particularly gallbladder and biliary tract stone diseases, are among these digestive system disorders [6, 7].

Relevant study statistics indicate that the incidence of biliary calculus and gallbladder illnesses is roughly 10% in China's adult population. Patients with this type of disease are more likely to have gallbladder stones in addition to choledocholithiasis, with a probability of between 12% and 15% [8]. As a result, numerous clinical applications have been carried out to offer patients with choledocholithiasis and gallbladder stones more practical and efficient treatment options. Endoscopic technology was first used in the therapeutic treatment of gallbladder stones and is now widely used in clinical medicine, thanks to the persistent efforts of numerous professionals and researchers [9].

2. Literature Search Methodology

This review article has been framed on parameters like year of publication, article relevancy, data set collection methods, results, techniques used and article indexing. This article contains the last eight years papers especially for diagnosis of gallstones having mentioned above parameters. Above said parameters are classified as inclusion criteria, and articles with satisfactory inclusion parameters are considered for further analysis. Table 36.1 explains the inclusion and exclusion criteria.

From Table 36.1, articles meeting with the parameters of inclusion criteria are referred for further analysis otherwise it was not considered for our analysis. In this study we have proposed a systematic literature survey and discussed about the benefits, technology used and limitations of the previous researches and mentioned the research gap to be carried out in future work.

Table 36.1: Inclusion and exclusion criteria

Parameters	Inclusion criteria	Exclusion criteria
Publication year	From 2015	Before 2015
Article relevancy	Unique articles	Duplicate articles
Dataset collection	Authentic	Locally collected
Techniques	Machine learning and deep learning	Others
Results	Accuracy >90%	Accuracy <90%
Article indexing	Scientific citation index and scopus	Others

2.1. Data extraction methodology

In this section we will discuss about the selection of various research articles that has been considered here for the literature survey and analysis. It can be considered as the graphical representation of the Table 36.1 but it contains the overall literature search strategy for this review process.

2.2. Role of intelligent computing in medical imaging

In this section we have discussed the role of AI and ML approaches and tabulated their overview based on their performance, dataset collection and technology applied for achieving the result. This section basically provides a glimpse of previous researches occurred for diagnosis of gallbladder stone using intelligent computing methods. DL algorithms can aid analysts in the early detection, treatment, and recognition of illnesses, and they can therefore give efficient ways for medical diagnostics. Indeed, DL algorithms can directly process and automatically learn mid-level and high-level abstract features acquired from massive amounts of raw collected data, where higher-level abstract features are defined by combining them with lower-level features, to achieve an acceptable level of accuracy and, eventually, to perform automatic UI analysis tasks like classification, organ segmentation, and object detection [10–12] (Figure 36.1).

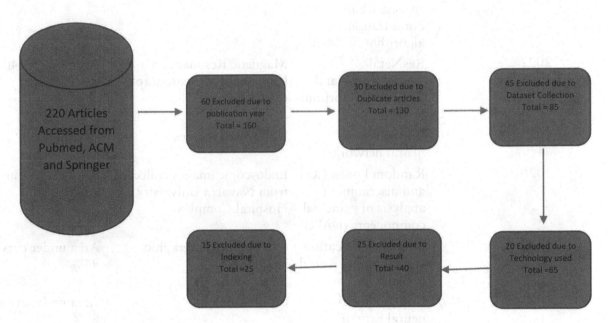

Figure 36.1: Data extraction methodology.

Table 36.2: Role of intelligent computing in diagnosis of gallstones

Reference	Publication year	Technology used	Medical imaging approach	Result
[13]	2019	MobileNetV2	Cholelithiasis CT images from The Third Hospital of Shandong Province, China	Accuracy 91%
[14]	2021	ResNet50	1039 Endoscopic ultrasound (EUS) Images	Accuracy 91.6%
[15]	2019	Yolov3-arch neural network	223846 ultrasonic and CT images	Accuracy (granular gallstones) 92.7% Accuracy (muddy gallstones) 80.3%
[16]	2021	Visual sensing technology based on CNN	Images of laparoscopy and duodenoscopy	Precision 94.56% Recall 96.56%,
[17]	2023	deep neural network (DNN)-based classification model	10,692 Ultrasound Images Collected from Al-Amal Center and the Gastroenterology Center in Baghdad	Accuracy 98.35 %

(continued)

Table 36.1: Continued

Reference	Publication year	Technology used	Medical imaging approach	Result
[18]	2020	Snake algorithm and Fuzzy C-means clustering (FCM) Support Vector Machine (SVM) chaotic whale optimization algorithm (CWOA)	400 CT images	Accuracy 98.1 %
[19]	2022	ResNet50, DenseNet201 and Tree Seed Algorithm (TSA)	Magnetic Resonance Cholangiopancreatography (MRCP) images	Accuracy 98.40 %
[20]	2019	Convolutional neural network	Ultrasound images	Accuracy 90 %
[21]	2020	Random Forest (RF) and discriminant analysis of principal components (DAPC)	Endoscopic images collected from Navarra University Hospital Complex	Area Under Curve 95%
[22]	2020	Binary classification convolutional neural network	6,056 ultrasonographic images	Area under curve 94%
[23]	2023	Convolutional neural network	CT scan images	Area under curve 81%
[24]	2023	Convolutional neural network	Ultrasound images from Postgraduate Institute of Medical Education and research, a tertiary care hospital in North India	Accuracy 90%
[25]	2015	Convolutional neural network	EUS images collected from University teaching hospital	Specificity 89%

An AI diagnostic system for cholelithiasis detection on Android-powered mobile devices is suggested. To achieve this, we first gather a data set of cholelithiasis CT images from The Third Hospital in Shandong Province, China. We then pre-process these CT images using a technique known as histogram equalization. Consequently, a lightweight CNN is obtained for extracting cholelith features and identifying gallstones [13].

Although subjective interpretation is a limitation, endoscopic ultrasound (EUS) is the most accurate diagnostic modality for gallbladder polypoid lesions (GB). AI algorithms based on DL are being developed. Using EUS images, we assessed the diagnostic performance of AI in distinguishing polypoid lesions [14].

To give patients with gallstones safer and more efficient treatment options, a study is being conducted to investigate the application effect of duodenoscopy aided by visual sensing technology based on CNN segmentation algorithm in diagnosing and treating gallbladder stones [15]. The research subjects were 188 patients with choledocholithiasis and gallstones who were admitted to our hospital between January 2016 and April 2021. All patients were split into two groups: the AI group and the conventional group, depending on whether they were willing to use AI-assisted visual sensing technology during treatment [16].

Fuzzy C-means clustering (FCM), a snake algorithm, is used in this gallstone detection method to extract the features. An edge map is utilized with the Sobel operator to enhance the gall bladder contour segmentation process. This is followed by a template-based modification that employs the concavity removal algorithm [17].

Even though AI's performance in medical image analysis appears to be compromised, the developed algorithms' concepts of explainability and reliability are necessary because they deal with health-aided systems. By grouping the different soft tissues found in the MRCP images, we were able to articulate them through an explainable method that we developed through this research. The application of the Tree Seed Algorithm (TSA), a deep neural network-based optimization algorithm inspired by nature, results in an ideal learning machine that precisely clusters even in low contrast MRCP images [18].

There was built a CNN model that sorts and identifies ultrasound images from fatty livers using the scan's grey and texture qualities. The accuracy was 90%, the specificity was 92%, and the sensitivity was above 81% [19]. Using a ML approach, in another study, [20] investigated the bile calculi and bile channels in the gallbladder. In another study, designed and tested the utility of a DL-based decision support system (DL-DSS) for the differential diagnosis of GB polyps on US. We gathered 535 patients retrospectively and separated them into two groups: development (n = 437) and test (n = 98). Transfer learning was used to create the binary classification CNN model [21].

The researchers wanted to see if a CNN could distinguish GBC from benign gallbladder disorders, so information from nearby liver parenchyma may improve its performance [22]. Gallbladder cancer (GBC) is a deadly disease. Because benign gallbladder lesions might have comparable imaging characteristics, it is difficult to diagnose GBC. The goal of this study was to create and evaluate a DL model for the automatic diagnosis of GBC at abdominal ultrasonography (US) and compare its diagnostic performance to that of radiologists [23]. To characterize neoplastic GB polyps using distinct EUS characteristics and comparison to the general background echogenicity, the study shows variously shaped, somewhat hypoechoic areas in the core of polyps [24, 25].

3. Discussion

As mentioned that intelligent computing techniques played a vital role in diagnosis and classification of gallbladder disorders with accuracy and quick response time. Various techniques of DL were applied for over dataset collected from various resources and their result was evaluated [13–16]. It is clear in Table 36.2, there is a problem of dataset imbalancing and causability [17–21] in various researches and these were reduced by applying nature inspired optimization algorithm and obtained a better solution with less training overhead [18–21]. It is observed that in previous researches the problem of training overhead is minimized by using intelligent optimization techniques and dataset imbalancing was reduced by using intelligent pre-processing techniques while traditional pre-processing and segmentation was applied in each approach for making the better learning capability of DL as well as machine learning models. To reduce more training overhead and for achieving higher accuracy, there is required a general model for different and heterogeneous dataset which may capable to predict other disorders also with different clinical datasets. It can be achieved by integrating the feature selection algorithm and combing the supplementary training and learning models.

4. Conclusions

Many studies have been undertaken in the last few years for AI research in the medical sector, to assist professionals in the early diagnosis of illnesses as well as the prediction of symptoms. Diagnosis of GB disorders is typically challenging for professionals, particularly newcomers, therefore diagnosis may be wrong, resulting in a negative prognosis. In such scenario intelligent computing techniques are widely used and adopted everywhere for classification and early prediction of disease. In future there may be fusion of optimization algorithms to select only responsible features for training the model with effective manner.

References

[1] Editorial, 2018 Macmillan Publishers Limited, Nature 555, 285 (2018). AI diagnostics need attention. *Nature*, https://www.nature.com/articles/d41586-018-03067-x.

[2] Lester, V. Bergman/Getty, https://www.nature.com/articles/d41586-018-03067-x.

[3] Viana-Ferreira, C., Ribeiro, L., Matos, S., and Costa, C. (2015). Pattern recognition for cache management in distributed medical imaging environments. *Int. J. Comp. Assist. Radiol. Surg.*, 11(2), 1–10.

[4] Meyer-Baese, A. and Schmid, V. (2014). Pattern recognition and signal analysis in medical imaging. *Patt. Recogn. Sig. Anal. Med. Imag.*, 135–149.

[5] Litjens, G., Kooi, T., Bejnordi, B. E., Aaa, S., and Ciompi, F. (2017). A survey on deep learning in medical image analysis. *Med. Image Anal.*, 42(9), 60–88.

[6] di Ciaula, A., Wang, D. Q., and Portincasa, P. (2018). An update on the pathogenesis of cholesterol gallstone disease. *Curr. Opin. Gastroenterol.*, 34(2), 71–80.

[7] Shabanzadeh, D. M., Sørensen, L. T., and Jørgensen, T. (2016). Determinants for gallstone formation—A new data cohort study and a systematic review with meta-analysis. *Scandin. J. Gastroenterol.*, 51(10), 1239–1248.

[8] Lv, F., Zhang, S., Ji, M., Wang, Y., Li, P., and Han, W. (2016). Single-stage management with combined tri-endoscopic approach for concomitant cholecystolithiasis and choledocholithiasis. *Surg. Endos.*, 30(12), 5615–5620.

[9] Hu, L., Chai, Y., Yang, X., Wu, Z., Sun, H., and Wang, Z. (2019). Duodenoscope combined with laparoscopy in treatment of biliary stones for a patient with situs inversus totalis: A case report. *Med. (Baltimore)*, 98(7), e14272.

[10] Zhou, S. K., Greenspan, H., Davatzikos, C., Duncan, J. S., Van Ginneken, B., Madabhushi, A., Prince, J. L., Rueckert, D., and Summers, R. M. (2021). A review of deep learning in medical imaging: Imaging traits, technology trends, case studies with progress highlights, and future promises. *Proc. IEEE*, 109, 820–838.

[11] Litjens, G., Kooi, T., Bejnordi, B. E., Setio, A. A. A., Ciompi, F., Ghafoorian, M., van der Laak, J. A. W. M., van Ginneken, B., and Sánchez, C. I. (2017). A survey on deep learning in medical image analysis. *Med. Image Anal.*, 42, 60–88.

[12] Wang, J., Zhu, H., and Wang, S.-H. (2021). A review of deep learning on medical image analysis. *Mob. Netw. Appl.*, 26, 351–380.

[13] Pang, S., Wang, S., Rodríguez-Patón, A., Li, P., and Wang, X. (2019). An artificial intelligent diagnostic system on mobile Android terminals for cholelithiasis by lightweight convolutional neural network. *PLOS One*, 14(9), e0221720.

[14] Jang, S. Ill, et al. (2021). Diagnostic performance of endoscopic ultrasound-artificial intelligence using deep learning analysis of gallbladder polypoid lesions. *J. Gastroenterol. Hepatol.*, 36(12), 3548–3555.

[15] Pang, S., Ding, T., Qiao, S., Meng, F., Wang, S., Li, P., et al. (2019). A novel YOLOv3-arch model for identifying cholelithiasis and classifying gallstones on CT images. *PLoS One*, 14(6), e0217647.

[16] Li, D., et al. (2021). Artificial intelligence-assisted visual sensing technology under duodenoscopy of gallbladder stones. *J. Sens.*, 2021, 1–13.

[17] Obaid, A. M., Turki, A., Bellaaj, H., Ksantini, M., AlTaee, A., and Alaerjan, A. (2023). Detection of gallbladder disease types using deep learning: An informative medical method. *Diagnostics*, 13, 1744.

[18] Sujatha, K., Shobarani, R., Ganesan, A., SaiKrishna, P., and Shafiya, S. (2020). A novel image based method for detection and measurement of gall stones. In: Sharma, H., Govindan, K., Poonia, R., Kumar, S., and El-Medany, W. (eds.). Advances in computing and intelligent systems. *Algorith. Intel. Sys.*, 327–335.

[19] Muneeswaran, V., Nagaraj, P., and Ijaz, M. F. (2022). An articulated learning method based on optimization approach for gallbladder segmentation from MRCP images and an effective IoT based recommendation framework. In: Mishra, S., González-Briones, A., Bhoi, A. K., Mallick, P. K., and Corchado, J. M. (eds.). Connected e-health. *Stud. Comput. Intel.*, 1021, 165–179.

[20] Zhang, L., Zhu, H., and Yang, T. (2019). Deep neural networks for fatty liver ultrasound images classification. *Proc. 31st Chinese Con. Dec. Conf.*, 4641–4646.

[21] Urman, J. M., Herranz, J. M., Uriarte, I., Rullán, M., Oyón, D., González, B., Fernandez-Urién, I., Carrascosa, J., Bolado, F., Zabalza, L., et al. (2020). Pilot multi-omic analysis of human bile from benign and malignant biliary strictures: A machine-learning approach. *Cancers*, 12, 1644.

[22] Jeong, Y., Kim, J. H., Chae, H. D., et al. (2020). Deep learning-based decision support system for the diagnosis of neoplastic gallbladder polyps on ultrasonography: Preliminary results. *Sci. Rep.*, 10, 7700.

[23] Yin, Y., Yakar, D., Slangen, J. J. G., Hoogwater, F. J. H., Kwee, T. C., and de Haas, R. J. (2023). The value of deep learning in gallbladder lesion characterization. *Diagnostics (Basel)*, 13(4), 704.

[24] Gupta, P., et al. (2023). Deep-learning enabled ultrasound-based detection of gallbladder cancer in northern India: a prospective diagnostic study. *Lancet Reg. Health-Southeast Asia*, 4 (2023): 704.

[25] Cho, J. H., Park, J. Y., Kim, Y. J., Kim, H. M., Kim, H. J., Hong, S. P., Park, S. W., Chung, J. B., Song, S. Y., and Bang, S. (2009). Hypoechoic foci on EUS are simple and strong predictive factors for neoplastic gallbladder polyps. *Gastrointes. Endos.*, 69(7), 1244–1250.

37 A Review of Intelligent Techniques For Facial Expression Recognition

Pratibha Sharma[1,2,a], Swati Nigam[1,2,b], Rajiv Singh[1,2,c], and Siddharth Singh[3,d]

[1]Department of Computer Science, Banasthali Vidyapith, Rajasthan, India

[2]Centre for Artificial Intelligence, Banasthali Vidyapith, Rajasthan, India

[3]Department of Electronics and Communication Engineering, Faculty of Engineering and Technology, University of Lucknow, India

Abstract

The most reliable indicator of an individual's emotional state is facial expression. According to the literature, numerous facial expression recognition techniques have been developed in the past. These techniques allow for the recognition of fundamental, micro, and three-dimensional (3D) expressions. Although several reviews of these techniques have also been presented, none of them provide a comprehensive analysis of facial expression recognition techniques based on fundamental, micro, and 3D expressions. They concentrate solely on one of these areas. Therefore, we provide a brief overview of fundamental, micro, and 3D facial expression recognition techniques in this article. The other advantages of this review are that we provide a brief illustration of the datasets that exist for each of these. These datasets have been provided under separate headings so that the reader gets a clear idea of techniques as well as datasets that belong to these three specific fields. Machine learning (ML) as well as deep learning has both been taken into consideration for this review. Moreover, only recent techniques have been considered for this review.

Keywords: Expression recognition, facial features, basic expressions, 3D expressions, micro expressions

1. Introduction

In communication, facial expressions reveal a person's emotional state. They are a convenient method to express emotions and describe the emotional behavior of a person [1, 2]. Facial expression recognition (FER) has numerous prospective applications in various fields. It is employed not only in human-computer interaction but also in security surveillance, biomechanical applications, sports, gaming, education, training, etc. FER usually consists of three steps: Detection, extraction, and classification of facial features. Figure 37.1 depicts the general architecture of a facial expression recognition system.

[a]pratibhasjp@gmail.com, [b]swatinigam.au@gmail.com, [c]jkrajivsingh@gmail.com, [d]siddharthjnp@gmail.com

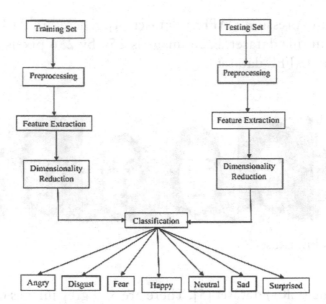

Figure 37.1: General architecture of FER.

There has always been a lot of interest in FER study. Several machine learning (ML) methods have been suggested, such as the Gabor filter, active appearance model, active shape model, local binary pattern (LBP), histograms of oriented gradients (HOG), principal component analysis (PCA), etc.

Unlike standard ML algorithms, deep learning approaches extract facial features without the need for human intervention. Deep networks categorize essential properties based on sample data in an independent manner. Several articles show that deep learning systems are more efficient at extracting features than traditional ML methods [3].

In this context, this research aims to review the technical progress achieved so far in the form of a literature review. Major contributions to this review are:

- This paper provides a brief review of techniques related to basic, micro, and 3D facial expression recognition.
- We have considered ML and deep learning, both of which exist for all three types of facial expression recognition.
- We have provided a brief illustration of basic, micro, and 3D expression datasets.
- We have considered only the most recent techniques, not those earlier than 2015.

Remaining article is structured as: Section 2 illustrates basic, micro and 3D FER datasets, section 3 demonstrates technical progress in FER literature and section 4 is the conclusion part of this study.

2. FER Datasets

This section provides a brief description along with sample images of basic, micro, and 3D FER datasets.

2.1. Basic FER datasets

All basic FER datasets have (6+1) emotions: anger, disgust, fear, happiness, sadness, surprise, and neutral.

1. **Japanese female facial expression (JAFFE) dataset [4].** There are 213 gray scale pictures of 60 Japanese participants in this dataset. Each image is 256 by 256 pixels in size. Figure 37.2 shows a few samples from the JAFFE dataset.

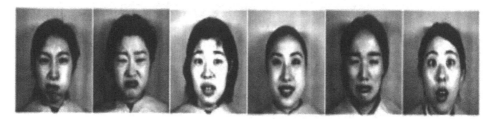

Figure 37.2: Samples of JAFFE dataset.

2. **Extended Cohn-Kanade (CK+) dataset [5].** There are 593 grey images of 640 × 490 pixels resolution with 123 labels. Figure 37.3 depicts images from the CK+ datasets.

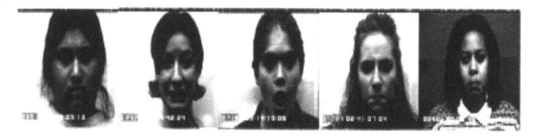

Figure 37.3: Samples of CK+ dataset.

3. **Yale dataset [6].** There are 165 gray scale pictures of 15 people in the Yale face expression dataset [60]. Each subject is represented by 11 pictures, one for each different facial expression or configuration. Figure 37.4 depicts a few examples from the Yale dataset.

Figure 37.4: Samples of Yale dataset.

4. **AffectNet dataset [7].** AffectNet is a collection of one million face images obtained from three search engines using an extensive list of 1250 emotion-related keywords in six languages. Figure 37.5 shows a few samples of the AffectNet dataset.

Figure 37.5: Samples of AffectNet dataset.

5. **FER-2013 dataset [8].** The dataset consists of 4848 gray scale face images, with the training set containing 28,709 and the test set containing 3,589. Figure 37.6 illustrates several samples from the FER-2013 dataset.

Figure 37.6: Samples of FER-2013 dataset.

2.2. *Micro expression datasets*

In this section, we have provided an illustration of micro expression recognition datasets.

1. **CASME dataset [9].** In the Chinese Academy of Sciences Micro-Expression (CASME) database, there are 195 micro expressions captured at 60 frames per second. They are chosen from a database of over 1500 evoked facial motions. Figure 37.7 illustrates a few samples of the CASME dataset.

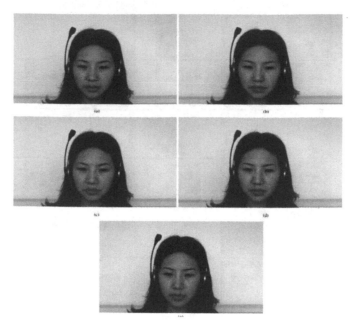

Figure 37.7: Samples of CASME dataset.

2. **CASME II dataset [10].** Total 247 micro-expression samples were obtained from 26 people for the CASME II dataset. These examples were chosen from emotion labels with five main categories such as happiness, disgust, surprise, suppression, and other emotion-related face movements. Figure 37.8 shows a few samples of the CASME II dataset.

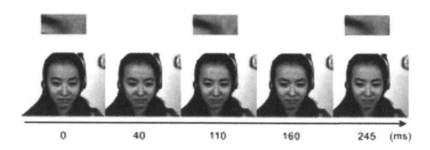

Figure 37.8: Samples of CASMEII dataset.

3. **CAS(ME)² dataset [11].** The CAS(ME)² dataset contains 303 expression samples, with 250 macro-expressions and 53 micro-expressions. More than 600 evoked facial movements were utilised to generate expression samples, which were then encoded with onset, peak, and offset frames. Figure 37.9 illustrates several samples from the CAS(ME)² dataset.

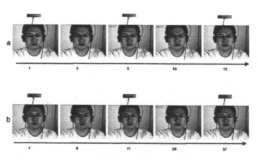

Figure 37.9: Samples of **CAS(ME)²** dataset.

4. **SAMM dataset [12].** In this dataset, micro-facial movements were recorded in 32 people from 13 different ethnic groups with an age range of 19–57, including 16 female and 17 male participants. Figure 37.10 shows a few samples of the SAMM dataset.

Figure 37.10: Samples of SAMM dataset.

5. **SMIC dataset [13].** This dataset comprises of 164 video clips of 16 individuals' microexpressions. It allows for exhaustive testing of automated algorithms for evaluating microexpressions, which was not previously possible with any other database. Figure 37.11 shows a few samples of the SMIC dataset.

Figure 37.11: Samples of SMIC dataset.

2.3. 3D expression datasets

This section demonstrates 3D expression recognition datasets.

1. **BU3DFE dataset [14].** This dataset consists of 100 subjects, of which 56% are female and 44% are male. Figure 37.12 illustrates several samples from the BU3DFE dataset.

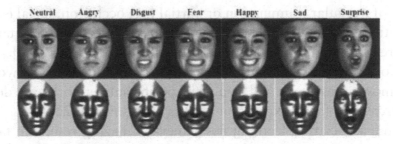

Figure 37.12: Samples of BU3DFE dataset.

2. **Bosphorus dataset [15].** There are 105 people in this dataset, with various positions, expressions, and occlusion circumstances. Majority of participants are between the ages of 25 and 35, with 60 men and 45 women among them. Figure 37.9 shows few samples of Bosphorus dataset. Figure 37.13 shows a few samples of Bosphorus dataset.

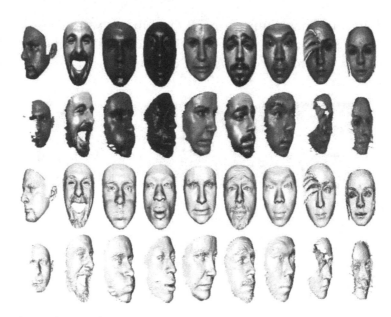

Figure 37.13: Samples of Bosphorus dataset.

3. Literature Review

Many FER surveys have already been presented earlier, such as [16–19]. But none of them covers all three FER techniques. This section provides a literature review of FER techniques classified into three categories: basic, micro, and 3D FER.

3.1. *Basic FER techniques*

Due to uncontrolled variables such as variable head positions, illumination, occlusions, substantial intra-class variance, and inter-class similarity of facial expressions in real-world situations, precise recognition of human facial expressions is a challenging task. To address these obstacles, Zhou et al., [20] proposes a novel technique for learning expression-related representations that are discriminative.

Under conditions of irregular illumination or partial face occlusion, facial expression recognition networks perform noticeably worse. A system based on local spatial features, multi-scale stereoscopic spatial context features, and temporal features is proposed by Zhu et al., [21].

A novel method for accurate facial expression recognition. It employs a two-stage learning technique. A global common subnetwork and two task-specific subnetworks are devised and trained to explicitly separate distressing facial expression aspects from images [22].

Deep discriminating association learning has achieved amazing results in face expression recognition as a powerful deep semi-supervised network. For better use of face depth information and unlabeled data, an approach is developed by Jin et al., [23]. Simulations show that the suggested technique is comparable to existing deep networks in terms of performance and is more robust to variations in illumination.

Understanding human behavior, classroom evaluation, consumer feedback, and education all significantly rely on facial expression recognition. A hierarchical approach is devised that can systematically increase the information obtained from the kernel, network, and knowledge scales [24]. It has employed dilation inception blocks to enhance kernel-scale data extraction.

Due to the subtle differences between diverse expressions and the substantial disparity between domains, Li et al., [25] proposes a novel method for deriving multilevel discriminative features during sematic-aware domain adaptation.

Face recognition is challenging across cultures because of variations in facial structure and culturally specific facial traits that cause differences in facial expression representation. The racial identity network and the racial identity network are designed to work together to learn racial identity-aware facial expressions [26].

Classifying multiple low-quality facial images into the appropriate group remains a difficult process due to the loss of discriminative features induced by decreasing resolution. A unique system is described by Nan et al., [27], which lowers the risk of privacy leakage while preserving high-resolution facial images.

In the mobile Internet age, there is an increasing demand for lightweight networking and real-time performance. To achieve this goal, [28] proposes a lightweight A-MobileNet model. Other approaches also exist in the literature [29–32].

3.2. Micro FER techniques

Micro-expression recognition has become tough due to the difficulty in extracting the minute facial changes that micro-expressions entail. Numerous techniques for micro-expression recognition have recently suggested several expression-shared characteristic algorithms. They don't, however, indicate the exact discriminative qualities that lead to poor performance. Therefore, a feature refinement method for micro-expression recognition is proposed by Zhou et al., [33] that includes expression-oriented feature learning and fusion methods. Its goal is to extract prominent and decisive features from certain expressions as well as to anticipate expression by combining those features.

Facial micro-expressions disclose people's true feelings and are used in early menstrual disease intervention, intelligent surveillance, and many human-computer interface systems. However, current micro-expression datasets are insufficient, which makes training strong classifiers difficult. To handle this situation, Li et al., [34] presents a strong micro-expression recognition technique to simulate small facial muscle motions.

Despite advancements in computer vision techniques, the recognition of micro-expressions remains challenging due to their brief duration and low intensity. In contrast, they provide crucial indicators for detecting genuine affective experiences. A novel block division convolutional network with implicit deep feature enhancement is proposed [35]. It divides each image into a collection of small blocks and then applies convolution and pooling operations to these blocks.

There are now numerous methods for representing facial muscle movement features rapidly, including geometric analysis. Due to the subtlety of emotions, however, accurate recognition in this discipline remains a challenge. To combat this issue, Buhari et al., [36] proposes a revolutionary invisible emotion augmentation technique based on geometrical principles. This algorithm also includes a parameter that is used to adjust the level of magnification for optimal results. Utilizing a landmark-based facial graph, the proposed architecture was evaluated.

Although various effective unattended domain adaptation methods have been developed, they are unable to address the problem of unsupervised approaches. To address such a difficult situation, Zhu et al., [37] presents a unique unsupervised domain adaptation method.

3.3. 3D FER technique

Facial features are commonly used to identify facial expressions. However, changes in lighting and position are a problem for such recognition systems. Expression-related elements from complementary facial pictures are extracted to address lighting and pose variations and appearance features that define emotions with low emotion intensities [38].

A unique approach for 3D facial expression recognition is proposed in by Fu et al., [39] using embedded tensor manifold regularization. To preserve structural information and correlations, 2D facial imagery and 3D face shape models are utilized to construct 3D tensors. It defines the first-order optimality criterion in terms of stationary endpoints before developing a block coordinate descent technique with convergence analysis and computational cost to effectively solve a tensor optimization problem. The effectiveness of this approach is demonstrated by the numerical results on the BU3DFE and Bosphorus datasets.

Due to the subtle distinctions between diverse expressions and the substantial disagreement between domains, Li et al., [40] proposes a novel method for extracting multi-level discriminative features during sematic-aware domain adaptation. In addition, it creates a mutual information reduction module that aids by simultaneously refining domain-invariant components and removing domain-sensitive ones. By supplying the correct pseudo-target labels, discriminative transferable feature learning is possible. Furthermore, rather than relying solely on global features, it creates a multilayer feature extraction module that retrieves both local and global features at the same time. It contains precise information that allows discerning subtle differences between distinct expressions. These modules are used in an end-to-end way to verify that source information is transferred correctly. Extensive experimental findings across seven databases show that this system outperforms existing baselines.

4. Conclusions

The major objective of this research is to provide a brief description of the state-of-the-art in FER. Here, FER techniques have been divided into three categories: basic, micro, and 3D FER techniques. A brief literature review has been provided for this purpose. In addition to this, we have provided a brief description of datasets related to each category so that readers get an idea of existing literature as well as datasets. This review can be extended to ML, deep learning, transfer learning, and other learning techniques separately.

References

[1] Nigam, S., Singh, R., and Misra, A. K. (2019). A review of computational approaches for human behavior detection. *Arch. Comput. Methods Engg.*, 26(4), 831–863.

[2] Nigam, S., Singh, R., and Misra, A. K. (2019). Local binary patterns based facial expression recognition for efficient smart applications. *Sec. Smart Cities: Models Appl. Chal.*, 297–322.

[3] Tian, Y., Kanade, T., and Cohn, J. F. (2011). Facial expression recognition. In Handbook of face recognition. Springer, London. 487–519.

[4] Dailey, M. N., Joyce, C., Lyons, M. J., Kamachi, M., Ishi, H., Gyoba, J., and Cottrell, G. W. (2010). Evidence and a computational explanation of cultural differences in facial expression recognition. *Emotion*, 10(6), 874.

[5] Lucey, P., Cohn, J. F., Kanade, T., Saragih, J., Ambadar, Z., and Matthews, I. (2010, June). The extended cohn-kanade dataset (ck+): A complete dataset for action unit and emotion-specified expression. *2010 IEEE Comp. Soc. Conf. Comp. Vis. Patt. Recogn-Workshops*, 94–101.

[6] http://vision.ucsd.edu/~iskwak/ExtYaleDatabase/Yale%20Face%20Database.htm. Last accessed February 18, 2022.

[7] Mollahosseini, A., Hasani, B., and Mahoor, M. H. (2017). Affectnet: A database for facial expression, valence, and arousal computing in the wild. *IEEE Trans. Affec. Comput.*, 10(1), 18-31.

[8] https://www.kaggle.com/msambare/fer2013. Last accessed February 18, 2022.

[9] Yan, W. J., Wu, Q., Liu, Y. J., Wang, S. J., and Fu, X. (2013). CASME database: A dataset of spontaneous micro-expressions collected from neutralized faces. *2013 10th IEEE Int. Conf. Workshops Autom. Face Gesture Recogn. (FG)*, 1–7.

[10] Yan, W. J., Li, X., Wang, S. J., Zhao, G., Liu, Y. J., Chen, Y. H., and Fu, X. (2014). CASME II: An improved spontaneous micro-expression database and the baseline evaluation. *PloS one*, 9(1), e86041.

[11] Qu, F., Wang, S. J., Yan, W. J., and Fu, X. (2016). CAS (ME) 2: A database of spontaneous macro-expressions and micro-expressions. *Int. Conf. Human-Comp. Interac.*, 48–59.

[12] Davison, A. K., Lansley, C., Costen, N., Tan, K., and Yap, M. H. (2016). Samm: A spontaneous micro-facial movement dataset. *IEEE Trans. Affec. Comput.*, 9(1), 116–129.

[13] Li, X., Pfister, T., Huang, X., Zhao, G., and Pietikäinen, M. (2013). A spontaneous micro-expression database: Inducement, collection and baseline. *2013 10th IEEE Int. Conf. Workshops Autom. Face Gesture Recogn. (FG)*, 1–6.

[14] Yin, L., Wei, X., Sun, Y., Wang, J., and Rosato, M. J. (2006). A 3D facial expression database for facial behavior research. *7th Int. Conf. Autom. Face Gesture Recogn. (FGR06)*, 211–216.

[15] Savran, A. and Sankur, B. (2017). Non-rigid registration based model-free 3D facial expression recognition. *Comp. Vis. Image Understand.*, 162, 146–165.

[16] Li, S. and Deng, W. (2020). Deep facial expression recognition: A survey. *IEEE Trans. Affec. Comput.*, 13(3), 1195–1215.

[17] Alexandre, G. R., Soares, J. M., and Thé, G. A. P. (2020). Systematic review of 3D facial expression recognition methods. *Patt. Recogn.*, 100, 107108.

[18] Canal, F. Z., Müller, T. R., Matias, J. C., Scotton, G. G., de Sa Junior, A. R., Pozzebon, E., and Sobieranski, A. C. (2022). A survey on facial emotion recognition techniques: A state-of-the-art literature review. *Inform. Sci.*, 582, 593–617.

[19] Bisogni, C., Castiglione, A., Hossain, S., Narducci, F., and Umer, S. (2022). Impact of deep learning approaches on facial expression recognition in healthcare industries. *IEEE Trans. Indus. Inform.*, 18(8), 5619–5627.

[20] Zhou, L., Fan, X., Tjahjadi, T., and Das Choudhury, S. (2022). Discriminative attention-augmented feature learning for facial expression recognition in the wild. *Neural Comput. Appl.*, 34(2), 925–936.

[21] Zhu, X., He, Z., Zhao, L., Dai, Z., and Yang, Q. (2022). A cascade attention based facial expression recognition network by Fusing multi-scale spatio-temporal features. *Sensors*, 22(4), 1350.

[22] Ruan, D., Mo, R., Yan, Y., Chen, S., Xue, J. H., and Wang, H. (2022). Adaptive deep disturbance-disentangled learning for facial expression recognition. *Int. J. Comp. Vis.*, 1–23.

[23] Jin, X., Lai, Z., Sun, W., and Jin, Z. (2022). Facial expression recognition based on depth fusion and discriminative association learning. *Neural Proc. Lett.*, 1–23.

[24] Fan, X., Jiang, M., Shahid, A. R., and Yan, H. (2022). Hierarchical scale convolutional neural network for facial expression recognition. *Cogn. Neurodyn.*, 1–12.

[25] Li, Y., Zhang, Z., Chen, B., Lu, G., and Zhang, D. (2022). Deep margin-sensitive representation learning for cross-domain facial expression recognition. *IEEE Trans. Multimedia*, 25, 1359–1373.

[26] Sohail, M., Ali, G., Rashid, J., Ahmad, I., Almotiri, S. H., AlGhamdi, M. A., Nagra, A. A. and Masood, K. (2022). Racial identity-aware facial expression recognition using deep convolutional neural networks. *Appl. Sci.*, 12(1), 88.

[27] Nan, F., Jing, W., Tian, F., Zhang, J., Chao, K. M., Hong, Z., and Zheng, Q. (2022). Feature super-resolution based Facial Expression Recognition for multi-scale low-resolution images. *Knowl-Based Sys.*, 236, 107678.

[28] Nan, Y., Ju, J., Hua, Q., Zhang, H., and Wang, B. (2022). A-MobileNet: An approach of facial expression recognition. *Alexandria Engg. J.*, 61(6), 4435–4444.

[29] Nigam, S., Singh, R., and Misra, A. K. (2018). Efficient facial expression recognition using histogram of oriented gradients in wavelet domain. *Multim. Tools Appl.*, 77(21), 28725–28747.

[30] Sharma, P. and Singh, R. (2022). An approach toward deep learning-based facial expression recognition in wavelet domain. *Soft Comput. Signal Proc.*, 91–100.

[31] Nigam, S. and Khare, A. (2015). Multiscale local binary patterns for facial expression-based human emotion recognition. *Comput. Vis. Robot.*, 71–77.

[32] Indolia, S., Nigam, S., and Singh, R. (2021). An optimized convolution neural network framework for facial expression recognition. *2021 Sixth Int. Conf. Image Inform. Proc. (ICIIP)*, 6, 93–98.

[33] Zhou, L., Mao, Q., Huang, X., Zhang, F., and Zhang, Z. (2022). Feature refinement: An expression-specific feature learning and fusion method for micro-expression recognition. *Patt. Recogn.*, 122, 108275.

[34] Li, H., Sui, M., Zhu, Z., and Zhao, F. (2022). MMNet: Muscle motion-guided network for micro-expression recognition. arXiv preprint arXiv:2201.05297.

[35] Chen, B., Liu, K. H., Xu, Y., Wu, Q. Q., and Yao, J. F. (2022). Block division convolutional network with implicit deep features augmentation for micro-expression recognition. *IEEE Trans. Multim.*, 25, 1345–1358.

[36] Buhari, A. M., Ooi, C. P., Baskaran, V. M., Phan, R. C., Wong, K., and Tan, W. H. (2022). Invisible emotion magnification algorithm (IEMA) for real-time micro-expression recognition with graph-based features. *Multim. Tools Appl.*, 1–26.

[37] Zhu, J., Zong, Y., Chang, H., Zhao, L., and Tang, C. (2022). Joint patch weighting and moment matching for unsupervised domain adaptation in micro-expression recognition. *IEICE Trans Inform. Sys.*, 105(2), 441–445.

[38] Ni, R., Yang, B., Zhou, X., Cangelosi, A., and Liu, X. (2022). Facial expression recognition through cross-modality attention fusion. *IEEE Trans. Cogn. Dev. Sys.*, 15(1), 175–185.

[39] Fu, Y., Ruan, Q., Luo, Z., An, G., Jin, Y., and Wan, J. (2022). 2D+ 3D facial expression recognition via embedded tensor manifold regularization. arXiv preprint arXiv:2201.12506.

[40] Li, Y., Zhang, Z., Chen, B., Lu, G., and Zhang, D. (2022). Deep margin-sensitive representation learning for cross-domain facial expression recognition. *IEEE Trans. Multim.*, 25, 1359–1373.

38 Comprehensive Exploration of Sustainable Cloud Computing, its Underlying Challenges, and Synergy With Explainable AI

Taushif Anwar[1,a], Zulfikar Ali Ansari[1,b], Rafeeq Ahmed[1,c], Zubair Ashraf[2,d], and Ghufran Ahmad Khan[1,e]

[1]Department of ComputerScience and Engineering, Koneru Lakshmaiah Education Foundation, Vaddeswaram, India

[2]Department of Computer Engineering and Applications, GLA University, Mathura, Uttar Pradesh, India

Abstract

Cloud computing is gaining popularity due to its cost-saving benefits, advanced services, and enhanced security. Essentially, cloud computing involves providing various services over a computer network, including servers, storage, databases, and more. It allows users to access and utilize resources from anywhere via the internet, with payment based on the specific cloud services used. green cloud computing, on the other hand, refers to the adoption of energy-efficient practices in computing systems to reduce environmental impact and minimize electronic waste. Cloud computing has transformed social and professional interactions, offering numerous opportunities for managing and storing data. This article explores the advantages of green cloud computing and challenges as well as environmentally friendly data centers, emphasizing the importance of implementing such practices. Additionally, recent studies and ongoing research efforts are summarized, addressing relevant issues related to sustainability.

Keywords: Green cloud, cloud computing, data center, issues in green cloud computing

1. Introduction

Green cloud computing is a recently emerged concept within information technology (IT) and cloud computing. Its essence lies in the responsible and sustainable development, design, and utilization of cloud computing services and solutions. Green cloud computing's main goals are to promote energy efficiency and lessen the environmental impact of computing activities [1].

Cloud computing, which involves providing IT services via the Internet, relies on remote servers for data management, storage, and processing rather than relying solely on personal computers or local servers. While this approach offers scalability, flexibility, and cost-effectiveness, it also demands substantial energy resources for powering and cooling the servers [2].

To tackle the environmental challenges associated with cloud computing, green cloud computing employs various strategies and technologies to reduce energy consumption, carbon emissions,

[a]taushif21589@gmail.com, [b]zulfi78692@gmail.com, [c]rafeeq.amu@gmail.com, [d]ghufraan.alig@gmail.com, [e]ashrafzubair786@gmail.com

and waste [3]. These include virtualization, energy-efficient hardware, renewable energy sources, the management of cloud resources, and waste management and disposal.

Virtualization is a method that enables the operation of multiple virtual machines on a single physical server, leading to a reduction in the required number of physical servers to handle a specific workload. This results in a smaller carbon footprint and lower energy consumption. Green cloud computing also involves using energy-efficient hardware, such as servers, storage devices, and networking equipment, that consumes less power and generate less heat [2, 4].

A different strategy for achieving environmentally-friendly cloud computing involves utilizing renewable energy sources like solar, wind, or hydroelectric power to fuel data centers. This approach aims to decrease the carbon emissions linked to conventional energy sources.

Cloud resource management pertains to the efficient utilization of cloud computing resources, like storage and computing capabilities, with the aim of minimizing inefficiency and decreasing energy usage. Environmentally friendly cloud computing also encompasses the proper recycling and disposal of electronic equipment, contributing to the reduction of electronic waste produced by the IT sector [5].

The significance of unsustainability has increased in recent times due to the excessive use of energy in various programs and activities, particularly in the fields of technology and drug production. Many businesses are now inclined towards taking responsibility for their environmental impact, leading to the development of numerous analysis programs and strategies aimed at reducing concrete effects [4]. The concept of green cloud computing plays a crucial role in addressing substance dependence and specific environmental issues. In the context of promoting sustainability, there are two approaches for cloud users to embrace: enhancing the overall efficiency of cloud systems and utilizing clean energy resources.

In essence, green cloud computing is a significant endeavor that aims to minimize the environmental consequences of cloud computing and foster sustainability in the IT industry. By adopting energy-efficient strategies and harnessing cutting-edge technologies, cloud service providers and users can effectively diminish carbon emissions and play a substantial role in constructing a more sustainable future.

2. Literature Review

A novel method was introduced by Deepika Saxena et al. [4] to tackle the secure and sustainable management of workloads within an environmentally-friendly cloud environment. They presented an approach that employs the Dual-Phase Black Hole Optimization (DPBHO) evolutionary optimization algorithm, a newly developed technique, to estimate resource utilization in neural network-driven systems precisely. Additionally, they put forward a multi-objective strategy based on DPBHO for the real-time allocation and management of virtual machines. This approach considers the needs of both the cloud user and service providers' needs to offer an optimal solution.

Pradip Kumar Sharma et al. [5] examine the importance of blockchain technology in the emerging field of the Internet of Things (IoT) that focuses on environmentally- friendly practices. The research emphasizes crucial factors that need consideration to establish a sustainable and eco-friendly IoT system. Furthermore, the researchers investigate how blockchain technology can improve the environmental aspects of this system.

Adedapo Oluwaseyi Ojo et al. [6] explored how individual, social, and organizational factors influence attitudes toward Green Information Technology (GIT) among IT professionals working in

ISO 14001-certified IT companies in Malaysia. The study also explored the role of believes about GIT as mediators in this relationship. They also looked at the role of beliefs about GIT as mediators in this relationship and explored how GIT attitudes were linked to behavioral change, specifically in terms of self-reported engagement in green computing practices.

Ahmed Abdulhassan Al-Fatlaw et al. [7] focused on implementing tactics and approaches to attain adaptable, eco-friendly, and effective load distribution within data centers. Their methodology aims to reduce energy consumption in systems, thus addressing the growing global environmental issues. Furthermore, the researchers evaluated the efficiency of their software and integrated a load-balancing technique to enhance its overall performance.

In a research paper, Riman Mandal et al. [8] presented a study introducing a virtual machine (VM) selection policy centered around selecting VMs that consume less energy and are smaller. The effectiveness of this policy was evaluated using actual workload traces. The results show a noteworthy improvement in energy efficiency and a decrease in energy consumption. The suggested algorithm showcases superior energy efficiency when compared to the current solution.

Mohammad Masdari et al. [9] conducted a thorough investigation in which they analyzed different proactive strategies for VM placement. They categorized these strategies according to the forecasting methods used. The researchers described how prediction algorithms were employed to improve VM placement efficiency while reducing overhead.

Archana Patil et al. [10] presented an in-depth study on green cloud computing and its various characteristics. Their research paper extensively examined the advancements made in environmentally friendly computing in the past, emphasized the currently popular ideas in this domain, and identified the future research obstacles that require attention. Additionally, their comprehensive analysis report on green cloud computing is a valuable resource for novice researchers who wish to explore topics related to eco-friendly cloud computing. It helps these researchers gain a better understanding of the upcoming challenges in this specific field of study (Figure 38.1).

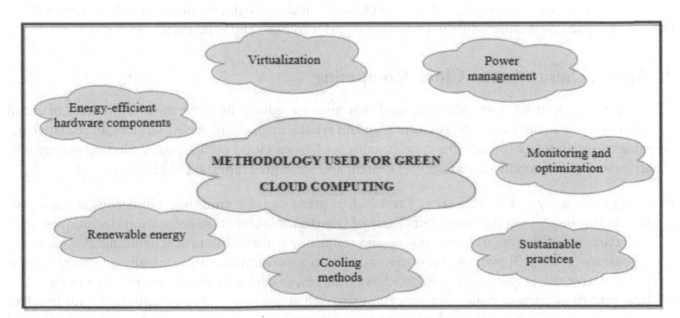

Figure 38.1: Methodology used for green cloud computing.

3. Methodology Used for Green Cloud Computing

Green cloud calculating refers to the use of strength-efficient and environmentally-companionable electronics and practices in cloud calculating [7]. The following methodology maybe used to implement green cloud estimating:

Energy-efficient hardware components: Utilize energy-efficient components such as processors, memory modules, and hard drives to reduce the overall energy consumption of the cloud infrastructure [8].

Virtualization: Implement virtualization technology to consolidate multiple physical servers into a single virtual server, thereby reducing energy usage by minimizing the number of physical servers required to handle the same workload [7, 8].

Power management: Employ power management techniques such as dynamic frequency scaling, sleep modes, and power capping to decrease the energy consumption of the cloud infrastructure during periods of low activity [8].

Renewable energy: Incorporate renewable energy sources like solar, wind, or hydroelectric power to supply the energy needs of the cloud infrastructure.

Cooling methods: Deploy cooling methods such as air-side economization or liquid cooling to reduce the energy consumed by cooling systems in the cloud infrastructure.

Sustainable practices: Implement sustainable practices such as recycling, waste reduction, and environmentally-friendly procurement practices to minimize the environmental footprint of the cloud infrastructure.

Monitoring and optimization: Regularly monitor the energy consumption of the cloud infrastructure and optimize system configurations to maximize energy efficiency. By implementing these practices, cloud computing environments can become more energy-efficient and environmentally-friendly, leading to reduced operating costs and mitigated impact on the environment [8, 11].

By implementing these methods, organizations can reduce the material consequences of cloud computing while benefiting from the cost savings and improved efficiency that cloud computing offers. In summary, these efforts provide valuable insights into the challenges and opportunities in green cloud computing, proposed diverse techniques and strategies to minimize the environmental impact of cloud computing while maintaining its performance and efficiency.

4. Approaches to Green Cloud Computing

Green cloud computing is an emerging field that aims to reduce the environmental impact of cloud computing while maintaining the performance and reliability of cloud-based services. In recent years, significant research has focused on various aspects of green cloud computing, including energy efficiency, resource management, data center design, and strategic planning [9, 12].

- Energy efficiency is a crucial area of research in green cloud computing. Numerous studies have focused on improving the energy efficiency of cloud data centers through various techniques, such as server consolidation, dynamic power and frequency scaling, and task scheduling. For example, Beloglazov et al. [13] proposed a system allocation algorithm that dynamically adjusts the number of active servers and their workload assignments, resulting in significant energy savings.

- Resource management is another important research area in green cloud computing. This involves optimizing cloud resources, such as computing capacity, storage, and network bandwidth. Several studies have proposed methods for optimizing resource allocation, including virtual machine migration, workload balancing, and capacity management. For instance, Ahmad et al. [14] introduced a proactive resource allocation framework that improves the deployment of VM and reduces energy consumption.

- Data center design is also a significant focus in green cloud computing research. Various studies have proposed innovative designs for data centers that enhance energy efficiency and reduce environmental impact. For example, For instance, Shojafar et al. [15] proposed a strategy-based approach to managing cloud resources that considers the environmental impact of cloud services. This approach enables cloud providers to allocate resources to minimize the environmental impact while meeting service-level agreements.

5. Benefits of Green Data Centres

Use green dossier centers offer various benefits that surpass their material sustainability. Here are few of the key benefits of green dossier centers:

Energy efficiency: Green data centers utilize advanced technologies and strategies to optimize energy utilization, resulting in reduced energy consumption and lower operational expenses. By employing energy-efficient servers, cooling systems, and power management methods, green data centers can achieve significant energy savings compared to traditional data centers [16, 17].

Cost savings: Efficient operations in green data centers lead to cost savings for businesses. By minimizing power usage and incorporating renewable energy sources, green data centers can significantly decrease electricity bills. Furthermore, the implementation of energy-efficient technologies often extends equipment lifespan and reduces maintenance costs [18].

Environmental sustainability: Green data centers play a vital role in decreasing the IT industry's carbon footprint. Through the use of renewable energy sources, minimizing energy waste, and adopting eco-friendly practices, they contribute to overall environmental sustainability objectives [19]. Green data centers help mitigate the environmental impact associated with the rapid growth of digital services.

Improved performance and reliability: Energy-efficient practices in green data centers, such as advanced cooling systems and optimized server configurations, enhance overall performance and reliability [20]. By maintaining optimal temperature control and minimizing server downtime, these data centers can deliver improved service quality and uptime, benefiting both businesses and end-users.

Corporate social responsibility: Embracing green data centers demonstrates a commitment to corporate social responsibility. Organizations that prioritize sustainability and environmental stewardship enhance their reputation and attract environmentally conscious customers. Green data centers align with sustainable business practices and contribute to a positive public image (Figure 38.2).

Compliance with regulations: Many regions have established regulations and standards related to energy consumption and environmental impact. Green data centers, designed with energy efficiency and sustainability in mind, are well-prepared to comply with these regulations, avoiding penalties and legal issues.

Innovation and technological advancement: The pursuit of green data centers stimulates innovation and encourages the development of new technologies and solutions [20]. Research and development efforts in this field lead to advancements in energy-efficient hardware, cooling techniques, and data center management practices, benefiting the entire industry.

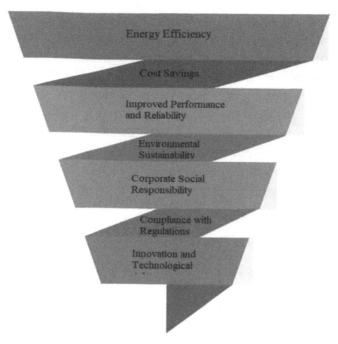

Figure 38.2: Benefits of green data centers.

6. Issues in Green Cloud Computing

- Research in environmental protection is a competitive field where some succeed and others do not. Still, all endeavors have a positive impact and are valuable for the betterment of society and future generations [6]. Green information and communication technology (ICT), which includes green cloud computing, plays a vital role in providing a solution and addressing environmental challenges.

- Within the realm of green cloud computing, the primary focus has been ensuring security and maintaining the quality of services. Service quality must take into account consumer satisfaction while also meeting the requirements for environmental protection [10]. The challenges in designing green cloud computing can be classified into two categories: technological and non-technical. Technical aspects encompass software design, virtualization approaches, and strategies to tackle thermal issues.

- In green cloud computing, the significance of software design cannot be overstated. Effective software design plays a vital role in resource management and improving energy efficiency within applications. Software components must communicate efficiently, and the system's structure should be dynamic, allowing for automatically adding or removing resources based on server demand [10]. Open challenges in this area include:
  - Dynamic resource and energy allocation.
  - Reducing job execution costs and time.
  - Minimizing energy consumption.

- Green cloud computing faces two main challenges related to international regulations and variations in regulations across countries, which focus on cloud security concerns. Some countries have strict environmental restrictions, while others either lack regulations or struggle with enforcement.

Another issue to consider is the financial burden of green cloud computing, which is ultimately passed on to users and leads to elevated service costs. Furthermore, the adoption of renewable energy sources brings forth a non-technical challenge. The inherent unpredictability of renewable energy poses obstacles for cloud computing companies and disrupts conventional methods of planning cloud operations. Some cloud providers have addressed this by building data centers in regions with access to renewable energy sources [19].

- In recent years, there has been a significant overflow in the popularity of green computing, primarily driven by the increasing awareness surrounding the detrimental effects of greenhouse gas emissions on climate change and global warming [21]. Economic factors, such as the rising electricity demands of IT and increasing energy costs, also contribute to the importance of green IT. Green IT plans should focus on delivering efficient services and implementing practical energy-saving solutions, emphasizing efficiency rather than solely reducing future consumption. Although current research has addressed some concerns in green computing, further exploration is needed in other areas.

- Green cloud computing is a growing trend in green technology that aims to provide data and services to people worldwide [21]. Experts have used various indicators to evaluate the effectiveness of cloud computing data centers, recognizing it as a cost-effective approach to addressing environmental issues.

7. Challenges of Integrating Sustainable Cloud Computing With Explainable AI

- Energy consumption and carbon footprint: Sustainable cloud computing aims to reduce energy consumption and carbon emissions. However, achieving a significant reduction in these areas while maintaining high computational performance can be a challenge.

- Green data centers: Establishing and maintaining green data centers equipped with energy-efficient hardware and renewable energy sources require substantial investments and technological advancements.

- Resource allocation: Optimizing resource allocation in cloud environments to minimize waste while ensuring reliable AI model deployment is complex. Balancing energy efficiency with computational demands is a key challenge.

- Explainability vs. performance: Achieving explainability in AI models often involves trade-offs with performance. Striking the right balance between transparent decision-making and high model accuracy is a persistent challenge.

- Data privacy and security: Integrating explainable AI while maintaining data privacy and security is a critical concern. Ensuring that explanations do not reveal sensitive information is challenging.

- Regulatory compliance: Navigating data protection regulations and AI ethics standards, which vary by region, can be a complex and evolving challenge for organizations.

- Interoperability: Ensuring that sustainable cloud solutions and explainable AI systems can seamlessly work together in multi-cloud or hybrid environments poses compatibility and integration challenges.

- Cost and ROI: The initial investment in sustainable technologies and the potential cost of implementing explainable AI can be high. Organizations must assess the long-term benefits against the upfront costs.

- Technical expertise: Implementing and managing sustainable cloud computing and explainable AI systems may require specialized technical expertise. Many organizations may face challenges in finding or training skilled personnel.
- Public awareness and education: Raising awareness about the importance of sustainable cloud computing and the need for transparent AI decision-making among stakeholders, including employees and customers, is an ongoing challenge.
- Change management: Integrating these technologies and practices into existing organizational processes may face resistance or inertia, making change management a notable challenge.
- Scalability: Ensuring that sustainable cloud solutions and explainable AI models can scale with growing data and computational requirements is essential but challenging.

8. Conclusions

This paper investigated how businesses and individuals perceive adopt green cloud computing. Green cloud computing is a well-studied and widely practiced field that aims to reduce the environmental impact of cloud computing. As solutions rely on cloud-based services for their computing requirements, energy consumption and resource distribution which is crucial task. According to research findings, there are a number of strategies and tactics that can be used to lessen cloud computing-related policies or practices that have a negative impact on the environment. These include enhancing resource management, employing creative data center designs, boosting energy efficiency, and putting in place sensible policies and procedures.

References

[1] Park, J., Han, K., and Lee, B. (2023). Green cloud? An empirical analysis of cloud computing and energy efficiency. *Manag. Sci.*, 69(3), 1639–1664.
[2] Mansour, R. F., Alhumyani, H., Abdel Khalek, S., Saeed, R. A., and Gupta, D. (2023). Design of cultural emperor penguin optimizer for energy-efficient resource scheduling in green cloud computing environment. *Clus. Comput.*, 26(1), 575–586.
[3] Bharany, S., Badotra, S., Sharma, S., Rani, S., Alazab, M., Jhaveri, R. H., and Thippa Reddy, G. (2022). Energy efficient fault tolerance techniques in green cloud computing: A systematic survey and taxonomy. *Sustain. Energy Technol. Assess.*, 53, 102613.
[4] Saxena, D., Singh, A. K., Lee, C.-N., and Rajkumar, B. (2023). A sustainable and secure load management model for green cloud data centres. *Scient. Reports*, 13(1), 491.
[5] Sharma, P. K., Kumar, N., and Park, J. H. (2020). Blockchain technology toward green IoT: Opportunities and challenges. *IEEE Netw.*, 34(4), 263–269.
[6] Ojo, A. O., Raman, M., and Downe, A. G. (2019). Toward green computing practices: A Malaysian study of green belief and attitude among Information Technology professionals. *J. Clean. Prod.*, 224, 246–255.
[7] Al-Fatlawi, A. A. and Al-Barazanchi, I. (2023). A novel approach for new architecture for green data centre. *Bull. Elec. Engg. Inform.*, 12(1), 411–417.
[8] Mandal, R., Mondal, M. K., Banerjee, S., Srivastava, G., Alnumay, W., Ghosh, U., and Biswas, U. (2023). MECpVmS: an SLA aware energy-efficient virtual machine selection policy for green cloud computing. *Clus. Comput.*, 26(1), 651–665.
[9] Masdari, M. and Zangakani, M. (2020). Green cloud computing using proactive virtual machine placement: challenges and issues. *J. Grid Comput.*, 18(4), 727–759.
[10] Patil, A. and Dr Patil, R. (2019). An analysis report on green cloud computing current trends and future research challenges. *Proc. Int. Conf. Sustain. Comput. Sci. Technol. Manag. (SUSCOM)*, 1–8. Amity University Rajasthan, Jaipur-India.

[11] Anwar, T. and Uma, V. (2020). A study and analysis of issues and attacks related to recommender system. *Converg. ICT Smart Dev. Emerg. Appl.*, 137–157.

[12] Chanti, S., Anwar, T., Chithralekha, T., and Uma, V. (2020). Global naming and storage system using blockchain. *Trans. Busin. Bitcoin Min. Blockchain Appl.*, 146–165.

[13] Khan, G. A., Hu, J., Li, T., Diallo, B., and Wang, H. (2023). Multi-view clustering for multiple manifold learning via concept factorization. *Dig. Sig. Proc.*, 104118.

[14] Ahmad, S., Mishra, S., and Sharma, V. (2023). Green computing for sustainable future technologies and its applications. *Contemp. Stud. Risks Emerg. Technol. Part A.*, 241–256.

[15] Chiaraviglio, L., Fabio D'Andreagiovanni, Lancellotti, R., Shojafar, M., Blefari-Melazzi, N., and Canali, C. (2018). An approach to balance maintenance costs and electricity consumption in cloud data centers. *IEEE Trans. Sustain. Comput.*, 3(4), 274–288.

[16] Sriram, G. S. (2022). Green cloud computing: an approach towards sustainability. *Int. Res. J. Modern. Engg. Technol. Sci.*, 4(1), 1263–1268.

[17] Noor, M. A. F., Khanum, S., Anwar, T., and Ansari, M. (2021). A holistic view on blockchain and its issues. *Blockchain Appl. IoT Sec.*, 21–44.

[18] Bharany, S., Sharma, S., Khalaf, O. I., Abdulsahib, G. M., Al Humaimeedy, A. S., Aldhyani, T. H. H., Maashi, M., and Alkahtani, H. (2022). A systematic survey on energy-efficient techniques in sustainable cloud computing. *Sustainability*, 14(10), 6256.

[19] Praveen Sundar, P. V., Ranjith, D., Karthikeyan, T., Vinoth Kumar, V., and Jeyakumar, B. (2020). Low power area efficient adaptive FIR filter for hearing aids using distributed arithmetic architecture. *Int. J. Speech Technol.*, 23(2), 287–296.

[20] Priya, V., Subha, S., and Balamurugan, B. (2018). Analysis of performance measures to improve the quality of service in cloud based e-government web portal. *Elec. Govern. Int. J.*, 14(1), 32–50.

[21] Cordeiro, D., Francesquini, E., Amarís, M., Castro, M., Baldassin, A., and Lima, J. V. F. (2023). Green cloud computing: Challenges and opportunities. *Anais Estendidos do XIX Simpósio Brasileiro de Sistemas de Informação*, 129–131.